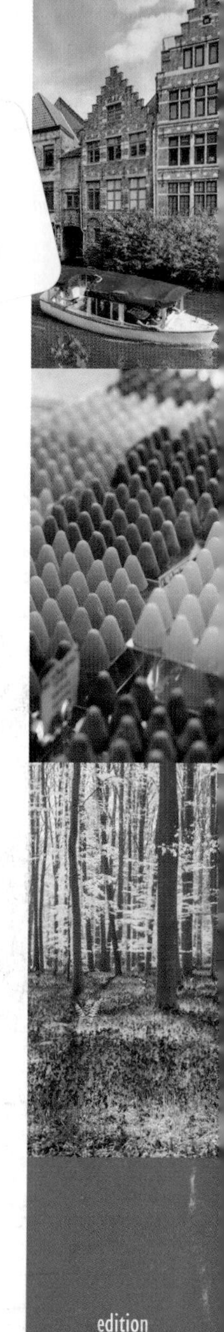

Northern Belgium

Flanders with Brussels, Bruges, Ghent & Antwerp

the Bradt Travel Guide

Emma Thomson

Updated by
Clodagh Kinsella

edition
2

www.bradtguides.com

Bradt Travel Guides Ltd, UK
The Globe Pequot Press Inc, USA

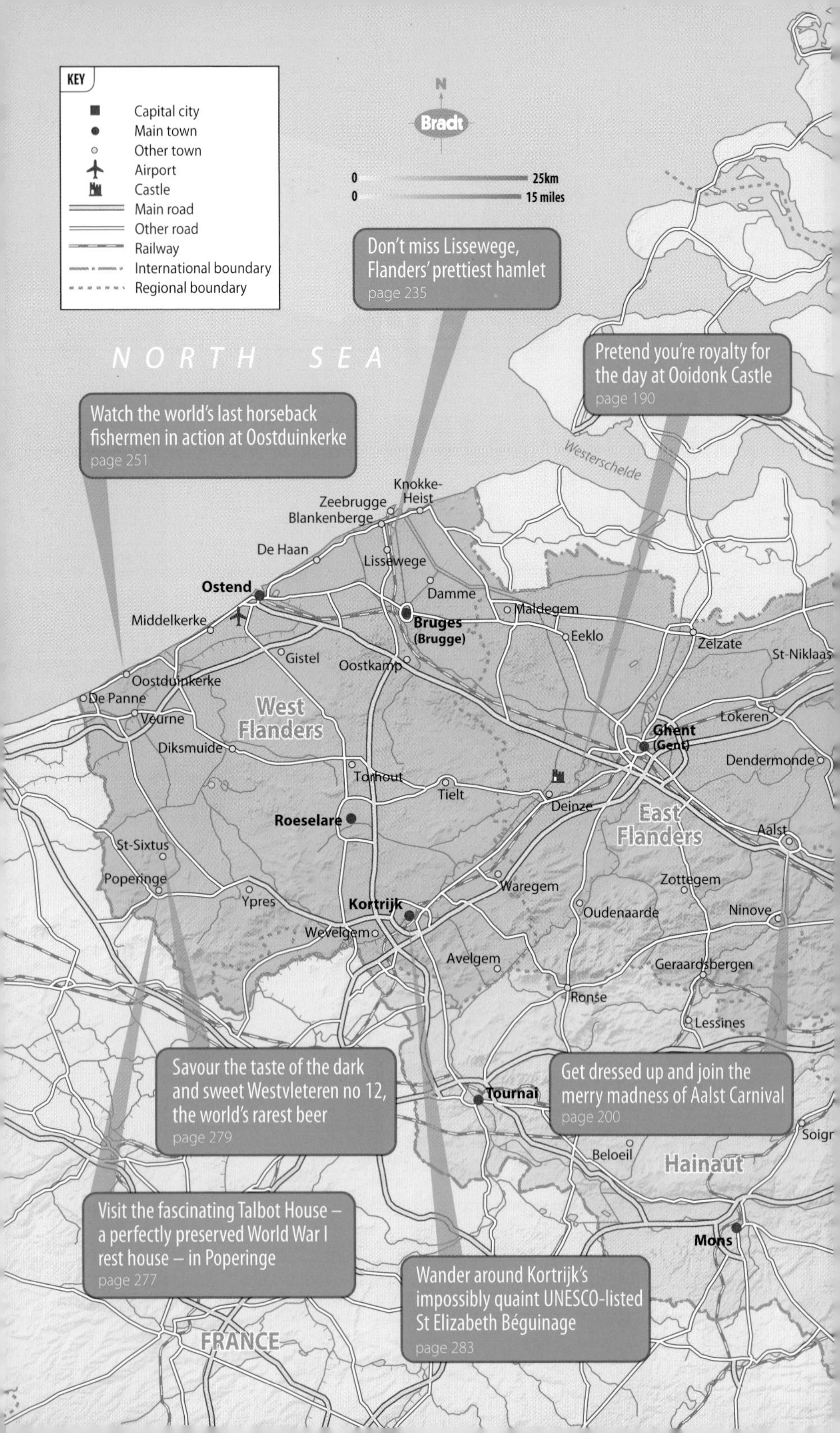
KEY
Capital city
Main town
Other town
Airport
Castle
Main road
Other road
Railway
International boundary
Regional boundary
N
Bradt
0 25km
0 15 miles
NORTH SEA
Don't miss Lissewege, Flanders' prettiest hamlet
page 235
Pretend you're royalty for the day at Ooidonk Castle
page 190
Watch the world's last horseback fishermen in action at Oostduinkerke
page 251
Westerschelde
Knokke-Heist
Zeebrugge
Blankenberge
De Haan
Lissewege
Ostend
Damme
Maldegem
Bruges (Brugge)
Middelkerke
Eeklo
Zelzate
St-Niklaas
Gistel
Oostkamp
Oostduinkerke
De Panne
Veurne
West Flanders
Ghent (Gent)
Lokeren
Diksmuide
Dendermonde
Torhout
Tielt
Deinze
East Flanders
Roeselare
Aalst
St-Sixtus
Poperinge
Ypres
Waregem
Zottegem
Kortrijk
Oudenaarde
Ninove
Wevelgem
Avelgem
Geraardsbergen
Ronse
Lessines
Savour the taste of the dark and sweet Westvleteren no 12, the world's rarest beer
page 279
Tournai
Get dressed up and join the merry madness of Aalst Carnival
page 200
Soign
Beloeil
Hainaut
Visit the fascinating Talbot House – a perfectly preserved World War I rest house – in Poperinge
page 277
Mons
Wander around Kortrijk's impossibly quaint UNESCO-listed St Elizabeth Béguinage
page 283
FRANCE

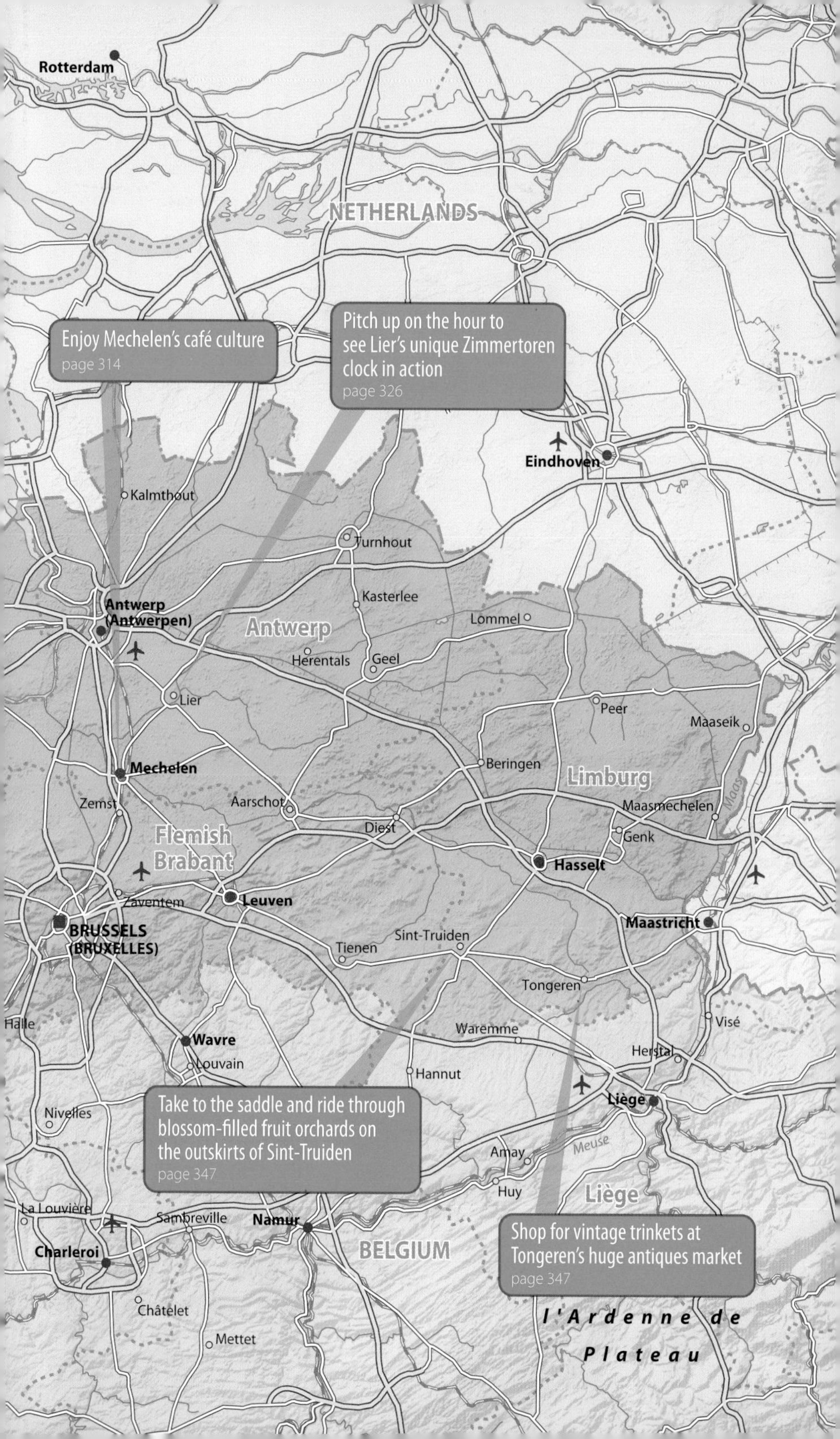
Enjoy Mechelen's café culture
page 314
Pitch up on the hour to see Lier's unique Zimmertoren clock in action
page 326
Take to the saddle and ride through blossom-filled fruit orchards on the outskirts of Sint-Truiden
page 347
Shop for vintage trinkets at Tongeren's huge antiques market
page 347
Rotterdam
NETHERLANDS
Eindhoven
Kalmthout
Turnhout
Kasterlee
Antwerp (Antwerpen)
Antwerp
Lommel
Herentals
Geel
Lier
Peer
Maaseik
Beringen
Mechelen
Limburg
Zemst
Aarschot
Maasmechelen
Maas
Diest
Genk
Flemish Brabant
Hasselt
Zaventem
Leuven
BRUSSELS (BRUXELLES)
Maastricht
Sint-Truiden
Tienen
Tongeren
Halle
Visé
Waremme
Wavre
Herstal
Louvain
Hannut
Liège
Nivelles
Meuse
Amay
Huy
Liège
La Louvière
Sambreville
Namur
Charleroi
BELGIUM
Châtelet
l'Ardenne de Plateau
Mettet

Northern Belgium Don't miss...

Medieval city centres
Marvel at the ancient architecture of medieval cloth towns, including Ghent's picture-perfect city centre
(BH/S) page 163

Sightseeing from the saddle
The whole region is criss-crossed with cycling paths, like this scenic landscape in Zottegem, East Flanders
(TD/S) page 59

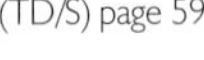

UNESCO-listed *begijnhofs*
Unique to Flanders and the Netherlands, these peaceful idylls are steeped in history (JDH/TB) page 19

Local festivals and traditions
Join the merry madness of a live concert or carnival, such as Dendermonde's decennial Ros Beiaard (W) page 196

World War I sites
The atrocities of World War I played out in Flanders' fields. Pay your respects at Lijssenthoek, Belgium's second-largest cemetery for Commonwealth forces (VF) page 279

Northern Belgium in colour

In summertime, Flanders puts on a technicolour show: take in the vivid guildhouses of celebrated Markt square, Bruges (*above* M303/S; page 211) and the stunning scenery of Brussels's Mont des Arts (*below* S-F/S; page 114)

right **Lier's hand-built Zimmertoren features 13 clocks, which tell you everything from the tides to the phases of the moon** (ET) page 326

below **The Manneken Pis, Belgium's most beloved icon, captures the country's surreal streak** (VF) page 101

bottom **Ghent's Gravensteen, or Castle of the Counts, has a fascinatingly horrible history** (TD/S) page 182

left A handful of the 54,896 soldiers' names inscribed on the Menin Gate, Ypres (ET) page 269

below left Fallen heroes: photos of soldiers who have passed through Talbot House, a World War I resthouse and B&B in Poperinge (ET) page 277

below right Rebuilt World War I trenches, Hill 62 (VS/S) page 272

AUTHOR

Emma Thomson is an award-winning travel writer and photographer, who lived in Belgium for a decade and writes about the country for international newspapers, magazines and publishers (print and online). The first edition of *Flanders: The Bradt Travel Guide* won Best Guidebook at the 2012 British Guild of Travel Writer Members' Awards. As a country specialist, Emma is consulted on everything ranging from where to find the best chips to booking the hippest hotels. She has also presented for the Belgian TV show *Fans of Flanders* and been interviewed by Peter Greenberg for Worldwide Radio aboard the Eurostar.

UPDATER

Clodagh Kinsella is a freelance travel and culture writer who contributes to international magazines and newspapers including the *Guardian*, *The Independent*, *BBC Travel* and *Condé Nast Traveler*. The editor-at-large of *Gogo City Guides*, she moved to Belgium seven years ago, and has been exploring the country's quirks and corners ever since, often reporting on obscure cultural events or famous Flemings for the national airline's on-board magazine. She currently lives in Antwerp, in a building named after Rubens's first wife.

PUBLISHER'S FOREWORD

Adrian Phillips, Publishing Director

There's much to be said for a place that produces some of the world's best beer and chocolate! But, believe it or not, Northern Belgium has even more to tempt you. Emma Thomson offers a genuine insider's view, having lived in a Flemish village with her sheep and chickens, and she's been able to take us to towns and villages that brim with traditional character and colour. Comprehensively updated by Clodagh Kinsella, this is an entertaining, informative and above all joyful book built on knowledge and love; we hope it inspires you to look beyond the typical cities on the tourist trail.

Second edition published October 2019
First published 2012 (previously entitled *Flanders: Northern Belgium*)
Bradt Travel Guides Ltd
31a High Street, Chesham, Buckinghamshire, HP5 1BW, England
www.bradtguides.com
Print edition published in the USA by The Globe Pequot Press Inc,
PO Box 480, Guilford, Connecticut 06437-0480

Project Manager: Heather Haynes
Cover research: Pepi Bluck, Perfect Picture

ISBN: 978 1 78477 088 4

British Library Cataloguing in Publication Data
A catalogue record for this book is available from the British Library

Photographs Alamy Stock Photos: Arterra Picture Library (APL/A); Getty Images: Westend61 (W61/G); Agnese Sanvito (AS); Shutterstock.com: Beketoff (B/S), Thomas Dekiere (TD/S), Botond Horvath (BH/S), littlewormy (l/S), Mapics (M/S), Martin M303 (M303/S), RIRF Stock (RIRF/S), S-F (S-F/S), Vaughan Sam (VS/S), sam100 (s100/S); Superstock (SS); Emma Thomson (ET); Toerisme Brugge (TB): Jan D'Hondt (JDH/TB); VISITFLANDERS (VF); Volksbunde Deutsche Kriegsgräberfürsorge (VDK); Wikipedia (W)
Front cover The old town of Bruges in the evening, featuring the Rozenhoedkaai, the canal and the belfry tower (W61/G)
Back cover Lindenmolen windmill in Diest, Flemish Brabant (s100/S); Benedictine nuns at the Princely Béguinage Ten Wijngaarde, Bruges (VF)
Title page Flower-lined canal, Ghent historic centre (M/S); Coloured cuberdon sweets, Ghent (VF); Hallerbos bluebell forest in Halle, Flemish Brabant (RIRF/S)
Text photos page 60: Cycling sign (ET); page 273: Aerial photographs of Passchendaele (W); page 275: German soldiers of 238 Reserve Infantry Regiment (VDK)

Maps David McCutcheon FBCart.S; colour relief base by Nick Rowland FRGS

Typeset by D & N Publishing, Baydon, Wiltshire; Ian Spick, Bradt Travel Guides Ltd; www.dataworks.co.in
Production managed by Jellyfish Print Solutions; printed in India
Digital conversion by www.dataworks.co.in

Acknowledgements

EMMA THOMSON Thanks to Hilary Bradt and Adrian Phillips for commissioning the guide and my original project-managing team: Tricia Hayne, Sally Brock, David McCutcheon, Fiona Dale, Greg Dickinson, Anna Moores and Tim Webb.

An enormous *dank u wel* to Anita Rampall at Visit Flanders and the fantastic press people at the individual tourist boards at the time, especially Nathalie De Neve and Freya Sackx (Visit Ghent), Igor Daems (Visit Antwerp), Pierre Massart (Visit Brussels), Florie Wilberts (Mechelen Tourism), Nancy Brouwers (Leuven Tourism), Petra Delvaux (Ypres Tourism), Isabelle D'Hondt (Ostend Tourism) and Anne De Meerleer (Bruges Tourism).

To the characters I met along the way, including Mark Bode and the monks of Sint-Sixtus Abbey, Elizabeth Evans, Evgenia Paparouni, Deken Roger van Bockstaele, Trees Coene and Genevra Charsley.

Thanks and love to my Flemish family and friends for all their support, especially Aunt Louise for sharing her wartime stories. But above all to Bart Wijnant – for everything.

CLODAGH KINSELLA I'd like to thank Kim Bonduelle and Jochen Van Rooy (SNCB) and the incredibly enthusiastic, professional and patient tourist board representatives, notably: Ellen Hubert (Visit Antwerp), Ann Plovie (Visit Bruges), Pierre Massart (Visit Brussels), Veerle Lenaerts (Visit Mechelen), Annik Altruy (Visit Leuven), Lynn Meyvaert (Visit Ghent), Fernand Vanrobaeys (Visit Ypres) and Steven De Backer (Tourism East-Flanders). Thanks also to Raïsa Qvick (Westtoer) and Ronny Luyckx (Visit Limburg) for driving this non-driver around their respective regions – *and* on their days off too.

DEDICATION

For Bart – forever my heart and home.

Contents

LIST OF MAPS

AUTHOR'S STORY

Like all good stories, mine starts in a bar. Not a Flemish one, mind you, but the slightly more prosaic setting of Watford, north London. I was working as a cocktail bartender and one day in walked our new boss: a Flemish fellow called Bart – and that, as they say, was that. Within a month I was standing in Brussels's Grand-Place gawking at the gold-fringed guildhouses winking in the sun – a convert.

That was 16 years ago and, in truth, I've been researching this guide ever since: jotting down a great restaurant or some nook-and-cranny bar on each successive trip. Researching this guide proper, then, was a treat because it allowed me to delve deeper than ever before. However, it also made me nervous. From the get-go I was acutely aware of the stereotypes equated with 'boring' Belgium and her northern Flanders region. My former Bradt colleagues were quick with the quips: 'Flanders? I think I've driven through it on the way to Germany' or 'Quick, quick … name five famous Flemings!' I feared it would be an uphill struggle to convince everyone to the contrary. But I want to state it loudly here: Flanders is nothing like the clichés. She remains quirky in some quarters but achingly hip in others. In fact, her curious blend of character has won the hearts – and pens – of many a heavyweight travel writer.

So, no cajoling required: Flanders surprises at every turn. Its main cities are epicentres of culture and you could easily spend all your time visiting just these. But where possible, take the time to explore the outer towns and villages away from the regular tourist trail – they give an excellent insight into real Flemish life and its driving values. Throughout the guide I've applied Bradt's off-the-beaten-track ethos, steering clear of chain hotels and bland eateries and instead focusing on places that are classic, enchanting or quirky in character. So consider this guide a key, if you will, with which to unlock and ease open the yeasty tavern door and join the merry madness inside. My hope is that the guide will make a 'flanderophile' of you before you can finish your first beer.

FEEDBACK REQUEST AND UPDATES WEBSITE

At Bradt Travel Guides we're aware that guidebooks start to go out of date on the day they're published – and that you, our readers, are out there in the field doing research of your own. You'll find out before us when a fine new family-run hotel opens or a favourite restaurant changes hands and goes downhill. So why not write and tell us about your experiences? Contact us at **e** info@bradtguides.com. We will forward emails to the author who may post updates on the Bradt website at **w** bradtupdates.com/northernbelgium. Alternatively, you can add a review of the book to **w** bradtguides.com or Amazon.

Introduction

The Flemish have a saying: 'you can't sell the skin off a bear before it's shot.' Visitors would do well to abide by this when considering the merits of visiting Flanders. For too long Belgium's northern region has been sold out as 'dull,' 'small-minded' and 'characterless.' Flanders is anything but. It may lack the pomp and pride of French regions, or the self-assuredness of German states, but Flanders has a good thing going and doesn't feel the need to boast.

Invaded, occupied and ransacked, it has been the site of numerous battles between successive foreign powers over the centuries, but it is no longer just a stepping stone between France and Germany. The tables have turned. Brussels is home to NATO headquarters and the European Union and frequently hailed as Europe's business capital, while towns such as Antwerp and Zeebrugge are pulling in the heavyweights of European industry. This influx of wealth has propelled the region forward and progress is everywhere. But these achievements fail to capture what draws her fans back to her cobbled streets and cosy cafés time and time again. Flanders' appeal lies in its ability to satisfy life's fundamental desires: thirsts are quenched (or drenched?) with the choice of over 800 beers, hungry tummies are filled with home-cooked food, and bodies tired from wandering can sink into the four-postered comfort of a welcoming bed and breakfast. Take the time to experience the heavy, warm whiff of the yeast-filled air in the brasseries; to taste the custard-filled creations of the patisseries, and feast upon the works of world-renowned artists and cartoonists.

Recent reappraisals have redefined Flanders; what was once criticised as fuddy-duddy is now considered hip. Its refreshing mix of cosmopolitan towns and rural villages allows you to spend one day enjoying galleries, theatre, dinners and dancing 'til dawn amid Art Nouveau districts and medieval town squares, and the next visiting rural communities where life slips back a gear.

But why a guide to Flanders, not Belgium? Well, while the whole country is worth exploration, Flanders has its own unique character which sets it apart from the south. The region is small, but it's brimming with such a wealth of things to do that it warrants individual attention. This is, of course, thanks to the grit and good humour of its citizens who have influenced world culture in more ways than common opinion allows for. Few know that Hollywood starlet Audrey Hepburn hails from Brussels; that the Big Bang theory was actually devised by Leuven professor and priest Georges Lemaître in 1927; and that Flanders hosted the first European Gull Screeching Championship and is home to Walter Arfeuille, a man who can pull eight railway coaches with his teeth. Such quirks set Flanders apart from its neighbours and place it in a league of its own. She is not a perfect place, but one you quickly learn to love because of her eccentricities, not in spite of them.

Having visited Flanders countless times now, I've learned to stop shooting bears. Every trip offers up something new. Prepare to develop a life-long devotion.

HOW TO USE THIS GUIDE

AUTHOR'S FAVOURITES Finding genuinely characterful accommodation or that unmissable off-the-beaten-track café can be difficult, so the author has chosen a few of her favourite places throughout the country to point you in the right direction. These 'author's favourites' are marked with a ✷.

PRICE CODES Throughout this guide we have used price codes to indicate the cost of those places to stay and eat listed in the guide. For a key to these price codes, see page 44 for accommodation and page 45 for restaurants.

BIKE RENTAL Information about renting bikes can be found under the *Tourist information* sections within each chapter.

MAPS

Keys and symbols Maps include alphabetical keys covering the locations of those places to stay, eat or drink that are featured in the book. Note that regional maps may not show all hotels and restaurants in the area: other establishments may be located in towns shown on the map.

Grids and grid references Several maps use gridlines to allow easy location of sites. Map grid references are listed in square brackets after the name of the place or site of interest in the text, with page number followed by grid number, eg: [84 C3].

FOLLOW BRADT

For the latest news, special offers and competitions, subscribe to the Bradt newsletter via the website **w** bradtguides.com and follow Bradt on:

- BradtTravelGuides
- @BradtGuides
- @bradtguides
- bradtguides
- bradtguides

Part One

GENERAL INFORMATION

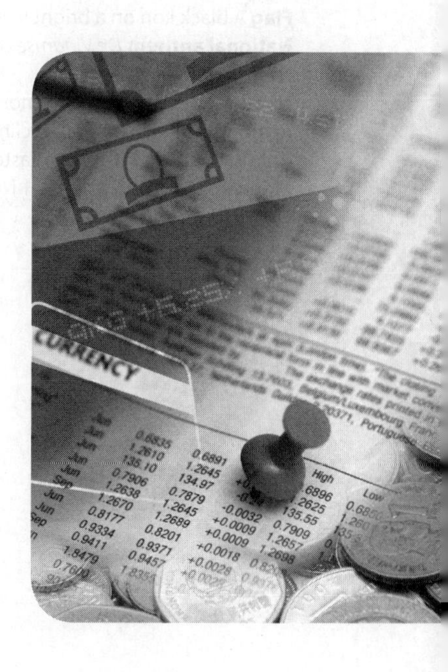

NORTHERN BELGIUM AT A GLANCE

Location Northern Belgium, western Europe
Neighbouring countries France, Germany, Luxembourg, Netherlands
Size/area 13,522km^2
Climate Temperate (mild winters, cool summers)
Status Federal parliamentary democracy under a constitutional monarchy
Population 6.6 million
Life expectancy Men: 80; women: 84.3
Capital Brussels (2.1 million)
Other main towns Bruges, Ghent, Antwerp
Economy Exports: chemicals, minerals, transport equipment, plastic, pharmaceuticals
GDP per capita €38,288
Languages Flanders: Dutch; Brussels: officially bilingual (Dutch & French) but over 60% of residents speak French as their native language
Religion Christian 60% (50% Roman Catholic, 10% Protestant), 5% Islam
Currency Euro (€)
Exchange rate £1=€1.10; US$1=€0.88 (July 2019)
National airline/airport Brussels Airlines/Brussels Airport Zaventem
International telephone code +32
Time GMT+1
Electrical voltage 230v AC/50Hz
Weights and measures Metric
Flag A black lion on a bright yellow background
National anthem *De Vlaamse Leeuw* ('The Flemish Lion')
National flower Red poppy
National bird/animal Common kestrel
National sports Football, cycling, tennis
Public holidays 1 January, Easter Monday, 1 May, Ascension Day, Whit Monday, 21 July, 15 August, 1 November, 11 November, 25 December

1

Background Information

GEOGRAPHY

Flanders – or Northern Belgium – sits at the heart of western Europe, shares its northern border with the Netherlands and has a 67km coastline lapped by the North Sea. You can drive from east to west in 2 hours and 30 minutes, and north to south in an hour. Flanders surrounds Brussels, which is its own independent region.

The landscape is characterised by pancake-flat coastal plains that convert to marshy areas, or polders, as you move inland. These areas sit below sea level and are drained by canals. East Flanders' southern fringes boast an area of gently rolling hills, nicknamed the Flemish Ardennes, which backs on to the fertile farming grounds of Pajottenland in the Flemish Brabant region. In the northeast is the Kempen, studded with pine forests and moorland and the site of Hoge Kempen, Flanders' only national park.

Water is a huge part of Flanders' make-up. The region is crisscrossed with rivers, providing watery highways for early traders. The largest of these is the Scheldt, which arrives in Flanders just south of Oudenaarde, detours via Ghent and rumbles out to sea at Antwerp.

CLIMATE

Notorious for its four-seasons-in-one-day climate, Flanders lies on the same latitude as the south of England and experiences similar weather patterns – it is the luck of the draw as to whether it will be a summer of heatwaves, or one of endless rain, though the latter has tended to dominate of late (just don't say global warming). From spring (Mar–May) to autumn (Sep–Nov) you can expect temperatures to fluctuate between 14°C and 6°C and cool, sunny days to be intermingled with overcast, drizzly days. During summer, temperatures hover around the 20°C mark, but in winter (Dec–Feb), when the Baltic breezes come whistling down uninterrupted from the North Pole, temperatures plummet, rarely rising above 6°C and occasionally dropping to –5°C. However, even the darkest days have their splendour, and there's something rather romantic about dashing from café to café across soaked but sparkling cobblestone streets.

TEMPERATURE TABLE FOR BRUSSELS

	Jan	Feb	Mar	Apr	May	Jun	Jul	Aug	Sep	Oct	Nov	Dec
Max°C	4	7	10	14	18	22	23	22	21	15	9	6
Min°C	–1	0	2	5	8	11	12	12	11	7	3	0

As a guide, July tends to be the hottest month, January the coolest, November the wettest and February the driest. During summer, the sun rises between 05.00 and 06.00 and doesn't set until 22.00. During winter, the days shorten considerably – sunrise is between 07.00 and 08.00 and sunset between 16.00 and 17.00.

NATURAL HISTORY

Until 1989 there was no environmental planning in Flanders. Large swathes of the countryside were intensively farmed, leaving only pockets of protected areas, like Het Zwin (page 238), the Westhoek dunes (page 254) and Hoge Kempen National Park (page 344). You'll see lots of cows, horses, sheep – even the odd farmed llama – but sightings of wild mammals are rare. However, NGOs such as Natuurpunt have striven to raise awareness and implement conservation programmes and it seems to be working. After a long absence, foxes and wild cats are making a comeback across the region; in 2018, a wolf was spotted in Flanders for the first time in a century, reflecting a wider mainland European trend.

Throughout West Flanders and Brussels there are populations of red squirrel, hedgehog and dwarf bat and even a colony of Siberian chipmunks in the Forêt de Soignes, south of the capital. The waterways of Flanders are home to a thriving population of beavers – one briefly became a tourist attraction in Leuven – and Limburg has healthy populations of badger and the hazel dormouse.

Many birds use the country as a rest stop during their annual migration. One of the best places to see them is the Het Zwin wetlands and marshes on the coast east of Knokke-Heist. Seabirds include the Mediterranean, Icelandic and great black-backed gulls, curlew, sandpiper, grey heron, storks and the rarely seen shoveller.

Coastal dunes support much of the plant life found in Flanders – the Westhoek Nature Reserve just past De Panne is the only area on the coast where nearly all dune vegetation appears before your eyes in one unbroken landscape. The main concentration of woodland is in the pine forests of Hoge Kempen National Park, whose mix of forest and moorland is home to deer, snakes, frogs, toads and goshawks.

HISTORY

The history of Flanders is the history of Belgium, and as far as countries go Belgium is comparatively new. Up until 1830, when it gained its independence, the country was lumped together with Luxembourg and the Netherlands. Collectively they formed the Low Countries and suffered as the pawns of successive foreign powers. These powers played tug of war over boundaries and carved up the land to form the borders that define the countries today.

ANTIQUITY In 500BC three tribal groups covered the area: the southern-dwelling Celtic Belgae, the coastal-dwelling Germanic Frisians and the Batavians who settled in the southern Netherlands. It was these tribes that Roman General **Julius Caesar** (100–44BC) encountered during his invasion of Gaul (western Europe) in 58BC. He fought and defeated only the Celtic tribes and incorporated their land as a province of Rome under the name Gallia Belgica, including towns like Tongeren (*Aduatuca Tungrorum*). The area, which comprised much of present-day Flanders and the Netherlands, was granted to the Germanic Franks – a group of Germanic tribes under forced conscription by the Romans. When the Roman Empire began to lose its grip in the north in AD500, the Franks took over, spawning the Merovingian dynasty. The long-haired kings' lazy attitude towards ruling cost them dearly and they were quickly succeeded by the Carolingians, once mayors of the Merovingian palaces, who rose to assume power. The dynasty was named after its greatest leader Carolus Magnus, better known as **Charlemagne** or 'Charles the Great' (AD742–814), who was crowned Holy Roman Emperor in AD800. When his son, Louis the Pious, died unexpectedly, inheritance laws decreed that his lands be divided between Charlemagne's three grandsons. Three years of civil war ensued until the **Treaty of Verdun** was drawn up in AD843, which carved the emperor's portion of the territory into the early divisions of France, the Low Countries and Germany, and Italy. As a result of the treaty, Flanders remained part of the Germanic Frankish lands and the remainder of the Low Countries belonged to the Roman Empire. It is at this point that the basis of Belgium's current language divide was formed. Throughout the Middle Ages, the northern part of Belgium became increasingly Germanic in parlance, while the south, overseen by the Romans, was exposed to Latin dialects.

ROMANESQUE PERIOD As the threat from raiding Vikings increased, local lords and counts capitalised on the fragile authority exercised by the French kings and German emperors, and assumed control of the towns in which they lived, forming feudal states that closely resemble today's regional divisions, including the County of Flanders, the Duchy of Brabant and the Duchy of Limburg. Opportunistic characters, such as **Baldwin the Iron Arm** – who took control of Flanders by kidnapping and marrying the French king's daughter and then blackmailing him with the threat of a Norman alliance – consolidated their powers and gained autonomy often through strength of purse, not arms.

The end of the Romanesque period saw the decline of feudalism and the rise of economic prosperity, particularly in towns like Bruges, Ghent and Ypres, which not only increased their trade of Flemish cloth with merchants from Spain, Venice and Genoa, but also benefited from the newly established **Hanseatic League**. This alliance of trading guilds created a monopoly across the Baltic Sea and improved commerce with Russia, Bulgaria and England.

The influx of wealth drew a dividing line between the local counts and the merchants and craftsmen who had gained a stronger economic foothold by uniting to form guilds. Friction arose when the guilds, in an attempt to maintain the delivery of vital raw materials from England, began to resist centralist French policies and side with the English in conflicts between the two countries. In one

JACOB VAN ARTEVELDE (1290–1345)

Known affectionately as the 'Brewer of Ghent', Artevelde hailed from a wealthy weaving family and rose to fame during the Hundred Years War. When feuds between England and France began to affect the wool trade, Artevelde appealed to the English King Edward III to maintain regular shipments of raw materials, on the basis that the allied cloth towns of Bruges, Ypres and Ghent were neutral. His act of defiance angered the Count of Flanders and the French King Phillip IV, but unexpectedly their efforts to restrain him failed and the Count was forced to sign a treaty recognising the partnership. As a result, the textile towns flourished. However, his friendship with Edward III provoked jealousy among his peers, and when rumours surfaced that he planned to replace the existing Count of Flanders with Edward III's son, riots broke out. During the uprising, Artevelde fell into the crowd and was murdered by an angry mob. A statue of him stands on Ghent's Vrijdagmarkt.

particular incident, the French King, **Philip IV 'the Fair'** (1268–1314), forcibly removed the Count of Flanders, Guy of Dampierre, and exiled the citizens of Bruges in an attempt to suppress the uprisings. However, on the morning of 18 May 1302, the residents returned to the city and murdered as many Frenchmen as they could find in a retaliation recorded as the **Brugse Metten** (page 214). Two months later, near Kortrijk, Philip IV launched his offensive against an army of furious Flemings and lost in the **Battle of the Golden Spurs** – so-called for the 600 golden spurs collected from the French knights killed in battle. The defeat marked a significant development in Flemish political independence and is considered by many as the key to why Dutch is still spoken in Flanders today.

GOLDEN AGE OF THE BURGUNDIANS Amid the sporadic struggles of the **Hundred Years War** (1337–1453) – in which England and France respectively tried to pursue and retain the French throne – the stalemate between regional lords and French or German rulers was broken with the arrival in 1419 of **Philip the Good** (1396–1467). The first Duke of Burgundy, he inherited lands from the recently deceased Count of Flanders and in quick succession expanded these territories which spread from the modern-day Netherlands through Belgium into Germany. During his reign, the work of the Flemish Primitives, like Jan van Eyck and Rogier van der Weyden, flourished, and the breathtaking Grand-Place in Brussels was constructed.

Philip's son, **Charles the Bold** (1433–77), was considered the last 'great duke', but his reign was cut short when he was struck in the head by a spear at the Battle of Nancy on 5 January 1477. At the age of 20 his daughter and heir, **Mary of Burgundy** (1457–82), was thrust into the political limelight and forced by the French king to sign the 'Great Privilege' charter. This restored civic rights to Flanders, Brabant etc, effectively undoing her grandfather's attempts to create a centralised state.

THE HABSBURGS As the only heiress of the rich Burgundian Empire, Mary was not short of marriage proposals, but after much deliberation she chose the Habsburg **Maximilian of Austria** (1459–1519). For a time tensions with the French eased, but these were quickly revived when, after five short years of marriage, Mary fell from her horse and died, leaving Maximilian in charge. After countless struggles, the Duke finally squashed French rule of Burgundy and added the lands to the growing Habsburg Empire. Maximilian's first son, **Philip the Handsome** (1478–1506), died of typhoid fever before he could inherit the throne, which passed to Philip's second child, **Charles V** (1500–58). Born in Ghent, Charles was a linguist, lover of ladies and nephew of Catherine of Aragon, Henry VIII's first wife. As a ruler, he united the 17 provinces governed by the Habsburg and Burgundian families and the Spanish Castilian and Aragonese crowns. He was only six when his father died, so for a period of nine years his aunt, **Margaret of Austria** (1480–1530), controlled his empire. In 1519 Charles took over; aged 20 he was the most powerful ruler in Europe and his empire was enormous. He ruled Spain and her New World territories, Germany, Austria, Sardinia, Sicily, Belgium and the Netherlands, and spent much of his life travelling between his lands, defending them against the expansionist French.

Residents were outraged at the high taxes used to fund the wars fought by their absent king, and the burghers rebelled. They were quickly suppressed, but realising the revolts would continue, Charles tactfully granted autonomy to the 17 provinces of the Netherlands. In 1553, an exhausted Charles returned to the Netherlands. Two years later he relinquished his titles and divided the realm by leaving the Spanish throne and rule of the Netherlands to his son **Philip II** (1527–98) and the crown of the Holy Roman Empire to his younger brother **Ferdinand I** (1503–64).

THE REVOLT OF THE NETHERLANDS Born in northern Spain, Philip II had spent barely four years in the Low Countries and lacked the emotional attachment his father had formed to the land. When his father died, Philip left his second wife – the Catholic Mary Tudor, Henry VIII's eldest daughter and Queen of England – and returned to Spain, deciding to rule the Low Countries from a distance. Disgusted by the rise of Protestantism in the territories, Philip employed the Spanish Inquisition to crush heretics and quickly passed his responsibilities on to his sister **Margaret of Parma**, Charles V's illegitimate daughter. For eight years she ruled from Brussels with the assistance of Cardinal Granvelle, struggling to calm the storm of religious discontent.

Meanwhile, **William of Orange-Nassau** – loyal subject of Charles V – found himself siding with the opposition. Despite being a Catholic, he believed in religious tolerance and was outraged at Philip's persecution of Protestants. In response, he joined other Protestant-sympathetic nobles and formed the **Confederacy of Noblemen**. Together, in April 1565, they submitted a petition that called upon Margaret to moderate the King's anti-Protestant policies. Their appeal was dismissed, and they resorted to violence. Churches throughout the Low Countries were vandalised, their reliquaries, shrines and stained-glass windows smashed in riots labelled the **Iconoclastic Fury**.

In an attempt to quash the religious uprising, Philip dispatched his general, the **Duke of Alba**, along with 10,000 soldiers. Assisted by the Inquisition, General Alba established the **Council of Troubles** (commonly known as the 'Council of Blood' for the thousands it tried and sentenced to death) to try those who had taken part in the Fury. Among those summoned before the council were William and his cohorts, the Counts of Hoorn and Egmont. The counts were tried, condemned and executed on Brussels's Grand-Place, but William failed to appear, so Philip declared him an outlaw, seized all his property and put a price of 25,000 crowns on his head.

With nothing to lose, William embarked upon a series of attacks along the river Meuse. Having gained a foothold in the Low Countries, he finally entered Brussels, victorious, in 1576. The **Pacification of Ghent**, an agreement assuring religious freedom for all, was signed, but Catholics in the south were less than keen to unite with William and the squabbles continued. Philip II capitalised on the fragmentation and sent Margaret's son, **Alexander Farnese**, to provoke discord between the Protestants and Catholics. Renowned for his cunning and powers of persuasion, Farnese convinced the southern territories to sign the **Treaty of Arras** on 6 January 1579, which promised to remove garrisons of foreign troops from the towns, in return for sworn allegiance to Philip II and the Catholic faith. Barely three weeks later, in an effort to counterbalance this treaty, seven of the northern provinces met to sign the **Union of Utrecht**. The alliance formed the United Provinces, which refused to acknowledge Spanish rule; instead they appointed William as their first *stadhouder*, or governor. These divided territories became known as the Spanish Netherlands and the United Provinces. William enjoyed a short term in office, before he was assassinated in July 1584.

SPANISH RULE (1579–1713) When Philip II died in 1598, **Philip III** (1578–1621) inherited his father's Spanish throne while his favourite daughter **Infanta Isabella** (1566–1633) and her husband **Albert Archduke of Austria** assumed control of the Spanish Netherlands. Under their rule, the area enjoyed a much-needed period of peace and prosperity. The arrival of silk-weaving, lace-making and diamond-processing revived the land's economic wealth and the arts received royal patronage.

Conscious of her father's anti-Protestant policies, Isabella attempted to wage war against the Protestant north, but with little success – so, in 1609, she agreed to a ceasefire in the **Twelve Years Truce**. The agreement temporarily granted the United Provinces their independence and over 100,000 Protestants and anti-Spanish thinkers fled north.

When **Philip IV** (1605–65) became king at the age of 16 he revived the wars against the Protestants. He suffered a series of defeats that lost him lands in the southern part of the Netherlands and compelled him to sign the **Peace of Westphalia** (also known as the Treaty of Münster) in 1648. The treaty ended the **Thirty Years War** and formally acknowledged the independence of the United Provinces.

However, French King **Louis XIV** (1638–1715) was still intent on adding the Spanish Netherlands to his territories and embarked on a number of sieges, the worst of which, in August 1695, left Brussels's city centre, including the Grand-Place, in ruins. Events continued to go well for Louis when **Charles II** (1661–1700) – the last of the Spanish Habsburgs – died, leaving no heir. The crown passed to **Philip, Duke of Anjou** (1683–1746), who also happened to be Louis XIV's grandson. The United Provinces, England, Sweden and Austria among other states knew it was only a matter of time before Louis pressured his grandson into handing the Spanish Netherlands over to France. Fearful of French domination, the countries formed an alliance and drove French troops out of the Netherlands in the **War of Spanish Succession** (1701–13). Utterly defeated, France signed the **Treaty of Utrecht** in 1713, which allowed the Duke of Anjou to keep his Spanish crown, but entrusted the rule of the Spanish Netherlands and the Holy Roman Empire to **Charles VI** (1685–1740), who belonged to the Austrian Habsburgs.

AUSTRIAN RULE (1713–94) Unfortunately, Charles VI produced no male heir either. Well aware of the inherent problems the accession of his eldest daughter **Maria Theresa** (1717–80) would cause, he announced in 1713 a pragmatic sanction that encouraged the major powers to agree to her ruling. Upon his death, however, the sanction was ignored and several contestants came forward disputing Maria's right to the throne. The disputes escalated into the **War of the Austrian Succession**, which involved most of Europe and the Spanish colonies. The distraction left the country open to invasion and France naturally obliged, managing to occupy much of the Netherlands by 1744. However, after eight years of conflict, Britain (Austria's ally) finally convinced France to sign the **Treaty of Aix-la-Chapelle**, which restored the Austrian Netherlands to Maria Theresa.

During the war, Maria had made her only sister, Maria Anna, and brother-in-law, Charles Alexander of Lorraine (1712–80), governors of the Austrian Netherlands, which went on to enjoy a period of economic prosperity. When Charles and Maria Theresa both died in 1780, her son, **Joseph II** (1741–90), assumed full control of the Empire. Unlike his Roman Catholic mother, Joseph had been heavily influenced by the Age of Enlightenment sweeping through Europe and he quickly embarked on a prolific programme of reforms. He overhauled the education and public health systems, issued the **Patent of Toleration** in 1781 that granted Protestants freedom of worship, and moved the government from Brussels to Vienna, declaring German the official language. Although many of his reforms were of benefit to the neglected poor, his radical moves created uneasiness and two groups of opposition emerged: the Catholic conservatives led by **Henri van der Noot**, who opposed Enlightenment and longed to return to an absolute government; and a second group, led by **Jean Vonck**, who opposed the idea of a single monarch and wished to expel the Habsburgs in favour of a liberal state. Joseph attempted to quell the unrest but, unexpectedly, the parties united to defeat the Austrian army near Antwerp in a retaliation known as the **Brabant Revolution**. Riding high on their success, the parties were quick to form their own congress, with van der Noot at its head, and to declare the formation of the independent United States of Belgium. When Joseph died in 1790, his brother **Leopold II** (1747–92) wasted no time in dispatching troops to disband the Revolution and crush the fledgling attempts at Belgian nationhood; within a year the country had been pulled back into the Empire.

FRENCH RULE (1794–1830) Leopold's reign was cut short when France declared war against Austria and Prussia. Despite Leopold's best efforts, Austria was absorbed into French territories in 1794. The Habsburg dynasty had fallen and for a time it seemed Belgium was without a ruler. But by 1795, Belgium and the Netherlands had been overpowered by the French and renamed the Batavian Republic. When Napoleon Bonaparte assumed power in 1799, he brought many improvements to the area; he rebuilt damaged docks and forced the Netherlands to relinquish control of the Scheldt, thereby opening up trade again. Furthermore, France's dependency on Belgian imports boosted the economy, breathing new life into the textile industries.

Despite the financial benefits, the populace were indignant with the French occupation and when conscription was introduced in 1797, to support Napoleon's campaigns abroad, numerous (unsuccessful) revolts were launched. Soon enough, the **Holy Alliance**, a peace-keeping coalition, was formed between Russia, Austria, Prussia and eventually England. Together, in June 1815, they met and defeated Napoleon on the battlefield at **Waterloo**. The Batavian Republic was dissolved and Belgians celebrated their apparent freedom.

THE UNITED KINGDOM OF THE NETHERLANDS (1815–31) Their celebrations were short-lived. No sooner had they removed one ruler than they were saddled with another. After Napoleon's defeat at Waterloo, the **Congress of Vienna** (1814–15) met to redraw the political boundaries of the continent. It was decided that the old United Provinces should be joined with the Spanish/Austrian Netherlands to create the United Kingdom of the Netherlands and ruled by **Frederick William of Orange (William I)** (1771–1843). Patience and tolerance among the Belgians was wearing thin and William lacked tact. His decisions to make Dutch the official language, secularise church-controlled schools and refuse fair representation in parliament to the dominant south left the populace furious.

INDEPENDENCE (1830–1900) Frustrations came to a head on the evening of 25 August 1830, during a performance of French composer Daniel Auber's new opera *La Muette de Portici*. The story is one of revolution against the Spanish in 1647 and it was not long before the Belgians saw the parallels with their own situation. Imbued with nationalist vigour, citizens rushed from the Théâtre de la Monnaie into the streets of Brussels and raised the flag of Brabant over the Hôtel de Ville in the Grand-Place. Uprisings like this spread in waves throughout the country and William quickly sent in the army to quash the rebels. He was successful in Hasselt and Leuven, but when Dutch troops arrived in Brussels on 23 September, four days of street fighting ensued. After bloody brawls the Dutch were finally surrounded by the nationalists and forced to make a quick retreat. The provisional government wasted no time in declaring independence on 4 October 1830. With William poised for war, the provisional government appealed to other European powers to recognise the independent Kingdom of Belgium. Great Britain and France acquiesced and at the **London Conference** in 1831 the country's independence was recognised for the first time, on the proviso that Belgium remain a neutral state and not enter into any alliances with surrounding powers.

The government then had to find a suitable king to rule their constitutional monarchy. They offered the throne to the German Prince **Leopold of Saxe-Coburg** (1790–1865), uncle and advisor to Britain's Queen Victoria. He was sworn in as King Leopold I of the Belgians on 21 July 1831. Two weeks later, a disgruntled William invaded, but Leopold managed to keep his troops at bay. These skirmishes lasted for eight years until William finally gave up in 1839 and signed a treaty acknowledging Belgium's independence.

Leopold I immediately set about regenerating the economic strength of his new country. The Société Générale bank (now BNP Paribas Fortis) was revived and financed work on roads, canals and mainland Europe's first public railway line, between Brussels and Mechelen. These improved transport links created enormous industrial growth.

When **Leopold II** (1835–1909) succeeded his father in 1865, he continued his programme of national development. Antwerp became an international port and railroad companies were contracted to build lines throughout Europe and in China and South America. In Brussels the proceeds financed the filling-in of the river Senne to clean up the surrounding slums, the construction of the vast Palais de Justice and Musées Royaux des Beaux-Arts de Belgique, and – for the 50th anniversary of Belgium's independence – the imposing Parc du Cinquantenaire.

However, Leopold was still not satisfied. He wanted Belgium to stand tall among other European nations, but was hindered by a government that controlled the treasury's purse strings. Frustrated with their lack of vision, he began to look elsewhere for alternative means of finance. The 'Scramble for Africa' was looming, and Leopold joined the race for the unconquered jungles of the Dark Continent.

THE HEART OF DARKNESS

> They grabbed what they could get for the sake of what was to be got. It was just robbery with violence, aggravated murder on a great scale, and men going blind at it – as is very proper for those who tackle a darkness. The conquest of the earth, which mostly means taking it away from those who have a different complexion or slightly flatter noses than ourselves, is not a pretty thing when you look into it too much.
>
> *Heart of Darkness*, Joseph Conrad

Leopold was cunning, secretive and hell-bent on his pursuit of an African colony, laying meticulous plans towards its attainment. On 12 September 1876 he hosted a conference in Brussels to persuade prominent European explorers and geographers to back the foundation of the **Association Internationale Africaine** (AIA). Its aim? To suppress the slave trade, civilise the natives and create bases from which to chart and explore the continent. Leopold assured the assembly that 'Belgium may be a small country, but she is happy and contented with her lot; I have no other ambition than to serve her well.' Neal Ascherson, author of *The King Incorporated*, writes that the aims he outlined at the conference were merely 'a smokescreen to confuse stronger nations while he laid the foundations of a colony'. Leopold was elected as the first AIA chairman and once the meeting was adjourned he wasted no time in sourcing an explorer who could found potential 'bases' for the Belgian committee of the AIA to work from.

The Welsh-born journalist and explorer **Henry Morton Stanley** (1841–1904) was by this time at the height of his fame; he had just returned from an expedition to Africa to locate the missing Scottish missionary Dr Livingstone. Known among the Congolese as *Bula Matari*, 'Breaker of Rocks', Stanley favoured firearms when it came to making 'agreements' with local tribes. Leopold was impressed and invited

Stanley to Brussels. Stanley initially declined but returned six months later and agreed to Leopold's plan.

After a while the AIA was forgotten; other nations had now also realised that the economic benefits of colonial ventures outweighed the philanthropic opportunities and the association soon fractured and dissipated. Leopold then created the **Association Internationale du Congo** (AIC). Stanley, along with the rest of the world, remained unaware of the change. The similarity in name to the AIA was no coincidence; Leopold deliberately blurred the lines between the two organisations until it was assumed that the AIC was a remodelled version of the AIA. Leopold was now in personal control of the AIC, and financed the entire venture from his own pocket.

By 1884, Stanley had acquired an enormous chunk of central Africa through bribery and brute force and Leopold renamed it the **Congo Free State**. However, Leopold still faced challenges from France and Portugal and must have been relieved when later that year the **Berlin Conference** was held and Belgium's authority over the region was formally recognised.

By 1890 news of the atrocities taking place in the colonies had reached the ears of the European press and continued pressure from outraged liberalist and socialist groups forced Leopold to hand the colony over to the Belgian government in 1908. Life for the Congolese improved almost immediately and the Congo became one of the richest countries in Africa. However, apartheid still existed and rumblings of independence grew to a roar once World War II had ended. Belgium offered it on the condition of a three-to four-year transition period, ostensibly to prevent the Congolese administration from collapsing, but more realistically to prolong the immense revenue Belgium received from the mining of diamonds and gold. But after riots broke out in protest, the Belgian government quickly gave in and granted the Republic of Congo independence on 30 June 1960.

This insalubrious chapter in Belgian history continues to cast a long shadow. Just as Leopold himself erased traces of his exploits at the time, burning Congo state records for eight days straight after the handover, so Belgian authorities have kept the matter swept under the carpet. As recently as 2018, the United Nations strongly criticised the country for failing to address or take responsibility for its colonial past, following the relaunch of the controversial Royal Museum for Central Africa in Tervuren. One can only hope for a proper reckoning soon.

WORLD WAR I (1914–18) On 4 August 1914, at 9 o'clock in the morning, German troops breached Belgian neutrality and marched across the countries' shared eastern border, embarking on the first phase of the **Schlieffen Plan**. This sweeping attack from the northeast relied on speed and was designed to surprise and capture French forces guarding the French–German border. Without an army, France would be forced to surrender.

The might of the German army eventually overwhelmed Belgium's attempts at resistance and by the end of 1914 the majority of the country was under German occupation. However, **King Albert I** (1875–1934) did succeed in defending a small portion of the northwestern corner of the country that lay behind the river Yser, and from Veurne he and the army plotted their attempts to reclaim their homeland.

The unexpected verve of Belgium's resistance delayed German troops for over a month and with it they lost the element of surprise. French troops re-engaged and four years of trench warfare ensued. The town of Ypres was obliterated while, in the nearby **Ypres Salient**, Belgian, British, French, Canadian and ANZAC troops found themselves surrounded by German soldiers, with both sides suffering catastrophic losses for the sake of gaining a few hundred metres of land that was quickly lost during the next offensive.

Meanwhile, the rest of Belgium struggled under German occupation. Forced to relinquish their crops, stores of wood and often their homes, they endeavoured to make life for the Germans as difficult as possible. After the Allies' decisive **Hundred Days Offensive** Kaiser Wilhelm abdicated, and Germany finally agreed to a ceasefire on 11 November 1918.

BETWEEN THE WARS As a reward for their efforts in the fight against Germany, King Albert granted suffrage to the working-class population (although women were still denied), established new social laws that would provide workers with financial security during periods of unemployment and old age, and reduced the working day from 12 hours, seven days a week to 8 hours, six days a week.

LIFE UNDER GERMAN OCCUPATION

Louise Wijnant has lived in Liedekerke all her life. Situated just south of Aalst, the small village invited more interest from the Germans than usual during World War II because of its radio station hidden in the nearby forest. The shack was the only facility in the area capable of receiving long-distance radio messages from the UK and US, and the Germans were keen to intercept any communication. One lunchtime, as we sat around her dining-room table eating pancakes, she told me, in her booming voice, what life had been like as a child during the war:

'I was seven years old when the war started. I had one set of clothes and used to run around barefoot. We couldn't afford electricity, so used petrol lamps instead. At first we weren't really affected, but then food supplies began to run low and the rations tickets they issued were never enough to feed everyone. Instead of registering our goats and sheep, we began to hide them in the woods – that was our 'black market' for meat.

When I was nine, mum used to let me sneak up to the railway tracks at midnight with my brother, to collect coal that had fallen off the back of the wagons. One night, when we were just 100m from home, we heard voices. We threw ourselves to the ground, listening. After several minutes of hearing nothing, we decided to get up. But, as my brother wandered off into the darkness, two German police emerged from the shadows and caught me with my sack of coal. I thought they would confiscate it as usual, but instead they asked me where I lived. I silently pointed to my house a hundred yards away, fearing worse punishment, but to my surprise they let me go! I think they must have taken pity on me for dragging it all that way.

When the bombs started to fall, we were lucky to have connections with the White Brigade, who warned us when the attacks might begin, so we could board up our windows. My mother owes her life to them. She was caught smuggling bread and threatened with deportation to the German work camps, so they hid the whole family. Luckily, Belgium was liberated 14 days later.

The world seemed to turn inside out after the war. There was so much of everything; everyone screamed with excitement the first time someone got a radio. We have come such a long way. I remember walking with my father, fantasising about the idea of space travel and yet, miraculously, he managed to see the first Shuttle launch before he died.'

By 1929 Belgium, along with the rest of Europe and North America, was experiencing the full effects of the **Great Depression**. The period was also characterised by a dip in democracy. Groups of disgruntled Flemish felt that, despite bearing the brunt of the fighting during World War I, government policy still favoured Wallonia (the French-speaking southern region of the country). They were tired of French dominance and called for a unilingual Flanders and bilingual Brussels, which the government grudgingly granted in 1930.

Four years later, Albert I – the nation's beloved 'Soldier King' – fell to his death rock-climbing in Namur. The country was devastated, but briefly found solace in the beautiful face of **Princess Astrid of Sweden** (1905–35), who rose to become queen when Albert's son **Leopold III** (1901–83) inherited the throne. Her disregard of stuffy royal protocol and down-to-earth demeanour made her the most beloved queen in Belgian history and her sudden death in a car crash left the nation numb. Leopold had lost control of their car as they drove towards their villa in Switzerland, causing it to plunge into a nearby ravine.

Leopold had little time to grieve: **Adolf Hitler**'s (1889–1945) rise to power in Germany was giving everyone cause for concern and, in 1936, in an attempt to prevent Belgium from becoming embroiled in another war, Leopold reasserted the country's neutrality.

WORLD WAR II (1939–45) Germany once again ignored Belgium's neutral status and after invading Poland, Norway and Denmark, Hitler turned his attentions to Belgium, France and the Netherlands. He invaded on 10 May 1940 with a series of air attacks that left the country reeling. Within days, Leopold had surrendered without resistance and effectively made himself a prisoner of war by deciding to stay at the Royal Palace in Brussels, where he was held under house arrest until he was deported to Germany in 1944. The bewildered Belgian government meanwhile fled to Paris and later to London to support the Allied war effort.

In 1944, three months after the D-Day landings at Normandy, Belgium was liberated. Germany made one final counter-attack at the **Battle of the Bulge** in the Ardennes, before capitulating on 8 May 1945. The same month, the American army liberated Leopold. However, as a confessed anti-Semite, he was among the thousands believed to have collaborated with the enemy – in his case through treasonous meetings with Hitler at Berchtesgaden. He was forbidden from returning to Belgium and spent the next five years in exile in Switzerland, while his brother **Prince Charles** took up regency. Leopold was eventually cleared of the accusations and returned to power briefly in July 1950, but abdicated a year later following protests, leaving his 21-year-old son **Baudouin** (1930–93) in charge.

MODERN BELGIUM The death of his mother when he was only five and a childhood spent in exile seemed to make Baudouin wise beyond his years. The young king succeeded where his father had not in renewing public support for the monarchy and maintaining a united nation that had been showing signs of fragmentation.

After the war, under the **Marshall Plan**, the US offered aid to the European countries hit hardest by the fighting. Belgium (and Luxembourg) benefited to the tune of US$777 million and the money went into the construction of skyscrapers, self-service supermarkets, and highways so well lit that their network could be seen from space. Things improved further when Brussels was chosen as the headquarters of the **North Atlantic Treaty Organisation** (**NATO**) in 1949 and, two years later, as the provisional seat of the **European Coal and Steel Community**, the precursor of the **European Union** (**EU**). This blossoming of Belgium was displayed for all the world to see at World's Fair **Expo '58**, for which the famous Atomium (page 129) was constructed. In 1960 Baudouin was forced to relinquish control of the Congo, and later of Rwanda and Burundi.

His biggest challenge, though, lay closer to home. The ever-widening gap between Walloon and Flemish thought had created a chasm between government parties and revived problems of a linguistic divide. On top of this, Flanders' economy was flourishing on the back of its new light industries, while the unwanted heavy industries prevalent in the south caused the region to sink further into depression. These events combined to bring tensions to a head and after several strikes, the country was divided into a federal state in 1993 in a series of constitutional revisions that were finalised in 2001. Today, everything from films to government speeches must be presented in two languages, yet despite the apparent compromise, politicians continue to push for entirely separate communities. For now, though, Belgium remains the 'heart of Europe' – albeit a troubled heart.

GOVERNMENT AND POLITICS

Despite being one of the smallest countries in the EU, Belgium is armed to the teeth when it comes to constitutional matters. To ensure fairness and maintain neutrality between the three administrative areas (Flanders, Wallonia and the capital region Brussels), ten provinces and over 500 local authorities, powers of decision-making have been divided and subdivided until the federal government was left with responsibility for major issues like defence, foreign affairs, justice, national budget, taxes and social security. All laws relating to the environment, transport (except Belgian railways), agriculture, energy etc, rest with the individual regional governments, while policies for education and culture are controlled by local communities. There is an overlap of administration in Brussels. The regional and local government are entirely autonomous and conduct their own elections, and their ministers have equal status with the federal party members. If you're confused, don't worry: most of the politicians are, too, and are equipped with a personal advisor to cut it all back to basics for them. The system borders on the ludicrous and is highly ineffectual.

Put simply, Belgium is governed as a federal parliamentary democracy under a constitutional monarch. Like Australia, the country's policies are decided by a coalition government, while the king – Philippe, as of 2013, when King Albert II abdicated – has theoretical authority to form and dissolve governments, but no real executive power. Federal elections are held every four years, regional and community elections every five years and local elections every six years. Belgium has the oldest existing compulsory voting system in the world.

Following a general election in June 2010, Belgium was famously unable to form a government owing to long-running divisions between Walloon and Flemish parties. When, on 6 December 2011, French-speaking bow-tie-wearing Socialist Elio Di Rupo was elected as prime minister, it ended 589 days of political deadlock – a record-breaking 'accolade' passed to Northern Ireland in 2018.

The 2014 elections saw the formation of a centre-right coalition government led by Prime Minister Charles Michel – the first time the separatist N-VA (New Flemish Alliance) had participated; it has since risen to become the largest party in Belgium. After a crisis regarding a migration agreement, the N-VA left the government and Michel ultimately resigned in December 2018, making way for a caretaker government. Amid continuing tensions and the rise of populist parties, federal, regional and European elections have just taken place at the time of writing, with the far-right Vlaams Belang party finishing second to the N-VA in Flanders

EUROPEAN UNION

The roots of today's political and economic union of nation states, known as the EU, were largely inspired by a speech made by Winston Churchill in 1946. World War II had ended a year before and the fear of a reoccurrence was fresh in the minds of all politicians. Churchill suggested that a 'United States of Europe' would consolidate the continent's future and safeguard against more wars. Four years later, French foreign minister Robert Schuman and international economist Jean Monnet presented a proposal outlining the joint management of France's and Germany's coal and steel industries. The proposal was solidified in 1951 by the Treaty of Paris and was extended to include Italy, Belgium, Luxembourg and the Netherlands. The European Coal and Steel Community (ECSC) heralded the birth of the EU, which gained its current name in 1993.

Today, Brussels is the principal seat of the EU, housing the lion's share of the EU's seven institutions: the European Commission, the Council of the European Union, the European Council, and the most important seat of the European Parliament. Other institutions are located in Frankfurt, Strasbourg and Luxembourg – the latter home to the European Court of Justice.

Since its inception, the EU has established border-free travel in much of the continent under the Schengen Agreement, implemented a single currency – the euro – thus facilitating travel and stabilising trade, and prevented war for over six decades. However, sceptics accuse the EU of being a bundle of red tape, riddled with unaccountability and corruption – one key argument that fed into the Brexit saga involving the UK's departure from the union. The feelings of ill will have also spread into Brussels society, which criticises the international community for being insular and holds it responsible for rising house prices and the demolition of elegant residential neighbourhoods in favour of modern EU buildings.

– but whether or not a government will have been formed by the time this guide appears is anyone's guess!

ECONOMY

Flanders was one of the first European areas to undergo an industrial revolution and the development of ports and railways created an exceptionally efficient transport network. The manufacturing of textiles brought great wealth until the 1840s, when Flanders entered a depression. After World War II, regeneration money provided by the US Marshall Plan (page 13) was poured into the development of the north and, after transferring to 'light' industries, production in Flanders caught up with, and quickly overtook, Wallonia's coal industry. The level of heavy industry once required in the south never returned and today Wallonia still suffers from 10% unemployment, over double that of Flanders, which provides almost 60% of the country's GDP. To make matters worse, Flanders is forced to pour €7 billion a year into the Wallonian economy to keep it afloat.

Flanders' main exports, which are booming, are automobiles, food, petroleum products, iron and steel, and diamonds – accounting for 10% of Belgian output, and revolving around Antwerp, also Europe's second-biggest port. The majority of trade is with neighbouring markets. In 2018, the KOF Swiss Economic Institute ranked Belgium as the most globalised country in the world.

PEOPLE

For visitors as well as expats, the Flemish can seem to be a bit of an enigma – almost more easily pigeon-holed by what they're not (not as loud and blunt as the Dutch, that's for sure) than what they are. One persuasive stereotype relates to their domesticity: often quoted as being born *met een baksteen in de maag* ('with a brick in their stomachs'), they seek the suburban dream of a self-built house, children and car, though increasing numbers are opting to skip the marriage part, enjoying many of the same rights as married couples. Many Flemish do, however, remain in the town in which they were born to be close to relatives, and roles are often traditional. But don't be fooled: if the Belgian man is the head of the family, the woman is the neck that can turn the head any way she chooses. Women are not expected to change their maiden names if they get married and there are egalitarian laws permitting men to take paternity leave to help their partners after the birth of a baby.

The much-mocked linguistic frictions between the northern Flemish and southern-dwelling Walloons figure far less in daily life than the press might suggest, though the separatist movement shows no sign of abating, and nationalist sentiment is strong. Most people identify themselves as Flemish or Walloon ahead of any Belgian nationality, but regional identification is also prevalent, whether you're a 'proud' *Antwerpenaar* or a 'rebellious' *Gentenaar*. While Walloons look up to France, the same can't be said of the Flemish, who regularly exchange (comic) barbs with the Dutch like combative siblings. But if, like the Dutch, you have labelled the Flemish as ineffectual/stubborn/bad drivers etc, then you're missing the point. Make an effort, and break through that initial phlegmatism, and you'll discover a people who rejoice in the good life – that'll be their Burgundian roots – be it having a few beers or a hearty feed, have a strong Surrealist streak, and make brilliantly loyal pals.

LANGUAGE

Flemish, or *Vlaams*, is a Dutch dialect based on the Frankish introduced by the conquering Franks following the decline of the Roman Empire. Its roots are predominantly Germanic, but over time different regions developed varied dialects. Linguists dispute the exact scope of these, but four main groups are commonly identified: West Flemish, East Flemish, Brabantian and Limburgish. Brussels also has its own dialect, associated with the outer communes, and often heard in the Marolles district, though it's endangered now.

Residents of East and West Flanders tend to pronounce 'h' and 'g' sounds much more softly than their Brabantian neighbours, while Limburgians have a sing-song element to their dialect. All are increasingly adding English loanwords to their street Flemish. Another tendency is to add '-je' (singular), '-jes' (plural) and '-ken' at the end of a noun to imply a familiarity or fondness. For example, friends refer to me as 'Emmaken', instead of 'Emma'. The Flemish also often string several words together to create one long word, so you might need *uithoudingsdvermogen* (stamina) to wrap your tongue around all those vowels.

The Flemish delight in the fact that these dialects afford them some fun with their Dutch neighbours. In schools, Flemish children are taught Dutch and as a result speak perfect *Nederlands*, but the Dutch are left in the dark when it comes to understanding Flemish dialects. Add to this the variation of words and accents between towns, even villages, and things get really interesting. Even within a distance of 2km, the names of items (particularly culinary ones) change. For example, the *millefeuille* pastry found in bakeries is referred to as *booksken* in Denderhoutem, *glascaken* in Denderleeuw and *veleken* in Liedekerke.

Having said all that, the Flemish mostly speak excellent English (not least thanks to TV and films) and youngsters in particular jump between the two languages with enviable ease. Another brainteaser is the change in spelling of place names on road signs between the two regions. For a list of the most common name changes, see box, page 40.

THE LINGUISTIC DIVIDE

> If I were king, I would send all the Flemings to Wallonia and all the Walloons to Flanders for six months. Like military service. They would live with a family and that would solve all our ethnic and linguistic problems very fast. Because everybody's tooth aches in the same way, everybody loves their mother, everybody loves or hates spinach. And those are the things that really count.
>
> Jacques Brel

If only the politicians saw things as simply as Jacques Brel. Undeniable, discussed to death and at times looming on a fast-approaching horizon, the linguistic divide between the Dutch-speaking Flemish and the French-speaking Walloons – that's not even including the German-speaking community in east Belgium – has almost come to define Belgium, as much as it threatens to tear it apart. The roots of the division can be traced back to the Middle Ages when the Treaty of Verdun carved Charlemagne's lands between his three grandsons (page 5). Flanders became part of the Germanic Frankish lands, while the remainder of the Low Countries belonged to the Roman Empire and was exposed to Latin dialects. During the Burgundian Empire, French became the official language of the court and Flemish remained the tongue of the working class. Despite the formation of the Belgian state in 1831, it was not until 1967 that the Flemish fight to equalise the status between the two languages was granted – tensions having been underscored yet again during World War I, when exclusively French-speaking officers could not be understood by the Flemish soldiers, sometimes with disastrous effect.

With nationalist sentiment resurgent in the era of Donald Trump and Brexit, and separatist movements also in the headlines, the linguistic divide is unlikely to resolve itself any time soon. The increasing sway of groups such as the New Flemish Alliance, which seeks a 'velvet' or non-violent seccession from Wallonia, cannot be ignored, but the problem of bilingual Brussels, caught between the two regions and claimed by both, may prove to be intractable.

RELIGION

Catholicism became the religion of the masses during the Spanish occupation (1579–1713) and to this day 60% of Flanders' population identifies as Christian (50% Roman Catholic and 10% Protestant). While most towns hold an annual religious procession, church attendance has dropped by more than half since the late 1990s, and around 30% of the population identifies as either atheist or agnostic, on par with other western European nations.

Stemming from immigration agreements signed with Morocco, Turkey, Algeria and Tunisia from the 1960s, Islam has increased in the country and today 5% of the population identifies as Muslim. Antwerp is probably the country's most religiously diverse city, home to a healthy percentage of Moroccan immigrants and one of the most observant Jewish communities in western Europe; Jews first arrived in

Belgium during the 12th and 13th centuries, after being expelled from France and England when persecution hit its peak during the Crusades, and are based predominantly around the diamond district. Numbers of Hindus, Buddhists and Jains – the latter also active in the diamond sector – are also on the rise in Belgium.

CULTURE

Flanders' contribution to the arts is far-reaching and rather fantastic. From architectural firsts and world-renowned artists to iconic comic strips, the region is brimming with talent old and new.

LITERATURE The Belgian Revolution that led to the establishment of the country brought with it a firm anti-Dutch sentiment, with the language relegated to the rank of a patois. This denial of Flemish as an official language provoked protests and spawned a number of literary societies, kickstarting a transition that would eventually see it being credited in its own right. One of the first works to contest the inequality was **Hendrik Conscience**'s (1812–83) *In 't Wonderjaer 1566*, published in 1837. Disgusted that he'd written the novel in Flemish instead of French, his father threw him out of the family home and a penniless Conscience was forced to wander the streets of Antwerp. He had the last laugh though; eminent painter Wappers presented him to the royal court and in 1845 he was made a knight of the Order of Leopold. Conscience's historical romances – notably *De Leeuw van Vlaanderen* (*The Lion of Flanders*), in 1838, about the Flemish victory over the French at the Battle of the Golden Spurs – helped kickstart the Flemish literary movement.

With his novels about the harsh lives of peasants, **Cyriel Buysse** (1859–1932) was Flanders' own Émile Zola. Lier-born autodidact **Felix Timmermans** (1886–1947) meanwhile lifted regionalism to the highest level, being nominated for the Nobel Prize three times.

The 20th century gave rise to the 'big three' of Flemish literature, starting with **Willem Elsschot** (1882–1960), an Antwerp ad agency owner whose laconic novels depict the life of the bourgeoisie. Flemish novels often have a heavy dose of social engagement; journalist and erotica collector **Louis-Paul Boon** (1912–79) mixed that with literary experimentalism to become a Flemish-language James Joyce, best known for his 1953 masterpiece *De Kapellekensbaan* (*Chapel Road*), about a girl, Ondine, who wants to escape the industrial town of Aalst in the 19th century. The giant of Flemish literature is writer, poet, playwright and painter **Hugo Claus** (1929–2008). Hailing from Bruges, his seminal 1983 work *Het Verdriet van België* (*The Sorrow of Belgium*) tells the story of a Flemish child caught up in the German occupation of Belgium during World War II.

Prominent Flemish writers since then include: **Stefan Hertmans** (1951–), whose 2013 *Oorlog en terpentijn* (*War and Turpentine*) brings to life his grandfather's reflections on World War I; **Tom Lanoye** (1958–), whose novel *Sprakeloos* (2009) ranks among Flanders' most beloved classics; and the caustic **Dimitri Verhulst** (1972–) often hailed as Louis-Paul Boon's literary descendant. Breakout star **Lize Spit** (1988–), author of twisted thriller *Het Smelt* (*It Melts*), has had the rights to her work snapped up by numerous countries – but many Flemish authors (like Dutch) have been lost to translation, their Francophone counterparts stealing the limelight. **Georges Simenon** (1903–89), creator of detective Maigret, is foremost among them.

POETRY Two names dominate 19th-century poetry: **Maurice Maeterlinck** (1862–1949) and Emile Verhaeren. Maeterlinck became an overnight success with his first

BEGIJNHOFS (BÉGUINAGES)

These walled islands of religious seclusion cropped up throughout the Low Countries during the 13th century. Comprised of a cluster of terraced homes arranged around a central garden and chapel, béguinages were founded by pious sisterhoods of Catholic women who wished to serve God without having to take vows, give up their property or retire from the world. According to one interpretation, the networks of support arose following an increase in the number of women left as widows after the Crusades or disease took their husbands; another view holds that, with marriage occurring later and less than previously believed, single women were moving to new cities to find work, and béguinages answered their social and economic needs, while providing personal independence – not an easy thing for a woman to have then. In that light, it's not too much of a stretch to claim them as a very early proto-feminist movement.

Making vows of chastity and obedience – but not of poverty – to the Groot Juffrouw or Mother Superior, the béguines tended the gardens, washed wool for weavers, worked in the on-site brewery and infirmary and prayed three times daily, but they were free to break their vows and leave at any time. The popularity of these self-sufficient communities allowed the sisterhood to pick and choose between applicants. Thus admission to the order was often extended to those who could afford to make donations to the financially independent community. These well-off residents occupied the larger rooms within the complex and spent their time caring for the elderly and sick and weaving lace. Flanders' 13 béguinages are UNESCO-listed. The prettiest can be found in Leuven, Lier, Turnhout, Tongeren, Diest, Kortrijk and Dendermonde.

play *La Princesse Maleine* in 1889, and is the only Belgian to have won the Nobel Prize for Literature. **Emile Verhaeren** (1855–1916) trained as a lawyer, but tried only two cases before turning to literature. Inspired by the works of Flemish painters like Jacob Jordaens and David Teniers, he published his first set of poems, *Les Flamandes*, in 1883. They are still admired for their raw and provocative depiction of Flemish life. Roman Catholic priest **Guido Gezelle** (1830–99) is famous for his use of the West Flemish dialect, his works often inspired by his mystic love of God.

Minimalist **Roland Jooris** (1936–) and **Herman De Coninck** (1944–97), known for his song-like parlando poetry, are considered part of a Flemish new realist wave, demanding more focus on reality. Many contemporary authors including Hertmans have also written poetry, while Lanoye previously served as Antwerp city poet – a role also offered in other major cities that reflects poetry's shift into the public sphere.

PAINTING

The Flemish Primitives Confined to the pages of illuminated manuscripts for over 700 years, Flemish art leapt from the shadows at the beginning of the 15th century. This early Netherlandish painting flourished for over two centuries and was pioneered by a group of painters known as the Flemish Primitives – so-called for their experimentation with oil paint instead of the traditional tempera – whose work represented the transition from Middle Ages Gothic art to Renaissance. They pioneered the two or three painted wooden panels known as diptychs and triptychs. Artists began signing their works for the first time and became celebrities in their

MADONNA STATUES

In every city and small village you will no doubt spy statues of the Virgin Mary and Child housed in small alcoves built into the sides of buildings or street corners. The practice originated in the early 15th century during the Counter Reformation, when Catholicism was experiencing a revival. The aim of specialist orders, like the Jesuits, was to bring piety back to the people and they built these statues to remind residents of the one true religion.

own right. One of the first – and best – was court painter and advisor to Philip the Good, **Jan van Eyck** (1390–1441). By mixing oils with turpentine, he was able to layer the paint thinner than ever before; the effects were luminous and allowed him to produce works of unparalleled detail and realism. A resident of Bruges for most of his life, van Eyck produced a number of paintings that offered insight into courtly life, including the intriguing *Arnolfini Portrait* (now housed in London's National Gallery). His seminal work was the world-famous, oft-stolen polyptych *The Adoration of the Mystic Lamb* (page 178), which will star in a Ghent-based 'van Eyck Year' programme in 2020.

Van Eyck was eventually eclipsed by his pupil, **Rogier van der Weyden** (1400–64), who became Brussels's *stadsschilder* (official town painter) in 1436. His most famous works were the *Justice of Trajan* and *Justice of Herkenbald* retables that once hung in the Golden Chamber of Brussels's town hall, but were destroyed during the French bombardment of 1695. His greatest follower was **Hans Memling** (1430–94), a German-born artist who carried on the tradition of his teacher van der Weyden's painting. Today, the Sint-Janshospitaal in Bruges houses superlative examples of his work, including his masterpiece the *Shrine of St Ursula*. Another of van der Weyden's understudies, **Dieric Bouts** (1410–75), rose to become city painter of Leuven in 1468. He was one of the first artists to experiment with the single vanishing point. This method of creating depth and perspective can be seen in his celebrated panel *The Last Supper*, which appears in the *Altarpiece of the Holy Sacrament*.

Gerard David (1460–1523) became Bruges's leading painter following Memling's death; his paintings cross the final bridge between Gothic and Renaissance art. You can find his works at the Groeningemuseum and Onze-Lieve-Vrouwekerk in Bruges.

Renaissance By the early 16th century the trickle of Renaissance influence had built to a tidal wave that swept through the Flemish art world. The period also witnessed the decline of cloth towns like Bruges and Ghent as important centres of art, whose epicentre moved to the booming port town of Antwerp.

Among the first to explore this hybrid of styles was **Quinten Matsijs** (1464–1530). The former ironsmith drew from the works of Dieric Bouts and van der Weyden, and his paintings show the same attention to detail, crisp outline and transparent, luminous layering of paint. However, his work also extends to hazy landscapes reminiscent of Leonardo da Vinci, and is infused with a strong personal religious fervour. Emotions are wrought upon the faces of his subjects, occasionally tipping into the grotesque, as seen in the comical and perturbing *Ugly Duchess* (now in the National Gallery in London).

Matsijs's collaborator and close friend **Joachim Patinir** (1480–1524) was renowned for his fantastical landscapes, effectively inventing the panoramic northern Renaissance 'world landscape' and showing little interest in the figures in his paintings.

Jan Gossaert (1478–1532) was one of the first artists to visit Italy in person. He brought back techniques like *sfumato* – a hazing or blurring of layers between paint to create a 'smoky' effect – and started using softer grey tones, instead of the bright colours favoured by the Flemish Primitives; he was also the first to introduce mythological nude figures into his paintings.

The work of **Pieter Bruegel the Elder** (1525–69) dominates the latter half of the 16th century. He was a fan of Hieronymous Bosch and several of his paintings are informed by Bosch's fascination with the grotesque, most notably *The Triumph of Death*. An accomplished landscape artist, he is praised for immortalising folk culture in his paintings of village life. In 2019–20, several exhibitions in Brussels will mark the 450th anniversary of his death – an event which came too early for him to teach his sons **Pieter Brueghel the Younger** (1564–1638) and **Jan 'Velvet' Brueghel** (1568–1625); their grandmother is believed to have been their first teacher. Partly to differentiate themselves from him, both reinserted into their surnames the 'h' he had dropped. While both sons are known for making copies of their father's peasant scenes, Pieter has lately been acclaimed as an innovator in his own right; Jan meanwhile carved his own path, focusing on landscapes and still life.

Baroque The Baroque period of Flemish art is often referred to as the 'Age of Rubens'. Raised in Antwerp, **Peter Paul Rubens** (1577–1640) kept Flemish art at the forefront of the cultural scene until the mid 17th century. Having visited Italy, and studied the techniques of masters such as Caravaggio, he returned to Antwerp and was appointed court painter to the Spanish rulers Infanta Isabella and Archduke Albert. Shortly after, he painted the exquisite triptych, *The Raising of the Cross*, and a year later *The Descent from the Cross*; both now hang in Antwerp's Onze-Lieve-Vrouwekathedraal.

While Renaissance work focused on encapsulating the moment immediately preceding an event, Baroque art centred on the moment of drama itself. Rich colours, the effect of *chiaroscuro* – the bold contrast between light and dark – and figures with muscular detail (often amply fleshed female nudes) all combined to give the works incredible dynamism. This new exuberance created ripples of excitement among artists and Rubens developed a loyal following. Those of note include **Anthony van Dyck** (1599–1641), who rose to become Rubens's best pupil, later employed as court painter to King Charles I. Famed for his portraits of the royal family, van Dyck lived like a prince in London until his death; his remains are interred in St Paul's Cathedral.

Dean of the Antwerp artists' guild, **Jacob Jordaens** (1593–1678) was employed by Rubens several times to convert his sketches into life-sized drawings, and after Rubens's death in 1640, succeeded him as the leading artist in town.

Alongside Baroque, genre painting, which captured the less poetic realities of everyday life, was beginning to emerge. At its helm was **Adriaen Brouwer** (1605–38). Brouwer by name, brewer by nature, he was a notorious drunk, but his familiarity with the taverns gave him intimate knowledge of his subject matter. His lively brushwork and muted earthy tones brought pub brawls to life and immortalised the ruddy-cheeked peasants that featured in them.

Frans Snijders (1579–1657) studied under Pieter Brueghel the Younger and after experimenting with still life moved on to painting animals, often in pursuit of a hunt. His awareness of composition and uncanny ability to capture the texture of an animal's fur were greatly admired – he was one of the first specialist *animaliers* – and frequently contributed to the works of Rubens and Jordaens.

Neoclassicism and Impressionism Following Rubens's death the crown of artistic significance shifted from Flanders to France, and Neoclassicist **Jacques-Louis David** (1748–1825), whose most famous work, *The Death of Marat*, is housed in the Musées Royaux des Beaux-Arts de Belgique in Brussels. When Belgium achieved independence in 1830, there was an upswell of nationalist pride and artists sought new ways of defining their art. Social and industrial developments towards the end of the century inspired the work of painter and sculptor **Constantin Meunier** (1831–1905), known for his portraits of labourers, dock- and mine-workers. Impressed by the works of Monet and Renoir, **Théo van Rysselberghe** (1862–1926) dabbled in Impressionism, but abandoned it upon seeing Pointillist works of art in Paris. He brought the technique back to Belgium, much to the annoyance of fellow Les XX (see box, page 24) member **James Ensor** (1860–1949). The latter, resident in Ostend for most of his life, was a key figure in Expressionism and Surrealism, often tipping into the world of the macabre. Much of his work,

COMIC STRIPS

Praised as the ninth art, the comic strip – *bande-dessinée* in French – has a huge following in Belgium, as in France. Prior to World War II, comic strips appeared as daily sketches at the back of newspapers, but shortage of paper forced publishers to relegate them to a weekly colour-spread. For the first time cartoonists could develop storyboards of substance and plot. The format was much preferred by readers and the weekly colour-spread stuck. The first comic strip to gain international acclaim was *The Adventures of Tintin*, penned by Hergé (see Georges Remi, page 372). Numerous others followed in his footsteps, borrowing his trademark, flat-looking *ligne claire*, and often making their debut in the famous comic magazine *Spirou*, launched in 1938. While *Spirou* is still holding steady, Belgian comics have had to adapt to changing times and technologies; leading publishers Lombard and Dupuis have targeted graphic novels and older customers, while comics have gone from a cult affair into a serious tourist business, with a museum (page 107) and comic-strip walking trail in Brussels. It's not just about nostalgia though – Brecht Evens's (1986–) sublime graphic novels have recently made a splash abroad – and many classic Belgian cartoons continue to evolve. Here are ten essential series:

BLAKE ET MORTIMER Created by Edgar P Jacobs (1904–87), the series first appeared at the front of the *Tintin* comic magazine. Apparently, the characters – a British scientist and his MI5 friend – were modelled on two of Jacobs's friends.

BOULE ET BILL This quaint strip first appeared in *Spirou* in 1959 and was an attempt to create a European take on *Peanuts*. It features a typical family, including the seven-year-old Boule and his cocker spaniel Bill, and was co-created by Schaerbeek-born Jean Roba (1930–2006), who later passed the series to his assistant Laurent Verron.

LE CHAT/DE KAT Philippe Geluck's strip devoted to an anthropomorphic, obese, besuited cat was published in *Le Soir* newspaper from 1983 until 2013. A dedicated Brussels museum is in the pipeline, and should be open by 2020.

LARGO WINCH Philippe Francq and Jean Van Hamme's tale of a Yugoslavian-born hero who becomes the head of the gigantic W group after his father's murder including the masterpiece *Christ's Entry into Brussels*, was seen as scandalous at the time, though he is now considered a pioneer.

Symbolism, Fauvism, Expressionism and Surrealism The late 19th century saw the rise of Symbolism alongside Impressionism, largely as an antithesis to realism and the materialist attitude of an industrialising world. Prominent Belgian artists in the field include **Fernand Khnopff** (1858–1921), a member of Les XX who admired the pre-Raphaelites and brought similar dreamlike qualities to his paintings; and the self-taught Ostend artist **Léon Spilliaert** (1881–1946), whose sickly and reclusive existence is echoed in the lone silhouettes that people his abstract, alien landscapes.

The 20th century witnessed the arrival – albeit short-lived – of Fauvism, led by Henri Matisse. Distorting reality to reflect emotion, and employing a bold, arbitrary use of colour, unfussy lines and an exaggerated perspective, painter and sculptor **Rik Wouters** (1882–1916) was Belgium's most notable advocate.

and has to grapple with the corrupt finance world. Van Hamme is also behind the hugely successful Norse-influenced comic book *Thorgal*.

LES SCHTROUMPFS/DE SMURFEN Pierre Culliford aka Peyo's sky-blue humanoids, living in an enchanted forest and facing off against pesky foe Gargamel, have spawned a vast empire spanning a long-running US TV series, numerous films – including a girl Smurfs spin-off – theme parks and countless collector items. There's even a Spanish village, Júzcar, painted in Smurf-blue livery.

LUCKY LUKE Cowboy and keeper of the peace Lucky Luke, with his faithful steed Jolly Jumper and dim-witted dog Rantanplan, encounter real-life Western greats like Calamity Jane and Billy the Kid. Drawn for over 50 years by Maurice De Bevère (1923–2001) – pen name Morris – it was taken over by French artist Achdé in 2003.

QUICK ET FLUPKE Another creation of Hergé, this one following the escapades of two *bruxellois* street urchins. It featured in *Le Petit Vingtième* from 1930, but Hergé abandoned it to concentrate on the hugely successful *The Adventures of Tintin*.

NERO The bald, medallion-sporting, flawed yet loveable protagonist Nero and Porsche-driving detective van Zwam appeared in Flemish newspapers between 1947 and 2002. Creator Marc Sleen (1922–2016) was a huge fan of Africa and wildlife; both passions cropped up in his storyboards.

SUSKE EN WISKE Known as *Spike and Suzy* in English and *Willy and Wanda* in the US, the orphan and heroine team were created by Willy Vandersteen (1913–90) and still appear in Belgian newspaper *De Standaard*. One of the best-selling comics in Flanders alongside *Jommeke*, though the latter is hardly known outside the region.

URBANUS This highly absurd strip is written by, and based on the life of, Flemish comedian and singer Urbanus (1949–), who appears as his 11- or 12-year-old self – albeit with a beard! The first story was published in 1982 and it's still going strong.

LES XX

Formed in 1883, Les XX was a group of avant-garde painters, designers and sculptors who set up an annual exhibition showcasing the work of 20 selected international artists, in the hope of inspiring new artistic developments throughout Europe. Its 11 founding members included the likes of James Ensor, whose earlier rejection by various salons was a contributing factor in the group's formation, Théo van Rysselberge and Symbolist Fernand Khnopff. They soon invited a further nine members and became known collectively as *les vingtistes.* For a time, their annual exhibitions attracted Europe's elite – the artists they showcased included Monet, Gauguin, Cézanne and van Gogh. However, their success was short-lived. Ensor left the group after arguments with fellow XX member van Rysselberge, and amid mounting disparagements from art critics, Les XX disbanded in 1893, before reforming as La Libre Esthétique, more oriented towards the decorative arts.

Expressionism continued to strengthen in Belgium, led by painter and sculptor **Constant Permeke** (1886–1952). Although wounded in World War I and banned from making 'degenerate art' during World War II by the Germans, Permeke was heavily productive during the intervening years. His success was such that the old 1,000 Belgian franc note bore his picture.

By the 1920s Surrealism had overtaken Expressionism in a big way, forcing onlookers to think in new ways with its unexpected juxtapositions. Perhaps the most famous proponent is **René Magritte** (1898–1967), best known for *The Treachery of Images*, the famous pipe that's not really a pipe. Also associated with Surrealism was **Paul Delvaux** (1897–1994), whose oneiric paintings, inspired by Giorgio de Chirico, consistently featured seemingly hypnotised female nudes in railway stations or wandering amid classical buildings.

Modern art After World War II, Belgian art tipped into the abstract. These post-war avant-garde artists soon joined together to form **La Jeune Peinture Belge**, from which the current Belgian Art Prize stems. Upon its demise, a larger-scale movement was founded encompassing artists from three European cities (Copenhagen, Brussels and Amsterdam). Nicknamed CoBrA, the movement advocated lively brushwork and vibrant colours, drawing on children's painting. Belgium's most famous exponent is Brussels-born **Pierre Alechinsky** (1927–), who often works in ink.

Working independently was **Marcel Broodthaers** (1924–76), a jack-of-all-trades who was primarily a poet until the age of 40, and whose first exhibition encased unsold copies of his latest poetry book! His witty and conceptual works persistently sought to give material form to language, and his immersive 'décors' often unified his previous works with borrowed objects. Another *sui generis* artist was **Henri van Herwegen** (1940–), better known as Panamarenko, whose madcap sculptures were modelled around the Greek mythological figure Icarus and rarely ever worked – his former Antwerp studio is now open for visits (page 310).

The most prominent Belgian artists working today include **Michaël Borremans** (1963–), whose painting style draws on 18th-century art as well as the work of Manet and Degas, and Antwerp-based **Luc Tuymans** (1958–), who is widely viewed as one of the world's most influential painters. A former bouncer and railway guard, he revived painting at a time when it was deeply unfashionable, turning his harsh, elegant gaze on subjects like the Holocaust and Belgian Congo, and often basing his work on existing materials such as photos. He's regularly to be seen propping up the bars in his hometown.

PHOTOGRAPHY Belgium is bursting with talented photographers, several of whom are represented by the legendary Magnum photo agency: **Harry Gruyaert** (1941–), a Kodak Prize winner known for his images of India, Morocco and Egypt, as well as his vibrant use of colour; **Carl de Keyzer** (1958–), whose subjects have included the collapse of the Soviet Union and marginal social groups; and **Bieke Depoorter** (1986–), whose intimate series often draw on random encounters, and who forms part of a bold new wave of talent including **Max Pinckers** (1988–), who mixes staged and documentary scenes.

FILM AND TELEVISION There was a time when Belgian cinema meant **Jean-Claude Van Damme** (1960–), Audrey Hepburn (born in Brussels, if to a Dutch mother) or – more credibly – Wallonian award-winners the Dardennes brothers, but now the industry is booming. Francophone movies traditionally dominated, but now Flanders has the momentum, with a more regulated industry bringing funding and a tax shelter that has spurred investments in audio-visual productions.

For many the breakout film was *Rundskop* (*Bullhead*, 2011), a brooding tale about the West Flemish beef trade which made the names of star **Matthias Schoenaerts** (1977–) and director **Michaël R. Roskam** (1972–). *The Broken Circle Breakdown* (2012), about blue-grass musicians whose daughter gets cancer, also won an Oscar nomination for director **Felix van Groeningen** (1977–). All three have gone on to Hollywood careers, and they're not alone: young Flemish duo **Adil El Arbi** (1988–) and **Bilall Fallah** (1986–) sprang to fame on the back of *Black* (2012), a sensational Brussels love story set amid rival gangs, and have been signed on to direct the next franchise of *Beverly Hills Cop*. **Lukas Dhont** (1991–) is the latest to win acclaim for *Girl* (2018), about a transgender ballerina.

This success has also extended to television, with Flemish directors helming hit international series such as *The Fall* and *House of Cards* (**Jakob Verbruggen**) and *Peaky Blinders* (**Tim Mielants**). The latter was also behind Antwerp-based homegrown hit *Cordon* – one of numerous Flemish series devoured by foreign audiences. Flanders hosts a handful of film festivals during the year (page 52).

ARCHITECTURE AND DESIGN Flanders' rich architectural heritage ranges from the 13th-century Romanesque and Gothic to 18th-century Baroque and 19th- and early 20th-century Art Nouveau. Visit today and you'll find a haphazard, but always charming, mixture of medieval houses next to modern steel and glass constructions.

Flanders' oldest and most celebrated architectural feats are its towering belfries and secluded béguinages (see box, page 19). They cropped up during the 13th and 15th centuries when the trading of cloth created an economic boom that also financed the Grand-Place in Brussels and many of the region's Gothic cathedrals and town halls; the most impressive examples of these can be seen, respectively, in Antwerp and Leuven.

The counter-Reformation of the 16th–17th centuries ushered in the Italian Baroque style. Characterised by twisted columns, arching domes and elaborate ornamentation, it was quickly adopted and given a Flemish twist by artists and architects and imaginatively renamed Flemish Baroque. The guildhouses of the Grand-Place were rebuilt in this style following Louis XIV's attack in 1695, while Antwerp's Sint-Carolus Borromeuskerk is a true Baroque beauty.

Following independence in 1830, Leopold I was keen to elevate Brussels's cityscape to the same level as Paris, so ordered the construction of numerous buildings. Among those commissioned were the magnificent Galeries Royales Saint-Hubert, famed for their arched glass-paned roof, and the labyrinthine Palais de Justice, at one time the largest building in Europe, and much admired by Hitler.

Towards the end of the century, Art Nouveau was in full swing. Influencing everything from buildings to bedroom furniture, the movement was characterised by the use of wrought iron, glass, marble and wood decorated with leaves and flowers in flowing, sinuous lines. Architects of note include **Paul Saintenoy** (1862–1952), responsible for the elegant Old England department store in Brussels which now houses the Musical Instrument Museum, **Henry van de Velde** (1863–1957), **Paul Hankar** (1859–1901) and the legendary **Victor Horta** (1861–1947). His most famous constructions include Hôtel Tassel, Hôtel Solvay, the greenhouses at Laeken (which he designed with Hankar) and the old *magasins* Waucquez, which now house the Belgian Comic Strip Center.

Leopold II's pride-boosting commissions included **Antwerp Centraal Station** (page 308), often considered to be one of the finest railway hubs in the world. Modern architectural design was meanwhile heralded by the city's **Boerentoren** (Farmers' Tower), completed in 1932, and Europe's first skyscraper. This was soon followed in Brussels by the space-age **Atomium** (page 129), a magnified iron-crystal molecule which became the icon of the 1958 World's Fair, and an enduring symbol of Belgium.

The Atomium was the undoubted exception in a notorious period of ***bruxellisation*** from the run-up to Expo '58 until the 1970s, when the capital adopted an increasingly grey, concrete shroud. Significant old buildings were torn down pell-mell to make way for new highways and office blocks, many for the nascent European Community, behind questionable-looking institutions such as the cruciform-shaped **Berlaymont** ('Berlaymonster') building.

More positively, in subsequent decades celebrity architects such as Richard Rogers and Zaha Hadid have sprinkled their magic dust on Antwerp, while Flemish architects such as minimalist **Vincent van Duysen** (1962–) have risen to the summit of their profession. On the interior design front, Flanders is renowned, with the godfather of the scene being international tastemaker **Axel Vervoordt** (1947–), a former antiques dealer who saved Antwerp's medieval Vlaeykensgang alley from demolition, before his rough-yet-refined aesthetic won commissions from stars like Kanye West and Robert De Niro.

PERFORMING ARTS

Theatre Flanders had no famous playwrights or major repertory theatre until relatively recently. An early light was the aforementioned Cyriel Buysse (page 18); Flanders' best-known playwright is Hugo Claus, who wrote some 70 plays alongside his novels and poems. Multi-tasking poet/novelist/playwrights have continued to dominate, with Tom Lanoye, for instance, often writing for Guy Cassiers's well-respected **Toneelhuis** in Antwerp, which mixes adaptations of the literary canon with more socially engaged work. Other notable companies include fellow city theatre **NT Gent**, whose new director Milo Rau has already started to shake things up. Another, frequently controversial, figure is playwright and leading contemporary artist **Jan Fabre** (1958–), who hit the headlines when he threw live cats in the air during a shoot, and when he staged a 24-hour theatrical orgy, *Mount Olympus*, in 2017. At the top of the pile is director **Ivo van Hove** (1958–), head of the Toneelgroep Amsterdam, and beloved for his experimental, ultra-modern approach.

Dance Since the 1980s, Flanders' dance scene has quite literally burst on to the stage from nowhere. Its genesis dates back to 1961 when, in the wake of the World's Fair, the director of La Monnaie asked French choreographer Maurice Béjart to form a company in Brussels – the result being the influential Ballet du XXe Siècle. Dance and theatre-makers wouldn't look back, rejecting conservatoires for fine arts academies; the term the 'Flemish Wave' was coined in the 1980s to describe the work of a radical group of choreographers and directors (including Fabre and Cassiers, see opposite) who were working at the limits of their traditions. In dance, **Anne Teresa De Keersmaeker** (1960–) formed her company Rosas, which went on to have a huge influence on the contemporary scene. Another Flemish Wave member, **Wim Vandekeybus** (1955–), is associated with raw physical dance performances, with members of his company Ultima Vez hurling themselves at each other or across the stage. Trained at De Keersmaeker's dance school P.A.R.T.S, **Sidi Larbi Cherkaoui** (1976–) has meanwhile won acclaim for his mix of hybrid forms of movement and intense theatricality, and currently helms the Royal Ballet of Flanders.

Music At a cultural crossroads between the Netherlands, France and Germany, with the input of immigrants from the Democratic Republic of Congo and beyond, Belgium has a surprisingly dynamic music scene, reflected in its rich array of outdoor festivals and concerts (page 52). Here is a brief rundown of its major contributions.

Jazz Given that one Belgian (Adolphe Sax) invented the saxophone, and another – Django Reinhardt – invented a genre (gypsy swing), it's no surprise that the country has heavily influenced the jazz scene. Brussels-born **Jean-Baptiste 'Toots' Thielemans** (1922–) achieved fame for his accomplished harmonica playing and virtuoso whistling, going on to become a member of Charlie Parker's All-Stars band and recording with all the greats. The region's love of jazz still runs strong and numerous jazz festivals are hosted every year, among them the world-renowned Ghent Jazz Festival (page 54) and Brussels Jazz Weekend (page 53).

Folk Before leaving for America, Thielemans was part of **Bobbejaan Schoepen's** (1925–2010) backing band. Schoepen was a superb whistler, who ditched his all-singing-all-dancing vaudeville act in favour of American country music. During the 1950s his supporting acts included Jacques Brel. From the late 1960s there was a vivid revival of the folk genre in Belgium.

Chanson In 1956 Belgian singer-songwriter **Jacques Brel** (page 370) arrived on the Parisian music scene and saved Belgian music from falling into obscurity. His breakout hit *Quand on n'a que l'amour* was troubadour in style and tone, but he quickly moved on to explore more complex themes and compositions and his highly literate, poetic and theatrical songs bewitched first France and then the world.

Classical music The territory that is now Belgium played a major role in European polyphony in the 15th and 16th centuries. Cut to 1970, and leading Ghent-born conductor and J S Bach specialist Philippe Herreweghe founded the ensemble **Collegium Vocale Gent**, which has become world-renowned for its authentic, historically informed performances – notably of Baroque works – using original instruments. Herreweghe regularly conducts at Antwerp's Queen Elisabeth Hall (page 298).

Electronic music Since the early 20th century, Belgium has embraced dance music, beginning with tea dances and soon extending to barrel organs such as the **Decap** which played instead of live bands and followed instructions from strips of perforated cardboard. By the 1960s, American soul records were pouring into the country, DJs were springing up, and the **Popcorn** scene, named after a Sunday party in East Flanders, was born. Fast-forward 20 years and – way before Berlin or Ibiza – Belgium was Europe's hottest electronic music hub, spawning the influential **New Beat** movement, mixing synthesisers with acid and Chicago house sounds. Records were released at lightning pace, featuring the movement's iconic smiley logo, and clubs popped up at the side of motorways to cater to crazily dressed hordes of fans coming from far and wide. This period gave rise to the band **Front 242**, who pioneered a style called electronic body music. In the 2000s, Ghent brothers **Soulwax**, also active as 2Many DJs, broke into the mainstream, while **Dimitri Vegas & Like Mike**, who grew up in the tiny Flemish town of Willebroek, regularly rank on DJ Mag's top 100 DJs poll, and are ambassadors of Belgian mega-festival Tomorrowland (page 54).

Pop and rock Uncategorisable, annoying but mega-catchy, **Plastic Bertrand's** parody of punk and new wave created a massive hit in *Ça plane pour moi* in 1978. Flanders is also fond of pop group **Clouseau**, who shot to fame with their song *Anne* after participating in tryouts for the 1989 Eurovision Song Contest; **Sandra Kim** remains the only Belgian winner for her 1987 entry *J'aime la vie*, which came when she was just 13. Jette-born Max Colombie has received tributes from the likes of Elton John for the electro-pop music he makes under the name of **Oscar and the Wolf**, while other well-known pop acts include half-Congolese half-Belgian rapper **Baloji**, singer-songwriter **Selah Sue** and Etterbeek-born **Stromae**, aka Paul van Hever, a nattily dressed, formidably eloquent pop star influenced by Brel, best known for his hit song *Alors en Danse*.

NORTHERN BELGIUM ONLINE

For additional online content, articles, photos and more on Northern Belgium, why not visit w bradtguides.com/northernbelgium?

2

Practical Information

WHEN TO VISIT

Flanders is best visited during spring and summer, or just before Christmas. From March to May the countryside is alive with newborn lambs and calves, and orchards are filled with blossoms; July and August are marked by an impressive array of music and folk festivals and parades; and come December romantic Christmas markets line cobblestone squares (see box, page 57). There are a few provisos: avoid the coast during winter when it becomes a series of ghost towns whipped by gale-force winds and rain; be aware that from mid-November to February many of the smaller towns – and the World War I memorial sites – tend to go into hibernation; and that in July and August you'll be battling the selfie sticks in Bruges, so plan your trip accordingly.

HIGHLIGHTS

***THE ADORATION OF THE MYSTIC LAMB*, GHENT** Come face to face with the world's most frequently stolen painting, shining after a lengthy restoration. See page 178.

OOSTDUINKERKE'S HORSEBACK SHRIMP FISHERMEN Watch the world's last horseback fishermen trawling the North Sea shallows for grey shrimp – and try a few too. See page 251.

SINT-ELIZABETH BEGIJNHOF Wander around Kortrijk's impossibly quaint UNESCO-listed béguinage, learning about the lives of the pioneering female béguines. See page 283.

TRY THE WORLD'S RAREST BEER Savour the taste of the dark and sweet Westvleteren no 12, brewed by the monks of Sint-Sixtus Abbey and only available at their abbey café. See page 279.

MECHELEN Enjoy the café culture, carillon concerts and museums of this buzzing but often overlooked town. See page 311.

TALBOT HOUSE, POPERINGE Reflect on the past at this perfectly preserved World War I resthouse that's as touching as the cemeteries. Learn about Tubby, the jolly proprietor, and the men who stayed here. See page 277.

CYCLE AROUND SINT-TRUIDEN Take to the saddle in springtime and ride through blossom-filled fruit orchards, stocking up on fresh strawberries, apples and pears as you go. See page 345.

LISSEWEGE Don't miss Flanders' prettiest hamlet, made up of whitewashed cottages concealing good restaurants and homely B&Bs. See page 235.

OOIDONK CASTLE Pretend you're royalty for the day at this fairytale castle, complete with moat and drawbridge. See page 190.

TONGEREN Shop for vintage trinkets at the huge antiques market in Flanders' oldest town – and visit an award-winning museum. See page 347.

AALST Get dressed up and join the merry madness of Aalst Carnival, which features a street parade, a bonfire and lots of cross-dressing and drinking. See box, page 200.

LIER Pitch up on the hour to see Lier's unique Zimmertoren clock in action. See page 326.

SUGGESTED ITINERARIES

It doesn't take very long to go anywhere in Flanders. All the major cities are roughly a 40-minute train ride from one another and, as a result, it's possible to fit quite a lot into a short trip. I've included a Classic Tour, covering the major cities, but also several itineraries based around a series of themes designed to introduce you to the real Flanders, and allow you to mix and match as you see fit. Don't cram too much in; allow enough time to enjoy a beer while sunning yourself on a terrace, or linger over a really good meal.

CLASSIC TOUR (TEN DAYS)

Brussels Spend a few days in the lively capital getting an art fix, visiting classic bars and admiring the Art Nouveau Ixelles district (page 65).

Antwerp Take the pulse of Belgium's fashionable second city, browsing boutiques, exploring Rubens's palazzo and visiting the world's only UNESCO-listed museum (page 287).

Ghent Medieval grandeur meets buzzing bars in this underrated city, home to fine restaurants and the intense *The Adoration of the Mystic Lamb* (page 163).

Bruges Spend at least a night in this famous, picture-postcard city, juggling searing Flemish Primitivism, winding canals and windmills (page 211).

Ostend Take the 15-minute train ride from Bruges to explore the most dynamic Flemish coastal town, with its beguiling Ensor artworks, Modernist architecture and delicious *moules-frites*. Then zip along the coast via the world's longest tramline (page 241).

BEER Beer pilgrims can visit the following breweries: De Cantillon and Brussels Beer Project in the capital, De Halve Maan in Bruges, De Dolle Brouwers near Diksmuide, Het Anker in Mechelen, De Koninck in Antwerp and De Vrede café in Westvleteren. It makes sense to chime a visit with one of Belgium's beer festivals; April is beer month in Leuven (page 52) with three events dedicated to the brown stuff.

CYCLING Flanders' most famous cycle race, the Ronde van Vlaanderen (Tour of Flanders), is associated with the towns of Geraardsbergen and Oudenaarde. The latter has a dedicated cycling museum, as does Roeselare. Great cycle routes include: the Bruges to Damme canal, from which you can access the entire North Sea coastline; the orchard-filled Haspengouw region near Sint-Truiden; and Limburg, where you can cycle amid swans at Cycling Through Water (page 344).

WORLD WAR I World War I sites and cemeteries are clustered in West Flanders around the town of Ypres, where you'll want to visit the In Flanders Field Museum and Menin Gate, before heading on to the battlefields of the Ypres Salient. Other major sites are Poperinge, 10 minutes by train from Ypres; low-key Diksmuide, home to the IJzertoren monument and museum, and Dodengang (Trench of Death). Add in Veurne, and Nieuwpoort, hosting a brilliant museum recounting how intentional flooding here stopped the German advance during World War I.

OFF THE BEATEN TRACK To experience a real slice of Flemish life, add quaint Lissewege and Lier to your itinerary, follow in witches' footsteps in Laarne, and visit Baarle-Hertog, the world's most Baroque border town.

TOURIST INFORMATION

The tourism infrastructure in Flanders is superb and the range of publications produced to help guide visitors around the region is vast. Even the smallest of villages has an information kiosk where you can find everything from where to stay and eat to local events. I have provided the tourist information offices for each city and town within the individual listings, but if you would like to do some research ahead of a visit, the website of the official tourist board (w visitflanders.com) is a wonderful starting point.

TOUR OPERATORS

Flanders is a popular weekend-break destination and you can easily find deals on flights to and hotels in the major cities and towns via short-break operators and travel companies such as Eurostar. Here is a list of operators including ones with a specialist slant.

UK

Gold Crest 01943 433 457; w gold-crest.com. Coach holidays to Ghent, Brussels, Antwerp, Bruges & Ostend, plus beer festival tours & Christmas market trips.

Martin Randall Travel 020 8742 3355; w martinrandall.com. Leading cultural tour specialist offering art- & war-themed circuits led by experts; accommodation is mainly in 4-star hotels.

Osprey Holidays 0131 243 8098; w ospreyholidays.com. Independent short-break operator that offers value-for-money packages inc chocolate & battlefields tours. Wide range of accommodation options to choose from.

Railbookers 020 3780 2222; w railbookers.co.uk. Arranges travel to & accommodation in all of Flanders' main cities.

Shortbreaks 0844 482 2977; w short-breaks.com. Market-leader offering city breaks to Antwerp, Brussels, Bruges, Leuven, Mechelen, Ostend & Ghent with an emphasis on posh hotel stays & lots of add-ons (restaurants, concert tickets).

Thomas Cook 01733 224 330; w thomascook.com. Well-established agency that organises city breaks to Bruges & Brussels, as well as car hire, travel insurance & foreign currency.

SPECIALIST TOUR OPERATORS

UK

Freedom Treks 01273 334 066; **w** freedomtreks.co.uk. Provides an array of guided/self-guided bike tours, inc a fun bike & boat trip where you stay on a succession of vessels while cycling into Flanders from Amsterdam.

Hooked on Cycling 01506 635 399; **w** hookedoncycling.co.uk. Offers 2 self-guided bicycle tours of Flanders: Brussels–Bruges & through West Flanders via Ypres, Poperinge, Diksmuide & Bruges.

US

Beer Trips +1 406 531 9109; **w** beertrips.com. This American operator runs annual trips taking in Flemish breweries & the 'great beers' of Belgium.

In Trend +1 845 510 9630; **w** intrend.com. Chocolate-themed private tours visiting Brussels, Bruges & Antwerp for seriously sweet-toothed travellers.

Belgium

Go4cycling **m** +32 496 40 42 89; **w** go4cycling.com. Offers very exclusive biking holidays where you can try the cyclo version of the Tour of Flanders (takes place the day before & open to non-professionals), but also get in some sightseeing.

Holiday Pride +32 2 502 73 77; **w** www.holidaypride.be. Tour operator offering a range of LGBT-friendly cruises & cultural trips in Flanders & beyond.

RED TAPE

SHORT STAYS Citizens from EU countries, Canada, Australia, New Zealand and the US do not require a visa to enter Belgium and are permitted to stay for 90 days, as long as you have three months left on your passport. If your country does not appear on this list, you must apply for a visa. At the time of writing, with the spectre of Brexit on the horizon, the situation for British travellers was unclear to say the least. In the case of a deal, Britons will not need a visa to visit the EU, but will need to buy pre-travel authorisation akin to the ESTA scheme in the US (this is unlikely to happen before 2021). If there's no deal, a visa may well be required. Check before travelling.

EMBASSIES AND CONSULATES

ABROAD

Australia 19 Arkana St, Yarralumla, Canberra, ACT 2600; +61 2 6273 2501; 07.00–12.30 & 13.00–16.00 Mon–Thu, 09.00–12.30 & 13.00–15.00 Fri

Canada 360 Albert St, 8th Flr, Suite 820, Ottawa, K1R 7X7; +1 613 236 7267; 09.00–13.00 & 14.00–15.00 Mon–Thu, 09.00–14.00 Fri

France 9 rue de Tilsitt, 75840 Paris Cedex 17; +33 1 44 09 39 39; 09.00–13.00 & 14.00–17.00 Mon–Fri by appointment only

Germany 52–3 Jägerstrasse, 10117 Berlin; +49 3020 6420; 09.00–noon Mon–Fri, afternoon by appointment

Ireland 1 Elgin Rd, Ballsbridge, Dublin 4; +353 1 631 5284; 09.00–13.00 & 14.00–15.00 Mon–Fri or by appointment

Luxembourg 4 rue des Girondins, Luxembourg 1626; +352 44 27 461; 09.00–14.00 Mon–Fri

Netherlands 11 Johan van Oldenbarneveltlaan, 2582 NE Den Haag; +31 70 312 34 56; 09.00–noon & 13.30–15.30 Mon & Wed–Thu, 09.30–noon Tue & Fri

UK 17 Grosvenor Cres, London SW1X 7EE; 020 7470 3700; variable depending on which department you need; check website

US 3330 Garfield St NW, Washington, DC 20008; +1 202 333 6900; 09.00–12.30 & 13.30–16.00 Mon–Fri

BRUSSELS

Australia 56 av des Arts; 02 286 05 00

Canada 58 av des Arts; 02 741 06 11

France 65 rue Ducale; 02 548 87 11

Germany 8–14 rue Jacques de Lalaing; 02 787 18 00

Ireland 50 rue Froissart; 02 282 34 00

Luxembourg 75 av de Cortenbergh; 02 737 57 00

Netherlands 4–10 av de Cortenbergh; 02 679 17 11
New Zealand 7th Flr, 9–31 av des Nerviens; 02 512 10 40
UK 10 av d'Auderghem; 02 287 82 11
US 27 bd du Régent; 02 811 40 00

GETTING THERE AND AWAY

Flanders is incredibly accessible. Bang in the middle of Europe and hugging the North Sea coastline, it can be reached by air, sea or land. It also helps that Brussels is a major business hub and, as a result, transport links have increased to meet the demand of international commuters. Companies are battling to provide competitive fares and travellers can benefit from these price wars.

BY AIR

From the UK and Ireland You can fly direct from London, Manchester, Birmingham, Bristol and Edinburgh and, in Ireland, direct from Dublin. Flights from the UK take about an hour; those from Ireland an hour and 40 minutes. Brussels has two major airports: **Brussels Airport Zaventem** (w brusselsairport.be) and **Brussels South Charleroi Airport** (w brussels-charleroi-airport.com). Zaventem is 13km northeast of Brussels and served by most major airlines, including national carrier Brussels Airlines. Outer-lying Charleroi is 60km south of the city, or around an hour's drive away, and serves budget airlines. For transfers to Brussels, see page 66.

Aer Lingus 0333 004 5000; w aerlingus.com. Flies direct from Dublin to Brussels Zaventem.
British Airways 0844 493 0787; w britishairways.com. The airline giant operates 6 flights a day, 7 days a week between Heathrow & Zaventem.
Brussels Airlines 0905 60 95 609; w brusselsairlines.com. Flies from Heathrow to Zaventem; rates often more competitive than BA.
Flybe 0371 70 02 000; w flybe.com. Offers direct flights from London Southend to Antwerp.
Logan Air 0344 800 2855; w loganair.co.uk. Have taken over flyBMI route between Newcastle & Brussels with departures Mon–Thu, as well as Fri & Sun eves.
Ryanair 0871 246 0000; w ryanair.com. Budget airline serving Charleroi from Edinburgh, Manchester & Glasgow, & Charleroi & Zaventem from Dublin.

From the US and Canada Direct flights from the US to Brussels are no longer hard to find, and there are also direct links from Canada. The most competitive rates start at just over US$300 for a week-long trip. Brussels Airlines (see above) serves Brussels from New York, Washington, DC and Toronto. Other companies flying direct to the Belgian capital include Air Canada from Montreal, United from New York, Chicago and Washington, DC; and Delta from New York and Atlanta. On average, flights from the east coast of the US and Canada to Brussels take around 7 hours.

Air Canada 888 247 2262; w aircanada.com. From Calgary, Halifax, Montreal, Ottawa, Toronto & Vancouver to Brussels via London.
American Airlines 800 433 7300; w aa.com. Chicago & New York (JFK) to Brussels.
Delta Airlines 800 241 4141; w delta.com. New York (JFK) & Atlanta to Brussels.
United Airlines 800 300 1547; w united.com. Washington to Brussels.

From the rest of the world Unfortunately, there are no direct flights to Belgium from Australia or New Zealand. The best option is to fly via Dubai or Doha; Emirates (w emirates.com), Etihad (w etihad.com) and Qatar Airways (w qatarairways.com) are the main competitors. Rates start as low as US$670 for a seven-day trip, and the journey takes a day. User-friendly Google Flights (w google.com/flights) offers an overview of the cheapest rates/routes.

BY FERRY Travel by boat has been heavily eclipsed by the faster Eurostar and Eurotunnel services, but if you're not in a rush, cross-Channel ferries can offer savings, especially for families. **P&O** (01304 86 30 00; w www.poferries.com) runs services from Dover to Calais, and an overnight service from Hull to Zeebrugge (the only UK to Belgium crossing now), while **DFDS Seaways** (0208 127 8303; w dfdsseaways.co.uk) sails from Dover to Calais and Dunkirk.

BY CAR To reach Belgium from the UK by car, either take a car ferry (see above) or **Eurotunnel** (w eurotunnel.com). This high-speed car train runs from Folkestone to Calais 24 hours a day, with up to four departures an hour during the day and every couple of hours between 23.00 and 06.00. The journey takes 35 minutes, then from Calais it's a 2-hour drive along the E40 to Brussels; De Panne is just 50 minutes away.

Fares for motorists and motorcyclists start at £30 each way; the cheapest rates are for overnights (up to two days) or short stays (up to five days). Journey times to Brussels from cities in neighbouring countries are as follows: Amsterdam (2hrs 30mins); Paris (4–5hrs); Cologne (2hrs 20mins); and Luxembourg City (2hrs 30mins).

BY TRAIN

From the UK **Eurostar** (w eurostar.com) runs up to ten services a day from St Pancras International to Bruxelles Midi/Brussel Zuid; the journey time is about 2 hours. There are three classes of ticket: Standard; Standard Premier, which includes a light meal; and Business Premier, which you can change or cancel for free. The cheapest returns start at £58; standard singles can run as high as £170 if booked last-minute. You can buy an 'Any Belgian Station' ticket for a small supplement, which includes an onward journey within Belgium; high-speed trains such as Thalys aren't included, and if you are heading to Brussels Airport Zaventem you'll have to pay a €5.25 'Diabolo' supplement each way either at a Belgian station or on board. They frequently run promotions combining rail travel and hotels, so check their website. For flexible travellers, Eurostar Snap (w snap.eurostar.com), launched in 2016, offers discount rates as low as £50 return. You can specify the day of travel and whether you want to leave in the morning or afternoon; 48 hours before departure, you will get an email with your allocated train. It's the luck of the draw so be prepared to travel at dawn or late; check their website for the latest promotions.

ARE YOU LEGAL?

When driving in Europe, you're legally required to carry headlamp converters, a warning triangle, GB plate (unless the registration plates have the GB logo on them), reflective vest, first-aid kit and fire extinguisher. If you are stopped and found to be missing any of the above you may be issued a hefty on-the-spot fine. Check the website w gov.uk for the latest requirements, which are likely to change after Brexit, and may well involve acquiring an international driving permit (IDP).

HI BELGIUM PASS

Since April 2017, in an effort to boost tourism across Belgium, Brussels Airlines has clubbed up with the national rail provider and individual attractions to offer the superbly good value Hi Belgium Pass. The pass (€149; w hibelgiumpass.brusselsairlines.com) includes a return flight from 50 cities in 18 countries across Europe – including five airports in the UK – to Brussels, unlimited train travel within the country, and vouchers for activities (museums, beer tasting etc) in two cities. You must fly out to Brussels between Thursday and Saturday, and return between Sunday and Tuesday. Vouchers cover activities in Antwerp, Brussels, Ghent, Leuven, Mechelen and Ypres, as well as Wallonia.

From France, Germany, Luxembourg and the Netherlands **Thalys** (w thalys.com) is the swiftest way to get from Paris, Cologne and Amsterdam to Bruxelles Midi/Brussel Zuid; it also serves Antwerp from Amsterdam, Schiphol Airport and Rotterdam. The journey from Paris to Brussels takes around 1½ hours; from Amsterdam it takes 2½ hours; from Cologne just under 2 hours. Thalys's low-cost subsidiary **Izy** (w izy.com) offers Brussels–Paris fares from just €10 one way, though I'd advise going for their standard seats (from €19) for a minimum of comfort. The service runs once a day during the week and twice a day at weekends; it takes 2½ hours. From Germany, aside from the Thalys, there are a number of high-speed trains (notably **ICE** trains) offering affordable rates and swift journey times; book through **Deutsche Bahn** (w bahn.de). Useful websites are w trainline.eu for price comparison and booking; and w b-europe.com, the international branch of Belgian train operator SNCB, which sells Eurostar, Thalys, TGV and ICE tickets, and often has excellent seasonal deals.

BY BUS

From the UK If you're prepared to put in the bum-numbing hours, **Eurolines** (w eurolines.co.uk), a division of National Express, offers daily departures from London Victoria coach station to Brussels and Antwerp. The journey takes 8½ hours, with fares from £30 return if booked well ahead. Cheaper still is German company **Flixbus** (w flixbus.co.uk), launched in 2013 to rival state railway Deutsche Bahn. It connects London and Bruges twice a day, taking a mere 6 hours; it also has daily services to Ghent, Antwerp and Brussels, and is useful if you're on a wider European jaunt, with direct links from Flanders to Paris, Amsterdam and beyond. UK–Belgium routes start from £9.99 for a single journey.

HEALTH *with Dr Felicity Nicholson*

There are no official vaccination requirements for entry into Flanders and no serious health issues to worry about. However, it is best to be up to date with the vaccinations recommended for Britain such as diphtheria, tetanus and polio – now given as the all-in-one vaccine Revaxis – that last for ten years and MMR. There has been an increase in the number of cases of measles in Europe so ensure that you have either had measles, mumps and rubella (the diseases) or have had two doses of the MMR vaccine. Other vaccinations would include hepatitis B for health-care workers, plus influenza and pneumococcal vaccines for the elderly and those at special risk. If you are walking in long grass, check yourself for ticks afterwards;

they may carry Lyme disease which manifests as a rash accompanied by a fever, headache, neck stiffness, painful muscles and joints, swollen lymph glands and fatigue. It is treatable with antibiotics if it is recognised at an early stage.

Residents of EU countries, including the UK and Ireland, should obtain a **European Health Insurance Card** (EHIC) (w www.ehic.org.uk) before travelling as it allows you to receive medical treatment at a reduced cost and sometimes for free. Order it online. The EHIC doesn't cover all eventualities, so you should still buy travel insurance that includes medical costs. The nature of the UK's departure from the EU was still hanging in the balance as we went to press, with access to health care when visiting an EU country likely to change imminently; given the above, purchasing travel insurance is advised.

PHARMACIES Pharmacies (*pharmacie/apotheek*) are easily identified by the illuminated green cross outside and usually open 09.00–18.00, though in some areas only during the week; at weekends, pharmacies post a sign in their window indicating the nearest on-duty branch. Note that you will have to go to a pharmacy to purchase even basic healthcare items/medicines including painkillers and cold remedies. You can check where your nearest pharmacy is at w pharmacie.be.

MEDICAL CARE In case of an emergency you can dial ☎ 112 free of charge from any phone. They can arrange an ambulance but it will be at your expense. Other useful numbers are: ☎ 101 (police); ☎ 100 (fire service/find your nearest on-call doctor); and ☎ 02 648 40 14 – a 24-hour community crisis/information service helpline in English. The majority of hospitals in Flanders have first-rate facilities and most staff speak English. Like Flemish nationals, you will have to pay for treatment upfront and reclaim a proportion of the costs later providing you have an EHIC card or travel insurance (see above).

SMOKING Since July 2011, smoking has been banned in all restaurants, cafés, bars, clubs and casinos in Belgium, with the exception of designated smoking rooms (the same rules apply for e-cigarettes). As of February 2019, smoking in vehicles while in the company of a minor has also been banned. Flanders has, however, traditionally been smoker-friendly, and it's not at all unusual to see bar owners turning a blind eye, particularly late at night.

SAFETY

Flanders is safe to visit. Like most places there are instances of bag-snatching, pickpocketing and very rarely mugging, and you should be vigilant if walking late at night in the vicinity of Brussel Zuid/Bruxelles Midi and Brussel Noord/Bruxelles Nord railway stations. As long as you aren't flashing huge sums of cash or leaving valuables exposed in the back seat of your car, you shouldn't encounter any problems. Nonetheless it's a good idea to make photocopies of your important documents, and to store them separately from the originals.

DRUGS The most frequently occurring drug in Flanders is cannabis. Currently it is legal for over-18s to possess up to 3g of the plant for personal consumption. However, those found to be under age or in possession of more than the specified amount will face fines and possibly prison sentences. Class A drugs are certainly present, especially in towns like Brussels, and likewise in Antwerp which has transformed in recent years into the continent's main entry point for South

American cocaine (most goes to the Netherlands). Penalties for possession and consumption of these drugs are severe.

TERRORISM There have been a number of high-profile attacks in recent years conducted by terrorists linked to Daesh, most notably on 22 March 2016, when co-ordinated attacks killed 32 and injured hundreds at Brussels Airport Zaventem and on the capital's metro system. Brussels's profile as the 'capital' of Europe and HQ to numerous international institutions like NATO and the EU will continue to make it vulnerable, but with a stepped-up police presence at transport hubs and in major cities, there's absolutely no reason to avoid travelling to Belgium or to feel unsafe once there. In fact, it's worth taking a leaf out of locals' notebooks: in the wake of an anti-terror lockdown in Brussels, when requested not to give away the police's positions, residents took to posting (often defiant) pictures of cats online instead! If you are worried, you can always check the FCO website w gov.uk/foreign-travel-advice for updates.

FOCUS ON SPECIFIC GROUPS

WOMEN TRAVELLERS You are highly unlikely to be hassled as a young woman travelling independently. Women are viewed as equals and the quiet nature of Flemish men means you will rarely encounter the Casanova types that may harass you elsewhere in continental Europe.

SENIOR TRAVELLERS Senior citizens are held in high respect in Flemish society and you can expect to be treated with courtesy. The great news is that over 60s will qualify for discounted ticket rates for many museums, theatres etc and benefit from reduced rail fares.

LGBT TRAVELLERS Belgium is recognised as one of the most progressive countries in the world when it comes to LGBT rights, having legalised same-sex marriage back in 2003 – it was the second country to do so – and same-sex adoption in 2006. While the LGBT flag flies at a slightly lower mast than in the Netherlands, there's a vibrant scene spanning dynamic Pride events and a healthy selection of gay-friendly bars, clubs and hotels in the main cities (see boxes, pages 88 and 297). The Brussels tourist board has meanwhile embraced this slice of the market, and regularly publishes information on LGBT-friendly parties or initiatives. For more information check out the websites below:

f **girlsheartbrussels** Covers Brussels from a female, feminist & queer perspective, runs pop-up bars & mini-breaks around Art Brussels fair.
w **rainbowhouse.be** Information centre & bar in Brussels that hosts movie nights, readings & debates. The best place to get tips for what's happening.
w **travelgay.com** The world's most visited LGBT site; has information on Flanders & Brussels.
w **www.holidaypride.be** Brussels-based travel agency for LGBT holiday packages.

TRAVELLING WITH KIDS Children are adored in Flanders and well catered for by most hotels and guesthouses, who usually have a family room and, if not, are happy to supply a cot or fold-away bed. Well-behaved tots are welcomed into most restaurants and cafés, and can usually enjoy dedicated kids' menus. Children also get a discount on public transport and at museums, with those under six usually going free – you'll also find family ticket deals. Child-friendly attractions include

TRAVELLING WITH A DISABILITY IN NORTHERN BELGIUM

In the run-up to the World War I centenary, the Flemish tourist board devoted considerable resources to improving accessibility, which had lagged behind other countries on the continent. The first accessibility study and guide was completed in 2013 for Flanders Fields and the Westhoek, followed by the coastal cities in 2015. Fast-forward to today, and Visit Flanders offers a huge array of English-language brochures covering day trips to Antwerp, Bruges, Leuven, Ghent and Mechelen, as well as accessible accommodation and access for the visually impaired. There is also a specific guide to choosing suitable transport to and from Flanders. A large proportion of buses and trams across the region (called 'More Mobile Lines') are now accessible, and wheelchair users no longer have to book in advance for these services. The network is likely to increase. While this marks a big improvement, certain parts of the infrastructure – rail, for instance – still have some way to go, and visitors are well advised to do some research in advance to make their visit as problem-free as possible. Here are some useful websites:

TRANSPORT

Bus and tram

w **delijn.be** Has an 'accessibility' tab that shows which lines are wheelchair-friendly.

w **navigeerenparkeer.be** (Flemish only, use Google Translate) provides a handy list of the parking spaces on the coast reserved for people with a disability.

By rail

Assistance can be arranged at stations if booked 24 hours in advance; call 02 52 82 828 or reserve online.

w **belgiantrain.be** Has a menu bar with a section dedicated to travellers with reduced mobility, & lists contact numbers & available facilities at each station.

General

w **visitflanders.com/en/accessibility** Provides an excellent all-round resource with a trip-planning tool, accessible day-trip brochures, accommodation etc.

w **www.gov.uk/guidance/foreign-travel-for-disabled-people** Gives general information about travelling for people with disabilities.

w **toevla.be** Details accessible accommodation, transport & tourist attractions in Flanders. Results can also be filtered to those with visual or auditory impairments.

w **handy.brussels** Searchable database with information about disability access in Brussels.

ZOO Antwerp (page 309), the Belgian Comic Strip Center (page 107), the Museum of Natural Sciences (page 117) and the Flemish coast.

TRAVELLING WITH PETS Taking your dog or cat on holiday shouldn't pose too many problems. You will need to carry a veterinarian certificate, issued at least 30 days before travel but no more than a year prior to entry, indicating the health status of the pet and proof of a rabies vaccination. Make sure you check the regulations of your airline carrier or ship, however. The Federal Public Service (w health.belgium.be) has a page with all the details.

WHAT TO TAKE

With such fickle weather, it's best to dress in layers that you can peel off and on as necessary. The dress code in Flanders is casual and relaxed; even when it comes to a night out, smart jeans or trousers, boots and a top, rather than high heels and diamonds, will suffice. This is of course a general rule, and you'll see plenty of Louis Vuitton-sporting sophisticates in the more chic cities such as Antwerp. During the winter, a hat, scarf, gloves and windproof/waterproof jacket are essential to ward off the biting northern winds. As to footwear, trainers or sturdy walking shoes are more practical among the cobblestone streets of the main towns and open fields found elsewhere. During the summer, you can switch the waterproof jacket for a light sweater or jacket and a T-shirt. Practical items that you should consider taking are a conversion plug (sockets are the European two-pin style), sunscreen and a compact umbrella.

MONEY

Belgium converted from the Belgian franc (BF) to the euro (€) in January 2002. Notes come in denominations of €500, €200, €100, €50, €20, €10 and €5. Coins in circulation include the €2 and €1 with mock silver centre and outer gold band; the gold-coloured 50, 20, 10 cents; and copper-coloured 5, 2 and 1 cents. ATMs are commonplace in all cities and towns and most accept major debit and credit cards, although be warned that the majority of banks at home will charge a commission fee for withdrawals made abroad (some don't charge for purchases). At the time of going to print, the exchange rate was €1: $1.10/£0.88; check the currency conversion website (w xe.com) for the latest rates. While Belgium has been hailed as a pioneer in its move towards becoming a 'cash-free society', in reality, even in bigger cities, many businesses take cash only, so make sure that you have some money to hand for such eventualities.

TIPPING Tipping is not expected in Flanders – it's somewhat more common in Wallonia – because a service charge is automatically added to any restaurant, hotel or taxi bill. Only leave something extra if you were really impressed; a few euros will suffice.

BUDGETING

When it comes to expenses, Flanders is on par with most western European areas. Costs are inevitably higher in the main cities and accommodation rates are inflated during the summer high season. The trick is to visit the main cities at weekends when businessmen decamp and rates drop significantly, especially in Brussels, and make use of the discounts hotels offer for stays of three or more days. Entry to some Brussels museums is free on the first Wednesday of the month. You can also save money with the City Cards on offer in Brussels, Ghent, Bruges and Antwerp (see various boxes on pages 95, 177, 226, 237, 300, 340 and 350). Try dining in fancier restaurants at lunchtime when they offer a discounted two- or three-course *dagmenu* (daily menu), or opt for the *dagschotel* (dish of the day) in run-of-the-mill restaurants. The prices quoted below are based on a daily spend per person, on the assumption that two people will be sharing a room.

SCRIMP AND SAVE Those on a tight budget can scrape by on €50 (£44/US$57) by staying in hostels or camping, visiting free sites of interest, having a large *dagschotel* at lunch, snacking on *frites* at night and enjoying the odd beer in a time-forgotten *estaminet*. To further lower costs you'll need to couchsurf (w couchsurfing.com).

MAKING DO For €80 (£70/US$90) you can sleep in a two-star hotel or decent Airbnb, and have change for a light lunch, entry to a museum and a modest two-course dinner in a back-street brasserie.

ABLE TO CHOOSE Those who can afford to loosen the belt a little will, for €140 (£123/US$160), be able to sleep in style at a boutique B&B, visit several museums or a show, dine at a decent restaurant and still have change for a few snacks throughout the day.

AFFLUENT Spending €250 (£219/US$283) will buy a high-star hotel room, treats such as a horse-drawn carriage tour of the town, and a lunch and dinner you can linger over, and leave a nice kitty at the end of the evening to spend on some deceptively strong Belgian beers.

MONEY NO OBJECT If you can afford to spend more than €300 (£263/ US$240) a day, you'll have access to the very best hotels, enjoy first-rate cuisine at a Michelin-starred restaurant and take in an opera or dance show in your finest new Belgian-designer outfit.

GETTING AROUND

The public transport system in Flanders is exemplary. Trains and buses service every corner of the country and, what's more, they nearly always arrive on time.

BY CAR Belgian drivers get a lot of bad press and I've certainly seen evidence to back this up, but on the flipside, Belgian highways are some of the best in Europe, are toll-free and, until energy-saving measures were put into place, so well lit at night that you could see them from space. Naturally, you will encounter some irks: Antwerp and Brussels often figure at the top of lists of Europe's most traffic-congested cities, so make an effort to avoid them at rush hour. Then, of course, there are the road signs that switch from one language to another (see table, below). However, with a little preparation and bravado, travelling by car will give you the freedom to get off track and discover sights, or that special restaurant, that would otherwise pass you by as you stare out of the window of the train.

PLACE NAMES

Most place names have French and Flemish variations. The list here highlights the main alternatives:

CITY	FLEMISH	FRENCH
Antwerp	Antwerpen	Anvers
Bruges	Brugge	Bruges
Brussels	Brussel	Bruxelles
Ghent	Gent	Gand
Leuven	Leuven	Louvain
Mechelen	Mechelen	Malines
Ostend	Oostende	Ostende
Ypres	Ieper	Ypres
Aalst	Aalst	Alost
Tongeren	Tongeren	Tongres

PRIORITÉ À DROITE

The 'priority to the right' principle, which exists in most European towns, states that, in the absence of road markings, drivers must give way to cars joining a road from the right, even if they have stopped at a road junction or to wait for pedestrians. Exceptions to this include roundabouts, motorways, roads signposted with an orange diamond within a white background, and when drivers are attempting to join a road having gone the wrong way down a one-way street. Clear as mud?

Road rules You must drive on the right-hand side of the road, overtake on the left, give way to traffic already on roundabouts and observe the *priorité à droite* (see box, above). Trams have priority over other traffic. Speed limits range from 120km/h (75mph) on motorways to 50km/h (31mph) in towns, but be aware that 90km/h (56mph) is often allowed outside built-up areas and that near schools the speed limit drops to 30km/h (20mph).

Fuel Rates in Belgium are average to favourable compared with its immediate neighbours when it comes to petrol; for diesel, however, it is among the most expensive in the EU zone.

Car hire Rental companies (all the usual suspects, including Avis, Hertz, Budget, Europcar, Dollar and Sixt) operate at airports and in selected railway stations. Costs begin from as little as €200 per week; check the website w autoeurope.com for the best deals. Drivers will need to be over 21 and have been driving for at least a year; drivers under 25 may incur a young-driver surcharge.

BY TRAIN Trains are operated by the excellent national railway company SNCB-NMBS (☎ 02 528 28 28; w belgiantrain.be), with services starting at 05.00 and ending at midnight. Tickets may be bought online, or at the station; avoid the premium for buying them on board if you can. Fares are relatively low. Antwerp to Poperinge, for instance, which is one of the longest direct journeys in Flanders, costs €21 one way; Ghent to Brussels is €9. It's worth planning trips for the weekend when return tickets are half-price (you must depart after 19.00 on Friday). Those under 26 can travel anywhere in Belgium except Brussels Airport Zaventem for €6.60 each way, while seniors (aged 65+) pay only €6.80 for a same-day return

LOW-EMISSION ZONES

Since 2017, Low-Emission Zones (LEZ) have been introduced in Antwerp and Brussels; Ghent is planning to follow suit in January 2020. If you're intending to drive to these cities it is mandatory to register your vehicle and check whether it is allowed to enter a given zone. Only cars from Belgium or the Netherlands do not need to register, providing that they meet the guidelines; cars from all other countries must do so, preferably at least ten days in advance. Check the website w lez-belgium.be for full details; given the different regulations governing each area, the process is not necessarily straightforward. If your car does not meet requirements, you may be able to purchase a day pass. Otherwise you will need to hire a vehicle locally.

DECIPHERING TRAIN TIMETABLES

Strange codes appear in the left-hand margin of all train timetables (and next to the list of trains on departure boards), and if you happen to miss the small print you could be in for a long journey.

L – stands for 'locale' and indicates trains that will stop at every single village on the way to your destination, via Timbuktu. Suffice to say, they are painfully slow and should be avoided unless absolutely necessary to get where you're going.

IC – The InterCity is an express service, stopping at all the main cities.

anywhere in Belgium, as long as they leave after 09.00 on weekdays. Up to four children under 12 also travel free when accompanied by an adult. Seats cannot be reserved. Most stations have coin-operated luggage lockers. Bicycles are allowed on trains; buy a one-trip card (€5) or day card (€8). Folding bikes are free.

Rail passes If you are going to be taking several journeys you are likely better off buying a rail pass.

Go Pass 10 For those under 26 this €53 pass (valid for a year) allows you to take ten single second-class trips between any two Belgian stations. It's not registered in your name, so friends can share it.

Rail Pass Equivalent to the Go Pass but for those over 25, this pass allows ten single journeys between any two Belgian stations. A second-class pass costs €83; a first-class pass is €128.

Key Card Offers ten short single trips for the bargain price of €24 (second class) and €31 (first class), provided you travel within a designated area. Look at the website (w belgiantrain.be) or ask at a station for details.

B-Excursion Combines rail travel with entrance to a nationwide attraction of your choice and any connecting buses, metros or trams. Prices vary depending on distance and attractions you want to visit.

BY METRO, TRAM AND BUS All three are operated by **De Lijn** (w delijn.be) in Flanders and **STIB-MIVB** (w www.stib-mivb.be) in Brussels. Tram systems operate in Brussels, Ghent, Antwerp and on the Flemish coast. Unless you are heading to out-of-the-way attractions, or on a very tight budget, you will probably not need the bus, which works in harmony with the rail network. In all cases, you can buy tickets from dedicated kiosks, from automatic ticket machines or on board, though you will pay a premium for this. A day pass (*dagpas*) or multi-day pass is usually the cheapest option for travellers. Once on board, you will need to validate your ticket by punching it in the yellow machines situated at the front and by the doors.

BY TAXI Stands can be found outside most railway stations, airports and hotel entrances; outside of major cities it can be hard to hail a taxi in the street so ask your hotel for a reputable local company. I have included suggestions for taxi companies within the Brussels and Antwerp chapters. Fares are based on a meter; they begin with a fixed charge of €2.40 (€4.40 at night) and are then calculated at €1.80/km within the Brussels Capital Region and €2.70 elsewhere.

Uber This service is currently only operating in Brussels (page 67).

ACCOMMODATION

Flanders is bursting at the seams with exciting accommodation. You can sleep in a monastery one night and be lording it up in a 17th-century mansion the next. The gamut of beds on offer – from bunk to boudoir – ensures there are styles to suit all budgets and tastes, though inevitably this is going to be your main expense. The Benelux hotel classification was introduced in 1989 as a guide to quality and follows a blue-star rating of one to five. However, these awards are often a poor reflection of an establishment's true character because classification is not compulsory and officials follow tick lists of facilities (lifts, fire exits etc). Bearing in mind that where you stay can 'make or break' a trip, I have avoided chain hotels (they're not hard to find, with Ibis being the best-value and most prevalent), as they don't offer anything particularly memorable.

During the summer (May–September) and at Christmas, establishments get booked up very quickly, but it's advisable to book ahead in any case, especially given the free cancellation often offered by websites such as w booking.com. If you are travelling on a tight budget it pays to stay in the larger cities over the weekend, when rates drop in response to the mass exodus of businessmen heading home. Flanders has a huge array of Airbnb (w airbnb.com) properties that can also often work out cheaper, especially if you don't mind sharing a place.

HOTELS The medieval layout of Flanders' oldest towns and cities has thankfully prevented many mega-chains from squeezing in and as a result smaller establishments, oozing character, have managed to stay. Given the Flemish flair for design, boutique hotels are particularly exceptional, though you'll also find international luxury chains. Rates range from around €60 for a double in a low-end hotel outside of the major cities to €300 plus for a double in the top-end establishments.

QUIRKIEST STAYS IN FLANDERS

CasAnus Kemzeke, East Flanders; w verbekefoundation.com. You don't get weirder than sleeping in a giant polyester replica of an intestine. The extraordinary one-off apt is part of the Verbeke Foundation art museum.

Hotel Le Berger Brussels. A meticulously preserved 1930s *maison de rendezvous* (ooh la la!) where lovers once had their assignations, now turned into a fabulously characterful hotel (page 77).

Martin's Patershof Mechelen. A stunning deconsecrated neo-Gothic church where you breakfast by the eye-popping altar (page 314).

Station Racour Landen, Flemish Brabant; w stationracour.be. One for trainspotters: sleep in a former railway station, old railway carriage or railway worker's cottage – all aboard!

Wake up in art Knokke; w hotelvanbunnen.be. Rare chance to stay over in a real-life art gallery surrounded by prime Belgian modern art & design; book through the nearby Hotel van Bunnen.

ACCOMMODATION PRICE CODES

Accommodation listings are laid out in decreasing price order, in five categories, as shown in the following key (also on the inside front cover), which also gives an indication of prices. Prices are based on the cost of a double room per night in high season and generally include breakfast unless otherwise stated; city tax – usually no more than €2.50 per person per night – is not included.

Luxury	**€€€€€**	€251+
Upmarket	**€€€€**	€176–250
Mid-range	**€€€**	€101–175
Budget	**€€**	€51–100
Shoestring	**€**	<€50

BED & BREAKFAST (*CHAMBRES D'HÔTES/GASTENKAMERS*) From remote hamlets to big cities, Flanders excels at the B&B and I am a huge advocate. Whether or not your room is part of the proprietor's home, you'll avoid hotel anonymity and are likely to get brilliant local tips too. Often excellent value for money, prices range from €60 for a double to roughly €250 for an en-suite double in a luxury establishment. As with hotels, special rates are usually offered to those staying two or more nights. Conversely, some offer only a minimum two-night stay.

HOSTELS (*AUBERGES DE JEUNESSE/JEUGDHERBERGEN*) The extensive network of hostels throughout Flanders ensures that only in the smallest and most off-the-beaten-track towns will you be without a budget bed, whether young or not. Many are affiliated with Hostelling International, and run locally by Vlaamse Jeugdherbergen (**w** jeugdherbergen.be), so it makes sense to join the scheme before you go to avoid surcharges, though you can also do so on site. Dorm beds start at €20 (breakfast is usually included, but sheet and towel hire often cost extra); doubles start at €40. Flanders' hostel scene has come a long way, with some award-winning properties offering more boons than many hotels.

CAMPING Campsites are graded on a one- to five-star basis: five being the best, but one–two being the most common. Slightly gloomy places off-season, they come alive during summer with numerous activities on offer and entertainment programmes for kids. Prices are usually calculated on individual payments for a site, cost per adult, cost per child, any pets and a car. You will also pay extra for electricity and in some instances hot showers. I wouldn't advise camping rough. Flanders may be flat, but the majority is assigned to farming and you may anger local landowners.

EATING AND DRINKING

> Great restaurants are, of course, nothing but mouth-brothels. There is no point in going to them if one intends to keep one's belt buckled.
>
> Frédéric Raphael

Flanders might be best known for fries, beer and chocolate, but foodies have long since cottoned on to its dense concentration of Michelin stars – there are more starred restaurants in Bruges alone than in the whole of Denmark – and this

RESTAURANT PRICE CODES

Restaurant listings are laid out in decreasing price order, in five categories, as in the following key (also on the inside front cover), which also gives an indication of costs. Figures are based on the cost of a main meal (including tax) per person.

Expensive	€€€€€	€31+
Above average	€€€€	€25–30
Mid-range	€€€	€16–24
Cheap and cheerful	€€	€9–15
Rock bottom	€	<€8

trickles down to a huge glut of high-class bistros and, latterly, street-food pioneers reinventing traditional snacks. It's quite possible to let your nose and appetite guide you around the region, sampling fresh fish on the North Sea coast and beer-soaked stews in cosy, wood-panelled establishments in the countryside. When all this can be washed down with award-winning beers or a cheeky shot of *jenever*, the appeal of Flemish dining is irresistible – gastronomes prepare to let a notch out of your belt.

FOOD When it comes to dining, there are two types of Flanders meals: traditional meals based around meat and fish – often filling fodder that would have kept farm

FRITES

Flanders is famed for producing some of the finest cuisine in Europe but the not-so-humble chip is adored above all else. Even the smallest of villages houses at least one *frietkot* to cope with local demand, while the Belgian fry culture itself enjoys UNESCO's patronage (despite the name French fries, Belgium actually invented the genre). The secret to achieving the crunchy golden exterior and light and fluffy centre is freshness. Potatoes are sliced and cooked within 2 hours, fried in beef fat and allowed to cool before being fried a second time. Sadly, traditional *frietkot* caravans are disappearing – stamped out by planning laws and hygiene standards; meanwhile, though their shabbiness is part of the appeal, Brussels officials have recently set about commissioning architects to turn some of the capital's chip shacks into shiny, eco-friendly frites shrines.

Joints usually stay open until 23.00 or midnight and there's nothing better than leaving a bar and picking up piping-hot chips to tuck into on the way back to the hotel. Common sauces include mayonnaise (ultra-classic), *andalouse* (mayonnaise-based with tomato and basil), and the very popular *samourai* (taste-bud-tingling chilli, tomato and bell peppers). You can get a huge array of snacks to accompany your fries, ranging from *stoofvlees* to *kroketten* (croquettes – usually cheese, prawn or meat), *balletjes met tomaatensaus* (small meatballs in tomato sauce flavoured with herbs), *carbonade flamande* (sweet-sour beef and onion/beer stew) and the infamous *Bicky burger* (hamburger served with a special pickle sauce and deep-fried chip bits). *Brochettes* (kebabs) are also common. One of the most popular places to try frites is Maison Antoine in Brussels (page 83).

hands happy until dinner time in the old days – and the entirely different experience offered by fine-dining restaurants, which proliferate in villages, suburbs and cities. National favourites are undoubtedly *steak-frites* – the meat is of high quality and usually from a local butcher – and *mosselen-frieten/moules-frites;* mussels and other shellfish are in season between September and March, or – according to the adage – any month whose spelling contains an 'r'. In addition, most towns have their own specialities and I've included these under individual listings.

In winter, the Flemish like to tuck into *witloof in de oven* (chicory wrapped in ham and covered in a creamy cheese sauce); *waterzooi* (a broth containing fish/chicken and vegetables); *stoemp met prei* (mashed potato mixed with leeks); *stoofvlees* (beef stew made with brown beer); *konijn en pruinen* (rabbit cooked with prunes and

CHOCOLATE

Chocolate arrived in Europe in the 16th century when Christopher Columbus returned from his voyages to the New World and presented a handful of cocoa beans to Emperor Ferdinand and Infanta Isabella. Barely a year later, the first official shipment arrived in the docks of Seville and by the 17th century chocolate had become the most sought after luxury/medicinal item among European nobility.

Towards the end of the 18th and during the early 19th centuries, both Swiss and English chocolate makers were looking for new ways to enjoy chocolate and began reintroducing extracted cocoa butter to solidify the liquid and add alkali to neutralise the acidic flavour. These solid blocks first went on sale in 1847 and could be found in pharmacies, whose patrons recommended chocolate as a cure for stomach ache.

For years, chocolate production followed the same recipe until, in 1912 in Brussels, Jean Neuhaus created something entirely new that revolutionised the world of chocolate and made Belgium synonymous with chocolate excellence. Using the basic 'couverture' chocolate produced by chocolate makers, he crafted an individual chocolate designed to be eaten for pleasure. He filled these individual cups with flavoured creams, fruit, liquors or crushed-nut paste and named them *pralines*, after the sugared nuts favoured by the Marquis de Praslin. Originally served in paper cones, Neuhaus's wife developed the *ballotin*, a cardboard box that all confectioners use today to keep chocolates fresh. His original shop is still in situ in the Galeries Royales Saint-Hubert in Brussels (page 103) and every year at Easter and Christmas they produce elegant chocolate-inspired window displays.

Predictably, over the years traditional chocolate brands have been swallowed up by multi-national conglomerates – including famous *marques* such as Godiva, and acclaimed brands of more recent origin such as Galler, now owned by the Qatari royal family. Others have moved their production abroad, much to the consternation of Belgians, for whom chocolate is a matter of national pride. However, acting as a bulwark against that trend, there has been a resurgence of artisanal chocolatiers practising the cult of real chocolate, which is free from vegetable fats and contains at least 52%, and often 70%, pure cocoa solids. Of particular note are Pierre Marcolini, Frédéric Blondeel and – for his Willy Wonka-style flavour combinations – Dominique Persoone. And, while consumption is falling, the average Belgian still can't get enough of the stuff, scoffing an impressive 6kg a year.

BRUSSELS SPROUTS

Brits and Americans have the Belgians to thank for this Sunday roast staple. A mutation of the savoy cabbage, the Brussels sprout (*Brassica oleracea var gemmifera*) originated in Afghanistan, Iran and Pakistan. Its presence in Europe was first recorded in the early 1200s, when it was sold in markets in Brussels – supposedly where it picked up its common name. During the 16th century its popularity in Belgium spread to the rest of Europe and by the end of the 18th century it was being cultivated in England and France. North America didn't catch on until President Thomas Jefferson introduced it in 1812.

beer); and *paling in 't groen* (young eel cooked in a green sauce of spinach, sorrel, mint, thyme, tarragon, bay leaf and white wine).

In summer, menus feature the likes of *tomaat met grijze garnaalkes/tomate aux crevettes* (tomatoes stuffed with North Sea shrimp mixed with mayonnaise and ketchup) and *asperges op vlaamse wijze/asperges à la flamande* (white asparagus served in melted butter and with a crumbled boiled egg), which come into season at the end of May. If you are feeling really adventurous – vegetarians avert your eyes – you might like to try meaty specialties like *bloedworst* – literally 'blood sausage' – made from ground-pork leftovers, fat, breadcrumbs and pig's blood; *kop* (a chunky pâté made from ground beef and tongue and set in gelatine); *paardefilet* (horse steak); and, finally, *filet américan*, which sounds deceptively like a steak, but is actually a raw patty of beef mincemeat mixed with raw egg, onion, capers and a splash of Worcestershire sauce.

Snacks: sweet and savoury Wander down almost any street and your nose will crinkle as some delicious smell wafts by. Savoury bites include the inimitable frites (see box, page 45), meatballs (*ballekes/bouletten*), filled baguettes (*belegde broodjes*) and, especially in Brussels, the well-known *croque monsieur*. Bakers and *pâtissiers* offer sweeter treats, from delicate cream cakes and fruit tarts to custard-filled pastries. **Belgian waffles** need no introduction and come in two varieties: the Brussels and the Liège. The latter (and tastier) is a dense, doughy mixture laced with sugar and served piping hot. The yeast-leavened Brussels variety, on the other hand, may contain fewer calories but is similar in weight and taste to polystyrene, perhaps the reason why they cover it in icing sugar, chocolate sauce, ice cream or fruit. Also look out for the marzipan-flavoured *mattentaart* (see box, page 203), cinnamon-flavoured *speculaas* biscuits and Diksmuide's custard-filled *IJzerbollen*. Most cities produce chocolates referencing the nickname of inhabitants.

Vegetarians and vegans Meat is the main focus of most Flemish dishes, and while exclusively vegetarian restaurants are still scarce in the smaller towns and villages, veggie establishments are now to be found in the main cities, especially Ghent, which has the most vegetarian restaurants in Europe and where every Thursday is a city-wide meat-free day. Elsewhere it can be difficult if you're not a fan of pasta pesto or goat's cheese salads (sigh), but I've indicated veggie-friendly restaurants where possible.

DRINK **Beer** is to Belgium what wine is to France: a daily essential, with UNESCO recently recognising Belgium's entire beer tradition – from the brewing to the drinking – as a slice of intangible cultural heritage. With over 800 varieties, the production and consumption of beer are a source of national pride and their breadth

BEER *Tim Webb (co-author of* Good Beer Guide Belgium; **w** *camra.org.uk)*

Any beer drinker who comes to Flanders to drink lager such as the local Stella has missed the point. It is like wanting to sample the food and sticking with chips, or trying to see the region without leaving the motorways. International-brand lagers are like white sliced bread – simple, predictable, dull and everywhere. Flemish ones are no better than the rest.

The beers that make Belgian brewing world-famous come mainly in bottles, usually with a yeast sediment (so pour with care) and sometimes in a size (75cl) designed for sharing, like wine. Some come bearing a logo that reads 'Authentic Trappist Product', a sign that it is made within the confines of a Trappist abbey under the control of the Order. The monastic connection goes back to the days when abbeys were centres of scientific study, which included working out how a benign Almighty had enabled man to make alcohol out of anything that grows from the ground.

Whoever makes the beers, they come in just about every strength, shade and style imaginable. Each has its own glass, too, though this is mainly for marketing purposes.

Relatively well-known brands like Hoegaarden wheat beer, Belle Vue cherry beer, Leffe Blond and others have popularised Belgian brewing, but are not its finest achievements. What follows is a quick run through of Flanders' better brews.

WEST FLANDERS The Van Eecke and St Bernardus breweries of Watou, in the hop-growing area west of Poperinge, brew great beers in numerous styles under the Watou, Kapittel and St Bernardus brands. Nearby, the café opposite Sint-Sixtus Abbey's gates near Westvleteren (page 279) serves its remarkable Trappist ales.

Best local style Oak-aged ales like Rodenbach Grand Cru, Vichtenaar, Duchesse de Bougogne or Verzet Oud Bruin come mainly from around Kortrijk.

Brewery to visit De Dolle Brouwers at Esen, near Diksmuide (page 262), brewers of Oerbier and others.

LIMBURG The transformation of Limburg from the Flemish coalfield to a holiday area of forests and lakes brought with it a quiet revolution in beer-making, topped off by the arrival of the Trappist brewery at Achel, on the Dutch border.

Best local style Limburg brewers make light blonde ales with a distinctive hoppy character. Try Martens Sezoens, Bink Blond, Ops-Ale, Ter Dolen Blond or the draught blonde ale at the Achel cloister to get the drift.

Brewery to visit The loveliest brewery buildings in Flanders belong to Kerkom Brouwerij, near Sint-Truiden (469 Naamsesteenweg, Kerkom; ⏲ Apr–Oct 11.00–

and quality have had beer *aficionados* fizzing with delight for years. Like a fine wine – and treated with the same respect – the majority of these beers should be sipped slowly and savoured, which is no bad thing when alcohol percentages reach 12%.

Also high in the alcoholic stakes is ***jenever***, a juniper-flavoured spirit unique to Flanders and the Netherlands. Traditionally developed from the distillation

19.00 Wed–Sun, Nov–Mar 13.00–19.00 Thu–Sun). In summer they use the old farm buildings and in winter open their traditional 19th-century café. The brewer now makes his Bink beers elsewhere.

ANTWERP The crucible of the Belgian beer revolution is much revived in recent years. A *bolleke* of De Koninck is the toast of the city, while big blonde Duvel, from Breendonk near Puurs, struts its stubby-bottled stuff around the globe. For world-class craft beers drink Dochter Van de Korenaar from Baarle-Hertog (page 332).

Best local style The modern incarnations of the *dubbel* and *tripel* styles of ale have their origins in beers made at the abbey of Westmalle, northwest of Antwerp, while the last of the great Mechelen brown ales is Gouden Carolus Classic.

Brewery to visit Het Anker, in Mechelen, hosts informative brewery tours, and has a hotel and multi-storey bistro (pages 314 and 315).

BRUSSELS AND BRABANT The only Belgian beers with a European Union TSG (Traditional Speciality Guaranteed) certification are three types of Lambic beers called *oude g(u)euze*, *oude kriek* and *faro*. The *oude* distinguishes them from (often tacky) modern derivatives.

Best local style The building blocks of Lambic beers are musty, fungal, lactic, citrus concoctions called Lambics, made much like regular wheat beers but fermented by naturally occurring wild yeast for up to three years in oak casks. Expert blenders then mix these and bottle them, sparking new life to create clear, ultra-dry *oude g(u)euze*. Alternatively, they may be added to a cask filled with bucket-loads of hard, dry cherries, steeped for many months before bottling as *oude kriek*. Suspend disbelief and instruct your taste buds to ignore beer and think of traditional cider, or wild local wines from mountain villages. The best are from Cantillon, 3F (Drie Fonteinen), Boon, Oud Beersel, Hanssens and De Cam.

Brewery to visit The Cantillon brewery in Brussels (page 122) shows how Lambic is made and sells samples. There are public brewing days in March and November.

EAST FLANDERS Most of East Flanders' 20+ breweries produce good beers but, sadly, few let in visitors. And while brand names like Witkap, Pater Lieven, Valeir and Malheur usually indicate high quality, there is no longer a specific East Flanders style of beer. However, if there is such a thing as the nicest pub in Belgium, the Gulzigen Bok (48 Gentweg; ⌚ 17.00–late Wed, 11.00–late Thu–Sun) in Vurste, just south of Ghent, might just be it.

and fermentation of malt, this liver-warming drink comes in two varieties: *oude* (old) and *jonge* (young). In fact, the differentiation has nothing to do with age, but rather varying distillation recipes; younger jenevers are made from grain and are served chilled, tasting similar to vodka; old jenevers have a higher concentration of malt, are aromatic like whisky and are served at room temperature. Alcohol

BASIC BEER GLOSSARY

ABBEY BEER A beer that imitates the monastic brewing styles of the Trappist breweries. Some imitations are better than the originals.

ABV Alcohol by volume. Regular beers made in the English-speaking world are generally low alcohol at 4% abv; standard international beers are 5%; speciality beers range from 4% to 12% depending on the style.

ALE Beer that is fermented at room temperature and, ideally, continues to do so (Flemish: *op gist*; French: *sur lie*) in the cask or bottle, as in British 'real ale'.

DUBBEL (French: *double*) Medium-sweet brown ale of 6–7.5% abv.

G(U)EUZE Old pale ale. But see *oude g(u)euze* (below).

KRIEK Cherry alcopop with a beerish slant. But see also *oude kriek* (below).

LAGER Beer that is fermented below room temperature and, ideally, continues to mature in chilled vats for many weeks. Most do not.

LAMBIC Beer that is fermented very slowly by wild yeast, traditionally in oak casks, for anything from one to three years.

OUD BRUIN Oak-aged brown ale, usually of low–medium strength (5–7%), with a matured and sour character.

OUDE G(U)EUZE A mix of old and young Lambics plus a drop of sugar, refermented in champagne bottles for a year or more. Unique, brilliant and memorable.

OUDE KRIEK Lambic steeped with a boatload of cherries for several months, then bottled.

TRAPPIST Beer brewed at one of seven monasteries of the Trappist Order that are licensed to make beer. Six are in Belgium: Achel, Chimay, Orval, Rochefort, Westmalle and Westvleteren.

TRIPEL (French: *triple*) Strong, sweetish blonde beer style of 7.5–9.5% abv.

WHITE BEER (Flemish: *witbier*; French: *bière blanche*) Brewed with plenty of wheat in the mash, making it naturally cloudy with a fresh-bread sweetness. Lowish alcohol (4–5.5%) and often spiced with coriander and dried peel.

percentages range from a hefty 20% to a toe-curling 40%. Hasselt is particularly renowned for its production and has a dedicated museum (page 340). There are several specialist jenever bars scattered throughout the region and these have been mentioned in the bar listings. Surprisingly, northerly Flanders also has a modest sprinkle of vineyards, including **Genoels-Elderen** (page 351) on the outskirts of

Tongeren, and award-winning DIY outfit **Schorpion** (37 Kersendaelstraat, 3724 Vliermaal; m 0477 58 12 08), situated just outside Hasselt and renowned for its sparkling white wines.

Non-alcoholic drinks Belgians aren't keen on the hard water that flows through their taps, so most buy bottled water. In addition to this you'll find the usual array of fizzy drinks, as well as the omnipresent Cécémel, a syrupy chocolate shake. Flanders has very much joined the coffee revolution in recent years, and you won't struggle to find purveyors of slow-filter coffees and latte art.

RESTAURANTS, BRASSERIES AND CAFÉS The Flemish obsession with good cooking ensures standards are kept high, and even budget restaurants are unlikely to serve inedible food. Most offer a daily special (*dagschotel/plat du jour*) or day menu (*dagmenu*) that are excellent value for money. Also look to see if the restaurant bears a *Bib Gourmand* sign (usually posted beside the entrance); this Michelin qualification is a sign of good food sold at reasonable prices. The prevalence of eating out means popular venues do get very busy at weekends, so it's advisable to make a reservation, either by phone or online through portals such as w resto.be.

Compared to other European destinations, global mega-chains such as McDonald's and Starbucks have thankfully failed to conquer the Belgian market – largely due to the high minimum wage and business taxes. You will, however, find many branches of Belgium-born burger chain Quick, and superior healthy fast-food spot EXKi. The country's migrant population meanwhile ensures plenty of privately owned Chinese, Indian, Thai, Turkish, Italian, Greek and Japanese restaurants. I have tended only to include establishments that focus on Belgian cuisine in the restaurant listings, and in many cases suggested sites that will require a 'bit of a walk', but are well worth the effort if you want to get away from the tourist traps. Be aware that pricier restaurants often close in the afternoon, usually between 14.30 and 18.30, when they reopen for dinner, and that they stop serving early by European standards – at around 21.00 or 22.00. Many also close briefly to take their holidays in the first two weeks of January and perhaps the odd week in July or August.

PUBLIC HOLIDAYS

1 January	New Year's Day	Nieuwjaarsdag
March/April	Easter Monday	Paasmaandag

FLEMISH CAFÉS

In winter, Flemish cafés are snug dens in which to shelter from rain or biting cold; come summer, the doors are thrown open and tables and chairs assembled on the pavements so locals and tourists can enjoy the inimitable tradition known as *een terrasje doen* – 'doing a terrace'. If you're sitting inside, waiters usually expect you to set up a tab, whereas drinkers on the terrace tend to pay on a drink-by-drink basis. Closing time is determined by the last drinker, so there's plenty of time to nurse a heavy-duty beer. The Flemish refer to pubs as 'cafés', an umbrella term which also includes the *bruin café* (an old-fashioned, wood-panelled pub), the *eetcafé* (a café serving a small selection of meals) and the *volkscafé* (a people's café, populated by elderly locals, not strong on décor, and not on most tourists' radar).

1 May	Labour Day	Dag van de Arbeid
May	Ascension Day	Onze Lieve Heer Hemelvaar
May/June	Whit Monday	Tweede pinksterdag
21 July	National Day	Nationale feestdag
15 August	Assumption Day	OLV-Hemelvaart
1 November	All Saints' Day	Allerheiligen
11 November	Armistice Day	Wapenstilstand
25 December	Christmas Day	Kerstmis

EVENTS

Flanders' events calendar is jam-packed, reaching its zenith during the summer months when open-air music festivals dominate the social scene, and the *Gentse Feesten* (Ghent Festivities) sees 2 million tourists pour into Ghent. In addition, in February and March, most towns hold an annual carnival, entailing locals donning fancy dress and getting severely sloshed. The main religious festivals are Ommegang in Brussels and the Heilig-Bloedprocessie in Bruges. Here are some of the highlights.

JANUARY

Bommelsfeesten (w bommelsfeesten.be) Ronse kicks off the first carnival of the year on the second weekend of January.

Djangofollies (w djangofollies.be) Stalwart Flanders-wide festival fêting Belgium-born gypsy jazz maestro Django Reinhardt.

FEBRUARY

Aalst Carnaval Celebrates Aalst's town mascot *Voil Jeannetten* – a drunk transvestite – and features the *prince carnaval* who is allowed to 'rule' town for three days (see box, page 200).

MARCH

Anima (w animafestival.be) The Brussels International Animation Film Festival offers ten days of animated shorts, workshops etc.

Bal Rat Mort (Dead Rat Ball) (w ratmort.be) An extravagant fancy-dress affair held on the first Saturday of the month in Ostend casino, and co-founded in 1898 by artist James Ensor (page 370).

Brussels Art Nouveau & Art Deco Festival (BANAD) (w banad.brussels) Many of the capital's finest buildings aren't open to the public, but this biannual event allows you to sneak inside via guided tours on foot or by bike. Next edition: March 2021.

Krakelingen and Tonnekensbrand Held in Geraardsbergen on the last Sunday of February, this festival bids farewell to winter, with town dignitaries drinking red wine out of a silver chalice containing tiny live fish and throwing pretzels at the crowd (see box, page 202).

APRIL

Leuven Beer Weekends Over three weekends, Leuven goes beer-crazy, taking in the **Leuven Beer Innovation Festival** (w leuveninnovationbeerfestival.com), with its focus on innovative beers, the gourmet **Food & Hops** event (**w** leuvenbeerweekends.be) and epic **Zythos Beer Festival** (**w** zbf.be), with over 500 types of beer.

Ronde van Vlaanderen (Tour of Flanders) (**w** rondevanvlaanderen.be) The famous cycle race is held on the first Sunday in April, departing from Antwerp and finishing in Oudenaarde.

The Royal Greenhouses of Laeken (**w** monarchie.be) Brussels's 19th-century greenhouses have been opened to the public for three weeks each spring for over a century.

MAY

Belgian Pride (**w** pride.be) A colourful procession through Brussels's city centre on the second weekend in May, plus spin-off parties and festivals (Antwerp Pride takes place in August).

Brussels Jazz Weekend (**w** brusselsjazzweekend.be) Replacing the Brussels Jazz Marathon, this newish free festival offers a host of concerts in squares, bars and beyond from the centre to Ixelles.

Concours Reine Elisabeth (Queen Elisabeth Competition) (**w** cmireb.be) World-renowned classical music competition held in Brussels. Instrument categories change yearly: 2020 is for piano; 2021 is for cello.

Festival van Vlaanderen (Festival of Flanders) (**w** festival.be) Not one music festival but a handful of them across the Flemish region held from June to December. Notables include Bruges's MAfestival (August) and the Ghent Festival of Flanders (September–October).

Hanswijkprocessie (Procession of Our Lady of Hanswijk) (**w** hanswijkprocessie.org) Revolves around the veneration of the Virgin Mary, a statue of whom is believed to have cured a town plague. Held in Mechelen on the Sunday before Ascension Day.

Heilig Bloedprocessie (Procession of the Holy Blood) (**w** holyblood.com) Held in Bruges on Ascension Day, this important parade, dating from medieval times, sees a relic reportedly containing drops of Christ's blood borne through the town's streets.

Kattenstoet (**w** www.kattenstoet.be) Eccentric 'cat parade' held in Ypres every three years on the second Sunday of May (page 268).

Taste of Antwerp (**w** proeft.be) Star chefs grace this leading Belgian food festival, with dishes from €5–7.50; held early May.

JUNE

Brussels Film Festival (**w** bsff.be) Annual European cinema event attracting star guests; usually held in mid-June.

Brussels Ommegang (**w** ommegang.be) Between late June and early July, this important folkloric procession – held on the Grand-Place – takes the form of a historical re-enactment of the entry of Emperor Charles V into Brussels in 1549. Expect more than a thousand extras in period costumes, stilt walkers, puppets and jousting.

RetroRonde van Vlaanderen (w retroronde.be) Very fun vintage version of the Tour of Flanders held in early June with riders wearing Eddy Merckx-style jerseys and riding pre-1987 bikes.

Rock Werchter (w rockwerchter.be) On the outskirts of Leuven, this is one of Europe's most famous and reliably well-programmed rock festivals (last weekend in June).

Sand Sculpture Festival (w zandsculpturen.be) Taking place from late June until early September, a huge, family-friendly festival has been latterly held in Ostend and features sand-sculpted Disney characters created by 40 artists.

JULY

Boetprocessie (w boetprocessie.be) Unique Penitential Procession held on the last Sunday of July in Veurne (see box, page 257).

Bruxelles-les-Bains (w bruxelleslesbains.be) For five weeks between July and mid-August, 4,500 tonnes of North Sea sand are deposited on Brussels's quayside, transforming it into a 1km-long city beach lined with bars.

Cactusfestival (w cactusfestival.be) Established and relaxed one-stage music festival held in early July in Bruges's ultra-scenic Minnewaterpark, mixing genres from reggae to rock and pop.

Foire du Midi (w zuidfoor.be) Huge Brussels funfair that spreads along bd du Midi between Porte de Halle and Porte d'Anderlecht from mid-July to mid-August.

Ghent Festivities (w gentsefeesten.be) A must-see extravaganza of free open-air gigs and events (including Ghent Jazz Festival), street entertainers, food stands and parties that take over Ghent city centre for ten days in late July, drawing 2 million visitors. Includes the Procession of the Guild of the Noose–Bearers (page 166).

Tomorrowland (w tomorrowland.com) The world's largest electronic music festival, famed for its wacky themes and extravagant scenography. Held near Antwerp on the last two weekends of July.

Zomer van Antwerpen (w zva.be) Throughout July and August, Antwerp lays on pop-up bars, an open-air cinema and circus shows.

AUGUST

Brussels Flower Carpet (w flowercarpet.be) Every other year Brussels's entire Grand-Place is covered with an elaborate tapestry of thousands of begonias. Next edition: 13–16 August 2020.

Brussels Summer Festival (w bsf.be) Sprouting up around the place Royale mid month, a huge ten-day music bash that draws headline names.

Festival Dranouter (w festivaldranouter.be) Long-running folk music festival on the first weekend of the month south of Ypres. Bring a tent. Also has a De Panne spin-off in April.

Jazz Middelheim (w jazzmiddelheim.be) Founded in the late 1960s, this mid-August festival takes place in Antwerp's serene Park Den Brandt (page 311).

Meyboom (w meyboom.be) Wacky, wonderful folklore tradition going back to a medieval victory of Brussels over Leuven; a tree is paraded via the Grand-Place and erected on rue des Sables, with a brass band and puppets joining in. Falls on 9 August.

Pukkelpop (w pukkelpop.be) On the third weekend of August, this much-loved Hasselt music festival puts on a broad spectrum of acts from hip-hop to heavy metal.

WECANDANCE (w wecandance.be) The Belgian coast's trendiest music event animates Zeebrugge beach mid month.

SEPTEMBER

Beer and Hop Festival (w hoppefeesten.be) Three-day festival with a fun parade showcasing Poperinge's two major assets: hops and beer. Held on the third weekend of September every three years. The next is in 2020.

Belgian Beer Weekend (w belgianbrewers.be) Dozens of Belgian breweries descend on Brussels's Grand-Place on the first weekend of the month, luring 60,000 beer lovers.

Open Monumentendag (Open Monument Day) (w openmonumentendag.be) Over the last two weekends of September hundreds of protected monuments and historical buildings across Flanders are opened to the public free of charge.

OCTOBER

Hasseltse Jeneverfeesten (Hasselt Jenever Festival) (w jeneverfeesten.be) Hasselt – home of jenever – hosts this festival on the third weekend of October. Cafés throw open their doors, free samples abound, live music fills the air, history walks are hosted and even the fountains flow with jenever.

Film Fest Gent (w filmfestival.be) Major cinema rendezvous hosting over 100 films, and putting the spotlight on soundtracks.

Pompoenregatta (Pumpkin Regatta) (w pompoenregatta.be) Wacky races perfectly describe this bizarre annual event where participants canoe 100m in oversized pumpkins. Held the Sunday before Halloween in Kasterlee.

NOVEMBER

Ice Sculpture Festival (w icesculpture.be) Thousands of blocks of ice are deposited on Bruges's Stationsplein and transformed into frozen masterpieces. Late November to early January.

Six Days of Ghent (w sport.be/z6sdaagse) Huge indoor track cycling event, held in Ghent's Kuipke stadium on the third weekend of the month. Expect an incredible party atmosphere.

SINTERKLAAS

Being a child in Flanders is a good gig. Every year on 6 December Sinterklaas, the patron saint of children, pays a visit accompanied by a huge sack of presents and his faithful, un-PC helper Zwarte Piet. Originally a Turkish bishop, St Nicholas was renowned for saving children from a life of prostitution and resurrecting them from the dead. He wore a red bishop's robe, sported a long white beard, carried a big book containing every child's name and rode a white horse called Amerigo across the rooftops – sound familiar? He may have traded old Amerigo for Rudolph, but Sinterklaas is unmistakably the current mythical figure known as Santa Claus. The mix-up came about when English settlers arrived in New Amsterdam (modern-day New York) and mistook the Dutch pronunciation of 'Sinterklaas' for 'Santa Claus'.

According to legend, St Nicholas did not have numerous elves to help him; he had only one assistant, Zwarte Piet – the devil. During the 19th century, when the slave trade was at its peak, this element of the tale morphed into 'black Pete', an African servant. This idea was eventually replaced with the less emotive idea that Pete's face was blackened from soot after climbing down chimneys to deliver presents.

Today, Flemish kids still leave a shoe under the chimney or outside the front door in the hope that Sinterklaas will visit. If they have been good they will awake to find the shoe filled with chocolate, often shaped in the first letter of the child's name, or marzipan fruit, but if they have been bad the shoe will be filled with salt.

DECEMBER

Sinterklaas On the evening of 6 December Sinterklaas and his helper Zwarte Piet come to visit children, leaving sweets, chocolate and gifts. Special celebrations are held in the town of Sint-Niklaas (see box, above and page 192).

SHOPPING

Chocolate, beer and lace are the standard souvenirs, but Flanders offers a lot more. Why not pick up a discount diamond, some edgy Belgian fashion or vintage trinkets from a market? As a rule of thumb, most shops are open 10.00–18.00 Monday–Saturday. There are exceptions: on the first Sunday of the month, many shops throw open their doors and on the Flemish coast they open year-round on Sunday.

ART AND ANTIQUES As showcased by many upmarket B&Bs listed in this guide, there are numerous *objets d'art* and antiques floating around the markets of Flanders. Those with a keen eye can pick up everything from Art Nouveau lamps to Pointillist paintings – I know of a family aunt who even had wooden masks and spears brought over during the Belgian occupation of the Congo. Bargains are rare, but on the whole prices are fair. The best cities for antiques are Brussels and Tongeren. In Brussels the place for quality antiques is the place du Grand Sablon. This square hosts a long-running market every Saturday and Sunday, while streets leading off from here are home to numerous stores – of note is the Sablon Antiques Centre (39 pl du Grand Sablon) housing around 20 dealers. Cheaper items can be found along rue Blaes and at the place du Jeu de Balle flea market (page 110). Tongeren's Sunday antiques market is one of the largest in the Benelux and a prime hunting ground (page 347), while lovers of 20th-century design should head to Antwerp's Kloosterstraat (page 298).

BEER Flanders has around 1,500 different beer brands, ranging from famous names like Leffe to revered Westvleteren Trappist beer. Of course, the best place to buy them is from the breweries themselves (page 48). You can also buy them from specialist shops, which abound in Bruges and Brussels; recommended are the **Bottle Shop** (13 Wollestraat) in the former, and **Beer Mania** (page 91) in the latter. Nowadays, many tourist offices stock regional beers as well.

BISCUITS The Flemish love a good biscuit. By far the most popular is cinnamon-flavoured *speculaas* – a treat that appears in various guises, notably hand-shaped *Antwerpse handjes* (see box, page 296). Other regional biscuits to try are Diest's

CHRISTMAS MARKETS

Flanders loves a good Christmas market and from the end of November until early January, stalls pop up in the main squares of nearly every town. There's an inevitable amount of tat on offer, of course, but nothing beats mulled wine, warm waffles and the twinkle of fairly lights. Here is a list of the main players.

ANTWERP Stretching from Groenplaats – host to an ice rink – to the river Scheldt, where you'll find a Ferris wheel and ice-tubing track (the latter has also been known to pop up by the zoo), the Winter in Antwerp season (early December to early January) has plenty of artisanal stalls and music performances.

BRUGES Given its fame, Bruges's market can be underwhelming, but the tourist office is stepping up efforts to introduce more crafts, and the city itself is unbeatably atmospheric come Christmas. Pop into the ice sculpture festival by the railway station before browsing the stalls on Markt and Simon-Stevinplein. Usually 23 November to 1 January.

BRUSSELS Known as Plaisirs d'Hiver (w plaisirsdhiver.be), this is a market befitting the capital's status, with over 240 chalets snaking from the Grand-Place to place Sainte-Catherine. There are bold light and sound shows on the Grand-Place and food trucks clustered on the now pedestrianised rue Anspach. Runs late November to early January.

GHENT Like the city itself, Ghent's market remains underrated, but more people are cottoning on to its assets – namely smaller crowds than Brussels, an authentic market vibe with wooden huts radiating out from Sint-Baafsplein and, best of all, its superior, almost endless range of street-food stands. Mid-December to early January.

LEUVEN One of Belgium's cosiest markets: the stalls only remain for two weeks in mid-December, but are brilliant quality. During the *Wintertijd* (Winter season) events, they also lay on winter walks (pub tours, silence walks), concerts at Sint-Pieterskerk and a raft of food trucks in De Bruul park before New Year. Their nativity scene usually has real sheep, which is lovely. Early December to early January.

halve maantjes (page 158), Mechelen's *maneblussertjes* (page 314) and Geel's *Geels hartjes* (page 330).

CHOCOLATE Chocolate is the number one gift brought back from Flanders, with Brussels Airport Zaventem, perhaps unsurprisingly, the world's largest sales outlet for the sweet stuff. Brands like Godiva, Neuhaus and Leonidas are household names. However, for the real McCoy you need to seek out a master chocolatier like those listed in the box on page page 46 and on page 92. Many establishments sell pre-packed boxes, but it's much more fun to handpick your own chocolates. Specialist terms to look out for are *ganache* (chocolate, fresh cream and a stronger percentage of cocoa butter flavoured with cinnamon, coffee or liqueur); *gianduja* (milk chocolate and smooth hazelnut paste); and *praline* (chocolate mixed with finely chopped nuts or toffee).

COMICS Brussels is a mecca for fanboys. The highlight is a visit to the Belgian Comic Strip Center (page 107), which has a well-stocked gift shop. You can also follow a dedicated Comic Strip Trail – pick up a booklet at the tourist office. Filigranes (39 av des Arts) has a good English-language section, while in Antwerp, I recommend the brilliant Mekanik Strip (73 Sint-Jacobsmarkt).

DIAMONDS About 85% of the world's rough diamonds and 50% of all cut diamonds are traded in Antwerp, so if you're looking for a sparkler you could do a lot worse than coming to shop for it in this metropolitan city (see box, page 309).

FASHION Antwerp's unlikely status as an avant-garde fashion hub dates back to a group of designers known as the 'Antwerp Six', who graduated from the fashion department of the city's Royal Academy of Fine Arts in the 1980s, and whose members included Walter van Beirendonck, Dirk van Saene, Dirk Bikkembergs, Marina Yee, Ann Demeulemeester and Dries van Noten. Demeulemeester, known for her Gothic, minimal wares, and van Noten, celebrated for his elaborate patterns and cerebral approach, remain big names in the fashion world. Since the mid 1990s, Antwerp-based designer Raf Simons has enjoyed great acclaim for his own subculture-influenced menswear label, and taken on some of fashion's top jobs, including stints at Dior and Calvin Klein. If you're set on bagging Belgian fashion, Antwerp is a great place to do it, particularly during the biannual stock sales (see box, page 299), but for a wider choice you'll want to head to Brussels's fashion districts, which centre around rue Antoine Dansaert (vintage and independent brands) and the wide tree-lined avenue Louise (international luxury). Sales (*soldes/solden*) take place in January (by law 3 January is the earliest date) and July and offer up to a 70% discount.

ATTENDING THE FASHION GRADUATION SHOWS

Both the Antwerp fashion department (**w** antwerp-fashion.be) and Brussels's fashion school La Cambre (**w** lacambre.be) are renowned worldwide, with graduates going on to start their own brands or work behind the scenes at famous fashion houses. Unusually, bagging a ticket to their graduation shows is a simple process, and will offer you a great insight into Belgian fashion, as well as a supremely theatrical experience. Both events are simply called 'SHOW', and take place in early June; you'll find links to tickets on the schools' websites from April.

JENEVER An ancestor of gin, jenever stored in a traditional stoneware bottle makes an excellent gift. The main brands – Filliers, St-Pol and Smeets – are sold in most supermarkets, but for superior quality it's best to buy from specialist shops. The Jenevermuseum in Hasselt (page 340) is one such place; you can also try De Vagant café in Antwerp (page 296), which has an attached boutique.

LACE This medieval craft was applied almost exclusively to the robes of the clergy until the 16th century. Considered a luxury item, its popularity soared throughout the Low Countries and soon men and women who could afford it had added lace (*dentelle* in French, *kant* in Flemish) to the cuffs, hems and collars of their dresses and shirts. Its delicate white frills were sewn on to handkerchiefs, bed linen, tablecloths, hats, shawls and hair clips, and at the peak of its production around 50,000 lacemakers were employed in Flanders, many of them béguines. Despite cheap imports from the Far East dominating the market, the number of outlets specialising in local cotton bobbin lace is gradually rising, and local governments are supporting amateur clubs keen to keep the tradition alive. Price is determined according to the size and complexity of the design, as well as its heritage in the case of antique pieces. Finding the real deal can be hard, but you can't go wrong at 't Apostelientje in Bruges (page 223).

PHOTOGRAPHY

Belgium has a healthy photography festival scene, including the biennial Summer of Photography run by BOZAR in Brussels (next edition: 2020). Bruges is one of the most photogenic destinations in the world; for combined city tours and instruction, try **Photo Tour Brugge** (w phototourbrugge.com), run by the energetic Andy McSweeney. You'll be sure to get that perfect snap of the Rozenhoedkaai. Het Zwin nature reserve (page 238) and Hallerbos (page 153) are musts for nature photographers.

SPORT

The two national obsessions are cycling and football. Come the weekend, local pitches are filled with footie teams battling it out and the cycle paths are dotted with enthusiasts of all ages whizzing by in multi-coloured Lycra racing suits. During summer, the coastline also offers excellent opportunities for watersports.

CYCLING As the saying goes: 'Cycling is Flanders and Flanders is cycling'. It's part of the national psyche and reached fever pitch when Eddy 'The Cannibal' Merckx (page 372) exploded on to the scene in 1966 and started setting world records right, left and centre. Exploring the region by bike is an excellent way of discovering off-the-beaten-track villages – and it's easy thanks to the national network of waymarked cycling paths, known as ***fietsknooppuntennetwerk***. The majority of cycle paths are well maintained and safe, but watch out for the lanes that cross roundabouts and motorway exits and entrances. Cyclists have right of way in most circumstances, but remember to give way from the right and use hand signals when turning. Lock your bike when leaving it unattended, too. Tourist offices can furnish you with maps of local cycle routes, and I've suggested the best of these for most towns.

Most railway stations have a Fietspunt bike-hire shop which charges around €10 a day, and if they don't I've suggested alternative rental shops for each town. Antwerp and Brussels both have city-bike schemes. If you want to rent a bike for longer periods, Blue Bike (w blue-bike.com), inspired by the OV-Fiets system in the Netherlands, and connected to the rail network, offers very competitive rates – albeit with caveats; you have to take an annual subscription (€12.50/year and then pay a maximum of €3.15/24hr). You can sign up online or at selected bike points.

The region is famous for its cobbled classics held in spring, the most famous being the Tour of Flanders (page 53), held at the start of April. Other highlights include the one-day Omloop Het Nieuwsblad (w omloophetnieuwsblad.be), which opens the cycling season in late February and departs from Ghent, and the indoor Six Days of Ghent, held in November. The events are amazingly social, with whole villages turning out to cheer and whoop shouts of support as the fluorescent millipede of cyclists swooshes past.

Standard cycle route sign: the top number indicates which junction you're at, and the bottom two give you the direction for the next closest junction.

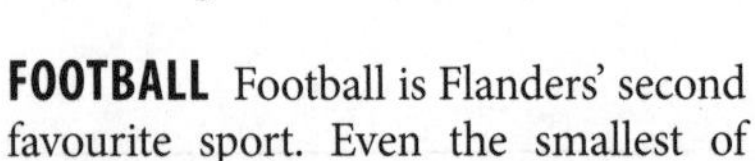

FOOTBALL Football is Flanders' second favourite sport. Even the smallest of towns has its own team and every Saturday the local fields are filled with players thrashing it out in the provincial leagues. The 34 teams making up the Belgian First Division A attract fierce followings; the two leading clubs are Anderlecht and Club Brugge – though bear in mind that these 'big teams' are on the same annual budget as those of England's smallest clubs. On the international level, Belgium's 'Red Devils' have enjoyed huge success in recent years – the so-called 'golden generation' finishing third at the 2018 World Cup. More than half the squad that performed during that event also play for the English Premier League, with captain Eden Hazard one of the most in-demand players in the world at the time of writing.

HIKING Hiking (*wandelen*) is incredibly popular in Flanders and all the tourist offices have well-signposted local routes you can follow. I have often included references to the best maps in each province.

MEDIA AND COMMUNICATIONS

NEWSPAPERS AND MAGAZINES Flanders' three most widely circulated newspapers are the regionally oriented *Gazet van Antwerpen*, *De Standaard* (centre-right broadsheet) and tabloid *Het Laatse Nieuws*. The main English-language publications are quarterly magazine and website *The Bulletin* (w thebulletin.be) and online-only papers *Flanders Today* (w flanderstoday.eu) and the *Brussels Times* (w brusselstimes.com). The major US political paper *POLITICO* (w politico.eu) set up a Brussels headquarters in 2015 and reports on the EU. Getting hold of English papers and magazines isn't too hard; most Relay shops in stations have a selection. The capital also publishes free *Metro* newspapers in Dutch and French, while if you want to get to grips with all things cool, take a look at the English-language website *The Word* (w thewordmagazine.com).

CINEMA The majority of mainstream films are shown in English (check that the listing features the VO – *version originale* – code alongside it) with Dutch or French subtitles. Dubbed films will bear the code VF – *version française.* The average ticket price is €8–9. The Cinenews website (w cinenews.be) provides listings in English.

TELEVISION Flanders' national television network is VRT. However, most of the region subscribes to cable TV providers such as Telenet, and this means you'll be able to watch English-language channels like BBC 1, BBC 2, National Geographic Channel and Discovery Channel.

RADIO You can easily stream a lot of content from British radio stations so long as you have a Wi-Fi connection; it's worth downloading BBC iPlayer before you go if you're likely to get homesick. Some stations may require the use of a VPN. Local stations include the youthful/alternative Studio Brussel (w stubru.be) or its classical sibling Klara (w klara.be).

TELEPHONES Belgium's international dialling code is 00 32. Emergency telephone numbers are noted on the inside front cover of this book. To call Flanders from abroad, input the international dialling code 0032, followed by the city code (minus the initial zero). Those calling from the US should dial 011 + 0032 + city code + required number. To call abroad from Flanders, enter the international dialling code of the required country followed by the domestic number – again you will have to omit the initial zero.

Mobile phones Flanders has good network coverage, and since the abolition of roaming fees in the EU on 15 June 2017, you won't rack up a fortune on data. If you'll be staying for a while, though, I do recommend buying a local SIM card, which has the added boon that you can pay for De Lijn buses and trams by text at cheaper rates. The market revolves around three firms: **Proximus** (w proximus.be), **Mobistar** (w mobistar.be) and **Base** (w base.be). Make sure that your phone is unlocked if you plan to replace your SIM card.

POST Belgium's national postal service is called bpost. Post offices are generally open 09.00–noon and 14.00–17.00 Monday to Friday, and 09.00–noon Saturday, and sell stamps and basic packaging materials. A stamp for a standard item sent to an address in Europe currently costs €1.46; within Belgium it's €0.95 (Non-Prior) and €1 (Prior). Sending a parcel of up to 5kg to neighbouring countries (UK, Germany, France, Luxembourg) is €16.40; double that for the rest of the EU. From experience, I find that the premium for sending goods registered is not worthwhile, and often takes longer than regular post. Postboxes are red and marked *post/poste.*

INTERNET Internet cafés are becoming a thing of the past, with almost all hotels and cafés offering free Wi-Fi, and most cities setting up free hotspots. Since 2017, the Brussels underground system has been hooked up to the network, while national rail company SNCB-NMBS has equipped many of its stations with free Wi-Fi – a number only set to grow. If you're in a bind, however, many tourist offices have a desktop computer hooked up to the internet that visitors can use.

BUSINESS The majority of Flemish are skilled linguists, often speaking Dutch, French and English fluently. As a result, the bulk of business in Brussels is conducted in English, though French is also common. Meetings are formal and punctuality is key, as is smart attire. It is considered rude to interrupt someone when they are speaking and Belgians will always let someone finish before giving their reply. The exchange of business cards is popular and it pays to have your details translated into French or Dutch depending on the region you are working in. Sensitivity to the language divide will be appreciated, so don't dive in with all those questions about the exact nature of tensions. And if you're invited to dinner by a colleague, try to finish everything on your plate – Belgians are generally thrifty.

BUYING PROPERTY

Houses for sale are marked '*te koop/à vendre*'. There are no restrictions on foreigners buying in Belgium, even non-residents. Properties are cheaper than in neighbouring countries. However, transaction costs (legal fees/registration tax) could add up to 25% of the purchase price, and if you sell within five years of purchase you also incur a heavy capital-gains tax (16.5%). Given the very favourable rates, many expats choose to rent instead. The best property search websites are **w** immo.vlan.be and **w** immoweb.be.

CULTURAL ETIQUETTE

The Flemish are exceptionally laid-back and you would have to commit a serious *faux pas* in order to create offence. However, being aware of local values and customs concerning behaviour, dress and body language will enrich your experience of the region and save you from a potentially embarrassing situation. I've listed a few social customs to help you create a quick rapport with locals.

THREE KISSES A handshake is satisfactory at formal meetings, but the Flemish do one better than the French when it comes to greeting friends or loved ones; they bestow three kisses on alternate cheeks. Younger generations and urbanites tend to prefer the more fashionable 'kiss the air', 'darling' variety; while the elderly generation and country residents plump for sturdy smackers on the recipient's cheek. Men may opt for the fail-proof handshake or, in younger circles, hug or kiss.

GIFT-GIVING The Flemish love giving gifts. When a baby is born, for example, the parents traditionally prepare cards and a small sack of *doopsuiker* (sugared chocolates) to give to visiting friends and family. Should you be invited to someone's house, it is customary to bring a small token of thanks; safe bets are flowers or pralines.

TABLE MANNERS If you are invited for dinner, punctual arrival is expected. It is also polite to wish everyone '*eet smakelijk*' before they start eating – it's the equivalent of *bon appétit*. Most Flemings are very hospitable and will dole out large portions; do your best to finish – it will make your host or hostess proud.

TRAVELLING POSITIVELY

If you enjoy your travels around Flanders and would like to give something back, I suggest making a donation to the **Commonwealth War Graves Commission** (**w** www.cwgc.org), which does an excellent and important job of maintaining the World War I cemeteries. You can pop into their office in Ypres (33 Menenstraat) to find out more. Alternatively, Poperinge-based **Talbot House** (page 277), which served as an everyman's club for British soldiers in World War I, preserves the past and its famous hospitality through an on-site museum and guesthouse. You can send them a cheque, use the PayPal donation button on their website, or even become a 'Talbotousian' – ask them for more details.

Part Two

THE GUIDE

3

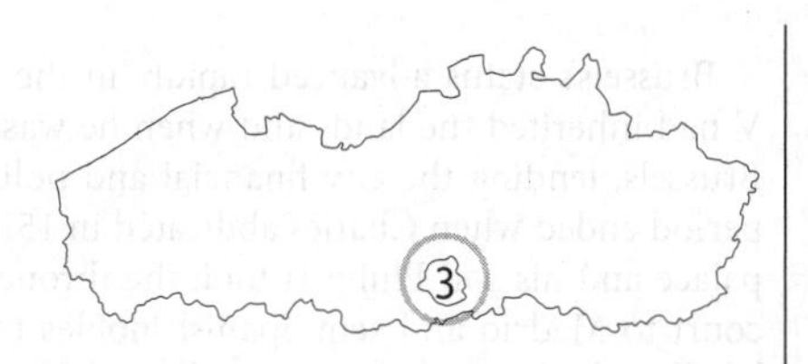

Brussels

A capital, an independent region, an island in a language-divide dispute, the centre of Europe and the seat of the European Union – Brussels wears many hats. Which side you see depends on the purpose of your visit, but most agree that the city is initially something of an enigma – and it's still common to hear people invoking its supposedly 'boring' reputation.

Situated at the centre of a cultural crossroads of Latinate and Germanic traditions, and home to 1.2 million people – almost 70% of whom are of foreign descent – Brussels is, perhaps surprisingly, the second most cosmopolitan city in the world after Dubai. Not classically chic like Paris, or hip and stately like Berlin, it can be hard to pigeonhole – much like its architecture, which is a mishmash of historic buildings and ultra-modern constructions. But conventional beauty is banal and Brussels's trump card is its multi-cultural make-up and small scale. Often described by residents – known as *Zinnekes* – as a village, Brussels is compact, easy to get around and not overwhelming like most European capitals.

It may be introverted – shy to share its secrets with those who live there, let alone with visiting strangers – but therein lies the appeal. All romantics know the exhilaration is in the chase and what better thrill than to pace her streets in search of what makes Brussels tick? Look among flea markets and award-winning kitchens of passionate, headstrong chefs, hang out in glorious Art Nouveau cafés and amble through intriguing residential communes. I guarantee that underneath the calm and composed surface you'll find the heartbeat of a city with an unmistakably Bohemian, eclectic spirit.

HISTORY

The capital began life on an island. St Géry, the Bishop of Cambrai, built a small chapel on a marshy mound in the river Senne and around it gathered a small settlement. The city's name doesn't enter the history books until the 10th century when Duke Charles of Lower Lotharingia (an area encompassing modern-day Belgium, parts of Germany and northern France) erected a fortress in a growing community called *Broeksel* – 'home on the marsh'.

By the 12th century, and under the rule of the feudal Dukes of Brabant, the town was beginning to flourish. It had become a popular stopover for merchants using the Bruges–Ghent–Cologne trading route and soon the marshes were drained to allow the town to expand. It was granted town rights in 1229 and, soon after, the first city walls were erected, encompassing the site of the city's founding, St Géry island, the Grand-Place, the original Cathédrale Saints-Michel-et-Gudule and the ducal palace of Coudenberg.

These were replaced over a century later, from 1356 to 1383, by medieval ramparts that covered a larger area and stayed in place until the 19th century. Today, they sit under the petit-ring motorway that encircles Brussels.

Brussels's status advanced rapidly in the 15th century. Child emperor Charles V had inherited the lands and when he wasn't waging war abroad, he ruled from Brussels, lending the city financial and political pulling power. This honeymoon period ended when Charles abdicated in 1555 at the (now destroyed) Coudenberg palace and his son Philip II took the throne. A Catholic zealot, Philip moved his court to Madrid and sent Spanish nobles to impose anti-Protestant edicts. Riots labelled the Iconoclastic Fury followed but were brutally crushed. Rebellion and a successful revolt led by William I Prince of Orange ensued and a Protestant government was kept in place until the end of the French Revolution, when Philip took the city back and consolidated its status as capital of the Spanish Netherlands. Squabbles with neighbouring France had been going on for centuries, but the most calamitous event by far came during the Nine Years War, when King Louis XVI's troops bombarded the city in 1695, destroying over 4,000 buildings including the majority of the medieval guildhouses on the Grand-Place – these were rebuilt five years later and are the examples on show today.

Control passed to the Austrian Habsburgs and later the French, whose rule ended when Napoleon was defeated at the Battle of Waterloo and forced to relinquish the area, which was incorporated into the new Kingdom of the Netherlands and ruled by William I. Unease over his rule erupted in revolt in 1830 (page 9) and soon enough an independent Belgian state was formed and Brussels chosen as its capital. With a renewed sense of national pride, Leopold I set about dismantling the city walls and constructing new, grand buildings. The trend was taken up with enthusiasm by Leopold II who poured profits from his colonies in the Congo into smartening up the city, laying down wide boulevards, clearing poverty-stricken areas and covering over the remainder of the disease-infested river Senne.

The capital was occupied by German troops during World Wars I and II, and has continued to modernise exponentially ever since. Since 1958, when the European Economic Community was born – Brussels hosted the World's Fair the same year – it has become the de facto capital of what is now called the EU, the process of 'Brusselisation' seeing landmark buildings make way for new roads and glass-and-steel constructions to house its swelling number of institutions. Its status as a region was finalised on 18 June 1989.

GETTING THERE AND AWAY

BY AIR Brussels has two airports: Brussels Airport Zaventem (**w** brusselsairport.be), and Brussels South Charleroi Airport (**w** brussels-charleroi-airport.com). Zaventem is located 13km northeast of Brussels and serves most major airlines, including national carrier Brussels Airlines. Charleroi is 60km south of the city and serves budget airlines; try to avoid it unless you're hiring a car as it's far-flung and ill-placed for exploring Flanders.

Getting to/from Brussels Airport Zaventem

By train The railway station is located in the basement (level –1). Trains depart every 15 minutes or so and take 17 minutes to reach the city centre, with stops at Brussel Noord/Bruxelles Nord, Brussel Centraal/Bruxelles Central and Brussel Zuid/Bruxelles Midi. Trains run from around 04.40–midnight; the journey costs €8.60 one way. You'll need to buy a ticket from the machine or ticket office and scan it to pass through the gates to the platforms. The same applies for your return journey to the airport, so hold on to your ticket when you exit the train.

By bus The bus station is located on the ground floor (level 0). There are two operators:

De Lijn w delijn.be. Operates an express service which drops you at Brussel Noord/Bruxelles Nord (buses 272/471) metro. It departs from platform A; a one-way ticket is €3.

MIVB/STIB w stib.be. Operates a 30-min express service from the airport to the EU Quarter. From Mon to Fri before 20.00 you need bus 12, & at the w/end or after 20.00 you need bus 21; all buses depart from platform C, where you'll find a GO ticket machine. A one-way fare from the machine costs €4.50, or it's €6 on board.

By taxi Taxis are always available outside the arrivals hall. A one-way fare to the city centre costs €40–50 and the journey takes 20–50 minutes depending on traffic. Despite ongoing wrangles, rideshare app **Uber**'s UberX service still serves the airport; cars will pick you up by the car park P1 on level 4/5 (choose which in the app).

Getting to/from Brussels South Charleroi Airport

By bus Flibco (w flibco.com) departs every 20–30 minutes for Bruxelles Midi/Brussel Zuid railway station. Buses run from 04.30 to 01.00 from the airport and coincide with flight timetables. A one-way ticket costs €17 (€14.20 online). The journey takes 55 minutes. The bus stop in Brussels is located on the corner of rue de France and rue de l'Instruction on the west side of Bruxelles Midi/Brussel Zuid station. Buses in the airport direction run from 03.30 to 22.30 every day. Flibco also offers direct connections to Antwerp (1hr 45mins), Ghent (1hr 20mins) and Bruges (2hr 10mins).

By train You'll need to catch TEC Bus A from the airport (turn left when you exit) to Charleroi railway station (🕘 20mins), from which there are direct trains to Brussels city centre (🕘 1hr). Opt for an airport ticket at the machine next to the bus stop (€15.50), which covers the cost of the bus and the train journeys to central Brussels.

By taxi A taxi rank is located outside the main terminal building. It's a (hefty) €90 or so from the airport to Brussels city centre, though companies often recruit passengers to share taxis if you don't mind waiting until the vehicle is full.

By shuttle Launched relatively recently, a direct shared-taxi service, or Super Shuttle, from Antwerp (w mysupershuttle.be; reserve at least 6 hours ahead) takes the pain out of the tiresome Charleroi journey; it costs €25, takes 90 minutes and has numerous departure times daily. It's most useful if you're departing or arriving at unsociable hours, when the train doesn't run.

BY TRAIN International trains like the Eurostar, Thalys and TGV arrive and depart from Bruxelles Midi/Brussel Zuid, while most domestic trains leave from Bruxelles Central/Brussel Centraal. For details of getting to Brussels by train, see page 34. See individual listings for details of how to get to other Flemish cities.

BY CAR See page 34. Note that Brussels is now a Low-Emission Zone so you will need to make sure your car is permitted to enter (see box, page 41).

BY BUS Brussels is very well connected by bus to many continental European cities (for arrival from London, see page 35). Eurolines (w eurolines.co.uk) and Flixbus (w flixbus.co.uk) both connect Brussels with a wide array of cities in neighbouring countries, and rates are very competitive.

STREET NAMES

Shared by Flanders and Wallonia, Brussels is officially bilingual and as part of the compromise street and commune names – along with press, sights etc – appear in both French and Flemish. However, French is spoken by 80% of Brussels residents, and for better or worse most visitors will have a better knowledge of French than Flemish, so to save a few trees I have used the French names throughout this chapter.

ORIENTATION

Central Brussels is encircled by the pentagon-shaped 'petit-ring' motorway (R20) that mirrors where the 14th-century city walls once stood. Within this sits the city centre, broadly divided in two by a wide north–south boulevard variously named Empereur, Impératrice and Berlaimont.

To the west of this axis is the **Lower Town**, originally a working-class area populated by Flemish speakers and still the commercial heart of the city, with a bewildering array of restaurants, hotels and cafés. Cramped, cobbled and still medieval in layout, the Lower Town revolves around the famous Grand-Place and nearby Manneken Pis, though the streets around foodie place Sainte-Catherine – beyond the pedestrianised, rather drab boulevard Anspach – are arguably more rewarding. North of the Grand-Place, main shopping street rue Neuve leads up to the towering office blocks of place Rogier and the Gare du Nord.

To the east of the city, where the ground begins to slope up, is the **Upper Town**, once home to the French-speaking elite who would keep watch on the minions below. The easiest way to access it is to take the covered walkway running through the Galerie Ravenstein arcade by Gare Centrale, and the open-air staircase running along the modern Mont des Arts. At the top you'll find stately rue Royale and rue de la Régence, forming the Upper Town's backbone and housing the superb Musées Royaux des Beaux Arts. Well-heeled antiques quarter Sablon and the immense Palais de Justice also lie within the Upper Town's scope.

The rest of the region's **19 communes** fan out from the petit-ring towards the second outer ring road (R0). Immediately attached are Art Nouveau hotspots Ixelles and Saint-Gilles; urbanised Etterbeek, abutting the EU quarter; Anderlecht, synonymous with Belgian football; and highly diverse, eclectic neighbourhoods Schaerbeek and Saint-Josse-ten-Noode. Further out lie the affluent suburbs of Uccle in the south, the green spaces of Woluwe-Saint-Pierre in the east, and in the northwest the smaller communes of Koekelberg and Jette.

GETTING AROUND

Brussels is best explored on foot: all the main sights are within a 1km radius of the Grand-Place. However, walking on cobblestones can become tiring, in which case you can make use of the city's public transport system. Run by STIB–MIVB (**w** stib.be) and combining buses, trams and the metro, most lines run from 05.00 to midnight.

TICKETS Tickets are valid on all three services (metro, bus and tram) and can be purchased at metro station ticket offices, GO self-service machines, tourist offices and newsagents, as well as on board buses and trams (more expensive). You can

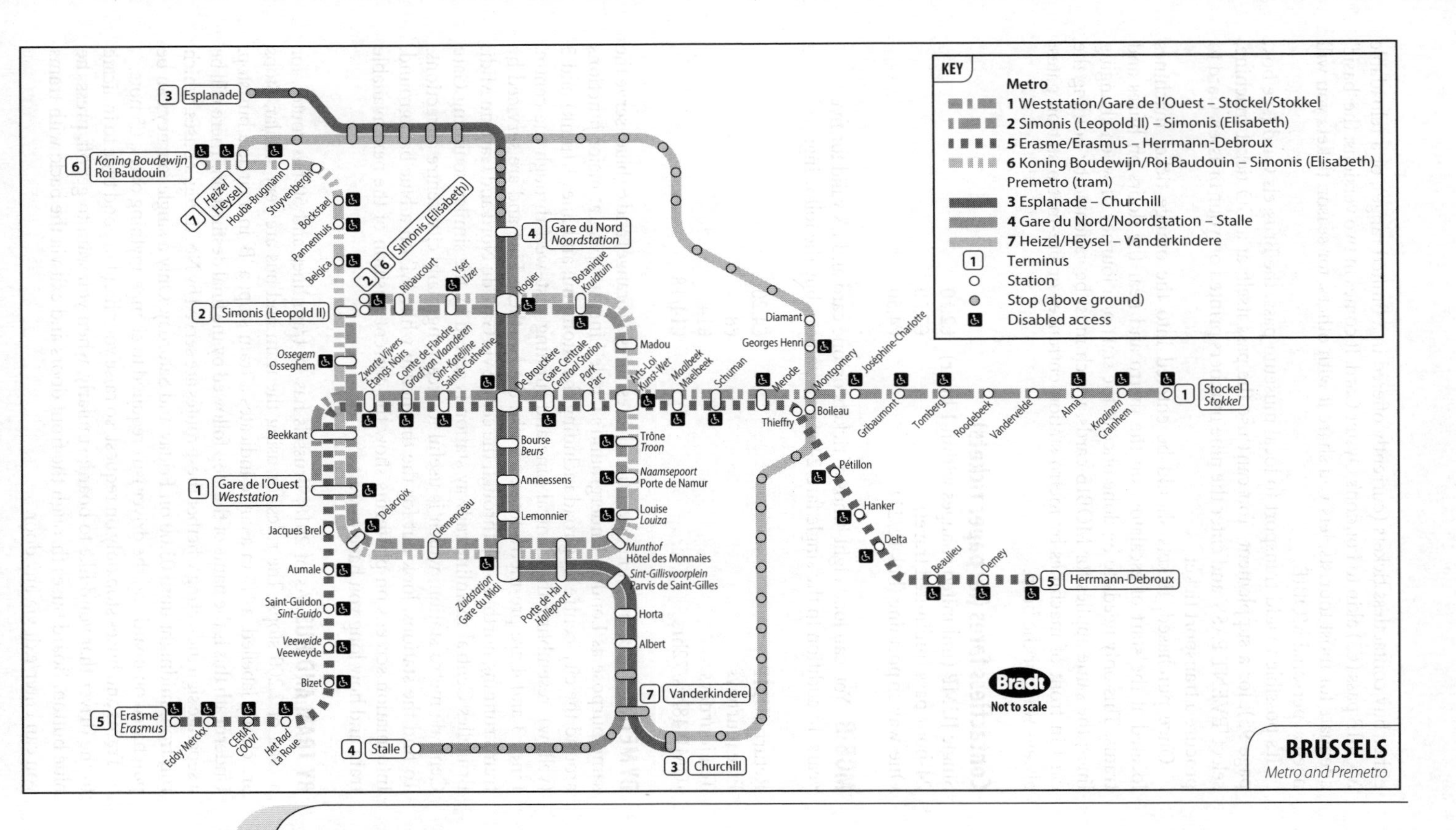
KEY
Metro
1 Weststation/Gare de l'Ouest – Stockel/Stokkel
2 Simonis (Leopold II) – Simonis (Elisabeth)
5 Erasme/Erasmus – Herrmann-Debroux
6 Koning Boudewijn/Roi Baudouin – Simonis (Elisabeth)
Premetro (tram)
3 Esplanade – Churchill
4 Gare du Nord/Noordstation – Stalle
7 Heizel/Heysel – Vanderkindere
Terminus
Station
Stop (above ground)
Disabled access
3 Esplanade
6 Koning Boudewijn Roi Baudouin
7 Heizel Heysel
Houba-Brugmann
Stuyvenbergh
Bockstael
Pannenhuis
Belgica
2 6 Simonis (Elisabeth)
Ribaucourt
Yser Ijzer
Rogier
4 Gare du Nord Noordstation
Botanique Kruidtuin
2 Simonis (Leopold II)
Ossegem Osseghem
Zwarte Vijvers Étangs Noirs
Comte de Flandre Graaf van Vlaanderen
Sint-Katelijne Sainte-Catherine
De Brouckère
Gare Centrale Centraal Station
Park Parc
Arts-Loi Kunst-Wet
Maalbeek Maelbeek
Schuman
Merode
Montgomery
Joséphine-Charlotte
Gribaumont
Tomberg
Roodebeek
Vandervelde
Alma
Kraainem Crainhem
1 Stockel Stokkel
Madou
Diamant
Georges Henri
Boileau
Thieffry
Beekkant
Bourse Beurs
Trône Troon
Naamsepoort Porte de Namur
1 Gare de l'Ouest Weststation
Anneessens
Louise Louiza
Lemonnier
Delacroix
Clemenceau
Jacques Brel
Munthof Hôtel des Monnaies
Aumale
Zuidstation Gare du Midi
Porte de Hal Hallepoort
Sint-Gillisvoorplein Parvis de Saint-Gilles
Saint-Guidon Sint-Guido
Horta
Veeweide Veeweyde
Albert
Bizet
7 Vanderkindere
5 Erasme Erasmus
Eddy Merckx
CERIA COOVI
Het Rad La Roue
4 Stalle
3 Churchill
Pétillon
Hanker
Delta
Beaulieu
Demey
5 Herrmann-Debroux
Bradt
Not to scale
BRUSSELS
Metro and Premetro

either buy contactless tickets (currently offered in a limited range), or a reloadable MOBIB pass (€5) akin to London's Oyster Card. It comes in two versions: the 'basic', adequate for most tourists, lets you share it with others; for season tickets you will need a 'personal MOBIB'.

It's possible to add transport to local museum pass, the Brussels Card (see box, page 95), for a supplement. You can't use the pass itself; at a GO ticket machine, select 'EVENT PASS' and enter the nine numbers printed on your Brussels Card to procure a transport ticket.

Once purchased, tickets should be entered into the orange ticket machines located at the start of escalators on the metro and near the doors on buses and trams. This only needs to be done once at the start of a journey or when changing lines; the same applies for MOBIB cards, which must be validated by holding the card in front of machines by metro station entrances or pre-metro station gates; always wait for the beep.

Contactless fares (ie: paper tickets)

Single JUMP (unlimited changes within 1 hour)	€2.10
24-hour pass (unlimited travel)	€7.50
One-way airport line (bus 12/21)	€4.50

MOBIB You can load eight kinds of tickets on one card and it's valid for five years. In addition to the single fare/24hr pass you can buy the following:

Return JUMP	€4.20
Five journeys	€8
Ten journeys	€14
JUMP 48hrs/72hrs	€14/18

BY METRO There are four conventional lines: lines 2 (orange) and 6 (blue) serve the same purpose as London Underground's Circle Line, stopping at major junctions around the city-centre ring road including the Atomium; and lines 1 (pink) and 5 (yellow), resembling the Central Line and running east–west through the centre. Lines 3 and 4 are pre-metro lines, act like the Northern Line and are serviced by trams running north–south through the centre via Gare du Nord and Gare du Midi. Bruxelles Central mainline railway station is served by the similar-sounding Gare Centrale metro station, which is useful for reaching many city-centre attractions. To find the stations, look out for the distinctive white 'M' on a blue background. Information screens on platforms show the current position of the next available train and how long you have to wait.

BY TRAM AND BUS As of 2018, Brussels has 18 tram lines and 50 bus routes, for a total of 2,200 stops. The rules for using the tram and bus are very similar. Stops are clearly labelled: a 'T' in a circle indicates a tram stop; a 'B' in a circle a bus stop. Underneath this is the name of the stop followed by the final destination. There will be a separate sign indicating whether these routes are served by Noctis night buses, which run from midnight until 03.00 on Friday and Saturday. Only a single journey can be purchased on board and the driver isn't required to change anything over a €5 note.

Trams and buses stop only on request, so raise your hand in good time to indicate to the driver that you'd like to board; similarly, when you want to get off, press the blue button. Board buses through the front doors and exit via the back; with trams you can enter/exit via any door.

UNDERGROUND ART GALLERY

The capital's somewhat dingy metro system is enlivened by 80 wonderful works of art. Launched 40 years ago by CAID (Commission Artistique des Infrastructures de Déplacement) to instil an appreciation of art in the public, the project covers all media from sculptures to photos and stained glass. Some of the most intriguing examples include Surrealist Paul Delvaux's 13m-long mural *Nos vieux trams bruxellois* at Bourse station; fragments of demolished Art Nouveau buildings, among them the twirly balustrades of architect Victor Horta's la Maison du Peuple, at Horta station; and two Hergé bas-reliefs (completed shortly before his death) at Stockel which feature over 140 characters from his *Tintin* albums. STIB sells a hefty €5 booklet, *Art in Brussels begins with the metro*, detailing the project and for sale at Brussels Tram Museum or the Standaard Boekhandel on place de la Monnaie; you can also download the PDF for free on their website.

BY BICYCLE City-bike rental scheme **Villo!** (☎ 078 05 11 10; w www.villo.be) has bike terminals dotted all around town, and runs 24 hours a day. Just slot in your bank card and away you go! As a visitor you can purchase a one-day (€1.60) or seven-day card (€8.20): the first half an hour is free and thereafter you pay anything from €0.50 to €2 per hour depending on how long you keep the bike. There are plans to add electric bikes to the scheme, perhaps before the end of 2019. Alternatively, **Pro Vélo** (15 rue des Londres, 1050 Ixelles; ☎ 02 502 73 55; w provelo.org; ⏲ 10.00–13.00 & 13.30–17.00 Mon & Wed–Fri, 13.00–17.00 Tue; Ⓜ Trône/Porte de Namur) is a government-run outfit offering bike rental (city bike €16/day, e-bike €28/day plus €300 deposit) and guided cycling tours from March to November.

BY TAXI A fixed charge of €2.40 (€4.40 at night) applies at the start of all journeys, and the fare is then calculated at €1.66/km within the Brussels-Capital Region or €2.70/km outside it. You'll be given a printed receipt at the end of your journey and tips are included. If you're hailing a taxi on the street, only use cars bearing the official yellow-and-blue Brussels taxi sign. The following are trusted companies: **Taxis Bleus** (☎ 02 268 00 00) and **Taxis Verts** (☎ 02 349 49 49); the latter has taxis equipped for passengers with disabilities at no extra charge.

TOURIST INFORMATION

Brussels – as an independent region – has its own dynamic tourist board, **Visit Brussels** (w visitbrussels.be), which has three outposts in the city.

ℹ Station Europe [118 A6] pl du Luxembourg; ☎ 02 513 89 40; ⏲ 09.00–18.00 Mon–Fri, 10.00–18.00 Sat–Sun. Newest outpost of Visit Brussels in the heart of the EU Quarter.

ℹ USE-IT [85 F1] 25 Galerie Ravenstein; w use-it.be; ⏲ 10.00–18.00 Mon–Sat. Superb non-profit information centre for young travellers. Their specially tailored free city maps to Brussels & beyond are full of off-the-beaten-track suggestions & local knowledge, & the young, fun team also offers free lockers, internet & coffee.

ℹ visit.brussels (BIP) [85 G2] 2–4 rue Royale; ☎ 02 513 89 40; ⏲ 09.00–18.00 Mon–Fri, 10.00–18.00 Sat–Sun & hols. The tourist board's main office sells a vast array of cycling maps (€2.50), city maps (€1.50) & themed guides including to Art Nouveau buildings (€5).

visit.brussels [94 D2] Hôtel de Ville, Grand-Place; 02 513 89 40; 09.00–18.00 daily. Small kiosk.

Visit Flanders [94 E2] 61 rue du Marché aux Herbes; m 0471 533 388; w flandersshop.be; Apr–Sep 10.00–18.00; Oct–Mar 10.00–17.00; closed 13.00–14.00 at w/end. Lavishly revamped in 2016, but more shop than office now, though they have basic information on the 6 'art cities' of Flanders (Brussels, Antwerp, Leuven, Mechelen, Bruges & Ghent).

WHERE TO STAY

Beds in Brussels are plentiful, but don't restrict your search to the options on offer around the Grand-Place. Staying beyond the petit-ring can be cheaper and more rewarding, with communes such as Ixelles and Saint-Gilles within easy reach of the sights. Brussels is busy all year round so it's advisable to book ahead, especially during the summer high season. Options run the gamut from stylish B&Bs to youth hostels and luxury hotels, though it's mid-range properties which especially impress here. If you have an early flight, numerous hotels near Zaventem lay on free shuttles; the Sheraton is right by the terminal (see w brusselsairport.be for a list).

LOWER AND UPPER TOWN

Luxury

Hotel Amigo [94 D3] (154 rooms, 19 suites) 1–3 rue de l'Amigo; 02 547 47 47; w roccofortehotels.com; Bourse. Equidistant between the Grand-Place & wee (pardon the pun) Manneken Pis, you couldn't stay any closer to the action. Built on the site of the old prison where Karl Marx & his wife were held before their expulsion. Part of the Rocco Forte chain, with designer Olga Polizzi's fingerprints all over its plush rooms decorated with Flemish fabrics, art & ceramics, including sketches of *Tintin* in the bathrooms (the Magritte Suite ups the ante). There's a fitness centre & restaurant, Bocconi (€€€€), for pricey Italian fare. B/fast €34. **€€€€€**

Upmarket

Le Dixseptième [94 F4] (37 rooms) 25 rue de la Madeleine; 02 517 17 17; w ledixseptieme.be; Gare Centrale. Sophisticated, characterful boutique hotel just minutes from the Grand-Place but remarkably restful – a real antidote to the chains. Grand public areas include a bar with a fireplace, & a 17th-century oak staircase (the building was reconstructed soon after the bombardment of Brussels in 1695, & became the Spanish ambassador's residence). **€€€–€€€€**

The Dominican [79 E6] (150 rooms) 9 rue Léopold; 02 203 08 08; w carlton.nl; De Brouckère. Swish design hotel – check out the flaming torches at the entrance – & former Dominican abbey whose main claim to fame is that painter Jacques-Louis David lived here from 1816 until 1825. They've achieved a good blend of old & new, & you won't miss out on mod cons – be it the buzzing bar/restaurant or sauna & steam room. **€€€–€€€€**

Le Plaza [79 E4] (190 rooms) 118–26 bd Adolphe Max; 02 278 01 00; w leplaza-brussels.be; Rogier. The city's oldest independent hotel – an Art Deco palace built by the architect behind the Villa Empain – still brims with class. Winston Churchill stayed here during World War II & during the 1960s & 1970s it became the go-to hotel for celebrities. The lobby's antiques, paintings, silk

INSIDER'S VIEW

Brussels can be a difficult city to fall in love with, so I highly recommend booking a free tour through Brussels Greeters (w visit.brussels/en/sites/greeters) – a network of locals who volunteer to show visitors around their town. It'll help you get under the skin of the place in no time and ensure you don't just stick to the well-beaten tourist routes.

rugs, sweeping staircases & marble floors set the scene, though the rooms could do with a bit of TLC. Service, however, is excellent. B/fast €29. **€€€–€€€€**

Mid-range

9 Hotel Central [79 F7] (47 rooms) 10 rue des Colonies; 02 504 99 10; w 9-hotel-central-brussels.be; Gare Centrale. Just behind Gare Centrale, a very solid boutique hotel from a small Paris- & Brussels-based chain (their website often runs deals). Slick, industrial-style rooms have exposed-brick walls & all mod cons; upgrade to a balcony room or add late check-out (15.00) for €20. B/fast €17, express b/fast €7.50. Their Sablon branch, modelled on a collector's apartment, is also excellent. **€€€**

Art de Séjour [94 A4] (4 rooms) 12 rue des Bogards; 02 513 97 55; w artdesejour.com; Anneessens. This Neoclassical townhouse is currently the best-reviewed B&B in all Brussels – hence the need to book way ahead if you want a chance to experience host Mario's seamless reception. There are 4 minimalist rooms – 1 for each floor – & a studio in the vast attic space, while b/fast (fresh orange juice, homemade croissants, eggs cooked to order) – takes place on linen-covered tables. **€€€**

* **B&B La Maison Haute** [94 D2] (4 rooms) 101 rue Haute; m 0475 69 21 32; w lamaisonhaute.be; Louise. You're hit by the scent of handmade soap from the ground-floor shop on entering this pitch-perfect B&B. A lot of care has gone into the individually styled rooms: the Vivienne has graphic wallpaper by designer Vivienne Westwood, & there's an all-white duplex suite with views of the Palais de Justice. I've rarely had a better b/fast in a B&B, & you're steps from the city's best antique shops & flea market. Doubles €115 inc b/fast; 2 nights min. **€€€**

Druum [78 A5] (6 rooms) 63 rue du Hublon; m 0472 05 42 40; w druum.be; Sainte-Catherine. A fascinating blend of art & history: housed in 1 of the 1st mansions built by a factory owner in the notorious *coin du diable* ('devil's corner') of Brussels, this one-off property has 6 distinct artist-designed rooms. The Permanent Room has a concrete bed for 4, while my favourite, HS63, looks to be mid-construction, with repurposed doors decorating the walls & an archive of recordings from the HS63 venue previously on the premises. Not strong on mod cons but just wonderful. **€€€**

The Hotel [85 F5] (420 rooms & suites) 38 bd de Waterloo; 02 504 11 11; w thehotel-brussels.be; Louise. Towering 94m above the Brussels skyline – it's 1 of the city's most iconic sights, if a tad less inspired than the Atomium – this high-rise hotel is a former Hilton stylishly relaunched in 2013. Since then VIPs like Obama (& his vast entourage) have enjoyed its minimal, contemporary rooms & dizzying 23rd-floor spa. Excellent b/fast (€20) spread an added boon. **€€€**

Hôtel des Galeries [94 F1] (23 rooms) 38 rue des Bouchers; 02 213 74 70; w hoteldesgaleries.be; Gare Centrale/De Brouckère. In the heart of the Galeries Royales Saint-Hubert shopping arcade, this very hospitable boutique hotel opened in 2013 & swiftly became a hit. Rooms have parquet floors, interesting design details & beautiful ceramic-tiled bathrooms; there are 3 duplex suites, 1 of which has its own footbridge! The open-kitchen restaurant (€€€€) serves seasonal bistronomy-style dishes; there's also a café. Check their website for the best deals – as low as €140 with b/fast in high season. **€€€**

Hotel Espérance [79 E4] (12 rooms) 1–3 rue du Finistère; 02 219 10 28; w hotel-esperance.be; De Brouckère. Wonderful 1930s Art Deco hotel which was saved from ruin & declared a listed building in 2008. Its tavern/b/fast room has hardly changed, while the rooms upstairs have been given a modern makeover. Ignore them, however, & plump for the original Art Deco room with its freestanding tub & gold taps – either request room 3 or look for the 'Deluxe Double Room' on booking sites. **€€–€€€**

Welcome Hotel [78 C5] (17 rooms) 23 quai au Bois à Brûler; 02 219 95 46; w hotelwelcome.com; Sainte-Catherine. I loved Hotel Welcome for its sense of fun. Rooms are named after countries where the owners – Sophie & Michel Smeesters – have travelled & are decorated with items they brought back. Don't let the wood-panelled lobby fool you: corridors of quirkiness await ... My favourites were the gargantuan 'Egyptian' suite, complete with gold mummy & 2-person jacuzzi; the standard azure 'Zanzibar' room with ornate doors from Stonetown; & the bright pink deluxe 'Bali' room. **€€€**

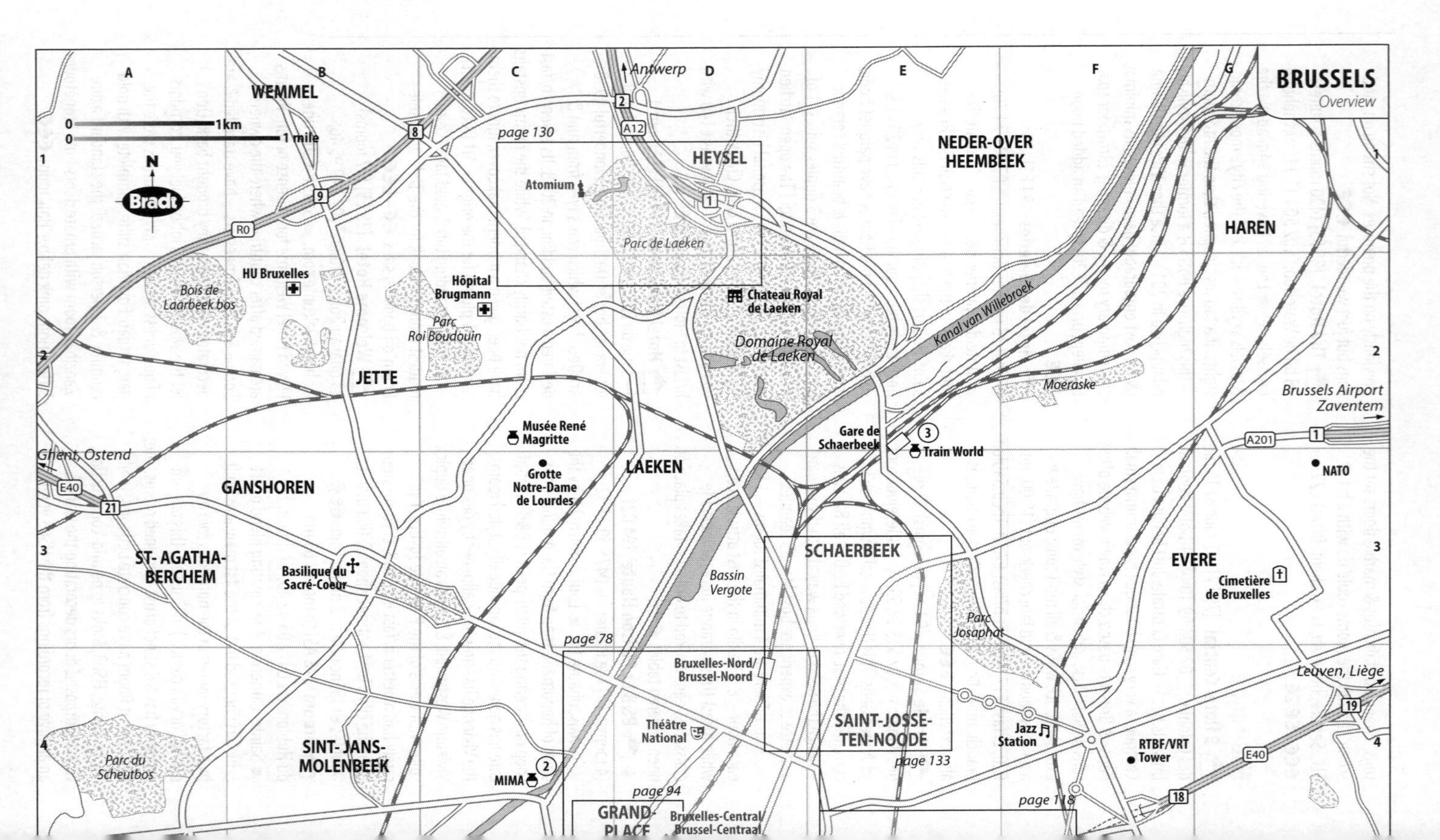
BRUSSELS
Overview
A
B
C
D
E
F
G
1
2
3
4
0
1km
0
1 mile
N
Bradt
WEMMEL
Antwerp
page 130
HEYSEL
Atomium
Parc de Laeken
NEDER-OVER
HEEMBEEK
HAREN
HU Bruxelles
Bois de
Laarbeek bos
Hôpital
Brugmann
Parc
Roi Boudouin
Chateau Royal
de Laeken
Domaine Royal
de Laeken
Kanal van Willebroek
Moeraske
JETTE
Brussels Airport
Zaventem
Musée René
Magritte
Gare de
Schaerbeek
Train World
Ghent, Ostend
Grotte
Notre-Dame
de Lourdes
LAEKEN
NATO
GANSHOREN
ST- AGATHA-
BERCHEM
Basilique du
Sacré-Coeur
SCHAERBEEK
Bassin
Vergote
EVERE
Cimetière
de Bruxelles
Parc
Josaphat
page 78
Bruxelles-Nord/
Brussel-Noord
Leuven, Liège
Théâtre
National
SAINT-JOSSE-
TEN-NOODE
Jazz
Station
RTBF/VRT
Tower
SINT- JANS-
MOLENBEEK
Parc du
Scheutbos
MIMA
page 133
page 94
page 118
GRAND-
PLACE
Bruxelles-Central
Brussel-Centraal
R0
E40
A12
A201

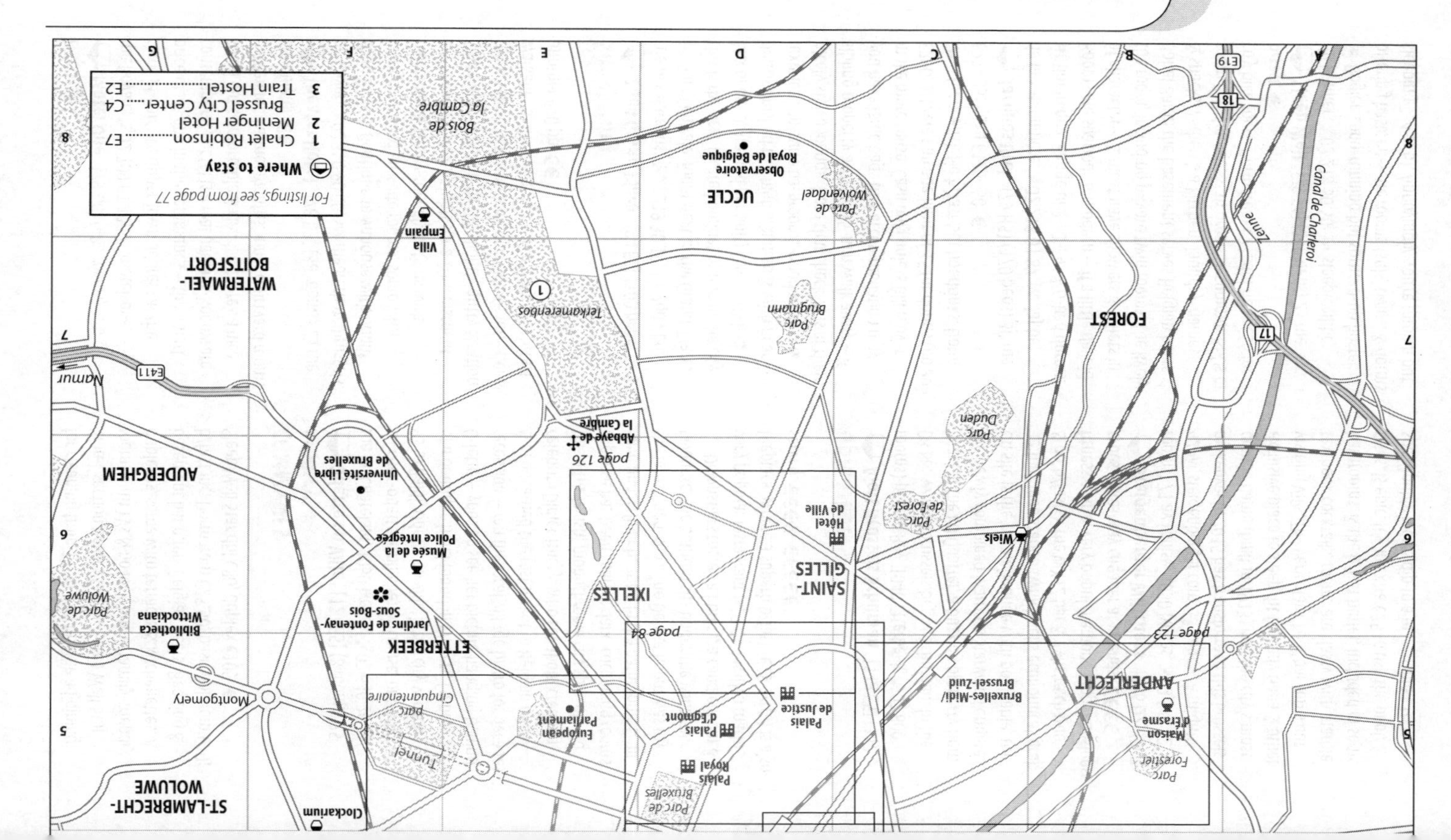
ST-LAMBRECHT-WOLUWE
AUDERGHEM
WATERMAEL-BOITSFORT
ETTERBEEK
IXELLES
SAINT-GILLES
UCCLE
FOREST
ANDERLECHT
Clockarium
Montgomery
Bibliotheca Wittockiana
Parc de Woluwe
Tunnel
parc Cinquantenaire
Jardins de Fontenay-Sous-Bois
Musée de la Police Intégrée
Université Libre de Bruxelles
European Parliament
Palais Royal
Palais d'Egmont
Parc de Bruxelles
Palais de Justice
Hôtel de Ville
page 84
page 126
page 123
Abbaye de la Cambre
Terkamerenbos
Villa Empain
Bois de la Cambre
Namur
E411
Parc de Forest
Parc Duden
Parc Brugmann
Parc de Wolvendael
Observatoire Royal de Belgique
Wiels
Bruxelles-Midi/ Brussel-Zuid
Maison d'Erasme
Parc Forestier
Zenne
Canal de Charleroi
E19
17
18
For listings, see from page 77
Where to stay
1 Chalet Robinson......E7
2 Meninger Hotel
Brussel City Center....C4
3 Train Hostel......E2
A
B
C
D
E
F
G
5
6
7
8

Budget

Motel One [79 G6] (489 rooms) 120 rue Royale; 02 209 61 10; w motel-one.com; Parc. An Upper Town address at the price of staying in the communes – this smart contemporary hotel is a real bargain. Rooms are small but comfortable & clean, & there's a nice garden for warmer months. Inner courtyard rooms are quieter. **€€**

Theater Hotel [78 D3] (38 rooms) 23 rue de Gaver; 02 350 90 00; w theaterhotelbrussels.com; Yser. Boutique townhouse with bright, straightforward en-suite rooms, some with balconies, & family-friendly options with kitchenettes. Stay 3 nights for a 20% discount. Some may be put off by the slightly gritty location, but it's close to the brilliant dockside Kaaitheater & walkable to the main sights. Dbl from €55; b/fast another €10 pp. **€€**

Shoestring

2Go4 Grand Place [94 E2] (100 beds) 6–8 rue des Harengs; 02 219 30 19; w 2go4.be; Gare Centrale. Right next to the Grand-Place, this is the best-located budget option in the city. Mix of quads (rented per unit) & 6- & 10-bed dorms finished to a high standard & with near luxurious en-suite bathrooms. Good kitchen & nicely styled lounge. Note that check-in is at their sibling property a 10- to 15-min walk away – if you have large bags that accommodation may make more sense. Cash only unless bill is over €200, & there's an age limit of 35 for dorms (no age limit for quads). No b/fast but hot drinks. Dorm €22–35; quad €120–50. **€**

Jacques Brel [79 H5] (170 beds) 30 rue de la Sablonnière; 02 218 01 87; w laj.be; Botanique. Range of 2-, 3-, 4- & 6-bed dorms. Rooms are spacious & modern – if a little devoid of character – & most have showers & toilets in the room, including private twin rooms. The lively Babel Bar in the basement serves Belgian beers & snacks, & there's a kitchen, laundry, games room & TV lounge. Staff organise summer BBQs or city bike tours. Dorm from €23, dbl from €56 inc b/fast. **€**

Sleep Well [79 F4] (240 beds) 23 rue du Damier; 02 218 50 50; w sleepwell.be; Rogier. Long-running but spruced-up hostel offering basic en-suite rooms (sgls, twins, & dorms sleeping 3, 4 or 6). Annoyingly, you're thrown out for cleaning from 11.00– 15.00. The adjoining 'hotel' section houses fancier 'Sleep Well Star' rooms with TVs & no lock-out, & family-friendly duplexes, some with terraces & kitchenettes. A basement bar offers Belgian beers. Bedding & b/fast inc. Dorm from €25.50, basic dbl from €70; Sleep Well Star dbl €80, duplex €105. **€**

COMMUNES

Luxury

Odette en Ville [127 E5] (8 rooms) 25 rue du Châtelain, 1050 Ixelles; 02 640 26 26; w chez-odetteenville.be; Louise, or tram 93 to Bailli. Odette 'en ville' is the city version of a boutique hotel found in Williers, France. Odette – you can see her picture hanging behind reception – ran the local village bistro for decades & bequeathed the restaurant to Belgian minor celebrity Didier Thiery, who set about creating this ultra-lavish, monochrome city spin-off. No expense has been spared: dark, cocooning rooms have under-floor heating in the bathrooms & all the latest mod-cons. The Deluxe Room was my favourite: the bathtub sits under the window.

Downstairs there's a library, a candlelit bar & very popular restaurant (€€€€) with a marble fireplace, where a superb b/fast (€25 extra) is also served. **€€€€–€€€€€**

Upmarket

Aloft Brussels Schuman [118 C5] (147 rooms) pl Jean Rey, 1040 Etterbeek; 02 800 08 88; w aloftbrussels.be; Schuman. In the heart of the EU Quarter, a buzzing property from the newly combined Marriott/Starwood empire. On site is the 're:mix' lounge with pool table, the 're:fuel' food station (which sells economical 'grab & go' b/fasts), the WXYZ bar & 24hr 're:charge' fitness centre. Very popular among hipper business types. Rates way cheaper at w/ends. **€€€€**

Steigenberger Wiltcher's [126 D2] (267 rooms) 71 av Louise, 1050 Ixelles; 02 542 42 42 w steigenberger.com; Louise. A mighty makeover in 2015 has transformed this Brussels grande dame (built in 1913) into the city's most exclusive place to sleep, fit for Lady Gaga & other visiting VIPs. The very glam 'Loui' bar turns out textbook cocktails, rooms are classy with marble bathrooms, & the b/fast buffet, included in some rates, is epic. It's an extra €25 to use the pool/spa. Double rooms dip to a reasonable €160 without b/fast, but can easily spiral far higher. **€€€–€€€€**

Mid-range

Maison Flagey [127 G6] (4 rooms, 1 suite) 39 av du Général de Gaulle, 1050 Ixelles; m 0496 24 28 23; w maisonflagey.com; tram 71 to Vijvers Elsene/81 to Flagey. Right by the genteel Ixelles Ponds, this stunning 1900 house is Art Nouveau heaven, having been sensitively converted to give it the necessary mod cons. Most rooms have terraces & beautiful original features, not least the Royal Suite's eye-popping shower mosaic & freestanding bath. B/fast (an added €10 pp) is served in a glorious 1st-floor room overlooking the ponds. Dbl from €140. **€€€**

Made in Louise [126 D3] (48 rooms) 40 rue Veydt, 1050 Ixelles; 02 537 40 33; w madeinlouise.com; Louise/tram 92 to Faider or 93 to Defacqz. Lovely Ixelles townhouse of note for its common areas (with ample free pastries & coffee) & service-oriented staff. Various categories of rooms; 'Charming' ones have funky wallpaper & elegant furnishings, but I'd stick with the simplest 'Cosy' rooms, which drop to €75. B/fast, included in some rates, is in a room overlooking a giant chess set. **€€–€€€**

Budget

✱ **Hotel Le Berger** [127 E1] (66 rooms) 24 rue du Berger, 1050 Ixelles; 02 510 83 40; w lebergerhotel.be; Porte de Namur. Unique chance to stay in a former *maison de rendez-vous* where men met their mistresses for champagne & assignations (fascinatingly, the double lift still in situ was so punters wouldn't run into anyone on exiting). Watch out – owing to its past some rooms have open bathrooms & toilets can be tiny, but you won't find anywhere else like it. Gorgeous kitsch décor in the common parts, which include a decadent bar serving food by popular Italian Vini Divini next door. Buffet b/fast €14; dbl from €55. **€€**

Hygge Hotel [126 D1] (50 rooms) 31–3 rue des Drapiers, 1050 Ixelles; 02 274 28 00; w hyggehotel.be; Louise. New Scandi-style hotel with appropriately serene (Instagrammable) wood- & wool-heavy décor, an impressive staircase & straightforward, stylish rooms (I love the blue-&-white tiles in the bathroom). Very fair rates – a dbl is €90 in high season. **€€**

Pantone Hotel [126 C2] (61 rooms) 1 pl Loix, 1060 Saint-Gilles; 02 541 48 98; w pantonehotel.com; Hôtel des Monnaies. Pantone's standardised colour-matching system is used by designers the world over, but this is the first time the concept has been applied to a hotel. All the rooms are a blank canvas in order to draw attention to the photograph mounted above each bed which features an obscure Brussels site magnified to emphasise the pure Pantone colours – arty, eh? Each floor has its own colour & when you check in they ask you what colour/mood you're in & assign you to a floor accordingly. Rooms ending in 6 all have panoramic views & a terrace. Dbl from €59. **€€**

Vintage Hotel [126 C2] (38 rooms) 45 rue Dejoncker, 1060 Saint-Gilles; 02 533 99 80; w vintagehotel.be; Louise/Hôtel des Monnaies. Old people's home turned retro boutique hotel. It's the attention to detail that – to quote Austin Powers – is rather 'groovy, baby', with psychedelic wallpaper, plastic orange phones & bubble lamps. More unusually, you can sleep in a vintage Airstream trailer built the same year as Expo '58! The trendy b/fast room doubles as a boutique wine bar. **€€**

Shoestring

BRXXL5 [84 A3] (50 rooms) 5 rue de Woeringen; 02 503 59 62; w brxxl5.com; Gare du Midi. A short stroll from both Gare du Midi & the centre, this slightly functional hostel is worth bearing in mind for its good-value rates. Range of private trpl & dbl rooms to 4- & 5-bed dorms, all with private bathrooms (dorms under 40s only). No kitchen but a microwave & vending machine, while a pool table & patio are among other amenities. Dorm €24–26, dbl €65, quad €90. **€**

Camping Ciel Ouvert [118 A7] (80 sites) 205 chaussée de Wavre, 1050 Ixelles; 02 640 79 67; Jul–Aug only; Trône. The only campsite in central Brussels (in Matonge, by the EU Quarter) is a small, leafy summer-only affair belonging to the St-Sacrement church in front of it. Thankfully the church bells don't chime during the night, but they do kick off at 07.00 so take earplugs. Simple showers & toilets are available, as well as a BBQ, & campervans can park outside. Adult/small tent €5, wide tent/parking €10, 50% off for under 12s. **€**

Meninger Hotel Brussel City Center [74 C4] (150 rooms) 33 quai du Hainaut,

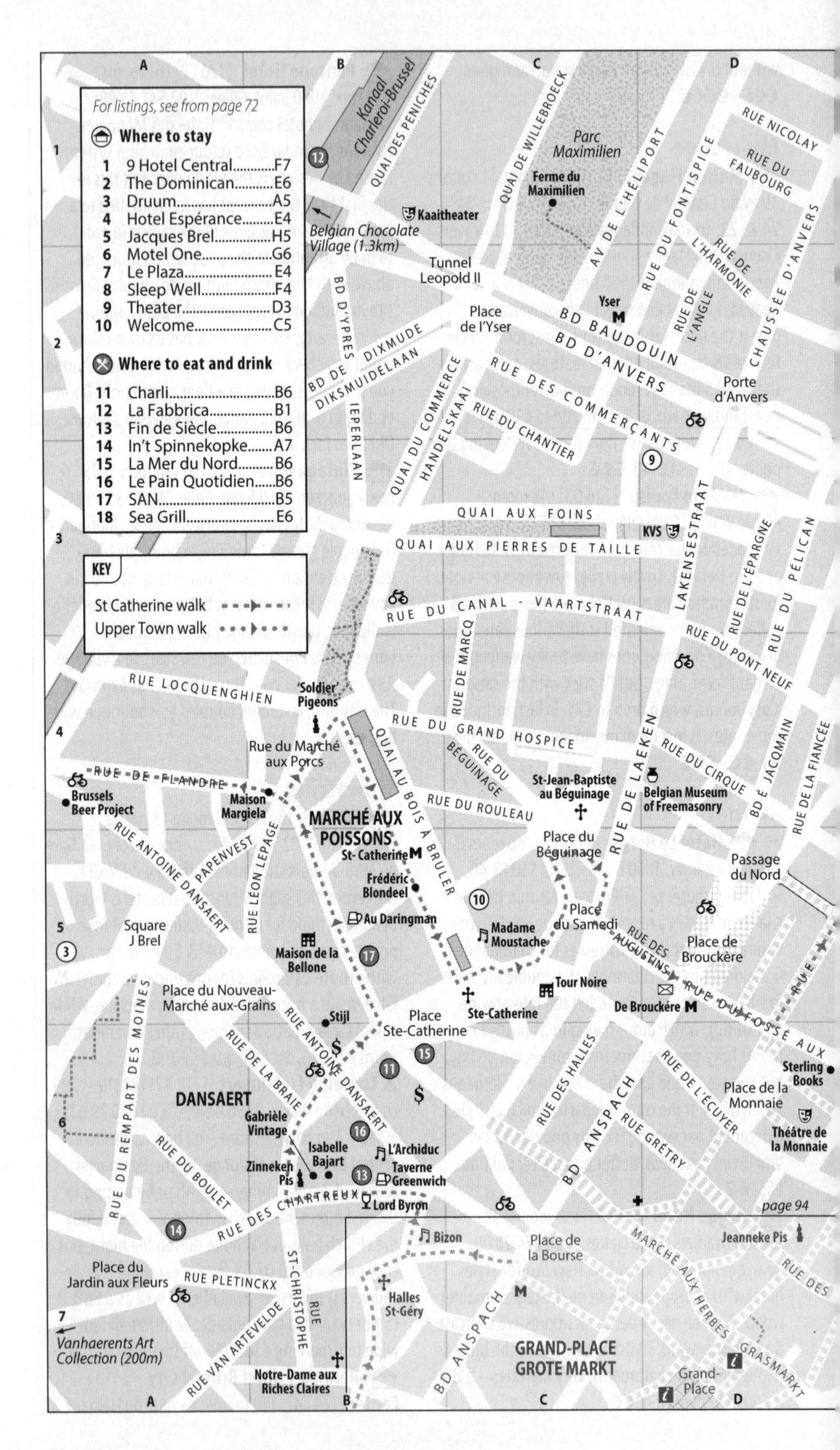

For listings, see from page 72
Where to stay
1 9 Hotel Central F7
2 The Dominican E6
3 Druum A5
4 Hotel Espérance E4
5 Jacques Brel H5
6 Motel One G6
7 Le Plaza E4
8 Sleep Well F4
9 Theater D3
10 Welcome C5
Where to eat and drink
11 Charli B6
12 La Fabbrica B1
13 Fin de Siècle B6
14 In't Spinnekopke A7
15 La Mer du Nord B6
16 Le Pain Quotidien B6
17 SAN B5
18 Sea Grill E6
KEY
St Catherine walk
Upper Town walk
Kanaal Charleroi-Brussel
Quai des Péniches
Parc Maximilien
Ferme du Maximilien
Kaaitheater
Belgian Chocolate Village (1.3km)
Tunnel Leopold II
Place de l'Yser
Yser
Bd Baudouin
Bd d'Anvers
Porte d'Anvers
Rue des Commerçants
Rue du Chantier
Quai aux Foins
Quai aux Pierres de Taille
KVS
Rue du Canal
Vaartstraat
Lakensestraat
Rue Locquenghien
'Soldier' Pigeons
Rue du Grand Hospice
Rue du Marché aux Porcs
Rue de Flandre
Brussels Beer Project
Maison Margiela
Marché aux Poissons
St-Catherine
Quai au Bois à Brûler
St-Jean-Baptiste au Béguinage
Belgian Museum of Freemasonry
Place du Béguinage
Rue de Laeken
Passage du Nord
Frédéric Blondeel
Au Daringman
Madame Moustache
Place du Samedi
Place de Brouckère
Square J Brel
Maison de la Bellone
Place du Nouveau-Marché aux-Grains
Tour Noire
Ste-Catherine
De Brouckère
Stijl
Place Ste-Catherine
Rue Antoine Dansaert
Dansaert
Gabrièle Vintage
Isabelle Bajart
Zinneken Pis
L'Archiduc
Taverne Greenwich
Lord Byron
Rue des Chartreux
Sterling Books
Place de la Monnaie
Théâtre de la Monnaie
Bd Anspach
Bizon
Place de la Bourse
Jeanneke Pis
Place du Jardin aux Fleurs
Rue Plétinckx
Halles St-Géry
Vanhaerents Art Collection (200m)
Notre-Dame aux Riches Claires
Grand-Place Grote Markt
Grand-Place
page 94

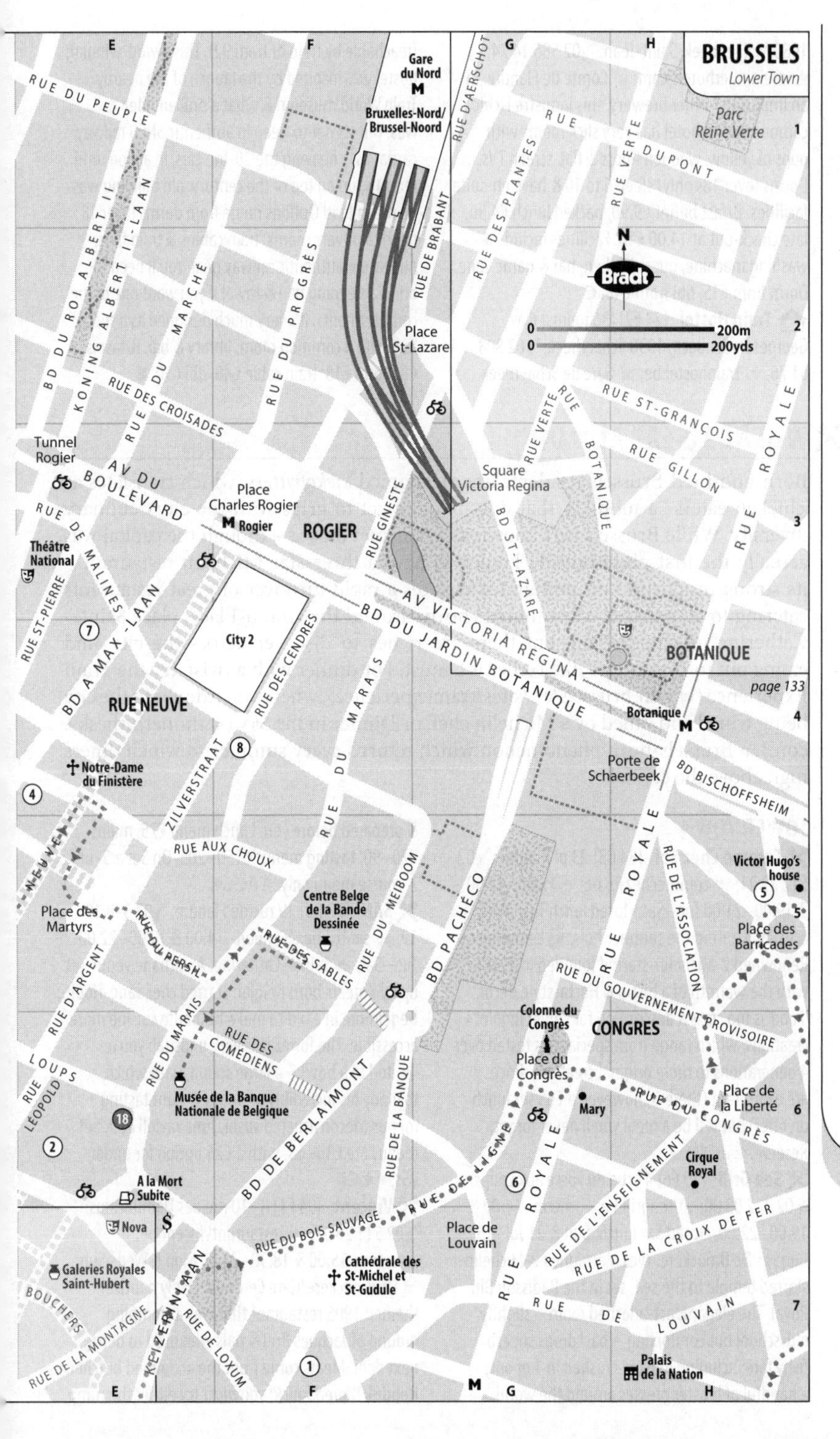

BRUSSELS
Lower Town
Gare du Nord
Bruxelles-Nord/ Brussel-Noord
Parc Reine Verte
RUE DU PEUPLE
RUE D'AERSCHOT
RUE DUPONT
RUE VERTE
RUE DES PLANTES
RUE DE BRABANT
BD DU ROI ALBERT II
KONING ALBERT II-LAAN
RUE DU MARCHÉ
RUE DU PROGRÈS
Place St-Lazare
200m
200yds
RUE DES CROISADES
RUE ST-FRANÇOIS
RUE ROYALE
RUE BOTANIQUE
RUE GILLON
Tunnel Rogier
AV DU BOULEVARD
Place Charles Rogier
Rogier
ROGIER
RUE GINESTE
Square Victoria Regina
BD ST-LAZARE
RUE DE MALINES
Théâtre National
AV VICTORIA REGINA
BD DU JARDIN BOTANIQUE
RUE ST-PIERRE
City 2
RUE DES CENDRES
BOTANIQUE
BD A MAX-LAAN
RUE NEUVE
RUE DU MARAIS
page 133
Botanique
Porte de Schaerbeek
BD BISCHOFFSHEIM
ZILVERSTRAAT
Notre-Dame du Finistère
RUE AUX CHOUX
NEUVE
RUE DU MEIBOOM
BD PACHECO
RUE DE L'ASSOCIATION
Victor Hugo's house
Place des Martyrs
Centre Belge de la Bande Dessinée
Place des Barricades
RUE DU PERSIL
RUE DES SABLES
RUE D'ARGENT
RUE DU GOUVERNEMENT PROVISOIRE
Colonne du Congrès
CONGRES
RUE DU MARAIS
RUE DES COMÉDIENS
Place du Congrès
LOUPS
RUE LEOPOLD
Musée de la Banque Nationale de Belgique
Mary
RUE DU CONGRÈS
Place de la Liberté
BD DE BERLAIMONT
RUE DE LA BANQUE
RUE DE LIGNE
RUE DE L'ENSEIGNEMENT
Cirque Royal
A la Mort Subite
Nova
RUE DU BOIS SAUVAGE
Place de Louvain
RUE DE LA CROIX DE FER
Galeries Royales Saint-Hubert
Cathédrale des St-Michel et St-Gudule
BOUCHERS
KEIZERINLAAN
RUE DE LOXUM
RUE DE LA MONTAGNE
RUE DE LOUVAIN
Palais de la Nation

1080 Moleenbeek-Saint-Jean; 02 588 14 74; w meiningerhotels.com; Comte de Flandre. In an imposing former brewery, this industrial-chic carbon-neutral hotel has very slick rooms with pops of yellow, wooden floors & flat-screen TVs. Dorms (over 18s only) sleep 6 to 10 & have en-suite facilities. B/fast buffet €9.90, packed lunch €4.50, late check-out at 14.00 €10. Facilities include a washing machine, guest kitchen, bar & game zone. Dorm from €15, dbl from €48. €

Train Hostel [74 E2] (36 rooms) 6 av Georges Rodenbach, 1030 Schaerbeek; 02 808 61 76; w trainhostel.be; Gare de Schaerbeek (reachable by train or tram 92). This award-winning hostel was inspired by the launch of the nearby Train World museum & what a brilliant idea it was. Guests get to sleep in authentic SNCB railway carriages – heaving the 30-ton cars, in action until recently, up on top of the century-old building was no mean feat! Options range from dorms (over 18 only) to private rooms, train cabins & train flats. All feature authentic railway gear. You'll need to bring a sleeping bag & towel if you want one of the compartments. It's very much designed as a social hub with a common room, library & bar. B/fast is €8. Dorm €18, train cabin €40, dbl €50. €

WHERE TO EAT AND DRINK

Born-and-bred Brussels residents are nicknamed *kiekefritters*, which translates as 'chicken eaters': a moniker that doesn't quite get to grips with the city's culinary diversity. While Brussels isn't known as a gourmet mecca – though the capital was actually the first place outside France to have a three-star Michelin restaurant – its strong proportion of immigrants ensures a rapid turnover of great restaurants catering to all palettes. Most tourists hover around the Grand-Place, place Sainte-Catherine or chic Sablon, but there are riches to discover across the city, and eating out in communes like Ixelles is a must. For dinner with a twist, try the Tram Experience (w visit.brussels/en/sites/tramexperience), where you ride about the city being wined and dined by a Michelin chef, or Dinner in the Sky (w dinnerinthesky.com), a Brussels-born phenomenon which returns every summer to winch diners high above the capital.

LOWER TOWN

Comme Chez Soi [84 B3] 23 pl Rouppe; 02 512 29 21; w commechezsoi.be; noon–13.30 & 19.00–21.00 Tue–Sat, closed lunch Tue–Wed & usually during the summer hols; Lemonnier. Renowned 2-Michelin-starred founded in 1926, with the warmth of a bistro & Horta-style décor. 'Food' is too crass a description for Lionel Rigolet's creations, which range from specialities tested over 4 generations to more original creations. Prices are exorbitant (there is, however, a €65 set lunch on offer) but it'll be a meal you'll never forget. Reserve. €€€€€

Sea Grill [79 E6] 47 rue du Fossé aux Loups; 02 212 08 00; w seagrill.be; noon–14.00 & 19.00–22.00, closed Sat lunch, Sun & 21 Jul–15 Aug; De Brouckère. Yves Mattagne's 2-Michelin-starred temple to the sea, set in the Radisson Blu Royal. The elegant, art-adorned room – slightly old-school but comforting – backdrops superb fishy fare including lobster, crushed in 1 of only a handful of lobster presses around the world, & prepared before you. Lunch menu €75, mains €70–90, tasting menus €150–205. On Sat a 5- or 7-course menu only. €€€€€

SAN [78 B5] 19 rue de Flandre; 02 318 19 19; w sanbxl.be; noon–14.00 & 19.00–22.00 Tue–Sat; Sainte-Catherine. An urbane venue set up by Korean-born Belgian starred chef Sang-Hoon Degeimbre in a bid to make his haute cuisine more accessible. The formula is very unusual: you're limited to a bowl & a large spoon, with which to enjoy his incredibly aromatic & light tasting menus (deconstructed sushi, tuna ravioli etc). Set menus are €36–65, with a €25 option for under 25s. €€€€

Vincent [94 F1] 8–10 rue des Dominicains; 02 511 26 07; w restaurantvincent.be; noon–15.00 & 18.30–23.00 Mon & Wed–Sun; De Brouckère/Gare Centrale. Lively nautical-themed 1905 restaurant that was a stomping ground of Jacques Brel & pals who used to booze next door. Meats come from the acclaimed butcher Hendrik Dierendonck; you *must* try either the rump steak flambéed in cream & alcohol on a table in front of you, or their mussels. €€€€

De L'Ogenblik [94 F1] 1 galerie des Princes; 02 503 00 00; w ogenblik.be; noon–14.30 & 19.00–midnight Mon–Sat; Gare Centrale. Created in 1969, & tucked away in the Galeries Royales Saint-Hubert, this marble-topped, wood-panelled bistro has a firm band of fans, drawn by its authentic bistro cuisine, timeless vibe & resident cat. €€€–€€€€

La Fabbrica [78 B1] 86c av du Port; 02 428 50 26; w lafabbrica.be; 11.30–15.00 Mon–Fri, 10.00–15.00 Sun; Ribaucourt. This one is for parents. Here you can b/fast with young kids & let them run amok & be as loud as they like enjoying craft tables & a bouncy castle, while you sip on good coffee & munch your avocado toast. €€€

In 't Spinnekopke [78 A7] 1 pl du Jardin aux Fleurs; 02 511 86 95; w spinnekopke.be; 18.00–23.00 Mon & Sat, noon–14.30 & 18.00–23.00 Tue–Fri; Bourse. The quaint & crooked 'little spider' house dates from 1762 & originally served as a post office, before being converted to a restaurant. The age-old Belgian classic serves all the favourites inc *tomate aux crevettes d'Ostende*, *lapin à la gueuze* & *waterzooi*, but excels at mussels recipes. There's a large selection of French wines – particularly Bordeaux – to choose from, & over 100 artisanal beers. €€€

Nüetnigenough [94 C3] 25 rue du Lombard; 02 513 78 84; w nuetnigenough.be; 17.00–22.30 Mon–Fri, noon-22.30 Sat & Sun. Does all the Belgian classics such as *stoemp* & vol-au-vent really well, but also some lovely experiments such as stewed lamb with chocolate beer. No reservations. €€€

Le Wine Bar des Marolles [84 D5] 198 rue Haute; m 0496 82 01 05; w winebarsablon.be; 19.00–22.00 Thu–Sun, also noon–15.00 Sat–Sun; Louise/Hôtel des Monnaies. Sommelier, wine broker, art connoisseur & chef Vincent Thomaes's much-loved institution moved from Sablon to rue Haute in 2007. Ingredients – mostly meaty – come almost entirely from small Belgian producers & are perfectly accompanied by the expert wines (let Vincent guide you) in a nice room with candles & Tiffany lamps. They do a soup & main for €15 at the w/end. €€€

Fin de Siècle [78 B6] 9 rue des Chartreux; 02 732 74 34; 16.30–23.45 Mon–Fri, 16.30–00.45 Sat–Sun; Bourse. Jam-packed on any day of the week, this stalwart bistro has a brilliantly lively atmosphere & turns out value-for money, hearty Belgian fare in traditional surroundings. No bookings accepted but that doesn't seem to deter anyone. €€

La Clef d'Or [84 C5] 21–2 pl du Jeu de Balle; 02 511 97 62; 05.00–17.00 Tue–Sun; Porte de Hal/Gare du Midi. Unassuming hangout by the pl du Jeu de Balle flea market with a distinct whiff of 'Belgitude'. Nothing fancy on the menu – eggs on toast, sandwiches & the like – but does the trick & it's fun to take in the bustling atmosphere. €

La Mer du Nord [78 B6] 45 rue St-Catherine; 02 513 11 92; w noordzeemerdunord.be; fish bar: 11.00–18.00 Tue–Sun; Sainte-Catherine. No longer an insider address, a bustling fish shack with limited seating where – rain or shine – you can tuck into a chilled glass of vino & fresh fishy snacks like steaming seafood soup, shrimp croquettes, fried calamari or razor clams, served on a tin plate & setting you back €2–8 per dish. Wonderful. €

Mr Falafel [84 B2] 53 bd Maurice Lemonnier; m 0493 34 64 12; noon–late; Anneessens. Tiny shop that doesn't look like much but serves the best falafel in town. It's made by an Egyptian chap called Shawkat & it's an absolute bargain. Comes with as much free salad as you like. €

Le Pain Quotidien [78 B6] 16 rue Antoine Dansaert; 02 502 23 61; w lepainquotidien.com; 07.00–19.00; Bourse. One of Belgium's big success stories, this is the original (slightly cramped) branch of the all-conquering chain, established in 1990 by Alain Coumont; the bread baked here follows a recipe he developed when he couldn't source decent *pain* for his diners. Fast-forward to today & the chain has 220 stores in 19 countries. Famous for their *table communale* – to encourage you to natter with your neighbours – & their *tartines* (open sandwiches) served on wooden boards. Still a great place for brunch. €€

Charli [78 B6] 34 rue Sainte-Catherine; 02 513 63 32; w charliboulangerie.com; 07.30–19.00 Mon–Sat, 08.00–13.30 Sun; Sainte-Catherine/Bourse. By common consent one of the very best boulangeries in Brussels, this is a superb spot for b/fast – including top-notch, buttery & flaky pastries (the *croissant aux amandes* is a favourite) & fine coffee. Prices are more than fair – though they only take cards for larger purchases, so have some cash on you. Limited seating. €

Tonton Garby [94 F4] 26 rue Duquesnoy; m 0484 29 02 16; 10.00–17.00 Mon–Fri; Gare Centrale. The snaking queues are the giveaway at this small shop, turning out the finest sandwiches in town. Less BLT than unusual combinations like the number 7, which melds cheese, cranberries & chorizo. Lovely owner who cares about his craft. A massive bargain to top it off. €

UPPER TOWN

Bozar Restaurant [85 G2] 3 rue Baron Horta; 02 503 00 00; w bozarrestaurant.be; noon–14.00 & 18.00–21.30 Tue–Fri, 18.00–21.45 Sat; Gare Centrale. Restored to its Art Deco splendour in 2010, this 1-Michelin-star haunt next to the namesake art museum, & designed by Victor Horta, has a line in French/Belgian classics (fish, game, steaks) whipped up by Karen Torosyan, an award-winning pie & pastry maker (male, by the way) on show in the open kitchen. Decent-value lunch menus. €€€€€

Le Rabassier [85 E3] 23 rue de Rollebeek; 02 502 04 00; w lerabassier.be; noon–13.30 & 19.00–20.45 Mon–Sat; Gare Centrale. Ranked among the very best restaurants in the city, this gastronomic surf & turf specialist (with a penchant for truffles) is well known for its exotic presentations & sublime flavour combinations – no-one can quite figure out why it doesn't have a star. Tasting menus from €78 to €155 for the black truffle version. Very few tables so you need to book. €€€€€

Les Petits Oignons [85 E4] 25 rue de la Régence; 02 511 76 15; w restaurant-petits-oignons-bruxelles.be; noon–14.30 & 19.00–22.00 or 23.00; Louise. Elegant brasserie serving fine French & Mediterranean food beloved by office workers but also those looking for a decent classically inflected meal. Has an extensive & well-considered wine list & good views over the surrounding streets. €€€

Claire Fontaine [85 E4] 3 rue Ernest Allard; 02 512 24 10; 11.00–19.00 Tue–Sat; Louise. A treasure trove for foodies. The counter of this delicatessen groans with quiches, flans, salads, freshly prepared sandwiches & cakes, all hand-cooked/-prepared by Claire, the owner. She's incredibly warm & greets regular clients with '*cou cou ma belle*'. There are a few tables on the pavement. €

COMMUNES

La Buvette [126 A6] 108 chaussée d'Alsemberg, 1060 Saint-Gilles; 02 534 13 03; w la-buvette.be; 19.30–23.00 Tue–Sat; Horta. The restaurant that every local foodie has on their bucket list, if they haven't already been. An old Art Deco butcher's, the casual fine dining spot (choose between 5- or 7-course tasting menus) cherrypicks overlooked ingredients & parlays them into small, sublime dishes with influences from around the world. €€€€

Au Vieux Bruxelles [85 H5/H6] 35 rue St-Boniface, 1050 Ixelles; 02 503 31 11; w auvieuxbruxelles.com; 18.30–23.30; Porte de Namur. Open since 1882, this utterly charming brasserie claims to serve the best chips in town alongside its array of typical Belgian dishes & *bruxellois* specialities (*carbonnade*, *waterzooi*). Recommended. €€€–€€€€

Chalet Robinson [75 E7] 1 sentier de l'Embarcadère; 02 372 92 92; w chaletrobinson.be; noon–23.00 Wed–Sat, 11.00–23.00 Sun; bus 41/136/137 to Vert Chasseur. Escape to an island in the heart of the city! Chalet Robinson is marooned in the middle of a lake in Bois de la Cambre & can be accessed only via a barge. The wooden cabin conceals an ultra-modern black-&-white interior, while the menu is standard but very serviceable brasserie fare. They rent out boats Apr–Oct for some pre- or post-prandial exercise. €€€–€€€€

La Quincaillerie [126 D6] 15 rue du Page, 1050 Ixelles; 02 533 98 33; w quincaillerie.be; noon–14.30 & 19.00–23.00 Mon–Fri, 19.00–23.00 Sat, 19.00–22.00 Sun; tram 51/bus 84 to Trinité. Stunning stalwart venue designed in Art Nouveau style by one of Victor Horta's disciples – the wrought-iron staircase & wooden storage drawers are something to behold. The good lunch deals are popular with business types, & specialities include seafood platters & oysters with crisp Sancerre to wash it down. €€€–€€€€

Le Zinneke [133 D4] 26 pl de la Patrie, 1030 Schaerbeek; 02 245 03 22; w lezinneke.be; noon–14.00 & 18.00–22.00 Wed–Thu &

Sun, noon–14.00 & 18.00–22.30 Sat–Sun; tram 25/62 to Patrie. Featured on the UK's *Travel Man* series, this wood-panelled institution is of note for its huge, plump 'golden' mussels cooked in 69 different ways – including the scary 'stinky feet' option & even more ominous 'Moules Genghis-Khan'. There's a good wine list to complement the crustaceans. €€€–€€€€

Be Positive [118 C6] 26 pl Jourdan, 1040 Etterbeek; 02 231 80 01; w be-positive.be; noon–19.00 Mon–Fri, noon–17.00 Sat, noon–14.00 Sun; Jourdan. Organic food shop that puts on a superb daily vegetarian buffet. Ideal if you've overdone it on the frites! €€€

Cool Bun [118 D3] 168 rue Stevin; 02 230 52 11; w cool-bun.be; noon–15.00 & 18.00–22.00 Mon–Fri, 18.00–22.30 Sat. Sometimes you just need a good burger & this is the best in the city. Smaller American slider-style buns with gourmet twists & matched with wines. €€€

* **Friture René** [123 B3] 14 pl de la Résistance, 1070 Anderlecht; 02 523 28 76; 11.45–14.00 & 18.00–21.30 Wed–Sun; Sainte-Guidon. Lovely, welcoming family-run restaurant beloved by locals & for good reason – the décor hits the perfect old-school note (lots of oak, tiled floor, chequered tablecloths) & the classics on the menu – mussels, oysters, superb hefty steaks, all with bottomless fries – are beyond reproach. €€€

Tero [126 C3] 1 rue St Bernard, 1060 Saint-Gilles; 02 347 79 46; w tero-restaurant.com; noon–14.00 & 19.00–22.00 Mon–Sat; Louise. Particularly excellent for vegetarians, this sleek Scandi-style spot in Saint-Gilles offers healthy but delicious small plates & sources ingredients from its own farm in Wallonia, drawing a cosmopolitan crowd. €€€

Sale, Pepe, Rosmarino [126 C2] 98 rue Berckmans, 1060 Saint-Gilles; 02 538 90 63; noon–15.00 & 19.00–midnight Mon–Fri, 19.00–midnight Sat; Hôtel des Monnaies. Beloved & very authentic Italian serving simple but exquisite dishes from eye-catching squid-ink linguine to superb antipasti. For both price & quality it's a real find. The walls are covered with drawings by a long-time patron who had Lucien Freud-esque habits, coming every day to eat, but sadly he has now passed away. €€

Maison Antoine [118 C7] 1 pl Jourdan, 1040 Etterbeek; 02 230 54 56; w maisonantoine.be; 11.30–01.00 Sun–Thu, 11.30–02.00 Fri–Sat; Schuman. One of the last traditional *fritkots* in the city – & hailed as the finest frites purveyor in the world by *The New York Times*, though that obviously invites detractors. Locals & tourists form long queues at lunchtime to scoff their fresh chips. Warm your hands on a paper cornet stuffed with chips & mayo or spicy Samouraï sauce & take them to Parc Léopold for an alfresco lunch. €

Café Belga [127 G4] 18 pl Eugène Flagey, 1050 Ixelles; 02 640 35 08; 08.00–02.00 Mon–Thu & Sun, 08.00–03.00 Fri–Sat; tram 81 to Flagey. Newly renovated spot on the ground floor of place Flagey's iconic Art Deco former broadcasting tower. Popular with a trendy international crowd from brunch to apero hour & late at night. Order at the bar & try to get a seat on the oversubscribed terrace. €€–€€€

Forcado [126 C5] 196 chaussée de Charleroi, 1060 Saint-Gilles; 02 539 00 19; w forcado.be; 10.00–18.00 Tue–Sun; tram 81/92 to Janson. If you want to refuel before exploring the Horta Museum, pop in to this delightful little café specialising in *pastéis de Belém*. Frequented by Portuguese (good sign), it offers a wide range of the custard creations from classic to a Portuguese & Belgian fusion speculaas version. Good strong coffee too. You pay at the counter & can then take away or sit in. €

L'Ultime Atome [85 H6] 14 rue St-Boniface, 1050 Ixelles; 02 513 48 84; w ultimeatome.be; 07.30–00.30 Mon–Thu, 07.30–01.00 Fri, 08.30–01.00 Sat, 09.30–00.30 Sun; Porte de Namur. Trendy (though not quite as trendy as once) brasserie filled with young international accents. Great décor – including a Mondrian-style bar – & multi-tasking menu, though it's especially popular for coffee & papers on Sunday mornings.

Le Verschueren [126 A3] 11 parvis Saint-Gilles, 1060 Saint-Gilles; 02 539 40 68; 08.00–02.00 Mon–Fri, 09.00–02.00 Sat–Sun; Porte de Hal. Dominating the hip Saint-Gilles quarter's main square, this much-loved bohemian hangout screams old-school Brussels, & has somehow kept its raggedy edge while the neighbourhood has gentrified. The thing to drink: the signature Verschueren Tripel, custom-brewed for the café by the Brasserie de la Senne.

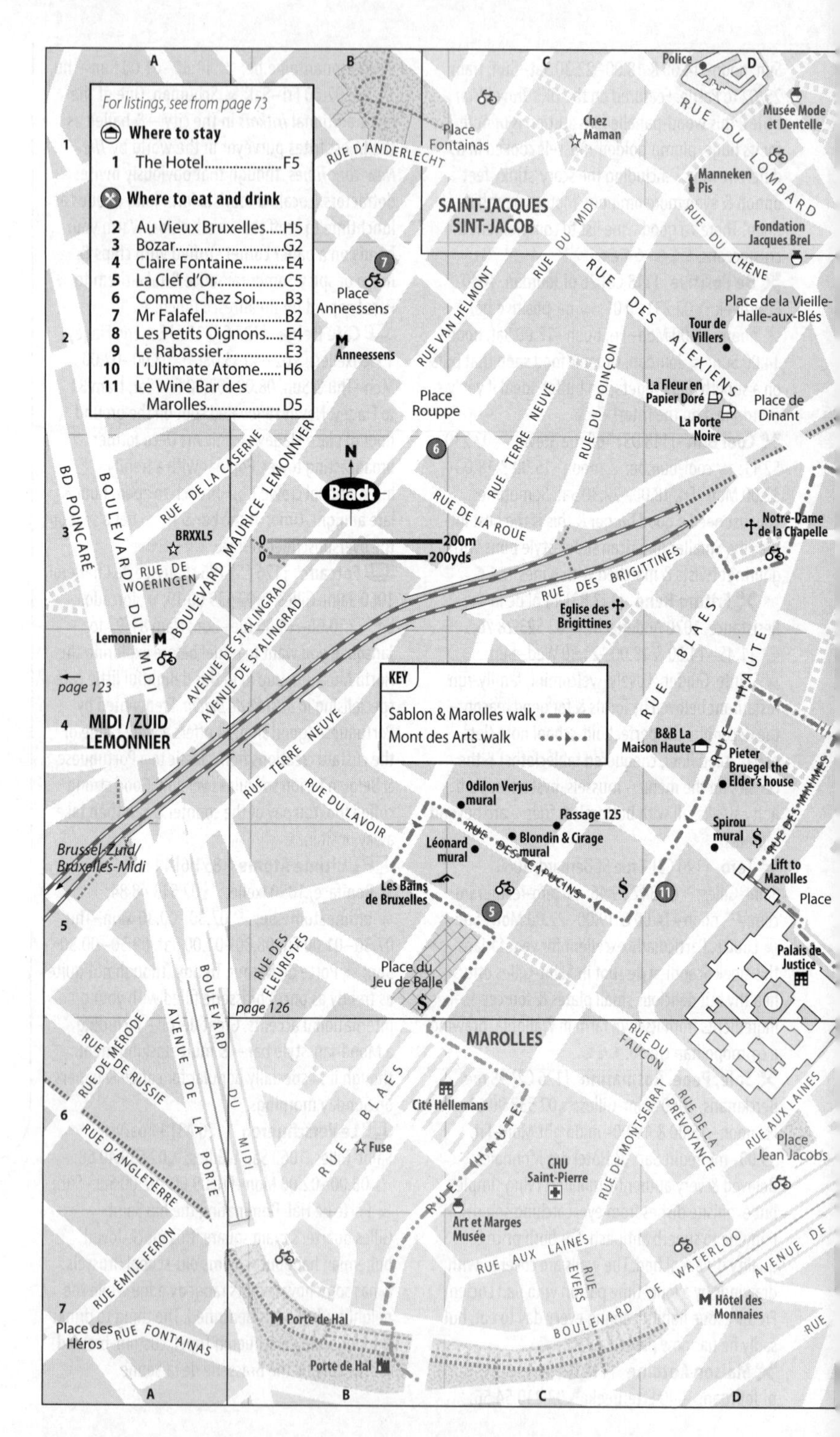
For listings, see from page 73
Where to stay
1 The Hotel.....F5
Where to eat and drink
2 Au Vieux Bruxelles.....H5
3 Bozar.....G2
4 Claire Fontaine.....E4
5 La Clef d'Or.....C5
6 Comme Chez Soi.....B3
7 Mr Falafel.....B2
8 Les Petits Oignons.....E4
9 Le Rabassier.....E3
10 L'Ultimate Atome.....H6
11 Le Wine Bar des Marolles.....D5
KEY
Sablon & Marolles walk
Mont des Arts walk
0 200m
0 200yds
Bradt
SAINT-JACQUES SINT-JACOB
MIDI / ZUID LEMONNIER
MAROLLES
Police
Musée Mode et Dentelle
Chez Maman
Place Fontainas
Manneken Pis
Fondation Jacques Brel
Place de la Vieille-Halle-aux-Blés
Tour de Villers
La Fleur en Papier Doré
La Porte Noire
Place de Dinant
Place Anneessens
Anneessens
Place Rouppe
Notre-Dame de la Chapelle
Eglise des Brigittines
BRXXL5
Lemonnier
page 123
B&B La Maison Haute
Pieter Bruegel the Elder's house
Odilon Verjus mural
Passage 125
Blondin & Cirage mural
Léonard mural
Spirou mural
Lift to Marolles
Place
Les Bains de Bruxelles
Palais de Justice
Brussel-Zuid/ Bruxelles-Midi
Place du Jeu de Balle
page 126
Cité Hellemans
Fuse
CHU Saint-Pierre
Art et Marges Musée
Place Jean Jacobs
Porte de Hal
Hôtel des Monnaies
Place des Héros
Rue d'Anderlecht
Rue du Lombard
Rue du Chêne
Rue du Midi
Rue des Alexiens
Rue Van Helmont
Rue du Poinçon
Rue Terre Neuve
Rue de la Roue
Rue des Brigittines
Rue Blaes
Rue Haute
Rue des Minimes
Rue de la Caserne
Rue de Woeringen
Bd Poincaré
Boulevard du Midi
Boulevard Maurice Lemonnier
Avenue de Stalingrad
Rue du Lavoir
Rue des Capucins
Rue des Fleuristes
Rue du Faucon
Rue de Montserrat
Rue de la Prévoyance
Rue aux Laines
Rue de Mérode
Rue de Russie
Avenue de la Porte
Rue d'Angleterre
Rue Émile Feron
Rue Fontainas
Rue Evers
Boulevard de Waterloo
Avenue de
Rue

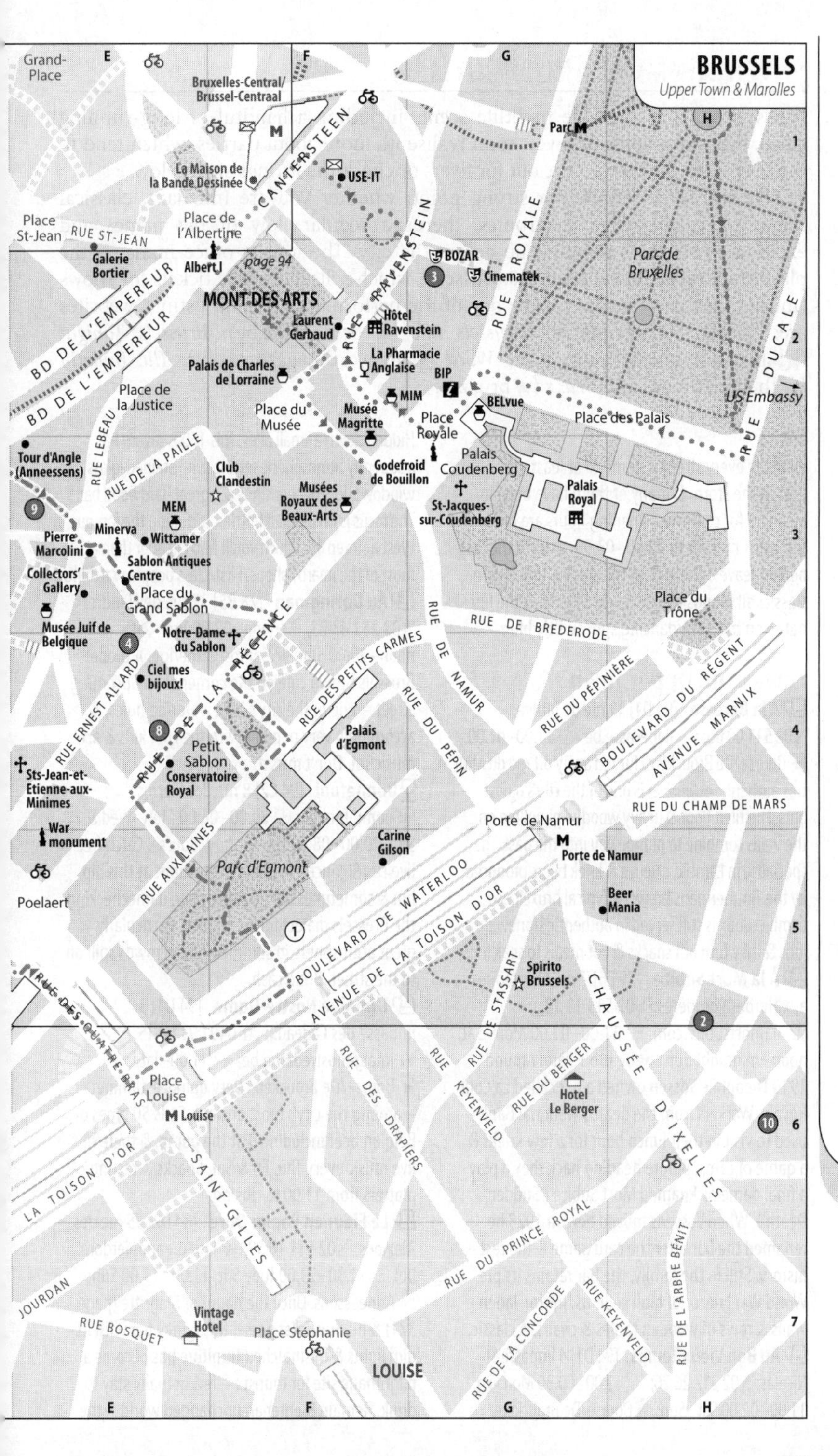

Brussels WHERE TO EAT AND DRINK

3

ENTERTAINMENT AND NIGHTLIFE

Brussels has a respectable nightlife scene, including a handful of long-running clubs, but stay a while and you soon realise it's more about parties, which tend to move around, so keep an eye out for flyers or check the listings sites below.

Live music is definitely a strong point: whether you are into jazz, classical music or cutting-edge electronics, there's a regular flow of big names and exciting newcomers popping up across the city. The tourist office manages the platform **Arsène 50** (w arsene50.brussels), which sells half-price tickets for shows (music, theatre, comedy) on the day of the performance. Useful listings websites are: *Agenda* (w agenda.be), *Brussels Life* (w brusselslife.be), *Brussels Tonight* (f BrusselsTonightEvents), *The Word* (w thewordmagazine.com), *The Bulletin* (w thebulletin.be) and *Bruzz* (w bruzz.be).

BARS

Virtually every street is home to at least one port in the storm & many of them have been in business for centuries. Opening hours are rarely set; most make it to 02.00–03.00, or until the last person leaves. These days the creaky, time-worn classics sit alongside cool cocktail bars, & the lines between bar/café/dancing spot swiftly blur.

Lower and Upper Town

À la Bécasse [94 D1] 11 rue de Tabora; 02 511 00 06; w alabecasse.be; 11.00–01.00; Bourse/De Brouckère. Tucked away off rue du Midi, this authentic *estaminet* is one of the city's oldest bars. The tiled floor & heavy wooden panelling on the walls combine to plunge you into the past. They specialise in Lambic, gueuze & kriek beers produced by the Timmermans brewery. Typical bruxellois Lambic-doux is still served in authentic stoneware jugs & they turn out snacks & hot meals to soak it up.

À la Mort Subite [79 E6] 7 rue Montagnes aux Herbes Potagères; 02 513 13 18; w alamortsubite.com; 11.00–01.00 Mon–Sat, noon–midnight Sun; De Brouckère. Around 1910 Théophile Vossen owned a bar called La Cour Royale. Workers from the nearby National Bank used to visit in their lunch hour for a few krieks & a game of cards. Before heading back they'd play a final game nicknamed Mort Subite ('Sudden Death'). When Vossens moved here in 1928 he renamed the bar after the card game & the rest is history. Still in the family, the bar retains its pre-World War I décor of high ceilings, mirror-laden walls & rows of wooden tables & chairs. A classic.

Au Bon Vieux Temps [94 D1] 4 impasse St-Nicolas; 02 217 26 26; 11.00–00.30 Mon–Fri, 11.00–02.00 Sat–Sun; Bourse/De Brouckère. Hidden down a small alley, this 1600s tavern has a superbly atmospheric setting with stained-glass windows, lots of beer signs & a great hardwood bar. The focus is on Belgian bottles, including the famous Westvleteren 12, which you'll find cheaper than at most of the nearby shops. First-class people watching.

Au Daringman [78 B5] 37 rue de Flandre; 02 251 43 23; noon–02.00 Tue–Sat, noon–20.00 Sun; Sainte-Catherine. A proper Brussels brown café on the corner of an upcoming street – one of the city's best watering holes, & accordingly very popular with the cool kids & art/music set. Don't miss it.

Bonnefooi [94 C2] 8 rue des Pierres; w bonnefooi.be; 20.00–06.00 Mon–Wed & Sun, 20.00–08.00 Thu–Sat; Bourse. Catch free live DJs & concerts almost every night at this hip, hot & sometimes hectic 2-floor bar, namechecking the Brussels dialect for 'by chance'. Particularly great atmosphere in summer when crowds spill on to the street. Bring cash.

L'Imaige Nostre-Dame [94 D1] 3 impasse des Cadeaux; m 0497 91 54 15; w imaigenostredame.be; 11.00–late; Bourse/De Brouckère. Very quirky estaminet – among the city's most ancient. Sells 50 types of Belgian beer including 9 at the pump, & there's live music every Thu, Fri & Sat. Snacks & tasting platters from 11.00 to closing.

La Fleur en Papier Doré [84 D2] 55 rue des Alexiens; 02 511 16 59; w lafleurenpapierdore.be; 11.30–23.00 Tue–Sat, 11.00–19.00 Sun; Anneessens. Once the haunt of Magritte (page 371) & his Surrealist posse, this quirky bar with its dim lights & mismatched furniture has become a pilgrimage site for tourists – few actually stay to drink. Remain & enter an unchanged world – the

TOP FIVE QUIRKIEST BARS

Bar 77 [127 H7] 437 av de la Couronne, 1050 Ixelles; m 0474 26 13 42; w bar77.be; 18.00–02.00 Mon–Wed, 18.00–03.00 Thu, 18.00–04.00 Fri, 18.00–midnight Sat. A bar without a bartender. Instead the beer pumps are in the centre of your table.

Le Cercueil [94 E2] 10–12 rue des Harengs; m 0497 12 45 65; 16.00–02.00 Mon–Thu, 13.00–04.00 Fri–Sat, 13.00–01.00 Sun. Kitsch den of coffin tables, cocktails served in skull mugs & metal music so loud you may want to join the dead.

Dolle Mol [94 E4] 52 rue des Eperonniers; m 0497 33 04 60; w dollemol.brussels; 15.00–midnight Tue–Sat. Resuscitated for a 4th time, this legendary bar prides itself on attracting anarchists & free-thinkers, including Tom Waits & Bob Dylan back in the day. Lots of events promised.

Goupil Le Fol [94 D3] 22 rue de la Violette; 02 511 13 96; w goupillefol.com; 16.00–02.00 daily. Formerly a brothel, this joint just off the Grand-Place is still dimly lit, but has a charming mish-mash of taxidermy, old books & a jukebox playing Jacques Brel.

New Chattouille [126 C4] 11 rue Tasson-Snel,1060 Saint-Gilles; w lenewchattouille.be; 17.00–21.00 Thu–Fri, 13.00–20.00 Sat–Sun. Japan's craze for cat cafés has reached the Belgian capital. Sip a beer & stroke away your stress amid new feline friends. Be comforted that the cats are from rescue shelter Maison de Suzy & ready for adoption.

walls are still littered with original newspaper cuttings, photos & paintings.

La Pharmacie Anglaise [85 F2] 66 Coudenberg; m 0489 56 07 36; w lapharmacieanglaise.com; 17.30–01.00 Tue–Thu, 17.30–02.00 Fri–Sat; Gare Centrale. Enough brown bars – this fancy cocktail den in an old apothecary's shop (hence the name) looks akin to a debauched British squire's quarters, decorated with oriental rugs & the bones of hapless creatures. Superb libations on offer though they don't come cheap.

La Porte Noire [84 D2] 67 rue des Alexiens; 02 511 78 87; w laportenoire.be; 17.00–02.00 Mon–Thu, 17.00–04.00 Fri–Sat; Anneessens. A few doors up from La Fleur en Papier Doré, but much less touristy, this underground pub is housed in the cellar of the former Alexiens monastery. Great buzz & hosts live bands every Thu & DJs on Sat.

Lord Byron [78 B6] 8 rue des Chartreux; 02 540 88 78; 17.00–02.00 Mon–Sat; Bourse. Considerably more under-the-radar than its famous neighbour, below, this arty, discreet bar is a great place for an intimate cocktail over superior tunes (Nina Simone, Lou Reed etc). The name isn't a tribute to the famed English poet but rather because no-one could pronounce the name of the Kosovan founder, Bajram.

Taverne Greenwich [78 B6] 7 rue des Chartreux; 02 540 88 78; w greenwich-cafe.be; noon–midnight; Bourse. This period classic was another of Magritte's beloved cafés – & who can blame him? Sadly, they've spruced things up in recent years, & the old locals playing chess have made way for a more commercially minded brasserie operation. Still, it's almost worth buying a drink just to check out the original Art Deco gents' toilets!

Communes

Moeder Lambic Original [126 A6] 68 rue de Savoie, 1060 Saint-Gilles; 02 544 16 19; w moederlambic.com; 16.00–02.00 Mon–Thu, 16.00–03.00 Fri, 10.30–03.00 Sat, 10.30–midnight Sun; tram 81/97 to Lombardie. This tiny, unpretentious corner café, established in the 1980s – it's usually preferred to 'Fontainas', its younger spin-off in the centre – is a firm favourite for its epic selection of brews, w/end brunch & hearty cheese boards. The staff are very friendly & more than happy to talk you through the 1,000-strong beer list.

La Belladone [126 C5] 17a rue Moris, 1060 Saint-Gilles; m 0471 42 90 45; 16.00–02.00 Mon–Sat, 15.00–01.00 Sun; tram 92/97 to Janson. Grand, charming Art Nouveau bar largely off the tourist trail. They are brilliantly knowledgeable about wine (reasonably priced) & turn out a great cocktail too. One of those places you hope everyone doesn't find out about.

LGBT+ NIGHTLIFE

The majority of LGBT bars – and rainbow flags – are congregated on and around rue du Marché au Charbon, near Bourse metro. It's here that you'll find **Maison Arc-en-Ciel** or 'The Rainbow House' [94 C3] (42 rue du Marché au Charbon; 02 503 59 90; w rainbowhouse.be; bar and exhibitions 19.00–late Wed–Sat), an information centre hosting movie nights, exhibitions, readings and parties in its bar. You'll also find pre- or post-dinner institution **Le Belgica** [94 C3] (32 rue du Marché au Charbon; w lebelgica.com; 20.00–01.00 Thu & Sun, 21.00–03.00 Fri–Sat), a small 1920s brown café that has welcomed the likes of Björk and John Galliano. On the corner of the street, relaxed, vintage-style café **Le Fontainas** [94 B4] (91 rue du Marché au Charbon; 02 503 31 12; 10.00–late Mon & Thu–Fri, 11.00–late Sat–Sun) attracts LGBT hipsters, with its bar snacks & vast terrace. Other magnets are pubby **La Réserve** [94 D1] (2 petite rue au Beurre; 02 511 66 06; 15.00–midnight), the city's oldest and most famous gay bar.

Chez Maman [94 B4] (7 rue des Grandes Carmes; 02 310 71 85; w chezmaman.be; 23.00–late Fri–Sat) hosts brilliantly fun drag shows and it gets colourful, crammed and hot. Watch out for their sporadic 'Cuir as Folk' party. Big events include Pride (w pride.be), held in May, November's Pink Screens film festival (w pinkscreens.org), and – a huge crowd-puller – the monthly techno party La Démence (w lademence.com) at Fuse (see below). Women were for a long time less well catered for, but that has changed hugely in recent years thanks to initiatives like magazine *Girls Like Us*, which has recently branched out into pop-up bars, and mainstay Catclub (w catclub.be), which throws glamorous parties in exotic or abandoned locations round town.

NIGHTCLUBS

☆ **C12** [94 F3] 116 rue Marché aux Herbes; w c12space.com; Gare Centrale; usually 22.00 or 23.00–late Fri–Sat. Hidden beneath Gare Centrale in what was once called the Horta Gallery, this very intriguing new multi-disciplinary platform is run by the Deep in House techno collective. Welcoming a mixed crowd (& very LGBT-friendly) they host art installations, live shows & vinyl markets, & have already drawn big names (eg Detroit's Theo Parrish) for their club nights. They offer a sizeable discount for entry before 01.00.

☆ **Club Clandestin** [85 F3] 20 rue Saint-Anne; m 0471 50 18 76; w clubclandestin.be; 20.00–late Fri–Sat; Gare Centrale. Not as much of a speakeasy as it sounds, this dapper 2-floor Sablon 'micro-club' attracts international expats – average age 30-something or above – & hosts occasional live shows, house & disco nights.

☆ **Fuse** [84 B6] 208 rue Blaes; 02 511 97 89; w fuse.be; 23.00–late Sat & special events; Porte de Hal. Marking its 25th birthday in 2019, this Marolles club has moved to the pole position of the capital's nightlife scene with its well-pitched electronic & techno programming. They run their own eponymous label & juggle upcoming talent with marquee names – you might catch Ghent's 2ManyDjs or a Detroit mainstay depending on the night you go.

☆ **Madame Moustache** [78 C5] 5–7 quai au Bois à Brûler; m 0489 784; w madamemoustache.be; 20.00–04.00 Tue–Fri (sunny days open from 14.00); Sainte-Catherine. This veteran is a winning hybrid of club & cabaret, with a wooden dance floor. All manner of live music & dancing but there's often a retro theme – be it rockabilly or '80s nights. Some events charge €8–10 entry.

☆ **Spirito Brussels** [85 G5] 18 rue de Stassart; m 0483 58 06 97; w spiritobrussels.com; 23.00–06.00 Fri–Sat; Porte de Namur. Housed in an old Anglican church, this swish decade-old club just oozes opulence – it has won awards for its looks. Expect an armada of bouncers

who will turn you away if you wear trainers. They have a VIP area if you really want to live it up.
☆ **ZODIAK** [94 E3] 10 rue du Marché aux Fromages; w zodiak.club; ⌚ 23.00–07.00 Fri–Sat; 🚇 Gare Centrale. Way less commercial than the locale would suggest, this new 3-floor club is cheap, friendly & has quite an underground vibe. No big names but quality programming centring on electronic acts.

LIVE MUSIC

♫ **Café Bizon** [94 B1] 7 rue du Pont de la Carpe; ☎ 02 502 46 99; w cafebizon.com; ⌚ 16.00–late Mon–Fri, 18.00–late Sat–Sun; 🚇 Bourse. Cosy blues bar with a 'living room' atmosphere, where you can sip on Bizon Blood vodka & listen to live performers most nights of the week, inc their famous jam sessions on Mon & acoustic nights on Wed. Concerts start around 21.30 & there's no charge.

♫ **Jazz Station** [74 F4] 193a–5 chaussée Leuven, 1210 Saint-Josse-ten-Noode; ☎ 02 733 13 78; w jazzstation.be; ⌚ concerts 18.00 Sat & 20.30 Mon–Fri; bus 318/351/410 to Clovis. Wonderful railway station conversion set up by the commune's jazz-drumming former mayor – trains still run below. It co-hosts the River Jazz Festival in Jan, offers cheap drinks & a wide-ranging programme of talks, workshops & concerts. On Sat, apero-concerts focusing on Belgian musicians, & on other days big band, singers nights & album releases. Entry usually €10, & under 12s go free.

♫ **L'Archiduc** [78 B6] 6 rue Antoine Dansaert; ☎ 02 512 06 52; w archiduc.net; ⌚ 16.00–05.00; 🚇 Bourse. Long a pillar of the Brussels social scene – ring the bell & you're ushered into an eye-popping room with a balcony & seats featuring fabric from the 1974 film *Murder on the Orient Express*. The piano in the centre belonged to Stan Brenders, the bar's founder & songwriter for Nat King Cole. Current owner Jean-Louis has been in charge for over 30 years & organises great free live concerts at w/ends (17.00) & occasional other days. Order the 'Cointreau–Teese', created by burlesque artiste Dita Von Teese.

♫ **Les Ateliers Claus** [126 A4] 16 rue Crickx, 1060 Saint-Gilles; ☎ 02 534 51 03; w lesateliersclaus.com; ⌚ 20.00–04.00 Mon–Sat; tram 81 to Guillaume Tell. Ghent import Frans Claus's beloved, slightly anarchic venue is the place to be for cutting-edge concerts spanning rock, experimental & electronic acts.

♫ **Recyclart** [84 C3] 13–15 rue de Manchester, 1080 Molenbeek; ☎ 02 502 57 34; kitchen ⌚ noon–15.00 Mon–Fri, bar ⌚ 10.00–16.00 Mon–Fri, check website for event times; 🚇 Delacroix. Long a pillar of the Brussels social scene, a multi-tasking non-profit venture whose café makes an effort to employ long-term jobseekers & reintegrate them into the market. It was kicked out of its long-time home in Bruxelles Chapelle station in 2018 & now occupies an ex-printing house in Molenbeek. It may return to its original location by the end of 2019. Mix of gigs, DJs & exhibitions.

♫ **Sounds** [127 F1] 28 rue de la Tulipe, 1050 Ixelles; ☎ 02 512 92 50; w soundsjazzclub.be; ⌚ 20.00–04.00 Mon–Sat; bus 71 to Fernand Cocq. This long thin jazz bar has been in situ since 1986 & books some of the genre's best talents to perform most nights of the week. Run by a husband-&-wife team: Sergio makes the cocktails, while Rosy turns out Italian food from 20.00. Concerts at 21.30.

CONCERT HALLS

🎭 **Ancienne Belgique (AB)** [94 B2] 110 bd Anspach; ☎ 02 548 24 24; w abconcerts.be; ⌚ closed Jul–Aug; 🚇 Bourse. One of Belgium's top concert venues, with a packed roster spanning everything from pop & rock to indie via South Korean acts & megastars like Neneh Cherry.

🎭 **Beursschouwburg** [94 B1] 20–8 rue Auguste Orts; ☎ 02 550 03 50; w beursschouwburg.be; 🚇 Bourse. Difficult to pigeonhole – part bar, part venue for films, theatre & abstract performance art, plus upstairs event space with a roof terrace for club nights & festivals. Young, socially conscious vibe (feminist & queer talks etc).

🎭 **Botanique** [79 H4] 236 rue Royale; 1210 Saint-Josse-ten-Noode; ☎ 02 218 37 32; w botanique.be; 🚇 Botanique. Very atmospheric – previously serving as the main orangery of the National Botanic Garden of Belgium, this cultural centre is one of the most intimate places to see a gig in the city – not least in the 250-capacity, circular Rotonde. Hosts the annual Les Nuits Botanique festival in spring.

🎭 **BOZAR** [85 G2] 23 rue Raventstein; ☎ 02 507 82 00; w bozar.be; 🚇 Gare Centrale. The heart of the arts in Brussels, this Art Nouveau venue was completed by Victor Horta in 1928 & sits mostly underground because its height was not allowed to disrupt the king's view of the Lower Town. Numerous velvet-seated halls play host to flamenco festivals, early music & jazz seasons & the National Orchestra of Belgium, resident here. Also hosts the finals of the Queen Elisabeth Music Competition.

Flagey [127 H4] pl Sainte-Croix, 1050 Ixelles; 02 641 10 20; w flagey.be; tram 81 to Flagey. With world-class acoustics – the soundtrack of silent film *The Artist* was recorded here – this ship-shaped Art Deco icon hosts the Brussels Philharmonic, & a classical- & jazz-centric programme that also extends to films & festivals.

La Monnaie [78 D6] 5 pl de la Monnaie; 02 229 12 11; w lamonnaie.be; De Brouckère. Site of the famous Belgian break for independence in 1830 (page 9), this federal opera house has a stunning auditorium & a good programme that includes dance recitals (famous company Rosas was once based here). Tickets (€10–160) are snapped up quickly so it's best to book in advance.

THEATRE

Kaaitheater [78 B1] 19 pl Sainctelette; 02 201 59 59; w kaaitheater.be. Occupies the iconic La Luna building, also hosts edgy theatre, dance & music, unusually sometimes in English.

KVS [78 D3] 7 quai aux Pierres de Taille; 02 210 11 12; w kvs.be. The Dutch-speaking counterpart to the Théâtre National.

Théâtre National de la Communauté française [79 E3] 111–15 bd Emile Jacqmain; 02 203 41 55; w theatrenational.be. One of Brussels's main theatres.

Théâtre Royal de Toone [94 E2] 66 rue du Marché aux Herbes; 02 513 54 86; w www.toone.be; shows 20.30 Thu–Sat, also 16.00 Sat, closed Jan. Puts on puppet shows, usually in French but sometimes in the *bruxellois* dialect.

CINEMA

Cinema Galeries [130 B2] 26 Galerie de la Reine; 02 514 74 98; w galeries.be; Gare Centrale. The old Cinema Arenberg in the chic Galeries Royales Saint-Hubert has made way for this appealing follow-up, focusing on art house flicks.

Cinematek [85 G2] 9 rue Baron Horta; 02 551 19 00; w cinematek.be; Gare Centrale. The official Royal Belgian Film Archive, with a library of 70,000+ titles – also happens to be the city's cheapest picture house with tickets for €4.

Nova [78 D5] 3 rue d'Arenberg; 02 511 24 77; w nova-cinema.org; De Brouckère. Very alternative, nicely dilapidated non-profit cinema staffed by volunteers. Works hard to promote little-known directors & regularly hosts adventurous festivals such as Offscreen. The hard wooden seats aren't comfortable but it's superbly atmospheric. Also has a bar.

SHOPPING

Brussels runs the gamut from open-air markets to posh 19th-century arcades and vintage boutiques. As you'd expect, the **Grand-Place** and environs are dominated by tatty souvenir shops, but the covered **Galeries Royales Saint-Hubert** nearby cut a more stylish silhouette, housing revered Belgian brands such as leather specialist Delvaux. South of the Grand-Place, **rue du Midi** is the go-to area for artists, philatelists and numismatists. Collectors also flock to **Sablon**, juggling pricey antiques with the city's densest array of chocolatiers, and design and flea-market quarter the **Marolles**, pivoting around rue Blaes and rue Haute. For high-end labels, head beyond the petit-ring to **avenue Louise** and **avenue de la Toison d'Or**, abounding in Chanel and co, while nearby **rue du Bailli** hosts lovely independent shops for one-off finds. For edgier wares, a short walk west of the Grand-Place is **rue Antoine Dansaert**, which has long been the place to pick up Belgian labels. The action has now spread on to neighbouring streets such as place du Nouveau Marché aux Grains.

Pedestrianised **rue Neuve** is the main artery for high-street brands, with **chaussée d'Ixelles** close behind. While on rue Neuve, pop in to the caryatid-adorned **Passage du Nord**, built in 1882 and lined with artisanal cigar and spirits shops.

CONTEMPORARY ART

There's scant space here to do justice to the capital's art scene, but suffice to say that it has been dubbed the 'new Berlin', with artists pouring into the city in recent years. If you visit in April, the Art Brussels (w artbrussels.be) fair is a veteran event that's well regarded internationally, with the New York import Independent (w independenthq.com) fair running simultaneously. During the sociable Brussels Gallery Weekend (w brusselsgalleryweekend.com) in early September, 30 or so galleries throw open their doors to mark the new season. To find out about openings, check w neca.brussels. I've included some of the major arts venues in the running text, but below are a few others worthy of a detour. The city has long lacked a major contemporary art showcase – this is set to change in 2022, when Paris's Pompidou Centre opens a spin-off, Kanal-Centre Pompidou.

La Patinore Royale [126 D3] 15 rue Veydt, 1060 Saint-Gilles; 02 533 03 90; w prvbgallery.com; 11.00–18.00 Tue–Sat; free; Louise. Known as the 'Royal Skating', this 1877 building was one of Europe's 1st roller-skating rinks, later becoming a weapons depot & Bugatti garage. Since 2015 it has housed the city's grandest exhibition space mixing solo shows & retrospectives.

MIMA (Millennium Iconoclast Museum of Art) [74 C4] 33 quai du Hainaut, 1080 Molenbeek-Saint-Jean; m 0472 61 03 51; w mimamuseum.be; 10.00–18.00 Wed–Fri, 11.00–19.00 Sat–Sun; adult/6–12/under 6 & Brussels Card €9.50/3/free; Comte de Flandre. Converted brewery in Molenbeek opened in 2016 & devoted to 'culture 2.0' (street art, graffiti, skateboarding).

Vanhaerents Art Collection [78 A7] 2 rue Anneessens; 02 511 50 77; w vanhaerentsartcollection.com; open to individuals 4 w/ends per year, reserve ahead, adult/12–18/under 12 €17/12/free; Sainte-Catherine. Superb private collection in a 3-floor industrial building from 1926. Laid out as an intimate 'viewing depot', the collection – augmented by temporary shows – includes Bruce Nauman, Jeff Koons, Bill Viola & Cindy Sherman.

ANTIQUES AND DESIGN

In the Sablon area, there are several antiques & design shops. Rue Blaes & rue Haute especially abound in secondhand & antiques shops.

Ciel mes bijoux! [85 E4] 5 rue Ernest Allard; 02 514 50 49; w cielmesbijoux.com; 11.00–18.30 Tue–Sun. Exhibits at major fairs, & has a wonderful selection of pre-owned designer bags, silk scarves & jewellery.

Collectors' Gallery [85 E3] 12 rue des Minimes; 02 511 46 13; w collectors-gallery.com; 11.00–18.30 Tue–Sat. Focuses on rare artist-designed jewellery, especially Scandinavians like Georg Jensen.

Passage 125 [84 C5] 125 rue Blaes. This is a temple of vintage cinema seats, jewellery & antiques.

Sablon Antiques Centre [85 E3] pl du Grand Sablon; w sablon-antiques-market.com; 09.00–17.00 Sat, 09.00–15.00 Sun. Small, but reliably high-quality antiques & jewellery.

BEER

Beer Mania [85 G5] 174–6 chaussée de Wavre, 1050 Ixelles; 02 512 17 88; w beermania.be; 11.00–21.00 Mon–Sat. This is a bar & shop with an epic selection.

Beer Planet [94 E1] 45 rue de la Fourche; m 0484 95 53 50; w beerplanet.eu; 13.00–21.00 Wed–Fri, 11.00–21.00 Sat–Sun. Combines a superb selection with helpful service.

De Biertempel [94 E2] 56b rue du Marché aux Herbes; 02 502 19 06; w biertempel.eu; 10.00–19.00. A tad pricey but strong on beer paraphernalia & brews.

BOOKS AND COMICS

The city's arcades are prime stomping grounds for bookworms.

La Boutique Tintin [94 E2] 13 rue de la Colline; 02 514 51 52; w boutique.tintin.com; noon–18.00 Mon, 10.00–18.00 Tue–Sat, 11.00–17.00 Sun. Tintin toys, books, you name it.
Forbidden Zone [126 B5] 25 rue de Tamines, 1050 Saint-Gilles; 02 534 63 67; w forbiddenzone.net; 12.30–19.00 Tue–Sat.
Comic geek heaven over 3 floors.
Galerie Bortier [85 E1/E2] 55 rue de la Madeleine; 09.00–18.00. Elegant covered passage abounding in secondhand books.
La Maison de la Bande Dessinée [94 G4] 1 bd de l'Impératrice; w maisondelabd.be; 02 502 94 68; 10.00–18.00 Tue–Sun. Big shop with comics in various languages.
Multi BD [94 B2] 122 bd Anspach; 10.30–19.00 Mon–Sat, 12.30–18.00 Sun. Enormous selection, plus figurines too.
Sterling Books [78 D6] 23 rue du Fossé aux Loups; 02 223 62 23; 10.00–18.30 Mon–Sat. Superbly stocked English-language specialist.
Tropismes [94 F1] 1 Galerie des Princes, Galeries Royales Saint-Hubert; 02 512 88 52; w tropismes.com; 11.00–18.30 Mon, 10.00–18.30 Tue–Thu, 10.00–19.30 Fri, 10.30–19.00 Sat, 13.30–18.30 Sun. Beautiful highbrow bookshop.

CHOCOLATE

The number one souvenir: make for the place du Grand Sablon area for the big names (Godiva, Leonidas) & more select brands.

Frédéric Blondeel [78 B5] 24 quai aux Briques; 02 512 77 12; w frederic-blondeel.be; 10.30–19.00. A new-wave star.
Laurent Gerbaud [85 F2] 2 rue Ravenstein; 02 511 16 02; w chocolatsgerbaud.be; 10.30–20.00. A second new-wave star.
Mary [79 G6] 73 rue Royale; 02 217 45 00; w marychoc.com; 10.00–18.00 Mon–Sat. A favourite of Belgian royals.
Pierre Marcolini [85 E3] 1 rue des Minimes; 02 514 12 06; w marcolini.be; 10.00–19.00. Celebrated chocolatier turning out high-end artisanal treats.
Wittamer [85 E3] 12–13 pl du Grand Sablon; 02 512 37 42; w wittamer.com; 09.00–18.00 Mon, 07.00–19.00 Tue–Sat, 07.00–18.30 Sun. Venerable pâtissier & chocolatier with 2 sablon shops & a café.

FASHION

Carine Gilson [85 F5] 26 bd de Waterloo; 02 289 51 47; w carinegilson.com; 10.00–18.30 Mon–Sat. Here lace is worked into sublime, stylish couture lingerie.
Gabriele Vintage [78 B6] 27 rue des Chartreux; 02 512 67 43; w gabrielevintage.com; 13.00–19.00 Mon–Tue, 11.00–19.00 Wed–Sat, noon–17.00 1st Sun of month. Excellent for authentic old wares from flapper dresses to top hats.
Isabelle Bajart [78 B6] 25 rue des Chartreux; 02 512 67 43; w isabellebajart.be; noon–19.00 Mon–Tue, 11.00–19.00 Wed–Sat. Vintage secondhand designer labels.
Maison Margiela [78 B4] 114 rue de Flandre; 02 223 75 20; w maisonmargiela.com; 10.30–18.30 Mon–Sat. Famously edgy Belgian clothes.
La Manufacture Belge de Dentelles [94 F2] 6–8 Galerie de la Reine; 02 511 44 77; w mbd.be; 10.30–18.00 Mon–Sat, 10.30–17.00 Sun. Great place for lace.
Stijl [78 B6] 74 rue Antoine Dansaert (women), 6 pl du Nouveau Marché aux Grains (men); 02 512 03 13, 02 513 42 50; w www.stijl.be; 10.30–18.30 Mon–Sat. Sonia Noël's pioneering boutique helped to make the street's name with its razor-sharp collection of Antwerp Six designers & subsequent homegrown talent.

MARKETS

Brussels was built upon the marketplace & the tradition is still thriving. **place Sainte-Catherine** hosts an organic-only market (07.30–15.00 Wed), **place du Châtelain** has a swinging evening food market (14.00–19.00 Wed) & the crowds flock to **place Flagey** for its multi-cultural foodie treats (07.00–13.30 Sat–Sun). For the city's **Christmas market**, see box, page 57.

Marché aux Puces [84 B5] pl du Jeu de Balle; w www.marcheauxpuces.be; 06.00–14.00 Mon–Fri, 6.00–15.00 Sat–Sun. Go on a w/end & you'll find a vast, sprawling bric-a-brac market covering the whole square with everything from retro crockery to clothes & commodes. A lovely way to spend a few hours.

Marché du Midi bd du Midi; 🕘 07.00–13.00 Sun. One of the biggest food markets in Europe, with more than 450 stalls selling sizzling chicken, tropical fruit, & specialities from Africa & the Mediterranean.

OTHER PRACTICALITIES

$ Banks KBC [78 B6] 9 rue du Vieux-Marché aux Grains, 🕘 09.00–12.30, afternoon by appointment only; [79 E6] 11 rue d'Arenberg, 🕘 09.00–12.30 & 13.30–16.30 Mon–Fri

Luggage storage Self-service lockers at all 3 main railway stations; €4.50/5/5.50 for small/medium/large for 24hrs. The service Nannybag (w nannybag.com) has many outposts across the city & charges €6/24hrs.

✚ Pharmacy Multipharma [78 C6] 37 rue du Marché aux Poulets; 🕘 09.30–18.30 Mon–Fri

✉ Post offices The main post office is 1–5 bd Anspach [78 D5]; 🕘 08.30–18.00 Mon–Fri, 10.00–16.00 Sat. There is also a branch in the Relay by Brussel Centraal/Bruxelles Central, 2 Carrefour de l'Europe; 🕘 06.00–19.00 Mon–Fri.

WHAT TO SEE AND DO

The list of things to see and do in Brussels is at times overwhelming, and many visitors – who only have a day or two in town – have a tendency to wander aimlessly without locating either the popular sites or lesser-known gems. With this in mind, rather than listing attractions by the traditional Lower and Upper Town categories, I've built them into a series of accessible walks which you can extend or condense as you see fit, visiting a museum here, or having a lazy lunch there. Beyond the petit-ring, the communes are often left out entirely from many guides – I've provided a short history for the main ones and listed their key sites; they're well worth a look if you have the time.

LOWER TOWN

Grand-Place and Bourse walk

Gare Centrale/Bourse; 2½hrs; see map, page 94

This classic walk around the old Lower Town starts in the city's mighty centrepiece. Declared '*le plus beau théâtre du monde*' ('the most beautiful theatre in the world') by French poet and playwright Jean Cocteau, the charm of the UNESCO-listed **Grand-Place** isn't diminished by the busloads of tourists who make it their first port of call. In summer, the cobbles are covered with people sipping beer and taking in the gold-leaf inlays of the guildhouses glowing in the afternoon sun, and in winter, short days bring on early moons that cast the stepped-gable roofs and spires in silhouette against an eerie night sky.

Originally marshland, the square was drained and became a marketplace in the 12th century – note the number of surrounding streets named after food: rue du Beurre (butter), rue Chair et Pain (meat and bread). As the economic wealth of the city grew, trade flourished and guilds set up home on the square. City administration and politics arrived when the Gothic **Hôtel de Ville** was built in the 15th century. From then on, the square witnessed numerous pivotal moments in the city's history. It was here that Charles V abdicated in favour of his son in 1555, here that the Duke of Alva had patriots Count Egmont and Hoorn publicly executed (page 7), and here that the town celebrated its pageants, tournaments and processions. However, much of that history was erased on the night of 13 August 1695. King Louis XIV of France was smarting from a Grand Alliance (a coalition – pitted against France

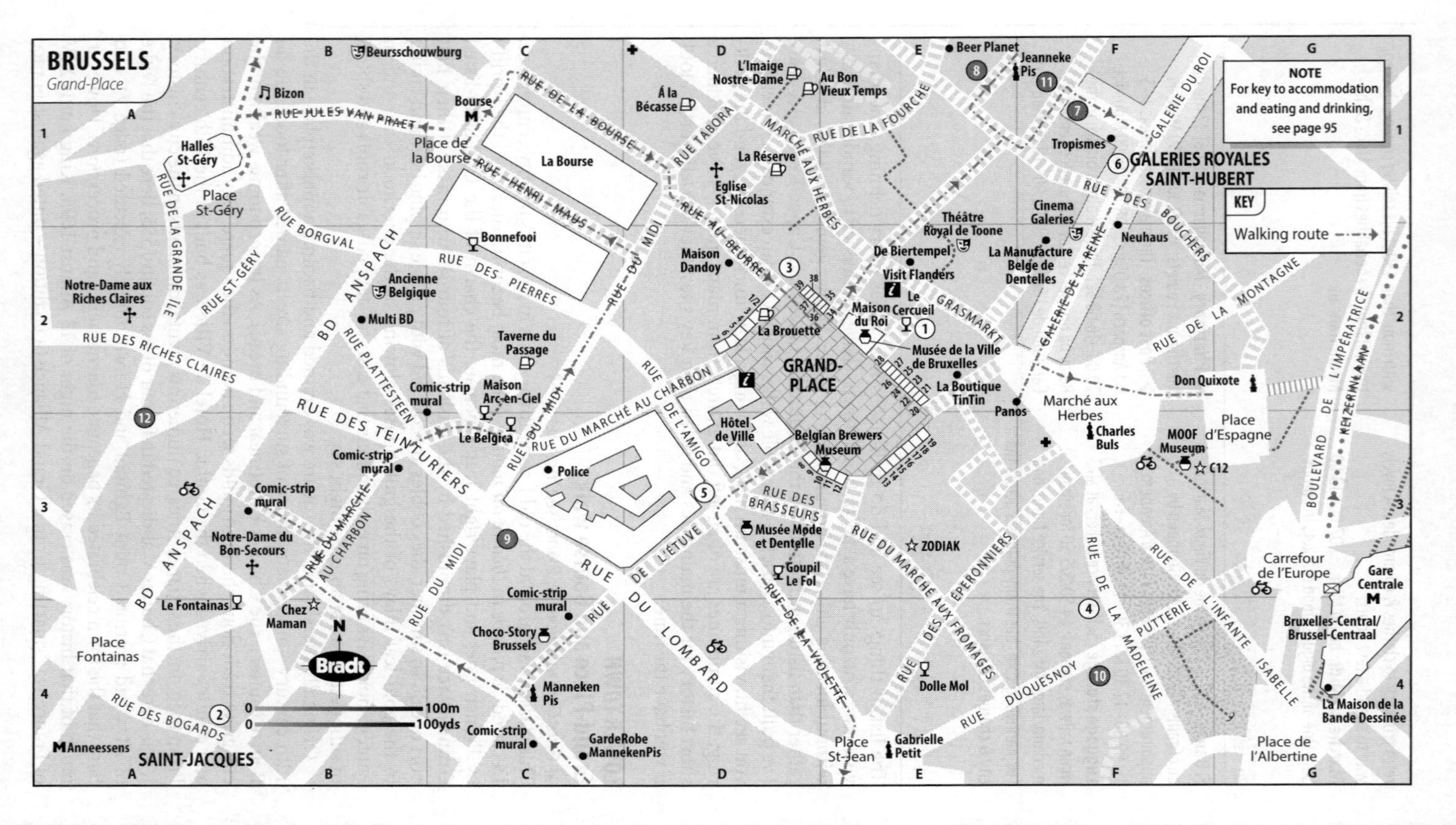

BRUSSELS
Grand-Place
NOTE
For key to accommodation and eating and drinking, see page 95
KEY
Walking route
GALERIES ROYALES SAINT-HUBERT
GRAND-PLACE
Beursschouwburg
Bizon
Bourse
Place de la Bourse
La Bourse
Halles St-Géry
Place St-Géry
Notre-Dame aux Riches Claires
Bonnefooi
Ancienne Belgique
Multi BD
Taverne du Passage
Comic-strip mural
Maison Arc-en-Ciel
Le Belgica
Police
Hôtel de Ville
Belgian Brewers Museum
La Brouette
Maison du Roi
Le Cercueil
Visit Flanders
De Biertempel
Musée de la Ville de Bruxelles
La Boutique TinTin
Panos
Théâtre Royal de Toone
La Manufacture Belge de Dentelles
Cinema Galeries
Neuhaus
Tropismes
Beer Planet
Jeanneke Pis
L'Imaige Nostre-Dame
Au Bon Vieux Temps
Á la Bécasse
La Réserve
Eglise St-Nicolas
Maison Dandoy
Marché aux Herbes
Charles Buls
Don Quixote
Place d'Espagne
MOOF Museum
C12
Carrefour de l'Europe
Gare Centrale
Bruxelles-Central/ Brussel-Centraal
La Maison de la Bande Dessinée
Place de l'Albertine
Musée Mode et Dentelle
Goupil Le Fol
ZODIAK
Dolle Mol
Gabrielle Petit
Place St-Jean
Notre-Dame du Bon-Secours
Le Fontainas
Chez Maman
Choco-Story Brussels
Manneken Pis
GardeRobe MannekenPis
Place Fontainas
Anneessens
SAINT-JACQUES
100m
100yds
Bradt
RUE JULES VAN PRAET
RUE DE LA BOURSE
RUE HENRI MAUS
RUE TABORA
RUE AU BEURRE
MARCHÉ AUX HERBES
RUE DE LA FOURCHE
GALERIE DU ROI
RUE DES BOUCHERS
GALERIE DE LA REINE
GRASMARKT
RUE DE LA MONTAGNE
BOULEVARD DE L'IMPÉRATRICE
KEIZERINLAAN
RUE DE LA GRANDE ÎLE
RUE ST-GÉRY
RUE BORGVAL
BD ANSPACH
RUE DES PIERRES
RUE DU MIDI
RUE DES RICHES CLAIRES
RUE PLATTESTEEN
RUE DES TEINTURIERS
RUE DU MARCHÉ AU CHARBON
RUE DE L'AMIGO
RUE DE L'ÉTUVE
RUE DU LOMBARD
RUE DES BRASSEURS
RUE DE LA VIOLETTE
RUE DU MARCHÉ AUX FROMAGES
RUE DES EPERONNIERS
RUE DUQUESNOY
RUE DE LA MADELEINE
PUTTERIE
RUE DE L'INFANTE ISABELLE
RUE DES BOGARDS

BRUSSELS *Grand-Place*
For listings, see from page 72

Where to stay

1 2Go4 Grand Place............ E2
2 Art de Séjour................... A4
3 B&B La Maison Haute......D2
4 Le Dixseptième................ F4
5 Hotel Amigo..................... D3
6 Hôtel des Galeries............ F1

Where to eat and drink

7 De L'Ogenblik..................... F1
8 Delirium Café..................... E1
9 Nüetnigenough.................. C3
10 Tonton Garby..................... F4
11 Vincent.............................. F1
12 Winehouse Osteria............ A3

– between England, Spain, the United Provinces and the Roman Empire) attack on French-occupied Namur, so in retaliation he ordered the Duke of Villeroy and 70,000 French soldiers to attack Brussels. The Duke fired cannons and mortars at the city in an unrelenting bombardment that lasted 36 hours. The damage was immense. Amazingly, the Hôtel de Ville façade survived the bombing, but only fragments of a select few guildhouses remained. Everything you see today was rebuilt from the ruins.

Guildhouses form the skeleton of the square. After the French bombardment, the city governor and councillors asked the guilds to submit plans for a rebuild, so the new-look square was a coherent blend of Italian and Flemish Baroque styles. The buildings were also required to be built with stone, not timber, to prevent another catastrophic outbreak of fire. The restoration took five years. Touch-ups have of course taken place since, the most productive of which was instigated by mayor Charles Buls between 1882 and 1923. A statue of him and his dog graces the place Agora, a short stroll east of the square.

Each façade bears an ornate blend of statues and reliefs – markings with a practical, as well as a decorative, use: house numbers were not applied until the French Revolution, so the reliefs were icons of the trade on offer. Start the walk on the west side of the square, at the rue au Beurre.

West side of the square

Nos 1 and 2 Le Roi d'Espagne – The King of Spain – was named in honour of Charles II, whose bust dominates the second-floor façade, to show allegiance and celebrate his victory at the Battle of Zenda in Turkey. The building belonged to the wealthy guild of bakers; from left to right, Force, Wheat, Wind, Fire, Water and Prudence, indispensable for bakers, are embodied by allegorical statues above the balustrades. St Aubert, patron saint of bakers, watches on.

No 3 La Brouette – The Wheelbarrow – dates from 1644 and belonged to the guild of the tallow merchants, who extracted goose fat needed by the tanners, though it

MAD FOR MUSEUMS?

If you're planning to visit several museums, it's worth buying the Brussels Card (w brusselscard.be). Available for 24, 48 or 72 hours (€27/35/43), the card grants you free access to 41 of the city's museums and includes a city map. It also gets you a 25% discount at participating restaurants, bars and shops. For a supplement, you can add public transport or travel on the Hop-on Hop-off buses. Buy it through the Visit Brussels website (you can print it out or download it on to your phone), at the tourist offices on the Grand-Place or place Royale, at the Visit Flanders shop or at select museums. Note that the pass offers no real savings for under 12s. A number of combi-tickets are also available, including one for the GardeRobe MannekenPis and Brussels City Museum.

TOP TEN QUIRKY MUSEUMS

MUSÉE DES ÉGOUTS (SEWER MUSEUM) [123 G1] Off-the-beaten-track museum allowing you to explore the city's underbelly: the sewer system, dating from 1867. Check out the weird array of objects that have washed up in the pipes or book ahead for a free monthly guided tour (page 122).

MUSÉE DE LA POLICE INTÉGRÉE (POLICE MUSEUM) [75 F6] (33 av de la Force Aérienne; 02 642 65 70; closed for renovation, contact for details; free; tram 7/25 to VUB) This largely overlooked museum was updating its exhibits – artefacts and even a helicopter charting the story of Belgium's federal police and beyond – as we went to press but will reopen during the lifetime of this guide.

GARDEROBE MANNEKENPIS [94 C4] Of recent vintage, this wacky museum is a must after visiting Brussels's most famous statue, the Manneken Pis. It houses a truly epic collection of his jaunty costumes (page 100).

BIBLIOTHECA WITTOCKIANA [75 G5] (23 rue du Bemel; 02 770 53 33; w wittockiana.org; 10.00–17.00 Tue–Sun; adult/student/1st Sun of month €5/3/free; tram 39/44 to Jules César) Hugely underrated private museum and library in a brutalist building that's dedicated to bookbinding, with exhibits dating back to the Renaissance. Temporary shows and workshops are reliably superb.

MOOF MUSEUM [94 F3] (Galerie Horta, 116 Marché aux Herbes; 02 207 79 92; w moofmuseum.be; Jul–Aug 10.00–18.00 Mon–Sun, Sep–Jun 10.00–18.00 Tue–Sun; adult/12–24/under 12/under 3 €10/7/3/free; Gare Centrale) Comic book heaven: a formidable collection of privately owned collector figurines – many of which will be obscure to all but die-hards – with special areas dedicated to manga, American and Flemish comics.

MEM – MUSEUM OF EROTICS AND MYTHOLOGY [85 E3] (32 rue Sainte-Anne; 02 514 03 53; w m-e-m.be; 14.00–20.00 Mon & Thu–Fri, 11.00–17.30 Sat–Sun; €10;

takes its name from the faint gold wheelbarrows above the door. The guild's patron saint St Gilles is represented at the top. The café here is among the square's best.

No 4 Le Sac – The Sack – was the carpenters' and coopers' guild, and the tools of their trade can be seen in reliefs on the second storey. Although the first two floors survived the bombardment, a third type of ancient Greek column was used to create consistency in the façade of the building. At the bottom sit examples of the plain and vertical Doric order; above this the scrolled tops of the Ionian column, and above this the newer ornate Corinthian order.

No 5 La Louve – The She Wolf – takes its name from the bas-relief that sits above the door and depicts a she wolf suckling the founders of Rome, Romulus and Remus, after they were left for dead on the river Tiber as babies. The house belonged to the archers' guild – look for the arrows on the balcony and the shield and helmet further up – and was the only façade to evade the bombardment of 1695. The phoenix on the roof was added after the rebuild to signify the rebirth of the Grand-Place. Statues of Truth, Falsehood, Peace and War can be seen on the second floor.

Gare Centrale) Created in 2012, this charming Sablon house has a brilliantly evocative collection of 800 erotic art pieces – not least its fascinating array of the small Japanese ivory sculptures known as netsuke.

BELGIAN MUSEUM OF FREEMASONRY [78 D4] (73 rue Laeken; 02 223 06 04; w mbfm.be/wp; 13.00–17.00 Tue–Fri, 13.00–16.30 Sat; adult/under 26/12–18/under 12 €6/4/2/free; De Brouckere) Thought the freemasons were a closed book? Not at this stately museum, run by the Belgian branch of the order, which works to dispel their reputation of secrecy. Jewels, books and regalia past and present trace the evolution of their ideas and current structures – fascinating!

MUSÉE D'ART FANTASTIQUE (MUSEUM OF FANTASTIC ART) [126 C6] (7 rue Américaine; m 0475 41 29 18; w fantastic-museum.be; May–Sep 14.00–17.00 Sat–Sun; €6/free 1st Sun of month; Gare du Midi) A cabinet of curiosities made flesh – this wonderfully atypical museum offers wildly bizarre exhibits from the biography of the Elephant Man to the 'Matto Grosso mummy'. They go all out for their popular Halloween festival too.

CLOCKARIUM MUSEUM [75 G5] (163 bd Auguste Reyers; 02 732 08 28; w clockarium.org; by guided visit only 15.05 Sun except school hols; adult/child €6/free; tram 7/25 to Diamant) In the 1920s and '30s the Art Deco faïence clock decorated every home in Belgium and Northern France. This museum, appropriately set in a stylish Art Deco house, pays tribute via 1,000 clocks.

MUSEUM OF THE BLACK SISTERS [74 B3] Set in Koekelberg's Basilica of the Sacred Heart, this small museum namechecks a religious congregation that sprang from a late branch of a medieval movement called Cellites, who primarily cared for the plague-stricken. It's worth a visit for its prime collection of Flemish art and silverware (page 128).

No 6 Le Cornet belonged to the boatmen's guild – a fanciful building dating from 1697. Note the gable, shaped like the stern of a galleon, and nautical paraphernalia decorating the frames of the lower windows. Charles II makes another cameo here: his head is in the medallion flanked by the four trade winds and two sailors.

No 7 Le Renard – The Fox – dates from 1699 and takes its name from the golden fox above the door. It was the guild of the haberdashers, as indicated by the four bas-reliefs that depict the various activities of the trade. Further up are five statues; the middle figure wearing a blindfold and holding the scales and sword symbolises fair trade and either side of her stand the four *known* continents – Australia was only discovered in the late 18th century. At the top is St Nicolas, who is patron saint of merchants.

South side of the square Turning back to the Grand-Place you come to the towering **Hôtel de Ville** [94 D2/3] (1 Grand-Place; 02 513 89 40; English tours 14.00 Wed, 10.00, 15.00 & 16.00 Sun; adult/under 12 €7/free, tickets sold same day only from 09.00 at the Visit Brussels office on the Grand-Place). The original *stadhuis* or town hall consisted of just the left wing and the square-topped belfry built in Gothic style between 1402 and 1421. Available funds led to the construction of the right wing and the ornate spire (which replaced the original belfry) in 1444–49, with the work being directed by popular architect Jan van Ruysbroeck. However, Charles the Bold's refusal to narrow the adjacent rue de la Tête d'Or prevented the building from reaching its proper length, and as a result the 96m tower does not appear to be placed centrally. Popular myth claims that the imbalance drove van Ruysbroeck to jump from the tower to his death. A copper statue of St Michael – the patron saint of Brussels – was placed at the pinnacle of the tower in 1455. Unfortunately, funds dried up before the 300 or so niches created for statues of the dukes and duchesses of Brabant could be filled, and they remained empty until French writer Victor Hugo rallied funds for their instalment in 1852. The ones in situ today are replacements; the originals are stowed in the Maison du Roi opposite.

After the French bombardment of 1695, all that was left of the Hôtel de Ville was the façade. The inside was gutted by fire and priceless archives and paintings, including the magnificent *Justice of Trajan* and *Justice of Herkenbald* retables by Flemish Primitive Rogier van der Weyden, were lost. It was during this final rebuild that two rear wings were built to form a complete quadrangle. If you wander into the central inner courtyard you will see a brass star set into the ground. Known as '**point zero**', this is supposedly the marker from which all distances in Belgium are measured. Also here are two fountains built to represent the main rivers that cross the country: the Meuse and Scheldt. Today the interior has regained its splendour and you can explore a series of lavishly decorated reception rooms, council offices and the superb Council Chamber (marriage hall).

No 8 L'Étoile – The Star. Originally home to the city magistrate, it was knocked down in 1850 and rebuilt in 1897, this time with a passageway connecting it to the Hôtel de Ville. Rumour has it that judges would stand at the windows of this gallery to watch public executions on the square. Set on the left-hand wall under the arch is a reclining bronze statue commemorating Everard 't Serclaes, who reclaimed the city for the Duke of Brabant after the Count of Flanders, Louis de Male, tried to seize it. Under the cover of night, on 24 October 1356, 't Serclaes scaled the façade of The Star and replaced Male's standard with that of the Duke, and went on to chase remaining invaders out of the city. He was hailed as a hero and made an alderman of the city five times. Parts of the escapade are highlighted in reliefs above his effigy, the latter kept shiny thanks to a tradition stating that good luck follows those who stroke it (rather odd given that Serclaes was ultimately assassinated by one of the Count's stooges in 1388).

No 9 Le Cygne – The Swan – once belonged to the guild of the butchers, and today houses La Maison du Cygne restaurant. However, during its golden days in the 19th century it was a café, famous for attracting political revolutionaries, including Karl Marx and Friedrich Engels who penned the *Communist Manifesto* and the first chapters of *Das Kapital* – the urtext for Communism – here before Marx was expelled for failing to pay his rent.

No 10 L'Arbre d'Or – The Golden Tree – or 'Maison des Brasseurs' is presided over somewhat arbitrarily by Charles of Lorraine, governer of the Austrian Netherlands, and his steed (a previous statue dropped off, so his was shunted in). The house belonged to the brewers' guild and is unique in that it still continues its role, housing the Belgian Brewers association – one of the oldest unions in the world. Inside is the rather lacklustre **Belgian Brewers Museum** [94 D3/E3] (10 Grand-Place; 02 511 49 87; w beermuseum.be; 10.00–17.00; adult/Brussels Card €5/free, cash only). A free beer is included, which for some may justify the entrance fee!

East side of the square

Nos 13–19 Maison des Ducs de Brabant – House of the Dukes of Brabant – appears to occupy a single, sprawling house but is in fact seven separate guild buildings sharing one façade, designed by Willem de Bruyn in 1698. Each of its 19 pillars bears the bust of a Duke of Brabant at its base.

North side of the square Besides La Maison du Roi, there are a few other highlights here.

Nos 24 and 25 La Chaloupe d'Or – or Golden Rowboat – belonged to the tailors' guild. A bust of their patron saint, St Barbara, sits above the doorway and on top is St Boniface, with a depiction of tailors' shears at his side.

Nos 26 and 27 Le Pigeon – The Pigeon – belonged to the painters' guild and was briefly home to exiled French writer Victor Hugo in 1852 (look for the plaque mounted on the façade), until criticism of his writings forced his move to Guernsey.

Nos 29–33 The neo-Gothic Maison du Roi – King's House in English, and *Broodhuis* in Dutch – takes its name from both its original incarnation, as a 13th-century bread hall, and its original owner, Charles V, who commissioned it in 1515. After the bombardment it was faithfully rebuilt in 16th-century style and now houses the **Musée de la Ville de Bruxelles** (**Brussels City Museum**) [94 E2] (02 279 43 50; w brusselscitymuseum.brussels; 10.00–17.00 Tue–Sun; adult/under 18, Brussels Card & 1st Sun of month €8/free). Masterpieces here include the sublimely detailed **Saluzzo altarpiece** (c.1500–10), typical folk painting the *Wedding Cortège*, now believed to be by Jan Brueghel the Elder rather than his more famous father Pieter, and – for popular appeal, if not aesthetics – the real Manneken Pis statue, designed by Jérôme Duquesnoy the Elder (the one nearby is a copy). You'll also find tapestries, city scale models and several of the Manneken's outfits – the rest are at the GardeRobe MannekenPis (page 100), included in the ticket price. The museum's VR experience (€2) recreating the 1695 bombardment is also very popular.

Leave the Grand-Place via rue Charles Buls Walk to **Hotel Amigo** (page 72), the site of the old city prison and whose name arose as the result of a mistaken translation. Known as *vrunte*, meaning 'enclosure' in Flemish, the Spanish took it to mean 'friend' and consequently applied the Spanish equivalent *amigo*, which is certainly less offputting for guests staying at the hotel today. Just opposite is Rose's Lace Boutique – look for the granite plaque devoted to French poet Paul Verlaine, who famously shot his lover Arthur Rimbaud here in 1873. Next – in order to avoid the tatty souvenir shops along rue de l'Étuve – turn into rue de la Violette directly opposite the hotel and visit the **Musée Mode et Dentelle** (**Fashion and Lace Museum**) [94 D3] (12 rue de la Violette; 02 213 44 50; w fashionandlacemuseum.brussels; 10.00–17.00 Tue–Sun; adult/under 18, Brussels Card & 1st Sun of month €8/free), with its excellent horde of 18th- and 19th-century Brussels lace and costumes, bolstered by newer acquisitions such as pieces by Belgian haute couture lingerie designer Carine Gilson. Temporary shows are well worth catching.

Continue until you reach place St-Jean. In the centre you will see a statue of **Gabrielle Petit** [94 E4], a young Walloon nurse who acted as a spy for the Allies in World War I. She was eventually caught by the German secret police, held at the Prison de St-Gilles and executed at the Tir National shooting range in Schaerbeek on 1 April 1916. From here, head south to place de la Vieille Halle aux Blés to visit the **Fondation Jacques Brel** (11 pl de la Vieille Halle aux Blés; ☎ 02 511 10 20; w fondationbrel.be; ⊕ 11.00–18.30 Tue–Sun; individual attractions €7, or €25 for all exhibits & audio walking tour), a wonderful multi-media library/museum honouring the *chansonnier* (page 370). They also run a great audio-guide walking tour (adult/under 12 €10/free) lasting 2 hours and 40 minutes; you can stop off for lunch en route and return the guide later – just ask. (You will find a plaque marking Brel's birthplace at 138 av du Diamant in Schaerbeek.)

Turn right into rue du Chêne You'll soon come to the quirky and fun **GardeRobe MannekenPis** [94 C4] (19 rue du Chêne; ☎ 02 514 53 97; w mannekenpis.brussels; ⊕ 10.00–17.00 Tue–Sun; adult/under 18 & 1st Sun of month €4/free, combi-ticket with Brussels City Museum €8), opened in 2017 and housing a sizeable array of the statue's 1000+ costumes, ranging wildly from Mozart to Mandela. Carry on down the street; on the left at no 9 is a mural depicting a scene from the **Olivier Rameau comic strip**, dreamt up during the hallucinogen-addled year of 1968, and at the end the crossroads that houses the beloved **Manneken Pis** himself [94 C4] – literally 'little man peeing' in the *bruxellois* dialect. While it's often voted rather overrated (he's very small and invariably surrounded by tourists), have a quick glimpse to check out what he's rocking today.

Before continuing the walk, take a quick detour to the right to 37 rue de l'Étuve for a well-known **Tintin mural** from *The Calculus Affair* in which the bequiffed hero, Snowy and Captain Haddock flee from danger down a fire escape. The long-running Musée du Cacao et du Chocolat – now **Choco-Story Brussels** [94 C3] – decamped here in February 2019 (41 rue de l'Étuve; ☎ 02 514 20 48; w choco-story-brussels.be; ⊕ 10.00–17.00; adult/12–26/6–11/under 6 €9.50/8.50/6.50/free). There's more of an accent on interactivity, with an audio guide, two-floor museum featuring chocolate dresses and chocolate sculptures, and – carried over from its former incarnation – popular demonstrations.

Head back to the Manneken Pis Turn right down rue des Grands-Carmes until you come out on to rue du Marché au Charbon. Once here, first turn to the left to visit **Notre-Dame du Bon-Secours** (**Our Lady of Assistance**) [94 B3] (91 rue du Marché au Charbon; ☎ 02 514 31 13; ⊕ 09.30–17.00). There was a chapel here in the 12th century, and soon a church, St-Jacques, serving as a resthouse for pilgrims on their way to visit the apostle's tomb in Compostela, Spain. It acquired its current name in the 17th century when a church tutor, Jacques Meeus, discovered a statue of the Virgin Mary. Crowds came again, funding an expansion from the 1660s to 1694. Barely a year later, much of it was destroyed by the 1695 French bombardment and a new church (the soot-blackened version that stands today) was rebuilt in Flemish Baroque style. It's an atmospheric spot – look for the emblems of the Compostela pilgrim (shell, water bottle, hat and staff) above the door and the 14th-century oak statue of the Virgin above the main altar.

Exiting the church, turn left and follow the street north. Have a quick glance at 9 rue du Bon Secours to see a scene from *Ric Hochet*, a **comic strip** published in *Tintin* magazine in the 1950s, then move on down rue du Marché au Charbon to see two more murals: the first, hidden behind a wall on the right-hand side of the road at no 60, features a scene from *Victor Sackville* by Francis Carin; the second, where rue Plattesteen begins, depicts Frank Pé's great creation, *Broussaille*. At this point a good lunch option is intimate Italian trattoria **Winehouse Osteria** [94 A3] (42 rue de la Grande-Île; ☎ 02 350 02 91; **w** wine-house.be; ⏰ noon–14.30 & 18.00–22.30 Mon–Fri, noon–22.30 Sat–Sun; **€€€**), a 3-minute walk west down rue des Teinturiers and rue Riches Claires, then left on rue de l'Eclipse. Afterwards, rejoin the pedestrianised boulevard Anspach and head north until you are standing in front of the old stock exchange, **La Bourse** [94 C1], in place de la Bourse or rejoin the walk at the comic-strip mural Broussaille. From here, proceed to the end of the road and turn left on to rue du Midi, then left along rue Henri Maus to reach La Bourse at the end of the road. An impressive Neo-classical building constructed in 1873, La Bourse is guarded by two lions and decorated with assorted nudes, cherubs and allegorical figures pertaining to Africa, Navigation and Industry – all smug reflections of the bourgeois mindset during Belgium's 19th-century economic boom. The building has been earmarked for a beer museum.

Turn down rue de la Bourse At the end of the street, skirt right into rue au Beurre to visit the **Église St-Nicolas (St Nicholas Church)** [94 D1] (1 rue au Beurre; ☎ 02 267 51 64; ⏰ 10.00–18.00 Mon–Sat, 09.30–18.30 Sun). Named after the patron saint of traders, St Nicolas is one of the city's oldest churches. Built in the 12th century – with an asymmetric layout avoiding a brook that once ran through the area – it has been restored numerous times, most recently in the 1950s. The

MANNEKEN PIS

The first mention of the Manneken Pis dates back to 1451, when the fountain was pivotal in the distribution of drinking water, 'peeing' into its double stone basin. Several legends surround the identity of the little boy: one cites him heroically putting out a fire by weeing on it, another relates the discovery of a lost nobleman's son eventually found peeing at this spot. We do know, however, that Jérôme Duquesnoy the Elder was commissioned in 1619 by city officials to make a bronze statue that would decorate the watering well and encapsulate the joie de vivre of Brussels residents. Whether it was a replica of an older version is unknown.

Since then the tiny 61cm-high icon has been stolen numerous times – most infamously in 1745, when French soldiers stashed him in a whorehouse, but were forced to return him when King Louis XV ordered a full-scale search and then knighted the statue to prevent him from being stolen again. In 1817 an ex-convict stole the statue for its bronze. He was apprehended, but not before poor Manneken had been smashed to smithereens. The thief was publicly branded on the Grand-Place and given a life sentence in a forced labour camp; the cast for the new Manneken Pis (the one that stands today) was forged from the broken pieces.

For centuries, it has been customary for visiting dignitaries to donate a costume to the wee urchin's enormous wardrobe and on special dates he gets a change of attire followed by a formal ceremony. Costumes of note include the Elvis Presley outfit fitted on 8 January and, from 21–25 December, Père Nöel. A full list of costume changes is posted in the Brussels City Museum (page 99); outfits are on show at his GardeRobe (see opposite).

main feature of note inside is a copper relic of the **Martyrs of Gorkum**, containing the remains of Catholic priests martyred by Protestants in Holland in 1572, but there are also works by Flemish painter/tapestry maker **Jean Van Orley**. Across the way is **Maison Dandoy** (31 rue au Beurre; ⏲ 09.30–22.00 Mon–Sat, 10.30–22.00 Sun), famous for its cinnamon speculaas biscuits.

Continue down the street towards the Grand-Place, taking the first left on the square: rue Chair et Pain. Pass puppet theatre **Toone** on your right (page 90), turn left at the end on to rue des Bouchers, then take the first right on to impasse de la Fidelité. This narrow street is home to **Jeanneke Pis** [94 E1], Manneken Pis's little sister. The squatting girl (now unfortunately behind bars due to vandals) was erected in 1987 by Denis-Adrien Debouvrie as a symbol of feminism. The famous **Delirium Café** [94 E1] (4 impasse de la Fidelité; 📞 02 514 44 34; **w** deliriumcafe.be; ⏲ 10.00–04.00 Mon–Sat, 10.00–02.00 Sun) is opposite if you need a pick-me-up.

Return to the rue des Bouchers Look for **no 26** (now Le Brueghel tavern). In 1960, the Commune Libre de l'Îlot Sacré – a protected islet centring around the Grand-Place – was established. It came off the back of fears, starting in the early 1950s, about the modernisation of the city centre and prospective widening of roads like rue des Bouchers in the run-up to the 1958 World's Fair. To preserve the area from such a fate and guard its folkloric character, a series of town-planning regulations were stipulated within the islet: no signboards and the restoration of façades with over 1m² of traditional stonemasonry.

TOP TEN MUST-SEES

GRAND-PLACE From beheadings to bombardments and begonia carpets, Brussels's centrepiece has seen it all. As stunning on an icy winter morning as during a summer sunset, when an orange glow glints off its guildhouses, there's little wonder this is most visitors' first pit stop (page 93).

MANNEKEN PIS Despite recently being voted one of the world's most overhyped tourist spots, it's not possible to visit the capital without taking in the famous Manneken. Yes, it's just a statue of a little boy peeing, but it's Belgium's proudest icon, and a glance is mandatory (see box, page 101).

MUSÉE MAGRITTE AND HOUSE Hosting the world's biggest collection of witty Belgian Surrealist René Magritte's works, the Musée Magritte (page 116) will challenge your view of the world. Follow it up with a visit to his birthplace, Jette, and the more intimate house museum, Musée René Magritte (page 128).

MUSÉE OLD MASTERS The backbone of the Musées Royaux des Beaux-Arts de Belgique, also housing the Musée Magritte (see above) and Fin-de-Siècle Museum (see below), houses a superlative collection of Flemish Primitive art, as well as masterpieces by Pieter Bruegel the Elder, Peter Paul Rubens and Jacob Jordaens (page 115).

FIN-DE-SIÈCLE MUSEUM Opened in 2013, this beguiling museum spans the years 1868 to 1914, when Belgium turned out world-class, memorably esoteric painters of the calibre of James Ensor, Fernand Khnopff and Léon Spilliaert (page 116).

Turn left down rue des Dominicains Continue until you reach the entrance to the **Galeries Royales Saint-Hubert** [94 F1] on your right. This glorious Neoclassical gem has the honour of being Europe's first shopping mall and was built by Jean-Pierre Cluysenaar in 1847. Its construction caused quite a controversy at the time – a resident died of shock when the bailiff informed him he would have to vacate his property and a shop owner even slit his throat in protest. Split into three sections – the Galerie du Roi, Galerie de la Reine and Galerie du Prince – the arcade takes its name from the St-Hubert passage that once connected rue du Marché aux Herbes and rue des Bouchers. When the covered galleries first opened, the refined clientele were charged 20 cents to wander beneath the stunning vaulted-glass ceiling and across the marble floors that today house the boutiques of designers including Delvaux and Akaso, who work with Ethiopian tribes; the legendary **Tropismes** bookshop (page 92); a superlative cinema (page 90); a classy hotel (page 73); and a selection of pricy eateries, including the famous writers' haunt **Taverne du Passage** [94 C2]. Perhaps most famous, though, is chocolatier **Neuhaus**, where the first praline was concocted in 1912 by Jean Neuhaus (see box, page 46).

Exit the Galerie de la Reine by Godiva Turn left and wander through place Agora, where a **statue of Brussels mayor Charles Buls** and his faithful mutt sits, and up the right-hand side of Hotel Ibis to **place d'Espagne**, which is dominated by a raised statue of the fanciful (and fictional) 'knight' **Don Quixote and his earthy squire Sancho Panza**, presumably because several reprints of the novel were

GALERIES ROYALES SAINT-HUBERT Shopping arcades don't come much grander than this Neoclassical icon – Europe's first mall. It doesn't just look good: here you'll find some of the city's top artisans, from leather brand Delvaux to chocolatier Neuhaus, inventor of the praline (see above).

CENTRE BELGE DE LA BANDE DESSINÉE From its setting in a Victor Horta-designed department store to the joyous permanent exhibition covering Hergé, the Smurfs and co, the Belgian Comic Strip Center covers the country's passion and flair for the ninth art with considerable aplomb. And it's brilliant fun (page 107).

MUSÉE HORTA The all-conquering Art Nouveau architect's signature is all over Brussels, but nowhere more so than in his four-floor former home and studio. From the wrought ironwork to the sinuous curves of the spiral stairway, it's a billboard for the genre's 'total' art style (page 134).

ATOMIUM Belgium's own Eiffel Tower: an unlikely homage to a magnified iron molecule which was created for the 1958 World's Fair. It's now such a beloved part of the cityscape that millions have been spent ensuring the towering set of silver balls – housing exhibitions and a restaurant – gleams to perfection (page 129).

HOUSE OF EUROPEAN HISTORY A visit to the newest and most satisfying of several local attractions devoted to the troubled European Union is surprisingly rewarding – taking in everything from the Greek myth of Europa to the EU's genesis and its status today (page 117).

published in Brussels during the 17th century. Also here is a sullen-looking statue of Béla Bartók (1881–1945), a Hungarian composer renowned for his folk music. From here you can either carry straight on and come out in front of Gare Centrale, or retrace your steps to place Agora and scout out the **commemorative plaque** situated on the corner of rue de la Colline (85 rue du Marché aux Herbes; currently a Panos outlet) to mark the sewing of the first two Belgian flags by Madame Abts on 26 August 1830.

Sainte-Catherine and beyond walk

Bourse; 2½ hrs; see maps, pages 94 and 78

On exiting Bourse metro station [94 C1], look for the **Paul Delvaux painting** *Nos vieux trams bruxellois* above the escalators (see box, page 71 for more metro art) and then head west along rue J van Praet to **place St-Géry**. Brussels's history began here when the Bishop of Cambrai founded a small chapel on this very spot – then an islet surrounded by the river Senne. A number of churches have since replaced the old St-Géry chapel, which was destroyed in AD800. When the last one was demolished under French rule in the late 18th century, the open space was made into a market square and at its centre they put a fountain and obelisk salvaged from Grimbergen Abbey. When architect Vanderheggen was commissioned to build a covered market hall in 1882, he was careful to build around the obelisk, and the Flemish Renaissance-style **Halles St-Géry** [94 A1] (1 pl St-Géry; 02 502 44 24; w hallessaintgery.be; 10.00–midnight, exhibitions until 18.00) are still in place today. The halls were abandoned after World War II and finally restored in the 1980s; initially they were earmarked to become chic covered markets, similar to London's Covent Garden, later serving as an information centre and now hosting a ground-floor café, and an exhibition and event space. The surrounding area is rather trendy and famous for its cafés and bars with sprawling terraces.

Walk to the west side of the square Pass under the arch – known as Au Lion d'Or Gate – to the left of Ô Lion d'Or restaurant. This leads to an inner courtyard that was once home to the brewery and bakery of Notre-Dame aux Riches Claires convent (see below). To the left, down some steps, is one of the **last open stretches of the river Senne**, which was covered in the mid 19th century to eliminate the diseases brewing in its fetid waters. Also on place St-Géry you'll find a **mural of famous comic book hero Nero** (see box, page 23) and his buddies rescuing a cat from a tree.

Turn the corner and walk down rue de la Grande Île until the next intersection. Here you will find **Notre-Dame aux Riches Claires** [78 B7] (23 rue des Riches-Claires; 02 213 00 65; 09.00–16.30), an elegant church in Flemish Renaissance style designed by Lucas Fayd'herbe (1617–97) in 1665. It was used as a hospital to treat soldiers wounded during the Belgian revolution. A fire in June 1989 destroyed large portions of the interior, including the church organ. Now restored, it's a central point for the Hispanic and Latino community in Brussels.

Return to place St-Géry and leave via the northeast exit located on the opposite side of the square. Known as rue du Pont de la Carpe, the street takes its name from a bridge that crossed the river Senne here until the mid 19th century. Take the first left on to rue des Chartreux and keep an eye open for Magritte's favourite café, the **Taverne Greenwich** (page 87) on the right-hand side, and, just after it, a **comic-strip mural of L'Ange de Sambre** by Yslaire. As you come to the corner of rue du Vieux Marché aux Grains, notice the statue of a dog cocking its leg against a bollard. Sculpted by popular artist Tom Frantzen, the mutt is known as **Zinneke Pis**

I SPY A SEASHELL

Throughout the Lower Town strange brass abalone (clam) shells are embedded into the pavement. These were the emblem of pilgrims travelling to visit the tomb of Apostle St James in Compostela, Spain. They mark a pilgrim route that has been in place since the Middle Ages and led travellers to sites on the pilgrimage trail.

[78 B6] and completes the Manneken and Jeanneke Pis 'family' of statues dotted around the city.

Turn right into rue du Vieux Marché aux Grains Follow the road all the way round, crossing the wide rue Antoine Dansaert (well-known for its fashion shops) and taking the first street on the left. Halfway along, on the left, is **Maison de la Bellone** [78 B5] (46 rue de Flandre; 02 513 33 33; w www.bellone.be; 09.00–15.00 Mon, 09.00–17.00 Tue–Fri). The stunning façade of this Baroque mansion is the definition of hidden gem. It was built in 1697 by Jan Cosyn, the sculptor responsible for the bust of King Charles II of Spain that decorates the bakers' guild on the Grand-Place, for arms-trader Nicolas Bally and his wife Gertrude de Smeth. Appropriately, the house is named after the Roman goddess of war, Bellona, whose bust sits above the doorway. Behind her is a scene depicting Austria's victory against the Turks in 1697. For unknown reasons, the building raced through a list of owners before Brussels mayor Charles Buls acquired it for the city in 1913. Since then, it has served as a police station and the offices of the Ommegang Society; today it sits resplendent under a glass dome and is home to theatre institute La Maison du Spectacle, which hosts concerts, workshops and exhibitions.

At this point it's a 5-minute walk west (via the Maison Margiela boutique, page 92) to **Brussels Beer Project** (**BBP**) [78 A4] (188 rue Antoine Dansaert; w beerproject.be; 14.00–22.00 Thu–Sat). Born in 2013, this craft brewery has injected new life into the Belgian beer scene – even their ultra-graphic labels look cool. Flash tours include a 15-minute visit and four beers (16.00 Thu–Fri, 14.00 & 15.00 Sat; €14 pp). They're currently plotting a second brewery in Anderlecht.

Rejoin rue de Flandre Take rue du Marché aux Porcs (from Maison de la Bellone turn left and take the third right; from BBP it's the second left) and walk towards the park. In the centre stands a bronze **statue dedicated to the 'soldier' pigeons** used to carry messages during World War I. Just south of this, between quai aux Briques and quai au Bois à Brûler, is a tree-lined plaza known as **Marché aux Poissons** [78 B5/6]. Up until 1853 the Willebroeck Canal flowed through these streets and was busy with barges delivering wares from Antwerp and the North Sea. The various street names – quai à la Houille (coal), quai à la Chaux (lime) and quai aux Barques (bricks) – give away the types of cargo on board and roughly where each was delivered at the docks. After frequent floodings the canal was filled in and the space used as a fish market (hence the current name). Although this closed in 1955, the area is still synonymous with seafood restaurants.

Continue to walk south along quai aux Briques until you reach **place Sainte-Catherine**. At the heart of this square stands **Église St-Catherine** (**St Catherine's Church**) [78 C5] (50 pl St-Catherine; m 0492 76 66 17; w eglisesaintecatherine.be; 09.00–20.00 Mon–Fri, 09.00–19.00 Sat–Sun). There was a church dedicated to St Catherine on this site in the 15th century, but the oldest remaining part today is the Baroque belfry, built in 1629. The rest of the church fell victim to rot caused by a series of floods from the Willebroeck Canal and was redesigned by architect Poelaert (of Palais de Justice fame), who modelled his design on the neo-Gothic St-Eustache church in Paris. By 1867 work was complete. Inside you'll find the legendary limestone 'black Virgin Mary' carrying the holy child. Dating from the 15th century, it was thrown in the Senne in 1744 by Protestants, but was found floating further downstream on a piece of earth and returned, albeit not before the limestone had turned an unorthodox shade of black. The church is keeping up with the times: in 2017 they hooked up with BBP to create the Ste Kat' beer, sold by cafés around the square. Proceeds go to the church's upkeep. To the east of the church is the **Tour Noire** (**Black Tower**) [78 C5], a remnant of the original city walls, and an incongruous sight amid its modern neighbours.

Leave place Sainte-Catherine Exit via place du Samedi and turn left on to rue du Cyprès, walking until you reach place du Béguinage, site of the **St-Jean-Baptiste du Béguinage** (**St John the Baptist at the Béguinage**) [78 C4] (pl du Béguinage; 02 217 87 42; 09.00–17.00 Mon–Fri, 11.00–17.00 Sat–Sun). This Flemish Baroque church is hailed as one of the prettiest in Belgium, and is the last remaining building of a béguinage that stood on this site from 1250. The self-sufficient béguines possessed large amounts of land in the surrounding area and enough income to build a Gothic church here in the 14th century. Both were razed by Calvinists towards the end of the 16th century and by the time funds were available to rebuild the church, the béguine community had started to shrink – changing times and high entry fees excluded all but the richest of women. Still, the church – built by Lucas Fayd'herbe (the architect behind Notre-Dame aux Riches Claires) – was completed in 1676 and outlasted the béguinage, which was dissolved in 1833. Of note is the huge Baroque pulpit featuring St Dominic condemning heresy and stamping on the odd heretic to drive home the point.

Heading south from **place du Béguinage**, continue along rue du Béguinage, cut right along rue de Laeken, and left down rue des Augustins until you reach major shopping hub **rue Neuve**. Head north and you'll soon reach the ornate but faded **Passage du Nord** – a covered walkway filled with cute specialist shops. After browsing here, return to rue Neuve and continue north, soon reaching the **Église Notre-Dame du Finistère (Church of Our Lady of Finistère)**.

Notre-Dame du Finistère (Church of Our Lady of Finistère) [79 E4] (76 rue Neuve; 02 217 52 52; 09.30–18.00 Mon–Fri, 10.00–19.00 Sat, 09.00–15.00 Sun) The medieval chapel that sat here originally was placed outside the 12th-century city walls – hence the name *finis terre,* 'end of the world'. The names of the surrounding streets, like rue au Choux (cabbages) and rue de la Blanchisserie (laundry), recall the activities that took place in the fields around the chapel, namely the planting of vegetables and the bleaching of sheets. In 1617, this land was bought by Hieronimus de Meester, who extended the street plan and named the central road nouvelle rue Notre Dame, which over the years was shortened to rue Neuve. Soon enough the small church could not cope with the rapidly expanding community and work on the Baroque version, which stands in place today, began in 1708. After a major mishap – a corrupt committee member legged it with construction funds – it was completed in 1730. The octangular belfry was added in 1828, and in 1862 another chapel was built to accommodate the church's prize possession – a statue of Notre-Dame du Bon Succès, believed to be from Aberdeen in Scotland.

On leaving the church, turn right Take the first left down rue Saint-Michel, arriving at the **place des Martyrs**. This Neoclassical square was created in 1778 and at its centre is a monument erected in memory of the Belgians who died in the fight for independence in 1830; their crypt lies below. Exit the square via rue du Persil, turn left into rue du Marais, and take the first right into rue des Sables. Halfway along this street is the **Centre Belge de la Bande Dessinée (The Belgian Comic Strip Center)** [79 F5] (20 rue des Sables; ☎ 02 219 19 80; w comicscenter.net; ⏲ 10.00–18.00; adult/12–25/under 12/Brussels Card €10/7/3.50/free), housed in the former Magasins Waucquez – a fabric and textiles shop designed by Victor Horta in 1906, and his sole surviving department store. The great vaulted-glass ceiling was intended to let the daylight pour in, so that ladies could see the true colours of the cottons and silks they were purchasing. Described by French writer Émile Zola as 'a palace of dreams', it's a heady tangle of twisted iron railings, tiered balconies and scrolled columns. The museum's permanent exhibitions cover the invention of the comic and legendary Belgian illustrators such as Hergé and Smurfs' creator Peyo. You'll find a vast reading room with over 3,000 albums to browse, a café and a well-stocked shop where you can pick up maps of the city's comic-strip trail.

Once outside, head back down rue des Sables and take the first left on to rue du Marais. You will quickly come to the **Musée de la Banque Nationale de Belgique (Museum of the National Bank of Belgium)** [79 E6] (57 rue Montagne aux Herbes Potagères; ☎ 02 221 22 06; w nbbmuseum.be; ⏲ 09.00–17.00 Mon–Fri; free inc audio guide). One of the few free museums in the city, the focus here is, of course, on money. Spend an hour learning about the stockmarkets, the secret features embedded in banknotes and the reason behind the conversion to the euro.

After finishing here, take the street opposite the Shaoshan restaurant – rue du Fossé aux Loups – then the first left on to rue Léopold, which brings you to the rear of the **Théâtre de la Monnaie** [78 D6] (5 pl de la Monnaie; ☎ 02 229 12 11; w lamonnaie.be; ⏲ guided tours 1st Sat of the month at noon, adult/under 12 €12/6), where this walk terminates. Site of the famous Belgian revolt in August 1830 (page 9) and the city's best opera performances (page 90), this grand Neoclassical building occupies the former location of the 15th-century Hôtel des Monnaies that served as the royal mint for the Dukes of Brabant. In 1817 it was replaced by an opera house that was destroyed by the revolt fires; the version that stands today was reconstructed by Joseph Poelaert in 1855 – although the Ionic columns and mantle were saved from the original theatre.

Sablon and Marolles walk

Anneessens; 3hrs; see map, page 84

This longer walk leads you through the well-to-do Sablon area and down-to-earth Marolles neighbourhood south of the city centre. While they were once poles apart – in the 17th century artisans working on the mansions in Sablon lived in the Marolles – the two areas feed into one another; more shop owners are snapping up cheap property in the latter, blurring the divide, though friendly Marolles still retains a working-class edge.

The walk begins outside **Notre-Dame de la Chapelle (Church of Our Lady of the Chapel)** [84 D3] (pl de la Chapelle; ⏲ 10.00–15.30 Mon & Wed–Sat). A must-see, this church – shining white after extensive renovation work in the 1990s – has one of the most impressive interiors in Brussels. A chapel was originally founded here in 1134, making it the oldest in the city. However, its chequered history has made it something of a mongrel, mixing a 12th-century Romanesque chancel and transept, a 15th-century Gothic nave and a Baroque belltower dating from 1699.

Inside the décor is predominantly flamboyant Gothic and features of note include the row of apostle statues mounted on the aisle columns and the ornate Baroque oak pulpit. More importantly, it is the burial place of Pieter Bruegel the Elder and his wife, who married here in 1563, and Frans Anneessens (1660–1719), who was beheaded on the Grand-Place for campaigning for civil rights during Austrian rule. There's a plaque in his memory in the Holy Sacrament chapel.

Turn right out of the church and head north along boulevard de l'Empereur. On your right you will soon spot **Tour Anneessens** aka **Tour d'Angle** [85 E3]. The round, brick tower and abutting wall are the last remnants of the 13th-century city walls. Frans Anneessens (see above) was imprisoned in this tower prior to his execution in 1719. Turn back towards place de la Chapelle, but take the first left into the cobbled **rue de Rollebeek**, lined with pavement cafés, restaurants and independent shops. Once you reach the end of the road, you can take a quick detour by turning right into rue de Minimes and visiting the **Musée Juif de Belgique** (**Jewish Museum of Belgium**) [85 E3] (21 rue des Minimes; 02 512 19 63; w www.mjb-jmb.org; 10.00–17.00 Tue–Fri, 10.00–18.00 Sat–Sun; adult/under 12 & Brussels Card €10/free). It contains a huge collection of religious paraphernalia telling the story of Jews in Belgium, including Judaica, bibles and and roughly 20,000 photographs. This is showcased in a permanent exhibition and fine temporary shows ranging from Amy Winehouse to Brussels immigration, the latter in response to a deadly shooting that took place at the museum in 2014, when a gunman with radical Islamist links killed four people.

Retrace your steps Enter the triangular **place du Grand Sablon**, skirted by antiques stores, restaurants and chocolatiers such as **Wittamer** (page 92). Named after the sandy road that led up to the city gates in the 13th century, the area's status was consolidated during the 14th century when the Sablon chapel was constructed. By the 15th century, the city walls had been expanded to encompass a now new-and-improved Gothic church, and the district was becoming popular with well-to-do citizens because of its proximity to the Palais d'Egmont. Today, the fashionable plaza hosts an antiques market (page 91). In the centre is the **Fountain of Minerva** [85 E3]. Dedicated to the Roman goddess of war, it was a gift from English earl (and exile) Thomas Bruce, a supporter of James II who lived on the square for many years and was buried in the Église des Brigittines. Head up the square to **Église Notre-Dame du Sablon** (**Church of Our Blessed Lady of Sablon**) [85 F4] (pl du Grand Sablon; 02 511 57 41; 09.00–18.30 Mon–Fri, 10.00–18.30 Sat–Sun) spread out before you. Its founding can be credited to one Beatrijs Soetkins, who stole a statue of the Virgin Mary from a church in Antwerp and brought it to Brussels, after (she claimed) a vision of the immaculate Mother had instructed her to do so. (This journey is re-enacted in the famous Ommegang procession held every summer; see page 53.) The archers' guild pooled funds to build a chapel that could house the statue in 1304, and soon enough the site had become a major stop on the Compostela pilgrimage route. It proved too small to accommodate the steady trickle of pilgrims, so the archers once again reached into their pockets and spent the late 15th and early 16th centuries converting the chapel into a splendid Gothic church. In fact, Charles the Bold married Margaret of York here in 1473, while work was still in progress. The enormous interior is warmed by the series of **stained-glass windows** that cast technicolour light into the shadows when the sun shines. The prettiest are the row of seven windows above the altar which recount the life of the Virgin Mary, and the rose window mounted on the left as you enter via the south entrance. Of particular interest is the privately funded funeral **chapel and crypt** (located in the north transept) of German nobles the Thurn und Taxis (or Tassis) family, who organised the first international (horse-fuelled) postal service out of Brussels, controlling the industry for almost two centuries.

Across the road from the church is **place du Petit Sablon**, a pretty and supremely tranquil landscaped garden severed from the main square by the construction of rue de la Régence in the late 19th century. Forty-eight statues representing the medieval guilds line its boundaries and at the centre stands a fountain topped with statues of the counts Egmont and Hoorn (page 7). At the back of the park, on the other side of rue des Petits Carmes, is the **Palais d'Egmont** [85 F4]. Closed to the public, it was built as a home for Count Egmont's mother, and today is used by the Belgian Ministry of Foreign Affairs.

Walk back down the other side of place du Petit Sablon Turn left on to rue de la Régence. Immediately on the left is the site of the Taxis family's former mansion now housing the neo-Renaissance **Conservatoire Royal de Bruxelles** (**Royal Conservatory of Brussels**) [85 E4] (30 rue de la Régence; ☎ 02 511 04 27; w conservatoire.be). It was built between 1872 and 1876 by Jean-Pierre Cluysenaar, the man behind the Galeries Royales Saint-Hubert, whose bust stands in the garden, hidden behind railings. Check the website for regular classical concerts and recitals.

Continue straight on, then turn left via rue Joseph Dupont to rue aux Laines and walk straight across the road into **Parc d'Egmont** [85 F5]. In front of you stands a replica Peter Pan statue gifted in 1924 by the children of London; the original sits in Kensington Gardens. On the left, peek over the railings to get a better look at the Palais d'Egmont. Leave the park via the east entrance on to boulevard de Waterloo, turn right and walk past designer shops, such as Hermès, Cartier and Louis Vuitton, until you reach place Louise. Keeping on the right-hand side, head to the far side of the roundabout and turn into rue des Quatre Bras on your right. This opens out on to place Poelaert [84/B D5/E5], at the centre of which stands an enormous monument [84 E5] dedicated to the Belgian soldiers who fought and died in World Wars I and II; you'll also spot an Anglo-Belgian war memorial honouring the support Belgians gave to British prisoners of war during World War I.

Palais de Justice (Law Courts) [84 D5] (1 pl Poelaert; ☎ 02 508 65 78) The Palais de Justice looms on the left of the place Poelaert. It was appropriately built on top of Galenberg or 'gallows hill' (a popular place for executions up until the 16th century) and placed here to cast a shadow over the Marolles district and remind the poor residents of what would befall them should they turn to a life of crime. Built between 1866 and 1883, it was – in its heyday – the largest building in the world. Architect Joseph Poelaert wanted to synthesise the whole of humanity in his design – unsurprisingly, perhaps, he died in a deranged state four years before completion amid rumours of a witch sticking pins into his effigy. Meanwhile, the building's budget spiralled out of control and entire neighbourhoods were uprooted to create the necessary space – a move that earned Poelaert the nickname of *skieven architek* or 'filthy architect' (still a form of slander today). The project is seen as the embodiment of 19th-century urban-planning lunacy.

Ascend the steps towards the entrance; on the left and right are giant plaques honouring kings Leopold I and II and Poelaert, and in front are forbidding brass doors. Renovations – started in 2003 and incredibly not due to complete until a futuristic-seeming 2040 – mean that large parts of the building are covered by scaffolding, but the inside retains its splendour and shows no traces of the fire started by German soldiers at the end of World War II. Sounds are lost in the vast central atrium and the 25 (predominantly empty) courtrooms. The building still serves as Belgium's Supreme Court of Law, and is open during working hours to lawyers meeting their clients. However, as long as you're quiet you're welcome to wander around and admire the mixture of Ancient Egyptian, Babylonian and Greek-Roman architectural styles, including columns as thick as tree trunks.

On exiting, turn to the left Take in the superb view of the city's skyline – you can make out the green dome of the Koekelberg Basilica in the centre, the Church of Our Lady of the Chapel behind that and, on the far right, the Atomium. Off to your left you'll see the free **glass lift** (🕘 07.00–23.30) that takes you down to the Marolles district 20m below. Until the late 19th century this working-class district thrived, but after the paving over of the Senne, factories closed down and it didn't revive until the 1980s, transforming into the city's most enjoyable, atmospheric (still slightly scruffy) antiques and design hub.

Once below, head behind the lift on to rue des Minimes where, at no 91, you'll find the **comic mural** 'passe-moi l'ciel'. Further up on the right is the soot-stained **Église Saint-Jean-et-Étienne-aux-Minimes** (**Church of St Jean and Etienne of the Minimes**) [85 E4] (62 rue des Minimes; 🕘 10.00–14.00 & 17.00–19.30 Tue–Fri, 08.30–13.30 Sat–Sun), which was built in the early 18th century for the Minim order of friars, and straddles Baroque and Neoclassical styles. Its whitewashed interior houses paintings by Jan Cosiers and its excellent acoustics are displayed during regular classical concerts.

Turn right as you exit the church and take the next left into rue du Temple. Descend the steps and then cut back left down rue Haute. Just after B&B La Maison Haute (page 73) you'll pass no 132, the gabled house where artist Pieter Bruegel the Elder lived and worked between 1563 and 1569 – look for the plaque. Keep walking south – have a quick glimpse at the **Spirou comic mural** [84 D5] on the square by the glass lift – and turn right into rue des Capucins. Here you'll find three murals: the first (no 23a) is Da Vinci caricature **Léonard** [84 C5], depicting the Palais de Justice; the second (no 15) is **Blondin and Cirage** [84 C5] – the former Tintin-like, the other his crazy buddy; the last (no 13) featuring the rotund and bearded missionary **Odilon Verjus** [84 C4] and sidekick Laurent offering a helping hand to an exotic beauty and her pet cheetah.

At the end of the street turn left Turn immediately left again on to rue de Chevreuil. You're met with another comic-strip scene – this one a sketch from Boule et Bill (195 rue du Chevreuil). Past this house, on the left, is **Les Bains de Bruxelles** [84 B5] (28 rue du Chevreuil; ☎ 02 511 24 68; 🕘 07.30–19.30 Mon–Thu, 07.30–20.00 Fri, 07.30–17.00 Sat; non-*bruxellois* adult/concession/under 3 €4/€2.30/free), the capital's last functioning public bathing house. A century ago, many households lacked private bathing facilities, and so were reliant on these public pools to get clean. Today the third-floor pool has large windows at one end offering unusual rooftop views of rue des Capucins. It's hardly smart, but certainly off the beaten track (take cash).

Immediately to the right of rue du Chevreuil is **place du Jeu de Balle** [84 B5/C5], named after the handball once played here, and site of a popular open-air flea market (🕘 07.00–14.00 Mon–Fri, 07.00–15.00 Sat–Sun) where you can browse for hours sorting the tat from the treasure. Leave via the southeastern corner by Au Mouton Bleu café, and walk along rue de la Rasière, which crosses half a dozen streets lined with uniform rows of brick tenements. Named **Cité Hellemans** [84 B6] after their architect, this social housing was built in 1913 and considered revolutionary at the time because each had ventilation and contained a flushing toilet. Rue de la Rasière leads you back on to rue Haute. From here turn right and walk south. You can see an array of outsider and brut art at the **Art et Marges Musée** [84 C6] (314 rue Haute; 02 533 94 90; w artetmarges.be; 11.00–18.00 Tue–Sun; adult/under 6 Brussels Card & 1st Sun of month €4/free), then continue south towards the ivy-covered, fairytale **Porte de Hal (Halle Gate)** [84 B7] (02 534 15 18; w www.kmkg-mrah.be; 09.30–17.00 Tue–Fri, 10.00–17.00 Sat–Sun; adult/under 18, Brussels Card & 1st Wed of month from 13.00 €7/free, inc audio guide), which dates from 1381 and is the last rampart of the city's seven medieval city gates. Stronghold of the fearsome Duke of Alva during Philip II's tyrannical reign, it was saved from demolition during Leopold II's expansion plans in the mid 19th century and opened to the public as a museum of weapons in 1847, making it one of Europe's first museums. Today it fills you in on what Brussels was like during the Middle Ages. There is an array of horse and human armour and the battlements offer sweeping views of the city. To return to the centre take the premetro from Porte de Hal, just off to the right. (The premetro refers to sections of the Brussels tramway network that run underground and at metro frequency.)

UPPER TOWN

Place Royale, Mont des Arts and Parc de Bruxelles walk

Gare Centrale; 4hrs; see maps, pages 78 and 84

This walk follows on well from the Sainte-Catherine route (page 104), which concludes nearby.

Start the walk at Gare Centrale [94 G3] Here you should locate the small passage between the Carrefour supermarket and Hilton hotel. Look up: in 2018, to mark their 60th anniversary, comic heroes The Smurfs got a huge **new mural** covering the roof of the passageway and drawing on Brussels tourist attractions. Turn back, cross the station square and head up the hill along boulevard de l'Impératrice; when you reach the park, cut across it to get to the commanding cathedral.

Cathédrale des Saint-Michel et Saint-Gudule (St Michael and St Gudula Cathedral) [79 F7] (pl St Gudule; 02 217 83 45; w cathedralisbruxellensis.be; 07.00–18.00 Mon–Fri, 08.00–17.00 Sat, 13.00–16.00 Sun; free; free guided tours in English 14.00 Sat, see w churchandtourismbrussels.be). A chapel dedicated to St Michael the Archangel – patron saint of travellers and of Brussels – already existed here in the 9th century. This was replaced by a Romanesque version in the 11th century and during the same period it gained its name when the relics of Brussels patroness St Gudule – a 7th-century figure who tended the poor and was famous for her dedication to prayer despite the devil playing tricks on her – were transferred here from the St-Géry chapel. Building of the current Gothic-style cathedral commenced in 1226 but took over 300 years to complete. As a result, the structure is a mixture of architectural styles: the 13th-century choir is the oldest part of the building; the triple-aisled nave dates from the 14th century; and the High Gothic façade with its two stone towers from the following century. Restoration work throughout the 1980s and 1990s uncovered preserved remnants of the old **Romanesque church and crypt** underneath the current choir (08.00–18.00; €1); the site is located to the left of the entrance and via a series of mirrors visitors can glimpse the old

'Westbau' (a section of the church reserved as a place of refuge for residents), the original round towers and the church entrance.

Inside, the first feature to catch your attention is the cathedral's magnificent **Baroque pulpit**, carved from a single chunk of oak by Antwerp sculptor Hendrik Verbruggen, and representing Adam and Eve being chased from the Garden of Eden. Above, the Virgin Mary and infant Jesus helpfully plunge a cross into the head of the serpent. Also of note are the **statues of the 12 apostles** that line the nave, sculpted by Jérôme Dusquesnoy the Younger (his father made the Manneken Pis currently installed by the Grand-Place) and Lucas Fayd'herbe, and some splendid Renaissance stained-glass windows, the most famous of which stands in the north transept and features Charles V and Isabelle of Portugal kneeling in front of the holy sacrament. Left of the choir is the **Chapel of the Blessed Sacrament of the Miracle**, which contains the church's **treasury** (🕘 10.00–12.30 & 14.00–17.00 Mon–Fri, 10.00–17.00 Sat, 14.00–17.00 Sun; adult/under 14 €2/free). Here superb stained-glass windows modelled on designs by painter Bernard van Orley recall episodes from the Miracle of the Blessed Sacrament – an anti-Semitic legend involving a Jew from Flanders stealing the consecrated Host from his church, before his fellow men attacked it with daggers, and his wife ultimately saved the day by bringing it to the cathedral. The other major draw here is the reliquary of the *True Cross*, also known as the ***Drahmal Cross***. The cathedral was promoted to its current status in 1962 and is used for royal weddings.

Continue the walk Take rue du bois Sauvage on the northern side of the cathedral and follow it north for 5 minutes until you reach place du Congrès. Standing tall on the left is the **Colonne du Congrès** [79 G6]. Another of Joseph Poelaert's creations, this 47m-high column commemorates the National Congress of 1830–1 that laid out the Belgian Constitution. A statue of Leopold I sits at the top and the figures seated at the four corners represent the four freedoms guaranteed under the constitution. The Belgian **Tomb of the Unknown Soldier** lies at its base, surrounded by an eternal flame; the World War I soldier buried here was selected by a veteran blinded in battle, and embodies all Belgian victims of the war.

Leave the square via rue du Congrès and when you reach place de la Liberté, take the first street on the left and walk north along rue de l'Association. Take the first right and follow rue de la Révolution to place des Barricades. On the eastern edge, at 4 place des Barricades, is the former family home of French writer **Victor Hugo**, who lived here from 1866 until 1871. A plaque outside bears his signature and engraved in gold are the words: *Je me sens le frère de tous les hommes et l'hôte de tous les peuples* ('I feel myself to be the brother of all men and the guest of all peoples'). After this, there's a brisk stroll south along rue du Nord, across place Surlet and down rue Ducale, until you come to the corner of Parc de Bruxelles. Have a glance at 51 rue Ducale (just across the road), where a plaque commemorates the 1816 stay of English Romantic poet **Lord George Byron** (1788–1824), fleeing an acrimonious separation with his wife. He is believed to have penned the third canto of his masterpiece *Childe Harold's Pilgrimage* here. Now skirt the park along rue de la Loi, passing the U-shaped **Palais de la Nation** (1–2 pl de la Nation), which hosts the Belgian House of Representatives. Cross the street and enter the **Parc de Bruxelles** [85 H1/2]. On the site of a former hunting ground of the Dukes of Brabant, this central 13ha park was laid out in the late 18th century, attacked by French revolutionary troops in 1793, and became a refuge for the army of the United Kingdom of the Netherlands during the struggle for independence. Despite its double row of lime trees it seems disappointingly bland given all that history. Fascinatingly, however, some see in its uniform design Masonic symbols like the compass and square: Charles of Lorraine, who commissioned the design, was a member. A small pool (in the bottom right-hand corner of the park) bearing the word 'Vitriol' – an acronym for the Latin saying *Visita Interiora Terrae Rectificando Invenies Occultum Lapidem*, which speaks of self-knowledge – further fuels the rumour mill.

Exit the park via the southeast corner In front of you stands the oblong **Palais des Académies (Palace of Academies)** (1 rue Ducale), which briefly served as the residence of the Prince of Orange until Belgian independence. Now walk along the wide place des Palais where, stretching out at the southern tip of Parc de Bruxelles, is the Palais Royal.

Palais Royal [85 G3] (pl des Palais; 02 551 20 20; w monarchie.be; mid-Jul–early-Sep 10.30–17.00 Tue–Sun, last entry 15.45; free) Less impressive than you might hope, the Royal Palace is not where Belgian royals live – that honour goes to Laeken (page 129) – but is instead where the king and queen receive guests. In the 1780s, under Austrian rule, four Neoclassical mansions were constructed here; King Leopold II was responsible for its present, more grandiose appearance. Inside is a maze of rooms lined with royal portraits, but of more interest are the modern interventions on show. In the **Hall of Mirrors,** originally intended as a Congolese tribute by King Leopold II, Jan Fabre is responsible for the stunning ceiling, *Heaven of Delight* (2002), studded with the wings of 1.4 million emerald Thai jewel beetles; the **Empire Room**'s *Les Fleurs de Palais Royal* (2004) features golden bowls filled with earth from each of the Belgian provinces, while artist Michaël Borremans and interior design maestro Axel Vervoordt collaborated on the unusual **Marshals' Room**, which also bears a clock by Lier's Louis Zimmer (page 326).

In one wing of the palace, occupying the former residence of Leopold II and Queen Astrid, is the **Musée BELvue** [85 G2] (7 pl des Palais; 02 500 45 54; w belvue.be; 09.30–17.00 Tue–Fri, 10.00–18.00 Sat–Sun; adult/18–25/under 18 Brussels Card €7/5/free, combi-ticket with Palais Coudenberg €12/8/free). Renovated in 2016, the museum relates the history of Belgium via an eclectic collection of objects ranging from a Magritte lithograph to a football signed by the Red Devils. Regrettably, there is scant mention of the Belgian Congo or World War I, and instead some EU propaganda – a bit of a missed trick given how genuinely fascinating Belgium's history is.

More worthy of a detour are the ruins of the **Palais Coudenberg (Coudenberg Palace)** [85 G2] (w coudenberg.brussels; same hours and rates as BELvue Museum, but open 10.00–18.00 daily in Jul–Aug), which shares a ticket desk with the BELvue Museum. This eerie archaeological site explores the remains of the enormous medieval Coudenberg Palace, which once stretched to what's now place Royale, and was home to the dukes of Brabant and Burgundy, Emperor Charles V, and the Archduke Albert and Archduchess Isabella. The majority of the palace was destroyed by fire in 1731 and what remains is a layout of under-lit brick walkways. The biggest rooms are the kitchens and larders that sat beneath the lavish **Aula Magna** banqueting hall built by Philip the Good in the 14th century, which hosted meetings held by the knights of the Order of the Golden Fleece and was where Emperor Charles V abdicated in 1555. Pick up the €3 audio guide to get the most out of a visit.

Exit into an underground alley This alley is by the unmissable, much-photographed Art Nouveau building which houses the **Musée des Instruments**

de Musique (Musical Instruments Museum, MIM) [85 F2] (2 rue Montagne de la Cour; ☎ 02 545 01 30; w mim.be; ⊙ 09.30–17.00 Tue–Fri, 10.00–17.00 Sat–Sun; adult/under 18, Brussels Card & 1st Wed of month from 13.00 €10/free). Built for the Old England clothing company in 1899, it now houses a world-class collection of 7,000-odd musical instruments – a fraction of which are spread over the four floors. Fancy headphones cued to play music that matches the instrument you're looking at really bring things to life – not least in the traditional instrument room on the first floor where you can listen to bagpipes, Tibetan bone instruments and African slit drums. Take your time and if you need a break the top-floor café serves fine fare with sublime city views, especially from the terrace. The top-floor auditorium usually hosts concerts on Tuesday from 12.30–13.30.

Continuing with the walk, turn right out of MIM and follow the road as it curves into rue Ravenstein. Look for the stepped gable of **Hôtel Ravenstein** (3 rue Ravenstein) set slightly back from the road on the right. Henry VIII's fourth wife, Anne of Cleves, was born in this aristocratic Gothic mansion. You'll quickly find yourself standing outside the **Palais des Beaux-Arts** or **BOZAR** [85 G2] (23 rue Ravenstein; ☎ 02 507 82 00; w bozar.be; ⊙ 10.00–18.00 Tue–Wed & Fri–Sun, 10.00–21.00 Thu). This fine arts centre contains a theatre and concert hall and high-profile temporary exhibitions (page 89). Work on the building started in 1922, and designer Victor Horta (page 371) is said to have been thoroughly miffed with city officials, who insisted that shops should line the street front on rue Ravenstein and that parts of the 'palace' should be sunk underground so the building would not obstruct the king's view of the Lower Town from the Palais Royal. In his memoirs Horta writes, 'Palace? That is not how I think of it: just an arts centre'.

Beyond the entrance to the building turn right down rue Baron Horta; look up at the side of the BOZAR building here to spot a plaque marking the former site of the **Pensionnat Heger**, a girls' boarding school. Novelists Emily and Charlotte Brontë taught English and music here in 1842 in return for French and German tuition and free board. Charlotte returned a year later and fell in love with the head of the school. Her first novel, *The Professor*, is believed to have been modelled on her experiences in Brussels, and its protagonist on Crimsworth. Further down on your right is the **Cinematek** (this used to be called the Musée du Cinema) (page 90).

Cross rue Ravenstein Walk into the covered **Galerie Ravenstein** arcade that emerges at the back of Gare Centrale. Now turn left and within 100m you'll reach place de l'Albertine. In the centre stands a demure Queen Elizabeth holding flowers and, opposite her, marking the beginning of the Mont des Arts, is **a statue of her popular husband, Albert I**, on horseback. To the left of him, a building suspended over an archway features a large **carillon clock** bearing 12 historical Belgian figures; they move on the hour and very diplomatically play Walloon and Flemish songs alternately.

Returning to the Albert I statue, you'll be looking across landscaped gardens and the **Mont des Arts**, the collective name given to the 16 museums and cultural sites covering this hill, all included in the Brussels Card (see box, page 95). This area marks the boundary between the Lower and Upper Towns. Walk through the gardens and up the steps and immediately turn right into rue du Musée, which opens on to place du Musée. Right beside you, shining white and concave, is the **Palais de Charles de Lorraine** [85 F2] (1 pl du Musée; ☎ 02 519 53 11; ⊙ closed for renovation until mid-October 2019; free). This grand building served as the home of Charles of Lorraine, governor of the Austrian Netherlands from 1744 to 1780 and an avid art and science enthusiast. Objects from his collection fill five stucco-

and silk-laden rooms, illustrating 18th-century life at the court of Brussels. The museum was due to reopen on 15 October 2019 for a major exhibition of Bruegel's prints (🕘 11.00–19.00 until 16 Feb 2020; adult/under 18 €12/free, inc audio guide) – part of a wider 'Bruegel Year' celebrating the artist. Next door to the palace is the lavish **Chapelle Protestante** (2 pl du Musée; ☎ 02 513 23 25; w eglisedumusee.be; 🕘 mass 10.30 Sun, also open Thu afternoon in summer or via private tours), a private chapel Lorraine had built in 1760. When Napoleon assumed power he handed it to the city's Protestant community, hence its name. King Leopold I attended services here, as did the Brontës.

Head back up the hill towards place Royale This square forms the heart of the Royal Quarter and peak of the Upper Town. You'll notice trams rattling around a **statue of crusade leader Godefroid de Bouillon** [85 G3] mounted on a noble steed and raising a flag on high. Erected in 1848, it marks the spot where he urged the Flemish to join his mission in capturing Jerusalem. The rest of the square has remained virtually unchanged since the late 18th century, when Charles of Lorraine employed Gilles Barnabé Guimard, a popular French architect of the day, to design a plaza that would sit on top of the ruins left by the fallen Coudenberg Palace (page 113).

Immediately on your right are the Musées Royaux des Beaux-Arts de Belgique.

Musées Royaux des Beaux-Arts de Belgique (Royal Museums of Fine Arts of Belgium) [85 F3] (3 rue de la Régence; ☎ 02 508 32 11; w fine-arts-museum.be; 🕘 10.00–17.00 Tue–Fri, 11.00–18.00 Sat–Sun; separate entry to Old Masters/Fin-de-Siècle or Magritte museums adult/under 19, Brussels Card, Eurostar 'Buy 1, get 1 free' & 1st Wed of month from 13.00 €10/free, combi-ticket with Musée Magritte €15/free, audio guide €4), are made up of the interconnected **Musée Old Masters**, **Musée Magritte** and **Musée Fin-de-Siècle** (notoriously, the museum's fine art collection has long lacked a proper showcase, though you can ask for a map of works at the information desk). Their combined artworks span seven centuries and form one of Europe's most complete collections. The former is world-famous for its comprehensive collection of Flemish Primitive (page 19) paintings. The main masterpieces to look for include: **Rogier van der Weyden**'s *Portrait of Anthony of Burgundy*, which depicts the illegitimate child of Philip the Good, who wears the chain of the Order of the Golden Fleece about his neck and holds an arrow to denote his membership of the archers' guild; two panels from **Dieric Bouts**'s *Justice of the Emperor Otto,* which captures the tale of a man falsely accused of adultery by a rejected empress, but who is proven innocent after death when his widow undergoes an ordeal by fire by holding a red-hot iron bar in her hand; **Hans Memling**'s *Martyrdom of St Sebastian*, commissioned by the archers' guild and depicting the saint oblivious to the firing squad's arrows; an assortment of paintings by **Hieronymus Bosch** including *Calvary with Donor*, depicting the crucifixion; Gerard David's beautiful *The Adoration of the Magi*; and *The Census at Bethlehem* painted by **Pieter Bruegel the Elder**, renowned for his earthy scenes of everyday life – here he ingeniously relocates Mary and Joseph from Judea to a wintry Brabant village. Moving on to the 17th century, you'll see plenty of big and bold paintings by **Peter Paul Rubens** (*Ascent to Calvary*, notably) and **Jacob Jordaens**, hugely in demand during his day. Among a scattering of 18th-century paintings, the highlight by far is Jacques-Louis David's iconic *Death of Marat*, depicting French Revolutionary hero Marat bleeding in his bath after being stabbed by Charlotte Corday.

Linked to the Old Masters Museum, the popular four-floor **Musée Magritte** [85 F3] (1 pl Royale; w musee-magritte-museum.be; ⌚10.00–17.00 Mon–Fri, 11.00–18.00 Sat–Sun; see page 115 for prices) honours prolific Belgian Surrealist René Magritte. The chronological display reunites works belonging to the Royal Museums of Fine Arts and Magritte's wife Georgette to create the world's most comprehensive collection of his oil paintings, drawings, sculptures, films and photographs, including *Olympia*, a nude portrait modelled on Georgette that was stolen in 2009 during the museum's first week of opening – but returned in 2012 after the €75,000 ransom was paid. Don't miss it! Sadly, quite a few of Magritte's masterpieces are located elsewhere, but you'll leave with a firm sense of his genius and wit.

A stairway leads down from the Magritte Museum to the **Musée Fin-de-Siècle** (see Musées Royaux des Beaux-Arts de Belgique, page 115, for practical details), opened in 2013 and dedicated to the supremely dynamic period between 1868 and 1914, when Belgium gave rise to artists like James Ensor, Fernand Khnopff and Léon Spilliaert, and the Brussels-based exhibitions of Les XX (see box, page 24). Highlights include a large array of paintings by **Constantin Meunier**, a gaggle of works by both French Impressionists (**Monet**, **Gauguin**, **Seurat**) and their Belgian counterparts (notably **Théo van Rysselberghe**) and a strong collection of Symbolist works. The gems here are the peculiar canvases of **Fernand Khnopff**, prone to repeatedly painting his sister Marguerite – most memorably and famously in *The Caress* (1896), where her head sits atop the body of a cheetah pawing at the waistband of an androgynous youth. Its sense of unresolved mystery is the embodiment of Symbolism, and no doubt a popular postcard!

The walk concludes on this enigmatic note. From here you can either head down the hill to Gare Centrale or pick up a quarter of the way through the Sablon and Marolles walk listed on page 107.

EU Quarter and Parc du Cinquantenaire walk

Trone/Malbeek; 3hrs; see map, page 118

Beyond the petit-ring but pivotal to city life is the EU Quarter. Until the late 19th century this area was rural farmland, but soon after Belgian independence, the new '**Leopold Quarter**' began to emerge between rue de la Loi and rue du Luxembourg, attracting the city's elite; in the 1880s, Leopold II requisitioned the former exercise grounds of the Civic Guards and the grand **Parc du Cinquantenaire** was born. Since the 1950s, the area has been progressively taken over by office blocks housing the **EU institutions.**

Start the walk at **place du Luxembourg** [118 A6], or 'Plux', a Neoclassical square that's a popular drinking spot for Eurocrats on a Thursday night (Trone and Malbeek metros are a 10-minute stroll away). In front of you, the former Brussels–Luxembourg railway station has morphed into **Station Europe** [118 A6] (page 71), an orientation point for visitors to the European Parliament. The Parliament itself begins on the other side of the visitor centre around futuristic square **Espace Léopold** [118 A6], dominated by the oval-shaped **Paul-Henri Spaak building** (43 rue Wiertz). Finished in 1997, it houses an enormous horseshoe-shaped debating chamber, the Hemicycle, and is nicknamed *Le Caprice des Dieux* ('whim of the gods') after a similarly shaped cheese – as well as EU hubris presumably.

Rarely has EU politics been more in the spotlight, and rarely has understanding its inner workings seemed more relevant amid the bluster of pro- and anti-European politicos. A good place to start is the slick, free **Parlamentarium** [118 A6] (60 rue Wiertz; 02 283 22 22; ⌚ 13.00–18.00 Mon, 09.00–18.00 Tue–Fri, 10.00–18.00

Sat–Sun; free inc audio guide) next to Station Europe, which takes you on an interactive journey through European law-making and the EU's evolution. It's high on propaganda, but if you want to find out about the 751 MEPs representing EU citizens or the tortures of decision-making, this is the place. Afterwards, cross to the other side of the square and follow the signs to the Hemicycle, passing down a flight of steps and curving around to the left past the flag-lined entrance of the Spaak building until you reach the park. You'll need to turn up 15 minutes before your chosen slot for free tours of the **Hemicycle**, also housed in the Spaak building (⌚ on the hour Sep–Jun 09.00–16.00 Mon–Thu, 09.00–11.00 Fri, Jul–Aug 09.00–16.00 Mon-Thu, 09.00–noon Fri; free inc audio guide); bring ID and expect queues – it's hugely popular with school groups. Tours are slightly cursory – the 30-minute audio-guide walks you through the building's art collection, and into the semi-circular chamber used to house the European Parliament's most important debates. If you'd like a more in-depth visit, you can either opt for a **briefing** (30–60mins) or visit during a **plenary session**, when debates are in full swing. Check the website (w europarl.europa.eu) for details.

Return the way you came and, after the Spaak building, take the first left on to rue Wiertz. Just after the entrance to the park is the former studio of 19th-century painter Antoine-Joseph Wiertz, now the **Musée Wiertz** [118 B7] (62 rue Vautier; ☎ 02 648 17 18; w fine-arts-museum.be; ⌚ 10.00–noon & 12.45–17.00 Tue–Fri; free). Wiertz was known for two things: his ego and his obsession with Rubens. He was so keen to be remembered that he conceived this museum well before his death, persuading the state to fund it in exchange for a bequest. A large display of his sculptures can be seen here, as well as his most famous canvases: *Les Grecs et les Troyens se disputant le corps de Patrocle* (*The Greeks and the Trojans fighting over the body of Patrocles*) and *La Belle Rosine* (*Two Girls*) – a macabre work in which a young girl faces a skeleton. Across the road are more skeletons at the **Musée des Sciences Naturelles** (**Museum of Natural Sciences**) [118 B7] (29 rue Vautier; ☎ 02 627 42 38; w naturalsciences.be; ⌚ 09.30–17.00 Tue–Fri, 10.00–18.00 Sat–Sun; adult/6–17/under 6, Brussels Card & 1st Wed of month from 13.00 €7/4.50/free). It's particularly famous for its collection of iguanodon skeletons, discovered by coal miners just west of Mons in 1878. Other highlights include the recent Gallery of Humankind, illustrating man's evolution via 25 hominid species and fascinating 3D models. In 2020 they will open a biodiversity and ecology gallery.

Head back out on to rue Vauthier and enter **Parc Léopold** [118 B6/C6], which overlooks a large pond and started life as a botanical garden and zoo, becoming popular with the local upper crust – until the zoo went bust owing to mismanagement. Follow the footpaths to the northern edge of the park and the **House of European History** [118 C5] (135 rue Belliard; ☎ 02 283 12 20; w historia-europa.ep.eu; ⌚ 13.00–18.00 Mon, 09.00–18.00 Tue–Fri, 10.00–18.00 Sat–Sun; free). Opened in 2017, this is the most satisfying of the attractions devoted to the EU, offering six floors of exhibits ranging from the ancient Greek myth of Europa to the formation of the EU and its embattled status today. After passing through security, head straight upstairs and swap your ID for an audio guide – available in every official EU language, naturally. I'd allot at least 2 hours to a visit. There's a great deal to see, and the sections dealing with the alternate swings towards nationalist sentiment (Nazi Germany, the recent migrant crisis) and pan-European solidarity are fascinating in the current climate.

Exit the building and cross place Jean-Rey, noting the mirrored façade of the Justus Lipsius building, housing the Council of the European Union. Head north along chaussée d'Etterbeek, soon arriving at Maelbeek metro station. The metro

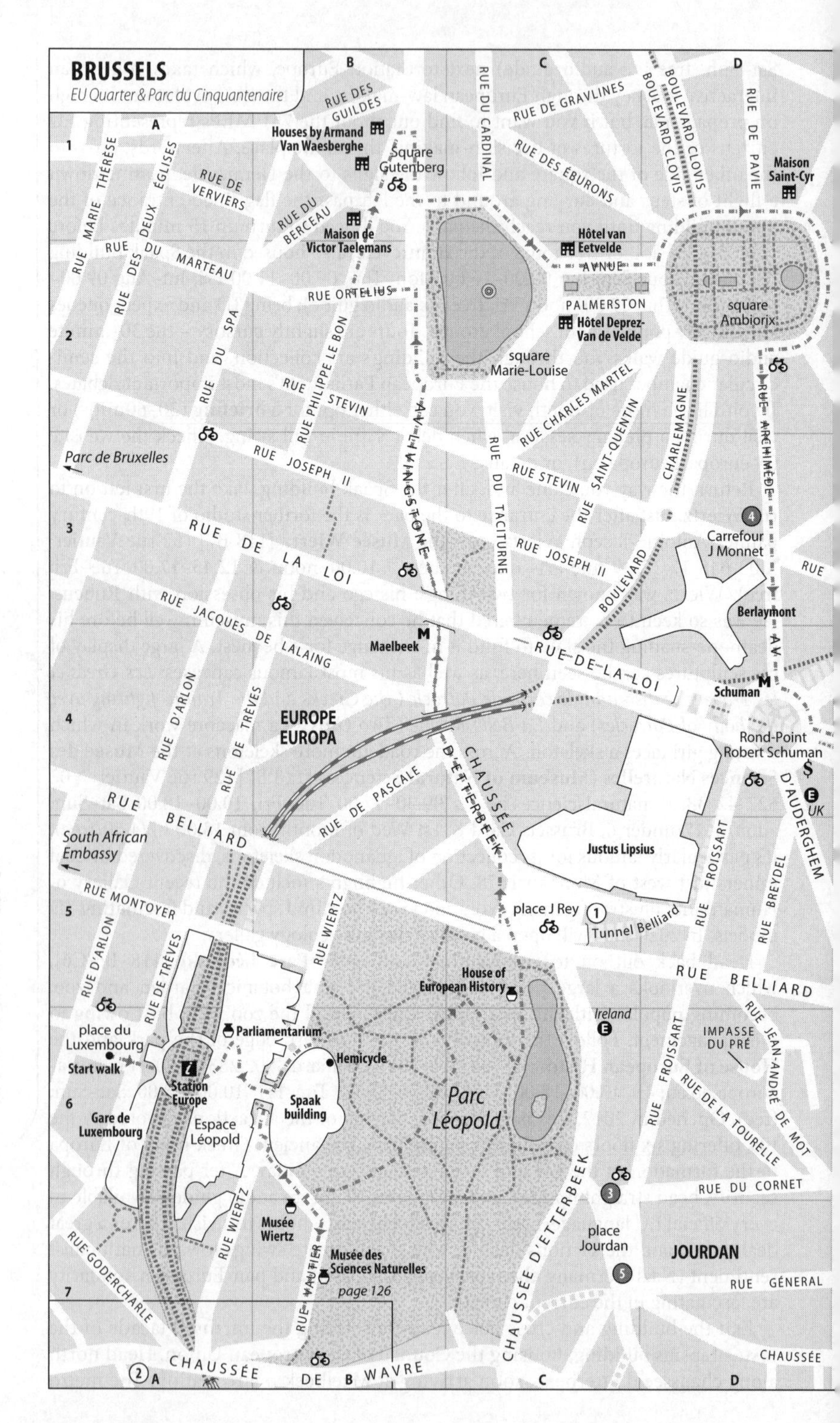
BRUSSELS
EU Quarter & Parc du Cinquantenaire
Houses by Armand Van Waesberghe
Square Gutenberg
Maison de Victor Taelemans
Hôtel van Eetvelde
Hôtel Deprez-Van de Velde
Maison Saint-Cyr
square Marie-Louise
square Ambiorix
Parc de Bruxelles
Carrefour J Monnet
Berlaymont
Maelbeek
Schuman
EUROPE EUROPA
Rond-Point Robert Schuman
UK
Justus Lipsius
South African Embassy
place J Rey
Tunnel Belliard
House of European History
Ireland
IMPASSE DU PRÉ
place du Luxembourg
Start walk
Parliamentarium
Hemicycle
Station Europe
Spaak building
Gare de Luxembourg
Espace Léopold
Parc Léopold
Musée Wiertz
Musée des Sciences Naturelles
page 126
place Jourdan
JOURDAN
RUE DES GUILDES
RUE DU CARDINAL
RUE DE GRAVLINES
BOULEVARD CLOVIS
RUE DE PAVIE
RUE MARIE THÉRÈSE
RUE DES DEUX ÉGLISES
RUE DE VERVIERS
RUE DU BERCEAU
RUE DES ÉBURONS
RUE DU MARTEAU
AVENUE PALMERSTON
RUE ORTELIUS
RUE DU SPA
RUE PHILIPPE LE BON
RUE STEVIN
AV LIVINGSTONE
RUE CHARLES MARTEL
RUE DU TACITURNE
RUE SAINT-QUENTIN
BOULEVARD CHARLEMAGNE
RUE ARCHIMÈDE
RUE JOSEPH II
RUE DE LA LOI
RUE JACQUES DE LALAING
RUE D'ARLON
RUE DE TRÈVES
CHAUSSÉE D'ETTERBEEK
RUE DE PASCALE
RUE BELLIARD
AV D'AUDERGHEM
RUE FROISSART
RUE BREYDEL
RUE MONTOYER
RUE WIERTZ
RUE JEAN-ANDRÉ DE MOT
RUE DE LA TOURELLE
RUE DU CORNET
RUE GODERCHARLE
RUE VAUTIER
RUE GÉNÉRAL
CHAUSSÉE DE WAVRE
CHAUSSÉE

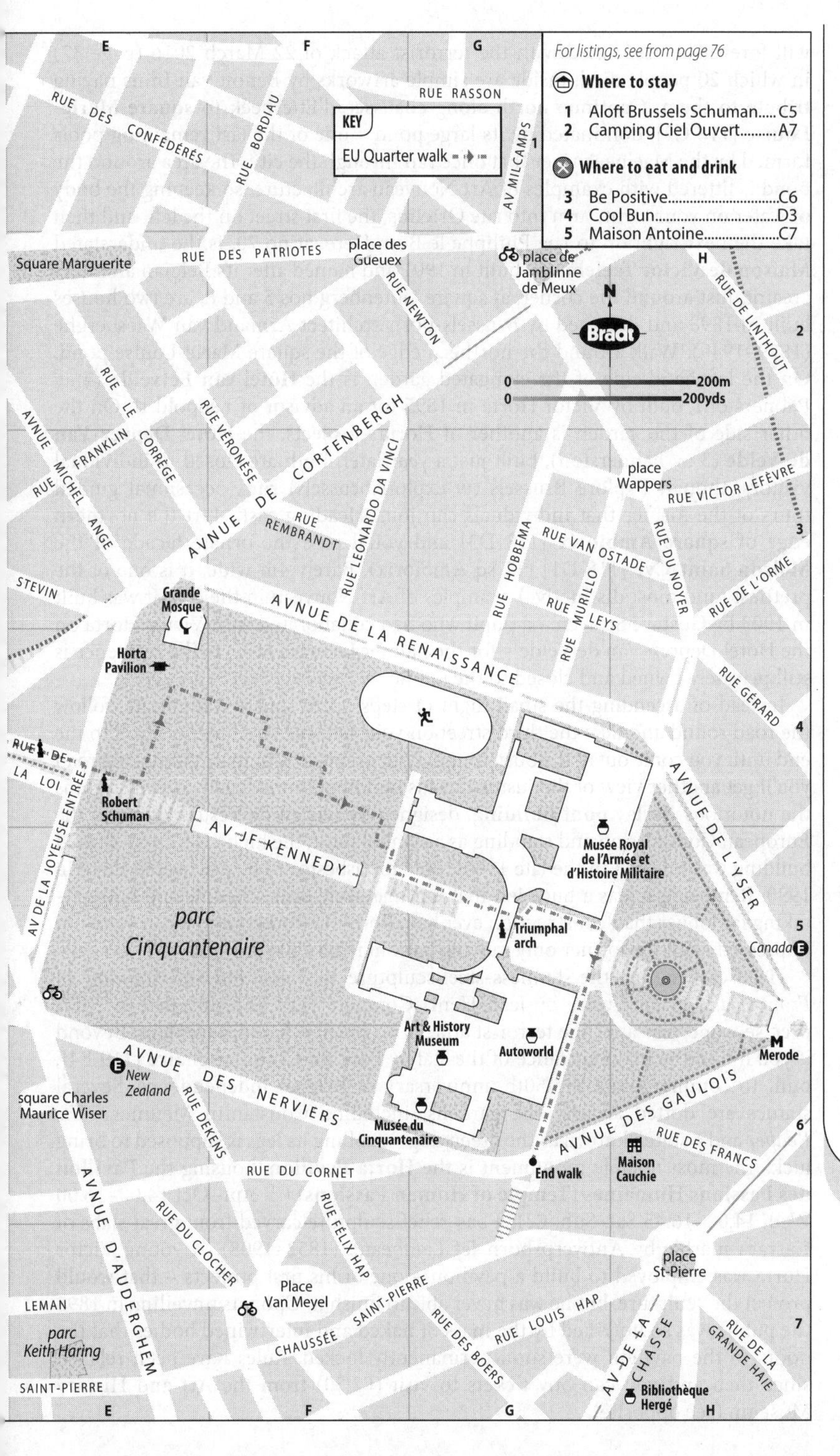
For listings, see from page 76
Where to stay
1 Aloft Brussels Schuman..... C5
2 Camping Ciel Ouvert.......... A7
Where to eat and drink
3 Be Positive..............................C6
4 Cool Bun...............................D3
5 Maison Antoine...................C7
KEY
EU Quarter walk
Bradt
0 200m
0 200yds
RUE RASSON
RUE DES CONFÉDÉRÉS
RUE BORDIAU
AV MILCAMPS
RUE DES PATRIOTES
Square Marguerite
place des Gueux
place de Jamblinne de Meux
RUE NEWTON
RUE DE LINTHOUT
RUE LE CORRÈGE
RUE FRANKLIN
AVNUE MICHEL ANGE
RUE VÉRONÈSE
AVNUE DE CORTENBERGH
RUE LEONARDO DA VINCI
RUE REMBRANDT
place Wappers
RUE VICTOR LEFÈVRE
RUE HOBBEMA
RUE VAN OSTADE
RUE DU NOYER
RUE DE L'ORME
RUE MURILLO
RUE LEYS
STEVIN
Grande Mosque
AVNUE DE LA RENAISSANCE
Horta Pavilion
RUE GÉRARD
RUE DE LA LOI
Robert Schuman
AV JF KENNEDY
AV DE LA JOYEUSE ENTRÉE
AVNUE DE L'YSER
Musée Royal de l'Armée et d'Histoire Militaire
Triumphal arch
parc Cinquantenaire
Canada
Art & History Museum
Autoworld
Merode
AVNUE DES NERVIERS
New Zealand
square Charles Maurice Wiser
RUE DEKENS
Musée du Cinquantenaire
AVNUE DES GAULOIS
RUE DES FRANCS
Maison Cauchie
End walk
RUE DU CORNET
AVNUE D'AUDERGHEM
RUE DU CLOCHER
RUE FÉLIX HAP
place St-Pierre
Place Van Meyel
CHAUSSÉE SAINT-PIERRE
RUE DES BOERS
RUE LOUIS HAP
AV DE LA CHASSE
RUE DE LA GRANDE HAIE
LEMAN
parc Keith Haring
SAINT-PIERRE
Bibliothèque Hergé
E F G H
1 2 3 4 5 6 7

will forever be associated with the terrorist attack of 22 March 2016 (page 37) in which 20 people died; inside are simple artworks by Benoît van Innis paying tribute to them. Continue north along chaussée d'Etterbeek to **square Marie-Louise** [118 C2], dominated by its large pond – one of the last remaining pools formed by the Maelbeek river that once ran through the city. The area around the pond is littered with examples of Art Nouveau architecture, so keeping the body of water on your right, turn into rue Ortelius, the first street on the left, and then take the next right on to rue Philippe le Bon. Here, at no 70, is the understated **Maison de Victor Taelemans**, built in 1901 and named after its Belgian architect creator. Just around the corner, at square Gutenberg nos 5 and 8, are two houses built in 1898 and designed by Brussels-born architect Armand van Waesberghe (1879–1949). Walk around the northern edge of the square Marie-Louise pond. On the left-hand side of the elongated garden is the **Hôtel van Eetvelde** (4 av Palmerston), built by Victor Horta in 1895 for an advisor of Leopold II. On the other side of the garden is another of Horta's projects, the **Hôtel Deprez-Van de Velde** (3 av Palmerston), built just a year later. Both are closed to individual visitors, though Explore Brussels (w explore.brussels) runs occasional guided tours of the former that individuals can join. Heading east, skirt the northern edge of **square Ambiorix** [118 D3] and you'll pass the ornate façade of the **Maison Saint-Cyr** [118 D1] (11 sq Ambiorix). Barely 4m wide, it is one of the prettiest (and most distinctive) examples of Art Nouveau in the city. It was built in 1903 by Gustave Straven – a pupil who had collaborated with Victor Horta on the Hôtel Deprez-Van de Velde – for the painter Léonard St-Cyr. The residence is still privately owned and closed to the public.

Instead of ascending the small flight of steps up to square Marguérite, follow the road round and take the third street on your left, rue Archimède. Stroll to the end until you come out at the busy roundabout on place Schuman. Across the road you'll get another view of the Justus Lipsius building. Immediately to your right is the notorious **Berlaymont building**, designed by Lucien de Vestel. Home to the European Commission and standing as a symbol for it, the high-rise, cross-shaped building was finished in the late 1960s, only for asbestos to be discovered there in 1990. Removing it was a huge job that ran massively over schedule and budget – taking far longer than construction ever had. Both EU workers and locals were not impressed, with the former only moving back in from 2004 onwards.

Head east, noting the stainless-steel sculpture *Wounded but Still Standing in Front of the Inconceivable* by Jean-Henri Compère [119 E6], unveiled in 2017, precisely one year after the terrorist attacks on Maelbeek and Zaventem. Beyond it you'll find the main entrance of the stately **Parc du Cinquantenaire** [119 E4], built to commemorate the 50th anniversary of Belgian independence. Several statues are dotted around the gardens, including Constantin Meunier's *The Reaper* and a statue known as the green dog – rubbing its legs is supposed to bring luck. The most notable monument is the **Horta Pavilion**, housing the **Pavillon des Passions Humaines (Temple of Human Passions)** (🕘 Apr–Oct 14.00–16.00 Wed, 14.00–16.45 Sat–Sun; €2), a bas-relief sculpture carved from great slabs of Carrara marble by Antwerp-born Jef Lambeaux (1852–1908). A young Victor Horta was employed to build a pavilion – one of his first projects – that would protect the sculpture, but he was never able to finish it. Upon its unveiling in 1898 the public was so horrified by the mass of naked and intertwined bodies that the doors to the pavilion were soon permanently locked. Rules have been relaxed since then and you can buy tickets to visit (€2.50) from the Art and History Museum (see opposite).

Next door to the pavilion is the **Grande Mosque** [119 E3/E4] – the oldest mosque in Belgium, which is appropriately housed in the Oriental pavilion used during the 1897 World's Fair, held here. The *pièce de la résistance* of the park, though, is the enormous **triumphal arch** [119 G5] that dominates its eastern end, topped by a bronze horse-drawn carriage that depicts Brabant raising the national flag. It's flanked by museums on both sides; a combi-ticket covers entry to all three.

Art and History Museum [119 G5] (10 Parc du Cinquantenaire; ☎ 02 741 73 31; **w** artandhistory.museum; 🕘 09.30–17.00 Tue–Fri, 10.00–17.00 Sat–Sun; adult/child €10/free, combi-ticket with Autworld and Art & History Museum €22) The former Cinquantenaire Museum morphed into the more literally named Art & History Museum in May 2018, seemingly in a bid to draw more tourists, unsure what it was all about. While its identity was still in a state of flux at the time of writing, its collections remain superb, running the gamut from Egyptian artefacts to European decorative arts and a standout display of Islamic art, ceramics and carpets.

Leaving the museum, make your way beneath the arch Turn right to visit **Autoworld** [119 G6] (11 Parc du Cinquantenaire; ☎ 02 736 41 65; **w** autoworld.be; 🕘 Apr–Sep & w/ends 10.00–18.00, Oct–Mar 10.00–17.00; adult/6–11/under 6 & Brussels Card €12/5/free, 3-museum combi-ticket €22). This enormous exhibition hall housed car and motorbike exhibitions in the early 20th century; since 1986 it has held the private collection of Ghislain Mahy, with a huge array of vintage vehicles ranging from early Cadillacs to a Rolls-Royce Silver Ghost and De Lorean sports car.

Now walk straight across the cobbles into the **Musée Royal de l'Armée et d'Histoire Militaire** (**Royal Museum of the Armed Forces and Military History**) [119 G5] (3 Parc du Cinquantenaire; ☎ 02 737 78 33; **w** klm-mra.be; 🕘 09.00–17.00 Tue–Sun; adult/6–18/under 6, Brussels Card & 1st Wed of month from 13.00 €10/8/free, 3-museum combi-ticket €22), a sprawling site covering military history from the Middle Ages to today. There's a particularly good **World War I** display, with an array of uniforms and weapons across two galleries, and tanks from World War II in the **courtyard**; at the time of writing, a new wing about Belgium's occupation and the liberation of Europe was in the works. From here you can take a free lift to the top of the triumphal arch for superb views over the city.

Exit the museum and follow the path situated to the right of Autoworld, which leads out on to avenue des Nerviens. After a few paces you will pass the entrance for the **Atelier de Moulage** (**Moulding Workshop**) (10 Parc du Cinquantenaire; ☎ 02 741 72 94; 🕘 13.30–16.00 Tue & Thu; free) on the right. Since 1876, artists here have made replicas of some of Europe's greatest sculptures. They're happy for you to walk about and you can buy various casts, with prices starting at €200. The walk ends here, but see the section on Etterbeek (page 124) if you would like to extend your visit of the area, and for more on Maison Cauchie, just next to the park.

COMMUNES

The city centre occupies just one of the region's 19 municipalities or 'communes'. The remainder are located outside the petit-ring, forming distinct districts whose tempo is determined by the broad array of ethnic groups that have settled there, lending the capital its multi-cultural DNA. Communes of most interest are covered below. In some cases attractions lie just outside the official commune borders, but I have included them where they are for practical reasons.

ANDERLECHT Saint-Guidon; see map, opposite

West of Bruxelles Midi/Brussel Zuid, the city's third-largest commune is most famous for its successful football team. Just a small village – famed for its cattle – in the 10th century, Anderlecht was incorporated into Brussels's territory in 1393 after Louis de Male, Count of Flanders, lost the Battle of Scheut to Joanna Duchess of Brabant. During the Middle Ages Anderlecht was well-known: the cult of St Guidon had attracted pilgrims en route to Santiago de Compostela and a clutch of famous residents – like Erasmus and the Duke of Aumale – had secured its reputation. Later it became an industrial centre known for its abbatoir, dating from 1888; though it's still in operation, the site now hosts a vast and colourful weekend market, as well as a new food hall. If you get hungry on your visit, you can also try the old-school **Friture René** (page 83).

Musée des Égouts (Sewer Museum) [123 G1] (Pavillons d'Octroi, Porte d'Anderlecht; 02 279 43 83; w sewermuseum.brussels; 10.00–17.00 Tue–Sat; adult/under 18 €8/free; tram: 51/82 to Pte d'Anderlecht) This under-the-radar, occasionally stinky spot takes you into the bowels of the city's sewer system, implemented at the same time as the fetid river Senne was filled in around 1867. There's a quirky display of objects that cropped up in the pipes, from wedding rings to revolvers. For a more comprehensive overview, there is a free guided tour at 14.30 and 15.30 on the first Saturday of the month – book ahead.

Maison d'Erasme (Erasmus House) [123A/B3] (31 rue du Formanoir; 02 521 13 83; w erasmushouse.museum; 10.00–18.00 Tue–Sun; €1.25 inc entry to the béguinage (see below) or free with Brussels Card; Saint-Guidon) A gem of a museum dedicated to the life and works of Dutch humanist and theologian Desiderius Erasmus of Rotterdam. An exceptional scholar, the Renaissance writer is best known for his translation of the New Testament from Greek into Latin. In 1521 he lived for five months in one of the Saint-Guidon collegial houses, before moving permanently to Switzerland. Today, the house contains a museum – highlights include a first edition of his seminal *In Praise of Folly* (1509) and Flemish Primitive artworks – plus a world-class library of Erasmus literature and a small garden filled with 16th-century medicinal plants believed to have been used by Erasmus himself.

Béguinage [123 A3] (8 rue du Chapelain; 10.00–noon & 14.00–17.00 Tue–Sun; €1.25, inc entry to Erasmus House; Saint-Guidon) The only surviving béguinage in Brussels (and Belgium's smallest) was built in 1252 from donations bestowed by a visiting canon. It has served as a museum since 1930, and contains assorted archaeological exhibits, religious art and a restored kitchen.

Collégiale Sts-Pierre-et-Guidon (Collegiate Church of St Peter and Guy) [123 A3] (pl de la Vaillance; 02 523 02 20; Saint-Guidon) Quoted as one of the prettiest churches in Brussels, the Gothic building that you see today was built by Jan van Ruysbroeck of Brussels town hall fame. Interred in the **crypt**, built at the time of the first Roman church here, is an unmarked tomb believed to be that of St Guy, an 11th-century priest who made a disastrous investment in a trading venture and embarked on a long pilgrimage, dying on his return home. A historical procession with giant puppets based on his life usually takes place on the second Tuesday in September (w anderlecht.be).

Gueuze Museum – Cantillon [123 F2] (56 rue Gheude; 02 521 49 28; w cantillon.be; 10.00–17.00 Mon–Tue & Thu–Sat; Clemenceau) Seventy years

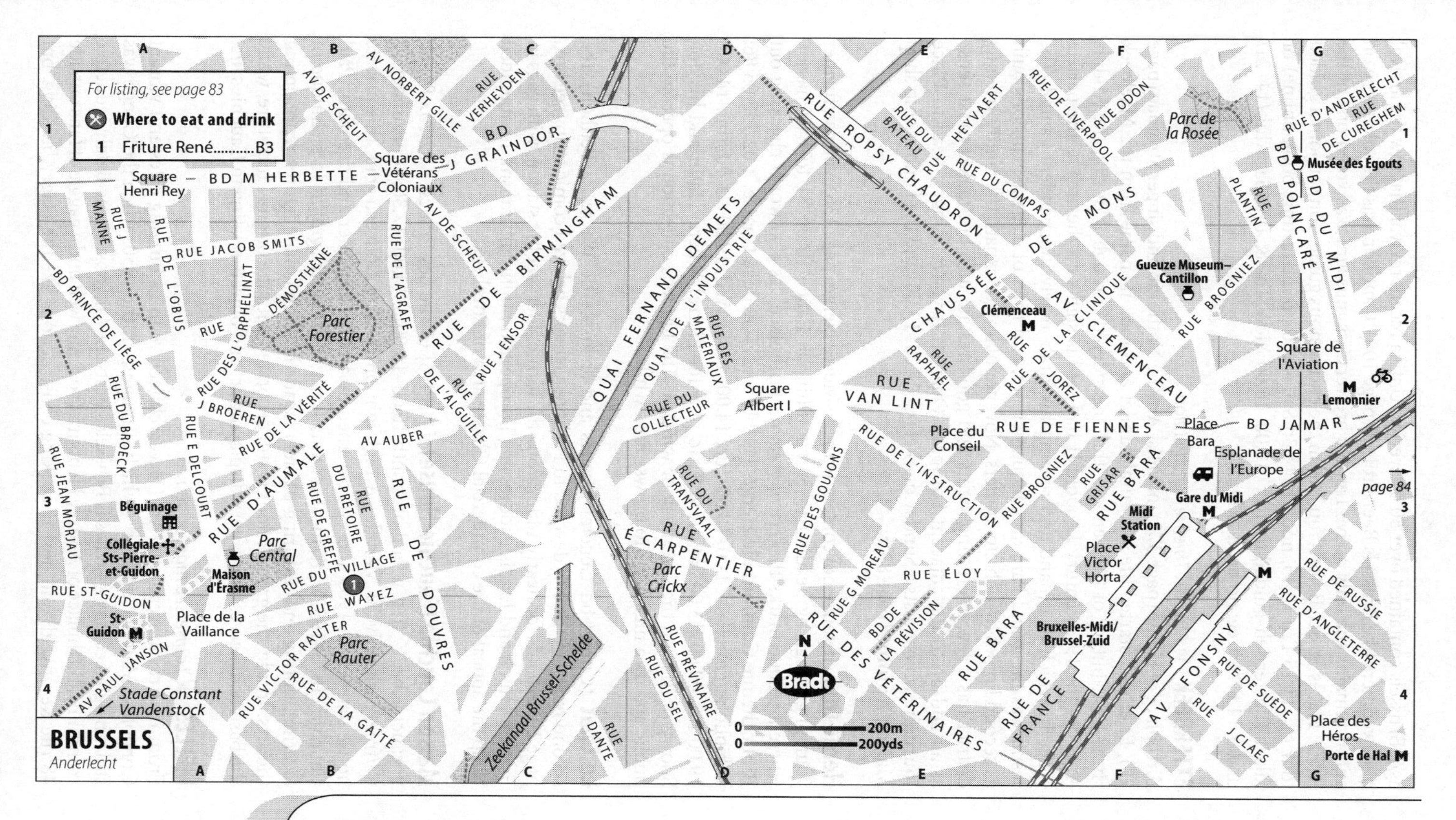
BRUSSELS
Anderlecht
For listing, see page 83
Where to eat and drink
1 Friture René..........B3
Square Henri Rey
BD M HERBETTE
Square des Vétérans Coloniaux
BD J GRAINDOR
AV NORBERT GILLE
RUE VERHEYDEN
AV DE SCHEUT
RUE DE BIRMINGHAM
QUAI FERNAND DEMETS
QUAI DE L'INDUSTRIE
RUE DES MATÉRIAUX
RUE DU COLLECTEUR
Square Albert I
RUE VAN LINT
RUE ROPSY CHAUDRON
CHAUSSÉE DE MONS
AV CLÉMENCEAU
RUE DE LA CLINIQUE
RUE JOREZ
RUE RAPHAËL
Clémenceau
RUE DE FIENNES
Place du Conseil
RUE DE L'INSTRUCTION
RUE BROGNIEZ
RUE GRISAR
RUE BARA
Place Bara
BD JAMAR
Esplanade de l'Europe
Gare du Midi
Midi Station
Place Victor Horta
Bruxelles-Midi/ Brussel-Zuid
AV FONSNY
RUE J CLAES
RUE DE SUÈDE
RUE D'ANGLETERRE
RUE DE RUSSIE
Place des Héros
Porte de Hal
Square de l'Aviation
Lemonnier
page 84
BD POINCARÉ
BD DU MIDI
RUE D'ANDERLECHT
RUE DE CUREGHEM
Musée des Égouts
RUE PLANTIN
Parc de la Rosée
RUE ODON
RUE DE LIVERPOOL
RUE HEYVAERT
RUE DU BATEAU
RUE DU COMPAS
Gueuze Museum–Cantillon
RUE BROGNIEZ
RUE J MANNE
RUE JACOB SMITS
RUE DE L'OBUS
BD PRINCE DE LIÈGE
RUE DÉMOSTHÈNE
RUE DES L'ORPHELINAT
Parc Forestier
RUE DE L'AGRAFE
RUE J ENSOR
RUE DE L'ALGUILLE
RUE J BROEREN
RUE DE LA VÉRITÉ
RUE DU BROECK
RUE E DELCOURT
RUE D'AUMALE
AV AUBER
RUE DE GREFFE
RUE DU PRÉTOIRE
RUE DE DOUVRES
RUE JEAN MORJAU
Béguinage
Collégiale Sts-Pierre-et-Guidon
Maison d'Érasme
Parc Central
RUE DU VILLAGE
RUE WAYEZ
RUE ST-GUIDON
St-Guidon
Place de la Vaillance
AV PAUL JANSON
Stade Constant Vandenstock
RUE VICTOR RAUTER
Parc Rauter
RUE DE LA GAÎTÉ
Zeekanaal Brussel-Schelde
RUE DANTE
RUE DU SEL
RUE PRÉVINAIRE
RUE É CARPENTIER
Parc Crickx
RUE DU TRANSVAAL
RUE DES GOUJONS
RUE G MOREAU
RUE ÉLOY
BD DE LA RÉVISION
RUE DES VÉTÉRINAIRES
RUE DE FRANCE
N
Bradt
0 200m
0 200yds

ago, Brussels contained over 50 breweries. Until a recent revival that saw the arrival of newcomers like Brussels Beer Project (page 105), Cantillon was the sole survivor, and it remains the only active Lambic brewery. Its museum was voted one of the '1,000 Places To See Before You Die' in the eponymous guide. You can join a guided tour (🕘 11.15 Fri, 10.45, noon & 14.30 Sat; €9.50 pp inc tasting; book online) or take a shorter self-guided tour (🕘 10.00–16.00 Mon–Tue & Thu–Sat adult/14–21/under 14 €7/6/free; no need to book).

ETTERBEEK *Mérode, Thieffrey and Pétillon*

Birthplace of Hergé (page 372), novelist Amélie Nothomb and singer Stromae (page 28), Etterbeek started life as a rural hamlet and took its name from the Maelbeek river – a tributary of the Senne – that meandered through it during the Middle Ages. By the 19th century Leopold II had set his sights on the area as the perfect space in which to expand and revamp his 'drab' newly independent capital. The result was the grand Parc du Cinquantenaire, and rows of elegant mansions built as second homes by rich city traders. Now popular with expats, the family-friendly district has a few interesting sights and good restaurants, but makes most sense as an add-on to the adjacent European Quarter. If you're hungry, head to **Place Jourdain**, which hosts a Sunday market (🕘 07.00–13.00) and the famous chip shop **Maison Antoine** (page 83).

Hergé tour If you're not content with the Musée Hergé (page 136), you can further your pilgrimage by heading to 33 rue Philippe Baucq (tram 81 to La Chasse), where a plaque marks the *Tintin* creator's birthplace. It's also worth checking out **Bibliothèque Communale Hergé** [119 H7] (211 av de la Chasse; 📞 02 735 05 86; w biblioherge.be; 🕘 14.00–18.00 Tue, 14.00–19.00 Wed, 10.00–18.00 Thu, 14.00–19.00 Fri, 09.00–13.00 Sat; tram 81 to pl Saint-Pierre), where Tintin and his dog Snowy peek from the second-floor window. The library's collection is open to the public and it's a nice place to browse for a while.

Le Chat (Cnr of bd Général Jacques and chaussée de Wavre; Pétillon) The second mural in the city devoted to Philippe Geluck's beloved comic strip (see box, page 22) extends for nearly 140m along the former Géruzet fire station, with gags in French, Dutch and English addressing Europe and multi-culturalism. It's intended to up the appeal of the commercial Chasse area of Etterbeek.

Maison Cauchie (Cauchie House) [119 H6] (5 rue des Francs; 📞 02 733 86 84; w cauchie.be; 🕘 first w/end of month 10.00–13.00 & 14.00–17.30; adult/under 12 €7/free, cash only; Mérode) A highlight on the Art Nouveau trail, this private house dates from 1905 and was designed by architect, painter and decorator Paul Cauchie (1875–1952). It's most famous for its distinctive *sgraffiti* (a technique of layering, tinting and texturing plaster) façade bearing female figures representing the arts. Inside, the ground floor is still decorated with the original furniture, while the basement serves as a gallery displaying art and objects relating to Cauchie's life.

IXELLES *Louise; see map, page 126*

From its Art Nouveau and Art Deco architecture to its buzzing cafés and vibrant Congolese Matongé quarter – which sprang up in the 1950s when the Congo was still a Belgian colony – Ixelles is Brussels's best-known, most immediately seductive commune. Birthplace of Audrey Hepburn (you may well find a gaggle of fans outside 48 rue Keyenveld) and host to striking constructions like the Flagey building, but also leafy ponds and a tranquil abbey, it abounds in wonderful boutiques, from the well-heeled avenue Louise to the one-off shops around place du Châtelain, also an after-work drinking spot.

Musée d'Ixelles [127 H3] (71 rue Jean van Volsem; ☎ 02 515 64 21; w musee-ixelles.be; ⏱ closed for renovation) This ex-slaughterhouse houses a fine 19th- and 20th-century art horde – though sadly it's shut for renovation until 2023.

Flagey [127 H4] (18 pl Flagey; tram 81 to Flagey) Nicknamed *le paquebot jaune* or 'yellow steamship' by locals, the mast of this Art Deco former radio broadcasting tower is highly distinctive. It was saved from demolition, and its conversion to a cultural centre has been a great success story for the commune. Café Belga (page 83) at its base is hugely popular with residents, also drawn by the square's daily market (⏱ 07.00–13.00), devoted to food in the week.

Hôtel Tassel [127 E4] (9 rue Paul-Emile Janson; tram 8/93 to Bailli) The UNESCO-listed Hôtel Tassel was built by Victor Horta for his friend Emile Tassel. Fresh from completing the Maison Autrique in Schaerbeek (page 132), and armed with a larger budget, Horta could finally implement the full extravagance of his designs. When the house was completed in 1894, its exquisite attention to detail caused a sensation and changed the face of architecture overnight, cementing Horta's celebrity status. Revolutionary features such as the central position of the front door, the large windows, columns and curved ironwork can be seen from the street. To see inside, you can either take an English tour with Explore Brussels (w explore.brussels) or visit during their biennial Art Nouveau and Art Deco BANAD festival (page 52).

Hôtel Solvay [127 F4] (224 av Louise; tram 8/93 to Bailli) The construction of this house was the result of a commission hot off the back of the success of the Hôtel Tassel. Built for Armand Solvay, son of the engineer and chemist Ernest Solvay, it was completed in 1898 and perhaps is best known for its low balcony that allowed the family to sit and watch those walking along trendy avenue Louise. In 2000 the house was added to the UNESCO World Heritage list. Tours are as above.

Musée Constantin Meunier (Constantin Meunier Museum) [127 F7] (59 rue de l'Abbaye; ☎ 02 648 44 49; w fine-arts-museum.be; ⏱ 10.00–noon & 12.45–17.00 Tue–Fri; free; tram 8/93 to Abbaye) A celebrated painter and sculptor, Meunier (1831–1905) commissioned the construction of this house at the height of his fame, with the sole intention that it should serve as his last residence and studio. The small museum was acquired by the state in 1936 and opened to visitors in 1939. It showcases over 150 paintings and drawings executed during the latter half of Meunier's life, when he began to focus on the burgeoning industrialisation in Belgium and, in particular, the mines in Wallonia. This later period of work inspired some of his greatest sculptures still dotted around Brussels today, including *Cheval à l'Abreuvoir* (*The Horse at the Pond*) on square Ambiorix. Meunier lies in the Cimetière d'Ixelles (see below).

Cimetière d'Ixelles (Ixelles Cemetery) [127 H7] (chaussée de Boondael; bus 95 to Thys) Set up for victims of a cholera outbreak in the early 19th century, this cemetery is the final resting place of a stellar line-up of history's greats, including Art Nouveau master Victor Horta, praline inventor Frédéric Neuhaus

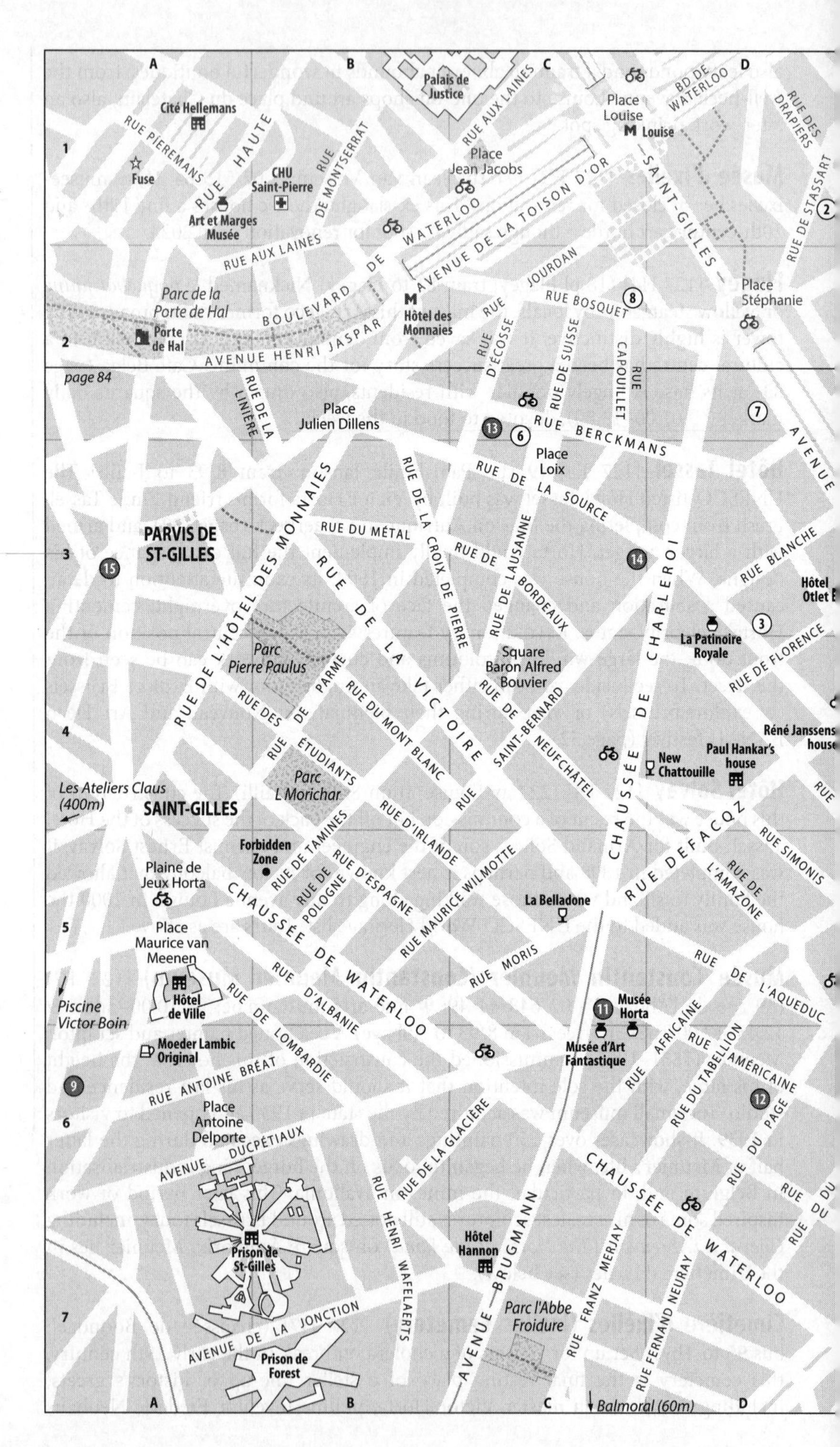

Palais de Justice
Place Louise
Louise
BD DE WATERLOO
RUE DES DRAPIERS
Cité Hellemans
RUE PIEREMANS
RUE HAUTE
Fuse
CHU Saint-Pierre
RUE DE MONTSERRAT
RUE AUX LAINES
Place Jean Jacobs
Art et Marges Musée
BOULEVARD DE WATERLOO
AVENUE DE LA TOISON D'OR
SAINT-GILLES
RUE DE STASSART
Parc de la Porte de Hal
Porte de Hal
AVENUE HENRI JASPAR
Hôtel des Monnaies
RUE JOURDAN
RUE BOSQUET
Place Stéphanie
RUE D'ÉCOSSE
RUE DE SUISSE
RUE CAPOUILLET
page 84
RUE DE LA LINIÈRE
Place Julien Dillens
RUE BERCKMANS
Place Loix
AVENUE
RUE DE LA SOURCE
RUE DU MÉTAL
RUE DE LA CROIX DE PIERRE
RUE DE LAUSANNE
RUE DE BORDEAUX
PARVIS DE ST-GILLES
RUE DE L'HÔTEL DES MONNAIES
RUE DE LA VICTOIRE
CHAUSSÉE DE CHARLEROI
RUE BLANCHE
Hôtel Otlet
La Patinoire Royale
RUE DE FLORENCE
Parc Pierre Paulus
Square Baron Alfred Bouvier
RUE DE PARME
RUE DES ÉTUDIANTS
RUE DU MONT BLANC
RUE SAINT-BERNARD
RUE DE NEUFCHÂTEL
Réné Janssens house
Paul Hankar's house
New Chattouille
Les Ateliers Claus (400m)
Parc L Morichar
SAINT-GILLES
RUE D'IRLANDE
RUE DEFACQZ
RUE SIMONIS
Forbidden Zone
RUE DE TAMINES
RUE DE POLOGNE
RUE D'ESPAGNE
RUE MAURICE WILMOTTE
RUE DE L'AMAZONE
Plaine de Jeux Horta
La Belladone
Place Maurice van Meenen
CHAUSSÉE DE WATERLOO
RUE MORIS
RUE DE L'AQUEDUC
RUE D'ALBANIE
Hôtel de Ville
Piscine Victor Boin
RUE DE LOMBARDIE
Musée Horta
Musée d'Art Fantastique
RUE AFRICAINE
RUE AMÉRICAINE
RUE DU TABELLION
Moeder Lambic Original
RUE ANTOINE BRÉAT
Place Antoine Delporte
AVENUE DUCPÉTIAUX
RUE DE LA GLACIÈRE
RUE DU PAGE
RUE HENRI WAFELAERTS
CHAUSSÉE DE WATERLOO
RUE DU
Prison de St-Gilles
AVENUE BRUGMANN
Hôtel Hannon
RUE FRANZ MERJAY
RUE FERNAND NEURAY
Parc l'Abbe Froidure
AVENUE DE LA JONCTION
Prison de Forest
Balmoral (60m)

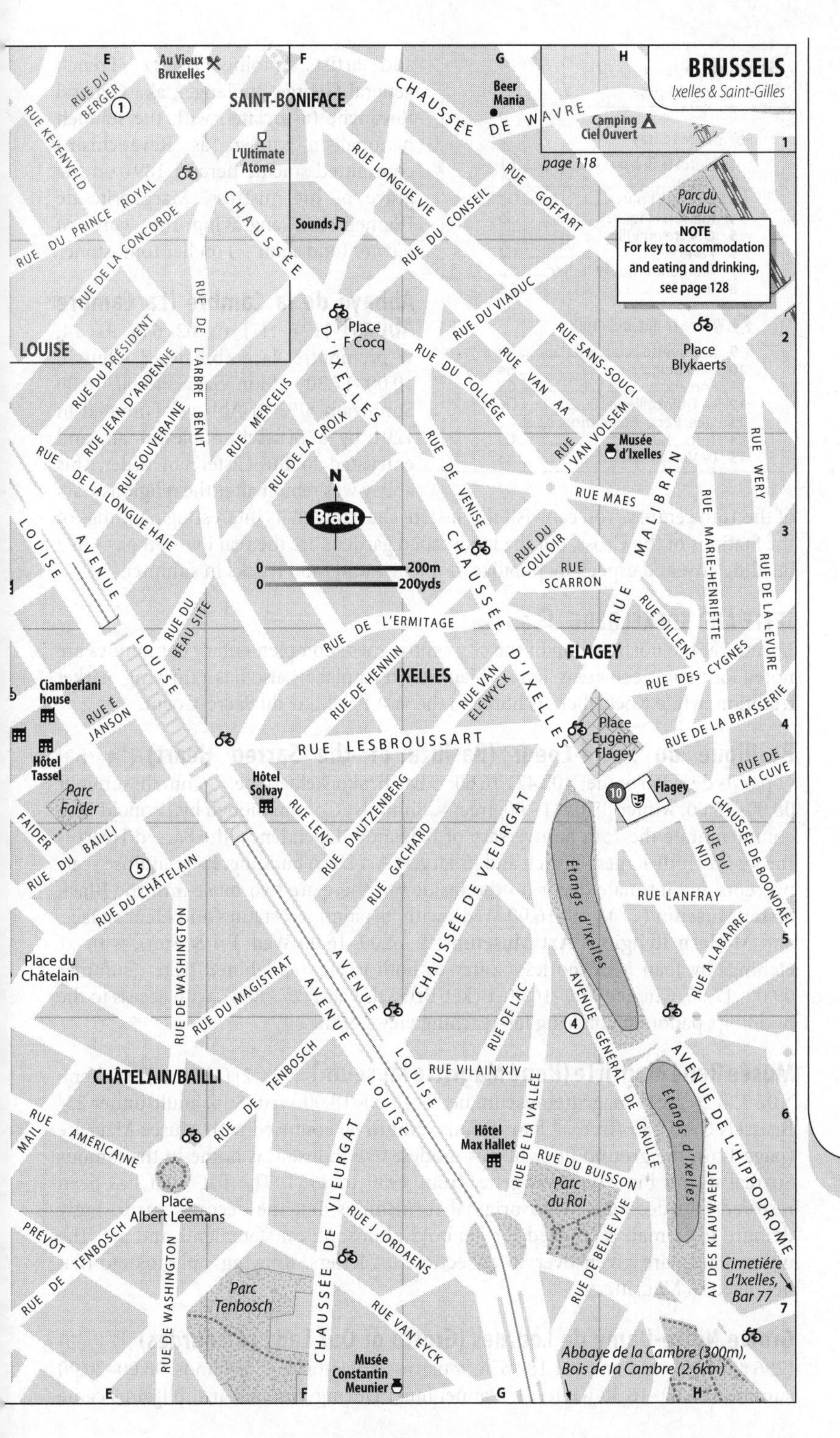
BRUSSELS
Ixelles & Saint-Gilles
NOTE
For key to accommodation and eating and drinking, see page 128
page 118
SAINT-BONIFACE
LOUISE
IXELLES
FLAGEY
CHÂTELAIN/BAILLI
Au Vieux Bruxelles
L'Ultimate Atome
Sounds
Beer Mania
Camping Ciel Ouvert
Parc du Viaduc
Place F Cocq
Place Blykaerts
Musée d'Ixelles
Place Eugène Flagey
Flagey
Ciamberlani house
Hôtel Tassel
Parc Faider
Hôtel Solvay
Place du Châtelain
Place Albert Leemans
Parc Tenbosch
Musée Constantin Meunier
Hôtel Max Hallet
Parc du Roi
Étangs d'Ixelles
Cimetière d'Ixelles, Bar 77
Abbaye de la Cambre (300m), Bois de la Cambre (2.6km)
0 200m
0 200yds
Bradt
N
CHAUSSÉE DE WAVRE
CHAUSSÉE D'IXELLES
CHAUSSÉE DE VLEURGAT
CHAUSSÉE DE BOONDAEL
AVENUE LOUISE
AVENUE GÉNÉRAL DE GAULLE
AVENUE DE L'HIPPODROME
AV DES KLAUWAERTS
RUE DU BERGER
RUE KEYENVELD
RUE DU PRINCE ROYAL
RUE DE LA CONCORDE
RUE DU PRÉSIDENT
RUE JEAN D'ARDENNE
RUE SOUVERAINE
RUE DE L'ARBRE BÉNIT
RUE DE LA LONGUE HAIE
RUE MERCELIS
RUE DE LA CROIX
RUE LONGUE VIE
RUE DU CONSEIL
RUE GOFFART
RUE DU VIADUC
RUE DU COLLÈGE
RUE VAN AA
RUE SANS-SOUCI
RUE J VAN VOLSEM
RUE MAES
RUE MALIBRAN
RUE WERY
RUE MARIE-HENRIETTE
RUE DE LA LEVURE
RUE DE VENISE
RUE DU COULOIR
RUE SCARRON
RUE DILLENS
RUE DES CYGNES
RUE DE LA BRASSERIE
RUE DE LA CUVE
RUE DU NID
RUE LANFRAY
RUE A LABARRE
RUE DU BEAU SITE
RUE DE L'ERMITAGE
RUE DE HENNIN
RUE VAN ELEWYCK
RUE É JANSON
RUE LESBROUSSART
RUE LENS
RUE DAUTZENBERG
RUE GACHARD
FAIDER
RUE DU BAILLI
RUE DU CHÂTELAIN
RUE DE WASHINGTON
RUE DU MAGISTRAT
RUE DE TENBOSCH
RUE VILAIN XIV
RUE DE LAC
RUE DE LA VALLÉE
RUE DU BUISSON
RUE DE BELLE VUE
RUE MAIL
RUE AMÉRICAINE
PRÉVÔT
RUE J JORDAENS
RUE VAN EYCK

BRUSSELS *Ixelles & St-Gilles*
For listings, see from page 76

Where to stay

1	Hotel le Berger	E1
2	Hygge	D1
3	Made in Louise	D3
4	Maison Flagey	G6
5	Odette en Ville	E5
6	Pantone	C2
7	Steigenberger Wiltcher's	D2
8	Vintage	C2

Where to eat and drink

9	La Buvette	A6
10	Café Belga	H4
11	Forcado	C5
12	La Quincaillerie	D6
13	Sale, Pepe, Rosmarino	C2
14	Tero	C3
15	Le Verschueren	A3

and artist Antoine Wiertz. French general George Boulanger, aka Général Revanche (associated with the staunch nationalism known as Revanchism) committed suicide here in 1891 on the grave of his mistress, Marguérite de Bonnemains, engraving the words *à bientôt* (and soon…) on her tombstone.

Abbaye de la Cambre (La Cambre Abbey) [127 H7] (02 648 91 14; w premontres-lacambre.be; church: 10.00–17.30 Mon–Sat, 13.00–18.00 Sun; tram 8/93 to Abbaye) Founded in 1201 by a Brussels noblewoman, and entrusted to the Cistercian order, this abbey was rebuilt after the religious wars of the 16th century. You can visit the austere church with its interesting paintings of the Stations of the Cross, but the landscaped gardens are the real joy – an oasis in a bustling city, and especially popular for picnics and food trucks in summer.

JETTE AND KOEKELBERG *Belgica*

Located at the northern tip of the city centre, these complementary communes are noted for their green areas. Jette – Magritte's birthplace – also has a thriving market tradition, while Koekelberg is home to the vast Basilique du Sacré-Coeur.

Basilique du Sacré-Coeur (Basilica of the Sacred Heart) [74 B3] (1 parvis de la Basilique; 02 421 16 60; w basilicakoekelberg.be; church: summer 08.00–18.00, winter 08.00–17.00; free; Simonis) Commissioned by Leopold II to commemorate the 75th anniversary of Belgian independence, the Sacred Heart is the world's fifth-largest church and its largest Art Deco building. Its grandiose scale prevents any intimate décor on the inside but there are two museums: the **Black Sister Museum** (14.00–16.00 Wed), with its paintings, statues and Flemish lace, and **Modern Religious Art Museum** (14.00–16.00 Wed–Fri & Sun), with 31 etchings by Joan Miró no less. Entry to both is via a combined ticket (summer 09.00–17.00, winter 10.00–16.00; ticket/Brussels Card €6/–40%), with access to the building's panorama offering far-reaching views of the city.

Musée René Magritte (René Magritte Museum) [74 C2] (135 rue Esseghem; 02 428 26 26; w magrittemuseum.be; 10.00–18.00 Wed–Sun; adult/under 23/ Brussels Card €8/6/free; Pannenhuis) Not to be confused with Musée Magritte (page 116), the ground floor of this modest townhouse was home to the famous Surrealist and his wife, Georgette, from 1930 to 1954. The flat itself has been restored and decorated with original furnishings, but the décor is surprisingly demure for a man renowned for his bold philosophical statements and art. The upper floors are given over to collections of letters, drawings, photos etc that belonged to Magritte.

Grotte Notre-Dame de Lourdes (Grotto of Our Lady of Lourdes) [74 C3] (296 rue Léopold I; m 0491 182 656; w paroissesdejette.be; grounds: 08.00–20.00 summer, 08.00–16.30 winter; Pannenhuis) During World War I, pilgrims came en masse to the little church that stood here to beg Our Lady of Lourdes to protect the soldiers. With so many visitors, the Father at the time decided to erect a grotto – with nearly 20,000 people attending its inauguration. Its popularity declined in the 1970s but it was happily saved from destruction by the locals, and is now run by volunteers.

Belgian Chocolate Village [78 A1] (20 rue de Neck; 02 420 70 76; belgianchocolatevillage.be; 09.00–18.00 Tue–Sun; adult/6–18/under 6 & Brussels Card €8/5/free; Heysel) Small but fun interactive chocolate museum whose highlights include a permanent exhibition of Brussels icons rendered – naturally – in chocolate. It's worth visiting just for the café, where you shouldn't miss the white hot chocolate (you can also book 15 days ahead for a chocolate-making workshop).

LAEKEN *Heysel/Stuyvenbergh*

A separate commune until 1921 but now part of the city of Brussels, Laeken houses the Belgian royal family's home and greenhouses, two follies constructed by Leopold II – the Chinese Pavilion and Japanese Tower – the celebrated Atomium and its new design-hub neighbour the ADAM museum.

Château Royal de Laeken (Royal Palace of Laeken) [130 G4] (av du Parc Royal; Bockstael then bus 53 to Serres Royales) The official home of the Belgian royal family, this Louis XVI-style palace was built as a summer residence for the governor of the Austrian Netherlands in 1784, and Napoleon later stayed here. While it's closed to the public, the nearby Serres royales de Laeken can be visited.

Serres royales de Laeken (Royal Greenhouses of Laeken) [130 G4] (av du Parc Royale; w monarchie.be; adult/under 12 €2.50/free; mid-Apr–early-May, see website) Open to the public for three weeks each spring, and worth seeing not only for the plants, just coming into bloom, but for the glass and metal Neoclassical structures themselves. Belgians flock from across the country to visit the site, so be prepared to queue. Opposite the royal estate, the glorious English-style **Parc de Laeken**, laid out by the architect of the Bois de La Cambre, stretches north towards the Heysel Plateau and Atomium.

Pavillon Chinois and Tour Japonaise (Chinese Pavilion and Japanese Tower) [130 G3] (44 av Jules van Praet; w kmkg-mrah.be; closed for renovation). In the northern corner of Parc de Laeken, just a 10-minute walk from the greenhouses, these out-of-place oriental buildings were also commissioned by Leopold II when he returned from the 1900 Paris World's Fair and wanted to erect something similar to impress visiting dignitaries. Sadly both buildings (and the nearby Museum of Japanese Art, which collectively formed the Museums of the Far East here) are closed for renovation, but it's still worth having a glimpse en route through the park.

Atomium [130 C2] (bd du Centenaire; 02 475 47 75; w atomium.be; 10.00–18.00; adult/>115cm/<115cm/Brussels Card €15/8/free/–25%; Heysel) Towering over the Heysel Plateau, Belgium's answer to the Eiffel Tower is a set of silver balls representing an iron molecule magnified 165 million times. Built for the 1958 World's Fair, the 102m-high sculpture was never intended to be permanent but has become such a familiar fixture on the Brussels skyline that

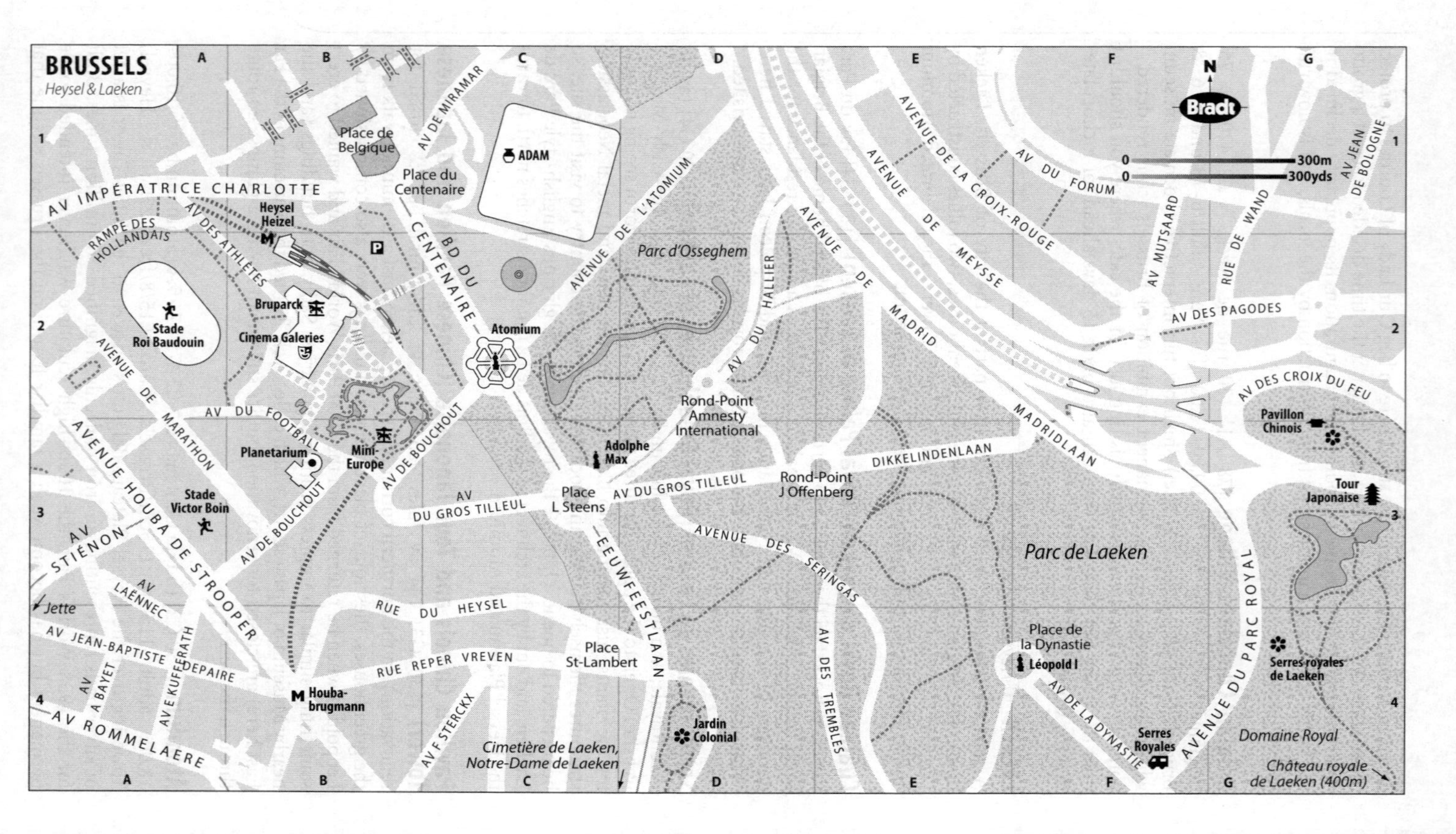
BRUSSELS
Heysel & Laeken
Bradt
N
0 300m
0 300yds
AV IMPÉRATRICE CHARLOTTE
RAMPE DES HOLLANDAIS
AV DES ATHLÈTES
Heysel Heizel
Place de Belgique
Place du Centenaire
AV DE MIRAMAR
ADAM
BD DU CENTENAIRE
AVENUE DE L'ATOMIUM
Parc d'Osseghem
Atomium
Stade Roi Baudouin
Bruparck
Cinema Galeries
AVENUE DE MARATHON
AV DU FOOTBALL
Planetarium
Mini-Europe
AV DE BOUCHOUT
Stade Victor Boin
AVENUE HOUBA DE STROOPER
AV STIÉNON
Jette
AV LAËNNEC
AV JEAN-BAPTISTE DEPAIRE
AV E KUFFERATH
AV A BAYET
AV ROMMELAERE
Houba-brugmann
RUE REPER VREVEN
RUE DU HEYSEL
AV F STERCKX
Cimetière de Laeken, Notre-Dame de Laeken
Place St-Lambert
EEUWFEESTLAAN
Jardin Colonial
Adolphe Max
Place L Steens
AV DU GROS TILLEUL
Rond-Point Amnesty International
AV DU HALLIER
Rond-Point J Offenberg
DIKKELINDENLAAN
AVENUE DES SERINGAS
AV DES TREMBLES
AVENUE DE MADRID
AVENUE DE MEYSSE
AVENUE DE LA CROIX-ROUGE
AV DU FORUM
AV MUTSAARD
RUE DE WAND
AV JEAN DE BOLOGNE
AV DES PAGODES
AV DES CROIX DU FEU
MADRIDLAAN
Pavillon Chinois
Tour Japonaise
Parc de Laeken
Place de la Dynastie
Léopold I
AV DE LA DYNASTIE
Serres Royales
AVENUE DU PARC ROYAL
Serres royales de Laeken
Domaine Royal
Château royale de Laeken (400m)
A B C D E F G
1 2 3 4

€27.5 million was raised to fund its renovation in 2006. It now includes an exhibition centre, classy restaurant (☎ 02 479 58 50; w atomiumrestaurant.be) and panoramic viewing station.

ADAM [130 C1] (pl de Belgique; ☎ 02 669 49 29; w adamuseum.be; ⏲ 10.00–18.00; adult/6–17/under 6 €10/8/free, or free with Atomium ticket, inc audio guide; Ⓜ Heysel) Celebrating 20th- and 21st-century design, this recently launched museum revolves around Brussels collector Philippe Decelle's one-off Plasticarium – a superb collection of pop objects from the iMAC to rare works by Joe Colombo and Ettore Sottsass. Fine temporary shows – eg: about nightclub design – are also included with your Atomium ticket.

Mini-Europe [130 B3] (Bruparck; ☎ 02 478 05 50; w minieurope.com; ⏲ Mar–Jun & Sep–Oct 09.30–18.00 daily; Jul–Aug 09.30–20.00 daily; Oct–early Jan 10.00–18.00 daily; adult/under 12/Brussels Card €15.80/11.80/2, combi-ticket with Atomium & ADAM €27.60/18.10) The leisure park at the foot of the Atomium; it features fun scale models of Europe's most famous landmarks, from Big Ben to the Colosseum.

SCHAERBEEK Ⓜ *Botanique; see map, page 133*

Nicknamed the Cité des anes – 'commune of the donkeys' – and bearing cherries on its coat of arms, the capital's largest municipality hails from country stock. After the 1830 revolution, Schaerbeek was granted independence from Brussels and development soon followed. By the end of the 19th century it was one of the most desirable districts for property, and Art Nouveau and Art Deco masters rushed to make their mark on the area. Interestingly, Jacques Brel (page 370) was born here, and Magritte (page 371) lived here at the end of his life.

An influx of Turkish immigrants during the latter half of the 20th century marked a turning point in the commune's reputation and, like Molenbeek, it was unwittingly thrust into the spotlight for all the wrong reasons in the wake of the 2016 terrorist attacks (page 37). But, with young couples and families attracted by low property prices and the area's authentic character, and a major new railway museum to shout about, its fortunes are on the rise. Visit now and you'll discover a diverse, unmistakably grand district where Art Nouveau hotspots have been restored, new art centres have thrown open their doors and contented residents kick back in the wonderful Parc Josaphat.

Maison Communale [133 C1] (pl Colignon; ⏲ 08.00–13.00 Mon–Wed & Fri, 08.00–19.00 Thu; free; tram 92 to Pogge) Schaerbeek's majestic town hall is considered one of the region's finest – it presumably offsets the bureaucratic tedium for expats (many English) applying for residency cards here! Built in Flemish Renaissance style in 1887, it was gutted by fire in 1911 but the façade is original. Note the cute donkey topiary out front, and then head inside – you're welcome to stroll around the sublime *salle des guichets* (ticket hall) and admire the many artworks on the ground floor. The commune runs free French tours every first Friday of the month and can arrange private English tours for €65 (☎ 02 240 34 82; e patrimoine@schaerbeek.be; w schaerbeek.be).

La Maison des Arts (House of Arts) [133 B3] (147 chaussée d'Haecht; ☎ 02 240 34 99; w lamaisondesarts.be; ⏲ house: 09.00–17.00 Mon–Fri & w/ends during exhibitions, garden: noon–17.00 summer, noon–15.00 winter; exhibitions free; Ⓜ Botanique or tram 25/92 to Robiano) This early 19th-century house – the old

Château Eenens-Terlinden, belonging to a rich cloth merchant – has been owned by the commune since the 1950s and now hosts exhibitions, installations and concerts. The ground-floor rooms have retained their original décor, while the back houses a pretty garden. Their sweet tucked-away bistro, **Estaminet** (m 0498 59 72 27; ⌚ noon–15.00; w lestami.net; €€), features furniture salvaged from a Jette café forced to close by Expo '58.

Les Halles de Schaerbeek [133 B3] (22b rue Royale St-Marie; ☎ 02 218 21 17; w halles.be; tram 25/92 to Robiano) Dating from 1865, this glass-and-steel structure once housed the commune's local food market. It was gutted by fire in 1898 and quickly rebuilt, but the effects of World War I slowed trade and competition from new 'luxury' stores led traders to abandon the hall entirely. Over the years it operated as a warehouse, workshop and car park until, in 1975, it was purchased by the Brussels French Cultural Committee. Today it's a hip venue for concerts, theatre and circus productions. Check the website for upcoming events. On the last Friday of May it also hosts a large public party, 'Neighbours' Day'.

Maison Autrique [133 C2] (266 chaussée de Haecht; ☎ 02 215 66 00; w autrique.be; ⌚ noon–18.00 Wed–Sun; ticket/Brussels Card €7/free; metrotram 92 to Église St-Servais). This dapper 1893 townhouse was Victor Horta's first independent project. He had just completed his internship with Alphonse Balat, creator of the Royal Greenhouses of Laeken, when Eugène Autrique – a friend and mechanical engineer at Solvay – commissioned Horta to build his family home. Despite the limitations of Autrique's small budget, you can see Horta's flirtation with aspects of the then nascent Art Nouveau style. It's extremely atmospheric to wander around, and the house is animated by installations and exhibitions. Not suitable for disabled travellers.

Distillerie Fovel [133 C3] (69 rue Thiefry; ☎ 02 215 58 15; ⌚ shop: 09.00–15.00 Mon–Fri; metrotram 25/62 to Coteaux) Makers of gin since 1863, the Fovel distillery is the oldest family-run company of its kind in the capital, marking its 150th anniversary in 2014. The commune sometimes advertises tours, but otherwise you'll need to get a group together; visits are €50. Alternatively, pop into their shop for bottles like the cherry-flavoured Griotte de Schaerbeek.

Musée Schaerbeekois de la Bière (Schaerbeek Beer Museum) [133 C2] (33–35 av Louis Bertrand; m 0470 81 43 00; w museeschaerbeekoisdelabiere.be; ⌚ 14.00–18.00 Wed & Sat; adult/under 14 €3/free; tram 92 to Église St-Servais) Forget the commercial beer museum on the Grand-Place and head to this ramshackle spot instead – a real labour of love established by locals in 1994, after they convinced commune officials to sign over the building, cajoled breweries to donate old machinery, and then trawled flea markets looking for paraphernalia. Today the collection exceeds 1,000 bottles and glasses, as well as copious beer posters and placards. The entry price includes a free beer – a natural choice is the local La Schaerbeekois.

Train World [133 C1] (5 pl Princesse Elisabeth; ☎ 02 224 74 98; w trainworld.com; ⌚ 10.00–17.00 Tue–Sun, last entry 15.30; adult/6–17/under 6 & Brussels Card €12/9/free, audio guide €2; Gare de Schaerbeek/tram 92) Set alongside Europe's first railway track, this high-profile new railway museum contains some superb historic Belgian locomotives and carriages, from the country's oldest preserved

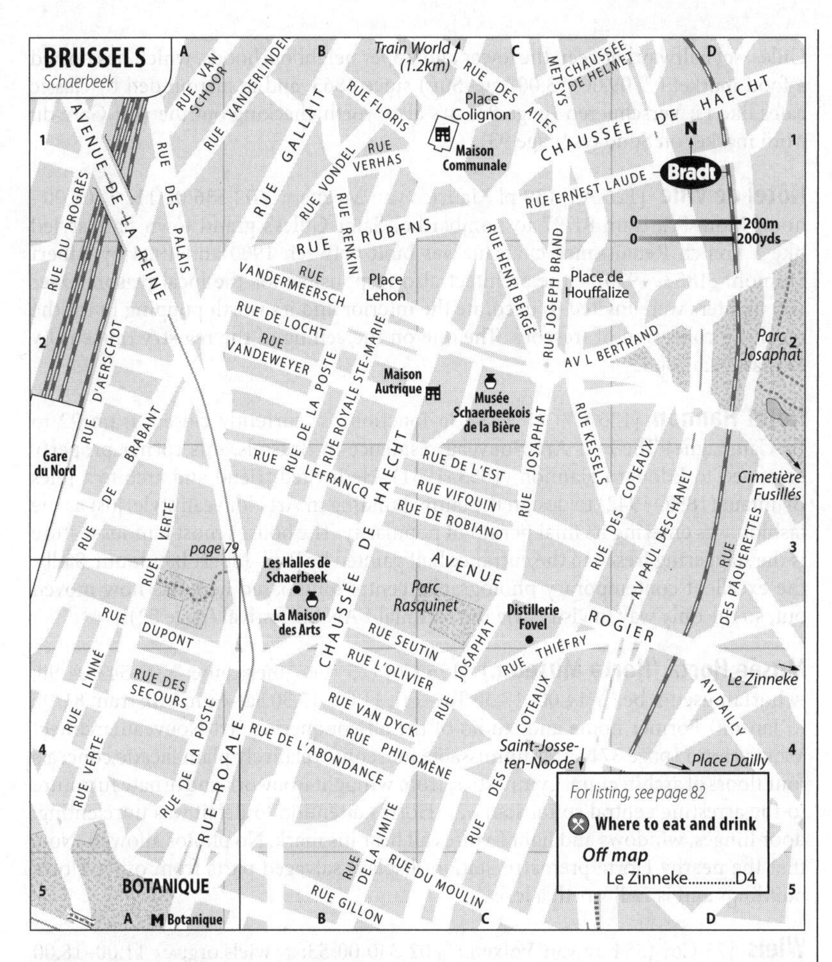

steam locomotive, the *Pays de Waes*, to the 'Type 12', which set a world speed record in 1939. The old Schaerbeek station, a listed monument, houses the ticket office. For the full effect, you can also stay overnight in nearby renovated railway carriages (page 80).

SAINT-GILLES *Porte de Hal; see map, page 126*

For centuries Saint-Gilles was called Obbrussel, 'Upper Brussels' – a quiet hamlet known for farming Brussels sprouts (inhabitants are known as *Kuulkappers* or 'cabbage-cutters'). It's still something of a village in the city, though today the local population – counting 130 nationalities, and skewed towards the young and arty – is more likely to be shopping for organic vegetable boxes. The area was mainly urbanised at the end of the 19th century – a time when Art Nouveau masters like Victor Horta were creating flamboyant buildings in the commune's elegant reaches. These remain at poles to the lower part of the commune, housing Bruxelles Midi/Brussel Zuid, the busiest train station in Belgium, which has resulted in massive but not always glamorous redevelopment. Today, however, more and more people are flocking to the area for its bohemian spirit, multi-cultural make-up and superb bar scene. Musts are the commune's lovely square, Le Parvis de Saint-

Gilles, set halfway between the lower and upper neighbourhoods, which has hosted a food market (⌚ 09.00–13.00 Tue–Sun) since 1865, and is surrounded by classic cafés like Le Verschueren (page 83). It's also worth checking out the vast Gare du Midi market on Sundays (page 93).

Hôtel de Ville [126 A5] (39 pl Maurice van Meenen; 02 536 02 11; ⌚ 08.00–noon Mon–Fri; tram 81/97 to Lombardie) Saint-Gilles's grand town hall, styled like a French Renaissance château, was built between 1900 and 1904 by Albert Dumont (1853–1920) – the architect also responsible for the local prison. Over 100 painters were invited to decorate the interior and it's worth popping in for the resulting collection of frescoes. The one on the ceiling of the registry office is by Fernand Khnopff.

Hôtel Hannon [126 C7] (1 av de la Jonction; ⌚ currently closed; tram 92 to La Campagne) The best Art Nouveau residence in Brussels, this corner property belonged to Edouard Hannon (1853–1931). He invited friend and architect Jules Brunfaut (1852–1942) to design the entire building in Art Nouveau style, just as the fashion was entering its final period of popularity. The house's most famous feature is the staggering fresco in the entrance hall painted by Paul-Albert Baudouin. Sadly, the excellent contemporary photography centre long based here has now moved out, so the only way to visit is via the biennial BANAD festival (page 52).

Musée Horta (Horta Museum) [126 C6] (25 rue Américaine; 02 543 04 90; w hortamuseum.be; ⌚ 14.00–17.30 Tue–Fri, 11.00–17.30 Sat–Sun; €10; tram 81/97 to Janson) Former home and studio of the all-conquering Art Nouveau architect Victor Horta (page 371), this unmissable museum's relatively plain façade conceals four floors of architectural gymnastics, from wrought ironwork and ornate furniture to the arresting central spiral stairway. Horta's attention to detail was unrelenting; door hinges, windows and light fixtures all bear his mark. No photos allowed. Note that the nearby Horta premetro station displays salvaged parts from other Horta buildings and is well worth a look.

Wiels [75 C6] (354 av van Volxem; 02 340 00 53; w wiels.org; ⌚ 11.00–18.00 Tue–Sun, late opening until 21.00 on the 1st & 3rd Wed of month; adult/under 12 & Brussels Card €10/free; tram 97 to Wiels) This monolithic former 1930s brewery is now Brussels's leading contemporary art institution. There's no permanent collection but rather occasionally daring, often Belgium-oriented temporary shows. The roof terrace (free to access) is a popular hangout spot in summer.

SAINT-JOSSE-TEN-NOODE *Botanique; see map, page 78*

The capital's smallest, most densely populated commune was once covered in vineyards but when Napoleon came to power he had them destroyed. Home to 153 nationalities of an average age of just 33, the commune wasn't always so diminutive – half its territory was siphoned off in 1853 and incorporated into the Leopold Quarter and Squares District in the current EU Quarter. It's known for its cultural centre and adjacent garden, and its jazzy rhythms – parlayed through many murals, the September St-Jazz-ten-Noode festival (w saintjazz.be) and Jazz Centre.

Ferme du Parc Maximilien (Maximilian Park Farm) [78 C1] (2 quai du Batelage; 02 201 56 09; w lafermeduparcmaximilien.be; ⌚ 10.00–17.00 Mon–Sat;

free; Yser) Under-the-radar city farm where kids can stroke sheep, donkeys and goats. A good place to unwind after sightseeing.

Botanique [79 H4] (236 rue Royale; 02 218 37 32; w botanique.be; Apr 08.00–18.45; May–Aug 08.00–20.45; Sep 08.00–19.45; Oct–Mar 08.00–17.45; Botanique) These Neoclassical botanical gardens were built between 1815 and 1830 and, with the National Botanical Garden of Belgium that was once located here now based in Meise, in the province of Flemish Brabant, the former orangery has turned into a popular cultural centre and gig venue (page 89). However, there's still evidence of its previous life: 6ha gardens in the English, French and Italian style; in spring, head to the latter to see the blossoming of 40 types of iris – the Brussels Capital Region's official flower.

Musée Charlier (Charlier Museum) (16 av des Arts; 02 220 26 91; w charliermuseum.be; noon–17.00 Mon–Thu, 10.00–13.00 Fri; adult/under 18 & Brussels Card €5/free; Madou) Classy art gallery in a Horta-renovated building displaying late 19th-century and early 20th-century Belgian art (James Ensor, Rik Wouters) alongside older furniture and objects. Try to coincide your visit with one of their regular concerts (see website).

UCCLE *Churchill*

As well as being the capital's second-largest commune, Uccle (meaning 'knoll' – it's hilly) is also the wealthiest, and so popular among French expats that it's almost a Paris suburb.

Musée van Buuren (Van Buuren Museum) (41 av Léo Errera; 02 343 48 51; w museumvanbuuren.com; 14.00–17.30 Mon & Wed–Sun; adult/under 12 €10/free; Churchill) Off-the-beaten-track gem. This stunning 1928 Art Deco house belonged to Alice and David van Buuren, who filled it with period furniture, sculptures, woodwork and paintings, including an original *Potato Peeler* sketch by van Gogh and a copy of Bruegel's *Landscape with the Fall of Icarus*. The landscaped gardens are incredibly romantic, with a labyrinth and heart-shaped secret garden.

Bois de la Cambre (La Cambre Woods) (tram 93 to Legrand, or tram 7 from Churchill) Originally part of the Fôret de Soignes south of the city centre, these woods were annexed to the city in 1842 and a tram line set up linking them to the centre, so residents could escape to a 'green' space at weekends. It's a lovely spot and comes alive with runners, cyclists and families picnicking in summer. There's a horseriding centre offering treks in the woods (w manege-lacambre.be), and a handful of restaurants such as Chalet Robinson (page 82).

Villa Empain [75 F8] (67 av Franklin Roosevelt; 02 627 52 30; w villaempain.com; 11.00–18.00 Tue–Sun; adult/12–25/under 12, Brussels Card & 1st Wed of month €10/4/free; tram 8/25 to Solbosch) Sublime 1930s Art Deco mansion built for the eponymous baron, then just 21. Empain wanted it to become an art museum, but it was repurposed by the Germans and Allies in World War II and later became a Soviet embassy before being snapped up by the Boghossian Foundation in 2008 and achieving its intended purpose. Hosts temporary shows about the decorative arts. Don't miss it.

While two of the following sites are over the border in Wallonia, I am including them owing to their proximity and likely interest to visitors.

TERVUREN

Musée Royale de l'Afrique Centrale (Royal Museum for Central Africa) (13 Leuvensesteenweg; ☎ 02 769 52 11; w www.africamuseum.be; ⌚ 11.00–17.00 Tue–Fri, 10.00–18.00 Sat–Sun; adult/18–26/under 18 & Brussels Card €12/4/free) King Leopold II set up this museum on his leafy royal estate essentially to boast about the colony he'd established in the Congo, filling it with plundered treasures. It was hoped that, after a recent five-year renovation, the museum might finally address this dark heritage, but sadly there is regrettably little on the subject – as lamented by UNESCO, which made a point of calling it out. Nonetheless, there is a token nod to Belgian brutality, and plenty of beauty on show – maps, photos, stuffed animals, African art, Henry Morton Stanley's expedition photographs – amounting to just 1% of the museum's collection.

Getting there and away From Bruxelles Central/Brussel Centraal take metro line 1 (direction: Stockel) to Montgomery station. Then take tram 44 until its last stop, Tervuren (⌚ 22mins) – the museum is across the road.

LOUVAIN-LA-NEUVE

Musée Hergé (26 rue du Labrador; ☎ 010 488 421; w museeherge.com; ⌚ 10.30–17.30 Tue–Fri, 10.00–18.00 Sat–Sun; adult/7–14/under 7 €12/5/free) South of Brussels in the student town of Louvain-la-Neuve is the remarkable Hergé Museum. Open since 2009, the building's dynamic architecture (by Pritzker Prize-winning Christian de Portzamparc) uses the same *ligne claire* that made Tintin universally recognisable. A free audio guide leads you through the fascinating multi-media collection of family albums, early doodles, original frames and interviews – much of it from the collection of Hergé's second wife.

Getting there and away During the week a direct train runs from Bruxelles Central/Brussel Centraal to Louvain-la-Neuve; at weekends you will have to change at Ottignies. The journey takes an hour; rail company SNCB offers a special B-Excursion rate including the train and museum admission. The museum is a short walk from the railway station.

WATERLOO This small town 18km south of Brussels is the site of the legendary Battle of Waterloo fought between the French, under Napoleon Bonaparte, and the English, led by the Duke of Wellington, on 18 June 1815. Napoleon's defeat ended 22 years of war and brought peace to Europe.

Getting there and away

By bus A bus journey takes longer than the train, but has the bonus of dropping you right outside the tourist information centre in Waterloo. Take TEC bus W (direction: Braine-l'Alleud) or 365 (direction: Charleroi) from outside the Ibis hotel on avenue Fonsny and alight at Waterloo Église; journey time 50 minutes. Ask for a one-day Horizon ticket (€10) which you can use to get to Waterloo, the battlefields and back to Brussels.

By train Catch the train from Bruxelles Midi/Brussel Zuid to Waterloo (⏲ every 15mins Mon–Fri, hourly Sat–Sun; 20mins). Alternatively, you can take a direct train to Braine-l'Alleud (⏲ every 15mins Mon-Fri, twice an hour Sat–Sun). From Braine-l'Alleud, you'll need to take bus W to get to the battlefield located 5 minutes away. From Waterloo station it's a 15-minute walk into town along rue de la Station. Coming back it's quicker to take the train from Braine-l'Alleud.

Tourist information

Tourist information 218 chaussée de Bruxelles; ☎ 02 352 09 10; w waterloo-tourisme.com; ⏲ Jun–Sep 09.30–18.00; Oct–May 10.00–17.00. Sells Pass 1815 (adult/7–17 €20/16, but due to rise in 2019) covering all the key attractions.

What to see and do

Musée Wellington (147 chaussée de Bruxelles; ☎ 02 357 28 60; w museewellington.be; ⏲ Apr–Sep 09.30–18.00; Oct–Mar 10.00–17.00; adult/7–17/under 7 & via Pass 1815 €7.50/6.50/free) Left of Waterloo's tourist information office, this 18th-century coaching inn was used as the headquarters of the British military during the campaign, and the Duke of Wellington is believed to have stayed here for two nights before the Battle of Waterloo. Its rooms – including Wellington's bedroom – and rare weapons are worth a visit before taking the bus to the Butte du Lion.

Waterloo Battlefield: Memorial 1815 (route du Lion; ☎ 02 385 19 12; w waterloo1815.be; ⏲ Apr–Jun & Sep–Oct 09.30–18.30, Jul–Aug 09.30–19.30, Nov–Mar 09.30–17.30; adult/10–17/under 10 €16/8/free, inc access to all 4 Memorial 1815 sites) Situated 3km south of Waterloo, Memorial 1815 sprouts up around the **Butte du Lion** (**Lion's Mound**) monument marking the front line of the battle between French and English troops. Here you'll find four attractions: **Memorial 1815**, a subterranean museum covering all aspects of the battle with a few original artefacts; the adjoining **Panorama**, a 110m-wide 1912 painting of the battle animated by a bellicose soundtrack; the **Lion's Mound**, built to a height of 100m by local women and topped by a gargantuan lion statue (there are superb views over the battlefield here); and the **Hougoumont farm**, a compound that played host to some of the worst fighting, and is reachable by a free shuttle-bus ride or on foot. I'd highly recommend visiting during the annual re-enactment in June (see website). A big one is held every five years; the next is scheduled for 2020.

Getting there and away From town, the bus stop for the battlefield is located opposite Musée Wellington. Take bus W and alight at Route de Nivelles, next to the Esso garage (⏲ every 20mins, but hourly on Sun; 12mins); the entrance is 500m away.

GAASBEEK

Kasteel van Gaasbeek (Gaasbeek Castle) (40 Kasteelstraat; ☎ 02 531 01 30; w kasteelvangaasbeek.be; ⏲ Apr–Oct 10.00–18.00 Tue–Sun, last entry 17.00; castle: adult/7–17/under 7 €10/2/free, inc audio guide) Ensconced in 17th-century parkland just 14km southwest of Brussels, the predecessor to the current castle here was part of the defence line of Brussels in the 13th century. It was repeatedly destroyed and rebuilt, enjoying a succession of aristocratic owners including Count Egmont (page 7) and Marquise Arconati Visconti, who thoroughly restored it in the 19th century and changed the interior to suit her tastes. You can visit her chambers and see temporary art exhibitions – a higher charge applies during shows – or enjoy the 49ha **park** (⏲ Nov–Mar 08.00–20.00, closes 17.00) full of historic buildings and housing a **garden museum** (🕘 May–Oct 10.00–18.00 Tue–Sun, closes 17.00 in Oct; adult/under 18 €5/free, or combi-ticket with castle €13) with rare fruit and vegetable species.

Getting there and away Bus 142 (direction: Leerbeek) departs from 🚆 Bruxelles Midi/Brussel Zuid and stops outside the castle (hourly Mon–Fri, every 2 hours Sat–Sun; 🕘 30mins). By car from Brussels, Ghent or Antwerp, take exit 15a off the R0 ring road (direction: Vlezenbeek) (14km; 🕘 20mins).

4

Flemish Brabant

Flemish Brabant envelops Brussels and is Flanders' smallest region. The university town of Leuven is its crown jewel and shouldn't be missed. To the east lies Hageland – a patchy area of woodland couched between the provincial towns of Tienen, Diest and Aarschot – and to the west Pajottenland, an area of rural farmland that produces excellent Lambic beers, asparagus and endives. Both provide lovely opportunities for cycling through proper Flemish countryside. All the tourist offices sell *Hageland* and *Pajottenland* cycling maps, linked to *Fietsknooppuntennetwerk* (try saying that after a few beers!), or a network of nodes that allows you to plan routes as long or short as you like. Straddle the saddle and explore a region studded with castles, watermills and two of Flanders' best-preserved béguinages.

LEUVEN

Compact, picturesque Leuven is the capital of the Flemish Brabant region and a bustling student city, its population swelling from around 100,000 to 150,000 residents during term time. Don't be fooled by its size: the stupendous architecture of Belgium's Oxford is testament to its illustrious history. From the 11th to the 13th centuries it was the stronghold of the Dukes of Brabant and flourished thanks to its thriving cloth trade. However, when the Duchy moved to Brussels and the trade of cloth fell into crisis, Leuven had to look for a new role. When John IV, Duke of Brabant, appealed to Pope Martin V to build a university in 1425, it changed the city's history forever, with the Catholic University of Leuven remaining a world-class institution. Today visitors can enjoy Leuven's celebrated Stadhuis, Belgium's largest béguinage, and a thriving beer culture spanning the famous Stella Artois brewery, part of AB Inbev, the world's biggest brewery conglomerate; microbrewery Domus; and three – yes, three – different beer events in April (page 52).

GETTING THERE AND AWAY

By car From Brussels, follow the E40 then the E314, taking exit 17 (direction: Winksele; 30km; ⌚ 35mins). If you're coming from the east, eg Hasselt, follow the E314 west and take exit 18 (direction: Herent; 60km; ⌚ 40mins). Note that you cannot drive in the historic city centre; Minckelersparking (94 J P Minckelersstraat; €6/24hr) is an affordable car park 10 minutes' walk from the Grote Markt.

By train Brussels (every 10mins Mon–Fri, 3 times an hour Sat–Sun; ⌚ 30mins); Antwerp (twice an hour; ⌚ 50mins/1hr 8mins); Bruges (twice an hour; ⌚ 1hr 30mins); Ghent (3 times an hour Mon–Fri, twice an hour Sat–Sun; ⌚ 1hr 5mins). The easiest way to get to Leuven is via direct trains from Brussels Airport Zaventem (twice an hour Mon–Fri, 3 times an hour Sat–Sun; ⌚ 15mins). The railway station and adjoining bus station are a 10-minute walk from the town centre.

COW SHOOTERS

Residents of Leuven are known as *De Koeienschieters* (The Cow Shooters) after an incident that occurred one night in 1691. Locals thought that they were under attack from the French and opened fire on their enemy. However, when day broke they realised the 'siege' had been nothing more than a herd of cows.

GETTING AROUND

On foot Leuven's historic city centre has been a pedestrian-only zone since 2016, and is a delightful place for a stroll.

By bike Leuven Leisure (see below) has an ample choice of bikes (€20/day) and cycling maps, including a self-guided pub crawl! There's also a Fietspunt at Leuven railway station (1 Prof R Van Overstraetenplein; 016 21 26 01; Apr–15 Oct 07.00–19.00 Mon–Fri, 08.30–17.00 Sat, 08.30–14.00 Sun; €10/day).

TOURIST INFORMATION

Tourist information [145 F7] 3 Naamsestraat; 016 20 30 20; w visitleuven.be; 10.00–17.00. This small office sells 2 versions of the ILUVLeuven pass: regular (€8), which includes a guided tour of the nearby Stadhuis, & entry to the Universiteitsbibliotheek & toren; & XL (€16), which adds entrance to M-Museum Leuven.

GUIDED TOURS

Leuven Leisure [145 G7] 5 Tiensestraat; 016 43 81 44; w leuvenleisure.com; 10.00–18.00 Wed–Fri, 10.00–19.00 Sat. Young, dynamic tour company offering beer walks & bike trips in Leuven & the surrounding area.

Beer tours

Stella Artois Brewery [144 E1] 20 Aarschotsesteenweg; English guided tours 15.00 Sat–Sun; adult/under 12 €8.50/free. The interactive tour leads you via the beer vats & bottling room, before a glass of the good stuff in their pub. Book through the tourist information office.

Domus Brauhaus [145 G7] 3 Jozef Vounckplein; 016 201 449; w domusbrauhaus.be; contact for timings; from €8 inc 2 beers. A microbrewery whose beer flows through pipes directly to their pub/restaurant in the shadow of the town hall. You can sample amber-coloured Nostra Domus, unfiltered lager Con Domus & a seasonal beer. Recommended if you do just 1 brewery tour.

WHERE TO STAY

The Fourth [145 F7] (42 rooms) 5 Grote Markt; 016 22 75 54; w th4th.com. A meeting place for guilds, a theatre, a bank … &, as of 2016, the city's newest, swishest hotel – set right on the main square in a very stately building. Rooms are ultra modern & self-consciously cool (with, alas, transparent bathroom doors – why do designers do this?!). Mezzanine suites have a kitchen, but that would be to miss the very glam on-site eatery, Tafelrond (€€€€). **€€€**

Martin's Klooster [144 B4] (103 rooms) 18 O L Vrouwstraat; 016 21 31 41; w martinshotels.com. Gorgeous gabled & beamed 4-star hotel dating back to 1531; Charles V's secretary lived here & it served as an Augustinian monastery. The Exceptional Suites in the former monastery part of the building are truly lovely, with fancy jacuzzi baths & 4-poster beds; other rooms are more modern. Fabulous bar & b/fast (€21, but €16 reserved in advance) seal the deal. **€€€**

Begijnhof Hotel [145 B8] (69 rooms) 15 Groot Begijnhof; 016 29 10 10; w bchotel.be. Grab the rare opportunity to stay in a béguinage – & Belgium's biggest at that. Rooms are rather functional, particularly in comparison to the exceptional garden/patio & setting, but there are plenty of boons: a bar/bistro for small plates, a sauna & what are frankly bargain rates (circa €60/ night). €€

Guesthouse Alizée [144 D3] (2 rooms) 41 Sint-Maartenstraat; m 0498 03 73 83; w bbalizee.be. Welcoming B&B with 2 rooms: North is en suite & pretty in pink, while South hugs the eaves & has a bathroom just across the hall. Central location but very peaceful, & lovely antique fixtures & fittings. Also a lounge with tea- & coffee-making facilities & a microwave oven. Min 3 nights. €€

Leuven City Hostel [145 F5] (10 rooms) 37 Ravenstraat; 016 84 30 33; w leuvencityhostel.com. New, very central hostel with clean en-suite twin, 4-, 6- or 7-bed rooms. There's a huge kitchen & pleasant patio, & you can buy a €7.50 b/fast at their budget hotel in the same building. Dorm bed €22, dbl €53. €

WHERE TO EAT AND DRINK

Zarza [144 F4] 92 Bondgenotenlaan; 016 20 50 05; w zarza.be; noon–13.30 & 18.30–21.00 Mon–Sat. High-quality, creative food in a fine setting – not least if you sit in the stunning city garden. Go à la carte or opt for 4- to 6-course menus (€58/75). A nice touch is their affordable 'Young Foodies' menu for under-30s. €€€€–€€€€€

Bistro Lust [144 C4] 14 Wieringstraat; 016 23 12 23; w bistrolust.be; noon–13.30 & 18.30–21.00 Tue–Fri, 18.30–21.00 Sat. Less humble bistro than upscale exemplar of the bistronomy trend, this classy mansion-set venture combines natural wines & very fine produce-led cuisine. Choose your main & they provide delicious seasonal sides. €€€–€€€€

Kokoon [145 G8] 1 's-Meiersstraat; 016 23 07 26; w kokoon.be; noon–14.30 & 18.00–22.00 Mon, Wed–Fri & Sun, 18.00–22.00 Sat. Just off main restaurant drag Muntstraat, a small spot offering very good value Belgian food &, unusually, also a selection of wok dishes – brilliant & arriving in huge portions! €€€

Rossi [145 F8] 2 Standonckstraat; 016 62 48 48; w ristoranterossi.be; noon–14.00 & 18.30–22.00 Tue–Sat. Don't be deterred by the basic décor; instead trust the sumptuous smells of garlic & red wine that emanate from the kitchen of this tiny, authentic Italian run by Slow Food representative Felice Miluzzi, voted best Italian chef in the country by Gault&Millau in 2018. He also has a pasta outlet at new foodie hub De Smidse (w desmidseleuven.be). €€€

Loving Hut [145 G7] 13 Rector De Somerplein; 016 84 47 02; w lovinghut.be; noon–20.00 Mon–Sat. Right in the centre, this minimal but cool Asian-accented veggie & vegan canteen, staffed by smiley students, is a safe bet for a fast & satisfying lunch – be it soya burgers, fresh soups or salads. You order at the counter & then get a buzzer alerting you when it's ready. €€

Grand Café De Hoorn [144 C1] 79 Sluisstraat; 016 79 54 75; w dehoorn.eu; 11.00–late Tue–Sat. On the site of former brewery De Hoorn, where the first Stella was brewed in 1926 (you eat overlooking the old copper kettles), this buzzing, industrial venue is a beacon in the upcoming Vaartkom neighbourhood (page 142). Burgers, pastas & pizza hit the mark. €€–€€€

Barbóék [145 F6] 17 Schrijnmakersstraat; 016 23 03 05; w barboek.be; 10.00–18.00 Mon–Sat. Wonderful, Tardis-like coffee bar/ bookshop with a vast selection of books, including an English shelf. Lovely atmosphere & plenty of places to perch over a chai latte or textbook coffee & pralines. €

De Werf [145 F8] 5 Hogesschoolplein; 016 23 73 14; w dewerf-leuven.be; 09.00–midnight Mon–Fri. Students love the large covered terrace at this friendly fixture, as well as the cheap wraps, quiches, salads & pastas. The green & red blankets on the backs of the chairs – in case you get cold – are a nice touch, as is the wacky décor referencing the café's name (meaning 'construction site'). €

ENTERTAINMENT AND NIGHTLIFE Leuven's nightlife is incredibly lively during the week thanks to its resident student population, but much quieter at weekends when they decamp home. Billed by the tourist board as 'Europe's longest bar', Oude Markt is the centre of revelries, its entire circumference lined by drinking holes, save for the odd pharmacy – presumably to hand out painkillers! Popular choices include

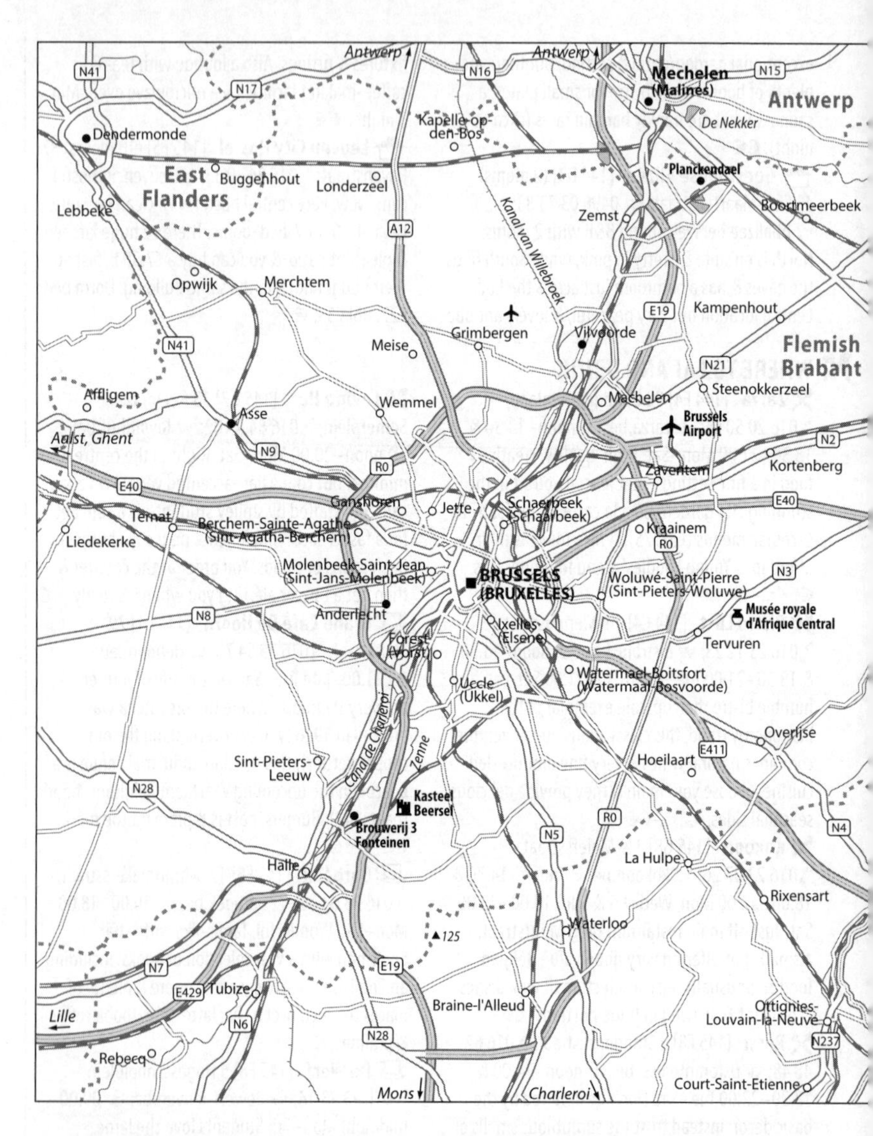

Café Belge (no 35), Origins Cocktail Bar (no 2) and De Giraf (no 38). These are mostly trendy, but there are still some atmospheric brown bars and cosy wine bars locally too – and in the north, canalside neighbourhood Vaartkom is changing at lightning speed, with new venues popping up all the time.

Pubs and bars

Café Commerce [145 E5] 16 Herbert Hooverplein; 016 22 55 78; w cafecommerce.be; 11.00–02.00 Mon–Thu, 08.30–03.00 Fri, 11.00–03.00 Sat. No-nonsense pub with a terrace near the university library which has been a local favourite for aeons. Freshly made soup & a wide choice of spaghetti to soak up the beers. Occasional gigs too.

De Fiere Margriet [145 F6] 11 Margarethaplein; m 0486 06 78 16; 14.00–02.00 daily. Fabulous time-capsule bar – down to the '80s soundtrack & creepy stuffed animals on the walls – with around 300 different beers,

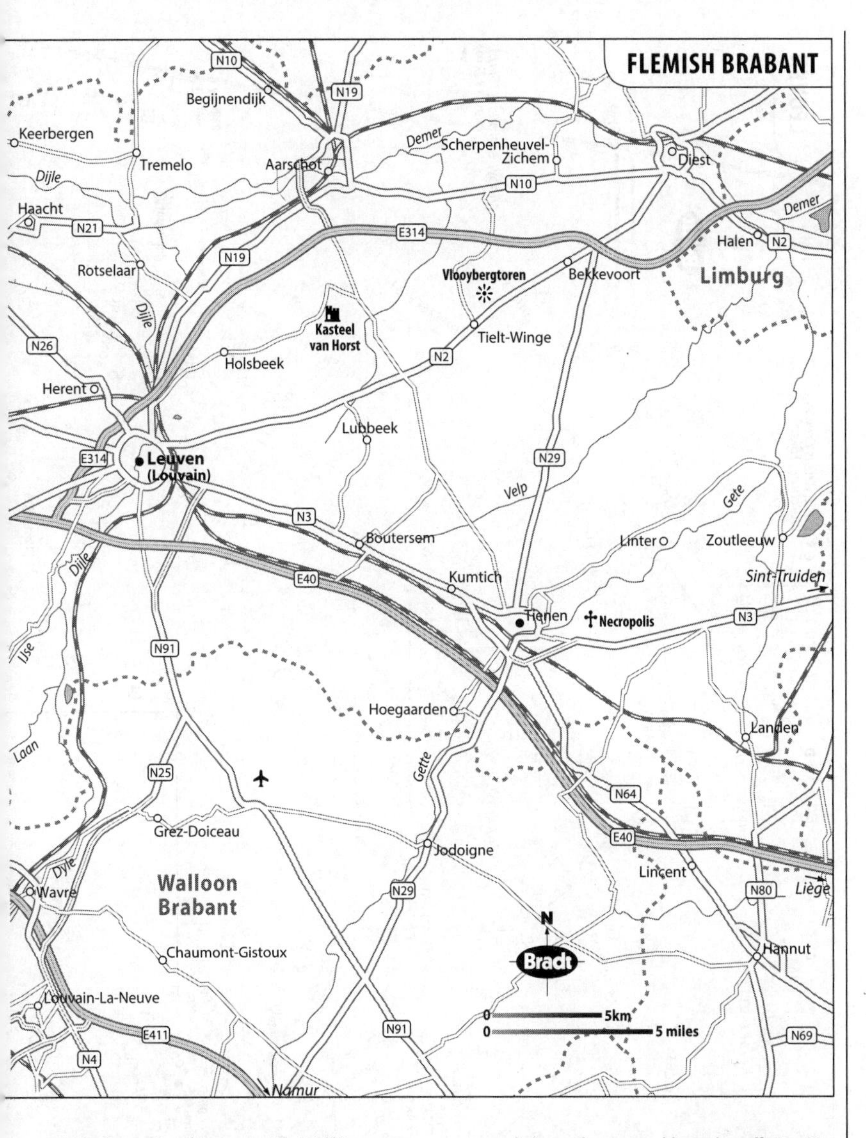

including regional brews such as Wolf & Broeder Jacob.

De Metafoor [145 C5] 34 Parijsstraat; **m** 0497 47 72 52; ⌚ 10.00–02.00 Mon–Sat, noon–02.00 Sun. Collapse on to the saggy leather couch underneath the old map on the wall, order a beer & strike up conversation with the locals at this charming brown bar, replete with dark-wood beams, tiled floor & witty décor.

Convento [144 C3] 87 Mechelsestraat; **m** 0468 51 71 35; **w** convento.be; ⌚ 10.00–22.00 Tue–Sat. This cosy wine shop & caterer has expanded over the years, adding a bar offering 20 wines by the glass (or pick a bottle from their shop) & local cheese & charcuterie. There's an excellent bistro on site too.

Theatres and concert halls

STUK [145 C7] 96 Naamsestraat; 016 32 03 20; **w** stuk.be. Rule-bending arts centre whose youthful new music programmer oversees a line-up of gigs & 'hybrid live acts without boundaries'. Also a great spot to catch dance performances, films & more. Very cool.

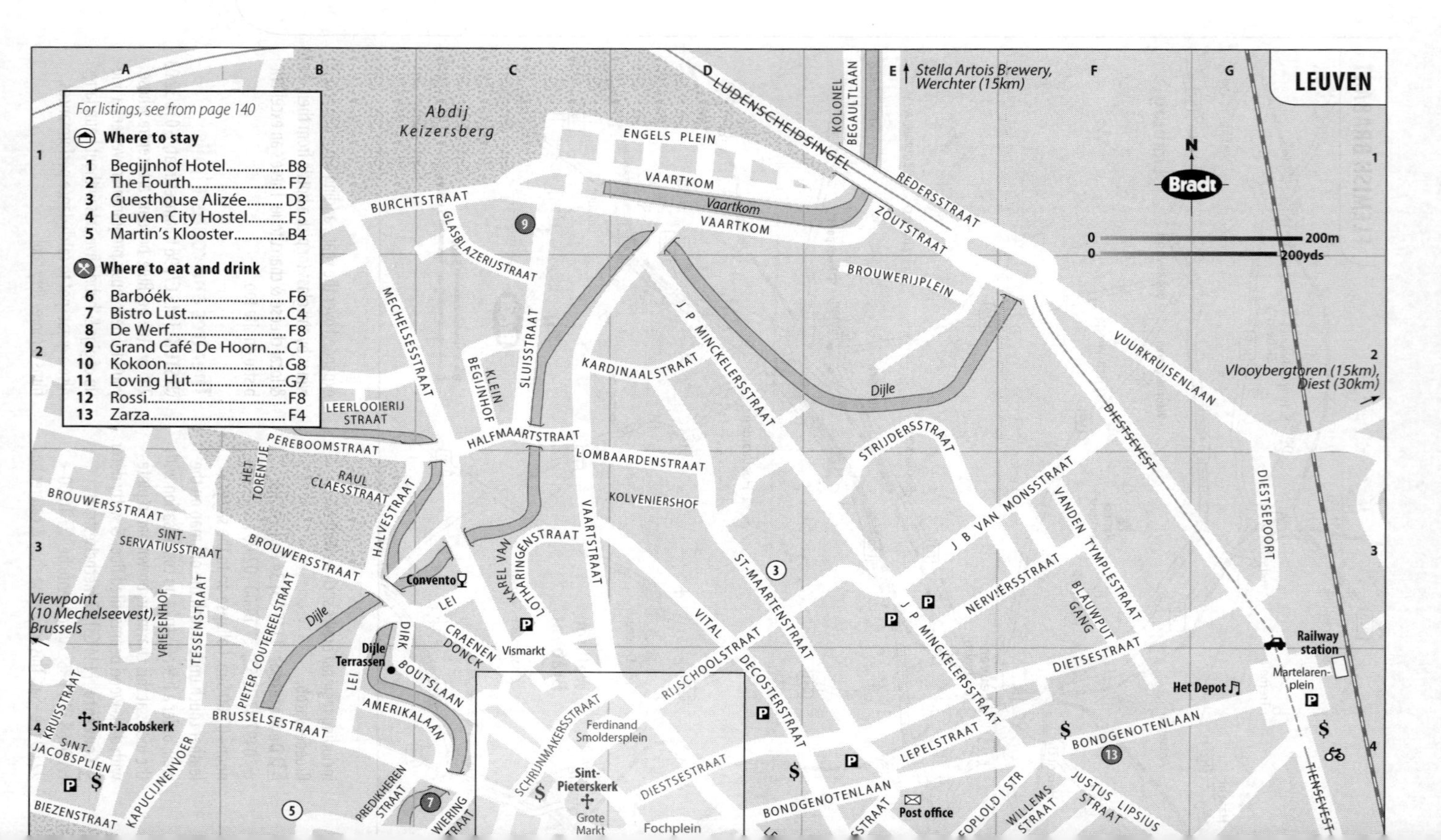
LEUVEN
For listings, see from page 140
Where to stay
1 Begijnhof Hotel B8
2 The Fourth F7
3 Guesthouse Alizée D3
4 Leuven City Hostel F5
5 Martin's Klooster B4
Where to eat and drink
6 Barbóék F6
7 Bistro Lust C4
8 De Werf F8
9 Grand Café De Hoorn C1
10 Kokoon G8
11 Loving Hut G7
12 Rossi F8
13 Zarza F4
Stella Artois Brewery, Werchter (15km)
Vlooybergtoren (15km), Diest (30km)
Viewpoint (10 Mechelseevest), Brussels
0 200m
0 200yds
Abdij Keizersberg
LUDENSCHEIDSINGEL
KOLONEL BEGAULTLAAN
REDERSSTRAAT
ZOUTSTRAAT
ENGELS PLEIN
VAARTKOM
Vaartkom
BURCHTSTRAAT
GLASBLAZERIJSTRAAT
BROUWERIJPLEIN
MECHELSESSTRAAT
SLUISSTRAAT
KLEIN BEGIJNHOF
KARDINAALSTRAAT
J P MINCKELERSSTRAAT
Dijle
VUURKRUISENLAAN
DIESTSEVEST
LEERLOOIERIJ STRAAT
PEREBOOMSTRAAT
HALFMAARTSTRAAT
LOMBAARDENSTRAAT
STRIJDERSSTRAAT
HET TORENTJE
RAUL CLAESSTRAAT
HALVESTRAAT
KOLVENIERSHOF
BROUWERSSTRAAT
SINT-SERVATIUSSTRAAT
KAREL VAN LOTHARINGENSTRAAT
VAARTSTRAAT
J B VAN MONSSTRAAT
VANDEN TYMPLESTRAAT
DIESTSEPOORT
Convento
LEI
ST-MAARTENSTRAAT
NERVIERSSTRAAT
BLAUWPUT GANG
VRIESENHOF
TESSENSTRAAT
PIETER COUTEREELSTRAAT
DIRK BOUTSLAAN
CRAENEN DONCK
Vismarkt
VITAL DECOSTERSTRAAT
RIJSCHOOLSTRAAT
Railway station
Dijle Terrassen
DIETSESTRAAT
Martelaren-plein
Het Depot
Sint-Jacobskerk
BRUSSELSESTRAAT
AMERIKALAAN
SCHRIJNMAKERSSTRAAT
Ferdinand Smoldersplein
LEPELSTRAAT
BONDGENOTENLAAN
KRUISSTRAAT
SINT-JACOBSPLIEN
KAPUCIJNENVOER
PREDIKHEREN STRAAT
WIERING STRAAT
Sint-Pieterskerk
Grote Markt
DIESTSESTRAAT
Fochplein
Post office
LEOPOLD I STR
WILLEMS STRAAT
JUSTUS LIPSIUS STRAAT
TIENSEVEST
BIEZENSTRAAT

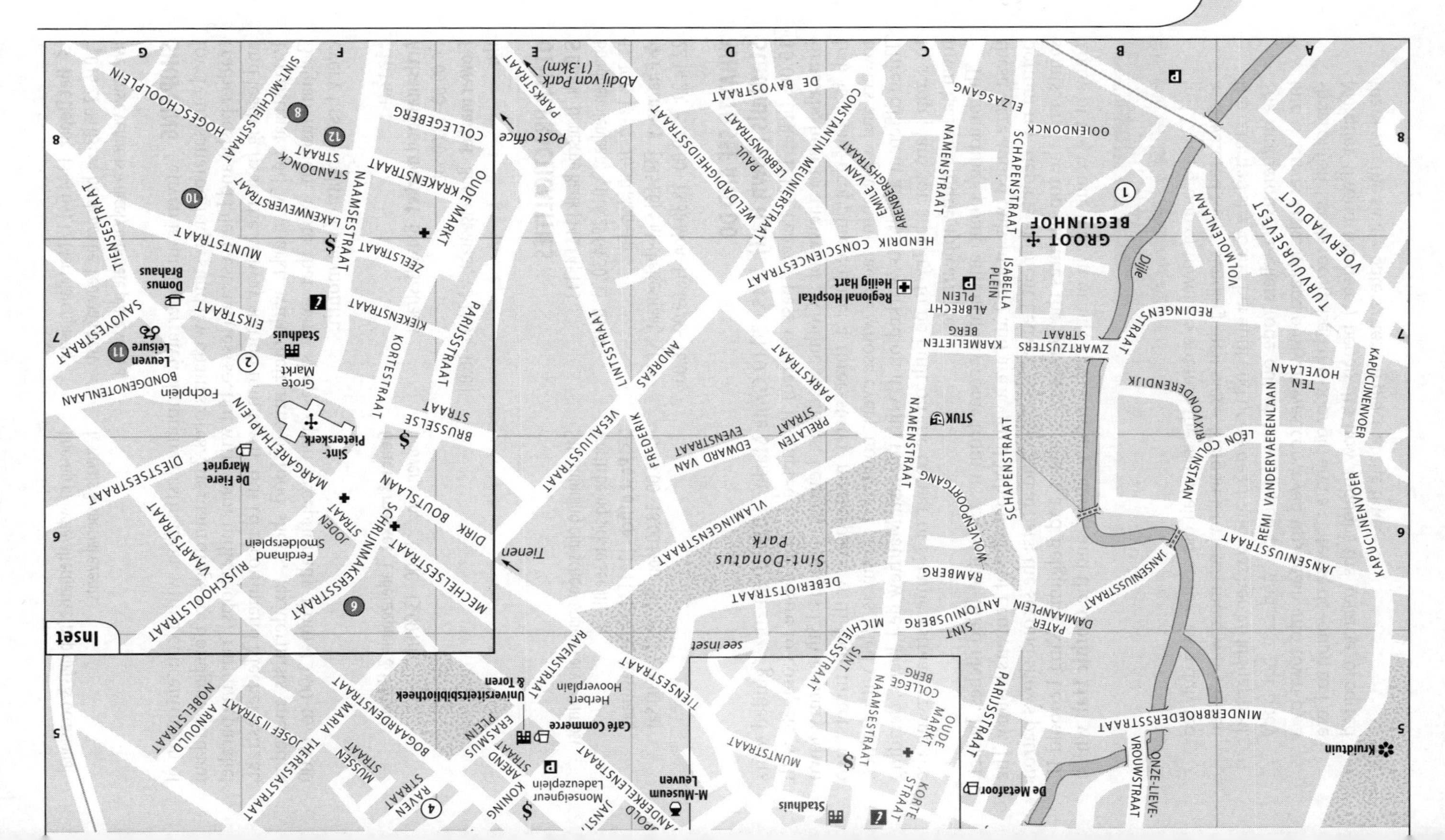
Inset
see inset
Sint-Donatus Park
Stadhuis
Grote Markt
Sint-Pieterskerk
De Fiere Margriet
Domus Brahaus
Leuven Leisure
Universiteitsbibliotheek & Toren
Café Commerce
M-Museum Leuven
De Metafoor
STUK
Regional Hospital Heilig Hart
GROOT BEGIJNHOF
Kruidtuin
Dijle
Tienen
Post office
Abdij van Park (1.3km)
Monseigneur Ladeuzeplein
Herbert Hooverplein
Fochplein
Ferdinand Smoldersplein
NAAMSESTRAAT
TIENSESTRAAT
MUNTSTRAAT
PARIJSSTRAAT
MINDERBROEDERSSTRAAT
SCHAPENSTRAAT
DEBERIOTSTRAAT
VLAMINGENSTRAAT
PARKSTRAAT
BRUSSELSE STRAAT
DIESTSESTRAAT
MECHELSESTRAAT
BONDGENOTENLAAN
HOGESCHOOLPLEIN
TURVUURSEVEST
VOERVIADUCT
KAPUCIJNENVOER
JANSENIUSSTRAAT
REDINGENSTRAAT

♫ **Het Depot** [144 G4] 12 Martelarenplein; ☎016 22 06 03; w hetdepot.be. Leuven's best live music venue is a nicely intimate place with a line-up of indie/alternative/pop gigs & occasional festivals & special events.

SHOPPING Leuven is an underrated shopping destination, with a concentration of lovely artisanal boutiques and few chain stores. The main drags are Bondgenotenlaan (rather posh) and Diestsestraat (less so, but with some indie shops), running parallel and leading from the railway station into town. But I'd recommend Mechelsestraat, Parijsstraat and Vismarkt, with their mix of food shops, taxidermists and edgy Belgian fashion. Note that many shops open exceptionally from 13.00 to 18.00 every first Sunday of the month.

Markets

Artisanal food market Brusselsestraat; ⏲ 09.00–18.00 Sat

Flower market Brusselsestraat; ⏲ 13.00–16.00 Thu

General market Ladeuzeplein & Herbert Hooverplein; ⏲ 07.00–13.00 Fri

OTHER PRACTICALITIES

$ **Bank** Deutsche Bank [144 F4] 113 Bondgenotenlaan; ☎016 29 04 30; ⏲ 09.00–12.30 & 13.30–16.30 Mon–Fri

✚ **Pharmacy** [145 F6] 5 Mechelsestraat; ☎016 22 14 29; ⏲ 09.00–18.30 Mon–Fri, 09.00–16.00 Sat. Stunning old-school apothecary – almost worth being sick to see it!

✉ **Post office** [144 E4] 12 Jan Stasstraat; ⏲ 09.00–18.00 Mon–Fri, 09.00–15.00 Sat

WHAT TO SEE AND DO

Stadhuis (Town Hall) [145 C5] (9 Grote Markt; ☎016 20 30 20; ⏲ guided tours 15.00; ticket/ILUVLeuven pass €4/free) Prompted by the desire to compete with Brussels, host to a jewel of a Gothic Stadhuis, Leuven's famous 15th-century town hall is a jaw-dropping edifice: a three-storey masterpiece with four turrets, two towers and a gleaming façade whose every nook and cranny is filled with statues. Three different architects worked on it, with the last, Matthew de Layens, deciding to scrap plans for a belfry to be built on the corner of Naamesestraat, giving the town hall its unique appearance.

The building's pomp and majesty come from its 236 statue-filled niches. In fact, these were added only in 1850 and are a visual Who's Who of Leuven's history. The bottom row depicts eminent Leuven scholars and artists; the second shows patron saints, and the top features the Dukes of Brabant and Belgium's King Leopold II. Tours of the venue take in ornate 19th-century salons, and the **Gothic Hall** which

PROUD MARGARET

In 1225, a group of travellers entered the inn of an old couple who duly fed and watered them, sending their niece, Margaret, to fetch more wine. When she returned she found her aunt and uncle dead, and was herself kidnapped. The murderous travellers rode out of town, raped her and cast her body into the river Dyle. Miraculously, it was conveyed upstream into town by a shoal of fish. Locals recognised the poor girl and an intense devotion to 'Fiere Margriet' (Proud Margaret) began. It's now thought the 'miracle' occurred thanks to the sluice-gate system in place at the time.

features an oak-beamed ceiling illustrating the life of Mary and Christ. Of most interest, however, are the four massive 19th-century paintings that line its walls and feature important city events. *Antonia van Roesmale elucidates the Bible* (1542) tells of a woman who wanted to read the Bible but, unable to understand Latin, unwittingly opted for a Dutch Protestant version. Emperor Charles V found out and had her buried alive in the Grote Markt. Such a pleasant, understanding chap! Another depicts the university's founding.

The archways on the back wall lead to the **small Gothic Hall** where your attention is stolen by the original Gothic star-vaulted ceiling and a copy of Dirk Bouts's *The Justice of Emperor Otto III* – the original hangs in the Royal Museums of Fine Arts of Belgium in Brussels (page 115). You can also now glimpse the Mayor's Office; the current mayor no longer works here, which is just as well as he now apparently feels liberated to have a computer, which had seemed anachronistic in such a splendid setting. Every third Saturday of the month you can also visit the cellars.

Back outside, across the square, is an irreverent statue of a young chap reading while sloshing liquid into his open skull. Known as **Fonske**, he's beloved by local university students, who like to think that it's booze that he's tipping into his cranium!

Sint-Pieterskerk (St Peter's Church) [145 F7] (Grote Markt; 🕘 10.00–16.30 Mon–Fri, 11.00–16.30 Sun, Oct–Mar closed Wed; free) In September 2019, this Gothic 15th-century church was due to reopen after refurbishment. Under the aegis of M-Museum Leuven, which manages its artworks, a new visitor display will offer free access to all its impressive artefacts, historically stored in the separate, paying treasury.

Construction on the church began in the 14th century, and overlapped with the town hall opposite; both buildings shared the same sequence of architects – Sulpitius van Vorst, Jan II Keldermans and Matheus de Layens (van Vorst, perhaps from the stress of the two jobs, died in 1448, before either was completed).

St Peter's suffered damage during the French Revolution and both World Wars, but thankfully its choir screen – the oldest in Belgium – survived. Its greatest asset is the masterful 15th-century triptych *The Last Supper* by Leuven town painter Dieric Bouts. It took him three years to complete the work, which makes full use of mathematical perspective – highly innovative for that time in the Low Countries. Rogier van der Weyden's *Edelheere Triptych* is also due to be relocated here from M-Museum Leuven to chime with the relaunch. In addition, don't miss a chapel dedicated to Proud Margaret, whose bones are housed in a neo-Gothic reliquary.

Universiteitsbibliotheek and Toren (University Library and Tower) [145 E5] (21 Monseigneur Ladeuzeplein; 016 32 46 60; **w** visitleuven.be; 🕘 10.00–19.00 Mon–Fri, 10.00–17.00 Sat–Sun; adult/under 12/ILUVLeuven pass €7/free/free) Turbulent barely covers the history of this striking, fully functional university library. Burnt down by the Germans during World War I – 300,000 volumes were destroyed, horrifying people abroad – it was rebuilt thanks to funding from America (mostly educational bodies, but also the NYPD) in the 1920s. Grand Central Terminal architect Whitney Warren was behind the design, intended to embody the idea of the Allies as good and the Germans as evil (an inscription 'Demolished by German fury, reconstructed with American gifts' was due to be included but later dropped). Despite this diplomacy, tragically the Germans again set fire to the building during World War II, and it had to be rebuilt once more. Visits lead you through the imposing **reading room**, and up the building's five-storey **tower**, which features an exhibition on the library's history. Unusually, the library tower houses a carillon with 63 bells and, during the academic year, on Tuesdays and Thursdays from 19.00 to 19.45, you can accompany the *carilloneur* up the stairs for a live concert (reserve ahead; **w** kuleuven.be/kunstenerfgoed/expo-events/carillon/carillonhome; €5).

M-Museum Leuven [145 D5] (28 Leopold Vanderkelenstraat; ✆ 016 27 29 29; **w** mleuven.be; ⌚ 11.00–18.00 Mon–Tue & Fri–Sun, 11.00–22.00 Thu; adult/under 26/18 & under/ILUVLeuven XL pass €12/5/free/free inc audio guide, last tickets 30mins before closing) The city is proud of its dynamic art museum, opened in 2009 and showcasing a mix of art from the Middle Ages to the present. The thought-provoking permanent collection on the first floor explores the politics of looking and collecting, explaining how the M-Museum's 52,000-object collection came to be, and expanding across a handful of rooms to terminate in fine 19th-century salons hosting applied arts gems. The crown jewel, Rogier van der Weyden's *The Seven Sacraments* altarpiece, will be reclaimed by Antwerp's KMSKA when it opens – possibly during the lifetime of this guide, though works have long been delayed.

Groot Begijnhof (Large Béguinage) [145 B7/B8] (Schapenstraat; free) A 10-minute walk south from the Grote Markt will lead you to Leuven's UNESCO-listed béguinage – the biggest in Belgium. This quiet world of cobblestones, red-brick houses and trickling streams was founded in 1205. It grew to accommodate 360 béguines (see box, page 19) before being abolished by the French in 1795. The béguines were allowed to stay, with the last one only moving out in 1988. The 'mini village' was restored between 1963 and 1990 and today the picturesque houses belong to the university, which lets them to lecturers and a few lucky postgraduate students.

Abdij van Park (Park Abbey) [145 E8] (7 Abdij van Park; ✆ 016 40 01 51; **w** abdijvanpark.be) A 20-minute walk further south (you can also catch buses 4/630, direction: Haasrode, or 5/6 direction: Wakkerzeel/Vaalbeek, from the bus station), this 42ha abbey was founded in 1129 shortly after the foundation of the Norbertine order. Norbertine monks continue to live here – amid one of the best-preserved abbey complexes in the Low Countries. The abbey will be undergoing renovation until at least 2022, but several sections are open to the public. You can take a 45-minute **abbey tour** (⌚ 14.00 Sat–Sun; adult/12–18/under 12 €10/5/free), visit museum **PARCUM** for temporary shows at the crossroads of religion, art and culture, or grab a bite at the brasserie set within a watermill, De Abdijmolen (**€€€**). It's a beautiful spot in summer, with plenty of signposted walking trails. A brand new Peace Carillon was also installed here during the Armistice centenary in November 2018; the city's original carillon historically stood on site but was later moved to St Peter's Cathedral – and, like many Flemish bells, destroyed by the

FANCY A STROLL?

Try walking through Leuven's Kruidtuin or Botanical Garden [145 A5] (30 Kapucijnenvoer; ⌚ May–Sep 08.00–20.00 Mon–Sat, 09.00–20.00 Sun; Oct–Apr 08.00–17.00 Mon–Sat, 09.00–17.00 Sun; free), which is Belgium's oldest (in fact, it predates Belgium's founding by almost a century), having been created by the university for students of medicine in 1738. Today the beautiful, relatively small complex houses several gardens, a greenhouse and plenty of benches to take a break from sightseeing.

Germans during World War I. Following a project between Leuven and the city of Neuss, where most of the German troops that ravaged Leuven came from, it is again resounding with messages of peace – so watch out for regular concerts.

Day trip

Vlooybergtoren (Vlooyberg Tower) (22 Oudepastoriestraat; ☎ 016 35 64 23; **w** tielt-winge.be; free) An M C Escher drawing made flesh, this spectacular 11m-high, 20m-long weathered-steel staircase was created in 2013 by creative studio Close to bone. Seeming to float in mid-air, and offering epic views of the countryside, it was designed to be resistant to vandalism – only to be heavily damaged by arson in 2018. You should be able to climb it again by the end of 2019.

Getting there and away Bus 370 (direction: Diest) runs from Leuven railway station to Tielt-Winge bus station (🕘 30mins), from which it's a 12-minute walk.

GRIMBERGEN

Only 12km north of Brussels, Grimbergen is actually part of Flemish Brabant and retains a small-town demeanour. Before beer enthusiasts start frothing at the mouth in anticipation, I should state that the famous Grimbergen Abbey beer has not been brewed here since the French Revolution; since 2008, Carlsberg has held the license to brew it, with Alken-Maes, south of Hasselt, responsible for production and distribution. The brewing giants pay the monks of the Norbertine abbey to use their name – a real travesty.

Nevertheless, this small town has a rich history dating back to when German Christian, Norbert of Xanten, and his group of monks founded the Grimbergen Abbey in 1128 – making it one of the oldest in Belgium. At that time, the town was ruled by the rich and powerful Grimbergen family, whose ruined castle can still be seen in Prinsenbos, the town park. However, disagreements with the Duke of Brabant led to the family losing their land, which later fell under the rule of the House of Orange-Nassau.

Part of the *Groene Gordel* – or Green Belt – surrounding Brussels, there are some lovely walks along the Maalbeek river and you should certainly try to visit the old watermills, Liermolen and Tommenmolen, on its banks.

Every year, on 13 May or the following Sunday, Grimbergen celebrates Sint-Servaasommegang, a pageant retelling the legend of the town's patron saint, St Servatius of Bulgaria.

GETTING THERE AND AWAY

By car From Brussels follow the N201 north, then the N277. Merge on to the A12, following signs for the E19/40 at the Strombeek-Bever interchange, then take exit 7 (direction: Grimbergen) (13km; 🕘 26mins).

By bus Three buses run from Brussel Noord bus station to Grimbergen town centre every 10 minutes, with the journey taking about 45 minutes: 231 (direction: Kapelle-op-den-Bos), 230 (direction: Humbeek) and 232 (direction: Grimbergen Verbrande Brug).

By train It's a 10-minute journey from Brussel Noord to Vilvoorde station, from where you can catch bus 821 (direction: Zaventem–Merchtem). Total journey time is about 35 minutes.

TOURIST INFORMATION

Tourist information 3 Prinsenstraat; 02 270 99 30; w www.grimbergen.be/toerisme; 09.00–noon Mon–Fri, also open 13.30–16.00 Tue–Thu. Small, ill-equipped office & the staff don't speak much English. It's worth hiring a guide (€50/2hrs, give at least 3 weeks' notice) so you can visit the beer museum housed in the old abbey. Alternatively, 3 walking routes are marked on the free town brochure: the *Prinsenwandeling* takes you past the Prinsenkasteel, the *Maalbeekwandeling* shows you how to get to Liermolen & Tommenmolen, & the Humbeekwandeling shows you 2 castles & a farm in nearby Humbeek village. The *Vier Dorpenroute* (4 villages cycling tour) takes you to all 4 villages in the Grimbergen municipality. Sadly, there's nowhere to rent bikes in town; Vilvoorde, 4km away, is the closest place to do so.

WHERE TO EAT AND DRINK

Tommenmolen 18 Tommenmolenstraat; 02 269 70 84; w tommenmolen.be; 11.00–21.30. Part of the MOT museum (see below), this 16th-century grain mill used to serve a more snacky menu, but the ex-owners of the local Lammekeshoeve restaurant have added proper Flemish bistro options to great effect (though you can still eat well for under €10 at lunch). Superb outdoor terrace caps it all. €€€

WHAT TO SEE AND DO

St-Servaasbasiliek (St Servatius Basilica) (1 Kerkplein; 02 272 40 60; w abdijgrimbergen.be; 07.00–19.00; free) Considered one of the most beautiful examples of Baroque architecture in Belgium and the Netherlands, this 17th-century abbey church is all that remains of the Grimbergen Abbey that was dissolved during the French Revolution. Immediately your eye is drawn to the soaring ceilings and baby-blue dome high above, and then to the main altar – a mass of black and Carrara marble whose centrepiece painting, the *Assumption of Mary*, is flanked by statues of the apostles Peter and Paul. Also of note are the ornate choirstalls and above them four paintings depicting episodes in the life of St Norbert, the founder of Grimbergen Abbey, and the Resurrection Memorial where Death (skeleton) and Time (old bearded man) hold a scroll listing the basilica's many abbots. The church boasts a 48-bell carillon and hosts regular concerts. In good weather, locals gather on the grass or grab a seat at the picnic table posted outside. In the abbey's old gatehouse, a **beer museum** has also been set up – it can be visited with a guide arranged through the tourist office.

Mira (20 Abdijstraat; 02 269 12 80; w mira.be; 14.00–18.00 Wed & Sun; adult/under 10 €3/free) Set up by a monk from the Norbertine abbey in 1967, this quaint observatory has several multi-media rooms, a weather station and a vast collection of historical astronomical instruments.

Prinsenkasteel (Prinsen Castle) (Princenbos; group tours offered Apr–Sep at €60/2hrs; arrange via MOT, see below) This impressive moat-surrounded castle with its own drawbridge, was built in the 17th century by Philip of Glymes, Prince of Grimbergen, whose tomb can be found in St Servatius Basilica. The castle was occupied by the Germans during World War II until fire left it ruined; it is now under the ownership of the city. Restoration has been ongoing for years, but must be progressing slowly – the only sign of life on the moat are dozens of rowdy geese and ducks.

MOT (Museum for Old Techniques) (20 Guldendal; 02 270 81 11; w mot.be; Apr–Sep 09.00–17.00 Mon–Fri, w/ends & public hols 14.00–18.00; adult/6–18/

under 6 €5/2/free) Despite having the dullest museum name ever conceived, MOT – spread across the 17th-century watermills Liermolen, Tommenmolen and Guldendal – is actually quite interesting and housed in wonderful buildings. Its collection mainly revolves around hand tools past and present. The **Guldendal**, which serves as the museum headquarters, offers smithing demonstrations. The former grain mills **Liermolen and Tommenmolen** (8 Vorststraat & 18 Tommenmolenstraat; ⌚ Apr–Sep 14.00–18.00 Sat–Sun & hols) sit in the north of town. During the tourist season, Liermolen puts on milling demos, while Tommenmolen has a lovely café.

Thermae Grimbergen (74 Wolvertemsesteenweg; 02 270 81 96; w thermae.com; ⌚ 10.30–23.00 Mon–Thu & Sun, 11.30–midnight Fri–Sat; day rate €27) Wonderful, recently renovated wellness centre with extensive sauna and pampering facilities indoors and outdoors, as well as trendy treatments like halotherapy (relaxing in a salt chamber). The wood sauna overlooks the abbey church. Much nudity but they have swimsuit sections, thankfully!

HALLE

Right up against the Flanders/Wallonia border, Halle lies 15km southwest of Brussels and is the main town of Pajottenland, an area of gently rolling farmland famous for its Lambic beers. The town was a major pilgrimage site from the 13th to the 15th centuries thanks to a miraculous statue of the Virgin Mary, and the church that grew up around it is still a big crowd-puller. In spring, Halle's forests are carpeted in bluebells, making for a stunning display; beer lovers should take the opportunity to make a pilgrimage to the renowned brewery 3 Fonteinen, which produces world-class gueuzes (strong, sparkling beer), and, not far away, the picture-perfect Kasteel van Beersel.

GETTING THERE AND AWAY

By car From Brussels follow the E19 south, take exit 21 (direction: Halle) and merge on to the E429/N203a (direction: Lille), then take exit for N6/Halle Centrum (20km; ⌚ 25mins).

By train Brussels (every 10mins Mon–Fri, every 20mins Sat–Sun; ⌚ 10mins).

TOURIST INFORMATION

Tourist information 1 Grote Markt; 02 365 98 50; w halle.be/toerisme; ⌚ Apr–Sep 09.00–noon & 13.00–16.00; Oct–Mar 09.00–noon & 13.30–16.00 Mon–Fri. Housed in the 17th-century town hall, this bright office has lots of information, but unfortunately mostly in Dutch & the women on the desk don't speak much English. Pick up some treats from their regional products stand.

Bike rental Fietspunt, 2 Vandenpeereboomstraat (railway station); 02 361 04 35; ⌚ 07.00–19.00 Mon–Fri; €10/day

WHERE TO STAY AND EAT In summer, the thing to eat is *plattekaas* (dark bread spread with cottage cheese and sprinkled with chopped radish) with a glass of local gueuze (page 49). Those with a sweet tooth should try *Halse krotten* (caramel sweets), which have their roots in pilgrimages, but also feature on the last day of the Halle Carnival (fourth weekend of Lent, usually March), when 5,000 of them are thrown through the windows of cafés on the Grote Markt! You can find all these and more at the well-stocked **Streekproducten Centrum** (3a Poststraat; 02 361 31 90; w streekproductencentrum.be; 09.00–18.00 Wed–Fri, 09.00–17.00 Sat).

Les Eleveurs (16 rooms) 1a Suikerkaai; 02 361 13 40; w les-eleveurs.be. Pleasant, modern rooms ranging from €125 for a standard to €165 for the 'luxury wellness' room with an infrared cabin. The on-site bistronomy restaurant (€€€–€€€€) is arguably Halle's best. Leafy terrace a boon. €€€

Restaurant de Kaai 12a Suikerkaai; 02 380 18 44; w restaurantdekaai.be; noon–14.00 & 18.30–22.00 Thu–Mon. On a nice canal a bit out of the centre, an outstanding fish restaurant – not cheap, but fish rarely is, & they offer good-value weekday specials. €€€€

Tes Tien En Tander 12 Maandagmarkt; m 0489 99 55 80; f; 08.00–18.00 Mon–Sat. Very cosy, country-style café right in the centre with a great range of coffees – though the most popular menu item is definitely the decadent chocolate milk. Lovely sweet treats too. €

WHAT TO SEE AND DO

Sint-Maartensbasiliek (St Martin's Basilica) (1 Grote Markt; 02 365 98 50; 09.00–noon & 13.30–16.00 Mon–Fri; Apr–Sep 09.00–noon & 13.00–16.00; free) Completely scrubbed up in 2015, this High Gothic church feels more like a cathedral – a sign of how rich Halle once was. The current church dates from 1409, but it's been a major site of pilgrimage since 1267 when Aleydis, a daughter of the Lord of Halle, gifted a statue of the Virgin Mary. Visits from princes and popes raised enough money to build this huge shrine, which is studded with interesting features.

Naturally, the main point of focus is the statue of Mary, or 'Black Madonna', kept on a plinth above the high altar. Legend has it she acquired her dark appearance during the siege of 1489 when she was placed on the city walls and, miraculously, caught cannonballs in her tiny lap – the gunpowder turning her black. These cannonballs are stored behind bars in a niche on the left as you enter the basilica.

Next your eye is drawn to the ornate pulpit, the base of which features Faith (woman holding the cross) and two angels destroying Sin, represented by rats and other vermin. The chapel off to the right is the Old Chapel of Adam and Eve, its altar laden with flowers and candles. Following the door to the left of the altar will take you round the back of the main altar, past all the side chapels, to the sacristy at the far end which marks the entrance to the crypt, whose treasures can be viewed on selected days.

Just before going down the short flight of stairs, look to your left to see the tiny tomb of Joachim, the son of French King Louis XI, tucked into the wall. Off to the right is the Trazegnies Chapel with a huge alabaster altarpiece depicting the seven sacraments, dating from 1467.

Finally, before leaving the church, have a peek at the 15th-century font in the baptistry in the chapel to the left of the exit. Made from beaten brass, its lid features figures of the 12 apostles, the patron saints St Maarten, St Hubert and St George on horseback and, at the very top, Christ being baptised in the river Jordan. Every Whit Sunday (last Sunday in May) at 15.00, Halle hosts Mariaprocessie (w mariaprocessie.be), when the statue of Mary is paraded through town.

Den AST (16 Meiboom; 02 365 97 70; w denasthalle.be; Apr–Sep 09.00–noon & 14.00–17.00 Wed–Fri, 14.00–17.00 Sun & public hols; adult/under 12 €3/free) The former Museum of Southwest Brabant rebranded and relocated in 2015 to this malting plant. A visit explores the malting process, holy Halle and festive Halle.

Day trips

Brouwerij 3 Fonteinen (47 Molenstraat, 1651 Lot; 02 306 71 03; w 3fonteinen.be; Wed–Thu 10.00–17.00, Fri–Sat 10.00–19.00; tours 10.30 Fri–Sat on reservation, email lambikodroom@3fonteinen.be; €15 pp inc 2 tastings) Run by Armand Debelder, a figurehead of Belgian Lambic beer, this brewery dates back to

1883, when it was also an inn. Despite major setbacks – notably the 'Thermostat Incident' in 2009, when they lost a year's worth of product – it continues to be renowned for its artisanal kriek (beer fermented with cherries) and gueuze; in 2016 they opened the Lambik-O-Droom: a tasting room and shop overlooking the barrel room, where you can also take tours. To get there, take the train from Halle to Lot (twice an hour, ⌚ 6mins) or Brussels (twice an hour, ⌚ 11mins), from where it's a short walk.

Hallerbos (Nijvelsesteenweg; **w** hallerbos.be) Just 5km southeast of Halle, this nature-rich woodland – home to pheasant, rabbit and deer – is famous for its springtime carpet of bluebells.

Getting there and away You can rent bicycles from Halle railway station (it's a 5km ride) or take the bus. During the week catch TEC bus 114 from outside Halle railway station (hourly; ⌚ 10mins) and get off at Halle Vlasmarkt. At the weekend, take De Lijn bus 156 (hourly; ⌚ 20mins) from the railway station and get off at Lembeek Congo; from there it's a 17-minute walk to the forest entrance. Alternatively, if you've got a car, take the N28 south from Halle and after passing Hall Horses Farm on your right, take the next left and follow Vlasmarktdreef across the motorway until you reach the woods. Alternatively, if you've got a car, take the N28 south from Halle, following signs for Dworp. After passing Ela Nijvel on your right, take the next left and follow Vlasmarktdreef across the motorway and the entrance is immediately on the right.

Kasteel van Beersel (Beersel Castle) (65 Lotsestraat, 1650 Beersel; ☎ 02 359 16 36; ⌚ Mar–Nov 11.00–17.00 Sat–Sun; Apr–May & Sep–Oct 13.00–17.00 Tue–Fri, 11.00–17.00 Sat–Sun; Jun–Aug 10.00–18.00 Tue–Sun; adult/under 12/under 3 €3/1/free) Straight from the pages of a fairytale, Beersel's feudal castle – complete with moat, drawbridge, parapets and portcullis – is remarkably well preserved and one of Flanders' prettiest. It sits 4.5km north of Halle and was built in 1300 by Jean II, Duke of Brabant, as an early defence line for Brussels. Kids will love exploring the spiral staircases, dingy dungeons and armoury. Be sure to point out its machicolations too – the openings through which stones and boiling oil were poured on to the heads of invaders. French poet and novelist Victor Hugo was suitably impressed with the place to compose a few lines in its honour, albeit lamenting its dilapidated state pre-restoration in the 20th century:

> He lies there in the valley, the mansion alone.
> The least noise was silent in its dreary poles.
> And every hour of the day sees a stone fall from its dark niche.
> The raven lodged in its ancient rooms.
> The owl reiterated his complaint there every night
> And the blade of grass between the cold tiles of its vast corridors.

If you like, you can have lunch at the relaxed Brasserie Kasteel Beersel (**w** brasseriekasteelbeersel.com; **€€€**) just around the corner.

AARSCHOT

Aarschot is largely left off visitors' itineraries, which is a shame because it's a great town to wander around, especially on Thursdays when the centre is lined

KASSELSTAMPERS

Residents of Aarschot are known as *kasselstampers* (cobblestone stampers) because in the past the town was repeatedly raided by thieves. Locals decided to hire guards, but were dismayed to find that the men constantly retreated to the pub during cold weather. To solve the problem, they forced the guards to wear clogs, so they could hear them patrolling the streets and be sure they were doing their job.

with market stalls. It grew up around the chocolate-coloured Demer river, which races underneath the wonderfully preserved 16th-century former grain mill Hertogenmolen. If you can, arrange to visit on 15 August when the town celebrates the **Sint-Rochusverlichting** (w sintrochusverlichting.be), as the centre is lit with thousands of tea lights, trams wend between sights until midnight, and there are plenty of music and dance performances.

A word of warning: when you pick up a map from the tourist information office you'll notice that the published street names don't match those pinned to the buildings; the latter are in the local dialect and trying to marry up the two will put your map-reading skills to the test! Here are a couple to give you a head start: Eeuwigheidsstraat is Kardinaal Mercierstraat, and Cabaretstraat is Martelarenstraat.

GETTING THERE AND AWAY

By car From Leuven follow the E314 north, taking exit 22 (20km; ⏲ 22mins); from Hasselt follow the E313 and E314 west, again taking exit 22 (48km; ⏲ 35mins).

By train Brussels (twice an hour Mon–Fri, via Leuven hourly Sat–Sun; ⏲ 40mins); Leuven (4 times an hour Mon–Fri, twice an hour Sat–Sun; ⏲ 13mins); Lier (twice an hour Mon–Fri, hourly Sat–Sun; ⏲ 30mins); Hasselt (3 times an hour Mon–Fri, twice an hour Sat–Sun; ⏲ 30mins).

TOURIST INFORMATION

Tourist information 103 Elisabethlaan; 016 56 97 05; w hetgasthuis.be/toerisme; ⏲ 09.00–noon & 13.00–16.30 Tue–Fri, 14.00–18.00 Sat–Sun. Very friendly office a 10-minute walk from the centre that houses the Stedelijkmuseum & a traditional-style bar.

Bike rental Velo, 18a Statieplein; 016 48 23 79; w velo.be; ⏲ Apr–mid-Oct 07.00–19.00 Mon–Fri, 08.30–17.00 Sat; €10/day

WHERE TO STAY AND EAT

Hotel Pluimpapaver (5 rooms) 51 Nopstal; 016 50 22 19; w pluimpapaver.be. Jasmina & Hans run this picturesque B&B just outside town & with stellar facilities: a cosy bar, 3- or 4-course dinners (except Sun) prepared by Jasmina, a wellness area & ample bike maps etc. Copious b/fast inc. €€€

's Hertogenmolens (25 rooms) 1a Demerstraat; 016 44 86 01; w lodge-hotels.be. Located in a beautifully restored 16th-century former watermill. Rooms successfully blend old & new, with exposed wooden beams & river views. The calm, upmarket brasserie (€€–€€€) is excellent. Well worth investigating the bargain overnight packages with dinner, b/fast & walking maps. €€

't Eetkafee 30 Jozef Tielemansstraat; 016 57 08 70; w eetcafe.be; ⏲ 17.00–23.00 Wed–Sun. Unpretentious eetcafé offering a global menu – woks, pasta, fajitas etc – at a great price. Nice patio & family-friendly. €€–€€€

WHAT TO SEE AND DO

Onze-Lieve-Vrouwekerk (Church of Our Lady) (Kardinaal Mercierstraat; ⌚ 09.00–noon; free) Built from the area's distinctive brown bricks, Aarschot's 15th-century church is very large considering the small size of the town, whose population was greatly diminished during an outbreak of the plague. Prior to this, the town flourished on the back of the Flanders–Rhineland trade route, which ran along the Demer river, and under the patronage of William de Croÿ, Lord of Aarschot, who became Charles V's tutor. Indeed, the emperor attended de Croÿ's funeral held at the church in 1521 before the body was moved to Leuven. The dim interior is lit only by the flicker of candles and the glint of stained-glass windows. Amazingly, it survived the Iconoclasm, but lost most of its treasures during Spanish raids, except a lavish wrought-iron chandelier designed by Quinten Matsijs.

Begijnhof (Béguinage) (⌚ daily) The town's original 13th-century béguinage was looted and burned during the 15th and 16th centuries by Austrians and later the Spanish. The béguines fled to Leuven, but returned in 1609 and built the brick buildings you see now. Unlike Flanders' other béguinages, it feels less of a lost world, as it's open to the road; notice the statues of saints over the doorways.

Stedelijkmuseum (City Museum) (103 Elisabethlaan, inside & same hours as tourist information office; free) The tourist office has obviously put a lot of effort into its town history museum, which starts with a caveman wearing trendy fur anklets and continues all the way up to the 20th century. Highlights include a room dedicated to Arthur Meulemans, an Aarschot-born composer who famously wrote the music for Bruges's Heilig-Bloedprocessie; a huge collection of shoe-making machines; and the sounds of market singer Rik Viool, who sang the local news to passers-by until the 1960s–70s. There's also a focus on Aarschot during the two World Wars, when it suffered hugely, and beer – you can play old café games in the attached Bruin Café. Since 2012, the latter has revived local beer Aarschotse Bruine, which stopped being brewed when the Tielemans brewery, on the banks of the Demer, closed in 1960.

Day trip

Kasteel van Horst (Horst Castle) (28 Horststraat, 3220 Holsbeek; ☎ 016 62 33 45; w kasteelvanhorst.be; ⌚ closed for restoration) Sitting calm and tranquil 10km south of Aarschot, this beautiful 15th-century moated castle has barely changed since the last owner, Maria-Anna van den Tympel, moved out in the 17th century. For now it is closed for restoration, but in tourist season volunteers run an information centre (⌚ mid-Apr–Sep 13.00–17.00 Wed–Sun) offering guided tours and hikes around the castle. Take lunch (and a Horst beer) at on-site restaurant **Het Wagenhuis** (☎ 016 62 35 84; w hetwagenhuis.be; ⌚ 11.30–23.30 Wed–Sun; €€€€). They do a very decadent – and pricey – brunch on Sunday from 11.00 until 13.00.

Getting there and away Take bus 310 (direction: Leuven) from the railway station to Sint-Pieters-Rode Horst (⌚ 10mins), from where the castle is a 10-minute walk. By car, follow the N223 south, turn right into Luttelkolen, then take the first right on to Horststraat (9km; ⌚ 15mins).

DIEST

For nearly 300 years, between 1499 and 1795, the attractive town of Diest was home to the Princes of Orange-Nassau – who still rule the Netherlands today. It

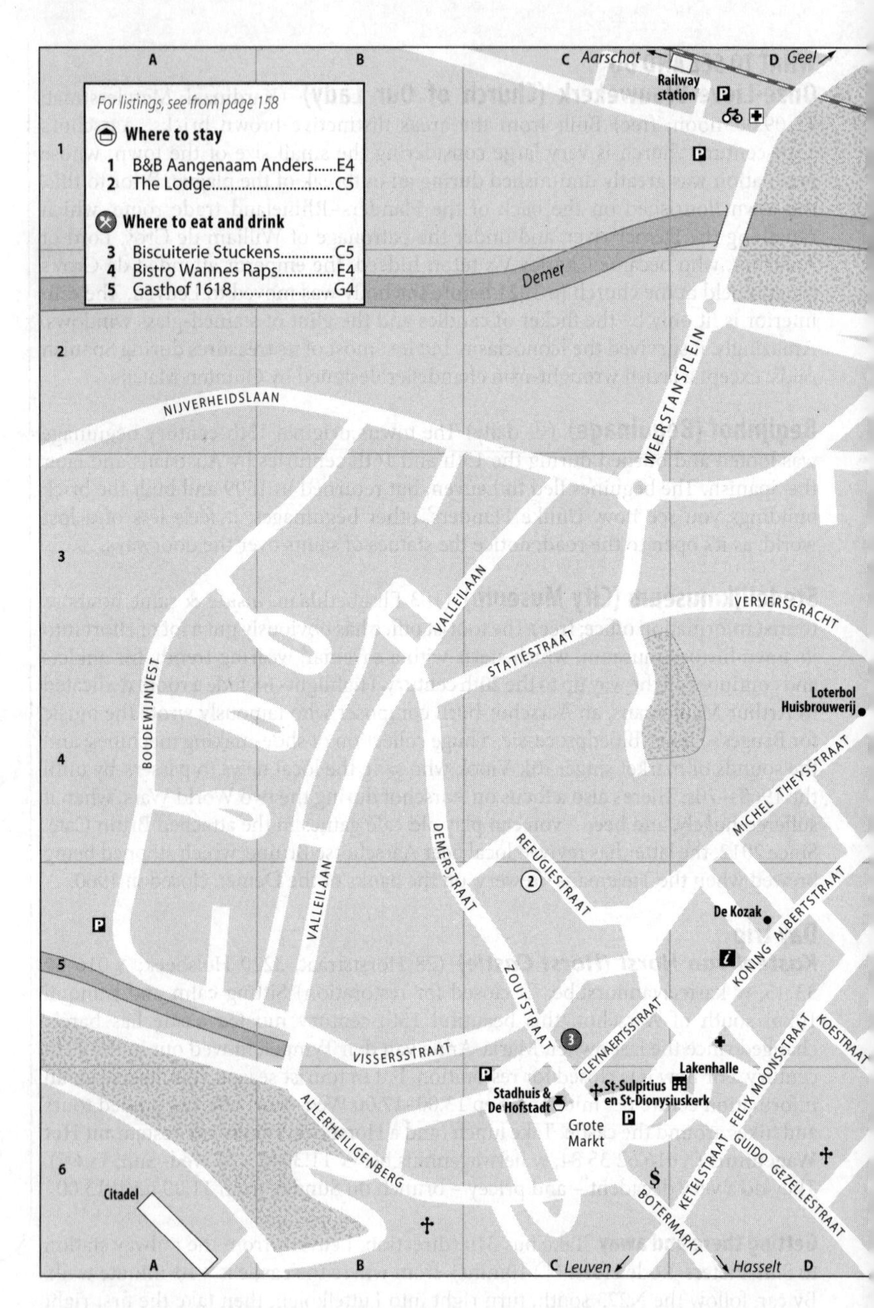

subsequently became known as the 'Orange City' and benefited from its location on the river Demer and the Cologne–Bruges trading route that operated along it. By the 16th century the linen trade had declined and the city's status nosedived as it was caught up in rebellions against the Spanish. Only under Austrian rule did stability and commerce return. The contorted Grote Markt is its main axis, but don't miss the béguinage – one of Flanders' finest.

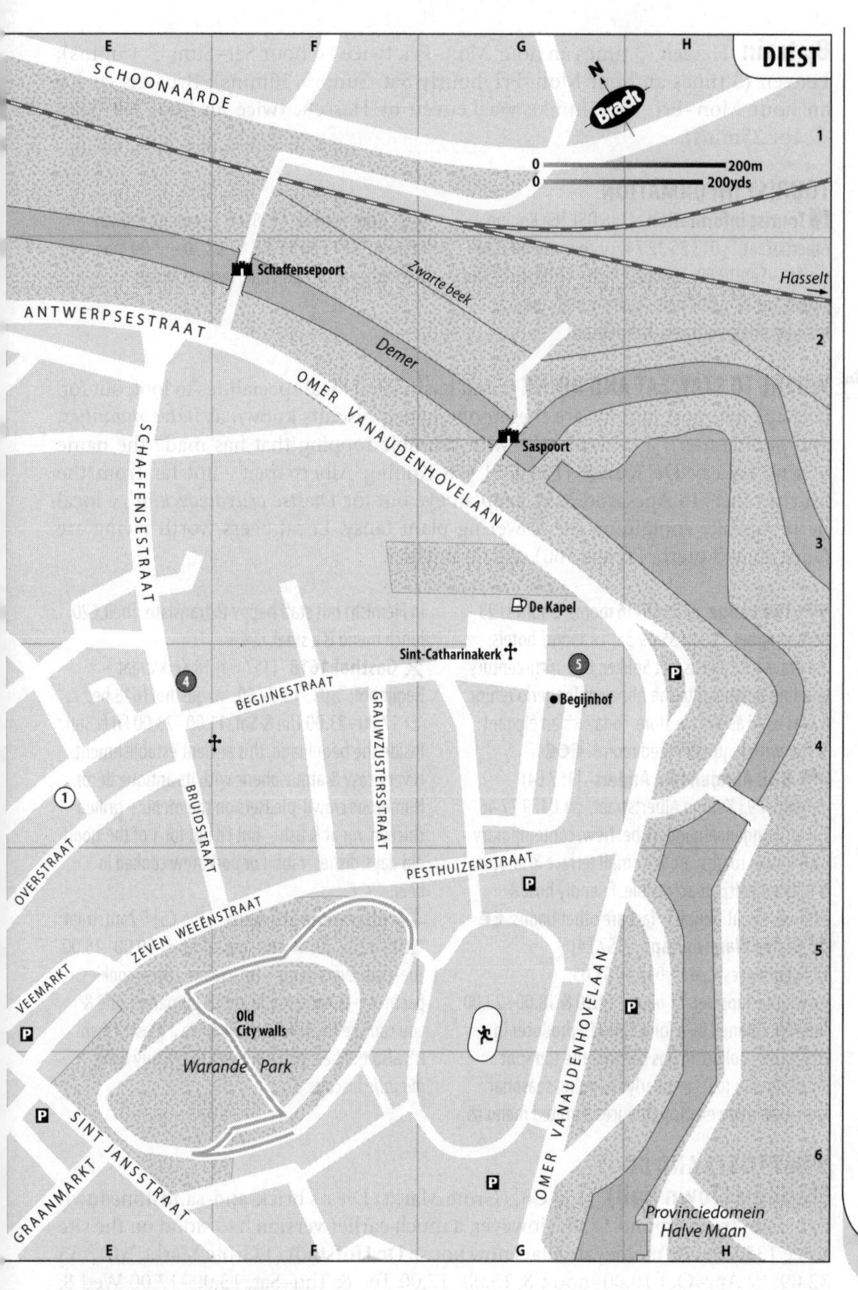

GETTING THERE AND AWAY

By car From Hasselt get on the E313 and in Lummen take the E314, then exit 25 (direction: Halen) (30km; ⌚ 23mins); from Leuven follow the E314, taking exit 24 (direction: Bekkevoort) (34km; ⌚ 30mins); from Tienen follow the N29 north (23km; ⌚ 30mins). You can park for free at the Citadel (Leuvensestraat), a 3-minute walk from town.

By train Hasselt (3 times an hour Mon–Fri, twice an hour Sat–Sun; ⏲ 15mins); Leuven (3 times an hour Mon–Fri, hourly Sat–Sun; ⏲ 30mins); Brussels (twice an hour Mon–Fri, ⏲ 45mins); via Leuven or Hasselt, twice an hour Sat–Sun, ⏲ 1hr 25mins).

TOURIST INFORMATION

Tourist information [156 D5] 16a Koning Albertstraat; ☎ 013 35 32 74; w toerismediest.be; ⏲ Apr–Sep 10.00–noon & 13.00–17.00; Oct–Mar closed Sun & public hols. A surprisingly large & modern office with very helpful staff.

Bike rental [156 D1] Fietspunt, railway station; ☎ 013 66 51 47; ⏲ 08.30–17.00 Mon–Fri; €10/day. For w/end visits, reserve ahead.

WHERE TO STAY, EAT AND DRINK Diest has several local specialities to look out for. Perhaps the most famous are the moon-shaped biscuits known as *halve maantjes*, and *patatjestaart*, a custard cake with crumble topping that has made the name of tiny bakery **De Kozak** [156 D5] (26 Koning Albertstraat), not far from the tourist office. In April and May, keep an eye out for *Diestse cruydtcoeck*; it's a local herb pancake containing the flowering plant tansy. Local beers worth trying are Gildenbier, Loterbol (page 160) and Oranjebier.

The Lodge [156 C5] (6 rooms, 2 suites) 23 Refugiestraat; ☎ 013 35 09 35; w lodge-hotels.be. Known locally as Het Spijker, this 16th-century building belonged to the Abbey of Tongerlo refuge & was used as a grain store. Today it's an elegant 3-star with high-ceilinged rooms. **€€€**

B&B Aangenaam Anders [157 E4] (3 rooms) 93 Koning Albertstraat; m 0479 77 46 77; w aangenaamanders.be. New, contemporary B&B with 3 rooms: 1 has a small terrace & another is fully wheelchair accessible. Friendly host & extensive continental b/fast are other boons. **€€**

Bistro Wannes Raps [157 E4] 17 Schaffensestraat; ☎ 013 30 58 05; w wannesraps.be; ⏲ noon–14.30 & 18.00–22.00 Tue–Fri. Opened by a long-time TV producer in 2012, this cool bistro has become the top spot locally owing to its regularly changing seasonal food with more exotic influences. Limited menu (& in Flemish) but staff happy to translate. Their €20 lunch menu is a steal. **€€€**

Gasthof 1618 [157 G4] 18 Kerkstraat – Begijnhof; ☎ 013 67 77 80; w gasthof1618.be; ⏲ 17.00–23.00 Thu & Sat, 11.00–23.00 Fri & Sun. Inside the béguinage, this ancient establishment is very cosy & atmospheric with its antique décor. Numerous crowd-pleasers on the menu – grilled chicken, meat & fish – but I'd opt for 1 of the 'good old days' dishes: rabbit or pork stew cooked in beer. **€€€**

Biscuiterie Stuckens [156 C5] 5 Zoutstraat; ☎ 013 32 52 20; w stuckens.com; ⏲ 09.00–18.00 Tue–Sat. Everything – ice-cream, cakes, cookies, pastries – is homemade at this upmarket café & you can see the bakers at work via a glass screen. It's also the best place in town to try/buy *halve maantje* biscuits. **€**

WHAT TO SEE AND DO

Stadhuis (Town Hall) [156 C6] (Grote Markt) Diest's brick-and-sandstone town hall dates from around 1730. However, a much earlier version had stood on the site since 1337 and its medieval cellars now house **De Hofstadt** (1 Grote Markt; ☎ 013 35 32 09; ⏲ Apr–Oct 10.00–noon & 13.00–17.00 Tue & Thu–Sat, 13.00–17.00 Wed & Sun; Nov–Mar 13.00–17.00 Tue–Sun; closed mid-Dec–mid-Jan; adult/under 12 €4/free, inc entrance to Museum voor Religieuze Kunst in St-Sulpitiuskerk), a museum devoted to the town's history and links to the House of Orange-Nassau. There's no audio guide, but ask for the laminated explanation sheets in English and start in the Gothic Hall. Here look for the 14th-century Virgin and Child statue – a copy of the original now stands in New York's Metropolitan Museum of Art – and five bells from the St Sulpitius Church carillon. On the left, the Orange-Nassau Room has portraits of René of Chalon, founder of the House of Orange-Nassau, and his wife, Anna of Lorraine, and next to these a painting of Philip William – whose tomb is found in St Sulpitius Church – lying in state in Brussels. Hanging on the back wall of the Linden Room you'll find Theodoor van Loon's *The Adoration of the Magi* (1645) and *The Presentation of Christ in the Temple and Simeon's Prophesy* (1635). The lovely *Esschius* triptych is in the Béguine Room, with its collection of household saints. Finally, in the dimly lit Treasure Chamber, are two remarkable 17th-century *Horti conclusi* – effectively 3D patchwork quilts – made by the *grauwzusters* of Diest (devout women who lived by the principles of St Francis but made no formal vow). You can also admire *The Annunciation*, a 1625 painting by Utrecht School artist Hendrik ter Brugghen included on the Flemish Masterpieces list.

Sint-Sulpitius en Sint-Dionysiuskerk (St Sulpitius and St Dionysius Church) [156 C6] (1 Grote Markt; ⌚ 15 May–15 Sep 14.00–17.00 Tue–Sun; free) Walk to the other side of the square to get a full view of Diest's main church, whose little tower is nicknamed the 'Mustard Pot'. It's unique thanks to its two-tone mishmash of red brick and white sandstone and because the construction became something of a farce, taking 18 architects 200 years to complete. The lavish interior has a number of treasures, most of which are held in the **Museum voor Religieuze Kunst** (**Museum of Religious Art**) (⌚ as above; €2, or combi-ticket with De Hofstadt €4). However, the main attraction here is the tomb of Filips Willem (Philip William), a Prince of Orange and Lord of Diest. He was kidnapped at the age of 13 and taken to Spain to be brought up as a strict Catholic, in retaliation for his father, William the Silent, ignoring the Spanish Duke of Alba's order to return to Brussels. Filips Willem didn't return until he was 42, but from then on he visited Diest regularly. On his death, after lying in state in Brussels, his embalmed body was buried between the choirstalls on 1 April 1618.

Lakenhalle (Cloth Hall) [156 D6] (Koning Albertstraat) Diest's 14th-century Cloth Hall was built at the height of the town's economic success, when its linen was found throughout western Europe and the trading of cattle and grain brought in huge sums of money. By the 17th century, trading had all but ceased and, over the years, the building was used as a school, an abattoir, a fire station and a festival hall; it's now an events venue. The 15th-century 'Holle Griet' cannon stands outside.

Warande [157 E6/F6] (Graanmarkt) On your way to the béguinage, take a detour through this fairly steep town park, studded with the remains of the old 19th-century city walls.

Begijnhof (Béguinage) [157 G4] (Begijnenstraat; free) Diest's 18th-century béguinage is wonderful to wander around, its chocolate-box cottages studded with original fixtures and hidden among them a B&B, a restaurant and a pub. Entering via the elaborate Baroque archway, you encounter the recently restored **Sint-Catharinakerk** (**St Catherine's Church**), dating from the 14th century. Around the back is **De Kapel** pub (Infermeriestraat 6; ☎ 013 33 33 70; w dekapel-diest.be; ⌚ 11.00–23.00 Tue–Sun) and, just down the lane, the atmospheric **Gasthof 1618** restaurant (see opposite). In the season it's worth visiting the information centre **In de Zevende Hemel** (21 Kerkstraat; ⌚ Apr–Sep 14.00–17.00 Sat–Sun; Oct–Mar 14.00–17.00 Sun). Every year, on the second Sunday in May, the béguinage hosts a **Begijnhoffeesten** (Béguinage Festival) with food and craft stalls to celebrate Mothers' Day, and at

19.00 on the first Sunday of September the streets and doorways are lined with tea lights, bathing the béguinage in gold.

Loterbol Huisbrouwerij [156 D4] (58a Michel Theysstraat; ☎ 013 77 10 07; w loterbol.be; ⌚ 16.00–midnight first Sat of month; free) Die-hard beer lovers will be pleased to hear that Belgium's smallest brewery – it produces around 650 crates a year – opens the doors of its on-site café the first Saturday of every month. You can try the Loterbol vat, a bitter banana-scented beer (6%), and the fruitier Blonde and Bruin (8%), and they often open up the brewing rooms too.

TIENEN

This oft-overlooked town has the biggest Grote Markt in Belgium after Sint-Niklaas, thanks largely to its status as a major market town during the Middle Ages. Most of the action now centres around this square, which still hosts a weekly market on Tuesdays and Fridays (⌚ 07.00–13.00) and is dominated by the former Justice of the Peace Court on the north side, the Onze-Lieve-Vrouwe-ten-Poelkerk on the east side and the flag-adorned town hall on the south side. The rose compass embedded in the pavement outside the town hall marks the spot where the town pillory once stood and where, macabrely, Belgium's last beheading took place in 1847. Now known as 'Sugar Town' thanks to the large sugarbeet-processing factory to the south, Tienen hosts the popular Suikerrock festival (w suikerrock.be) every July. Locals are known as *Tiense Kwèèkers* (Tienen Quackers), either owing to a local sexton's release of a duck – instead of the usual white dove, which he couldn't find – during Pentecost celebrations, or a failed ambush of rival city Leuven disrupted by pesky ducks!

GETTING THERE AND AWAY

By car From Leuven follow the N3 southeast (19km; ⌚ 30mins); from Hasselt take the N80 to Sint-Truiden and then follow the N3 west to Tienen (38km; ⌚ 45mins); from Diest follow the N29 south (23km; ⌚ 25mins). Paid parking is available on the Grote Markt; free parking on Sint-Jorisplein.

By train Leuven (every 10mins Mon–Fri, twice an hour Sat–Sun; ⌚ 15mins); Brussels (twice an hour; ⌚ 44mins); Hasselt (hourly; ⌚ 35mins). To get to the Grote Markt from the station, take Vierde Lansierslaan and at the end arc right slightly on to Leuvensestraat; follow it all the way to the northwestern edge of the main square.

TOURIST INFORMATION

Tourist information 6 Grote Markt; ☎ 016 80 57 38; w toerisme.tienen.be; ⌚ 10.00–17.00 Tue–Sun. A fabulously stocked *streekproducten* shop selling local Hageland produce & also doubling as the tourist office. Has walking & cycling maps. The fate of the former Sugar Museum next door was still undecided in 2019, but it's likely to become an exhibition space in the future.

WHAT TO SEE AND DO

Het Toreke (6 Grote Markt; ⌚ 10.00–17.00 Tue–Sun, last ticket 16.00; adult/under 26/under 6 €4/2/free) Intriguingly, the building which houses this museum served as the town prison for over a century, until the 1970s. It now contains an exhibition on Roman death and life rituals, drawing on Gallo-Roman treasures uncovered in local archaeology digs. The reconstruction of a Mithras temple and a Gallo-Roman tumulus grave are the eye-catchers. (If you're really intrigued, the tourist office sells a €9 Gallo-Roman cycling map leading you past major sites.)

Onze-Lieve-Vrouwe-ten-Poelkerk (Our Lady of the Lake Church) (Grote Markt) Marking the beginning of the Brabantine High Gothic style in Flanders, but predominantly Baroque on the inside, this church dates from the 14th and 15th centuries. It's named after a lake that once stood on the site and was drained to make way for the Grote Markt.

Sint-Germanuskerk (St Germanus Church) (36 Veemarkt) Beautiful church, expanded over the years from a 9th-century abbey church, on Tienen's original medieval market square. The 16th-century belfry houses a huge 54-bell carillon; in July and August you can listen to concerts every Wednesday night (🕘 20.00) – a listening post has been set up in the Apostle Courtyard, part of the original church graveyard! Visits to the UNESCO-listed tower are via guided tour only; reserve via the tourist office.

Necropolis (Pastorijstraat, Grimde; 🕘 08.30–17.00; free) The restored 13th-century St Peter's Church gained a new purpose in 1915, when around 140 Belgian soldiers who had fallen during the Great War were buried within the floor. A protected monument since 2002, it's also Belgium's first 'Silence Tourism' attraction. Getting there requires a 10-minute bike ride from town, or take bus 313 (direction: Tienen–St-Truiden) from Tienen Atheneum, just north of the Grote Markt, alighting at Tienen Tumuli (🕘 8mins). While you're there, have a look at the newly restored **De Drie Tumuli (Three Tumuli)** (Sint-Truidensesteenweg; 🕘 dawn–dusk), three roman burial hills built for Marcus Probius Burrus, a leading local citizen, and rich in archaeological gems.

SEND US YOUR SNAPS!

We'd love to follow your adventures using our *Northern Belgium* guide – why not tag us in your photos and stories via Twitter (@BradtGuides) and Instagram (@bradtguides)? Alternatively, you can upload your photos directly to the gallery on the Northern Belgium destination page via our website (**w** bradtguides.com/northernbelgium).

5

East Flanders

East Flanders – or *Oost Vlaanderen* – is my favourite region. Spend a few days in the vibrant regional capital of Ghent strolling the pretty cobbled streets and dining in some of Flanders' best restaurants, then head out into the countryside and have a go at the legendary Ronde van Vlaanderen cycling route, which runs from Oudenaarde to Geraardsbergen, where you can refuel on the delicious local *mattentaart*. In Sint-Niklaas learn about the legend of Reynard the Fox, and take the kids to see Sinterklaas's workshop; explore Ronse's rarely visited 13th-century Sint-Hermescrypte, and dance like a fool at Aalst Carnival (see box, page 200). Fans of beer and cycling might like to combine the two via the East Flanders tourist board's new Plan Bier (**w** planbier.be) campaign, which has resulted in an English Beer Guide (€9.95) featuring five cycling tours – one for each East Flanders region – and a Ghent walking route; myriad beer-themed cycling and walking brochures of the region are also available to download for free from their website.

GHENT (GENT)

Victor Hugo described Ghent as 'a kind of Venice of the North'. He wasn't exaggerating. Bruges may have more waterways, but it's far from an insider secret. Ghent, on the other hand, receives fewer visitors but has equally pretty medieval architecture and real Flemish residents, who are immensely proud of their buzzing, progressive university town – so proud that they're not really bothered if tourists visit or not. Actually, they've been a law unto themselves since Charles V's day, and this headstrong lot isn't about to start kowtowing to outsiders, which is only another incentive to visit. Trams rattle through the cobbled streets of a beautifully preserved city centre strong on boutique B&Bs and excellent restaurants, and home to fine and contemporary art museums, a triptych of béguinages and one world-famous, oft-stolen treasure: *The Adoration of the Mystic Lamb*, set to shine in 2020 via a new visitor centre when Ghent pulls out the stops to celebrate van Eyck year.

HISTORY Ghent's name is believed to be a derivative of the Celtic word 'ganda' meaning 'confluence', which perfectly describes its location at the confluence of the Scheldt and Leie rivers. A pivotal moment came in AD630, when French missionary St Amand founded two abbeys: St Pieter's and St Baaf's. A settlement grew around them and, despite a couple of Viking raids, the city flourished from the 11th century onwards. Originally, Ghent's wool industry was served by sheep reared on the fertile flats surrounding the rivers, but this was soon eclipsed by trade with England and the import of grain from northern France. The speed of trade improved further when Margaret of Constantinople, Countess of Flanders, gave permission for the Lieve canal to be dug in 1251, linking Ghent with Damme and

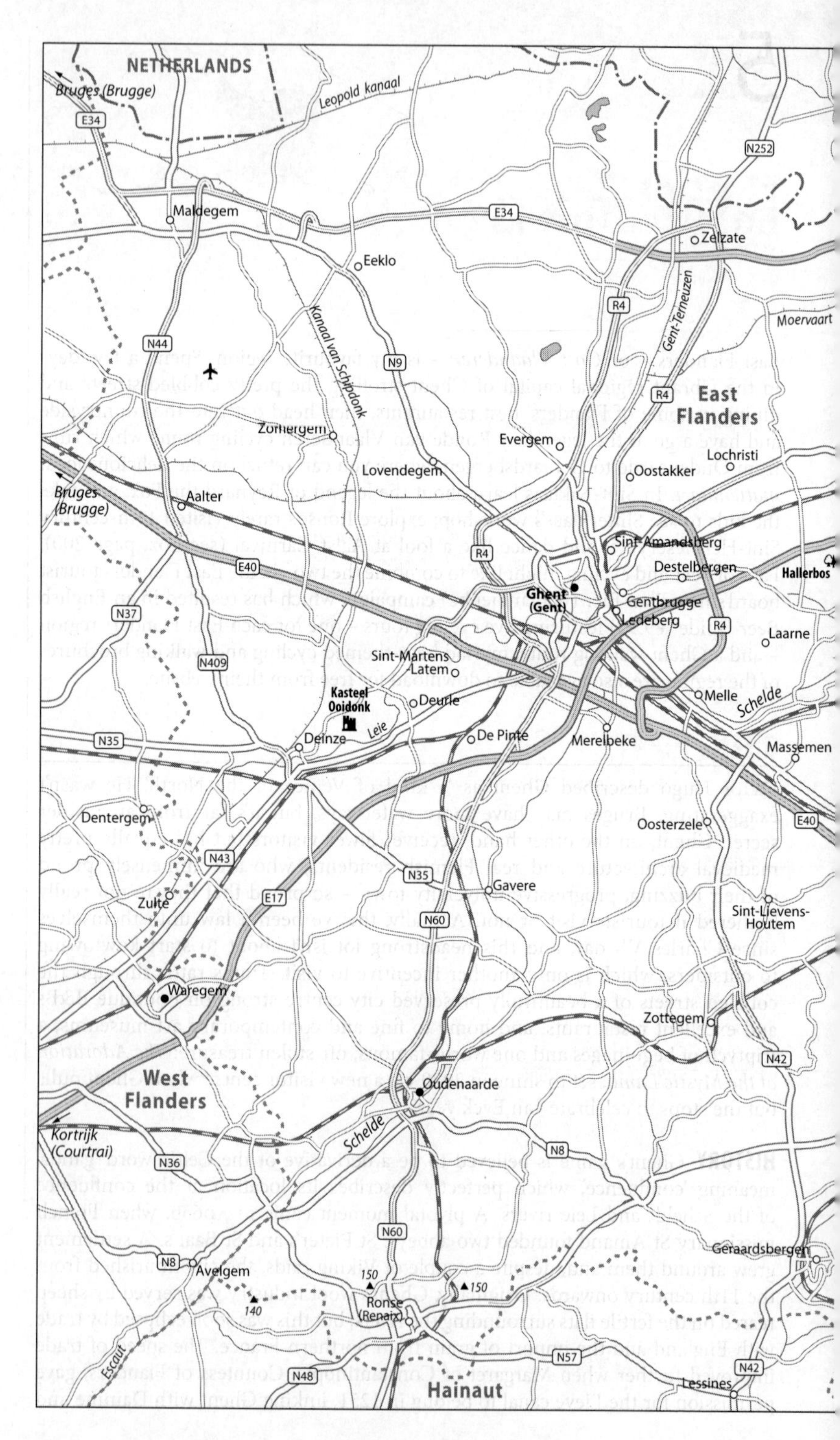
NETHERLANDS
Bruges (Brugge)
E34
Leopold kanaal
N252
Maldegem
E34
Zelzate
Eeklo
R4
Gent-Terneuzen
Moervaart
N44
Kanaal van Schipdonk
N9
R4
East Flanders
Zomergem
Evergem
Lochristi
Lovendegem
Oostakker
Bruges (Brugge)
Aalter
R4
Sint-Amandsberg
E40
Destelbergen
Hallerbos
Ghent (Gent)
Gentbrugge
N37
Ledeberg
R4
Laarne
N409
Sint-Martens-Latem
Kasteel Ooidonk
Deurle
Melle
Schelde
N35
Deinze
Leie
De Pinte
Merelbeke
Massemen
Dentergem
Oosterzele
E40
N43
N35
Gavere
Zulte
E17
Sint-Lievens-Houtem
N60
Waregem
Zottegem
N42
West Flanders
Oudenaarde
Kortrijk (Courtrai)
Schelde
N8
N36
N60
Geraardsbergen
N8
Avelgem
150
150
140
Ronse (Renaix)
Escaut
N57
N42
N48
Hainaut
Lessines

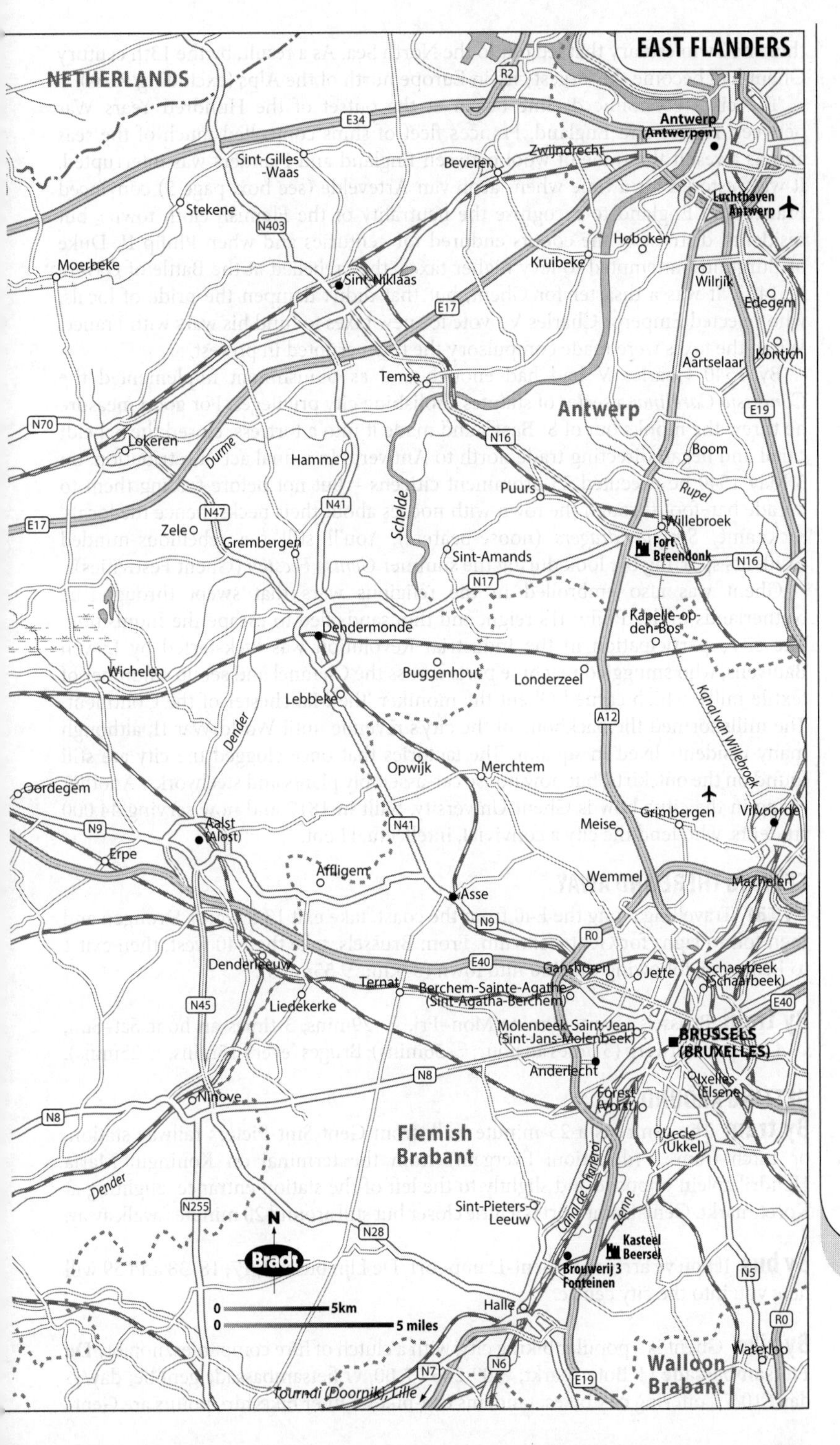
EAST FLANDERS
NETHERLANDS
R2
E34
Antwerp
(Antwerpen)
Sint-Gilles
-Waas
Beveren
Zwijndrecht
Luchthaven
Antwerp
Stekene
N403
Hoboken
Kruibeke
Moerbeke
Wilrijk
Sint-Niklaas
Edegem
E17
Aartselaar
Kontich
Temse
Antwerp
E19
N70
N16
Lokeren
Durme
Boom
Hamme
Puurs
Rupel
N41
N47
Willebroek
E17
Zele
Grembergen
Schelde
Fort
Breendonk
Sint-Amands
N16
N17
Kapelle-op-
den-Bos
Dendermonde
Wichelen
Buggenhout
Londerzeel
Lebbeke
Kanaal van Willebroek
Dender
A12
Opwijk
Merchtem
Oordegem
Grimbergen
Vilvoorde
N9
Aalst
(Alost)
Meise
N41
Erpe
Affligem
Wemmel
Machelen
Asse
N9
R0
E40
Ganshoren
Jette
Schaerbeek
(Schaarbeek)
Denderleeuw
Ternat
Berchem-Sainte-Agathe
(Sint-Agatha-Berchem)
E40
N45
Liedekerke
Molenbeek-Saint-Jean
(Sint-Jans-Molenbeek)
BRUSSELS
(BRUXELLES)
N8
Anderlecht
Ixelles
(Elsene)
Forest
(Vorst)
Ninove
N8
Flemish
Brabant
Uccle
(Ukkel)
Canal de Charleroi
Dender
Zenne
Sint-Pieters-
Leeuw
N255
N
N28
Kasteel
Beersel
Bradt
Brouwerij 3
Fonteinen
N5
0
5km
Halle
0
5 miles
R0
Waterloo
N7
N6
Walloon
Brabant
E19
Tournai (Doornik), Lille

thus the Zwin estuary that led out to the North Sea. As a result, by the 13th century Ghent had become the largest city in Europe north of the Alps (excluding Paris).

The city's economic decline began at the outset of the Hundred Years War between France and England. France's fleet of ships controlled much of the seas and as a result the trade of wool between England and Flanders was interrupted. It was restored for a time when Jacob van Artevelde (see box, page 5) convinced France and England to recognise the neutrality of the Flemish cloth towns, but residents' distrust of the counts endured for centuries and when Philip II, Duke of Burgundy, attempted to levy higher taxes, they rebelled at the Battle of Gavere in 1453. It was a disaster for Ghent, but that didn't dampen the pride of locals, who rejected Emperor Charles V's vote for new taxes to fund his wars with France. When the taxes were made compulsory the town erupted in protest.

By 1540 Charles V had had enough and as punishment implemented the *Concessio Carolina*: a series of statutes abolishing city privileges. For good measure he threw the monks out of St Baaf's and made it into a fortress, closed the Scheldt canal and began directing trade north to Antwerp. In a final act of retribution, on 3 May 1540 he executed 25 prominent citizens – but not before forcing them to parade barefoot through the town with nooses about their necks, hence the locals' nickname: *Stroppendragers* (noose-bearers). You'll still see rebellious-minded residents sporting the look during the summer *Gentse Feesten* (Ghent Festivities).

Ghent was also embroiled in the religious wars that swept through the Netherlands under Philip II's reign, and thousands fled to escape the Inquisition. The city's participation in the Industrial Revolution was kickstarted by Lieven Bauwens, who smuggled machine parts across the Channel and set up a number of textile mills, which earned Ghent the moniker 'the Manchester of the Continent'. The mills formed the backbone of the city's revenue until World War II, although many residents lived in squalor. The factories that once clogged the city are still found on the outskirts, but now house car-assembly plants and steelworks. Another string in the city's bow is Ghent University, built in 1817 and now serving 44,000 students, who lend the city a convivial, intellectual bent.

GETTING THERE AND AWAY

By car Travelling along the E40 from the coast, take exit 13 towards Drongen and then follow signs for Gent Centrum. From Brussels, take the E40 west, then exit 1 to Ledeberg, following the R40 into town (57km; ⏲ 55mins).

By train Brussels (every 10mins Mon–Fri, ⏲ 29mins; 3 times an hour Sat–Sun; ⏲ 42mins); Antwerp (3 times an hour; ⏲ 56mins); Bruges (every 15mins; ⏲ 25mins).

GETTING AROUND

By tram The centre is a 25-minute walk from Gent-Sint-Pieters railway station, or catch tram 1 (direction: Evergem) from the terminal on Koningin Maria Hendrikaplein opposite and slightly to the left of the station entrance, alighting at Korenmarkt. Gent-Dampoort is a little closer but still around 20 minutes' walk away.

By bus If you've arrived at Gent-Dampoort, De Lijn buses 3, 17, 18, 38 and 39 will take you into the city centre.

By bike Ghent is a popular biking city, with a clutch of hire companies, notably **De Fietsambassade** (1 Botermarkt; ☎ 09 266 77 00; w fietsambassade.gent.be; day/½ day €10/7), offering city bikes, tandems & e-bikes. Other bike-hire points are Gent-

Dampoort (next to the bicycle parking area/blue container; 07.00–19.00 Mon–Fri) and Gent-Sint-Pieters (south side of station; same hours as Dampoort, but also Mar–Oct 10.00–18.00 Sat). The tourist office sells themed cycling maps (€2), most rewardingly the 'Chateau route' leading to the Kasteel van Laarne (page 191).

TOURIST INFORMATION

Tourist information [172 A2] 5 Sint-Veerleplein; 09 266 56 60; w visitgent.be; 10.00–18.00. Hyper-modern glass-walled office on the Oude Vismijn with a multi-media touchscreen table & real humans to speak to also. By Starbucks in Gent-Sint-Pieters station [168 G3] is a digital info point with free city maps; you can consult FAQs & even make a video call to the main office. Very cutting-edge!

GUIDED TOURS

BeerWalk Departs from 2 Botermarkt; 09 233 76 89; w beerwalk.be. Discover Ghent's brewing tradition & history through beer goggles on 3hr walks (€39). You taste 5 regional beers inc rare Sint-Joris Blonde & Flemish Old-Style Sour Ale.

Bike Ghent m 0478 02 94 67; w bikeghent.be. Run by the enthusiastic Christophe, who takes you to off-the-beaten-track locations old & new on mountain bikes. The 3hr tours (€40) cover a lot of ground, but aren't too exhausting.

Gandante 9 Botermarkt; 09 375 31 61; m 0479 51 52 42; e info@gandante.be; w gandante.be. Guide association offering over 100 original tours inc – most exclusively – the Belfort, which is usually off-limits. The tours last approx 90mins & cost €90 (up to 25 people). Book by email at least 3 days in advance.

Gent Free Walking Tours m 0498 68 66 83; w gentfreewalkingtours.com. Depart from Hostel Uppelink (page 171) at 10.00, 13.00 & 18.30. Funny, informative volunteer guides have elevated this outfit into the most popular of its kind in town. Expect historical snippets & recommendations for the best spots to get fries & chocolate during the 2hr circuit. No need to book ahead.

Guide for Ghent m 474 84 28 03; w guide-for-ghent.com. Superb private tours shot through with art history insights, Flemish folklore & more by Russian-born Anna, who moved to Ghent in 1999 to study & never left. She offers highlights & Ghent Altarpiece tours (3hrs, €150) but can tailor things depending on interest.

Rederij De Gentenaer Groentenmaarkt (Vleeshuisbrug); Mar 11.00–16.00 w/ends, Apr–mid-Oct 10.30–18.30 daily, mid-Oct–Dec 11.00–16.00 daily; adult/under 12 €7.50/4.50. Departs every 15–20mins; journey time around 50mins. Offers lots of options, but the basic tour (included with the Ghent City Card) is a bargain. In Jan & Feb, tours are run by sister ship *Gent-Watertoerist* & depart from Graslei.

Vizit 1 Hof ten Walle; 09 233 76 89; w vizit.be. Born in Ghent in 1995 & now covering much of Belgium, this outfit offers culinary tours by foot, bike or boat: 'Nibbling through Ghent' (€16) takes you to speciality sweet, cheese & chocolate shops, & 'Amuse Gueule' (from €65) lets you try 4 courses in 4 different restaurants.

 **WHERE TO STAY** With over 35 hotels in the city centre, finding a place to sleep in Ghent isn't hard – whether you want to bed down in a plush mansion, an eco-friendly barge or (why not?) a shipping container. There's more good news: in comparison to Brussels, Antwerp and Bruges, prices at even the most upmarket of establishments are incredibly reasonable, while budget travellers are well catered for too: there's a campsite and a clutch of really impressive youth hostels to choose from.

Luxury

1898 The Post [172 A3] (37 rooms) 16 Graslei; 09 391 53 79; w zannierhotels.com. Set in Ghent's former post office – hence the name. Rooms & suites over the top 2 floors are filled with antiques & labelled by size, starting with dinky 'Stamp' rooms; the most romantic is the Tower Suite in the octagonal clock tower. The

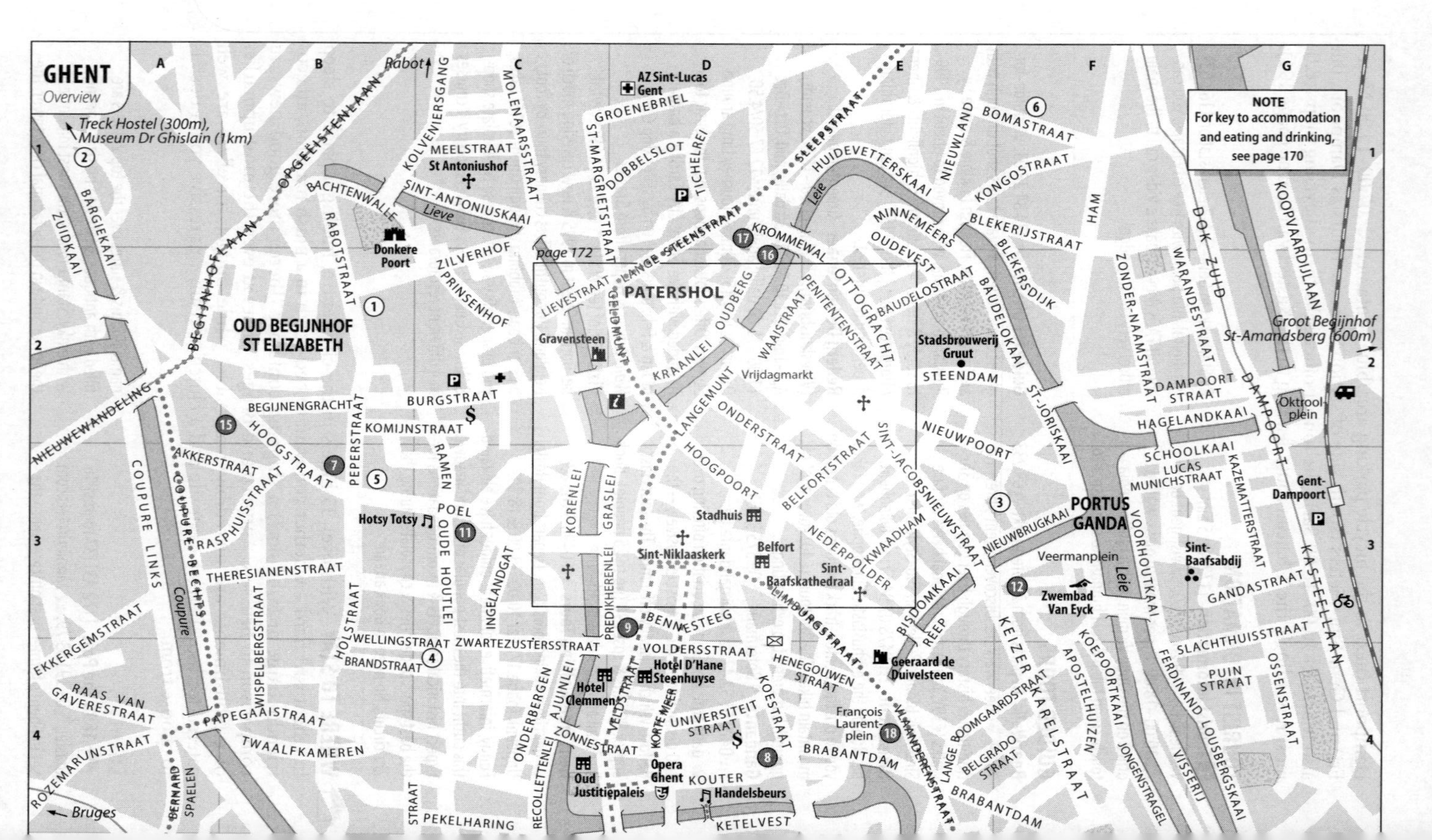
GHENT
Overview
Treck Hostel (300m), Museum Dr Ghislain (1km)
NOTE
For key to accommodation and eating and drinking, see page 170
page 172
Groot Begijnhof St-Amandsberg (600m)
Bruges
Rabot
A
B
C
D
E
F
G
1
2
3
4
ZUIDKAAI
BARGIEKAAI
OPGEEISTENLAAN
BEGIJNHOFLAAN
NIEUWEWANDELING
OUD BEGIJNHOF ST ELIZABETH
BACHTENWALLE
Donkere Poort
RABOTSTRAAT
KOLVENIERSGANG
MEELSTRAAT
St Antoniushof
SINT-ANTONIUSKAAI
Lieve
MOLENAARSSTRAAT
ZILVERHOF
PRINSENHOF
ST-MARGRIETSTRAAT
AZ Sint-Lucas Gent
GROENEBRIEL
DOBBELSLOT
TICHELREI
LANGE STEENSTRAAT
SLEEPSTRAAT
HUIDEVETTERSKAAI
Leie
NIEUWLAND
BOMASTRAAT
KONGOSTRAAT
HAM
MINNEMEERS
BLEKERIJSTRAAT
BLEKERSDIJK
KROMMEWAL
OUDEVEST
PATERSHOL
LIEVESTRAAT
GELDMUNT
OUDBERG
PENITENTENSTRAAT
OTTOGRACHT
BAUDELOSTRAAT
BAUDELOKAAI
Gravensteen
KRAANLEI
WAAISTRAAT
Vrijdagmarkt
Stadsbrouwerij Gruut
STEENDAM
ST-JORISKAAI
ZONDER-NAAMSTRAAT
WARANDESTRAAT
DOK ZUID
KOOPVAARDIJLAAN
DAMPOORT STRAAT
DAMPOORT
Oktrooi plein
HAGELANDKAAI
SCHOOLKAAI
LUCAS MUNICHSTRAAT
KAZEMATTERSTRAAT
Gent-Dampoort
BEGIJNENGRACHT
BURGSTRAAT
KOMIJNSTRAAT
HOOGSTRAAT
PEPERSTRAAT
AKKERSTRAAT
RAMEN
LANGEMUNT
ONDERSTRAAT
SINT-JACOBSNIEUWSTRAAT
NIEUWPOORT
HOOGPOORT
BELFORTSTRAAT
COUPURE LINKS
COUPURE RECHTS
Coupure
RASPHUISSTRAAT
POEL
Hotsy Totsy
OUDE HOUTLEI
KORENLEI
GRASLEI
Stadhuis
PORTUS GANDA
NIEUWBRUGKAAI
VOORHOUTKAAI
KASTEELLAAN
Sint-Niklaaskerk
Belfort
NEDERPOLDER
KWAADHAM
Veermanplein
Sint-Baafsabdij
THERESIANENSTRAAT
INGELANDGAT
PREDIKHERENLEI
Sint-Baafskathedraal
LIMBURGSTRAAT
BISDOMKAAI
REEP
Zwembad Van Eyck
GANDASTRAAT
EKKERGEMSTRAAT
HOLSTRAAT
WELLINGSTRAAT
ZWARTEZUSTERSSTRAAT
BENNESTEEG
VOLDERSSTRAAT
KEIZER KARELSTRAAT
SLACHTHUISSTRAAT
BRANDSTRAAT
WISPELBERGSTRAAT
ONDERBERGEN
AJUINLEI
Hotel Clemmen
VELDSTRAAT
Hotel D'Hane Steenhuyse
HENEGOUWEN STRAAT
Geeraard de Duivelsteen
KOEPOORTKAAI
APOSTELHUIZEN
FERDINAND LOUSBERGSKAAI
PUIN STRAAT
OSSENSTRAAT
RAAS VAN GAVERESTRAAT
PAPEGAAISTRAAT
UNIVERSITEIT STRAAT
KOESTRAAT
François Laurent-plein
VLAANDERENSTRAAT
LANGE BOOMGAARDSTRAAT
TWAALFKAMEREN
ZONNESTRAAT
KORTE MEER
BRABANTDAM
BELGRADO STRAAT
JONGENSTRAGEL
VISSERIJ
ROZEMARIJNSTRAAT
BERNARD SPAELEN
STRAAT
PEKELHARING
RECOLLETTENLEI
Oud Justitiepaleis
Opera Ghent
KOUTER
Handelsbeurs
KETELVEST
1
2
3
4
5
6
7
8
9
11
12
15
16
17
18

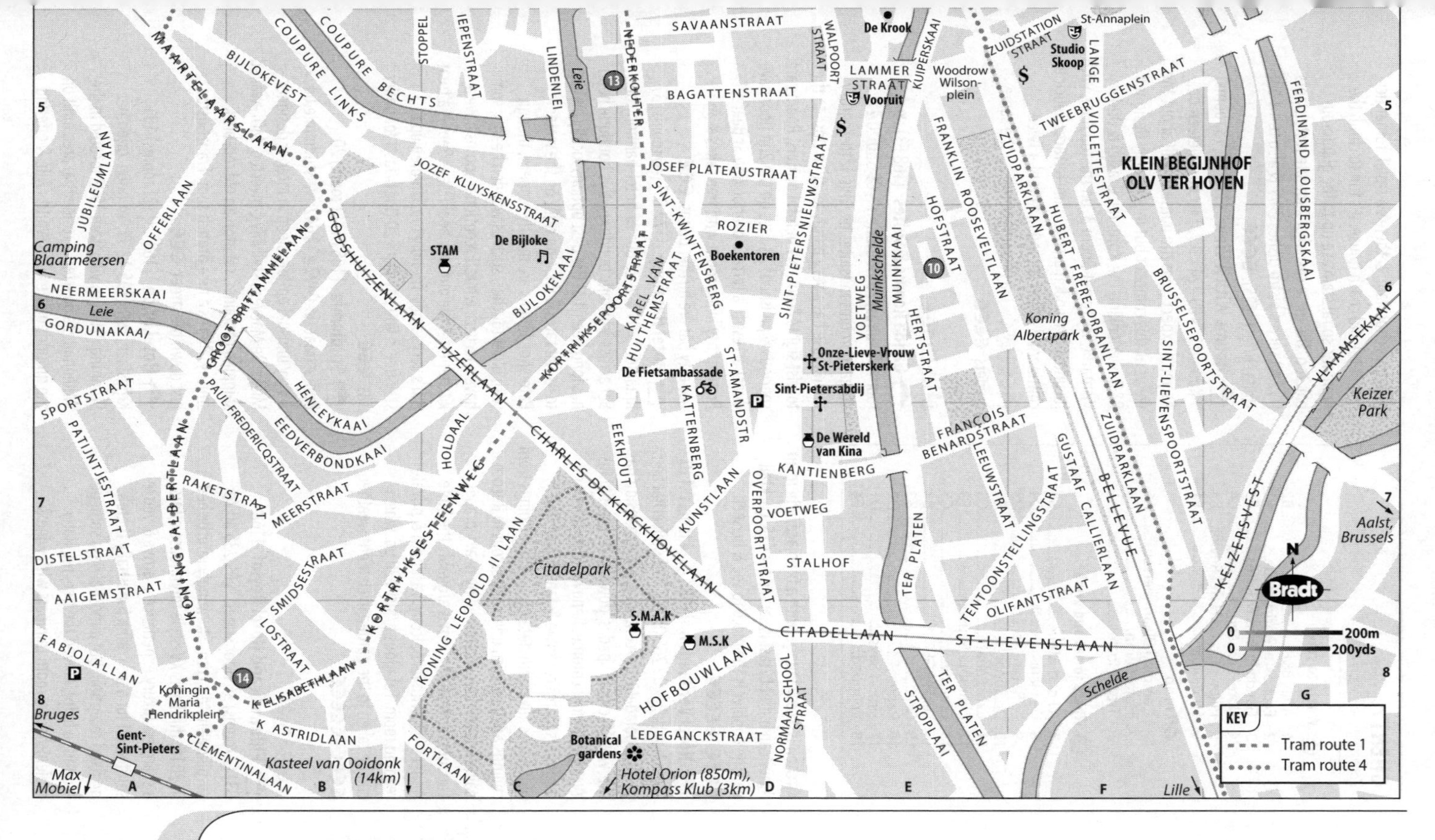
KEY
Tram route 1
Tram route 4
0 200m
0 200yds
N
Bradt
Aalst, Brussels
Keizer Park
VLAAMSEKAAI
FERDINAND LOUSBERGSKAAI
KLEIN BEGIJNHOF OLV TER HOYEN
KEIZERSVEST
BRUSSELSEPOORTSTRAAT
SINT-LIEVENSPOORTSTRAAT
ZUIDPARKLAAN
BELLEVUE
GUSTAAF CALLIERLAAN
HUBERT FRÈRE-ORBANLAAN
VIOLETTESTRAAT
LANGE
St-Annaplein
Studio Skoop
ZUIDSTATION STRAAT
TWEEBRUGGENSTRAAT
Koning Albertpark
Woodrow Wilson-plein
FRANKLIN ROOSEVELTLAAN
HOFSTRAAT
FRANÇOIS BENARDSTRAAT
LEEUWSTRAAT
TENTOONSTELLINGSTRAAT
OLIFANTSTRAAT
ST-LIEVENSLAAN
Schelde
Lille
TER PLATEN
STROPLAAI
KUIPERSKAAI
LAMMER STRAAT
De Krook
Vooruit
MUINKKAAI
Muinkschelde
HERTSTRAAT
VOETWEG
WALPOORT STRAAT
SINT-PIETERSNIEUWSTRAAT
Onze-Lieve-Vrouw St-Pieterskerk
Sint-Pietersabdij
De Wereld van Kina
KANTIENBERG
STALHOF
CITADELLAAN
NORMAALSCHOOL STRAAT
SAVAANSTRAAT
BAGATTENSTRAAT
JOSEF PLATEAUSTRAAT
ROZIER
Boekentoren
ST-AMANDSTR
OVERPOORTSTRAAT
SINT-KWINTENSBERG
De Fietsambassade
KATTERNBERG
KUNSTLAAN
M.S.K
HOFBOUWLAAN
LEDEGANCKSTRAAT
Hotel Orion (850m), Kompass Klub (3km)
NEDERKOUTER
KAREL VAN HULTHEMSTRAAT
KORTRIJKSEPOORTSTRAAT
EEKHOUT
CHARLES DE KERCKHOVELAAN
S.M.A.K
Citadelpark
Botanical gardens
Leie
LINDENLEI
BIJLOKEKAAI
De Bijloke
IEPENSTRAAT
STOPPEL
JOZEF KLUYSKENSSTRAAT
STAM
IJZERLAAN
HOLDAAL
KORTRIJKSESTEENWEG
KONING LEOPOLD II LAAN
FORTLAAN
COUPURE BECHTS
COUPURE LINKS
GODSHUIZENLAAN
HENLEYKAAI
EEDVERBONDKAAI
Kasteel van Ooidonk (14km)
BIJLOKEVEST
GROOT BRITTANNIELAAN
PAUL FREDERICQSTRAAT
MEERSTRAAT
SMIDSESTRAAT
LOSTRAAT
K ELISABETHLAAN
K ASTRIDLAAN
MAARTELAARSLAAN
RAKETSTRAAT
KONING ALBERTLAAN
Koningin Maria Hendrikplein
CLEMENTINALAAN
OFFERLAAN
Gent-Sint-Pieters
JUBILEUMLAAN
NEERMEERSKAAI
GORDUNAKAAI
SPORTSTRAAT
PATIJNTJESTRAAT
DISTELSTRAAT
AAIGEMSTRAAT
FABIOLALLAN
Camping Blaarmeersen
Bruges
Max Mobiel

GHENT *Overview*
For listings, see below

Where to stay

Where to eat and drink

Kitchen is a cosy lounge with a fireplace, where an American buffet b/fast is served for €25. Cocktail bar The Cobbler is the place to see & be seen. **€€€€–€€€€€**

Hôtel Verhaegen [168 C4] (4 rooms) 110 Oude Houtlei; 09 265 07 60; w hotelverhaegen.be. This palatial 18th-century private mansion has the 'wow' factor in spades, down to its prestigious Yves Klein monochrome. Renovated by interior designers Marc Vergauwe & Jan Rosseel, the building is alive with detail & lush furnishings from ceilings adorned with original frescoes to Rococo paintings & windows framed by heavy drapes. The most covetable room is arguably the Suite Années '40, with its balcony, vast bath & private reading room. Fabulous b/fast €20 pp, which can be taken in the garden in clement weather. **€€€€–€€€€€**

Upmarket

Pillows Grand Hotel Reylof [168 B3] (2 rooms) 36 Hoogstraat; 09 235 40 70; w pillowshotels.com. Stunningly refurbished in 2018, this Louis XV-style townhouse offers a seamless luxury experience – arrive & you're spirited off for a free drink (unusually there's no fixed reception, but almost always someone around to help). I loved the free, regularly replenished in-room minibars with wine & delicious chocolate, & there's a small, romantic spa in the old coach house. It's fun to climb the dramatic spiral staircase up to the glamorous bar, too. The more casual of 2 on-site restaurants (€€€) serves bistro dishes 24/7 & also turns out a stellar b/fast (€25). **€€€€**

Rooms With A View [172 A2] (3 rooms) 1 Korenlei; 09 224 00 73; w korenleieen.be. As you'd expect from the name, it's all about the views at this compact but ingeniously designed B&B overlooking the Korenlei, Graslei & Oude Vismarkt. Try to get Room 3, on the top floor, with its unusual wooden arch & mini-terrace. Delicious continental b/fast served in Korenlei Twee (€€€–€€€€), a restaurant run by the same owners. **€€€€**

Mid-range

Ganda Rooms & Suites [168 F3] (8 rooms & suites) 18 Houtbriel; 09 330 20 22; w gandaroomsandsuites.be. This 18th-century townhouse has a very handy location close to the tourist sights & notably helpful owners. Rooms are spacious & polished; 2 suites on the 2nd floor have direct access to a terrace overlooking St Baaf's. Proper, cosy living room with free cakes & an honesty bar are further boons. **€€€**

Hotel Harmony [172 B1] (40 rooms) 37 Kraanlei; 09 324 26 80; w hotel-harmony.be. Set across 3 historic buildings, this boutique hotel has long been 1 of the best options locally owing to its fair rates & location right on the water in Patershol. Rooms are mostly modern, though with older touches, such as wooden beams; some have a jacuzzi, while 'Exceptional' rooms have a kitchenette. The outdoor pool (May–Sep) is a treat, & it's very family-friendly too: children up to 3 stay free & you pay just €20 (inc b/fast) for under 18s. **€€€**

Studiomie [168 F1] (1 room) 20 Bomastraat m 0497 432 642; w studiomie.be. A very unusual option: sleep in interior designer Mieke De Maeyer's stylishly converted, MDF-walled shipping container, set atop an old red-brick smithy. There's a nice brunch spot, FranzGustav, just down the street. **€€€**

Hotel Orion [168 C8] (21 rooms) 181 Krijgslaan; 09 395 12 95; w hotel-orion.be. Stunning Art Deco villa from 1928 located in the 'Millionaires's Quarter', a residential area built on the grounds of the 1913 World's Fair, & offering an eye-popping mix of architectural styles. It's a bit outside the action – a 20-min tram ride into town – but worth it for huge rooms, friendly staff & a gorgeous pool & sauna (the former free, the latter €5/30mins). Continental b/fast is a snip at €12. **€€–€€€**

Budget

Atlas B&B [168 B2] (4 rooms) 40 Rabotstraat; 09 233 49 91; w atlasbb.be. Travel-themed mansion with 4 gorgeous rooms – a different continent for each – stuffed with objects relating to the destination; Africa has a 4-poster bed, sitting room & private bathroom. Cash only. They can also arrange babysitting. **€€**

The House of Edward [172 C1] (5 rooms) 17 Edward Anseeleplein; m 0477 78 64 60; w heirloom.be. Opened in 2016 – & since joined by a sibling property, the House of Trade – this is a real bargain: from around €75/night, you're mins from the centre & get to relax in clean, tastefully designed rooms (a studio has a kitchenette & private patio with sunbeds) featuring free movies & tea- & coffee-making facilities. Hassle-free: you receive a code to let yourself in & out. **€€**

Shoestring

Ecohostel Andromeda [168 A1] (18 beds) 35 Bargiekaai; m 0486 67 80 33; w ecohostel.be. All aboard! Liselot & her partner have lovingly converted this old barge into a hip eco-friendly hostel. All dirty water is siphoned upwards & filtered through the rooftop reed bed & the mattresses are made from 100% natural latex. Fun chalk messages in toilets, trust-operated fridge stocked with organic beers & hippy-style lounge with games & books. Organic b/fast inc. Dorm €23–25; dbl €68. **€**

Hostel Uppelink [172 A3] (9 rooms, 38 beds) 21 Sint-Michielsplein; 09 279 44 77; w hosteluppelink.com. Voted best hostel in Belgium by the Hoscar awards for an incredible 5 years running since it opened in 2012 – says it all. You get the best view in town (of the city's 3 medieval towers), use of a guest kitchen – alternatively, a buffet b/fast is €6 – & amazing amenities: they offer free English walking tours daily at 10.00 & 13.00, & beer tastings Tue & Thu at 18.00. If that wasn't enough, you can even rent a kayak! Dorm €16–20; dbl with bunk beds €50. **€**

Treck Hostel [168 A1] (9 caravans, 17 dorm beds, 2 tent pitches) 51 Groendreef; 09 310 76 20; w treckhostel.be. It's not often you get to stay in a 19th-century brick kiln – not least 1 filled with 9 cool themed caravans paying homage to Betty Boop graffiti etc (there are also 2 dorms & you can pitch your own tent – indoors, oddly). Grab a pint or Sun brunch at Treckhaak, the in-house bar. A 20–25min walk from the centre of town. Dorm €19; tent €15 pp; caravan from €35 pp. **€**

Camping Blaarmeersen [169 A6] (187 pitches, 8 cabins) 12 Zuiderlaan; 09 266 81 60; w gent.be/blaarmeersen. Part of an outdoor activity park, Ghent's 5-star campsite is a 25-min bus ride from the Korenmarkt. There's a tent meadow you can set up in & 8 very basic – but also very cheap – huts. Facilities include a shop, seasonal restaurant, café & laundry. Tent adult/5–12 €6–7.50/2.60–3.80; cabin €41. **€**

WHERE TO EAT AND DRINK Not so long ago eating out in Ghent was a nice enough experience, usually based around comforting classics such as *Gentse waterzooi* or *Gentse stoverij* (chicken/fish or beef stew). When it came to the higher end of things, however, there was nothing much to shout about. How times have changed, largely in the wake of 'Flemish Foodies' Kobe Desramaults, Jason Blanckaert and Olly Ceulenaere. Desramaults, who made his name with the Michelin-starred In De Wulf in West Flanders (now shut, alas), currently runs two highly acclaimed venues in Ghent (pages 172 and 173). But he's not alone: these days the city shelters six Michelin-starred restaurants and a host of creative bistros offering good-value deals.

That's not its only calling card: in carnivorous Flanders, Ghent styles itself as Europe's veggie capital, and every Thursday restaurants make an effort to up their vegetarian options. If you're hankering for a quick bite, head to Ghent's Turkish quarter on Sleepstraat. You'll also want to try *cuberdons* (little noses); these purple cone-shaped candies sparked a war between two rival sellers on Groentenmarkt – as covered by international newspapers – until one went too far and was banished!

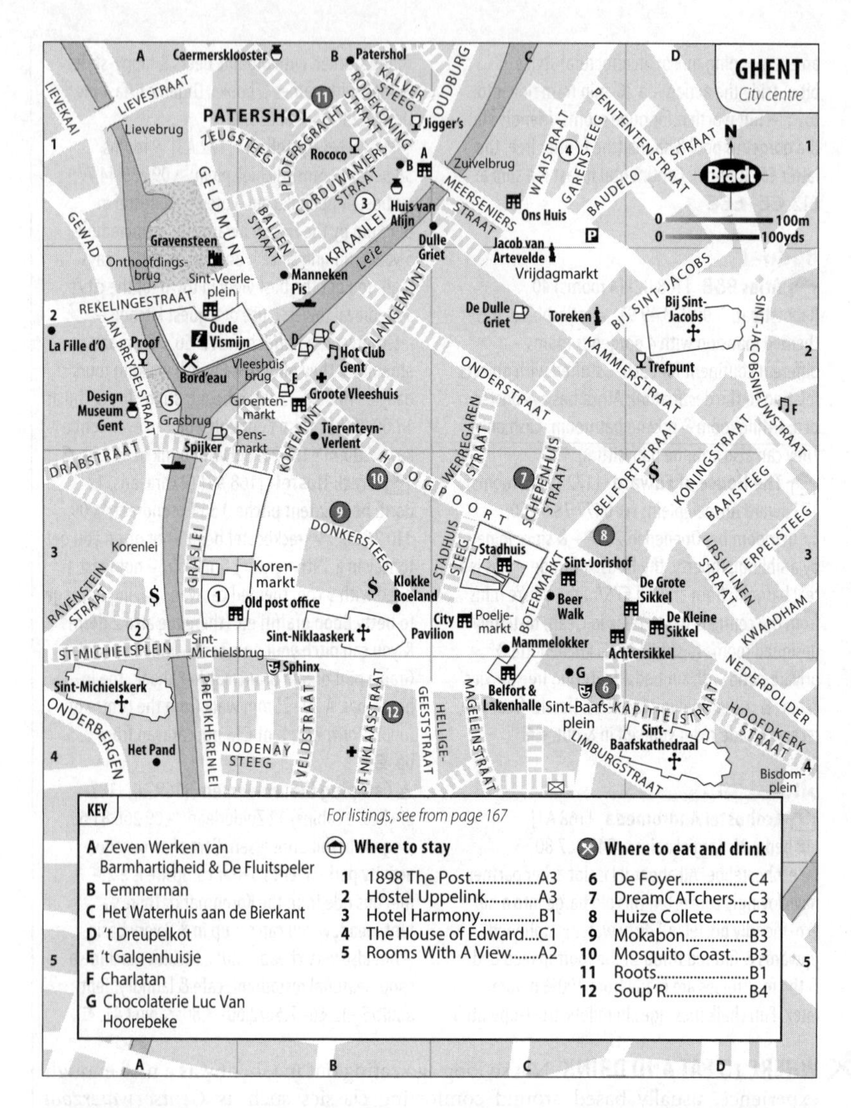

Restaurants

Expensive

Chambre Séparée [168 F3] 1 Keizer Karelstraat; **m** 0485 58 48 57; **w** chambreseparee.be; dinner Wed–Sat. First things first: this isn't a cheap experience, with the fixed (blind) menu coming in at an eye-watering €230 (more with drinks). However, for that you get 20 courses & the chance to be wowed by Flanders' hottest chef, Kobe Desramaults, alongside just 15 other diners at a time. All in the unusual setting of the city's Belgacom building, which will have to close for renovation around 2020, so best get in quick. €€€€€

Vrijmoed [168 E4] 22 Vlaanderenstraat; 09 279 99 77; **w** vrijmoed.be; Tue–Fri noon–13.30 & 19.00–21.30, Sat–Mon 19.00–21.30. A smart, contemporary townhouse is the setting for Ghent's sole 2-star restaurant, creatively splicing 'noble & inferior ingredients or product residues'. Non-carnivores will love the gourmet 'Pure Vegetables' fixed menus; there is also an à la carte (mains range from €40–90) & during the week you can sample the €55 lunch. €€€€€

OAK [168 B2] 167 Hoogstraat; 09 353 90 50; noon–13.30 & 19.00–20.30 Tue–Fri, noon–13.30 Sat. Brazilian/Italian chef Marcelo

Ballardin is behind this tiny, living room-style spot – one of Ghent's most highly regarded restaurants. You'll need to book 3 months ahead for his seasonal, globetrotting food: the 3-course lunch is €39; at night they serve 6- or 7-course menus (€80/95). If you can't get in, DOOR73 is a new sharing plates venue run by ex-OAK sous chef Eric. €€€€–€€€€€

Above average

A Food Affair [168 B3] 58 Hoogstraat; 09 224 18 05; 18.00–22.00 Tue–Sat. An 'eastern-inspired' restaurant run by Belgian chefs – it really shouldn't work, but this well-established Thai (est 2003) turns out divine flavours with just the right hit of spice & fragrance & they have a lovely romantic courtyard to the rear. €€€€

De Superette [169 E6] 29 Guldenspoorstraat; 09 278 08 08; w de-superette.be; 18.00–22.00 Wed–Fri, 10.00–16.00 & 18.00–22.00 Sat–Sun. Opened in 2015 by Kobe Desramaults (him again) & still very much the hippest place in town, this Brooklyn-style former launderette is now a multi-tasking bakery, restaurant & café. The pizzas are pricey, yes, but charred perfection & there are nice small plates to go with them. Impressively lives up to the hype & is especially fun at night when there's a real buzz (they also do w/end brunch). €€€–€€€€

Mid-range

De Foyer [172 C4] 17 Sint-Baafsplein; 09 234 13 54; w foyerntgent.be; 11.30–14.30 & 17.30–22.00 Wed–Fri, 10.30–21.30 Sat, 10.30–14.30 Sun. An elegant brasserie on the 1st floor of the National Theatre dishing up seafood, waterzooi & light bites. At its liveliest on Sun when an all-you-can-eat brunch is served. It's also very popular in summer when the windows are thrown open & lunch can be taken on the terrace overlooking Sint-Baafsplein – fight the locals for a table! €€€

Roots [172 B1] 5 Vrouwebroersstraat; 09 310 67 73; w rootsgent.be; noon–14.00 & 19.00–21.30 Mon–Fri. Tucked away in Patershol, this intimate venue is reputed for the best (5-course) lunch deal in town (€28, as against dinner, which is €55). Your cutlery is located in a drawer under the table, which is cute. As per the name, it's all about pure produce & a love of greenery that even shades dessert. €€€

Cheap and cheerful

Le Botaniste [168 D3] 13 Hoornstraat; 09 233 45 35; w lebotaniste.be; 11.30–21.00 Mon–Sat. Elegant pharmacy-style vegan restaurant offering customisable bowls (Asian-accented soup, curry, salad) plus vivid hummus plates & other incredibly tasty starters served in epic portions. Excellent €15 lunch deal. The owner runs a vineyard, so it's not just super-healthy smoothies to drink. €€

Greenway [169 C5] 42 Nederkouter; 09 269 07 69; w greenway.be; 11.00–22.00 Mon–Sat, 17.00–22.00 Sun. Pioneering mini-chain that helped to forge Ghent's veggie credentials; salads, wraps & curries, but the most hype is for the 'Beyond Burger' – 100% plant-based but freakily similar to the real thing. €€

Mosquito Coast [172 B3] 28 Hoogpoort; 09 224 37 20; w mosquitocoast.be; 11.00–late Tue–Sat, 15.00–late Sun. I always take friends to this laidback travellers' café for a glass of local aperitif Roomer – an elderflower-flavoured drink launched by two local brothers in 2004 to much acclaim. Has an extensive travel library, two terraces & a menu of filling chilli con carne, pastas & soups, as well as tapas by night. Go early & grab a comfy leather chair. €€

Shoestring

De Blauwe Kiosk [168 D4] Kouter; 0496 51 95 60; w deblauwekiosk.be; 10.00–16.00 Sun. Locals flock to this classy open-air stand – dating way back to 1885 – at w/ends for an indulgent snack of fresh oysters & champagne. Half a dozen molluscs sets you back €10. €

Lekker GEC [169 B8] 5–6 Koningen Maria Hendrikplein; 09 242 87 50; w lekkergec.com; 09.00–22.00 Mon–Fri, noon–22.00 Sat. A self-service restaurant dishing up delicious, 100% organic vegetarian meals. Now run as a co-op, it's had a social remit from the start, offering training to locals who have had trouble finding work. They also want to reduce waste: cost is by weight, to make you reflect on what you consume – & you really have to overload your plate to go above €10. €

Patiron [172 D2] 30 Sluizeken; 09 233 45 87; w patiron.be; 11.00–16.00 Tue–Sat. Lovely bio-café north of the centre where you should resist the temptation of the soups & opt for the house speciality: quiche, which is honoured through over 80 versions, including gluten-free. €

Soup'R [172 B4] 9 Sint-Niklaasstraat; 09 242 87 50; w soupr.be; 11.30–16.00 Tue–Sat. A choice of fantastic, warming soups served with delicious bread is unsurprisingly the main event at this cramped, popular spot, though their sandwiches are also highly regarded too. Expect a wait at peak times. €

Cafés

Simon Says [168 D1] 8 Sluizeken; 09 233 03 43; w simon-says.be; 09.00–18.00 Tue–Fri, 10.00–18.00 Sat–Sun. Charming coffee house run by Cardiff-born Simon Turner & his boyfriend Christopher. Panamarenko (page 24) drawings on the walls, gorgeous cheesecake & plenty of appealing b/fast options alongside quiches & salads for lunch. They also rent out 2 stylish bedrooms (**€€€**). €€

Café Labath [168 C3] 1 Oude Houtlei; 09 225 28 25; w cafelabath.be; 08.00–18.00 Mon–Fri, 09.00–18.00 Sat, 10.00–18.00 Sun. Local hangout with a magazine-friendly interior (funky tiled walls) but also 'slow' filter coffees & healthy b/fast & lunch options (granola, soup, daily specials). But forget being healthy: try the Malteser hot chocolate. Cards only. €

DreamCATchers [172 B3] 17 Schepenhuisstraat; 09 310 40 35; café 10.30–18.00 Wed–Thu & Sat, shop 13.00–18.00 Mon, Fri & Sun. Feline fans rejoice: the Japanese cat café trend made it to Ghent in 2016. A non-profit café, all the cats you see here are for adoption, & you can play with them & generally admire them over cat-themed drinks (catspressos, meaowcchiatos etc) & cakes – all vegan. They also have a shop stuffed with feline-related goodies. Reserve on the website before a visit as it can get busy, & not just with 4-legged friends. €

Huize Collete [172 C3] 6 Belfortstraat; m 0478 90 64 73; 09.00–19.00 Tue–Fri, 10.00–19.00 Sat–Sun. Named after co-owner Aline's mother, who kindly stumped up the cash to allow her & her friend to open this café/bookshop, which was inspired by their travels in England. The house specialities are sumptuous homemade cakes & hot chocolate made by melting lumps of top-quality chocolate into steaming milk – no cheap powders here! Upstairs there's a secondhand bookstore with sofas & tables usually hogged by students. €

Mokabon [172 B3] 35 Donkersteeg; 09 225 71 95; 09.00–18.30 Mon–Sat. In a tiny alley off Korenmarkt, this indie joint has quite some pedigree – a young Italian started a roastery & shop here in 1937, with space soon made for a café. Step through the door now &, after the heady rush of coffee hitting your nostrils, you'll find the gorgeous old-school interior intact. Limited seating & a few snacks, but this is all about the coffee – top-notch, potent & very reasonably priced. €

ENTERTAINMENT AND NIGHTLIFE All those students makes for a buzzing nightlife – especially when it comes to live music, be that gigs in atmospheric bars and concert halls every night, or several important festivals during the summer (page 52). If you want to drink in an eccentric, time-worn boozer, that's very much possible – but you can also have a world-class cocktail in a speakeasy-style venue. So colourful is the Ghent nightlife that there's even a film devoted to one of its most famous bars, the Charlatan (see opposite), but new venues are constantly popping up – and at the time of writing the city hosted Belgium's hottest new techno and house club.

Pubs

De Dulle Griet [172 C2] 50 Vrijdagmarkt; 09 224 24 55; 16.30–01.00 Mon, noon–01.00 Tue–Sat, noon–19.30 Sun. Named after the enormous 15th-century red cannon nearby, this bric-a-brac pub serves the biggest selection of beer in Ghent. The real draw is the 'shoe challenge': everyone who wants to drink the signature 1.2l Max beer, which comes in a special Kwak glass, has to give 1 shoe as a deposit, which is hoisted up to the ceiling in a basket & let down only when the glass is returned! Whether it was invented because the landlord was peeved at people nicking the glasses, or because it's just a genius marketing gimmick, it's a lot of fun.

't Dreupelkot [172 B2] 12 Groentenmarkt; 09 224 21 20; w dreupelkot.be; 16.00– late. Run by the inimitable Pol for over 30 years, this shabby waterside brown bar is the place to sample jenever (page 48). Furnishings are sparse (you seat yourself round upturned barrels) & you may have to wake Pol if he's sleeping in his armchair, but there are more than 200 flavours of schnapps on offer here, from garlic to grapefruit (watch out for the pepper – it's infamous).

Het Spijker [172 A2] 3 Pensmarkt; 09 329 44 40; 09.00–late. Cosy candlelit bar housed in a 12th-century building – the oldest on the street – that once stored grain reserves in case of an outbreak of famine. The terrace out the back has lovely views of the canal & is a real local favourite.

Het Waterhuis aan de Bierkant [172 B2] 9 Groentenmarkt; 09 225 06 80; 11.00–late. Situated right beside the river Leie, this pub is especially popular as a terrace-hopping spot in summer. It stocks over 160 types of beer & specialises in gueuze & kriek.

Bars

Jigger's [172 B1] 16 Oudburg; 09 335 70 25; w jiggers.be; 17.00–late Tue–Sat. Run by Olivier Jacobs, one of Belgium's top mixologists, this quirky speakeasy – the window has a stuffed fox sporting a monocle – has won a slew of awards over the years. There's a revolving menu of creative, seasonally inspired cocktails & Olivier's passion for foraging results in a lot of herb & flower infusions. The backyard is lovely in summer.

Proof [172 A2] 34 Jan Breydelstraat; m 0472 83 42 85; w proof.gent; 13.00–20.00 Thu–Sun. Billed as a 'tasting room', this very stylish bar is all about letting customers try out new spirits & wines. If you go for wine, for instance, you specify 'fresh & fruity', 'dry' etc & they'll pick something out for you. The extensive G&T list is the town's best & they also have a shop stocking cult spirits (mescal, pisco), which – unusually – you can buy in 5–20cl bottles to test them out.

Rococo [172 B1] 57 Corduwaniersstraat; 09 224 30 35; 22.00–late Tue–Sun. Romantic time-worn Patershol bar with candelabras on ancient wooden tables, an old piano in the corner & dried sausages hanging from a rack at the small bar presided over by the owner, Betty. The signature Liqueur d'Amour ignites passions!

Nightclubs

☆ **Kompass Klub** [169 C8] 717a Ottergemsesteenweg Zuid; w kompassklub.com; 23.00–07.00 Fri–Sat & occasional other days when gigs are on. Since opening in a factory near Ghent's football stadium in 2016 (it has its roots in earlier pop-ups) this has become the place to party locally, even winning honours as Belgium's best club at the 2018 Red Bull Elektropedia awards. Lures international techno & house DJs but makes room for homegrown talent too.

Live music

♫ **Charlatan** [172 D2] 6 Vlasmarkt; 09 224 24 57; w charlatan.be; 20.00–late Tue–Sun. Ghent's biggest live-music bar is a self-styled 'House of Ruin' deeply enmeshed with the city's nightlife scene – such is its legend that it even inspired a film, *Belgica*, by celebrated Flemish director Felix van Groeningen, whose father used to own it. Hosts a lot of gigs &, come 23.00 or so, things tend to morph into serious party mode, with DJs spinning tunes until dawn.

♫ **Hot Club Gent** [172 B2] Schuddevisstraatje; 09 256 71 99; w hotclub.gent; 17.00–late. Inspired by the famous 1930s Paris club of a similar name, this tucked-away nook was opened in 2005. Sadly, founder David De Rudder passed away in 2015, but long-serving staff took it under their wing & it's still hosting brilliant concerts – from Dixieland to gypsy swing – almost every night.

♫ **Hotsy Totsy** [168 C3] 1 Hoogstraat; 09 224 20 12; 18.00–late Mon–Fri, 20.00–late Sat–Sun. Inside a stepped-gabled house, this glorious bar – founded by the brothers of famous novelist Hugo Claus (page 18) no less – is usually humming with locals. Floral wallpaper & monochrome pictures of past acts contribute to the atmosphere & they host live jazz Oct–Apr most Thu nights, as well as stand-up comedy, poetry readings & even chanson nights.

♫ **Trefpunt** [172 D2] 18 Bij Sint-Jacobs; 09 225 36 76; w trefpunt.be; 17.00–late daily. The famous Ghent Festivities (page 54) started here in 1969 when Walter de Buck took to the stage of this bar with a couple of friends & their guitars. The lively local arts haunt hosts free concerts on Mon nights & paid events nearly every Thu & Fri, & is still active during the Ghent Festivities, when it tries to 'offer some resistance in a world where everything is increasingly about money'. Nicely done.

Concert halls

♫ **De Bijloke** [168 C5] 7 Bijlokekaai; ☎ 09 323 61 11; w bijloke.be; ⌚ ticket office: 13.00–17.00 Tue–Fri. Housed in the Gothic former infirmary of Bijlokeabdij, this magnificent renovated concert hall puts on respected classical & contemporary music concerts & is also associated with the Ghent Jazz Festival in July.

♫ **Handelsbeurs** [168 D4] 29 Kouter; ☎ 09 265 91 60; w handelsbeurs.be. Ghent's main concert hall has a pleasingly bombastic setting. Attracts top international rock & pop acts, but it's small enough to still feel intimate.

Opera Ghent [168 D4] 3 Schouwburgstraat; ☎ 070 22 02 02; w operaballet.be. No-expense-spared opera house built by 19th-century industrialists (the chandelier is an attraction in its own right) & hosting performances by the Vlaamse Opera (Flemish Opera) when they're not in Antwerp or on the road.

Vooruit [169 E5] 23 Sint-Pietersnieuwstraat; ☎ 09 267 28 28; w vooruit.be. This Art Nouveau building was built 1910–14 by the socialist party, keen to prove that they cared about workers' intellectual development. The colossal 'House of the People' soon flourished as an arts centre, but during World War II the Germans set up house there & kept livestock in the concert hall. Earmarked for demolition in the 1970s, it was thankfully saved & is now Ghent's most impressive multi-tasking arts venue, with a reliably eclectic programme of gigs, films & club nights, & a brilliantly atmospheric on-site bar/café.

Theatre

NT Gent [172 C4] 17 Sint-Baafsplein; ☎ 09 225 01 01; w ntgent.be. City theatre accommodating regional repertory company the Nederlands Toneel Gent (NTG). Offers mostly classical & contemporary theatre in Flemish, plus the odd English-language touring show. The De Foyer brasserie (page 173) is also on site.

Cinema

Sphinx [172 A3] 3 Sint-Michielshelling; ☎ 09 225 60 86; w sphinx-cinema.be. Small but appealing city-centre arthouse cinema with a good café; special discount rate of €6 on Mon night.

Studio Skoop [169 F5] 63 Sint-Annaplein; ☎ 09 225 08 45; w studioskoop.be. Opened in the 1970s & has 5 screens showing a mixture of mainstream, foreign-language & indie films. Nice old-school posters on the walls.

SHOPPING Ghent is not associated with a particular shopping highlight; it doesn't share Antwerp's monopoly on diamonds, or produce the lace long associated with Bruges. However, being home to Belgium's largest pedestrianised shopping area, browsing its boutiques and traditional stores is a relaxing, enjoyable affair. Langemunt and Veldstraat have long been the key shopping streets, mostly hosting the usual suspects; Onderbergen, parallel to Veldstraat, is quieter and more intriguing. Other areas to browse are the interconnecting Mageleinstraat, Volderstraat, Kalandenberg square and Koestraat. The streets around Vrijdagmarkt also contain some gems. Some of my favourite stores are listed below:

Chocolaterie Luc Van Hoorebeke [172 C4] 15 Sint-Baafsplein; ☎ 09 221 03 81; w chocolatesvanhoorebeke.be; ⌚ 10.00–18.00. Beautiful artisan chocolate shop active since 1982; you can often see Luc & his son Cédric – who runs his own shop at 1 Jan Breydelstraat – busy making the chocs in the basement, which is lovely.

La Fille d'O [172 A2] 21 Burgstraat; ☎ 09 334 80 10; w lafilledo.com; ⌚ 10.00–18.00 Mon–Sat. Very cool, contemporary lingerie by local designer Murielle Scherre, beloved by Lady Gaga among other stars. They don't just adopt a fake feminist posture, they live it – producing books & even the odd porn film celebrating women.

Groot Vleeshuis [172 B2] 7 Groentenmarkt; ☎ 09 223 23 24; w grootvleeshuis.be; ⌚ 10.00–18.00 Tue–Sun. The old meat market dates from 1419 & has a stunning oak ceiling. It sells over 175 regional food products & East Flanders specialities, inc spirit RoomeR. There's an atmospheric café (€€) too.

Tierenteyn-Verlent [172 B2] 3 Groentenmarkt; ☎ 09 225 83 36; ⌚ 10.00–18.00 Mon, 09.00–18.00 Tue–Fri, 09.30–18.00 Sat. This deli has been in situ since 1867 & is famous for its homemade

MAD FOR MUSEUMS?

The CityCard Ghent is brilliantly good value, and I'd strongly advise picking one up. Costing €30/48hrs or €35/72hrs, it includes free access to all the major sights – *and* many temporary exhibitions, which isn't always the case – as well as free tram and bus travel, one day's bike hire and a boat tour … now that's really quite impressive. Note that under 18s can get in free to most museums anyway, making the card somewhat redundant. The cards can be bought from the tourist information centre, the museums themselves, quite a few local hotels and De Lijn sales points.

mustard. It's pumped up from the cellars into a big wooden barrel & ladled into a jar of your choice. Be sure to buy a wooden spoon with it, otherwise the ingredients will 'split' when stirred – it's that fresh! The secret behind its bite is closely guarded, but I'm told it's definitely not horseradish!

Markets

Flea market Bij Sint-Jacobs/Beverhoutplein; ⌚ 08.00–13.00 Fri–Sun
Flower market Kouter; ⌚ 07.00–13.00 (small market daily, full market Sun)
Food markets General: Sint-Michielsplein; ⌚ 07.30–13.00 Fri; organic: Groentenmarkt, ⌚ 07.30–13.00 Fri

OTHER PRACTICALITIES

$ Bank [168 D4] KBC, 175 Kouter; ⌚ 09.00–16.30 Mon–Fri, 09.00–noon Sat
Luggage storage Gent-Sint-Pieters railway station & Gent-Dampoort both have left-luggage lockers.
✚ Pharmacy [172 B4] Apotheek Decloedt, 42 Sint-Niklaasstraat; ☎ 09 225 36 52; ⌚ 08.00–18.30 Mon–Sat
✉ Post office [172 C4] 55 Lange Kruisstraat; ⌚ 09.00–18.00 Mon–Fri, 09.00–15.00 Sat

WHAT TO SEE AND DO

City centre

Sint-Baafskathedraal (St Bavo's Cathedral) [172 D4] (Sint-Baafsplein; ☎ 09 269 20 45; **w** sintbaafskathedraal.be; ⌚ Apr–Oct 08.30–18.00 Mon–Sat, 10.00–18.00 Sun, Nov–Mar 08.30–17.00 Mon–Sat, 10.00–17.00 Sun; free) The oldest of Ghent's 59 churches, St Bavo's started life as a wooden chapel and originally went by the name of St Janskerk (St John's). As the city's wealth grew, so did the church, and despite his feuds with unruly locals, Emperor Charles V retained a soft spot for the church he was baptised in, donating money for its upkeep and expansion (the majority of the current exterior dates from the 16th century). However, by 1540 his patience had ended. He was short of buildings that could accommodate his Spanish soldiers posted to keep the citizens in check, so turfed out the monks living in St Bavo's Abbey in the east of town. They moved into St John's and the church adopted its current name – being elevated to cathedral status in 1559 by Pope Paul IV.

It's now home to a treasure trove of artworks. A good place to start is the dim **crypt**. While the relics here are mostly of limited interest, there are exceptions: Justus van Gent's mighty triptych *The Crucifixion of Christ*, and the silver reliquary of St Macarius gifted by the town of Mons, whose residents believed that it had saved them from a plague. Hanging opposite the crypt exit in the **north transept** is Rubens's enormous *St Baaf Enters the Monastery at Ghent* (1624). St Baaf was a 6th-century Frankish noble who abandoned his wild ways and converted to Catholicism when his wife died, accompanying St Amand on his missionary work before retiring to the woods outside Ghent. The moment of his conversion is captured in Rubens's painting – it is often said that St Baaf's face is actually that of Rubens. Also of note are the coats of arms of the Order of the Golden Fleece along the right aisle before the choir, and the monumental oak and marble Rococo pulpit.

In the De Villa chapel to the left of the entrance, behind bullet-proof glass, is the church's – and city's – greatest treasure: winged altarpiece ***The Adoration of the Mystic Lamb*** (🕘 Apr–Oct 09.30–17.00 Mon–Sat, 13.00–17.00 Sun; Nov–Mar 10.30–16.00 Mon–Sat, 13.00–16.00 Sun; adult/CityCard €4/free inc audio guide – otherwise an extra €1), completed on 6 May 1432 by Jan van Eyck (page 20) and his brother Hubrecht. Art historians are unable to distinguish who painted which bits, but it's clear that Jan added his name because he was the better known of the two. Regardless of ownership, it is considered to be the single most remarkable work of Flemish Primitive art. The pin-point accuracy and level of detail was far beyond what other painters were achieving at the time, and even more extraordinary is the luminosity of the paint – the brothers waited until it had begun to dry before applying it in thin layers – which is gleaming after a major restoration begun in 2012 by the Museum of Fine Arts Ghent (MSK). It is believed that around 40% of the work was overpainted after conception; restorers have made great strides reversing this, thereby revealing the softer face and true 'intense' gaze of the lamb, hidden for hundreds of years.

The lamb, in the centre, was a common symbol for Christ. The words of its best-known reference are found in the Gospel of St John (1:29) – 'Behold the Lamb of God, which taketh away the sin of the world!' – and are inscribed around the rim of the altar where the lamb stands. Above shines the light of the Holy Ghost and the city of Jerusalem; in front stands the Fountain of Life. Figures from the Old and New Testaments congregate in worship, including the brothers Cain and Abel off to the left. Sitting above, in the upper central panel, is God (again there's some debate about this), flanked by the Virgin Mary on the left and John the Baptist on the right. Either side of them are groups of angels making music in celebration. Amazingly, experts claim you can tell which notes the angels are singing by the varying shapes of their mouths. On the outer edges stand Adam and Eve.

The first stage of the painting's restoration was completed in October 2016, when the finished outer panels returned to St Bavo's Cathedral; it is hoped that, with restoration complete, the entire work will be reunited here in June 2020, after a huge van Eyck exhibition at the Museum voor Schone Kunsten,

THE WORLD'S MOST STOLEN PAINTING

Keeping the enormous Ghent Altarpiece together throughout history has proved a challenge to say the least: in fact, it's the world's most frequently stolen painting. It survived the riots of the 16th-century Iconoclastic Fury, but in 1794 the central panels were pilfered by French soldiers and taken to Paris. These were returned in 1815, but a year later the side panels were lifted and sold to a buyer in Prussia. It was 1920 before all the pieces were reunited, and then during World War II it was stolen by the Nazis – it was the artwork they craved most for a projected super-museum – and hidden in an Austrian salt mine, where it was found by the Monuments Men (of film fame), miners and a team of commandos in 1946. Sadly one of the panels – *De Rechtvaardige Pechters* (the Fair Judges) – is a copy; the original was carted off in 1934 and is still missing. New leads still crop up, so perhaps one day …

or M.S.K. (page 190). A brand-new visitor centre will bring both the painting and the cathedral to life thanks to the use of virtual-reality glasses. In the meantime, I strongly advise heading over to the MSK, where you can watch the restorers at work and glimpse some of the real panels not currently on display in the cathedral.

Belfort (Belfry) [172 C4] (Sint-Baafsplein; ☎ 09 375 31 61; w belfortgent.be; ⌚ 10.00–18.00; adult/19–25/under 19/CityCard €8/2.70/free/free) Construction of the town watchtower, a symbol of civic autonomy, began in 1313. Since 1377 it has been crowned with a copper dragon weathervane (you no longer see the original) believed to have been a gift from raiding Vikings who detached the mast from their ship and presented it to residents in admiration of their bravery; the current stone spire dates from 1913. Once upon a time, merchants would send boys up the tower to look for incoming trade ships and, until 1869, four guards – *kannenschijters* (can shitters) – would be posted there overnight to keep watch. The climb took so long that they were unable to descend if they needed the toilet, so instead they were given a pot in which to perform their nightly 'functions' – hence the memorable nickname.

The tower held the city's first carillon bell, known as **Klokke Roeland** (see below), which was cast in 1314, and melted into a carillon of 40 new bells – with the same name – in 1659. Today the current 53-bell carillon is hailed as one of the best in Belgium, and you can glimpse it after riding up the glass elevator to the top floor. You can't actually access the pinnacle, but the views over the square and rooftops of Ghent are still impressive, and the handy (free) app advertised at the entrance gives you more information. Gandante (page 167) also runs guided tours.

Lakenhalle (Cloth Hall) [172 C4] (18 Emile Braunplein) Serving as the entrance to the belfry, the cloth hall's construction was rather ill-timed: work on it came to an abrupt halt in 1441 when the textile trade dried up during the Hundred Years War. The basement was used as the city prison until 1902. Look for the relief on the upper façade: known as **Mammelokker**, it shows old Cimon, who was imprisoned by the Greek king and sentenced to death by starvation. However, months later he was still alive and well. Bemused, the guards decided to spy on his daughter, Pero, who visited him every day. To their amazement, they saw her breastfeeding her father. The king was so impressed by the ingenious plan that he freed Cimon.

Poeljemarkt [172 B/C3] Between the belfry, Stadhuis (page 187) and Sint-Niklaaskerk, the former Poeldermarkt – where rabbits, ducks and other poultry were once sold – houses three interesting sights. The most prominent by far is the **City Pavilion** (2012), a twin-peaked, open-sided structure designed by Flemish architects Robbrecht & Daem, also behind Bruges's concert hall (page 223). The barn-like structure, whose roof contains 1,600 small windows, split opinion as soon as it was unveiled and was quickly – and understandably – given the mocking nickname 'the sheep pen'! The **Klokke Roeland**, the largest of the belfry bells forged in 1659, developed a crack in 1914 when the bells began to be operated electrically and was later moved to this square. Since the construction of the City Pavilion, when the square was redesigned, it has been housed in a concrete stand next to Sint-Niklaaskerk. One side of it reveals famous local artist Michaël Borremans's small fresco ***De Maagd*** (**The Virgin**), with piercing light beams projecting from her eyes.

Sint-Niklaaskerk (St Nicholas's Church) [172 B3] (Cataloniëstraat; w sintniklaaskerk.be; ⌚ 14.00–17.00 Mon, 10.00–17.00 Tue–Sun; free) The Romanesque church built on this site in the 12th century was demolished in 1200 to make room for the present one. The congregation was made up almost entirely of merchants and guildsmen who worked nearby, and appropriately the church was consecrated in the name of St Nicholas – better known as Santa Claus – patron saint of merchants, sailors and children. The church tower was used as a lookout post until the belfry was built. Its central tower is unique, acting as a natural lantern as light tumbles on to the transept.

Korenmarkt and the old post office [172 B3] Stretching out in front of St Nicholas's is the cobbled Korenmarkt, a major tram nexus. Grain and corn unloaded at the nearby Graslei canal was sold here and horses would bring mail to and from the old post office, which sits opposite the church. Completed in 1909, it's a mixture of Gothic Revival and neo-Renaissance and heavily decorated with busts of the European heads of state who visited during the 1913 World's Fair (Florence Nightingale sits oddly among them). It now houses fashion shops, a grand branch of Le Pain Quotidien and trendy hotel 1898 The Post, opened in 2017 (page 167).

Sint-Michielsbrug (St Michael's Bridge) [172 A3] Leaving the Korenmarkt along Pakhuisstraat leads you to the Leie and this famous bridge, which offers great views of the guildhouses that line Graslei and, looking back, the city's three iconic towers belonging to St Nicholas's, the belfry and St Baaf's. Expect to see a fair few people taking selfies here, but don't be too impatient with them – it really is very pretty.

Sint-Michielskerk (St Michael's Church) [172 A4] (St-Michelsplein; ⌚ Apr–Sep 14.00–17.00 Mon–Fri; Oct 14.00–17.00 Sat; free) Next to the bridge stands this mighty church, whose construction was financed by the guild of brewers. Works started in 1440 and dragged on for almost 400 years – too much beer?! Designs for a 134m spire – one that would out-do Antwerp's Onze-Lieve-Vrouwekathedraal (123m) – were put in place, but a lack of funds left the church with its low, flat-topped roof. A stroke of luck actually: research has revealed that a higher tower would have toppled the whole thing. Its principal treasures are *The Crucifixion* (1630) in the north transept by Antoon van Dyck; Ghent-born Gaspar de Crayer's *Assumption of St Catherine*; and a copy of Michelangelo's *Madonna and Child* from Onze-Lieve-Vrouwekerk in Bruges.

Het Pand [172 A4] (Onderbergen 1) Adjoining St Michael's, this 13th-century building was home to the Predikheren or Ghent Dominican Friars. The grounds contained guesthouses and dormitories, as well as an infirmary, and a library housing a brilliant collection of medieval works. Sadly, the majority of these were thrown into the river by iconoclasts during the Fury; indeed, a local, Marius van Vaernewyck, wrote in his diary that so many volumes were discarded into the Leie that they rose above the water line to form a bridge enabling citizens to cross the river without getting wet. It was bought and restored by Ghent University in 1963 and now serves as a conference and exhibition hall (tours on request).

Hotels Clemmen and D'Hane-Steenhuyse [168 C4] At 82 Veldstraat, beautifully restored 18th-century patrician's house **Hotel Clemmen** (⌚ visits in tandem with Hotel D'Hane-Steenhuyse, below) belonged to one of Ghent's first textile barons, and is decorated in lavish Rococco and Classical style. Inside is a Chinese salon and reconstruction of the study of local Maurice Maeterlinck, who won the Nobel Prize for Literature. Wellington stayed here in 1815, handily allowing him to keep an eye on exiled French king Louis XVII, who was resident at the **Hotel D'Hane-Steenhuyse** (⏲ 14.00–18.00 Fri–Sun, free; or combi-tour with Hotel Clemmen 14.30 Fri–Sat; adult/under 19 €6/free) across the street! The highlight of the latter is the two-floor Italian ballroom. Get tickets at the on-site Uitbureau (82b Veldstraat; ☎ 09 233 77 88; w uitbureau.be; ⏲ 10.30–17.00 Mon–Fri, 10.30–16.00 Sat).

Oud Justitiepaleis (Law Courts) [168 C4] (23 Koophandelsplein) A little further south are the majestic Neoclassical law courts, dating from the 19th century – the façade was the only section to survive a fire in 1926. The triangular pediment on the south side of the building features the allegorical figure of Justice surrounded by lawyers, suspects and the guilty. These days the building only houses the Court of Appeal.

Graslei and Korenlei [172 A3] This stretch of canal was the city's first commercial port. Known as *Tusschen Brughen* (Between the Bridges), it became active in the 11th century, when Ghent had a grain staple right – meaning all grain imported into the County of Flanders had to pass through here, with boats leaving behind a quarter of their load.

Graslei The gabled guildhouses that line the banks of the canal have been well maintained and, on the Graslei side, from near right to far left, served as the following:

Gildehuis van de Vrije Schippers (Guildhouse of the Unfree Boatmen) (14 Graslei) The Free Boatmen had complete control of Ghent's waterways from the mid 14th to the mid 17th centuries. This meant all members of the Guildhouse of the Unfree Boatmen (page 182) had to hand over their goods to the brother guild on the outskirts of the city, and the Free Boatmen towed it into the centre. The guild decorated it with Ghent's coat of arms and a carving of a caravel – the type of ship Christopher Columbus was aboard when he discovered America.

Coorenmeterhuis (House of the Corn Measures) (12–13 Graslei) This fruit- and cartouche-laden building is where officials would keep track of the amount of grain delivered at the port and later sold at the city markets. By way of a standard measuring system they filled huge bronze tubs to the brim.

LET THERE BE LIGHT

Ghent is pretty by day, but come dark its iconic buildings and waterways are lit up to stunning, award-winning effect, with light picking out the most important monuments, streets and squares. The first light plan was designed in 1998, with the aim of providing sustainable lighting for the city, while making it safe for travellers and locals to trundle around; it's a far cry from the 18th century, when residents were ordered to carry a flaming torch with them if venturing out after the 22.00 curfew, or risk being arrested and interrogated for suspicious behaviour. Ask the tourist office for a Light Plan walking-tour map (5km; takes around 2hrs max).

Tolhuisje (Toll house) (11 Graslei) This slip of a building – Ghent's smallest – was where customs officers collected taxes on products passing through the port.

Spijker (Staple House) (10 Graslei) The squat Romanesque-style Spijker is the oldest building on the street. Dating from AD1200, it was built with grey Tournai limestone at a slant; this made it easier to haul sacks of grain, which didn't all fit on the ground floor, up the outside of the building. A fire in 1896 gutted the interior, but the façade and sidewalls remained intact. In keeping with the times, it's now a burger restaurant.

Den Enghel (The Angel) (8 Graslei) This six-turreted house had its façade replaced by the Guild of the Masons in 1912, but an angel with a banner was added to show the old name. It features four statues of the guild's patron saints, the Roman martyrs Severinus, Victorinus, Carpophorus and Severianus.

Korenlei Along Korenlei, on the opposite side of the river, is another row of historic houses. Those of most interest are noted below:

De Lintworm (The Tapeworm) (24 Korenlei) Flush against St Michael's Bridge, this Renaissance-style house is named after the long wagons used by the Guild of Beer Exporters that once occupied the premises.

De Zwaene (The Swan) (9 Korenlei) At the other end of the street, the Swan was the site of an old brewery. The building underwent extensive renovations in the 1940s, but parts of it still date from the 16th century.

Gildehuis van de Onvrije Schippers (Guildhouse of the Unfree Boatmen) (7 Korenlei) Situated diagonally opposite the Guild of Free Boatmen, this flamboyant Regency-style gabled house was built in 1739 and is littered with seafaring symbols such as dolphins, anchors and, at the very top, a caravel ship weathervane: an obvious boast of grandeur intended to impress the Free Boatmen.

Design Museum Gent [172 A2] (5 Jan Breydelstraat; 09 267 99 99; w designmuseumgent.be; 09.30–17.30 Mon–Tue & Thu–Fri, 10.00–18.00 Sat–Sun; adult/19–26/under 19/CityCard €8/2/free/free) Composed of two very different parts – the 18th-century Hotel de Connick and a modern extension – this is a brilliant place to come for some interior design inspiration. The collection comprises around 22,500 objects, spanning Art Nouveau gems and current design icons, but with a particular focus on Belgium's role on the international stage. Temporary shows are often excellent, while the permanent collection is showcased through rotating displays that are less thematic than designed to make objects pop. The museum has a particularly extensive range of work by Belgian minimalist Maarten Van Severen; it's also famed for having the zaniest bathroom in town – a building shaped like a giant loo roll, constructed as a jibe at the city after it reneged on promises to build a long-planned extension. With the expansion now approved (it will add a café and Belgian design shop), this much-loved symbol of Ghentian individualism will sadly get the flush.

Gravensteen (Castle of the Counts) [172 A2] (11 Sint-Veerleplein; 09 266 85 00; w gravensteen.stad.gent; 10.00–18.00; adult/19–26/under 19/CityCard

€10/6/free/free inc audio guide) The unlikely positioning of this moat-surrounded medieval fortress, right in the centre of town, makes it all the more impressive. Built in 1180 by Philip of Alsace to make the masses cower, it was modelled on the Krak des Chevaliers stronghold in Damascus, which Philip visited during the Crusades. For 150 years it served as the dark (and damp) seat of residence of the Counts of Flanders, but towards the beginning of the 14th century Charles V's new castle in the Prinsenhof quarter became the favoured residence of the counts when they weren't travelling around the country keeping an eye on their domain. It was still used to host the odd banquet and on one occasion, in 1445, a chapter of the Order of the Golden Fleece. After that it housed the counts' mint, but soon enough became the city prison and court of law. Grisly punishments, from flogging to burning at the stake, were administered either in the courtyard or on Sint-Veerleplein opposite; you'll find a large selection of torture instruments on the first floor. The castle's feared reputation hit a peak during the Inquisition under Philip II's reign and the 17th-century witch-hunts.

At the end of the 18th century the complex was sold to a private owner and converted to house two cotton mills, with workers living in the castle grounds or in shacks leant against the outer walls. These were all torn down in 1872, when the city bought the castle back and restored it. A new renovation and visitor infrastructure was in the works in 2019, but they have already introduced an audio tour by comedian Wouter Deprez, which is rather funny for the genre. The portions of most interest are the torture chambers, dank dungeons and the upper ramparts with good views over the city.

Onthoofdingsbrug (Decapitation Bridge) [172 A2] Beside the castle, this memorably titled bridge was named after the beheadings that took place here until the 16th century. Looking south (with the castle behind you) there is a row of houses on the right-hand bank. The fourth in line bears the last surviving wooden façade in the city and dates from the 16th century. It was painted yellow in honour of Isabella, Charles V's grandmother, who was associated with the colour after she refused to remove her yellowing vest until the siege of Granada was won.

Sint-Veerleplein [172 A2] The busy square on which the Castle of the Counts sits is named after patron saint St Pharaildis, commonly known as Veerle and sister to St Gudule (page 111), who remained a virgin until her death despite receiving beatings from the husband she was forced to marry. Other tales commonly link her to the miraculous resurrection of a goose. Legend has it a local villain stole and ate the bird, leaving only bones. Veerle prayed to God for its revival and the next morning it was clucking around her bedroom floor!

Round about are numerous façades dating from the 17th and 18th centuries. The most impressive is the **Oude Vismijn** (Old Fish Market), a grand Baroque gateway dominated by a statue of a trident-bearing Neptune. Below him are allegorical figures of the Scheldt (represented by a man) and Leie (woman) rivers. Fish was sold here until 1966, and after a period of dereliction it now houses the tourist information centre.

On the west side of the square – look for the public toilets sign! – are the remains of the **Het Wenemaerhospice** (Hospice Wenemaer), a hospital/almshouse founded in 1323 by rich cloth merchant Willem Wenemaer. The 15th-century façade, old entry porch and a passage are all that remain of the original building, but of most interest is the statue of St Laurence – the hospice's patron saint – above the doorway.

Groentenmarkt [172 B2] Just across the Leie, trams thread through this former vegetable market – the first commercial centre in the city outside the Graslei port. It started life as a fish market: canals once ran under the Groot Vleeshuis on the west side of the square, allowing the shipments of mussels and fish to be easily unloaded. It transferred to the sale of fruit and veg in the 18th century. The low-slung **Groot Vleeshuis** (**Great Butchers' Hall**) dates from the early 15th century and is the work of master-builder-of-the-times Gilles de Suttère. Here the Guild of Butchers graded the meat for sale until 1884. Today it houses a café and a shop promoting East Flanders specialities (page 176). Tacked on to the side is Ghent's smallest, cutest pub, **'t Galgenhuisje**, named after the gallows that once stood on the square.

Lievekaai and St Antoniuskaai [172 A1/168 C1] Wander 5 minutes north, back past the castle, to escape the crowds on these willow-lined quaysides. In the 13th century, the Lieve canal was dug up in order to create a direct link to the Zwin tidal inlet and sea. After that fell into disuse, part of the canal was filled, hence the current wide quay, whose name derives from the St Anthony archers' guild that once gathered here (symbols of shooters on the façade give the building away). Another highlight is the eye-popping **Brug der Keizerlijke Geneugten** (**Bridge of Imperial Pleasure**), built in 2000 by local artist and musician Walter De Buck (1934–2014) and decorated with sculptures nodding to legends about Charles V. Stand in the middle of the bridge for a great view of Rabot and old Augustinian monastery **St Antoniushof** [168 C1], with its tranquil gardens. Following the quay north leads you to the Prinsenhof quarter.

Prinsenhof

Prinsenhof Castle Once a lavish 300-room castle, Prinsenhof was the birthplace of Emperor Charles V (page 6), who took his first breaths within its walls on 24 February 1500. In the 12th century it was known as Hof ten Walle and owned by the Deputy Count of Flanders. It acquired its current name in the mid 14th century when it fell into the hands of Louis de Male, Count of Flanders. He was tired of the chilly and dark Castle of the Counts across town, so poured funds into the redecoration of Prinsenhof that now reached all the way to Burgstraat. In its prime, the residence hosted guests like Mary of Burgundy and English King William III. However, by the mid 17th century its heyday was over: sections were sold off and, like Gravensteen, it was filled with factories during the 18th century. Several industrial fires destroyed most of the castle and today the only remnant is the **Donkere Poort** (**Dark Gate**) [168 B1], which sits at the north end of Prinsenhofplein and bears a plaque showing a picture of the once-complete castle (its name is said to stem from its pollution by factories). The bottom rampart is original, but the brick upper levels were added in the 19th century. On the other side of the gate is a statue of a *stroppendrager* (page 166).

Oud Begijnhof St Elizabeth (Old St Elizabeth Béguinage) [168 B2] (Begijnhofdries; free) Ghent's largest béguinage was once a sprawling estate home to over 700 béguines who spun lace for sale. Like many others, it sprang up in the 13th century. Changes to the street layout in the 19th century led to several homes and gardens being bulldozed, so Duke Engelbert-Auguste Arenberg built the Groot Begijnhof St-Amandsberg (page 188) for the béguines, who moved there in 1874, leaving the St Elizabeth cottages as housing for the elderly. The best-preserved portions are clustered around Proveniersstersstraat; the area is today known as the 'holy corner' as there are four different churches in proximity.

above **Escape to the country – take to the saddle and explore poplar-lined canals** (ET) page 31

below **Board a boat tour of Bruges's romantic waterways** (SS) page 215

Be led around the region by your tastebuds: visit a brewery (*left* VF; page 48); try a glass of revered Westvleteren – the world's rarest beer (*below left* ET; page 279), or an ultra-strong 'tripel' produced by fellow Trappist brewery Westmalle (*below* VF; page 49) or the additive-free Oerbier by De Dolle Brouwers in Diksmuide (*bottom* ET; page 262)

Watch master chocolatiers at work (*right* VF; page 92)**; let local sweet treats like *Antwerpse handjes* melt in your mouth** (*bottom* VF; page 296)**; or gorge on a bowl of salty chips and mayo** (*below* VF; page 45)

above left **Bruges's Heilig-Bloedprocessie – when a vial containing a few drops of Christ's blood is paraded through the city – has been held every May for over 700 years** (TB) page 53

above right **Held in Antwerp, the music festival Tomorrowland is full of colourful displays** (VF) page 54

below **Join the tourist-free drunken revelry of Aalst Carnival** (ET) page 200

right Ypres's Kattenstoet parade celebrates all things feline (ET) page 268

below Free open-air bands, street entertainers, food stands and endless parties take over Ghent city centre for the last two weeks of July (APL/A) page 54

left See one of the world's last horseback shrimp fishermen in action at Oostduinkerke (ET) page 251

below The North Sea coast comes into its own in summer with festivals, art events and myriad sporting pursuits such as horseriding (B/S) page 236

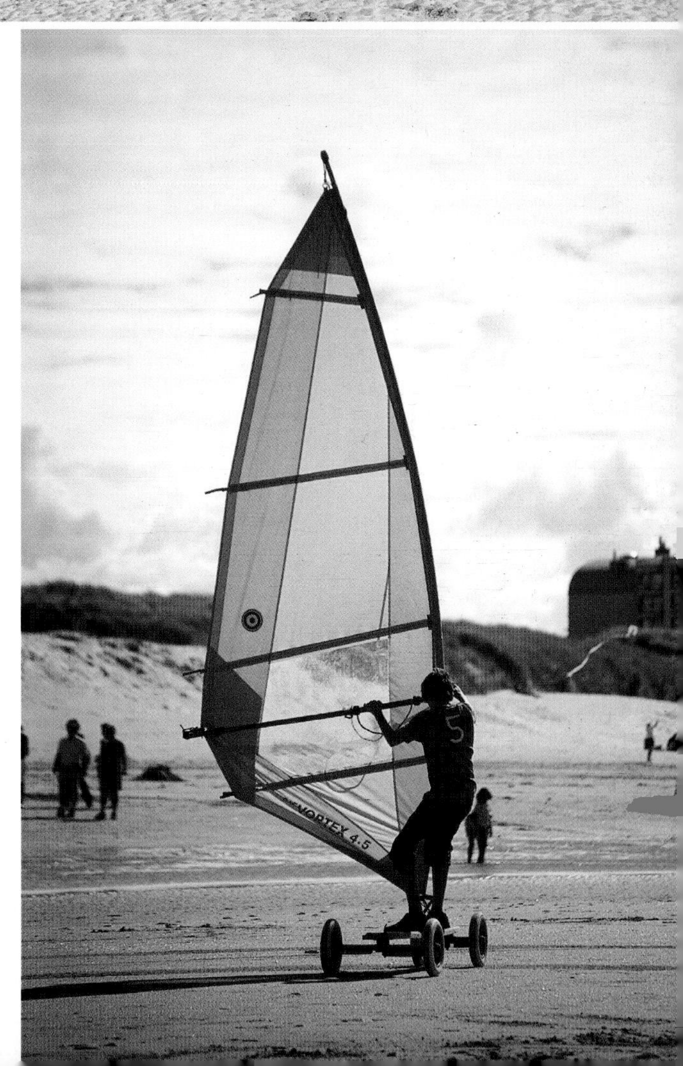

above Every few years, the Flemish coastal towns host Beaufort: a series of thought-provoking artworks scattered along the North Sea sands (ET) page 236

right Try your hand at sandsurfing in Middelkerke (ET) page 250

above left In Antwerp, Flemish folkloric trickster De Lange Wapper guards the medieval castle Het Steen (I/S) page 302

above The ultra-modern silver balls of the Atomium are modelled on an iron molecule (VF) page 129

below left Leuven's spectacular 15th-century town hall is covered with statues of famous Flemish figures (ET) page 146

below right The capital is littered with comic-book murals – including this one of Tintin and his loveable dog, Snowy (AS) page 100

Rabot [168 C1] (1 Opgeëistenlaan) A short stroll away, these two distinctive turreted towers guarding a stepped-gable building form the last of Ghent's city gates. The Lieve canal flowing through the town walls represented a weak spot for the city's defences; only by luck and a modest earth rampart did the citizens of Ghent ward off a 40-day siege launched on the city by Maximilian of Austria in 1488. To celebrate, these slightly more robust ramparts were built between 1489 and 1491.

Museum Dr Guislain (Dr Guislain Museum) [168 A1] (43 Jozef Guislainstraat; ☎ 09 398 69 50; **w** museumdrguislain.be; ⏱ 09.00–17.00 Tue–Fri, 13.00–17.00 Sat–Sun; adult/under 26/under 22/under 12/CityCard €8/3/1/free/free) Easily accessible via tram 1 (direction: Evergem/Wondelgem), this psychiatric hospital on the city's northern outskirts is the oldest in Belgium still in use today. The museum tells you about the pioneering doctor himself, as well as impressively tracing the history of psychiatry. Across the garden, you'll find an intriguing display of outsider art.

Patershol [172 B1] This tiny, maze-like medieval district – comprising just 13 streets – sits north of the city centre in the shadow of the Castle of the Counts. The quarter is named after an unremarkable blue door [172 B1] at the corner of Rodekoningstraat and Trommelstraat. Flemish for 'monk's arsehole' because of its small size, the low door was the entrance to a series of steps leading down to the waterside from which locals could draw their water. An ongoing refurbishment project has transformed the once working-class district into a hip neighbourhood with its fair share of desirable restaurants. It's the latest in a long line of transformations that have seen the area, bordered by Lange Steenstraat, Geldmunt, Kraanlei and Oudburg, go from the property of the Counts of Flanders to a district of magistrates and lawyers, followed by craftsmen and, in the 19th century, the working class, when houses where split into smaller units. Change came only in the 1980s, and now the picturesque district is one of the city's most popular tourist spots, playing host to a handful of sights:

Manneken Pis [172 B2] (17 Kraanlei) Above the doorway of this house, Ghent boasts its own statue of the miniature micturating boy famously attributed to Brussels. It's thought the small figure was a reference to the Tanners' Guild that often bought samples of strong urine to soften their leather hides.

Huis van Alijn (House of Alijn) [172 B1] (65 Kraanlei; ☎ 09 235 38 00; **w** huisvanalijn.be; ⏱ 09.00–17.00 Mon–Tue & Thu–Fri, 10.00–18.00 Sat–Sun; adult/19–26/under 19/CityCard €6/2/free/free) This U-shaped bundle of almshouses is the former 14th-century Alijn's Children Hospice. Their construction is attached to a Shakespearian-style story of scandal. Two boys – one from the Rijms family, the other from the Alijn family – had fallen in love with the same girl. Mad with jealousy, the young Rijm murdered Hendrik and Seger Alijn while they were at mass in St John's (the present-day St Bavo's). The Rijm family were banished, but a few years later given the option of a pardon by the count on the condition that they build a series of almhouses on land donated by the Alijn family. Despite its name, the hospice cared for elderly women who were chosen by a committee for pious or good behaviour. Bought by the city council in the 1950s, it's now a museum set on either side of a courtyard; above the reception you'll find temporary shows, while the permanent display (occasionally rotated) trots you through the months of the year while showcasing aspects of Flemish life through a variety of intriguing objects. Every Saturday there are afternoon puppet shows (🕘 Oct–May 14.30–16.00; €5); the complex also houses a quaint 19th-century tavern that serves Plumetje, a jenever served half and half (half cherry, half schnapps).

Zeven Werken van Barmhartigheid and De Fluitspeler [172 B1] (79 & 81 Kraanlei) Stop to admire the façades of these two terraced houses. The first, which belongs to Ghent's famous Temmerman sweet shop, is known as the **Seven Works of Mercy** and gets its name from the illustrations on the façade: burying the dead, ministering to prisoners, visiting the sick, feeding the hungry, giving drink to the thirsty, and clothing the naked; the seventh work, sheltering a stranger, was performed inside, as the building was originally an inn. On the corner is the mid-17th-century '**Flute Player**' house. Also known as **Het Vliegend Hert** (**The Flying Deer**), its bright-red terracotta reliefs depict female figures displaying the five senses: sight, smell, hearing, taste and touch. The reindeer in the middle of the top row symbolises new life. The three figures on the mantle are Faith, Hope and Charity.

Caermersklooster (Carmelite Friary) [172 B1] (14 Lange Steenstraat) The former Friary of the Calced Carmelites – an order of Roman Catholic monks – dates from the 13th century and reopened in January 2019 as an artist-run space led by the organisation Kunsthal Gent (w kunsthal.gent). Judging by the calibre of the inaugural programme, it looks like it's going to be a brilliant addition to the city.

Towards Vrijdagmarkt

Dulle Griet [172 C1] Cross the bridge from Patershol towards Vrijdagmarkt, and on the corner of Grootkanonplein you'll spot 'Mad Meg', a 5m-long, 12,500kg red cast-iron cannon that dates from the 15th century. It's the largest of its kind in Europe and was once capable of firing cannonballs weighing 250kg. It was made in Oudenaarde (page 206) and dragged all the way to Ghent, but alas the barrel split on the firing of the very first shot. Oudenaarde refused to offer a refund; naturally, relations between the two towns soured, and it's sat here, useless, ever since.

Vrijdagmarkt [172 C2] Named after the Friday market held here since 1199, this rangy square has been the stage for events good and bad over the centuries – from the official receptions of rulers and dignitaries to medieval jousting tournaments, tussles between guildhouses, public executions, and one memorable winter when 11-year-old Charles V – in celebration of his coronation – flooded the square with water, which froze to create an enormous skating rink.

The centre point is a straight-faced **statue of Jacob van Artevelde** (see box, page 5) addressing the crowds. The outskirts of the square are lined with 17th- and 18th-century gabled guildhouses, but disrupting the roofline in the north corner is **Ons Huis** [172 C1] (9 Vrijdagmarkt). This impressive building dates from 1900 and bears the embossed gold letters *Socialistische Werkervereenigingen* on its façade: it has served as the headquarters of the socialist labour union since 1902. Just like Vooruit (page 176), it points a finger at the bourgeoisie while cementing Ghent's unruly reputation. On the Kammerstraat side, 14th-century corner house **Toreken** [172 C2] is the oldest on the square, giving a sense of what it must have been like in medieval times.

Hoogpoort and Nederpolder [172 B–D3] Strolling along Langemunt brings you to Hoogpoort which, together with its add-on Nederpolder, forms the oldest street in town. Near its northern end it's bisected by **Werregarenstraat**, aka 'Graffiti Street', which was conceived as a temporary project for the 1995 Ghent Festivities, but has been gathering tags on almost a daily basis ever since. The show-stealer around here, however, is the **Stadhuis (Town Hall)** [172 C3] (1 Botermarkt). Construction of the ornate Gothic façade began in the late 15th century, but ground to a halt barely a quarter of the way through the build. Emperor Charles V's quibbles with the city residents had begun and as a punishment he retracted all the building funds – notice the still-unfilled statue niches. The 19 that are filled were installed only in the 19th and early 20th centuries, and those of Charles V and his aunt Margaret of Austria on the corner date from 2000. By the time sufficient funds had been saved to continue with the project, late-Gothic style was no longer in vogue and the remainder, facing Botermarkt, was completed in Renaissance style, giving the building a schizophrenic air. It still contains the offices of Ghent's burgomaster and alderman, but visitors are only allowed to explore the main rooms with a guide, including the *Pacificatiezaal*, or Court of Justice, with its distinctive blue-and-white tiled floor. It's said that crawling around it on your hands and knees would suffice as punishment instead of a pilgrimage to Jerusalem.

Across Botermarkt, on the corner, is the sandstone **Sint-Jorishof**, former guildhouse of the Crossbow Archers (who were responsible for defending the city) and site of the oldest hotel in western Europe – now a restaurant. The Flemish-Gothic building was inaugurated in 1477 by Mary of Burgundy, who laid the first stone and slept in one of the rooms still on offer at the fancy Cour St Georges hotel. A statue of dragon-slaying St George – the guild's patron saint – graces the top of the façade.

Geeraard de Duivelsteen (Castle of Gerald the Devil) [168 E4] (1 Geraard de Duivelstraat) This 13th-century Romanesque castle was named after its first owner, a knight called Geerard Vilain. His surname lent itself nicely to rumours of his diabolic behaviour: stories claim he beat his wife and plotted to murder his own son, so he could steal his pretty fiancée. The family property was sold in 1328 and has since served as a monastery, school, orphanage, madhouse and prison. It was sold back to the state in the late 19th century and until recently held government archives.

East of the centre

Stadsbrouwerij Gruut (Gruut Brewery) [168 E2] (1 Rembert Dodoensdreef; 09 269 02 69; **w** gruut.be; café: 14.00–18.00 Mon–Thu, 11.00–23.00 Fri–Sat, 14.00–19.00 Sun; Mar–Oct open from 11.00 Mon–Thu, otherwise same hours; tour €11 inc 3 tasters, or €16 inc local cheese & pâté) Tours of Ghent's decade-old brewery are normally reserved for groups, but if you email them (booking@gruut.be) they'll try to match you with an existing booking. In any case, you can always visit the café and try the Gruut Amber (6.6%), sweet and herby Blonde (5.5%), very light Wit (5%), light but mighty Inferno (9%), nutty Bruin (8%) or oft-changing special beer – all of them unique because a mixture of herbs (*grut*) is used instead of hops.

Portus Ganda [168 F3] (2 Veermanplein) At the confluence of the Scheldt and Leie rivers, where Ghent developed, this area was once concreted over to make way for cars, but has now been restored to its former glory. Park your pleasure yacht, stroll the boardwalk, prop up a table at a café, or do a few laps in Belgium's oldest swimming pool (built in 1896), the Art Deco **Zwembad Van Eyck** (1 Veermanplein). The marina is a great place to watch fireworks during the Ghent Festivities (page 54).

Sint-Baafsabdij (St Bavo's Abbey) [168 G3] (43 Voorhoutkaai; ⏲ Apr–Oct 14.00–18.00 Fri–Sun; free) One of two abbeys (the other was St Peter's, see opposite) founded by a missionary named Amand in AD630. Sadly, Amand's teachings weren't well received by locals: they drowned him in the nearby Scheldt and later named the church after his successor – a wealthy nobleman and landowner called Adlowinus who had taken the name Baaf when he entered the monastery, and who was elevated to the status of saint upon his death. When the Vikings arrived in AD879 they destroyed the abbey, and used the grounds as a base for raids throughout the country. When they left, the monks returned, rebuilt the abbey and adopted the Benedictine order. On the back of the wool industry, the abbey became rich and Ghent grew up around it – though, in revenge for the Ghent Uprising, Charles V ordered its demolition. Today shrubs surround the outline of the original Romanesque church, giving you an idea of its former grandeur. Most impressive is the intact refectory and its 12th-century vaulted timber roof, found up a flight of stairs above the north cloister. The room forms part of the **Museum voor Stenen Voorwerpen** (**Lapidary Museum**), which displays a collection of tombstones, among them the tomb of painter Hubert van Eyck, who contributed to the world-famous Ghent Altarpiece.

Groot Begijnhof St-Amandsberg (Great St Elizabeth Béguinage) [168 G2] (67 Groot Begijnhof; ☎ 09 228 23 08; **w** grootbegijnhof.be; ⏲ 06.30–21.30; free) Quite a trek from the city centre in St Amandsberg (it's easier to head there directly from Gent-Dampoort station) but well worth it, this is the newest of Ghent's three béguinages. It was built during the late 19th century to replace the Oud Begijnhof St Elizabeth (page 184) in the city centre, when the béguines were forced out under pressure from the liberal city government. Sadly, the on-site museum that gave you a glimpse of their way of life was shut as we went to press – hopefully this is temporary.

South of the centre Known as the ***Kunstenkwartier*** or **Arts Quarter**, the south of Ghent is dotted with museums, arts venues (such as Vooruit, page 176) and the city's parks, which cover the 2km stretch between Gent-Sint-Pieters station and the historic city centre. It's also home to the Ghent University campus.

De Krook [169 E5] (1 Miriam Makebaplein; ☎ 09 323 68 00; ⏲ 10.00–19.00 Mon–Wed & Fri–Sat, 10.00–21.00 Thu) Linking the centre and Arts Quarter, this hulking public library on a curve (or *krook*) in the river has a nice café; in 2020, they plan to add a rooftop eatery.

Stadmuseum Gent (STAM) [169 C6] (2 Godshuizenlaan; ☎ 09 267 14 00; **w** stamgent.be; ⏲ 09.00–17.00 Mon–Tue & Thu–Fri, 10.00–18.00 Sat–Sun; adult/under 26/under 19/CityCard €2/free/free, audio guide €3) This city history museum is the main attraction in the grounds of the sprawling **De Bijloke** site, which incorporates the remains of the 13th-century Cistercian Bijlokeabdij (Bijloke Abbey) and also now houses a renowned music centre. A visit to the artefact-stuffed permanent collection allows you to nose through the old abbey rooms, getting to grips with Ghent's rebellious streak, and also – best of all – the still unresolved theft of the Just Judges panel of *The Adoration of the Mystic Lamb* (page 178), which gets its own little section.

Boekentoren (Booktower) [169 D6] (9 Rozier) The University of Ghent's library and its distinctive 64m-high 'book tower' were designed by Art Nouveau master Henry van de Velde, who was a professor at the university between 1926 and 1936. Often hailed as the city's 'fourth tower' (after the three spires of St Bavo's, the Belfry and St Nicholas's Church), the building stocks some 3 million books.

Onze-Lieve-Vrouw St-Pieterskerk (Our Lady of St Peter's Church) [169 D6] (2 Sint-Pietersplein; 09 225 44 37; **w** mkgent.be; 10.00–17.15 Tue–Sat; Apr–Oct 10.00–12.30 & 14.30–20.00 Sun; Nov–Mar 10.00–12.30 & 18.00–20.00 Sun; free) A chapel dedicated to St Peter cropped up at roughly the same time as St Peter's Abbey (see below), but the Romanesque construction was demolished during the Iconoclasm and the version you see today is a Baroque masterpiece, also inspired by the Italian Renaissance flourishes of St Peter's in Rome. During the French Revolution it lost its function as an abbey church, and briefly served as a fine arts museum before morphing into a parish church. Inside, there are a number of excellent paintings, but of most interest are the tombs of five Counts of Flanders laid to rest under the Lady Chapel, and the remains of Isabella of Austria's tomb (sister of Emperor Charles V) in the far right-hand corner.

Sint-Pietersabdij (St Peter's Abbey) [169 E6] (9 Sint-Pietersplein; 09 243 97 30; 10.00–18.00 Tue–Sun; free entry to grounds, audio tour adult/19–26/under 19/CityCard €4/2/free/free) St Peter's is the other chapel founded by missionary St Amand in the 7th century. The abbey was partially destroyed on a number of occasions, first during Viking raids and later during the Iconoclasm. After each incident it was rebuilt and, as the preferred residence and burial site of the Counts of Flanders, it continued to grow into one of the richest and most important abbeys in the Low Countries. The brotherhood of Benedictine monks was finally expelled under French rule in 1796 and the abbey was sold at public auction. It was bought by the city and the grounds were used as army barracks until World War II. Part of the building now houses the **De Wereld van Kina (The World of Kina)** kids' natural history museum [169 D7] (14 Sint-Pietersplein; 09 244 73 73; **w** dewereldvankina.be; 09.00–17.00 Mon–Fri, 14.00–17.30 Sun; adult/19–25/under18/CityCard €3/2/free/free inc access to the garden), while at number 9 you can take a 1½hr audio tour of the abbey involving a murder mystery narrated by monk Alison or – for free – stroll about the ground floor, with its crypt and garden, which is intriguingly home to an active vineyard. The on-site café makes a point of employing people with disabilities, and is a nice place to stop for a beer.

Klein Begijnhof Onze-Lieve-Vrouw ter Hoyen (Small Béguinage Our Lady ter Hoyen) [169 F/G5] (235 Lange Violettestraat; **w** kleinbegijnhof-gent.be; 06.30–22.00) Ghent's third béguinage was established in 1234, but most of the buildings visible today date from the 17th century. The highlight of the central Baroque church is the 16th-century *Fountain of Life* polyptych painted by Lucas Horenbaut II. Located on the left-hand side of the church, the central panel features two fountains – the upper is the Fountain of Life, the lower is the Fountain of

Mercy – and to either side stand figures from the Old and New Testaments. The right panel depicts the Pope worshipping the Holy Sacrament of the Eucharist, and on the left King David pays homage to the ark of Jehovah. These days the béguinage is a residential site, and the former infirmary houses exhibitions.

Citadelpark [169 C7] Named after a fortress that stood here until the 1870s, this sizeable – rather hilly – park now has ponds, statues and a bandstand. It's most of interest, however, for hosting the city's two premier art museums.

Stedelijk Museum voor Actuele Kunst – S.M.A.K (Municipal Museum of Contemporary Art) [169 D8] (1 Jan Hoetplein, Citadelpark; 09 240 76 01; w smak.be; 09.30–17.30 Tue–Fri, 10.00–18.00 Sat–Sun; adult/under 18/CityCard €12/free/free) Housed in a former casino, this contemporary art museum is one of the most dynamic in Europe, let alone Flanders. The venue, which celebrated its twentieth birthday in May 2019, has an excellent permanent collection of works (ranging from expressionist art group CoBrA to pop art, conceptual art and radical Italian arte povera, via Warhol, Panamarenko and Beuys) which regularly changes in order to enter into dialogue with the daring temporary shows.

Museum voor Schone Kunsten – M.S.K. (Fine Arts Museum) [169 D8] (1 Fernand Scribedreef, Citadelpark; 09 323 67 00; w mskgent.be; 09.30–17.30 Mon–Fri, 10.00–18.00 Sat–Sun; adult/19–25/under18/CityCard €8/2/free/free) Opposite S.M.A.K, and occupying a regal building resembling a classical temple, the Fine Arts Museum displays around 350 permanent works of art dating from the Middle Ages to the first half of the 20th century. Make sure to pick up a floor plan from reception, and don't miss rooms 5 to 7, near the entrance, with a spread of works by Rubens and Jordaens, as well as the last suite of rooms – allocated a letter rather than a number – which takes you from pre-Impressionism to Surrealism. Note that, in the early months of 2020, Ghent will be honouring Flemish master van Eyck – subject of a 'van Eyck year' in Flanders – with a major exhibition pivoting around the restored *Ghent Altarpiece*, but also featuring exclusive loans.

Day trip

Kasteel van Ooidonk (Ooidonk Castle) (9 Ooidonkdreef; 09 282 26 38; w ooidonk.be; castle: Apr–15 Sep 14.00–17.30 Sun; gardens: Mar–Oct 13.00–18.00 Tue, 09.30–18.00 Wed–Sun; Nov–Feb 13.00–17.00 Tue, 10.00–17.00 Wed–Sun; castle: adult/under 12 €10/3, gardens: adult/child €2/0.50) People come from far and wide to visit Flanders' most complete, and beautiful, castle. Surrounded by a moat and rich woodland, Ooidonk Castle once belonged to Philippe II de Montmorency-Nivelle, also known as the Count Hoorn, who was executed on Brussels's Grand-Place alongside Count Egmont for resisting Spanish rule (page 7). The castle suffered extensive damage during the religious wars of 1579 and was rebuilt in the Flemish-Spanish style you see today. You're free to wander the lovely gardens all week, but the interior is only open at weekends because the current owner, Henri t'Kint de Roodenbeke, still lives in the castle. Its collection of period furniture, paintings, tapestries and silver is sumptuous. While in the area, I highly advise stopping off for creative Flemish classics at restaurant **Bachtekerke** (9 Bachtekerkstraat; 09 273 53 00; w bachtekerke.be; noon–14.30 & 18.00–22.30 Thu–Fri & Sun–Tues, 18.00–22.30 Sat; €€€), whose tree-lined terrace on the banks of the Leie river was voted the best in Belgium by Gault&Millau in 2018.

Getting there and away

By bus Take bus 14 (direction: Deinze) from Gent-Sint-Pieters station to Bachte-Maria-Leerne Mulderstraat (🕘 30mins), from where the castle is a 13-minute walk.

By car From Ghent follow the N466 southwest to Deinze, and after passing through the village of Sint-Martens-Leerne, turn left on to Leernsesteenweg, then left again on to Ooidonkdreef (14km; 🕘 23mins).

LAARNE

The leafy village of Laarne, 15km east of Ghent city centre, is full of hocus pocus. Along with the neighbouring village of Kalken, it was the site of witch burnings in 1607. In the early 21st century, a witches' guild was revived and, in between promoting the local Toverhekske beer, they have set up *heksenpad*, a 20km-long walk through the village that pinpoints the homes and meeting places of former witches.

GETTING THERE AND AWAY

By bus Bus 34 runs from Gent-Dampoort to Laarne Dorp (every 45mins; 🕘 32mins).

By car From Ghent take the E17 and turn off at the exit to Destelbergen. Merge on to the R4, then take exit 5 (direction: Laarne; 16km; 🕘 24mins).

TOURIST INFORMATION

Tourist information 2 Dorpsstraat; 09 365 46 25; w laarne.be/toerisme; 🕘 09.00–11.45 Mon & Thu, 09.00–11.45 & 14.00–18.45 Tue, 09.00–11.45 & 14.00–16.45 Wed, 09.00–12.45 Fri. Not an official tourist information office per se, but the staff in the town hall are happy to help & they sell the *heksenpad* walking route (€1.80).

WHAT TO SEE AND DO

Kasteel van Laarne (Laarne Castle) (5 Eekhoekstraat; 09 230 91 55; w slotvanlaarne.be; 🕘 guided tours May–Sep 15.00 Sun; Jul–Aug also 15.00 Thu; adult/child/under 6 €8/6/free) This looming medieval fortress complete with moat and turreted towers is among Belgium's finest. Built in the 13th century, it served as residence to Gerard of Zottegem when he returned from the Crusades in 1218. The fort protected a garrison of the Count of Flanders from sieges in 1362 and 1382, before falling under the private ownership of – variously – local lords, the De Vos family, the van Vilsterens, and later the Counts of Ribaucourt who donated it to the Koninklijke Vereniging voor Historische Woonsteden (Society for Historic Houses) in 1953. The houses on the corners of the first courtyard were occupied by coachmen, gardeners and chaplains; on the right, a fancy **restaurant** (09 230 71 78; w kasteelvanlaarne-rest.be; 🕘 noon–13.30 & 19.00–21.00 Wed–Sat, noon–14.00 Sun; €€€€€) occupies the old farm buildings. At the other end, across the bridge, is the grey-stone castle. Rooms of note include the Renaissance loggia, or entrance hall, whose large fireplace bears the crest of the van Vilsteren family and has paintings of Holy Roman Emperor Charles VI and his wife Elizabeth; and the Knight's Hall decorated with Brussels-made tapestries. Upstairs is the excellent Dallemagne collection of 17th- and 18th-century silverware.

SINT-NIKLAAS

Equidistant between Antwerp and Ghent, Sint-Niklaas belongs to Waasland, a formerly swampy region that served as the backdrop to the ancient fable of Reynard the Fox (see box, page 194). One claim to fame is that it boasts Belgium's largest Grote Markt, which hosts a weekly market every Thursday morning, and where, on the first complete weekend of September, dozens of hot-air balloons are launched during the Vredefeesten (Peace Festival) and subsequent three-day Villa Pace music festival.

Additionally, as you may have guessed, Sint-Niklaas is famous for being the hometown of Sinterklaas, otherwise known as Santa Claus. In 1217 the local clergy founded Sint-Nicolaas parish and dedicated it to the Greek bishop. Around this grew the cult of Sinterklaas. As well as boasting a huge statue of the saint outside the town hall, the city organises several events. The highlights are his arrival on the Grote Markt, around 15 November each year (enquire at the tourist office for exact dates), astride a white horse and complete with red velvet robes and a real long white beard; and a present workshop set up in the Salons (page 194). It's a great experience for both children and young-at-heart adults. Sint-Niklaas may not be an immediately pretty town, but it has some quirky charms if you spend a few hours getting to know it.

GETTING THERE AND AWAY

By car From Antwerp follow the E17 southwest and take exit 15 to Sint-Niklaas (25km; ⌚ 25mins). From Brussels follow the A12 north, take exit 7 and follow the N16 to Sint-Niklaas (45km; ⌚ 55mins). From Ghent follow the E17 northeast and take exit 15 (42km; ⌚ 33mins). There's a car park beneath the Grote Markt.

By train Antwerp (twice an hour; ⌚ 25mins); Ghent (twice an hour; ⌚ 31mins); Brussels (direct train hourly, or change in Antwerp/Ghent/Mechelen; ⌚ 1hr).

TOURIST INFORMATION

Tourist information 45 Grote Markt; ☎ 03 778 35 00; **w** ontdeksint-niklaas.be; ⌚, 15 May–15 Sep 09.00–noon & 13.00–17.00 Mon–Fri 10.00–16.00 Sat–Sun & hols; 16 Sep–14 May 09.00–noon & 13.00–17.00 Mon–Fri. Can arrange tours of various sites at €60/2hrs with a week's notice. Also sells combi-tickets (€9) for the town's 3 main attractions.

Bike rental Fietspunt, 2 Leopold II-laan (railway station); **m** 0493 51 64 76; **w** denazalee.be; ⌚ May–Sep 07.00–19.00 Mon–Fri, 09.00–13.00 Sat; €9/day

WHERE TO STAY AND EAT *Map, opposite*

Sint-Niklaas is heavily associated with the legend of Reynard the Fox, so it's only fitting that the local cake is named after him. The *Reynaertgebak* has a cake base, a thick layer of marzipan coated in chopped almonds and a disc bearing a picture of the tricksy fox on the top.

Hotel Moon (5 rooms, 2 suites) 18 Richard van Britsomstraat; ☎ 03 337 14 02; **w** hotelmoon.be. Fashionable & welcoming B&B with dark, dramatic suites & dbls with tea- & coffee-making facilities. **€€€**

Ibis (85 rooms) 2 Hemelaerstraat; ☎ 03 231 31 41; **w** ibishotel.com. I don't usually include chains, but this bright & modern Ibis outpost is definitely one of the best options in town, with clean rooms & a pleasant bar. **€€**

Brasserie 't Heerehuys 41 Casinostraat; ☎ 03 766 75 05; ⌚ 11.30–14.00 & 17.30–21.00 Wed–Sun. Classy brasserie with a lovely terrace. The menu does the classics well & the fondue

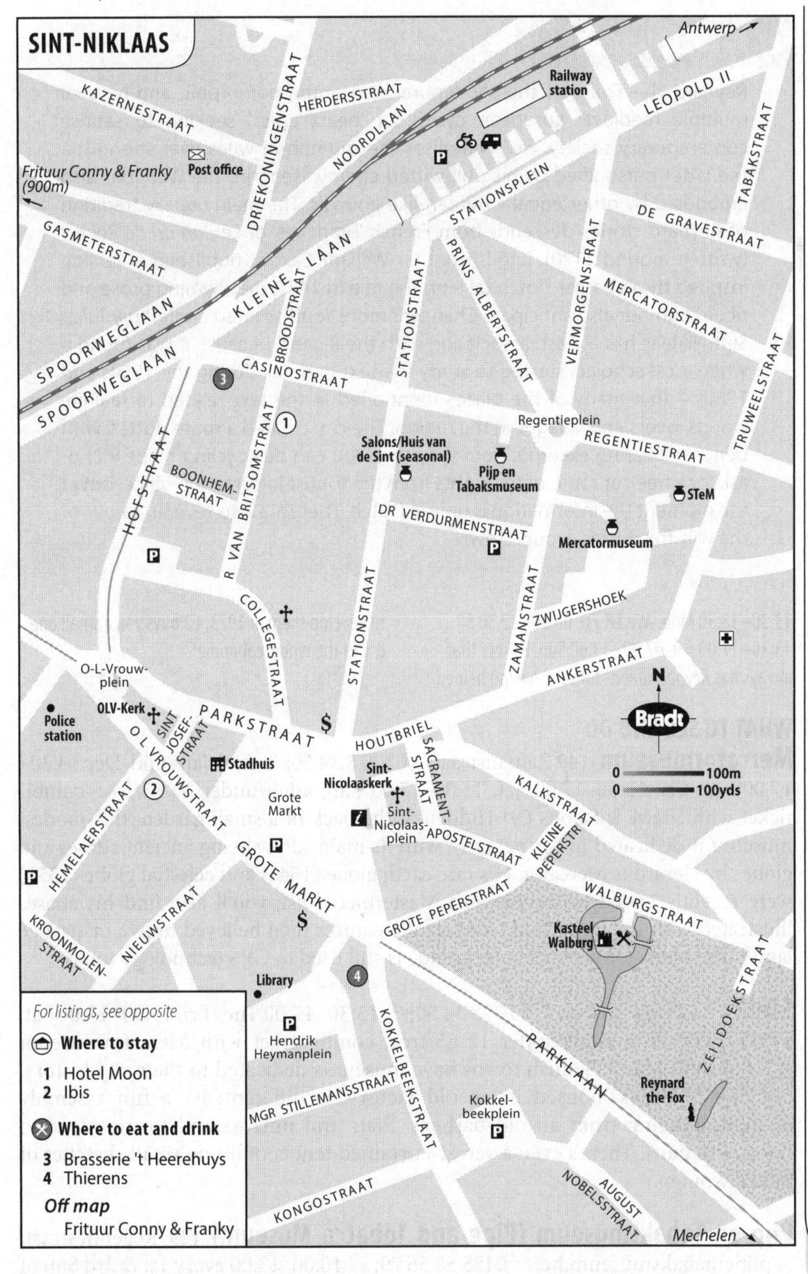

lunches (Sun) & dinners (Fri–Sun) are very popular indeed. €€€

Frituur Conny & Franky 325 Plezantstraat; **m** 0483 48 84 41; **w** frituurconnyenfranky.be; 17.00–22.00 Mon–Wed, 17.00–midnight Fri–Sat, 17.00–23.00 Sun. The main event – handcut & traditional – is brilliant at this humble chip joint, but the real joy is everything else: pulled-pork burgers, Philly-style cheese steaks & even goulash sides (not your usual *frituur* then). You won't leave hungry. €

Thierens 47 Kokkelbeekstraat; 03 776 15 80; **w** patisseriethierens.be; 06.30–12.30 &

REYNAERD DE VOS

Reynard the Fox was the sly, amoral and anthropomorphic anti-hero of multiple medieval European cycles, or 'beast epics', seeking to satirise contemporary society. He symbolises the triumph of wiles over strength – the latter personified by his dull-witted enemy, Isengrim the Wolf, but also embodied by other equally human-like animals. The main literary tradition of Reynard stories descends from French 'branches' of *Le Roman de Renart* (written around 1170). English printer William Caxton published a version inspired by an earlier Dutch take on the tale in 1481; the rhyming prose and ribald humour also anticipate Chaucer's more sophisticated *Canterbury Tales*. Sint-Niklaas has a close association with the legend because it was found – when local scholars started to study the text in detail during the 1950s and 1960s – that many of the places mentioned in the text related to real-life woods, rivers and villages in the region. The city created a route dotted with benches bearing excerpts from the story. You can buy cycling maps (€2) or ask for a free car route of the sights from the tourist information office, but at the moment the information is only in Dutch. There are also several statues of the wily fox dotted around town.

13.30–18.30 Mon–Wed & Fri, 06.30–12.30 & 13.30–17.00 Sat, 07.00–13.00 Sun. Bakery that always has *Reynaertgebak* for sale, having helped to develop them in 1973; €2 buys you a small one & €19 the whole caboodle!

WHAT TO SEE AND DO

Mercatormuseum (49 Zamanstraat; 03 778 34 50; mid-Jan–mid-Dec 13.30–17.00 Tue–Fri, 13.00–17.00 Sat, 11.00–17.00 Sun; adult/under 12 €5/free, combi-ticket with STeM & Salons €9) Hidden at the back of a small garden, this modest museum is dedicated to cartography, with its major draw being ancient atlases and globes by Gerardus Mercator. His rare earth globe (1541) and celestial globe (1551) were recently added to the Flemish Masterpieces list; you'll also find his atlases illustrated with the weird and wonderful creatures then believed to live in strange lands. The Mercator projection technique is still used in GPS technology today.

STeM (14 Zwijgershoek; 03 778 34 50; 13.30–17.00 Tue–Fri, 13.00–17.00 Sat, 11.00–17.00 Sun; adult/under 12 €5/free, combi-ticket with Mercatormuseum & Salons €9) Many Flemish towns have museums dedicated to their city history, but Sint-Niklaas's, housed in an old factory, is different: it's a fun assembly of items ranging from an old barber's chair and mirrorstand to mosaic-tiled floors and guns. There's even a velvet-curtained tent containing small sketches of naked women.

Pijp-en Tabaksmuseum (Pipe and Tobacco Museum) (29 Regentiestraat; w pijpentabaksmuseum.be; m 0485 58 56 79; 10.00–13.00 every 1st & 3rd Sun of the month; €3.50) Set back from the street down an alley, this history museum has a pipe collection dating from 1492 and owns the Low Countries's largest pipe, as well as the world's largest cigar (random, but fun).

Salons (85 Stationstraat; 03 778 34 50; mid-Jan–mid-Dec 13.30–17.00 Thu–Fri, 13.00–17.00 Sat, 11.00–17.00 Sun; adult/12–18 €2/1, combi-ticket with

STeM & Mercatormuseum €9) Most of the year this 1920s townhouse displays the city's small but rich collection of 16th- to 20th-century paintings, including works by Félicien Rops and Henri Evenepoel. However, in winter it dons its robes to morph into the **Huis van de Sint** – Father Christmas's workshop (⌚ 12 Nov–6 Dec 16.00–17.30 Mon–Tue & Thu–Fri, 14.00–17.30 Wed, 10.00–17.30 Sat–Sun; free). Kids can see Santa's bedroom, exercise room (!) and the present-manufacturing room.

DENDERMONDE

The small town of Dendermonde sits at the confluence of the Dender and Scheldt rivers and, consequently, has been a fortified town since the 12th century – archways can still be seen at the southern and northern ends of Leopold II-Laan. Like nearby Ghent, it grew wealthy on the back of the cloth trade and the money was poured into the construction of its town hall and Vleeshuis (Butcher's Hall). Sadly, these and large parts of the town were burnt by invading German troops during World War I, making Dendermonde one of seven so-called Belgian *Martelaarsteden* ('Martyr towns'). It's best known for its Ros Beiaard parade held every ten years (see box, page 196), but few know that, from the mid 19th to the mid 20th centuries, Dendermonde was home to an esteemed arts academy – one of Belgium's best – that schooled painters like Franz Courtens, whose paintings are on show in the town hall.

GETTING THERE AND AWAY

By car From Brussels follow signs for the R20 and continue on to the E40, taking exit 20 (direction: Ternat). Continue along the N285 and then the N47, which leads to Dendermonde (34km; ⌚ 50mins). From Ghent follow the E17 east and take exit 12 (direction: Lokeren), then follow the N47 south to Dendermonde (36km; ⌚ 35mins). From Aalst, follow the N406 north (16km; ⌚ 25mins).

By train Brussels (hourly; ⌚ 32mins); Ghent (hourly; ⌚ 25mins); Sint-Niklaas (via Lokeren, hourly; ⌚ 29mins).

TOURIST INFORMATION

Tourist information Stadhuis, Grote Markt; 052 21 39 56; w toerismedendermonde.be; Jun–Sep 11.00–17.30 Mon & Sat–Sun, 09.30–17.30 Tue–Fri, Oct–May 09.30–16.30 Tue–Fri, noon–16.30 Sat–Sun. Sells Reuzenroute & Ros Beiaardroute cycling maps (€2).

WHERE TO EAT AND DRINK

Local meaty treats to look out for are *Dendermondse paardenworstjes* (horse sausages) and *kopvlees* (pig's head pâté) served with mustard, which is tastier than it sounds, and the sweeter *Ros Beiaardkoekjes*. You may be able to pick some up at the weekly market held on Kerkstraat, Oude Vest and Brusselsestraat (⌚ 08.00–noon Mon). The award-winning Tripel Karmeliet and touristy Kwak are brewed by Brouwerij Bosteels in Buggenhout, 8km east of Dendermonde, while Dendermonde Tripel and Vicaris Tripel are produced in town.

Da Vinci 29 Koning Albertstraat; m 0475 92 58 35; w davincirestaurant.be; ⌚ 19.00–midnight Wed & Sat, noon–15.30 & 19.00–midnight Thu–Fri, noon–16.30 & 19.00–midnight Sun. The façade of this couple-run restaurant gives little clue as to the ambition of its food – be it the bargain 2-course market menu for Thu/Fri lunch (€27) or 4- to 5-course

ROS BEIAARD

The UNESCO-listed Ros Beiaard parade is held every decade in honour of a medieval folk song that recounts the tale of Charlemagne punishing the four sons of Aymon, Lord of Dendermonde, for fighting, by drowning their prized horse Beiaard – a beast reputedly able to understand human speech (and who somehow cheated death and lived eternally in the woods, ahem). Its centrepiece is an enormous oak horse measuring 5.2m long and 4.8m high and weighing a staggering 800kg. *Pijnders*, members of the Guild of Bearers, split into three groups of 12 men and take turns carrying the colossal horse through town. On its back sit four armour-clad brothers known as *heemskinderen*. It's a huge honour to be chosen because the rules of eligibility are very strict: the brothers must be the sons of Dendermonde residents, born in town, sequentially (ie no girls in between), and aged between seven and 21. This explains why it's held only once a decade! The next parade takes place on 24 May 2020 (w rosbeiaard.be), and will feature – as ever – more than 2,000 extras: take that Spielberg!

chef's menus on Sat night (€52+). Lovely garden in summer an asset. €€€€

Happy Days 33–7 Vlasmarkt; 052 57 79 77; w happydaysfan.be; 08.00–17.00 Mon, 08.30–17.00 Wed–Sat. Cheerful café with homely 1950s-inspired décor. Great for a buffet b/fast, fresh soup or hot chalkboard specials, or grab a homemade cake & the best coffee in town (a refill will set you back a princely €1). €€

Honky Tonk 12a Leopold II-laan; m 0478 92 80 70; w www.honkytonk.be; during concerts. Wonderful old-school jazz bar in a 19th-century army bunker that's been running since 1965. There are live events on Sat night around 20.30, generally every 2 weeks. The bar sits behind Jazz Center Flanders (13.30–16.30 Wed–Sat; free), which hosts exhibitions & has an epic jazz collection to listen to.

WHAT TO SEE AND DO

Stadhuis (Town Hall) (Grote Markt; same hours as tourist office; free) Dendermonde's symmetrical, recently renovated town hall, originally the storehouse of the weavers' guild, is very pretty in summer, with regional flags fluttering in the breeze. The original 14th-century version was destroyed during the bombardments of World War I – only fragments remain – and had to be rebuilt. You can collect an audio tour at the counter; the first floor boasts a number of paintings linked to the Dendermonde School of Art. Since 2018 it has also been possible to visit the **belfort** (€2 inc audio guide), which was awarded World Heritage status in 1999. Built in 1377, it once held the town's charters; it also houses a carillon with 49 bronze bells. When the hour strikes, the belfry plays the Ros Beiaard song – listen out for it.

In the entrance hall, look for the portrait of a chap sporting a heavy moustache and long sideburns. This is Polydore de Keyser. He was born in Dendermonde but moved to England in his teens, established a hotel and rose to become Lord Mayor of London (1887–88). Next enter the new part of the building, located to the left of the main staircase. In the *Renoutzaal* you'll find a painting of a frozen river by Franz Courtens, the most famous graduate of Dendermonde's School of Art. Back in the old part of the building, the small *Jumelagezaal* contains a trio of treasures: a wonderfully emotive plaster sculpture of kids fighting by Jef Lambeaux, a glass case containing the four suits of armour worn by the Ros Beiaard brothers (see box, above) and a huge painting commemorating the Ros Beiaard parade held when Polydore de Keyser visited in 1888. You can pick him out sitting in front of the town hall thanks to his red military attire. Also notice the Union Jack flags erected in his honour. Near the *Jumelagezaal* are three more paintings by Courtens: a view of the Royal Park of Laeken, men gathering hay and cows grazing.

Vleeshuismuseum (Butchers' Hall Museum) (23 Grote Markt; ⌚ Apr–Oct 09.30–12.30 & 13.00–18.00 Tue–Fri, 13.00–18.00 Sat–Sun; Nov–Mar w/end only; free) Across the square, it's easy to pick out the slender turret of the former Butchers' Hall, where meat was once sold on the ground floor. The current building is a reconstruction of a 15th-century version badly damaged in September 1914. It now houses an archaeology and town-history museum. Worth a visit, if just to see the skeleton of a 28,000-year-old mammoth – the town's oldest inhabitant, obviously!

Onze-Lieve-Vrouwekerk (Church of Our Lady) (Kerkstraat; ⌚ Apr–Sep 14.00–16.45 Sat–Sun; Jul–Aug 14.00–16.45 Tue–Sun; free) This splendid church proudly houses two paintings by Antony van Dyck – *The Adoration of the Shepherds* (in the north aisle) and *The Crucifixion* (in the baptistry) – and a 12th-century baptismal font crafted from blue Tournai marble. The tourist office can arrange guided tours.

Opposite the church entrance stands a statue of Pieter-Jan de Smet, a Roman Catholic priest who emigrated to America in the early 19th century. De Smet became well known in the US for successfully implementing the Treaty of Fort Laramie in 1868 between the government and American Indian clans. His statue stands outside Washington's Capitol; not bad for a local Dendermonde boy!

Sint-Alexiusbegijnhof (St Alexius Béguinage) (Brusselsestraat; free) It's easy to walk past the béguinage gateway buried between ING bank and Passerella clothes shop on Brusselsestraat. The cobbled path opens out to reveal a spacious triangular compound of 61 houses. No 11 retains its authentic béguine furnishings and can be visited, as can no 25 which belonged to Miss Ernestine De Bruyne – Dendermonde's last béguine, who died in 1975 – and now houses the **Begijnhofmuseum (Béguinage Museum)** (⌚ Apr–Oct 09.30–12.30 & 13.00–18.00 Tue–Fri, 13.00–18.00 Sat–Sun; Nov–Mar w/end only; free). Before you leave, pay your respects at Sint-Alexius cave at the back of the church, which is lit with prayer candles every evening.

AALST

Though it's the second-biggest city in East Flanders, Aalst is often bypassed by travellers en route from Ghent to Brussels – though there's one time of year when it *does* hog the spotlight: during its annual carnival (see box, page 200), which is held 40 days before Easter, and involves a great deal of beer and bad behaviour, along with all those fascinating traditional rites! Nonetheless, in the past few years, as new cafés and shops have appeared, the once marginal city has started to actively reposition itself – with Flemish papers even billing it as the region's next hipster hotspot!

Locals are known as *ajuinen* (onions) owing to the 19th-century onion plantation on the fertile river polders of the Dender – a nickname they flaunt because they feel it perfectly sums up their spicy, cutting humour. That wit is often put to work humbling Aalst's nemesis: Dendermonde. In the Middle Ages, Dendermonde levied high tolls on *Aalstenaars* using the river Dender; later Dendermonde got exclusive rights to load and unload goods in the region,

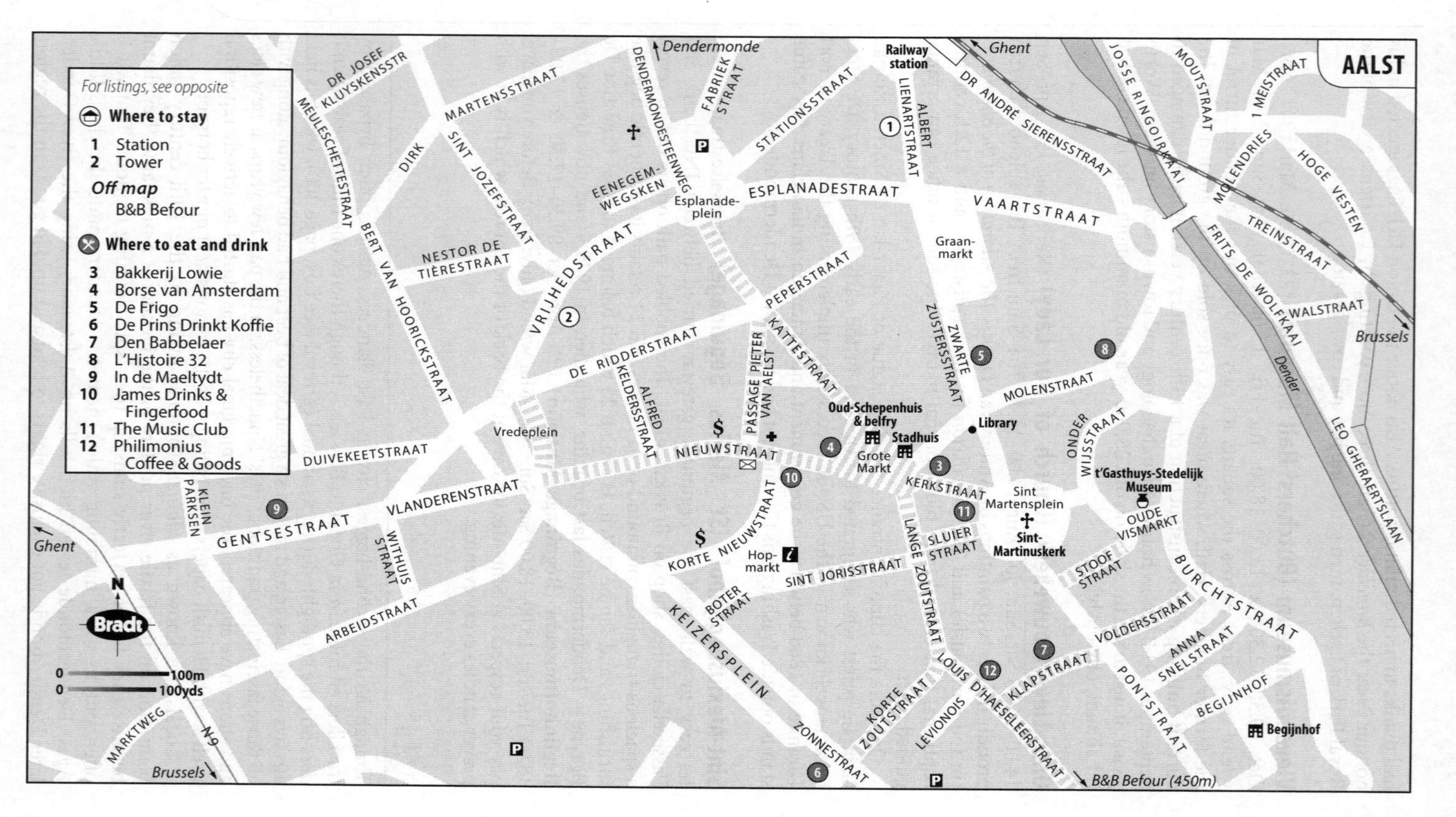

AALST
For listings, see opposite
Where to stay
1 Station
2 Tower
Off map
B&B Befour
Where to eat and drink
3 Bakkerij Lowie
4 Borse van Amsterdam
5 De Frigo
6 De Prins Drinkt Koffie
7 Den Babbelaer
8 L'Histoire 32
9 In de Maeltydt
10 James Drinks & Fingerfood
11 The Music Club
12 Philimonius Coffee & Goods
Bradt
N
0 100m
0 100yds
Railway station
Ghent
Brussels
Dendermonde
B&B Befour (450m)
Dender
Oud-Schepenhuis & belfry
Stadhuis
Grote Markt
Library
Sint Martensplein
Sint-Martinuskerk
t'Gasthuys-Stedelijk Museum
Begijnhof
Graanmarkt
Esplanadeplein
Hopmarkt
Vredeplein
JOSSE RINGOIRKAAI
MOUTSTRAAT
1 MEISTRAAT
MOLENDRIES
HOGE VESTEN
TREINSTRAAT
WALSTRAAT
FRITS DE WOLFKAAI
LEO GHERAERTSLAAN
DR ANDRÉ SIERENSSTRAAT
VAARTSTRAAT
ALBERT LIENARTSTRAAT
ESPLANADESTRAAT
STATIONSSTRAAT
FABRIEK STRAAT
DENDERMONDESTEENWEG
EENEGEM-WEGSKEN
VRIJHEDSTRAAT
MARTENSSTRAAT
SINT JOZEFSTRAAT
NESTOR DE TIÈRESTRAAT
DIRK
DR JOSEF KLUYSKENSSTR
MEULESCHETTESTRAAT
BERT VAN HOORICKSTRAAT
DE RIDDERSTRAAT
ALFRED KELDERSSTRAAT
PEPERSTRAAT
KATTESTRAAT
PASSAGE PIETER VAN AELST
NIEUWSTRAAT
KORTE NIEUWSTRAAT
BOTER STRAAT
KEIZERSPLEIN
ZWARTE ZUSTERSSTRAAT
MOLENSTRAAT
ONDER WIJSSTRAAT
OUDE VISMARKT
STOOF STRAAT
KERKSTRAAT
SLUIER STRAAT
LANGE ZOUTSTRAAT
SINT JORISSTRAAT
KORTE ZOUTSTRAAT
LEVIONOIS
ZONNESTRAAT
LOUIS D'HAESELEERSTRAAT
KLAPSTRAAT
VOLDERSSTRAAT
ANNA SNELSTRAAT
BURCHTSTRAAT
BEGIJNHOF
PONTSTRAAT
VLANDERENSTRAAT
DUIVEKEETSTRAAT
WITHUIS STRAAT
ARBEIDSTRAAT
GENTSESTRAAT
KLEIN PARKSEN
MARKTWEG
N9

severely affecting Aalst's trade. Dozens of songs and sayings have sprung up around the rivalry, each out-parodying the last, with jibes usually focusing on Dendermonde's beloved nag Ros Beiaard. Cycling fans should note that, in summer, just 24 hours after the climax of the Tour de France, famous riders from the competition descend on Aalst's market square for the start of Belgium's oldest post-Tour race (**w** criteriumaalst.be).

GETTING THERE AND AWAY

By car The seemingly neverending E40 runs from the coast right past Aalst; take exit 19.

By train Brussels (4 times an hour Mon–Fri, twice an hour Sat–Sun; ⌚ 33mins); Ghent (twice an hour; ⌚ 29mins); Bruges (via Gent-Sint-Pieters, 4 times an hour; ⌚ 1hr 10mins). Aalst railway station – designed by Jean-Pierre Cluysenaer, behind the Galeries Royales Saint-Hubert in Brussels (page 103) – is a short walk from the centre.

TOURIST INFORMATION

Tourist information 51 Hopmarkt; 053 72 38 80; **w** visit-aalst.be; ⌚ 09.00–17.00 Mon–Fri, 10.00–17.00 Sat, 13.00–17.00 Sun. Friendly office located in a big, modern glass cube. Offers a free English tourist booklet & fun 360° movie about Aalst. Guided tours (€60/2hrs) on request. Happy to provide details of local cycling routes (such as the Louis Paul Boon route, named after the famed local novelist).

WHERE TO STAY AND EAT *Map, opposite*

The city's speciality is *Aalsterse vlaaien*, a cinnamon-flavoured flan that's either eaten as is with a cup of coffee, or can serve as a sandwich spread – it's that soft and moist. The best place to try it is Bakkerij Lowie (page 200), which has launched DIY kits to counter the gradual ebbing of local knowledge about how to make it.

Tower Hotel (88 rooms) 62 Vrijheidstraat; 053 21 01 00; **w** towerhotelaalst.be. Central 4-star option with spacious rooms & a health club with sauna. B/fast on top floor features regional produce. **€€€€–€€€**

B&B Befour (4 rooms) 22 Felix De Hertstraat; 053 21 04 69; **w** befour.be. New, superior B&B located in a 1900 building that was originally a textile factory. The 4 big, modern rooms feature cool design touches & are named after former local mayors. There's a sauna & owner Bert speaks good English. **€€€**

Station Hotel (15 rooms) 14 Albert Lienartstraat; 053 77 58 20; **w** stationhotel-aalst.com. Set in a faded but glorious Baroque-style building stuffed with antiques & a minute from the station. Rooms have fridges & tea- & coffee-making facilities, & a generous b/fast (extra) is offered in a grand beamed dining room. Honesty bar & very helpful host – a bargain at €70/night. **€€**

L'Histoire 32 52 Molenstraat; **m** 0475 49 09 94; **w** lhistoire32.be; ⌚ noon–14.30 & 19.00–20.30 Wed–Fri, 19.00–20.30 Sat. Charming, creative fine-dining spot whose set menus – 4 courses for €55 or 5 for €65 – are really good value for cooking of this level. Service the opposite of stuffy. **€€€€€**

De Frigo 7a Zwarte Zustersstraat; 053 42 90 75; **w** defrigo.be; ⌚ noon–16.00 & 18.00–21.30 Tue–Sat. A restaurant in the back of a stunning butcher's – very much part of Aalst's cool new makeover. Carnivores salivate over beef & horsemeat cooked to perfection & served with fries, salad & several sauces. Nice cocktails to start & the *dame blanche* is a winner for dessert. Mains around €35. **€€€€–€€€€€**

Borse van Amsterdam 26 Grote Markt; 053 21 15 81; **w** borsevanamsterdam.be; ⌚ 09.30–21.30 Mon–Tue & Fri–Sat, 11.30–18.00 Sun. Left of the belfry, this upmarket brasserie occupies the beautifully restored former meat hall. Popular with lunching 'golden oldies', you can pop in for a pancake & coffee or a proper, good-value Flemish meal. €€€€

In de Maeltydt 91 Gentsestraat; 053 41 73 86; w indemaeltydt.com; 09.00–18.00 Mon–Tue & Thu, 09.00–14.00 Wed, 09.00–21.30 Fri–Sat. A café back in the 1920s & still run by the same family, this useful spot now operates as a restaurant focusing on organic, 'honest' produce. Basic b/fast is €7 & they have a good-value seasonal lunch deal. Caters to food intolerances. Cash only. €€–€€€

Philimonius Coffee & Goods 8 Louis D'Haeseleerstraat; m 0488 20 13 58; w www.philimonius.be; 10.00–17.30 Tue–Thu, 10.00–18.00 Fri–Sat, 14.00–18.00 Sun. Started as a webshop for handmade gifts – still on offer in its current guise as a coffee bar. Yes, it's very trendy, but they have a top barista, yummy cheesecake & their coffees (chai lattes & more obscure variants) look like art. €€€

De Prins Drinkt Koffie 2 Geraardsbergsestraat; m 0495 92 24 76; f DePrinsDrinktKoffie; 08.30–18.00 Mon & Thu–Sat, 13.00–18.00 Wed & Sun. Beautifully styled coffee bar with a unique selling point: it's run by Kris van Vaerenbergh, a former Aalst Carnival prince. Tarts & other goodies come courtesy of beloved Ghent-based Julie's House & they do a fabulous granola b/fast. €€

Bakkerij Lowie 16 Molenstraat; 053 77 43 00; w bakkerijlowie.be; 08.00–18.30 Mon–Tue & Thu–Sat. The best place to try *Aalsterse vlaaien*, though they also sell onion cakes & gimmicky choc onions as a nod to the local moniker. €

Den Babbelaer 3 Klapstraat; 053 77 58 96; 11.30–late Tue–Sat. A stone's throw from Aalst's (rather disappointing) béguinage, a very cosy vintage bar with a superb selection of regional beers, inc Gilladeken & Ondineke, brewed at De Glazen Toren brewery in the nearby town of Erpe-Mere. Also serves tapas.

James Drinks & Fingerfood 28 Grote Markt; w hijames.be; 16.00–22.00 Tue, noon–22.00 Wed, noon–23.00 Sun. The best cocktail bar in town – & run by a friend of the author, no less – this urbane joint offers inventive cocktails, palate-tempting boutique wines & lip-smacking nibbles to soak up the alcohol. A must.

The Music Club 11 Kerkstraat; m 0476 22 71 61; w themusicclub.be; Sep–Jun 16.00–late

AALST CARNIVAL

This relatively tourist-free folkloric feast dates back to the Middle Ages, when local rulers allowed the townsfolk to enjoy three days of no-rules debauchery prior to Ash Wednesday, the start of Lent. A word of warning: be prepared to party – this is a non-stop knees-up (think Rio Carnival on a Flemish scale) but it's not just that, with UNESCO recognising the event's intangible cultural heritage in 2010.

In 1851 townsfolk introduced the procession of flotillas that parade through town and mark the arrival of carnival. Local groups spend months preparing these floats, which take the mickey out of local figures and recent events – eg: a former mayor's holiday indiscretions or, in 2016, a float with a Trump-esque character demanding a wall between Aalst and Dendermonde (at Dendermonde's expense, of course)!

The procession starts on the Sunday/Monday before Ash Wednesday and ends with Aalst dignitaries throwing thousands of onions from the balcony of the town hall into the crowd, including one lucky golden onion. Tuesday is *Voil Jeanetten* – sure to stir up conversation. Men arrive dressed in stockings, corsets and birdcages, and stumble around on high heels drunkenly embracing each other (it's a nod to Aalst's working-class roots – in decades past, men couldn't afford fancy costumes, so dressed in their wives' old *schmatters*). As evening falls, everyone gathers on the Grote Markt and, with genuine tears of remorse, watches the Carnival Prince light a bonfire, signalling the end of the party.

Wed–Sun, Jul–Aug 16.00–late Wed–Sun & 18.00–late Mon. Jazzy bar in the house – with twee Swiss-style façade – where Priest Daens (see below) was born in 1839. Plump for a cocktail: if the 125 kinds on the menu don't suit, you can go bespoke.

WHAT TO SEE AND DO

Grote Markt Aalst's main square is dotted with several buildings of note. Standing tall is the Gothic **Oud-Schepenhuis** (**Aldermen's House**). Parts of it date back to 1225, making it the oldest of its kind in the Low Countries. The UNESCO-listed **belfry** on one corner was completed in 1460, and the next year fitted with a carillon by master craftsmen from Mechelen. Look for the inscription *Nec Spe, Nec Metu* ('Without hope, Without fear') below the statue reliefs; it's a quote by Spain's Philip II, who became Count of Aalst in 1595. Locals refer to the tower as *Tettentoeren* (Titty Tower) because of the raised balls that form the hour markers on the modern clock face, again showing their particular humour! The tourist office can arrange guided tours on request; there's free entry every third Sunday of the month.

The **statue of Dirk Martens** in front of the building has stood there since 1856. Thanks to the colour of the oxidised bronze, locals call him De Zwarte Man (the Black Man). In 1473 Martens developed the first printing press in the Southern Netherlands and published works by Christopher Columbus as well as Thomas More's *Utopia*. To the left of the Aldermen's House is the 17th-century **Borse van Amsterdam**; once the meat market, it's now an upmarket restaurant (page 199). To the right is the Neoclassical **Stadhuis** (**Town Hall**), erected in 1830. If you wander through its archway to an inner courtyard, you'll see a statue of Ondineke, a character from Louis Paul Boon's celebrated novel *De Kapellekensbaan*.

t'Gasthuys-Stedelijk Museum (13 Oude Vismarkt; ☎ 053 72 36 02; ⏱ 10.00–17.00 Tue–Fri, 14.00–18.00 Sat–Sun; free, explanations in Dutch only) Inside the town's only museum, on the first floor, is a lively exhibition about the history of the Aalst Carnival (see box, page 200) with old film footage and photos, a jukebox playing carnival tunes, a re-creation of a traditional *estaminet* (bar) and a line-up of the carnival 'princes'. Downstairs is the exhibition 'DNAalst', about the history of the town, and featuring local luminaries Dirk Martens, Valerius De Saedeleer (one of the chief artists in the early 20th-century, Modernist Latem school), priest Adolf Daens (known for his socio-political involvement) and Louis Paul Boon.

Sint-Martinuskerk (St Martin's Church) (5 Sint-Martensplein; ☎ 053 21 31 95; ⏱ winter 09.00–16.00, summer 09.00–17.00, closes 14.00 Fri; free) Aalst's neo-Gothic parish church is a real beauty. Work on the current building started in 1650 and, incredibly, is not due to finish until 2027! Inside it's bursting at the seams with no fewer than 22 chapels – each one belonging to a different guild – and over 400 artworks, notably Rubens's not-so-snappily titled *Christ Appointing St Rochus as Patron Saint of Plague Victims*.

GERAARDSBERGEN

The hilly town of Geraardsbergen (known as Grammont in French) sits at the southeastern edge of the Flemish Ardennes and is famous for its three Ms: the Muur, *mattentaart* (see box, page 203) and – the real – Manneken Pis. Amazingly, it's also believed to be Flanders' oldest city, with a charter dating from 1068. Later, on 29 May 1815, it enjoyed its 5 minutes of fame when the Duke of Wellington reviewed his troops in the fields surrounding the town prior to the pivotal Battle of Waterloo.

KRAKELINGEN

Every year, on the last Sunday of February, Geraardsbergen celebrates Krakelingen and Tonnekensbrand – a UNESCO-listed pagan procession that marks the end of winter. Townsfolk dress up in ye olde clothes and put together a parade recounting the town's history. It departs from outside Hunnegem church and climbs to the top of Oudenberg hill. From here town officials throw *krakelingen* (bagels) that have been blessed in Oudeberg Chapel to the crowds, city notables drink from glass bowls containing a dash of red wine and a live fish, and as evening falls the *Tonnekensbrand* (bonfire) is lit.

GETTING THERE AND AWAY

By car From Brussels follow the E40 west towards Ghent, taking exit 19 (Aalst). Then follow the N45 towards Geraardsbergen (50km; 58mins). From Ghent follow the E40 to Brussels, taking exit 17 (direction: Wetteren), then follow the N42 to Zottegem and Geraardsbergen (41km; 45mins). Free car parks are located on the edge of town, or there's paid parking in the centre; follow the P-route signs.

By train Aalst (hourly; 36mins); Ghent (hourly; 50mins); Brussels (hourly; 48mins).

TOURIST INFORMATION

Tourist information Markt; 054 43 72 89; w visitgeraardsbergen.be; 10.00–17.00. Bright, modern office with video, sound & even scent exhibits. Since 2016 the Manneken Pis has also finally got his own museum here (same hours as tourist information; free); you'll find the real statue – the one on Markt is a replica – & a huge array of his fabulous costumes.

WHERE TO STAY AND EAT

Grupello (11 rooms) 17 Verhaegenlaan; 054 41 60 07; w grupello-vijverhof.be. Landmark Art Nouveau building that was previously a luxury clothes shop, now an intimate hotel with modern en-suite rooms. Superb b/fast (especially cheese) served next to exquisite stained-glass windows. Swish brasserie (€€€) also on site with affordable half-board packages for cyclists. If you're going for the Tour of Flanders you'll need to book up to a year in advance. €€€

Bar Gidon 11 Markt; m 0477 59 16 02; 09.30–20.00 Mon, 10.00–21.00 Thu & Sun, 10.00–22.00 Fri & Sat. Much-loved local cycling café owned by ex-pro Frederic Penne & his girlfriend Els, the granddaughter of biking legend Albert Ritserveldt. Nostalgic vibe with bikes & jerseys on the wall. Also serves as the official fan club of double world champion Remco Evenpoel, who often pops in. €

WHAT TO SEE AND DO

Markt Perched on the slopes of Oudenberg hill, Geraardsbergen's old market square is a regal place. The **town hall** that sits on its northern flank has undergone several renovations. The current neo-Gothic façade dates from 1891. At its foot is the **Manneken Pis** fountain. Most people are familiar with Brussels's statue of the peeing boy (see box, page 101) but, in fact, Geraardsbergen's version dates from 1459, making it 160 years older. Like its counterpart in the capital, the statue has a wardrobe to rival any supermodel: more than 300 outfits gifted by various visiting dignitaries, some of which are on show at the tourist office.

To the left of the town hall are a copy of the **Marbol**, a Gothic-style fountain where the townsfolk used to draw their water, and the former **Lakenhalle (Cloth Hall)**, which now houses the tourist information centre.

To the east is the late-Gothic **Sint-Bartholomewskerk (St Bartholomew's Church)** (Markt; ⌚ Apr–Oct 08.30–18.00; Nov–Mar 08.30–16.00; free), which sprang up in 1476 but, again, has undergone several renovations. Inside, the Chapel of Our Lady holds a particularly beautiful triptych composed of rich reds, golds and greens. The chapel on the right behind the altar houses the relic of St Bartholomew in a silver chest whose lid is adorned with his bust and flanked by angels. It was moved here in 1515 from the Carthusian Monastery in Sint-Martens-Lierde, a relocation commemorated every year on 24 August (or the following Sunday) in the **Processie van Plaisance**, when the chest is paraded through town amid giants. Also worth a quick gander is the cute **Brandstraat** tunnel located on the south side of the square and, a short walk along Boerenhol and through the archway, the **Dierkosttoren**, the only tower remaining from the 12th-century city walls.

Oudenberg and De Muur Climbing the Oudenberg hill, which sits 110m above sea level, offers great views of the town and surrounding countryside. Leave the Markt via Hooiweg, keeping the church on your right. Soon you'll pass **Grupellopark**, which contains a statue of an elephant to commemorate those that lost their lives in the Belgian Congo (page 10) and, further up, a golden statue of an angel called **Heilig-Hartbeeld (Holy Heart)**. The park is named after local sculptor Gabriel Grupello, who was born on Pentitentenstraat in 1644.

Exiting the park, cross Pachtersstraat and make your way along the steep cobbled path known as **De Muur (The Wall)**, a mythic name in the cycling world. It long formed the penultimate, often decisive, climb of the **Tour of Flanders** cycle race; after being removed from the circuit when the finishing line relocated to Oudenaarde, it's now back, albeit some 95km from the end. Nonetheless, its killer cobbles ensure that every year, on the first Sunday of April, thousands come from all around to watch cyclists pit their wits and calf muscles against the punishing slope. On the crest of the hill sits the domed **Oudenbergkapel (Oudenberg Chapel)**. It was once a popular 17th-century pilgrimage site, but the current version only dates from 1905. Peek inside to see the 'thank you' plaques.

Geraardsbergse Musea (26 Collegestraat; ☎ 054 43 72 89; ⌚ 14.00–17.00 Tue–Sun; Oct–Mar 14.00–17.00 Sat–Sun; free) The town's foremost museum offers an overview of Geraardsbergen's industrial past, featuring rooms crammed with

MATTENTAART

Geraardsbergen is famous for its marzipan-flavoured *mattentaart*. They were first made during the Middle Ages as a way of putting soured milk to good use: the curds were mixed with eggs, sugar and almonds and covered in puff pastry. They are so beloved that they have their own dedicated song, feature in the *Guinness World Records* book and in 1985 became the first food to appear on a special-issue national stamp. Only bakers from Geraardsbergen and Lierde are allowed to sell *Geraardsbergse Mattentaart* and they must use local milk. Every year on the third Sunday in April, the town celebrates the curdled cake with festivities on the Markt. The tourist office has a *mattentaartkart* with recipes and a map of 24 local suppliers.

paraphernalia based on themes of tobacco, beer and lace. It's not exactly show-stopping stuff, but the room devoted to matchsticks (the first on the right) is worth a look. In 1850 a matchstick factory was established on Gaverstraat in the nearby village of Overboelare, which – at the height of its power – was the largest of its kind in the world, employing over 2,000 people. It closed in 1999.

Hunnegem and Oud-Hospitaal Along Gasthuisstraat you'll find the oldest hospital in Flanders. The appropriately named **Oud-Hospitaal** (**Old Hospital**) was built in 1238, but most sections now date from the 16th and 17th centuries. Also on site is a Rococo chapel and next to it the original spire of the Marbol fountain – a copy of which stands on the Markt. Later on it served as an orphanage, and today houses an arts academy. At the end of the street is the **Hunnegem** parish (⌚ visits by appointment only; enquire at tourist office). It was established in the 8th century, long before the town of Geraardsbergen grew around it. In the 17th century a group of Benedictine nuns built a convent next to the original Romanesque church.

Cycling If you want to have a go at tackling De Muur yourself, you can rent a bike from Danny Sport (456 Edingseweg; ☎ 054 58 97 52; **w** dannysport.be) and follow the 114km Ronde van Vlaanderen Route (€4) or the less draining, 46km Eddy Merckx bike route (€2), which gives you a taster of four famous slopes from the cycling classic plus information about cycling god Merckx.

RONSE

Ronse – or Renaix in French – is known as a 'facility town' because it lies mere metres from the Flanders/Wallonia border. Consequently, the locals switch easily back and forth between the two languages. However, it's a rather technical term for a rather quaint town, which boasts two century-old pubs and a remarkable 1,000 year-old crypt, which has to be one of Flanders' most overlooked treasures. During the 1920s and 1930s, Ronse was a textile hub, home to over 24,000 residents and a staggering 500 factories, one of which is now a museum. The trade brought great riches to the textile barons, who built themselves Art Nouveau and Art Deco mansions. One manufacturer, Valère Carpentier, even went so far as to employ master Art Nouveau architect Victor Horta to design his summerhouse, Villa Carpentier (9–11 Doorniksesteenweg). The town also kicks off the Flemish events calendar with *Bommelsfeesten* (**w** bommelsfeesten.be) on the second weekend after New Year. The next carnivals are: 11–13 January 2020; 9–11 January 2021; 8–10 January 2022.

GETTING THERE AND AWAY

By car From Aalst follow the N45, N8 and N48 to Ronse (45km; ⌚ 50mins). From Ghent follow the N60 south past Oudenaarde to Ronse (42km; ⌚ 45mins).

By train Oudenaarde (hourly; ⌚ 11mins); Ghent (hourly; ⌚ 50mins); Brussels (via Oudenaarde hourly Mon–Fri, ⌚ 1hr 13mins; via Ghent Sat–Sun, ⌚ 1hr 56mins).

TOURIST INFORMATION

Tourist information 2 De Biesestraat; ☎ 055 23 28 18; **w** visitronse.be; ⌚ Mar–Sep 10.00–17.00 Mon–Fri, 14.00–17.00 Sat–Sun; Dec–Feb 10.00–16.00 Mon–Fri. Housed in a lovely 15th-century compound known as 'De Hoge Mote', this information centre reopened in Sep 2018 after a major renovation & offers interactive panels, VR exhibits & films highlighting Sint-Hermes

& Ronse's development. Their €15 *smaak kaart* (taste card) takes in a protected café, a church & a regional eatery, & is available Wed–Sat.

Bike rental De Passage; 5 Sint-Martensstraat; 055 31 75 17; w depassageronse.be; 10.00–18.00 Wed–Sun. Has 5 electric bikes for rent (day/½ day €20/15) & sells cycling maps. It's part of new urban renewal project De Passage (see below) so ideal for picking up a picnic before you set out.

WHERE TO EAT AND DRINK

The town has its own microbrewery, Keun, and four local beers, parlayed through a gift box at the tourist office (€15): the high-malt Hoge Mote (6.1%), light brown Ronsischen Bommel (8.5%), dark Ronsischen Dubbel (7.4%) and amber Ronsischen Tripel (8%). Savour them with some Hoge Mote Bierkaas, a cheese submerged in the namesake beer for five days. You'll find them all at Brasserie Harmonie (see below). Since 2015 the Old St Martin's church, which was replaced by the New St Martin's church in the late 19th century, and later served as a sawmill, cinema and garage, has turned into foodie hub **De Passage** featuring **Passagio**.

Passagio 37 Sint-Martensstraat; m 0475 81 95 51; w ilpassaggio.be; 08.00–18.30 Mon–Fri, 07.30–18.00 Sat–Sun. La Bella Italia in Ronse's De Passage food court; twice a month the owners head to Italian farms to source produce – charcuterie, cheese, fresh pasta – which you can buy to take away or enjoy on site: choose what you want at the counter, get it weighed & then cart it off to the church nave, or profit from the terrace in summer. €€

Brasserie Harmonie 10 Grote Markt; 055 21 11 74; w brasserie-harmonie.be; 10.00–late. A classic pub on the main square, built around the turn of the 20th century & modelled on bars the rich textile barons had seen in Paris. German soldiers spent a lot of their downtime here during WWII.

Local Unique 25 Grote Markt; 055 21 38 00; 10.00–midnight. The walls of this spacious, century-old bar are filled with tiled mosaics & it's also the meeting place for participants in a wonderful, rarely seen, local sport: dove racing. Every w/end between Apr & Sep old men gather here with their best birds, waiting for the truck to take them to the starting line. Serves Ronse beers & *mattentaart*.

WHAT TO SEE AND DO

Sint-Hermescrypte (St Hermes's Crypt)

* (Sint-Hermesstraat; Mar–Sep 14.00–17.00 Tue–Sun; Oct–Nov 14.00–17.00 Sat–Sun, & also open 27–29 Dec & 3–5 January 13.00–16.00; adult/under 12 €5/free, combi-ticket with Must (page 206) €8) St Hermes is a rare Catholic saint: only five churches in Europe are dedicated to him. He was a Roman who converted to Christianity, and the decision landed him a lengthy jail sentence before he was beheaded. He became a martyr and the saint of mental illnesses thanks to his association with the head – or loss of it in his case. His relics came to Ronse in the 9th century. A church and crypt were built around the chest and throughout the Middle Ages pilgrims came from far and wide to be cured of depression, schizophrenia and epilepsy. The constant influx of travellers brought the town great wealth and status. This Romanesque church collapsed in 1267 – some of the remains still lie outside to the left of the crypt entrance – but parts of the 1089 crypt survive to this today; look for the jumbled bricks on the ceiling near the entrance. The **crypt** – which technically isn't a crypt because it sits above street level – was repaired and a new church built on top. It was given a new wing in 1517 that was constructed in the late-Gothic style, marked by the use of red brick.

To be eligible to enter, pilgrims had to complete two tasks. The first was a physical offering: they had to walk at least 25km on foot to reach the church, which stupidly meant Ronse locals couldn't enter. To solve the problem, they started the *Fiertelommegang*, a 32km procession around town that's still celebrated on Trinity Sunday when St Hermes's relic chest is paraded. Second, they had to make an offering of their own weight in goods or food. The system was actually fairly democratic since only the rich could afford to eat a lot and therefore weighed the most. Pilgrims were then allowed to enter the crypt and walk around the **relic chest**, touching it gently to absorb its healing powers (the wooden version on display today is a copy; the original was destroyed in the 16th-century religious wars). The sick would then take baths in water from the well in the centre of the crypt, symbolically washing away their sins, and also cleaning off actual dirt.

There are a number of interesting features to look out for. The walls are studded with slivers of terracotta, which are old Roman roof tiles, and at the back of the crypt is a support stone recovered from the church that collapsed. It stands on a pillar on the right-hand side. Look closely and you'll see it has a clear engraving of a vagina on it – a common fertility symbol.

Today, many people are dubious about the contents of relics like those of St Hermes, but some years ago the church had the whole box placed in a hospital scanner. Amazingly, the scan revealed the relic wasn't empty and did indeed contain human bones – not those of St Hermes, but of a man, woman and child. Who they are remains a mystery.

As you walk around you'll find basic information panels in English. A more detailed audio guide is also included with your ticket, but I'd advise hiring a real-life guide (€30/hr) via the tourist office, especially off-season, when it's the only way to get in.

Museum voor textiel – Must (Museum of Textiles) (St Hermess Crypt; ☎055 23 28 16; 🕘 via tour only Mar–Sep 15.30 Tue–Sun; Oct–Nov 15.30 Sat–Sun, 27–29 Dec & 3–5 Jan 14.30; adult/under 12 €5/free, combi-ticket with St Hermes's Crypt €8) Across the courtyard from the tourist information office, this former textile mill has over 40 looms of varying ages, all in working order. The curator will give you a demonstration so you can grasp the deafening level of noise the workers had to endure when there were hundreds of the machines all working at once. Notice the original triangular Rackham roof; the windows deliberately point north to allow the maximum amount of neutral light for the workers. To visit, you'll need to take an hour-long guided tour, or else hire a private guide via the tourist office (€45/1½hrs).

OUDENAARDE

Oudenaarde sits on the river Scheldt in the heart of the Flemish Ardennes, an area of rolling green hills studded with hamlets and woodland. Its riverside location allowed it to join the linen trade and the town flourished from the 11th century onwards. When the linen trade dipped, residents transferred their skills to tapestry-weaving and later silverwork, which lasted for over 300 years until the 18th century. The tapestries were highly admired and sold the world over, and it was during this period of prosperity that Oudenaarde's flamboyant-Gothic Stadhuis – which rivals those of Leuven and Brussels – was built.

The town was equally famous for its brewing industry, which remains a major asset. Local breweries converge on the Markt on the last weekend of June to celebrate Adriaen Brouwer Bierfeesten, a beer festival named after a local 17th-century artist famous for his paintings depicting peasant life.

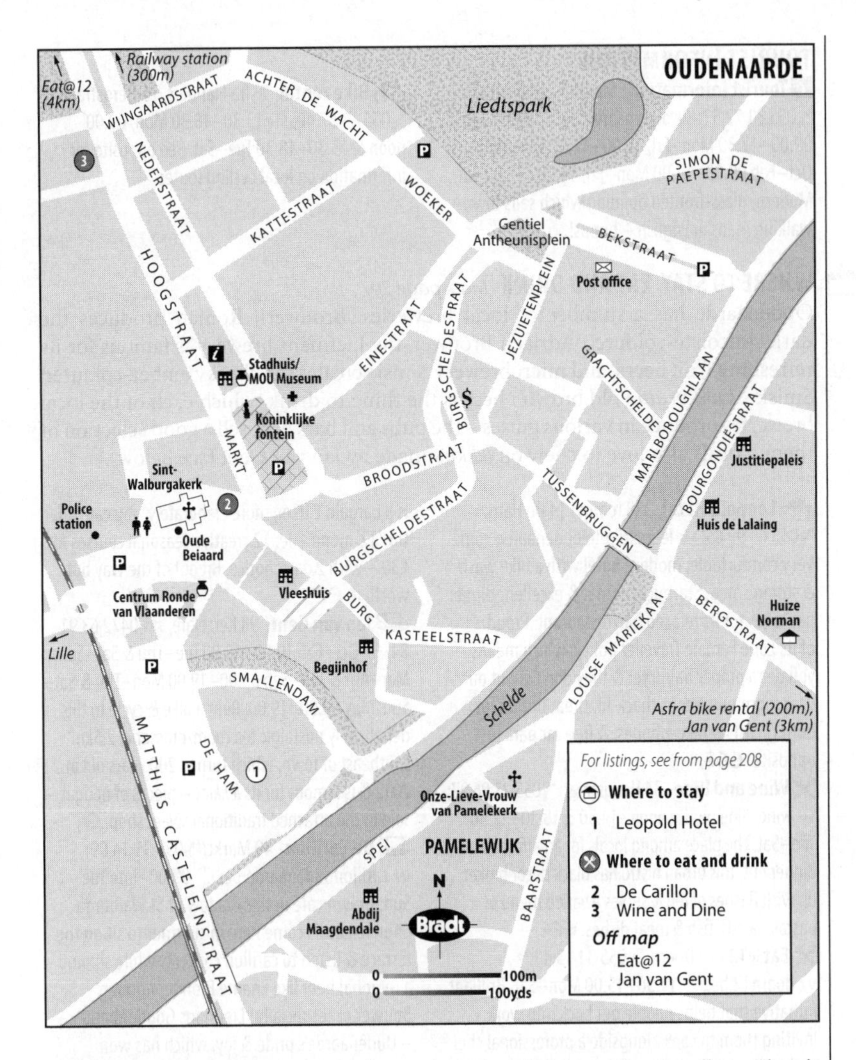

Despite this glorious history, Oudenaarde isn't well known by travellers. There's one popular time to go, however: during the Tour of Flanders, which nowadays terminates locally – something of a coup for the city. Be sure to book your accommodation well in advance if you plan to attend the April race.

GETTING THERE AND AWAY

By car From Brussels the fastest route is to take the E40 to Ghent, take the Zwijnaarde exit and merge on to the E17 (direction: Kortrijk). Soon after, take exit 8 (direction: De Pinte) and follow the N60 south to Oudenaarde (73km; ⌚ 1hr). From Aalst take the N9 west, then follow signs for the E40, continuing as above (50km; ⌚ 42mins).

By train Brussels (twice an hour Mon–Fri, ⌚ 55mins; hourly Sat–Sun, ⌚ 1hr 5mins); Ghent (twice an hour Mon–Fri, hourly Sat–Sun; ⌚ 30mins); Kortrijk (twice an hour Mon–Fri, hourly Sat–Sun; ⌚ 20mins).

TOURIST INFORMATION

Tourist information Stadhuis, Hoogstraat; 055 31 72 51; w oudenaarde.be; Mar–Sep 09.00–17.30 Mon–Fri, 10.00–17.30 Sat–Sun; Oct–Feb 09.00–17.00 Mon–Fri, 14.00–17.00 Sat. Modern, glass-fronted building which sells town walking maps in English – bonus!

Bike rental Asfra Flanders, 75 Bergstraat; 055 31 57 40; 13.30–18.30 Mon, 09.00–noon & 13.30–18.30 Tue–Sat. See opposite for information on local cycling routes.

WHERE TO STAY, EAT AND DRINK *Map, page 207*

Oudenaarde has a number of local breweries. Brouwerij Roman produces the dark chocolate-coloured Adriaen Brouwer, the Liefmans brewery is famous for its refreshing fruit beers, and microbrewery Smisje creates the cheeky amber-coloured Smiske. *Oud bruin* ('old brown') beer is the thing to drink, which each of the local breweries produce in various guises – the pubs and bars here sell a good selection of them. Locals also love to chew on *lekkies* made by Jan van Gent (see below).

Leopold Hotel (58 rooms) 14 De Ham; 055 69 99 65; w leopoldhoteloudenaarde.com. Very comfortable, modern hotel with a bike wash & storage area, Starbucks corner & excellent dinner packages for its relaxed bar/restaurant. Proud of its Lone Female Traveller policy, which means you get a proper hairdryer & they don't shout out your room number at check-in. Great option for both cyclists & bike-phobes, & free car park just opposite. €€€

Wine and Dine 34 Hoogstraat; 055 23 96 97; w wine-dine.be; noon–14.30 & 18.30–22.30 Tue–Sat. The place among locals for an affordable dinner out, this urban bistro has black décor broken up with flashes of red & serves a varied menu of pastas, salads, fish & meat dishes. €€€

Eat@12 12 Doorn; 055 31 13 45; w doorn12.be; 11.30–15.00 Mon–Sat. Brilliant initiative that helps people get back into work, inviting them to cook alongside a professional chef in this trendy venue. The set lunch (soup & a main) is a bargain €16 or, more elaborately, you can order the '12' menu – ie: 12 creative seasonal courses for €30 – with 2 days' notice. Bit out of the way but worth it. €€

Jan van Gent 98 Kerzelare; m 0472 63 91 84; Oct–Feb 10.00–18.00 Tue–Thu & Sat–Sun; Mar–Apr & Jun–Sep 09.00–19.00 Mon–Thu & Sat–Sun; May 09.00–19.00. Rent a bike & cycle to this delightfully nostalgic tea room/brasserie, 2.5km southeast of town, which turned 200 years old in 2012 & is famous for its *lekkies* – pieces of nougat – sold in the attached traditional sweet shop. €

De Carillon 49 Markt; 055 31 14 09; w carillonoudenaarde.be; 09.00–late Tue–Sun. Brown café in the shadow of St Walburga Church. Locals come here in summer to sit on the terrace & listen to carillon concerts while sipping a regional beer like Ename Blonde, Adriaen Bouwer or (especially) Liefmans Goudenband – Oudenaarde's pride & joy, which has won international medals. €

WHAT TO SEE AND DO

MOU Museum (Stadhuis, Markt; w mou-oudenaarde.be; Mar–Sep 09.30–17.30 Tue–Fri, 10.00–17.30 Sat–Sun; Oct–Feb 09.30–17.00 Tue–Fri, 14.00–17.00 Sat–Sun; adult/12–18/under 12 €6/1.50/free, inc audio guide) Standing tall and proud at the northern end of the Markt, Oudenaarde's ornate UNESCO-listed town hall cannot fail to impress. As of January 2019, it has housed the new MOU Museum, recalling the history of Oudenaarde and the Flemish Ardennes from the Middle Ages to today via interactive exhibits. The world-famous local tapestries – notably *verdures*, or vegetable carpets with pretty landscapes – and one of Flanders' largest silver collections, which is spread across three halls, are highlights.

Sint-Walburgakerk (St Walburga Church) (Sint-Walburgastraat; Apr–May & Oct 14.30–17.00 Tue & Sat, 10.00–11.00 & 14.30–17.00 Thu; Jun–Sep 14.30–

17.00 Tue–Wed & Fri–Sat, 10.00–noon & 14.30–17.00 Thu, 14.00–17.30 Sun; free) Perched on the southwestern edge of the Markt, this church topped with a carillon is in fact two churches joined at the transept: the choir, in dark-grey limestone, dates from the 13th century and the rest from the 15th century. The church lost most of its treasures during the religious wars but has a reasonable collection of statues and tapestries. There are carillon concerts on Sundays from noon to 13.00, and on Thursdays from 20.30 to 21.30 in July and August.

Centrum Ronde van Vlaanderen (Tour of Flanders Centre) (43 Markt; 055 33 99 33; w crvv.be; 10.00–18.00; adult/student/under 6 €12/6/free) Across the road from the church, this museum is dedicated to the illustrious Tour of Flanders and a must-see for cycling enthusiasts. Lots of newspaper clippings, footage and films, though not a huge amount in English. Relive the races by discussing them with the locals over a beer at the very pleasant on-site Peloton Café (€€–€€€). Three Tour of Flanders loops start from the door; they have a 'Ride Like a Pro' service where you can rent top-flight gear to really get in the spirit, *and* – excitingly – it's also possible to hire Tour of Flanders legend Johan Museeuw to take you around (if you have €275 to spare). Tip – Leopold Hotel guests get a €2.50 discount voucher on the entry price.

Begijnhof (Achterburg; summer 06.00–21.00, winter 06.00–19.00; free) Oudenaarde's béguines originally lived behind St Walburga Church and moved to this quaint enclave in 1449. A statue of St Rochus – the patron saint of plague victims – guards the entrance. The uniform rows of whitewashed buildings largely date from the 18th and 19th centuries. Wander round to the back to find the béguinage's minuscule, moody neo-Gothic chapel.

Beer With Oudenaarde serving as the beer capital of East Flanders, it's a brilliant place to go on a beer pilgrimage – perhaps combined with its other claim to fame, cycling (in moderation, obviously). The East Flanders tourist office recently published a 'Plan Beer Flemish Ardennes' brochure featuring four cycling routes and three walks via breweries and cafés in Oudenaarde and beyond (pick up a free printed version at the tourist office). If you have less time, the key breweries to visit are **Liefmans** (200 Aalstraat; 03 860 94 00; w liefmans.be; 2hr tours 10.00, 14.00 & 17.00 Mon–Sat; €12), which allows individual visitors to join pre-existing group tours, and **Brouwerij Roman** (105 Hauwaart; 055 45 54 01; w roman.be), which is Belgium's oldest family brewery, in action since 1545. Group tours run year-round in various languages, and you can sign up for a weekend slot (€8 pp inc a tasting and gift set) on the website.

Cycling Bang in the middle of the Flemish Ardennes and currently the terminus of the Tour of Flanders, Oudenaarde is one of the best towns in which to base yourself while tackling Flanders' most epic cycle rides. Have a go at the *Ronde van Vlaanderen* cycling route (€4) – available in three versions on one map – do a beer route (see above) or, for something easier, ie: flatter, try the two Scheldt River Valley routes (€2). You can download them all for free on the East Flanders tourist board's website (w tov.be/webshop), or pick up paper versions at the tourist office.

UPDATES WEBSITE

You can post your comments and recommendations, and read feedback and updates from other readers online at **w** bradtupdates.com/northernbelgium.

6

West Flanders

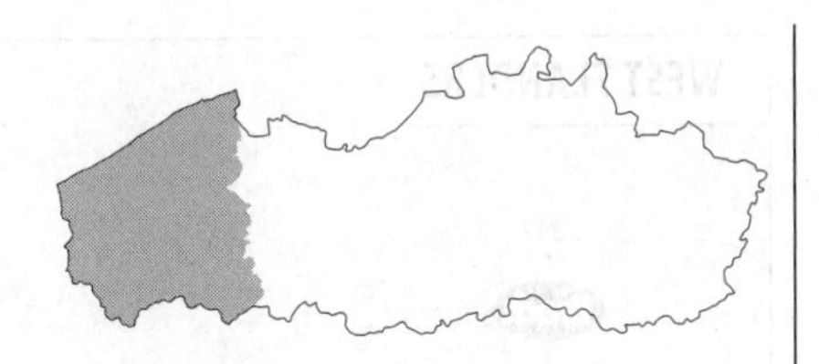

This coastal region is home to Flanders' most evocative place names: Bruges (Brugge), Ypres (Ieper), Passchendaele and Poperinge. The last three are famous for their involvement in World War I, which played out on the polders between coastal Nieuwpoort and Menen on the French border. Between 1914 and 1918, the fluctuating Western Front reduced many towns to rubble and left lasting scars on the landscape. It was a hellish period – the legacy of which has been carefully preserved by the War Graves Commission and Flemish Government, not least during the 2014–18 World War I centenary commemorations, which were marked by the launch of new visitor centres, large-scale installations and other tourist innovations.

Beyond these cities stretch flat green fields drained in the 10th century by the dykes still seen either side of the raised roads. These pathways join up to form some of the prettiest and most interesting cycling routes in the country, wending past working windmills, sleepy hamlets and picture-perfect villages like Damme and Lissewege.

Explore the romantic canals of Bruges, watch the North Sea fly by as you brave sandsailing at De Panne, step into the shoes of World War I soldiers at Poperinge's incomparable Talbot House, or taste the world's best beer at Sint-Sixtus Abbey. From sandy beaches to gritty war exhibits, this is perhaps Flanders' most rewarding region.

BRUGES

The capital of West Flanders, Bruges has long been a port of call for travellers, having risen to power owing to its direct link to the North Sea. When that connection was severed the city's fortunes foundered – only to revive in the 20th century when it cemented its reputation as a tourist hub. A spiderweb spun from spindly streets and framed by tranquil canals, Bruges's status as Europe's best-preserved medieval city attracts throngs of visitors in summer, but somehow that doesn't diminish its charms. From searing Flemish Primitivism – best displayed at the Groeningemuseum – to starred restaurants and moody churches like the Basiliek van het Heilig-Bloed, reputed to contain drops of Christ's blood, there's enough going on to fill a few days, but the best part is just strolling about and taking in the uncanny fairytale atmosphere.

HISTORY It's hard to overstate Bruges's importance. The city crops up in records as early as the 9th century, when Baldwin the Iron Arm, first Count of Flanders, built the first fort (*burg*) here and erected city walls to guard against Viking attacks. At that time the town was connected to the sea by a series of streams. These natural channels silted up in the 11th century, but fortunately a storm in 1134 caused the coastal plain to flood and form a new canal – the Zwin – that stretched to the current-day town of Damme.

By the 13th century these trade routes had expanded to cover the Mediterranean, and there was widespread demand for wool brought from England and woven into fine cloth. However, the influx of economic wealth encouraged the French king,

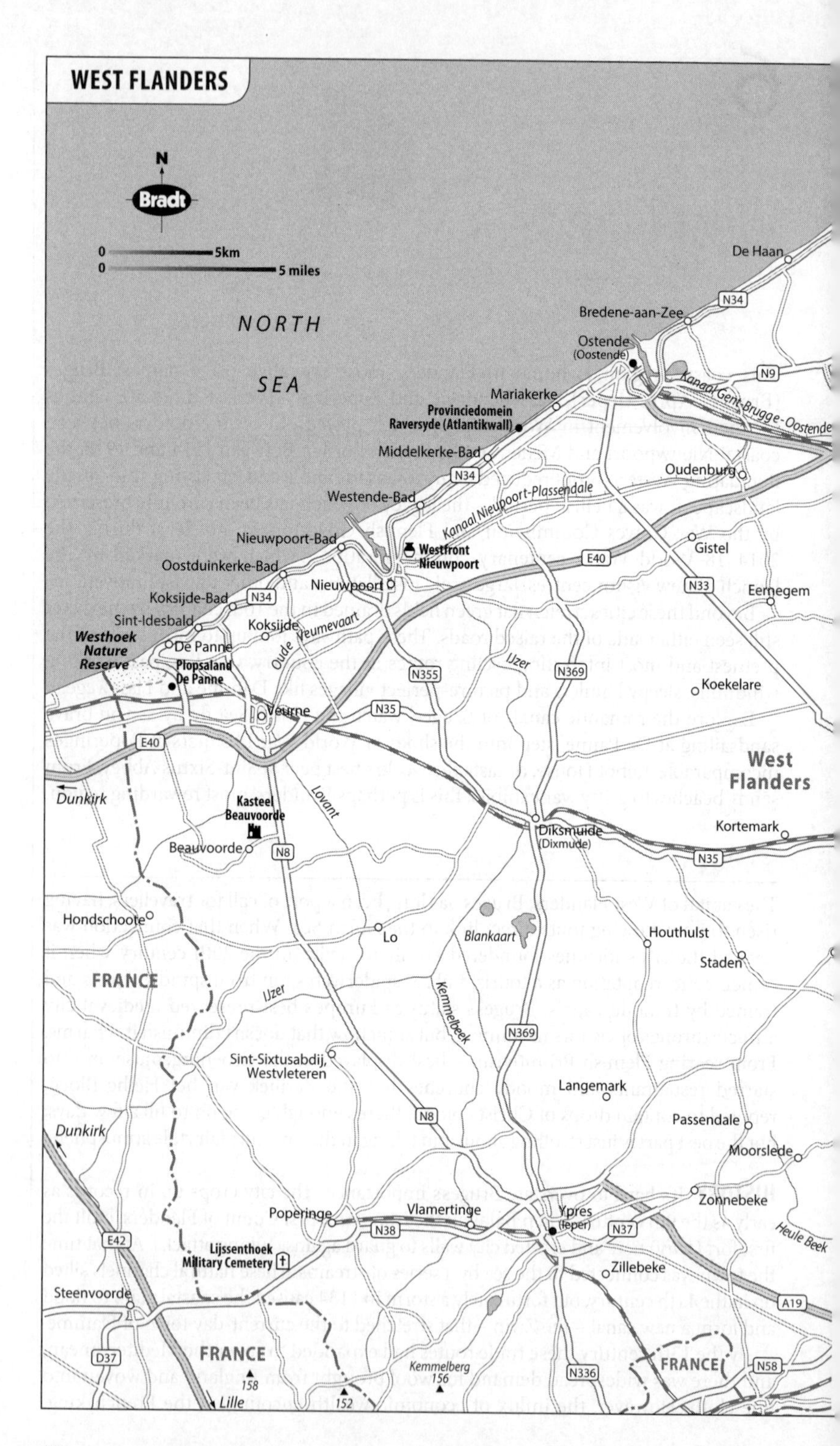
WEST FLANDERS
N
Bradt
0 5km
0 5 miles
NORTH
SEA
De Haan
N34
Bredene-aan-Zee
Ostende
(Oostende)
N9
Kanaal Gent-Brugge-Oostende
Mariakerke
Provinciedomein
Raversyde (Atlantikwall)
Middelkerke-Bad
Oudenburg
N34
Kanaal Nieupoort-Plassendale
Westende-Bad
Nieuwpoort-Bad
Westfront
Nieuwpoort
Gistel
E40
Oostduinkerke-Bad
Nieuwpoort
N33
Eernegem
Koksijde-Bad
N34
Sint-Idesbald
Koksijde
Oude Veurnevaart
Westhoek
Nature
Reserve
De Panne
Plopsaland
De Panne
IJzer
N355
N369
Koekelare
N35
Veurne
E40
West
Flanders
Dunkirk
Lovant
Kasteel
Beauvoorde
Diksmuide
(Dixmude)
Kortemark
Beauvoorde
N8
N35
Hondschoote
Lo
Blankaart
Houthulst
Staden
FRANCE
IJzer
Kemmelbeek
N369
Sint-Sixtusabdij,
Westvleteren
Langemark
N8
Passendale
Dunkirk
Moorslede
Zonnebeke
Poperinge
Vlamertinge
Ypres
(Ieper)
N38
N37
Heule Beek
E42
Lijssenthoek
Military Cemetery
Zillebeke
Steenvoorde
A19
D37
FRANCE
Kemmelberg
156
FRANCE
N58
N336
158
152
Lille

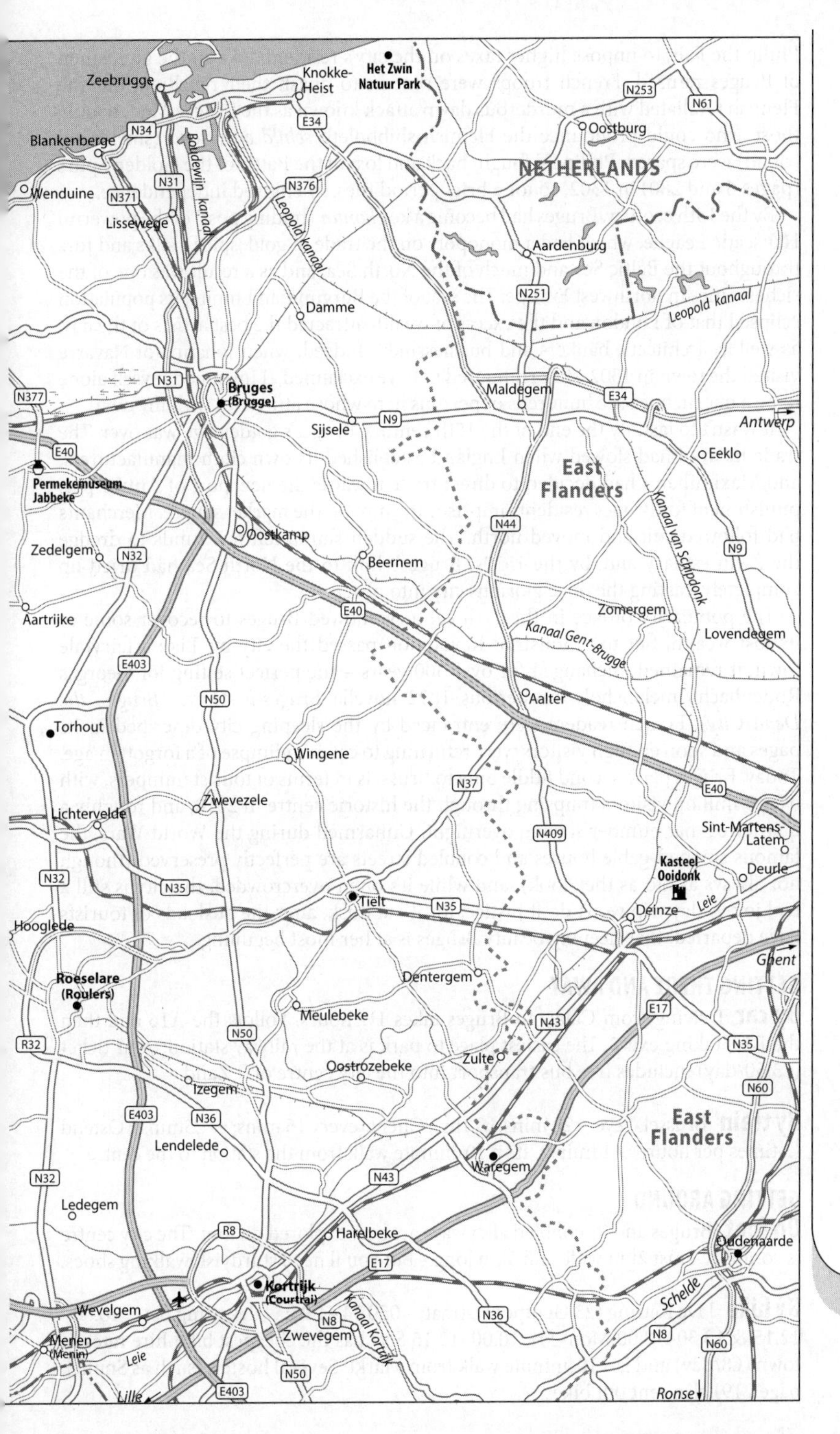
Zeebrugge
Knokke-Heist
Het Zwin Natuur Park
Blankenberge
Boudewijn kanaal
Oostburg
NETHERLANDS
Wenduine
Lissewege
Leopold kanaal
Aardenburg
Damme
Leopold kanaal
Bruges (Brugge)
Maldegem
Sijsele
Antwerp
Eeklo
Permekemuseum Jabbeke
East Flanders
Kanaal van Schipdonk
Oostkamp
Zedelgem
Beernem
Zomergem
Aartrijke
Kanaal Gent-Brugge
Lovendegem
Aalter
Torhout
Wingene
Zwevezele
Lichtervelde
Sint-Martens-Latem
Kasteel Ooidonk
Deurle
Tielt
Deinze
Leie
Hooglede
Ghent
Dentergem
Roeselare (Roulers)
Meulebeke
Zulte
Oostrozebeke
Izegem
East Flanders
Lendelede
Waregem
Ledegem
Harelbeke
Oudenaarde
Kortrijk (Courtrai)
Wevelgem
Scheldle
Kanaal Kortrijk
Zwevegem
Menen (Menin)
Leie
Lille
Ronse
N253
N61
E34
N34
N31
N376
N371
N251
N377
N9
E40
N44
N32
N9
E403
N50
N37
N409
N35
N32
N43
E17
N50
R32
N35
N60
N36
N43
R8
E17
N8
N36
N8
N60
N50
E403

Philip the Fair, to impose higher taxes on the city's residents. When the guildsmen of Bruges refused, French troops were sent in to quash their rebellion, but the Flemish retaliated with a murderous dawn attack known as the Brugse Metten; only those who could pronounce the Flemish shibboleth *schild en vriend* (shield and friend) were spared. Philip IV fought back and lost in the Battle of the Golden Spurs (pages 6 and 280) in 1302, so for a brief period the city enjoyed independence.

By the 14th century, Bruges had become a key *kontor* (trading post) of the powerful Hanseatic League, which had a monopoly on the trade of gold, spices, silks and furs throughout the Baltic Sea and much of the North Sea, and as a result was one of the richest cities in northwest Europe. The seat of the Burgundian Empire, its population eclipsed that of London and the excess of wealth attracted the best artists of the day, as well as architects, bankers and businessmen. Indeed, when Johanna of Navarre visited the town in 1302, she's rumoured to have exclaimed, 'I imagined myself alone to be a queen, but I see hundreds of persons here whose attire vies with my own.'

It wasn't to last. By the end of the 15th century Bruges's golden age was over. The trade in wool had slowed when England established its own cloth manufacturers, and Maximilian I had decided to direct trade towards the new port of Antwerp as punishment for Bruges residents imprisoning him on the market square. Merchants had followed suit and moved north. The sudden slump left few funds to dredge the Zwin estuary and, by the 1530s, Bruges's link to the North Sea had dried up completely, casting the once glorious city into obscurity.

The popularity of lace in the 17th century allowed Bruges to recover some of its lost wealth, but the Industrial Revolution passed the city by. Like a fairytale town, it remained unchanged for over 300 years – the perfect setting for Georges Rodenbach's melancholy, mysterious 1892 novella *Bruges-la-Morte* (*Bruges, the Dead City*). French readers were entranced by the sleeping city described in its pages and soon enough visitors were returning to catch a glimpse of a forgotten age. Today, Bruges plays second fiddle only to Brussels in terms of tourist numbers, with over 8 million visitors traipsing through the historic centre in 2018, and roughly a quarter of that number staying overnight. Unharmed during the World Wars, the famous stepped-gable houses and cobbled streets are perfectly preserved (though not always as old as they look), and while it's often overcrowded, the city is still a real joy. A day trip won't do it justice, for it's at dusk, after the busloads of tourists have departed, that sleeping beauty Bruges is at her most beguiling.

GETTING THERE AND AWAY

By car Driving from Calais to Bruges takes 1½ hours. Follow the A16 and then the E40, taking exit 7. The easiest place to park is at the railway station; your ticket (€3.50/day) includes free bus transport into the city centre or 't Zand.

By train Brussels (every 20 mins; ⌚ 1hr); Ghent (every 15 mins; ⌚ 25mins); Ostend (3 times per hour; ⌚ 14mins). It's a 10-minute walk from the station to the centre.

GETTING AROUND

On foot Bruges and its cobbled alleyways are best explored on foot. The city centre is compact – just 2km wide and 3km long – but you'll need sturdyish walking shoes.

By bike l De Ketting (23 Gentpoortstraat; 050 34 41 96; w deketting.be; ⌚ 10.00–12.15 & 13.30–18.00 Mon–Fri, 10.00–12.15 Sat) has the cheapest bike-hire rates in town (€8/day) and is a 10-minute walk from Markt. Several hostels (such as Snuffel, page 219) also rent out bikes.

By boat Half-hour boat tours depart from five points along the canal – see map on page 212 for locations – and run between March and November, as well as on clement off-season days (🕘 10.00–18.00; adult/4–11/under 4 €10/6/free).

By bus The bus station is situated outside the railway station. Buses 4, 13 and 14 stop by 't Zand tourist office and by Markt square. Tickets (one-way €3/valid for 1hr) can be bought from the De Lijn office by the station, or at vending machines.

By horse-drawn carriage Bruges is famous for its romantic horse-drawn carriage tours. You can hail one on the Markt (or Burg on Wednesday mornings) and the driver will clop around town for half an hour, with a 5-minute stop at the béguinage, giving a running commentary on what you're seeing, before returning to the starting point. A carriage holds up to five people and costs €50 per tour, paid to the driver.

TOURIST INFORMATION

Historium [217 D5] Markt; 050 44 46 46; w visitbruges.be; 🕘 10.00–17.00

Main office [217 B6] In&Uit, Concertgebouw (Concert Hall) on 't Zand; 050 44 46 46; w visitbruges.be; 🕘 10.00–17.00 Mon–Sat, 10.00–14.00 Sun. Here you can book myriad tickets for events & tours.

Railway station [217 B8] in the corridor to the platforms; 050 44 46 46; w visitbruges.be; 🕘 10.00–17.00

GUIDED TOURS

City bus tour [217 D5] Markt; 050 35 50 24; w citytour.be. Minibuses depart every half hour from 10.00 for a 50min highlights tour; 🕘 Jan & Nov–Dec they run until 16.00, 1–9 Feb until 16.30, 10–28 Feb until 17.00, 1–15 Mar & 16–31 Oct until 17.30, 16 Mar–30 Apr & 1–15 Oct until 18.00 , May–Sep until 19.00; adult/ 6–11/under 6 €20/15/free, inc audio commentary.

Koninklijke Gidsenbond [221 E3] 3 Kleine Hertsbergestraat; 050 33 22 33; w bruges-guides.com. The veteran Royal Guides' Association runs a series of themed private walking tours – think women's walks or maritime Bruges – & also covers Damme (page 232). They charge €80–90/2hrs.

Legends of Bruges Free Walking Tour Runs daytime tours (🕘 11.30 & 14.00, but also 09:45 Apr–Dec & 10.30 Dec), night tours (🕘 20.00) & foodie tours (🕘 11.00 Tue–Sun, but w/end only Jan–Mar) led by fun guides in historical costume; you pay what you feel they deserve & they don't press it. Start by the statue on Markt.

Pink Bear 050 61 66 86; w pinkbear.be. Runs scenic guided bike tours through the polders to the village of Damme, stopping for beer & waffles; departs under the Belfort on Markt at 10.25 & returns at 14.00; adult/under 25/ bring your own bike/under 8 €27/25/18/free.

QuasiMundo [217 E5] Predikherenstraat 28; 050 33 07 75; w quasimundo.com. Run 2½hr guided bike tours departing from their shop daily at 10.00 (reserve ahead & come 10mins early); adult/13–19/6–12/under 6 in a baby seat €30/26/15/5.

WHERE TO STAY Tucked among the winding medieval streets of Bruges are some exciting, one-off sleeping options. Large chains simply can't squeeze into the narrow corridors between canals and, as a result, exclusive B&Bs (w brugge-bedandbreakfast.com) have proliferated. However, even with several hundred lodging options on offer, supply can't keep up with demand at Christmas and in summer, when it's essential to book ahead.

Luxury

Brugsche Suites [216 B3] (3 suites) 20 Koningin Elisabethlaan; m 0473 80 31 53; w brugschesuites.be. The unassuming plain-white façade of this townhouse conceals a riot of colour within courtesy of the antiques dealer & interior designer owner. Highlights of the lavish interior include motif wallpaper, ancient portraits, tapestry

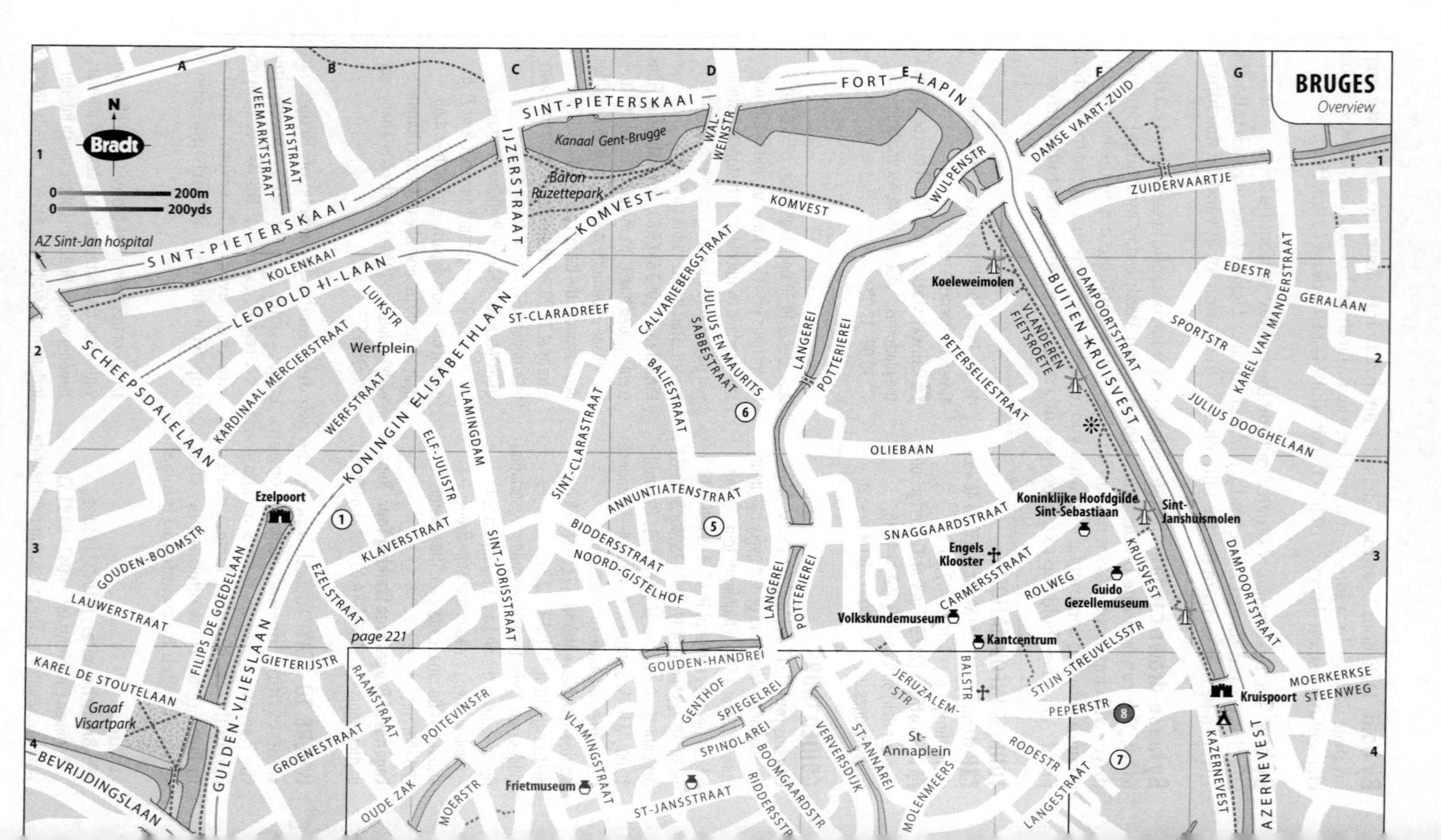

BRUGES
Overview
Bradt
N
200m
200yds
AZ Sint-Jan hospital
VEEMARKTSTRAAT
VAARTSTRAAT
SINT-PIETERSKAAI
KOLENKAAI
LEOPOLD II-LAAN
IJZERSTRAAT
Kanaal Gent-Brugge
Baron Ruzettepark
KOMVEST
WAL-WEINSTR
FORT LAPIN
WULPENSTR
DAMSE VAART-ZUID
ZUIDERVAARTJE
EDESTR
GERALAAN
KAREL VAN MANDERSTRAAT
SPORTSTR
JULIUS DOOGHELAAN
DAMPOORTSTRAAT
BUITEN KRUISVEST
VLAANDEREN FIETSROETE
Koeleweimolen
PETERSELIESTRAAT
LANGEREI
POTTERIEREI
OLIEBAAN
JULIUS EN MAURITS SABBESTRAAT
CALVARIEBERGSTRAAT
BALIESTRAAT
ST-CLARADREEF
LUIKSTR
Werfplein
KARDINAAL MERCIERSTRAAT
WERFSTRAAT
SCHEEPSDALELAAN
KONINGIN ELISABETHLAAN
VLAMINGDAM
ELF-JULISTR
SINT-CLARASTRAAT
ANNUNTIATENSTRAAT
SNAGGAARDSTRAAT
Koninklijke Hoofdgilde Sint-Sebastiaan
Sint-Janshuismolen
Engels Klooster
CARMERSSTRAAT
ROLWEG
KRUISVEST
Guido Gezellemuseum
Volkskundemuseum
Kantcentrum
Ezelpoort
KLAVERSTRAAT
BIDDERSSTRAAT
NOORD-GISTELHOF
SINT-JORISSTRAAT
EZELSTRAAT
page 221
GOUDEN-BOOMSTR
LAUWERSTRAAT
FILIPS DE GOEDELAAN
GULDEN-VLIESLAAN
GIETERIJSTR
KAREL DE STOUTELAAN
Graaf Visartpark
BEVRIJDINGSLAAN
GROENESTRAAT
RAAMSTRAAT
POITEVINSTR
OUDE ZAK
MOERSTR
Frietmuseum
VLAMINGSTRAAT
GOUDEN-HANDREI
GENTHOF
SPIEGELREI
SPINOLAREI
ST-JANSSTRAAT
BOOMGAARDSTR
RIDDERSSTR
VERVERSDIJK
ST-ANNAREI
St-Annaplein
MOLENMEERS
JERUZALEM-STR
BALSTR
STIJN STREUVELSSTR
PEPERSTR
RODESTR
LANGESTRAAT
Kruispoort
MOERKERKSE STEENWEG
KAZERNEVEST

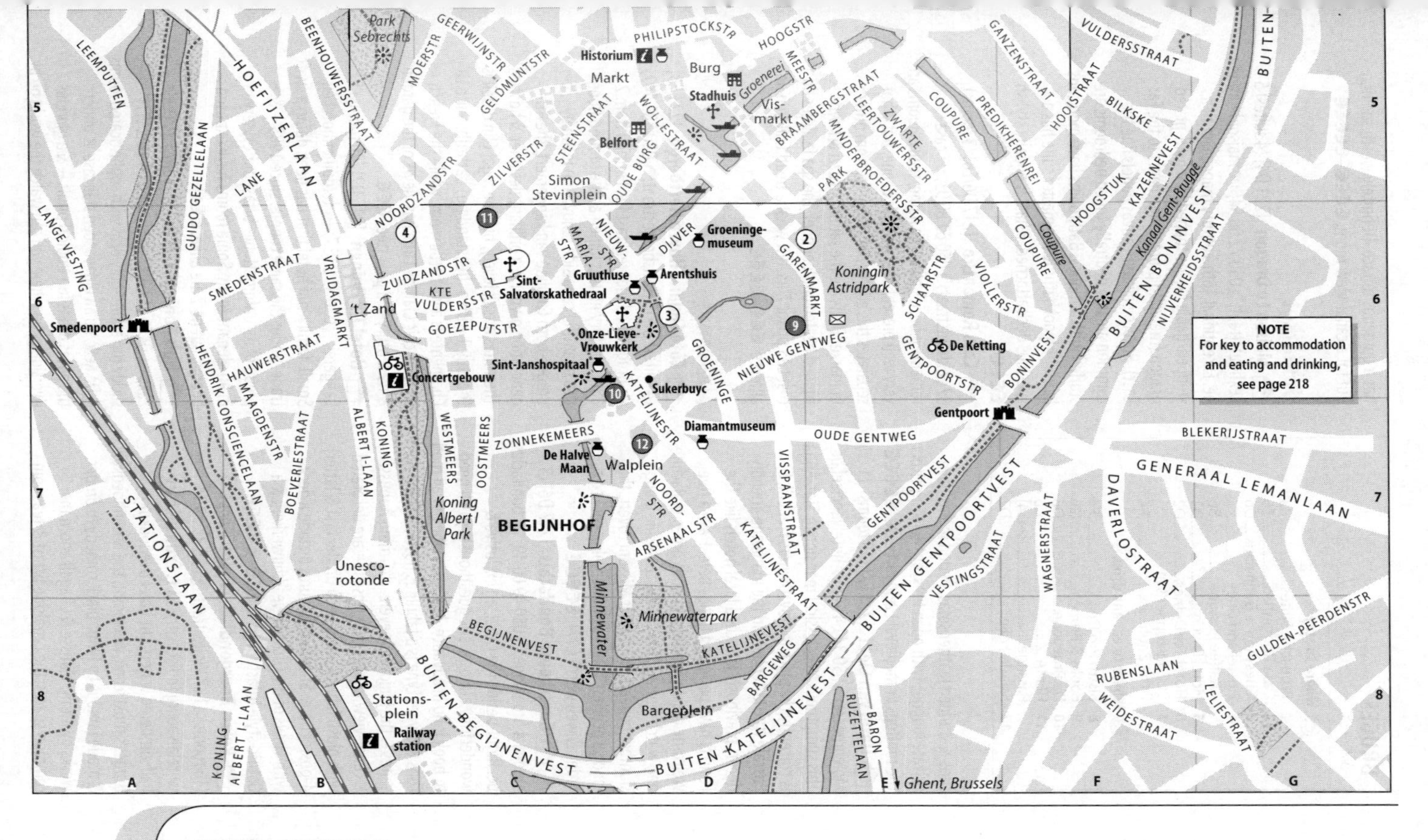
NOTE
For key to accommodation and eating and drinking, see page 218
Park Sebrechts
LEEMPUTTEN
HOEFIJZERLAAN
BEENHOUWERSSTRAAT
MOERSTR
GEERWIJNSTR
GELDMUNTSTR
PHILIPSTOCKSTR
Historium
Markt
Burg
Stadhuis
Groenerei
HOOGSTR
MEESTR
Vismarkt
BRAAMBERGSTRAAT
LEERTOUWERSSTR
ZWARTE
MINDERBROEDERSSTR
PARK
COUPURE
PREDIKHERENREI
GANZENSTRAAT
HOOISTRAAT
VULDERSSTRAAT
BILKSKE
BUITEN
GUIDO GEZELLELAAN
LANE
ZILVERSTR
STEENSTRAAT
Belfort
WOLLESTRAAT
OUDE BURG
Simon Stevinplein
NOORDZANDSTR
HOOGSTUK
KAZERNEVEST
Kanaal Gent-Brugge
BUITEN BONINVEST
NIJVERHEIDSSTRAAT
Coupure
LANGE VESTING
SMEDENSTRAAT
VRIJDAGMARKT
ZUIDZANDSTR
KTE VULDERSSTR
Sint-Salvatorskathedraal
NIEUW-STR
MARIA-STR
DIJVER
Groeningemuseum
Gruuthuse
Arentshuis
GARENMARKT
Koningin Astridpark
SCHAARSTR
VIOLLERSTR
Smedenpoort
't Zand
GOEZEPUTSTR
Onze-Lieve-Vrouwkerk
GROENINGE
NIEUWE GENTWEG
De Ketting
GENTPOORTSTR
BONINVEST
HAUWERSTRAAT
HENDRIK CONSCIENCELAAN
MAAGDENSTR
Concertgebouw
Sint-Janshospitaal
KATELIJNESTR
Sukerbuyc
Gentpoort
BOEVERIESTRAAT
ALBERT I-LAAN
KONING
WESTMEERS
OOSTMEERS
ZONNEKEMEERS
Diamantmuseum
OUDE GENTWEG
BLEKERIJSTRAAT
De Halve Maan
Walplein
VISSPAANSTRAAT
GENERAAL LEMANLAAN
STATIONSLAAN
Koning Albert I Park
BEGIJNHOF
NOORD-STR
ARSENAALSTR
KATELIJNESTRAAT
GENTPOORTVEST
BUITEN GENTPOORTVEST
VESTINGSTRAAT
WAGNERSTRAAT
DAVERLOSTRAAT
Unesco-rotonde
Minnewater
Minnewaterpark
BEGIJNENVEST
KATELIJNEVEST
BARGEWEG
GULDEN-PEERDENSTR
RUBENSLAAN
Stationsplein
Railway station
BUITEN BEGIJNENVEST
Bargeplein
BUITEN KATELIJNEVEST
RUZETTELAAN
BARON
WEIDESTRAAT
LELIESTRAAT
KONING ALBERT I-LAAN
Ghent, Brussels
A
B
C
D
E
F
G
5
6
7
8
2
3
4
9
10
11
12

BRUGES *Overview*
For listings, see from page 215

rugs & studded leather sofas. Period rooms have private lounges with open fires, overlooking either the rooftops or medieval Ezelpoort gate. €€€€€

Hotel van Cleef [221 F2] (15 rooms) 11 Molenmeers; 050 34 64 14; w hotelvancleef.be. This sumptuous Neoclassical mansion in Sint-Anna is currently *the* place to stay. Owners Frederik & Pascale (the latter behind the magazine-friendly décor) previously launched local hotels like The Pand & have perfected things here. Have a free welcome cocktail in the gorgeous green malachite bar, watch vintage flicks in the canalside lounge, slumber beneath Hermès or Missoni covers, then enjoy a peerless b/fast (continental or cooked to order, & well worth €17). €€€€€

* **Guesthouse Bonifacius** [217 D6] (3 rooms) 4 Groeninge; 050 49 00 49; w bonifacius.be. Right beside the canal, an exclusive & wonderfully atmospheric guesthouse; you'll need to book long in advance. Medieval vibe but all mod cons & owner Lyne is a fabulous hostess. The 3 suites – the junior Guinevere, charming Aubusson & canal-view master Clair Obscur – are decorated with plush fabrics, antiques & (in the first & latter) 4-poster beds. Standout features include a deck with views of the Onze-Lieve-Vrouwerkerk & a Gothic-style b/fast room. €€€€–€€€€€

Relais Bourgondisch Cruyce [221 D4] (16 rooms) 41–7 Wollestraat; 050 33 79 26; w relaisbourgondischcruyce.be. Extraordinary half-timbered waterfront hotel overlooking Bruges's most iconic viewpoint, the Rozenhoedkaai, & made famous by filmic black comedy *In Bruges*. Works by Klimt, Matisse & Chagall adorn the common spaces; the canalside b/fast & tea room has a gorgeous terrace. Definitely worth shelling out for a canal-view room. €€€€–€€€€€

Upmarket

Maison Le Dragon [221 D4] (4 suites) 5 Eekhoutstraat; 050 72 06 54; w maisonledragon.be. Exceptional 16th-century mansion with a stepped-gable façade topped by a gold-plated dragon (meant to protect merchants to the Far East). Rococo painted-canvas panels line the common areas & neutrally toned bedrooms are stuffed with antiques. Bathrooms have mod cons like whirlpool baths & the master suite has a spacious deck attached. B/fast is equally stylish. €€€€

Casa Romantico [217 D6/E6] (3 rooms) 37 Eekhoutstraat; 050 67 80 93; w casa-romantico.be. It's all in the name, really. Rooms are very well presented & it smells divine, but what separates this adults-only property from other upmarket B&Bs are the sauna, jacuzzi & lawn-fringed heated outdoor pool. The spa facilities do cost €35 pp for 2hrs, but what a treat! Children not allowed. €€€–€€€€

Mid-range

Côté Canal – Huyze Hertberge [221 E3] (4 suites) 8–10 Hertsbergestraat; 050 333 542; w bruges-bedandbreakfast.be. Formed from 2 18th-century houses joined at the ground floor, this beautiful canalside renovation is run by Bruges-born Caroline van Langeraert, the 4th-generation owner & a brilliant designer & hostess. The suites are all lovely, but the regal Clin d'Oeil is the only 1 with a (freestanding) bathtub. Suite La Charpente is a vast attic room, while the French shabby-chic Clair de Lune has views of the garden & its century-old pear tree. €€€

Hotel Ter Duinen [216 D2] (20 rooms) 52 Langerei; 050 33 04 37; w terduinenhotel.eu. Small, family-run hotel that has been doing a swift trade, under the same couple, since 1983 – & is proud of its 'unforgettable' b/fast buffet, served in an elegant room. Some rooms have exposed beams, but no 2 are alike. €€€

Huis Koning [221 A2] (4 rooms) 25 Oude Zak; m 0476 25 08 12; w huiskoning.be. Very slickly run adults-only B&B with sophisticated rooms – De Kelk, up an old wooden staircase, is under the eaves & has fun tropical prints – & a glorious riverside patio where you can watch the world go by or enjoy an extensive b/fast buffet (inc in the price) with home-baked bread. Min 2 nights. €€€

Budget

B&B Poppy's [221 F1] (2 rooms) 6 Sint-Annaplein; m 0473 78 45 33; w poppys-brugge.be. Very welcoming hosts, Iris & Peter, are ready with the tips & welcome drinks at this lovely, quiet B&B in an authentically preserved 19th-century house. Luxury room Cupid has a canopy bed & clawfoot tub; standard Little Bear is slightly less frilly with a mezzanine bathroom. Gargantuan b/fast served in a stately dining room. Sadly, the owners' dog, the namesake Poppy, passed away in 2018. €€–€€€

Hotel Fevery [216 D3] (10 rooms) 3 Collaert Mansionstraat; 050 33 12 69; w hotelfevery.be. Stellar option offering wonderful value for money. A fairtrade b/fast is part of the impressive eco-credentials (it was the first local hotel to win 'Green Key' status). Standard doubles are nice, but a small supplement gets you the attic room with a balcony; there's also a family duplex with connecting rooms. €€

Hostel and Gran Kaffee Passage [217 B6] (10 rooms) 26–8 Dweerstraat; 050 34 02 32; w passagebruges.com. A long-term favourite with backpackers thanks to its lovely Art Deco grand café, serving very good (& affordable) Belgian classics. They no longer offer dorm beds, so options are now limited to basic but comfortable dbls (€66), trpls & quads with shared bathrooms or an en-suite family room sleeping 4. Expect a bit of noise – it's right above the restaurant. €€

Shoestring

St Christopher's at the Bauhaus [216 F4] (22 rooms) 133–7 Langestraat; 050 34 10 93; w bauhaus.be. Downstairs a welcoming, vibrant Belgian beer bar with multiple happy hours; upstairs a blend of dorms (some with new-generation hi-tech 'POD' beds kitted out with power sockets & luggage storage), private rooms & long-stay (4 nights min) apts with fully equipped kitchens. Bedding & b/fast inc. Dorm beds €16.90–24.90, 2-bunk room €57, dbl €67. €

Snuffel Hostel [221 A1] (120 beds) 42 Ezelstraat; 050 33 31 33; w snuffel.one. Smartest hostel in Bruges – a non-profit that looks more like a minimal-chic hotel. Rooms range from 2- to 6-bed (inc 2 just for women) & come with or without en-suite bathrooms. There's a guest kitchen, laundry & lively bar offering 25 Belgian beers. They regularly put on gigs, exhibitions & special summer activities. Oh, & it's minutes from Markt. Dorm €16–18, dbl €48–52, inc b/fast. €

WHERE TO EAT AND DRINK Flanders' most touristy town has lots of restaurants and quality runs the full gamut. If you can't resist perching at the cafés on Markt and 't Zand (do try to though!) just have a coffee there, and then head into the maze of surrounding streets for atmospheric bistros, in which Bruges abounds, or full-on gastronomic flights of fancy. With six Michelin-starred restaurants (mostly French with a twist) the city is a contender for Belgium's gourmet capital – and a great place to treat yourself.

Restaurants

Expensive

Le Mystique [221 C2] 11 Niklaas Desparsstraat; 050 44 44 45; w lemystique.be; 18.30–21.30 Tue–Sat, closed 13–23 Jan, 14 Jul–7 Aug & 3–20 Nov. Just wow! If you like to dine in a place that looks as good as the food tastes, try this ultra-opulent restaurant attached to the Relais & Châteaux-owned Hotel Heritage, & just back from Markt. Their set menus run from €79–105, but they also do a rather reasonable à la carte, & the veggie option is as fancy as it gets. Expect to be treated like a king. €€€€€

Zet'joe [221 F3] 11 Langestraat; 050 33 82 59; w zetjoe.be; noon–14.00 & 19.00–21.00 Tue–Sat, closed 1st 2 wks Jan, 1st 3 wks Jul, 1st wk Sep. Gourmets were distraught when Belgian luminary Geert van Hecke shuttered his legendary Bruges 3-star restaurant De Karmeliet in 2016 – but, rather than hang up his chef's whites, he launched this smaller, more stylish follow-up. While it's less formal than De Karmeliet, it already has a star of its own, & the master's classical creations don't come cheap, being parlayed in tasting menus (watch out, on Sat they only serve the €136 'Brugge Die Scone' menu). A 3-course lunch is a more viable €56, while van Hecke's son

Louis runs a humbler bistro, Refter, around the back. €€€€€

Above average

Bistro de Schaar [221 G4] 2 Hooistraat; 050 33 59 79; w bistrodeschaar.be; noon–14.15 & 18.00–22.00 Mon, Tue & Fri–Sun. Look for the charming bronze scissors hanging above the door & enter this rustic restaurant famous for its steak & fish cooked over an open fire. Lovely terrace overlooking the canal. €€€€

De Stove [221 B3] 4 Kleine Sint-Amandsstraat; 050 33 78 35; w restaurantdestove.be; 11.45–14.00 & 17.45–21.00 Mon–Tue & Fri–Sun. Long-time owners Gino & Erica handed over the baton to Nico Vandendriessche & Debbie Devos in 2017, & this oft-heralded townhouse venture continues to do a swift trade – for good reason. Chef Debbie turns out fine Flemish classics (game, fish, rustic pâtés) while Nico is a charming host. Romantic & only 20 covers; booking in advance essential for dinner. €€€–€€€€

✷ **De Vlaamsche Pot** [221 A4] 3–5 Helmstraat; 050 34 00 86; w devlaamschepot.be; 17.30–22.00 Wed–Fri, noon–22.00 Sat–Sun. This gingham-laden terraced house has been turning out hearty Flemish fare for decades. It's famous for its waterzooi, but I'd also recommend the *stoofvlees* or *witloof* in de oven washed down with Brugse Zot beer. Only local produce is used – rabbit & blue-white beef from West-Flemish farmers & fresh fish from Zeebrugge – & they also do pancakes & waffles. It's worth peeking into the kitchen as you enter to see the chefs at work. Reserve ahead or regret it! €€€–€€€€

Mid-range

Bistro Pro Deo [216 F4] 161 Langestraat; 050 33 73 55; w bistroprodeo.be; 11.45–13.45 & 18.00–21.30 Tue–Fri, 18.00–22.00 Sat. Lovely, quirkily decorated Sint-Anna gem. Chef Kristof, a Lambretta scooter-riding jazz & soul DJ, turns out hearty *stoofvlees* – served with a second helping in a silver pot, crisp fries & salad – Howlin' Wolf burgers, stuffed jacket potatoes & mussels, while his wife Nathalie, a licensed city guide, charms guests in 4 languages. Great choice for solo diners. €€€

Breydel de Coninck [221 D3] 24 Breidelstraat; 050 33 97 46; w restaurant-breydel.be; noon–14.30 & 18.30–21.30 Thu–Tue. Run by a local family for nearly 6 decades, & right in the heart of the action between Burg & Markt, this casual but appealing spot is the place to try mussels & chips. €€€

Cheap and cheerful

Passage [217 B6] 26 Dweersstraat; 050 34 02 32; w passagebruges.com; 17.00–20.00 Tue–Thu, 17.00–23.00 Fri, noon–23.00 Sat, 17.30–22.00 Sun. A well-worn tourist spot, this Art Deco restaurant still deserves a mention because, despite the numerous buttocks grazing the upright wooden chairs, the tasty food & cheap beer are served at unbeatable prices. Lovely at night when lit with candles. €€

Salade Folle [217 D7] 13–14 Walplein; w saladefolle.com; 050 34 94 43; 11.45–14.00 Mon–Sat, & also 17.45–21.00 Thu–Sat. A fresh, bright café that provides a rare alternative to the meaty fare on offer elsewhere in Bruges with its reliably good, veggie-friendly salads, wraps, burgers, quiches & pastas. €€

Shoestring

Café de Gilde [221 C4] 19 Oude Burg; 050 44 41 17; f CafeDeGildeBrugge; 11.30–20.00 Mon–Sat afternoon (kitchen closes 14.30). Unfussy, buzzing Belgian bar that's reassuringly popular with the locals at lunch. Go for the €10 menu of the day (soup, a main – stew, pasta etc – & coffee). €

BRUGES *City centre*

For listings, see from page 218

Where to stay

1	B&B Poppy's	F1
2	Côté Canal – Huyze Hertberge	E3
3	Hotel van Cleef	F2
4	Huis Koning	A2
5	Maison Le Dragon	D4
6	Relais Bourgondisch Cruyce	D4
7	Snuffel Hostel	A1

Where to eat and drink

8	Bistro de Schaar	G4
9	Breydel de Coninck	D3
10	Café de Gilde	C4
11	Choco Jungle Bar	C2
12	Da Vinci	B3
13	De Stove	B3
14	De Vlaamsche Pot	A4
15	Le Mystique	C2
16	Pas Partout	F4
17	Sanseveria Bagelsalon	E3
18	Zet'joe	F3

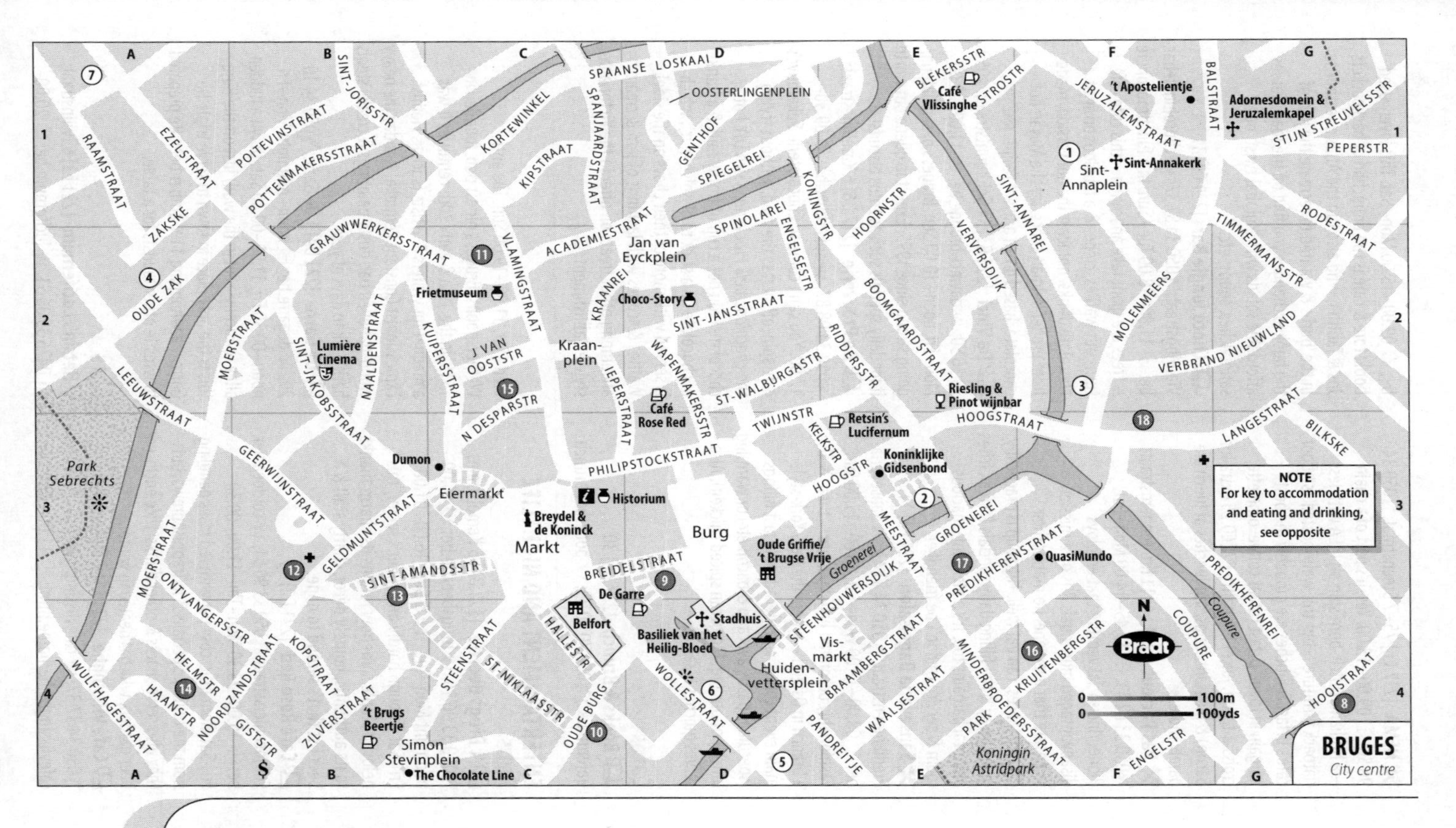
BRUGES
City centre
NOTE
For key to accommodation and eating and drinking, see opposite
Markt
Burg
Eiermarkt
Kraan-
plein
Jan van
Eyckplein
Sint-
Annaplein
Simon
Stevinplein
Vis-
markt
Huiden-
vettersplein
Park
Sebrechts
Koningin
Astridpark
Coupure
Groenerei
Belfort
Stadhuis
Basiliek van het
Heilig-Bloed
Oude Griffie/
't Brugse Vrije
Historium
Breydel &
de Koninck
De Garre
Café
Rose Red
Choco-Story
Frietmuseum
Lumière
Cinema
Dumon
'tBrugs
Beertje
The Chocolate Line
Retsin's
Lucifernum
Koninklijke
Gidsenbond
Riesling &
Pinot wijnbar
Café
Vlissinghe
't Apostelientje
Adornesdomein &
Jeruzalemkapel
Sint-Annakerk
QuasiMundo
SPAANSE LOSKAAI
OOSTERLINGENPLEIN
GENTHOF
SPIEGELREI
SPINOLAREI
KONINGSTR
ENGELSESTR
HOORNSTR
SINT-JORISSTR
POITEVINSTRAAT
POTTENMAKERSSTRAAT
EZELSTRAAT
RAAMSTRAAT
ZAKSKE
OUDE ZAK
GRAUWWERKERSSTRAAT
KORTEWINKEL
KIPSTRAAT
SPANJAARDSTRAAT
ACADEMIESTRAAT
VLAMINGSTRAAT
KRAANREI
SINT-JANSSTRAAT
J VAN OOSTSTR
KUIPERSSTRAAT
NAALDENSTRAAT
SINT-JAKOBSSTRAAT
MOERSTRAAT
LEEUWSTRAAT
GEERWIJNSTRAAT
N DESPARSTR
IEPERSTRAAT
WAPENMAKERSSTR
ST-WALBURGASTR
RIDDERSSTR
BOOMGAARDSTRAAT
TWIJNSTR
KELKSTR
PHILIPSTOCKSTRAAT
HOOGSTR
HOOGSTRAAT
GELDMUNTSTRAAT
SINT-AMANDSSTR
BREIDELSTRAAT
HALLESTR
STEENSTRAAT
ST-NIKLAASSTR
OUDE BURG
WOLLESTRAAT
ONTVANGERSSTR
KOPSTRAAT
HELMSTR
HAANSTR
NOORDZANDSTRAAT
GISTSTR
ZILVERSTRAAT
WULFHAGESTRAAT
MEESTRAAT
GROENEREI
STEENHOUWERSDIJK
BRAAMBERGSTRAAT
PANDREITJE
WAALSESTRAAT
MINDERBROEDERSSTRAAT
PARK
KRUITENBERGSTR
PREDIKHERENSTRAAT
PREDIKHERENREI
COUPURE
ENGELSTR
HOOISTRAAT
BILKSKE
LANGESTRAAT
VERBRAND NIEUWLAND
MOLENMEERS
VERVERSDIJK
SINT-ANNAREI
BLEKERSSTR
STROSTR
JERUZALEMSTRAAT
BALSTRAAT
STIJN STREUVELSSTR
PEPERSTR
RODESTRAAT
TIMMERMANSSTR
N
Bradt
0 100m
0 100yds

HEMA [217 C6] 75–7 Steenstraat; 050 34 96 56; 09.00–18.00. Yes, it's part of a chain – a brilliant, Dutch-born spin on IKEA with less flatpack furniture – but this well-located 1st-floor café's b/fast & lunches are probably the best bargain in town. B/fast (great coffee, omelette, croissant, jam, juice) is a paltry €2 (€0.25 extra for bacon) & pleasant soups/sandwiches at lunch are barely more. €

Pas Partout [221 F4] 11 Kruitenbergstraat; 050 33 62 43; 11.45–14.00 Mon–Sat. Pioneering social venture that employs disadvantaged individuals & is on a mission to ensure that everyone, no matter their circumstances, can eat well. The soup is practically given away & the filling daily specials & steak frites are total bargains too. It's a pleasant, spacious room & service couldn't be friendlier. €

Sanseveria Bagelsalon [221 E3] 11 Predikherenstraat; 050 34 81 43; w sanseveria.be; 08.00–17.00 Wed–Sat, 10.00–15.00 Sun. Fashionably decorated bagel parlour – there is also a branch in Ostend – where the New York-style main event comes with decadent b/fast fillings (speculaas paste, avocado & bacon etc) or warming lunch options (eg: Moroccan spiced chicken). Also serves quiches & salads. €

Cafés

Books & Brunch [217 D6] 30 Garenmarkt; 050 70 90 79; w booksandbrunch.be; 09.00–15.00 Mon–Sat. This lovely used bookstore & café is the brainchild of backpackers Jos & Tabitha, who also run the Atlas guesthouse in the 'burbs & wanted to recreate the joys of the book exchanges you find on the road. Serves affordable salads with a global twist, open sandwiches, soups, etc. €

Choco Jungle Bar [221 C2] 31 Vlamingstraat; 050 34 87 37; w chocojunglebar.be; 11.00–18.00 Tue–Sun. In a fun atmosphere – trees & a giant fake anaconda – this cute café turns out waffles, crêpes & a fabulous array of chocolate drinks, not least the hot version, made from proper Belgian chocs. Try the Mayan hot chocolate, based on an ancient recipe. €€

Da Vinci [221 B3] 34 Geldmuntstraat; 050 33 36 50; w davinci-brugge.be; 11.00–22.00 Mon–Fri, noon–10.00 Sun. Bruges's best gelateria, going strong since 1995. Expect to queue but worth it for daily specials such as Lotus biscuits! €

De Proeverie [217 D6] 6 Katelijnestraat; 050 33 08 87; w sukerbuyc.be; 09.30–17.00. You can't come to Chocolaterie Sukerbuyc's café spin-off, across the road, without trying the *chocolademelk Proeverie*, a rich DIY hot chocolate (you get a cup of frothy milk & a hunk of chocolate on a stick to dissolve in it), which is served with more of their chocs on the side! Waffles & scones with lashings of jam & cream are among other treats on offer in the Victoriana-style establishment. €

ENTERTAINMENT AND NIGHTLIFE

Pubs

't Brugs Beertje [221 B4] 5 Kemelstraat; 050 33 96 16; w brugsbeertje.be; 16.00–midnight Mon–Tue, Thu & Sun, 16.00–01.00 Fri–Sat. Though hardly an insider's secret, this beloved staple somehow retains its charm thanks to its authentic, homely décor, chatty staff & a beer list that's second to none.

Café Rose Red [221 D2] 16 Cordoeaniersstraat; 050 33 90 51; w cordoeanier.be; 15.00–23.30 Mon–Thu, 11.00–00.30 Fri–Sat. Romantic, cosy bar with red roses dangling from the ceiling. Specialises in Trappist brews, but they also serve snacks & other drinks. Nice enclosed beer garden, which is heated in winter.

Café Vlissinghe [221 E1] 2 Blekersstraat; 050 34 37 37; w cafevlissinghe.be/cafevlissinghe.be/home.html; 11.00–22.00 Wed–Sat, 11.00–19.00 Sun. The anti-Wetherspoons: Bruges's oldest pub, founded in 1515. In the 19th & early 20th centuries it was a magnet for writers & artists (such as Flemish Expressionist Constant Permeke) & today the heavy wood-panelled bar, dusty paintings & creaky stools hark back to days of yore.

De Garre [221 D4] 1 De Garre; 050 34 10 29; w degarre.be; noon–midnight Mon–Fri, noon–00.30 Fri, 11.00–00.30 Sat. Down a hidden alley (basically a slit in the wall) just off the Burg, this is the only place in town to serve triple De Garre – a whopping 11% amber beer. Be prepared to wrestle other tourists for a table.

Bars

Retsin's Lucifernum [221 E3] 6 Twijnstraat; m 0476 35 06 51; w lucifernum.be; 20.00–

23.00 Sun. It's hardly ever open, but do dress up & visit this bizarre bar if you can. Once famous among locals for its debauched drink-fuelled parties, the mansion belongs to Willy Retzin, who now serves quiet cocktails & entertains the crowds among his enormous collection of spooky, occasionally bad taste paintings, religious icons & statues (think a portrait of Hitler). You get entrance & a drink for €10. Every first Fri of the month they also run the 'Bal des Novices' (⌚ 20.00, reserve ahead, black-&-white dress code for men, women 'dressed in light').

Riesling & Pinot wijnbar [221 E2] 33 Hoogstraat; ☎ 050 84 23 97; **w** riesling-pinot.be; ⌚ 15.00–11.00 Tue–Fri, noon–23.00 Sat–Sun. This superb wine bar is a godsend for beer-phobes, with kind, knowledgeable staff & fabulous German wines by the glass. After a charcuterie platter you may blow off your dinner plans.

Cinemas and concert halls

Concertgebouw [217 B6] 34 't Zand; ☎ 050 47 69 99; **w** concertgebouw.be. Built to mark Bruges's year as European Capital of Culture back in 2002, a state-of-the-art cultural centre for contemporary dance, classical music & pop & rock concerts. Watch out for the early music MAfestival in Aug & December Dance.

Lumière Cinema [221 B2] 36 Sint-Jakobsstraat; ☎ 050 34 34 65; **w** lumierecinema.be. Beloved 3-screen cinema showing arthouse & cult flicks. Old-world atmosphere but recently renovated. The smallest screen seats just 47.

SHOPPING Lace and chocolate – while Bruges's shopping scene isn't limited to these two things, it does do best when it comes to the classics. Sifting the unique boutiques from the chaff isn't easy, but here are some personal recommendations to start you off. For lace, the quaint Sint-Anna boutique **'t Apostelientje** [221 F1] (11 Balstraat; ⌚ 10.00–noon & 13.15–17.00 Wed–Sat, 10.00–13.00 Sun, 13.00–17.00 Tue), just metres from the Kantcentrum (Lace Museum), is as authentic as it gets. All its pieces – doilies, collars – are handmade, with some dating back to the 16th century.

Of the city's 60 chocolate shops, my favourites are the family-run **Sukerbuyc** [217 D6] (5 Katelijnestraat; ⌚ 10.00–17.00), traditional **Dumon** [221 C3] (16 Eiermarkt; ⌚ 10.00–18.00 Mon–Sat, 10.00–17.00 Sun) and local hero Dominique Persoone's Willy Wonka-esque **The Chocolate Line** [221 B4] (19 Simon Stevinplein; ⌚ 09.30–18.30 Tue–Sat, 10.30–18.30 Sun–Mon), with its pleasingly oddball flavours such as bacon or tobacco.

Markets

Fish market Vismarkt; ⌚ 08.00–13.30 Wed–Sat. Smaller these days but still fun, & featuring fresh catch from the sea around Zeebrugge.

Flea market Dijver; ⌚ Mid-Mar–mid-Nov 10.00–18.00 Sat–Sun & Jun–Sep 10.00–18.00 Fri

Food and flowers Markt, ⌚ 08.00–13.30 Wed

General market 't Zand, ⌚ 08.00–13.30 Sat

OTHER PRACTICALITIES

$ Bank [221 B4] KBC, 34 Zilverstraat, ⌚ 09.30–noon & 13.30–16.30 Mon–Fri, 09.00–noon Sat. You'll also find many cash points in central Bruges, just off Markt.

Luggage storage Located in the passage left of the main station entrance; €3.50/4.50/5.50 for small/medium/large self-service locker.

+ Pharmacy [221 B3] 32 Geldmuntstraat; ☎ 050 33 34 37; **w** apotheekneyt.be; ⌚ 09.00–13.00 & 13.30–18.30 Mon–Wed & Fri, 09.00–13.00 Thu, 10.00–17.00 Sat

Post office [217 B6] 57–9 Smedenstraat, ⌚ 09.00–18.00 Mon–Fri, 09.00–15.00 Sat. The central post office is currently a bit of a schlepp west of the centre.

WHAT TO SEE AND DO

Het Zand [217 B6] One of the town's oldest squares, 't Zand takes its name from the sand dunes that 13th-century settlers started building on (until AD700 the sea reached as far as the city's western gates). Today it's host to the state-of-the-art **Concertgebouw (Concert Hall)** (34 't Zand; w concertgebouw.be) in the southeast corner. Downstairs is tourist information centre In&Uit; you can also follow the fun **Concertgebouwcircuit** (⌚ 14.00–18.00 Wed–Sat, 10.00–14.00 Sun; adult/6–26/under 6 €8/4/free), which takes you behind the scenes of the building via scattered artworks and musical interventions featuring Luc Tuymans and Edgar Varèse.

Markt [221 C3] Come summer, the city's central market square, an 8-minute walk away, throngs with tourists and clattering horse-drawn carriages. As the domain of guildsmen, the Markt was the commercial and social focal point of Bruges. It's not as old as it looks: following two major fires at the end of the 14th and 16th centuries, the city decided to replace the original medieval wooden houses with brick; those in place today are reconstructions dating from the 18th to the 20th centuries. The building with the richest history is 16 Markt, where the guildsmen of Bruges imprisoned the soon-to-be emperor Maximilian I for three months in 1488 – only for Maximilian to spend the rest of his reign directing trade north to the port of Antwerp. The late-Gothic corner house 'Bouchoute' (now the Meridian 3 tea room), topped by a shining gold-leaf ball, refers to Bruges professor Quetelet, who resolved the problem of poor timekeeping in Belgium by drawing a meridian on the ground and setting up an infallible 'noonday' hand. The meridian ran diagonally over the Markt and is now marked by copper nails. When the shadow of the golden ball falls on the meridian, it is precisely noon.

In the middle of the square stand the statues of butcher Jan Breydel and weaver Pieter de Coninck, who participated in the Battle of the Golden Spurs (pages 6 and 280) against French rule in 1302. Their statue overlooks the Provincial Court; until the late 18th century, a covered water hall stood here, and ships would sail right up to the building to unload their wares. The premises now house the silly but fun **Historium** [221 C3] (1 Markt; ☎ 050 27 03 11; w historium.be; ⌚ 10.00–18.00), with virtual-reality headset tours of Golden Age Bruges, and a love story-themed tour animating a Jan van Eyck painting. There's an on-site 'Duvelorium' bar whose balcony has prime views of the Markt. Since January 2019, you can now climb 145 steps to the top of the building's tower.

Belfort [221 C4] (⌚ 09.30–18.00, last tickets 16.15; adult/6–25/under 6/Musea Brugge Card €12/10/free/free) Bruges's belfry, which stands sentry over the Markt, took over three centuries to complete. The foundations date from the 13th century and stretch up to the first four ramparts of the tower. However, a lack of funds put building on hold until the 14th century, when the rest of the tower was completed, and the final octagonal steeple was added between 1482 and 1486. For approximately three centuries a wooden spire also stood atop the steeple, but after being destroyed by fire for a second time in 1741, it was never rebuilt. Now standing at a respectable 83m (and leaning close to a metre to the east), the belfry offers bracing views over the city. Visitors who wish to climb the 366 steep, notably narrow steps can pause to regain their breath at the **Treasury Room**, whose wooden box with ten locks originally held the town documents and could only be opened when the mayor and nine appointed town officials were present with their individually assigned keys. Climb higher and you pass the **Carillon Chamber**, which controls the tower's 47 bells played at regular carillon concerts (⌚ mid Sep–mid Jun 11.00–noon Wed & Sat–Sun, mid-Jun–mid-Sep 11.00–noon Wed & Sat–Sun, 21.00 Mon & Wed). I'd highly advise coming close to opening or closing time to avoid the crowds – it's a bit of a squeeze trying to get up when there are hordes of visitors simultaneously descending the steps.

The Burg [221 D3] Set just to the southeast of Markt, down Breidelstraat, is the smaller but arguably more majestic Burg square. It was here that the city was born, when Baldwin the Iron Arm, the first Count of Flanders, built the castle from which the square takes its name to guard against invading Normans and Vikings during the 9th century. Today, vestiges of St Donatian's Cathedral, which fell in 1799, are buried under – and integrated into – the Crowne Plaza Hotel at the north end of the square. Incidentally, visitors can see the remains of the choir gallery in the hotel's cellar. The ruins were uncovered in 1988 during excavations for the proposed hotel car park.

Stadhuis [221 D4] (12 Burg; ◷ 09.30–17.00; ☎ 050 44 87 43; adult/18–25/under 18/Musea Brugge Card €6/5/free/free, inc audio guide & entry to Het Brugse Vrije; see below) Construction of Bruges's Gothic town hall began in 1376, making it one of the oldest in Belgium. The 49 statues that decorate the elaborate sandstone façade are relatively new (1989), the originals having been destroyed by French revolutionaries in 1792. The majority of them depict the Counts and Countesses of Flanders, but the bottom row features biblical figures. You'll find a booklet with the full list inside.

The highlight of the interior is the dramatic **Gotische Zaal (Gothic Hall)**, whose exquisite vaulted polychrome wooden ceiling dates from 1402. Twelve vault-keys, depicting scenes from the New Testament, appear where the ribs of the arches converge, and where the arches meet the walls you will see 16 consoles illustrating the 12 months and four natural elements. The original 1410 paintings were replaced by frescoes created by Flemish artists Albert and Juliaan De Vriendt between 1895 and 1905. They depict pivotal events in the city's history, including the foundation of the Order of the Golden Fleece by Philip the Good in 1430 and Diederik d'Alsace bringing the relic of the Holy Blood to the church of St Basil in 1150.

Oude Griffie (Civil Registry) [221 D3] (11a Burg, ◷ closed to public) To the left of, and in stark contrast to, the Gothic town hall is the civil registry. Built between 1535 and 1537 to house municipal records, its vibrant Renaissance façade features ornate scrolled gables topped by bronze statues of Justice, Aaron and Moses.

Het Brugse Vrije (Liberty of Bruges) [221 D3] (11 Burg; ◷ 09.30–17.00; entry free with town hall ticket/Musea Brugge Card) Adjacent to the Civil Registry is the Burg's second-largest building, which served as a court of justice between 1795 and 1984, and now holds the city archives. One room of the former palace, the **Aldermen's Room**, remains, and is the main draw for visitors for a very good reason: its phenomenal 16th-century oak, marble and alabaster chimneypiece, taking up over a third of the wall space. Overseen by Lanceloot Blondeel (1496–1561), it commemorates Charles V's victory against the French at Pavia in 1525. The free audio guide talks you through it.

Basiliek van het Heilig-Bloed (Basilica of the Holy Blood) [221 D4] (15 Burg; ☎ 050 33 67 92; w holyblood.com; ◷ 09.00–12.30 & 14.00–17.30; treasury €2.50) Tucked discreetly into the southeast corner of the square sits the Basilica of the Holy Blood. Named after the holy relic it houses, this 12th-century church is composed of two parts: the lower, Romanesque St Basil's Chapel – bereft of decoration bar a statue of the Virgin Mary dating from 1300; and upstairs a moody neo-Gothic chapel. Here, within a silver tabernacle, you will find an intricately designed rock-crystal phial purported to contain a cloth stained with a few drops of blood and water washed from the body of Christ by Joseph of Arimathea. Local legend has it that it was brought back to the city by Flemish count Diederik d'Alsace, but it is more likely that it was acquired during the sacking of Constantinople in 1204. Whatever its provenance, it remains an object of great veneration, paraded through town every year on Ascension Day during the Holy Blood Procession (buy tickets for the parade at the tourist information office). While you don't need to pay to see the phial, there is a charge for the small but impressive **Schatkamer** (**Treasury**), where you can find the shrine that holds the phial of the Holy Blood during the procession.

Along and around Dijver Leaving the Burg via Blinde Ezelstraat (Blind Donkey Street) to the left of the town hall – look back to admire the ornate archway you've come through – cross the canal, coming out on **Vismarkt** [221 E4], where fish is still sold under the covered arcade from Wednesday to Saturday. Turning right brings you to the old tanners' square, **Huidenvettersplein** [221 D4], which served the poor – no sea fish for them but cheaper freshwater fish, once weighed via the post in the middle of the square. Continuing west leads you to Rozenhoedkaai, where salt traders once loaded and unloaded goods, and where selfie sticks now congregate to capture what is officially the most photographed spot in Bruges. Escape the madness by continuing along Dijver, passing the **College of Europe** (nos 9–11), where would-be politicians take masters in European studies, and arriving at the marquee Groeningemuseum.

Groeningemuseum (Groeninge Museum) ✷ [217 D6] (12 Dijver; 🕘 09.30–17.00; adult/18–25/under 18/Musea Brugge Card €12/10/free/free inc audio guide & entry to Arentshuis) Housing the world's most complete collection of Flemish Primitive artworks, this is Bruges's must-see museum. Rooms are allocated to subsequent artistic movements like Flemish Expressionism, Surrealism etc, but the spotlight understandably rests on the rotating display of early Flemish masterpieces, characterised by their pinpoint realism and supremely

MAD FOR MUSEUMS?

Sadly, the previous Bruges City Card was abolished in 2016 for mysterious reasons, so your best bet is therefore the Musea Brugge Card (adult/18–25 €28/22), which grants free access to 14 municipal attractions, as follows: the Archeologiemuseum, Arentshuis, Belfort, Brugse Vrije, Gentpoort, Gezellemuseum, Groeningemuseum, Gruuthusemuseum, OLV-Kerk, OLV-ter-Potterie, Sint-Janshospitaal, Sint-Janshuismolen, Stadhuis and Volkskundemuseum. The card is valid for three consecutive days – you can visit as many times as you like – and can be bought at participating museums (except the Sint-Janshuismolen and Brugse Vrije), as well as the information points at 't Zand and in the Historium. The city also sells a number of combi-tickets as follows:

- Historium/Groeningemuseum (€22, buy at the Historium)
- Kantcentrum/ Volkskundemuseum (€10)
- Choco-Story/Diamond Museum (€17)
- Choco-Story/Lumina Domestica/Belgian Fries Museum (adult/6–11/under 6 €16.50/13.50/free). You can combine two of these three above for a reduced rate.

tactile qualities, found in the first few rooms. Look for the following, using the free floor plan as your guide:

Hieronymous Bosch's teeming triptych *The Last Judgement*. Heaven is depicted in the left panel, hell in the right, and in the middle, earth. This central panel is perhaps the most disturbing: filled with mayhem and lewd sexual imagery – the harp and the bagpipes were well-known references to sexual organs – Bosch makes his opinions of the stupidity of the human race clear.

The enormous and equally graphic *The Judgement of Cambyses* (1498), painted by **Gerard David** (page 20), tells the story of the corrupt judge Sisamnes, who was sentenced to be flayed alive by the Persian king after accepting a bribe. It is interesting to note David's experiment with perspective and the lack of knowledge of human anatomy at the time – veins and sinew do not lie directly beneath the skin.

Jan van Eyck's *Portrait of Margareta van Eyck* (1439) – featuring van Eyck's rather plain-looking 33-year-old wife – and *Madonna with Canon Joris van der Paele* (1436), which depicts the commissioner, van der Paele, dressed in white on the right. Noteworthy features include the reflective armour worn by St George (also on the right) and the texture of the blue velvet robe worn by St Donatian who stands on the left.

Also of note is **Hans Memling**'s *Moreel Triptych* (1484), whose central panel features patron saint St Christopher carrying the Christ child on his shoulders. He is flanked by St Maurus (left) and St Gilles (right), and on the side panels kneel the commissioners of the painting, Moreel and his wife Barbara van Vlaenderberch, and their children.

Alongside the portraits of rich citizens for which he was best known, you'll find leading 16th-century artist **Pieter Pourbus**'s interpretation of the *Last Judgement* (1551). Depicting the physicality of the fight between angels and demons over human souls, it strongly reflects the wars of religion, or Reformation, sweeping through Europe at the time. Look for his signature, which can just be made out on the stone in the bottom right of the painting.

Additional highlights are the monumental Expressionist works of **Constant Permeke**, whose wartime experiences fed into his drab representations of workers (invariably with ginormous feet), and **Gustave van de Woestijne**'s equally gargantuan *Last Supper*. On the Surrealist front, you'll find uncanny works by **Paul Delvaux**, **René Magritte** and **Marcel Broodthaers**.

Arentshuis [217 D6] (16 Dijver; 🕘 09.30–17.00 Tue–Sun; adult/18–25/under 18/Musea Brugge Card €6/5/free/free) The ground floor of this 18th-century mansion is used as an overspill gallery for local municipal museums, chiefly the Groeninge Museum, as well as hosting temporary exhibitions. The first floor exhibits the etchings, paintings and carpets of versatile Welsh – but Bruges-born – artist Frank Brangwyn (1867–1956). Inspired by the Orientalism art movement, Brangwyn travelled as far as South Africa in search of different colour palettes, but is better remembered for his versatility with different media. He worked as an official UK war artist during World War I, but retained strong links with Belgium and was made an honorary citizen in 1936. At the foot of Arentspark you'll find **St Bonifaciusbrug**; this picturesque bridge might look medieval but surprisingly only dates back to 1910.

Gruuthusemuseum [217 D6] (17 Dijver; ☎ 050 44 87 43; 🕘 check **w** museabrugge.be for opening hours & prices) In May 2019 this Gothic palace was due to reopen after extensive renovations. Inside, the idea is to tell the story of

Bruges through diverse antiques and objects – the museum's applied arts collection spans the 13th to the 19th centuries. Highlights include an impressive horde of tapestries, as well as lace, sculpture, furniture and silver. The most famous object is a painted terracotta bust of Charles V. A new reception pavilion offering tourist information and booking services is also planned for the new complex.

Onze-Lieve-Vrouwekerk (Church of Our Lady) [217 D6] (Mariastraat; 050 44 87 43 09.30–17.00 Mon–Sat, 13.30–17.00 Sun; church: free; chancel: adult/18–25/under 18/Musea Brugge Card €6/5/free/free) Sitting beside the Gruuthuse you cannot miss Our Lady – thanks in large part to her 115m steeple (the tallest brick tower in the Low Countries). The church is a hotchpotch of Gothic and Romanesque architecture, but its star attraction is Michelangelo's surprisingly small statue of the *Madonna and Child*, featured in the George Clooney film *The Monuments Men*. Carved from one solid piece of Carrara marble, it was commissioned by the Bishop of Siena, but banker and friend Giovanni Mouscron fell so deeply in love with the High Renaissance-style sculpture that he begged Michelangelo to sell it to him instead. The master artist finally acquiesced when a price of 4,000 florins was named and Mouscron returned to Bruges with the only Michelangelo to leave Italy during his lifetime; the bishop eventually received a similar, but inferior, version. Michelangelo's depiction of the mother and child is unique when compared to the popular renditions of a virginal maiden smiling down upon her holy infant child: Michelangelo's Mary stares vacantly at onlookers, seemingly unaware of the child at her feet and devoid of the usual royal crown, while the infant Christ is empty-handed (he usually carries a cross) and seems to be on the verge of toddling away from his mother. The effect serves to humanise these holy figures. Also worth a look, in the **chancel**, are the exquisite 16th-century ceremonial tombs of Charles the Bold and his daughter Maria of Burgundy, with a pair of dogs nestled at her feet. Large-scale renovations were due to continue throughout 2019, with a discount on the chancel price in the meantime.

Sint-Janshospitaal (St John's Hospital) [217 C6] (38 Mariastraat; 050 44 87 43; 09.30–17.00 Tue–Sun; adult/18–25/under 18/Musea Brugge Card €12/10/free/free, inc audio guide) A haven for the sick and a resting place for pilgrims until the 19th century, this medieval site (founded in 1150) is one of the oldest preserved hospitals in Europe. The stone-arched former ward contains a museum filled with paintings and *objets d'art* documenting the hospital's history and a chapel with six works by the most famous Flemish Primitive, Hans Memling (page 20). Just before the chapel entrance, and foremost among them, is the *Reliquary of St Ursula*, a miniature wooden Gothic church depicting the story of Breton princess St Ursula on six panels. Legend has it she was murdered, alongside the 11,000 virgins accompanying her on a pilgrimage, by Huns near Cologne for refusing to abandon her faith. Nearby are two triptychs, *Lamentation* and *Adoration of the Magi*. Inside the chapel proper you will find the impressive *Mystical Marriage of St Catherine* triptych (aka the Saint John Altarpiece). *Diptych with Our Lady and Maarten van Nieuwenhoven* and *Portrait of a Young Woman* (aka *Sibylla Sambetha*), both in the side chapel, are fine examples of Memling's portrait skills. Afterwards, don't forget to head outside the building, turn left and enter the courtyard round the corner, to take in the old apothecary and herb garden, with its wonderful collection of old potion bottles and ex-votos.

Sint-Salvatorskathedraal (St Salvator's Cathedral) [217 C6] (Steenstraat; **w** sintsalvator.be; 10.00–13.00 & 14.00–17.30 Mon–Fri, 10.00–

13.00 & 14.00–15.30 Sat, 11.30–noon & 14.00–17.00 Sun; free) When the St Donatius Church on the Burg was destroyed in the 18th century, the Holy Saviour Church – the city's oldest Gothic parish church – was upgraded to the status of cathedral to take its place. To fit its new role, it was rebuilt in Romanesque style by English architect William Chantrell. Its most important treasures, like Dieric Bouts's and Hugo van der Goes's *The Martyrdom of St Hippolytus,* are housed in the **Schatkamer** (**Treasury**) (🕘 14.00–17.00 Mon–Fri & Sun), but several Flemish tapestries, works of art (not least a set of eight paintings by Jan van Orley) and tombs can be found inside the church.

Diamantmuseum (Diamond Museum) [217 D7] (43 Katelijnestraat; ☎ 050 34 20 56; 🕘 10.30–17.30; **w** diamondmuseum.be; adult/6–12/under 6 €9.50/8.50/free, inc diamond-polishing demonstration) Less ritzy than Antwerp's new diamond museum, but perhaps stronger on detail, this modestly sized spot traces the city's early entanglement with the carbon sparklers – including the invention of diamond-polishing by Lodewijk van Berquem, working under the jewel-hungry Dukes of Burgundy – before it lost its trade to Antwerp in the 16th century. A lab allows you to get to grips with the eight key characteristics of diamonds, and there are diamond-polishing demos at weekends (and weekdays from April to October) at 12.15 and 15.15.

De Halve Maan [217 C7] (26 Walplein; ☎ 050 44 42 22; **w** halvemaan.be; 🕘 guided 45min tours on the hour 11.00–16.00 Mon–Fri & Sun, 11.00–17.00 Sat, adult/6–12/under 6 €12/6/free; 'XL' (90min) tour 14.15, adult/6–12/under 6 €21/6.50/free) Bruges was once home to a handful of working breweries, but until the 2015 relaunch of **Bourgogne des Flandres** (**w** bourgognedesflandres.be), the soul survivor was De Halve Maan ('Half Moon'), which first crops up in record books in 1564! The current business was established in 1856 by Leon Maes and, incredibly, remains in the family. Maes's great, great, great, great-granddaughter developed the Straffe Hendrik and her son, Xavier, the blonde Brugse Zot (see box, below). You can try both in the converted maltery and bottling room, which now acts as a brasserie (€€€). In 2016 the brewery made international headlines when it launched the **world's first beer pipeline**, flowing over 3km underground from the brewery to their bottling plant outside the city, without damaging the medieval architecture above it. There's a peephole showing a section of the pipeline in the archway by the entrance. Regular tours include a Brugse Zot; if you're really keen, upgrade to their XL tour, where you get to taste three beers in the cellar.

CLOWNING AROUND

Take a sip of the beer produced by Bruges's De Halve Maan brewery and you'll notice the name on the label – Brugse Zot. Translating as 'Bruges Fool', it refers to the city's inhabitants. Legend has it the name was bestowed on them by Maximilian of Austria in the 15th century. The story goes that, in order to please the duke, a colourful procession of fools and merrymakers was assembled to welcome his arrival into the city. As the festivities drew to a close the residents of Bruges put forward their request for a new lunatic asylum, to which Maximilian replied: 'I have seen nothing but fools here today. Bruges is one great lunatic asylum!'

Begijnhof [217 C7] (24–30 Begijnhof; ☎ 050 33 00 11; ⏲ 06.30–18.30; free) Come spring, golden daffodils carpet the lightly wooded gardens of Bruges's lovely béguinage (see box, page 19), or 'Princely Béguinage Ten Wijngaerde' to give it its full dues. Established by Margaret of Constantinople, Countess of Flanders, in 1245, the medieval compound is one of the best-preserved in Belgium and like the others was designated a UNESCO World Heritage site in 1998. Now, with the béguines all gone, it's home to a handful of Benedictine nuns, whom you might spot in the Baroque *begijnhofkerk* church, where you are immediately assailed by a canvas on the high altar featuring the béguinage's patron saint – Elizabeth of Hungary – kneeling before a crucifix. The only other house here open to the public is the *begijnhuisje,* which serves as a **museum** (⏲10.00–17.00; adult/child €2/1) whose handful of preserved rooms give a good idea of what béguine life might have been like. Look out for the traditional béguine cupboard or *schapraai* in the dining room; from top to bottom its three compartments housed china, a dining table and a larder.

Minnewater [217 D8] Dubbed the 'lake of love' by writer Victor Hugo (the epithet has stuck and quite rightly so; see box, below), this willow-lined pond started out as the mooring place for barges sailing between Bruges and Ghent. The stone lockhouse at its head is actually a 19th-century reconstruction, but the Poertoren, on the west bank at the far end of the lake, dates from 1398 and was once part of the city wall, used to store gunpowder (the name translates as 'powder tower'). A footbridge here leads east to Minnewaterpark, or around to the old city gates; in the east, **Gentpoort** [217 E7/F7] (Gentpoortstraat; ⏲ 09.00–12.30 & 13.30–17.00 Tue–Sun; adult/18–25/under 18/Musea Brugge Card €4/3/free/free) houses a museum on how the gates were built, and the imports and exports that were ferried through them.

North and east of the city centre A 5-minute walk north of Markt, pretty **Jan van Eyckplein** [221 D2] was the Manhattan of Burgundian Bruges, where ships moored, loaded and unloaded, and tolls were paid. The square revolves around a statue of artist Jan van Eyck erected in 1878; on its north side, at nos 1–2, you'll find the 15th-century **Tolhuis**, whose Renaissance façade bears the coat of arms of the Dukes of Luxembourg, responsible for levying tolls. From the 13th to the 15th centuries, when Bruges was a key trading centre between the Hansa territories of Scandinavia, England and Germany, Spanish merchants plied their trade on **Spaanse Loskaai** [221 D1]; Easterners on **Oosterlingenplein** [221 D1]. To really

THE LEGEND OF MINNA AND MOREN

According to folklore, Minnewater lake is named after star-crossed lovers. During the Roman rule of Gaul, Bruges was just a small village. Among the inhabitants was a girl named Minna, who had fallen in love with Stromberg, a warrior from a neighbouring tribe. Her father disapproved of the match, and set in place an arranged marriage for the girl. Distraught, Minna fled to the nearby forest; when Stromberg returned from battle he raced to find her but it was too late – exhausted and malnourished, she died in his arms. The inconsolable Moren carried her body to a dried-up lake and then burst the banks of the nearby dyke, burying her body and naming the lake Minnewater as a symbol of their everlasting love.

escape the crowds, head east from here across the water to **Sint-Anna**, a former working-class neighbourhood filled with windmills, convents, churches and museums with a very different feel to the centre.

Choco-Story [221 D2] (2 Wijnzakstraat; 050 61 22 37; w choco-story.be; Sep–Jun 10.00–17.00; Jul–Aug 10.00–18.00; adult/6–11/under 6 €9.50/5.50/free) Housed in the 15th-century Maison de Croon, this informative museum covers the cocoa bean's migration from the hands of the Aztecs and Mayans (who used cocoa as currency) to the clutches of the Spanish, who introduced the luxury into the royal courts of Europe. Belgium's links to the trade are also discussed. The best bits of course are the liberal free samples throughout, and the chocolate-making demo on the ground floor.

Frietmuseum [221 C2] (33 Vlamingstraat; 050 34 01 50; w frietmuseum.be; 10.00–17.00; adult/6–11/under 6 €7/5/free) Dedicated solely to the humble chip, this three-floor museum charts the potato's peaty Peruvian roots, with emphasis on French fries – actually Belgian, of course! Like its sister museum, Choco-Story, the highlight is munching freshly cooked frites in the basement (you get a nominal discount with your ticket) but I also loved the kitsch chip paraphernalia upstairs.

Adornesdomein and Jeruzalemkapel ✷ [221 G1] (3 Peperstraat; 050 33 88 83; w adornes.com; Oct–Mar 10.00–17.00 Mon–Sat; Apr–Sep 10.00–17.00 Mon–Fri, 10.00–18.00 Sat; adult/7–25/under 6 €8/4/free) Refreshingly different in structure, and unforgettably evocative inside, the Jerusalem Chapel is a copy of the Holy Sepulchre in Jerusalem. The altarpiece is decorated with skulls and ladders and the small chapel at the back contains a replica of Christ's tomb, including a model of his corpse. In the old almshouses behind, a mini-museum charts the history of the Adornes family, who built the church and still run it – they're now on the 17th generation. You can make yourself a drink and snack in the lovely Scottish Lounge, using its honour system.

Kantcentrum (Lace Centre) [216 E3] (16 Balstraat; 050 33 00 72; w kantcentrum.eu; 09.30–17.00 Mon–Sat; adult/12–25/under 12 €6/5/free) Housed in the renovated lace school of the Sisters of the Immaculate Conception, this museum has an exhibition about the story of Bruges lace – once famous worldwide, but stymied by the arrival of machine-made lace in the 1840s – on the ground floor, which is also host to a shop. Upstairs catch demonstrations (14.00–17.00) or year-round lace-making workshops. If you want to buy some lace, at this point you're just metres from the superb 't Apostelientje (page 223).

Volkskundemuseum (Museum of Folk Life) [216 E3] (43 Balstraat; 050 44 87 43; 09.30–17.00 Tue–Sun; adult/18–25/under 18/Musea Brugge Card €6/5/free/free) Housed in a row of 17th-century almshouses, this charming series of rooms decked out in yesteryear décor recreates traditional scenes from the 19th and early 20th centuries. These include a classroom, a pharmacy, a hatter's workshop and, best of all, a confectioner's (fresh sweets are prepared here on the first and third Thursday afternoon of the month). Before leaving, duck into the museum pub, De Zwarte Kat, which is named after Bruges literary society 'Chat Noir', active around 1900. Ask the barman to set off the 1910 honky-tonk piano, and watch out for resident museum puss Aristide!

Guido Gezellemuseum [216 F3] (64 Rolweg; ☎ 050 44 87 43; ⏲ 09.30–12.30 & 13.30–17.00 Tue–Sun; adult/18–25/under 18/Musea Brugge Card €4/3/free/free) The life and works of celebrated poet-priest Guido Gezelle (1830–99) are documented in the house where he was born, his father Pieter serving as the gardener at the time. His poetry, exploring nature and nationalism, is predictably pious, but he also had a flair for sound and metaphor and is believed to have invented over 150,000 words to augment the Flemish vocabulary. A Jan Fabre work, *The Man Who Gives a Light*, adorns the romantic garden. Interestingly, Gezelle once ran the local Engels Klooster (see below), and also died there.

Koninklijke Hoofdgilde Sint-Sebastiaan (St Sebastian's Archers' Guild) [216 F3] (174 Carmersstraat; ☎ 050 33 16 26; w sebastiaansgilde.be; ⏲ Apr–Sep 10.00–noon Tue–Thu, 14.00–17.00 Sat; Oct–Mar 14.00–17.00 Tue–Thu & Sat; €3) Distinguishable by its Rapunzel-like tower, this archers' guild has existed for over 600 years – unprecedented in the world. King Charles II became a member during his banishment from England, and got the idea for his Grenadier Guards, who helped him to retake the throne. Ever since, all British sovereigns have been honorary members (including the Queen and, most recently, Prince Charles, who joined in 1980). Fascinating tours take in the grand **Koningszaal (King's Room)** lined with portraits of guild members, the covered shooting gallery and the garden, where members take aim at a 32m-high tower (they used to shoot at the sails of windmills on the brim of the hill). Reserve in advance – and ring the bell when you get there; the door isn't open.

Engels Klooster (English Convent) [216 E3] (85 Carmersstraat; ☎ 050 33 24 24; w the-english-convent.be; ⏲ 14.00–15.30 & 16.15–17.30 Mon–Thu & Sat; free) A hidden gem, this convent was founded by five English nuns in 1629; many English women had fled to Leuven during the persecutions in 16th-century England, including Thomas More's adopted granddaughter. As their numbers grew, they were given permission by the Bishop of Bruges, Henry van Susteren, to build a new church, completed in 1739. The resident nuns – numbering six, all in their eighties and following the rule of St Augustine – will happily show you around the Baroque church and, if you're lucky like me, break into song to demonstrate the fine acoustics. The chapel contains a portrait and relic (the cervical vertebra) of Thomas More.

Sint-Janshuismolen (St John's House Mill) [216 F3] (Kruisvest; ☎ 050 44 87 43; ⏲ Apr–Sep 09.30–12.30 & 13.30–17.00 Tue–Sun; adult/18–25/under 18/ Musea Brugge Card €4/3/free/free) Windmills have graced Bruges's ramparts since the city walls were built in the 13th century. Four remain, with St John's House Mill, dating from 1770, the only one still active and in its original location. In season the millers can show you around.

AROUND BRUGES

DAMME The beautiful village of Damme presents the perfect postcard of Flemish life: a small cobbled market square lined with ancient buildings, an atmospheric church and traditional restaurants all surrounded by waterways – it even has its own windmill, whose red sails turn gently in the coastal breeze. As an added bonus, it's also a book town – similar to Hay-on-Wye in the UK – with nine independent bookshops to browse through and a bi-monthly book market.

The village sprang up in the 12th century when the Het Zwin creek was created and Bruges dug a canal to meet it and gain access to the North Sea. Halfway between the two, Damme handled the import of everything from grain to herring. The village was razed in 1213, but locals – determined to start again – erected the Onze-Lieve-Vrouw-Hemelvaartkerk and established Sint-Janshospitaal (once housing a museum, its fate was unclear at the time of writing). The town hall was built in 1468 with the last of the money just as the Het Zwin canal was silting up. Damme was largely untouched by World War I, but fighting came very close in 1944 when the Battle of Mill was fought at Moerkerke, just 5km to the east.

Getting there and away

By boat During the Easter holidays, at weekends in April and Tuesday to Saturday from May to September, the *Lamme Goedzak* (w bootdamme-brugge.be; adult/3–11 €10.50/9, return €14.50/11.50) sails between Bruges and Damme. Departs Bruges (31 Noorwegse Kaai) at noon, 14.00, 16.00 & 18.00, and Damme (12 Damse Vaart-Zuid, opposite the windmill) at 11.00, 13.00, 15.00 & 17.00. Sailing time 35 minutes.

By bike If you're staying in Bruges, I highly recommend cycling to Damme. It's a simple 5km route along Noorweegse Kaai, and you cycle next to the canal through lovely sections of poplar-lined paths, then put your bike on the boat for the return leg.

By bus Bus 43 departs from Bruges railway station (16.33 & 17.33 Mon–Wed & Thu–Fri, 12.33 Wed) and from 't Zand (3 minutes later). The journey time is 12–30 minutes. From Damme, buses depart for Bruges from the main square (07.37 & 18.15 Mon–Wed & Thu–Fri, 13.12 Wed). From April to September you can combine a boat and bus ride to and from the *Lamme Goedzak* jetty. Otherwise, call the Belbus (059 56 52 56).

By car From Bruges follow signs for the N374 then take Damse Vaart-Zuid north (7km; 12mins). Damme is also around an hour's drive from Antwerp and Ghent.

Tourist information

Tourist information 3 Jabob van Maerlantstraat; 050 28 86 10; w visitdamme.be; 09.30–12.30 & 13.00–17.00 Mon–Fri, Sep–Easter hols open afternoon only at w/ends) Inside the Huyse de Grote Sterre, a 15th-century patrician house that belonged to the Spanish governor, this modern tourist information office can organise a guide (€75/2hrs) who can arrange for you to visit the windmill out of season. It houses the Uilenspiegelmuseum on the 2nd floor & has a permanent exhibition about Damme's creation, the Zwin landscape & forts. Also offers bike rental (€12/day or €7/½ day).

Where to eat and drink

Two local products to look out for here: Damse Mokke, a cheese similar to Camembert, and Uilenspiegel (8%) beer. You can find both at Tijl & Nele (page 234).

De Damse Poort 29 Kerkstraat; 050 35 32 75; w damsepoort.be; noon–14.30 & 18.00–21.00 Fri–Tue. 1900s house serving Flemish classics like *paling in 't groen* & *stoofvlees*. Also has a tea room for pancakes & ice creams (15.00–17.00) & a wonderful terrace in summer. €€€

Tante Marie 38 Kerkstraat; 050 35 45 03; w tantemarie.be; 10.00–18.00. Upmarket tea room/brasserie that makes its own jams & pastries. For lunch their speciality is *drie hartige gerechtjes*: a trio of small savoury dishes, usually inc their homemade croquettes. Decadent Sun b/fast until 11.00. €€€

Tijl & Nele 2 Jabob van Maerlantstraat; 050 35 71 92; **w** tijlennele-damme.be; 10.00–17.00, closed Fri Easter–Sep & Thu–Fri Oct–Easter. Low-key sandwich & gift shop run by Debbie & Bert, who also rent bikes for €12/day. €

Other practicalities

$ Bank There's an ATM concealed in a niche on the right-hand side of the town hall; look for a flight of stairs leading down from street level.

Shopping

Markets There is a general market on the Markt (08.00–noon Thu) & every 2nd Sun there's a book market in the town hall & on the Markt.

What to see and do

Stadhuis (Markt; only during exhibitions & book fairs) Built in 1464, the Gothic town hall is studded with six statues: Philip of Alsace; Joan and Margaret of Constantinople; Philip of Thiette; and Charles the Bold and his wife Margaret of York, who were married just around the corner at Huis St Jean d'Angély (13 Jacob van Maerlantstraat) in 1468. On the right flank of the building, two stones protrude from the wall: they were punishment stones which wrong-doing women, (men were given an alternative punishment) had to wear around their necks while walking around the marketplace; a public form of embarrassment similar to the stocks. A **statue of Jacob van Maerlant** – a Damme local who rose to become the greatest Flemish poet of the 13th century – stands outside.

Onze-Lieve-Vrouw-Hemelvaartkerk (Our Lady of the Assumption Church) (Kerkstraat; Apr–Sep 13.30–17.00; free) Bulky 14th-century church, made all the more impressive by the attached ruins of its nave, transept and spire – pulled down in 1725. You can climb the 43m-high tower (adult/under 12/under 5 €2/1/free) for great views, and inside is the tombstone of Jacob van Maerland, which, from 1300 to 1600, was believed to be the grave of Till Uilenspiegel (see below) until it was determined he was a fictional character. You can pay €15 to visit the church outside opening hours.

Uilenspiegelmuseum (3 Jabob van Maerlantstraat; 050 28 86 10; **w** visitdamme.be; 09.30–12.30 & 13.00–17.00 Mon–Fri, Sep–Easter hols open afternoon only at w/ends; €2.50) Till Eulenspiegel is a character from an ancient Germanic fable. The first written version of the tale was penned in 1500 by Hermann Bote, a resident of Damme, who portrayed Till as a villain who stood for everything society shouldn't be. However, this story was eclipsed by the version Charles de Coster wrote in 1867, which depicts Thyl Ulenspiegel – note the change in spelling – as a loveable rogue: a trickster who fights for freedom and has adventures with his girlfriend Nele and best friend Lamme Goedsak. The museum explores these different takes on the character and displays engravings, books, sculptures and paintings modelled on Till.

Schellemolen (Damse Vaart-West; Apr–Sep 09.30–12.30 & 13.00–18.00 Sat–Sun; free) Whether you arrive by boat, bike or car, this windmill catches your eye as soon as you enter Damme. It was built in 1867 on the site of an earlier wooden mill. Outside the usual opening hours, a guided visit (€19) can be arranged by the tourist office.

Terra Flamma (17 Jacob van Maerlantstraat; ⌚10.30–18.30 Mon–Tue & Thu–Sun, closed during school hols) This small pottery studio is owned by Bart and Marina Missiaen, who produce the ceramic bowls, mugs and vases themselves (they launched pottery courses in 2016). You can even see them at the wheel!

Cycling The area surrounding Damme is wonderful to explore by bike. There's a free map on the back of the tourist information leaflet that takes you past the tiny but typically Flemish villages of Hoeke and Oostkerke.

LISSEWEGE Just north of Bruges, Lissewege is a tiny conglomeration of whitewashed cottages nestled around an ancient Gothic church. It's one of Flanders' prettiest villages and home to a close-knit community of 2,400 inhabitants. However, this number can seem considerably greater during summer when groups of locals and tourists stop off for lunch during cycling tours of the surrounding polders, or potter about open-air exhibition *Statues in the White Village* (**w** beeldenroute.be), when over 100 artists create works strewing Lissewege's most picturesque spots. Visit at the beginning of September when the season is dying down and you'll be able to wander its cobbled streets in peace. I guarantee you'll start enviously eyeing up the *Te Koop* ('For sale') signs in some of the cottage windows.

Getting there and away

By car From Bruges take the N9 northwest, merge on to the N31 and follow it to Lissewege (11km; ⌚ 15mins).

By train Bruges (hourly; ⌚ 7–14mins).

Tourist information

Tourist information 5 Oude Pastoriestraat; 050 55 29 55 ; **w** lissewege.be; ⌚ May–Jun, public hols & last 2 w/ends Sep 14.00–17.30 Sat–Sun, Jul–mid-Sep 14.00–17.30. Informal information centre shared with the local police & town administration. In 1 of the back rooms they have 7 oil paintings depicting the village & surrounding polders; the venue also hosts the Saints' Museum (adult/under 12 €2/1) where you can see a sizeable collection of antique statues of patron saints.

Where to stay and eat

Lisdodde (3 rooms) 1 Oude Pastoriestraat; **m** 0476 97 51 40; **w** lisdodde.be. Lore Brouns & her daughter Eva run this fresh, modern B&B behind the church. It was planned as a retirement dream for Lore & her husband, but when he was sadly killed in a construction accident, Lore decided to go ahead anyway. She's done a great job: rooms (inc a stunning attic) are painted in calming shades & have wonderful views of the polder meadows out back. **€€€**

De Goedendag 2 Lisseweegs Vaartje; 050 54 53 35; **w** degoedendag.be; ⌚ noon–22.00. Pleasingly old-school restaurant (& very good hotel) serving authentic Flemish dishes & fresh fish. The generous array of set options include the weekly menu (amuse-bouche, starter, main, cheese or dessert for €38) & business lunch (€27), which are especially worth a look. **€€€€**

Ô d'Chatô 18 Stationstraat; **m** 0468 49 12 75; **w** odchato.be; ⌚ noon–20.00 Wed–Thu, noon–21.00 Fri–Sat, noon–18.00 Sun. Wine shop, bistro & art gallery all rolled into 1 – & the former railway station building has one of Lissewege's top terraces come summer too. **€€€**

Den Ouden Toren 3 Willem van Saeftingestraat; 050 54 40 86; ⌚ 10.00–02.00 Mon–Tue & Thu–Sat, 09.30–02.00 Sun. Characterful folk café voted the best in the wider Bruges region for its perennial buzz, low prices & extensive terrace. **€**

What to see and do

Onze-Lieve-Vrouw-Bezoekingkerk (Our Lady of Visitation) (Onder de Toren; ⌚ Jan–Apr 10.00–17.00, summer 10.00–18.00; free) The flat-topped tower of Our Lady church can be seen for miles around. She stands amid a collection of large marble tombstones, in the centre of the village, and dates from the 13th century. She's unusually big for such a small village because she was one of the first pit stops for pilgrims on their way to Santiago de Compostela in Spain. They came to see the miraculous statue of Our Lady of Visitation, and their offerings to Our Lady allowed the church to be extended several times. The current statue, carrying Jesus, is made of lime wood; the original was destroyed by Iconoclasts in 1586. Every first Sunday of May she's paraded in a Rococo chair from the church to Ter Doest barn (see below). Also on show are Jan Maes's *Adoration of St James in Compostela,* painted in 1665, and 13 panels spread across both sidewalls depicting Christ's crucifixion. Unusually, explanations of the artworks are given in English. It's also possible to climb the 264 steps of the **church tower** (m 0495 38 70 95; ⌚ last 2 w/ends in Jun, Jul & Aug, & first 2 w/ends in Sep 14.30–17.30, otherwise by appointment only; adult/child €2/0.50), which affords great views over the landscape.

Ter Doest (4 Ter Doeststraat; ⌚ 10.00–18.00; free) I highly recommend the 15-minute walk along country roads to visit this enormous Cistercian oak-beamed barn which, amazingly, dates from 1280. It is all that remains of a once-impressive abbey affiliated with Koksijde's Abdijmuseum Ten Duinen (page 252) and is a spectacular setting for concerts during Bruges's early music MA festival in August. The compound also now houses the memorable hotel and restaurant **Hof Ter Doest** (w terdoest.be).

Getting there and away On exiting the church, you'll notice the road forks: follow the road on the right, then take the tarmac-covered Ter Doeststraat, the first street on the left, and follow it for 1km. Turn right when you reach a small side chapel; you'll see the barn 300m away.

THE FLEMISH COAST

Most guidebooks give the Flemish coastline a bad write-up, though that's a tad lazy. In the 1900s, it was *the* holiday destination for northern Europe's rich and famous. King Leopold I regularly holidayed here with his wife and poured money into the development of Ostend. Belle-Époque mansions sprang up and the sweeping beaches were dotted with wooden beach huts. Today, the beach huts remain but the mansions have ceded to drab high-rise apartment blocks; only smaller towns like Knokke and De Haan have escaped the hands of contractors. However, the coast's heritage is only hidden, not lost. You can see the world's last shrimp fishermen trawling the shallows on horseback in Oostduinkerke, visit the medieval remains of Ten Duinenabdij and pay your respects at World War I sites. The area also boasts a jam-packed calendar of summer events, from music festivals to giant sand sculptures. Adinkerke even hosted the world's first Gull Screeching Impersonation Championships in 2019! Not forgetting the popular Beaufort triennial, when huge sculptures are dotted along the coast. Over 30 works from past editions have remained in situ, forming a de facto coastal art park; by late 2019, a dedicated cycle route leading you from one to the next will be on sale in the local tourist offices. The next triennial runs from March to September 2021.

One of the region's most tourist-friendly initiatives is the Kusttram: running the entire 67km length of the coast, it's the longest tram line in the world, beaches

MAD FOR MUSEUMS?

If you're planning on doing a bit of tourism along the Belgian coast, currently your best option is the Kustpas (w kustpas.be), which offers discounts of up to €250 (if you were really determined to take in every single sight) and covers the entire region. While we're only talking about a discount of a couple of euros per attraction in the main, it's hard to feel resentful given that the pass is completely free. Register on the website to download it. Some Flemish coast hotels also stock printed copies of the pass with a map of attractions, so keep an eye out.

blurring as you hop from one municipality to the next. However, it would be a shame to miss the scenic, dune-backed hikes on offer here – or the excellent promenade that runs the length of the coast and is tailormade for cyclists. As of 2016, the region's cycling network has been impressively rejigged; the tourist offices sell a selection of bike maps, including the indispensable *De Kust* (€8), or a compendium of four regional maps (€25). Unfortunately, you can't yet rent bikes from one town and drop them off in another, so you'll need to return to your starting point, or fork out the extra couple of euros to take your bike on the coast tram.

So, does the Flemish coastline rival the French Riviera? Perhaps not, but you won't be short of glamour in arty Knokke (see below), and in summer many towns launch beach bars where you can drink fancy cocktails with your feet in the sand. But linger a while and you'll find that the Flemish coast has its own charm: fabulous fish restaurants, endless watersports and the nostalgic air of how holidays used to be.

KNOKKE-HEIST Set foot in Belgium's very own Saint-Tropez and you'll soon be astonished by the amount of Mercedes and Porsches whizzing by. As indicated by the hyphen, Knokke and Heist (aka Heist-aan-Zee) are two separate towns spanning the beaches and villages of Duinbergen, Albertstrand and, east of Knokke, Het Zoute. Exclusive boutiques – most open on Sunday, unusually – sit alongside the most concentrated array of art galleries in Belgium outside Antwerp and Brussels: a dose of creativity that helps to offset the glitz and fake tans. The restaurants along this stretch serve the best seafood on the coast thanks to their proximity to Zeebrugge, with 20 Michelin stars within a 25km radius. And then there's the stunning Zwin Natuur Park reserve, which sits right up against the Dutch border and has a new visitor centre spotlighting the birds that pause here during their peregrinations.

Getting there and away On the coast tram (see box, page 238), alight at Heldenplein for the centre of Heist, Duinbergen for Albertstrand, and Station for Knokke. You can also reach Knokke-Heist (with stops in Heist, Duinbergen and Knokke) by train from Bruges (hourly; ⌚ 21mins).

Tourist information

Heist 22 Knokkestraat; 050 63 03 80; w myknokke-heist.be; ⌚ Easter–Oct school hols, plus Christmas & March school hols 09.00–12.30 & 13.30–17.30; all other periods same hours but w/end only.

Knokke 660 Zeedijk-Knokke; 050 63 03 80; w myknokke-heist.be; ⌚ 08.30–18.00. Knokke has the handier of 2 local offices: a large, modern affair where you can book hotel rooms, organise a guide (€60/2hrs) or buy maps: bike route *Riante Polder* (46km; €2) includes Damme (page 232) & the hamlet of Oostkerke, while hiking trail *Zwinwandelroute* (12km; €2) takes you through the Zwin's dunes & polders.

KUSTTRAM

De Lijn operates a cheap-as-chips (or should that be frites?) tram service that visits an epic 68 destinations along the entire 67km stretch of the North Sea coast. Trams run every 20 minutes during winter and every 10 minutes in summer. A day pass (adult/child €6/4) allows you unlimited hops on and off within a 24hr period; you can extend it to three, five or seven days (adult €12/17/24, child €8/12/16), or even bring your bike on board for €2 extra; a single journey costs €3. The first time you use the pass, you'll need to validate it on board using the automatic machines. Tickets can be bought on the tram, but are cheaper when purchased from De Lijn outlets.

Bike rental Cyclo Cars Kurt, 13 Zeewindstraat; 50 61 31 15; **w** rentabike.be. Very professional, well-stocked outfit with good rates for weekly rentals. Classic bike €12/½ day, €22/day, e-bike €24/40.

What to see and do An old primary school houses the **For Freedom Museum** (91–3 Ramskapellestraat; 050 68 71 30; **w** forfreedommuseum.be; Easter hols–mid-Nov 10.00–17.00 daily, mid-Nov–Easter 10.00–17.00 Sat–Sun; adult/Kustpas/7–12/under 7 €10/8.50/6/free inc audio guide; combi-ticket with Sincfala €11), a very engaging spot housing three private collections of World War II memorabilia, ranging from uniforms to unearthed aircraft remnants. There's more history on show at **Sincfala** (140 Pannenstraat; 050 53 07 30; **w** sincfala.be; 10.00–noon & 14.00–17.30; adult/Kustpas/6–26/under 6 €3.50/1.75/1/free), which covers the local fishing industry and life on the coast in the 19th century. However, the main attraction here is **Het Zwin Natuur Park** (8 Graaf Léon Lippensdreef; 050 60 70 86; **w** zwin.be; Jan–Feb 10.00–17.00 Sat–Sun, Mar & Oct–Dec 10.00–17.00 Wed–Sun, Apr–Jun & Sep 10.00–18.00 Tue–Sun, Jul–Aug 10.00–18.00; adult/Kustpas/6–17/under 6 €12/10/5/free), a 222ha wetland reserve attracting various species of birds on their way to winter nesting grounds. When you arrive at the new visitor centre you're given a bird ID card, and get to know your allocated species via interactive installations. Visit in April and you have a good chance of seeing stork chicks, while in December the herons descend. Also sharing the land are mouse-eared bats, foxes, Polish horses and highland ponies and cattle. There's a sheltered viewing centre overlooking the mud flats and salt marshes.

ZEEBRUGGE To this day, residents of Bruges still regard the port town of Zeebrugge (literally 'sea Brugge') as an adjunct to the city. The town is dominated by a huge international port, which handles one of Europe's largest fish markets as well as the delivery of cars and agricultural products; a new cruise terminal meanwhile receives 400,000 passengers annually – half German, and a quarter British travellers from Hull (page 34). Zeebrugge was the site of two major historical events. The first was the Zeebrugge Raid of 23 April 1918, when the British Navy sank two concrete-filled cruisers at the mouth of the port to prevent German U-boats – which presented a serious threat to Allied shipping – from leaving. The second was the 1987 Zeebrugge ferry disaster when the MS *Herald of Free Enterprise* capsized and 193 passengers drowned.

Getting there and away On the coast tram from Knokke (3 times an hour; 23mins) or Blankenberge (3 times an hour; 17mins), alight at Zeebrugge-Kerk or Zeebrugge-Strandwijk. During July, August and at weekends, direct trains from Bruges (every 2 hours; ⌚ 28mins) stop at Zeebrugge-Strandwijk; during the week they stop at Zeebrugge-dorp (hourly; ⌚ 19mins). If you come by car, unusually you can park right by the beach for free.

Tourist information

Tourist information Zeedijk Badengebouw; 050 44 46 46; w visitbruges.be/en/kust/zeebrugge; ⌚ Jul–Aug, Easter hols & Whit w/end 10.00–13.30 & 14.00–18.00. Outside these hours visit the Bruges office, page 215.

Where to stay and eat

Hotel Atlas (18 rooms) Brusselstraat 13–15; 050 54 54 19; w hotelatlas.be. Friendly family-run hotel just 20m from the beach, offering decent-sized, polished rooms, a good fresh continental b/fast buffet & free parking. **€€€**

Brasserie Nelson 24 Vismijnstraat; 050 54 59 54; w brasserienelson.be; ⌚ noon–15.00 & 18.00–22.00 Fri–Tue. First-rate fish restaurant down the road from the Seafront complex (see below) & just opposite the fish market – hence the fresh scampi, scallops, sole, prawns, etc. **€€€€**

Café 't Werftje Werfkaai 29; m 0497 55 30 10; w twerftje.be; ⌚ 07.15–midnight Mon & Thu–Sun (kitchen closes 21.00–22.00 in summer). Zeebrugge's oldest restaurant – in action since 1905 – & nicely renovated in 2015. The seafood is all good, but go for the award-winning shrimp croquettes. No reservations. **€€€€**

What to see and do Zeebrugge is keen to dispel its reputation as 'just an international port', but aside from the **beach** (tram stop: Strandwijk), which can lay claim to being the widest on the coast, and is never full even in high season, its attractions are rather low key. You can, however, enjoy a fine fishy meal, visit an old fishermen's pub or have a go at kitesurfing – Zeebrugge is a real mecca for pros, who drop into the Icarus Surfclub (w icarussurfclub.be). Slightly less bracing activities include 75-minute **boat tours** of the harbour, passing a naval base, mighty container ships and a giant lock (Tijdokstraat; 059 70 62 94; w havenrondvaarten.be; ⌚ Apr–mid-Oct 14.00 Sat–Sun, Jul–Aug 14.00 & 16.00, 1–20 Aug extra departure at 11.00; adult/3–11/2 & under €12.50/10.50/free); and **Seafront** (7 Vismijnstraat; 050 55 14 15; w seafront.be; ⌚ Sep–Jun 10.00–17.00, Jul–Aug 10.00–18.00; adult/under 12/Kustpas €13.50/9.50/€2 discount for up to 5 people), a converted fish market now hosting a maritime theme park with a lightship, Russian submarine and exhibits on the port's heritage. In mid-August, Zeebrugge plays hosts to festival WECANDANCE (page 55).

BLANKENBERGE Blankenberge is to Flanders what Blackpool is to northwest England. During summer, the coast's second-largest town is filled with noisy bars and restaurants and its 2km-long seafront crowded with people. It's not everyone's cup of tea, but it's a good place for kids thanks to a clutch of animal-themed attractions and the huge range of sports on offer.

Getting there and away On the coast tram alight at Blankenberge-Station or Blankenberge-Pier. You can also arrive by train from Bruges (hourly; ⌚ 13mins).

Tourist information

Tourist information 2 Hoogstraat; 050 63 66 20; w visit-blankenberge.be; ⌚ Oct–Mar 09.00–noon & 13.30–17.00 Mon–Sat; Apr–Jun & Sep 09.00–noon & 13.30–17.00; Jul–Aug 09.00–18.00. Can arrange many land- & water-based sports & sells walking maps of the Uitkerkse polder nature reserve.

What to see and do

Sea Life (116 Koning Albert I-laan; 050 42 43 00; **w** visitsealife.com/blankenberge; Jan–Mar & late-Oct–Dec 10.00–17.00; Apr–Jun 10.00–18.00; Jul–Aug 10.00–19.00; Sep–late-Oct 10.00–17.00 Mon–Fri, 10.00–18.00 Sat–Sun; adult/3–11/Kustpas €18.50/16/15) Kids will love the penguin corner, seals (they've rescued over 400) and turtles at Sea Life, which has the added boon of opening 364 days a year.

ZOO Serpentarium (146 Zeedijk; 050 42 31 62; **w** serpentarium.be; Jan–Mar & Oct 13.00–17.00 Mon–Fri, 10.00–17.00 Sat–Sun; Apr–Jun & Sep 10.00–17.30; Jul–Aug 10.00–18.30; Nov 10.00–17.00 Sat–Sun; Dec school hols 10.00–17.00; adult/Kustpas/under 18/under 18 with Kustpas/under 3 €12/10/8/6.80/free, combi-ticket with Sea Life €20.50) Children will also enjoy seeing the slithery creatures on show at ZOO Serpentarium.

Belgium Pier (261 Zeedijk; **w** belgiumpier.be) The highlight of the seafront and unique in the country, Blankenberge's pier has a long history. Built in 1894, it was set alight in World War I, before the current concrete pier you see was built in 1933. Stroll 365m down it and you'll find an Art Deco brasserie (**€€€**) with lovely views.

Huisje van Majutte (10 Breydelstraat; **m** 0486 06 17 80; **w** majutte.be; low season 14.00–18.00 Wed–Sat, 11.00–18.00 Sun, high season 11.00–23.00 Wed–Sat, 11.00–18.00 Sun; free but you must buy a snack or drink) This typical late 18th-century fisherman's cottage – stoop to enter – is uniquely well preserved, and the current owners, who took over in 2015, are incredibly passionate about sharing its history as well as that of the local fishing industry. After exploring the curious objects in the house, you can sample some regional produce – be it beer or delicious *slufferkoeken* (flat cakes with brown sugar once consumed by crew members).

Belle Époque Centre (24 Elizabethstraat; 050 636 640; **w** www.belleepoquecentrum.be; 14.00–17.00 Tue–Sun, Jul–Aug open until 18.00; adult/Kustpas/under 26 €4/2/2.50) This elegant museum, set in three Belle-Époque villas, revisits Blankenberge's heyday: the period from 1870 to 1914, when it became a key seaside resort, gaining attractions such as the casino and pier. They run regular free walks, and you can also hire a guide to explore themes such as Art Nouveau.

DE HAAN A complete contrast to Blankenberge, dune-bordered De Haan is one of the few coastal towns to have escaped high-rise development. There's not much to do beyond profiting from the excellent beach and promenade, but if you're looking for somewhere quiet to stay, De Haan is your place. You'll be following in famous footsteps: in 1933 Albert Einstein lived here for a short while. You'll find a statue of him on Normandiëlaan and his old abode, Villa Savoyarde, on de Shakespearelaan. Architecture fans can admire de Concessiewijk, a neighbourhood of white Anglo-Norman villas that are highly popular with German homeowners.

Getting there and away On the coast tram alight at De Haan-Aan Zee for the centre; De Haan is easily reached from Ostend (21mins) and Blankenberge (24mins).

Tourist information

Bike rental Fietsen André, 9 Leopold II-laan; 059 23 37 89; **w** fietsenandre.be; 09.00–17.30 Tue–Sat. Has an assortment of kids' bikes, tandems & electric bikes.

i De Haan Haan-Aan Zee tram stop; 059 24 21 35; w visitdehaan.be; Apr–Oct 09.30–noon & 13.30–17.00; Jul–Aug 09.30–18.00; Nov–Mar 09.30–noon & 13.30–16.00 Mon–Sat, 10.00–14.00 Sun

What to see and do Rent a bike, purchase the *Oude Dijken* cycling map (43km; €2) from the tourist information office and visit the old polder villages of Vlissegem and Klemskerke, roughly 2km and 7km inland from De Haan. The 157ha nature reserve **De Duinbossen**, to the east of De Haan, is a proper forest sprouting right next to the beach and lovely to explore. Buy the *Duinbossenwandelroute* hiking map (10.3km; €2) from the tourist office; starting and ending at De Haan tram station; it takes you through the forest and Concessiewijk. You walk along the beach until you reach Wenduine, where the **Spioenkop** is a striking red-roofed viewing point once used by customs officers, and offering lovely views. You can explore the dunes en route back.

OSTEND (OOSTENDE) The largest city on the Flemish coast began as a village on an island called Testerep but when the sea level dropped during the Middle Ages it became part of the mainland. By the 15th century this small fishing village was doing very well for itself, but it hit the jackpot in 1722 when local merchants established the Oostendse Compagnie, a fleet that traded with the East and West Indies. Despite the riches it brought, the company was closed in 1731 as part of the Treaty of Vienna, when the Austrian Netherlands joined forces with Britain against the French and Spanish. Ostend's reinvention as a seaside resort started not long after, and by 1850 it was the playground of the European aristocracy. The construction of the Brussels–Ostend railway line allowed for easier access to the town from 1838, and shortly afterwards a Dover–Ostend ferry route was established.

Today, the 'pearl' of the Flemish coastline has lost some of its shimmer, but it's a likeable, bustling place with first-class restaurants, snug bars and a great art museum, as well as an annual sand sculpture festival (page 54). Owing to its strategic location midway along the Belgian coast, it's also an ideal base from which to explore other coastal towns. Painter James Ensor lived here all his life and, fascinatingly, soul legend Marvin Gaye called the town home for a few months as well (see box, page 249).

Getting there and away

By car From Calais (95km; 1hr 12mins) or Dunkirk (56km; 50mins) follow the E40, then take exit 5 (direction: Gistel) and continue on the N33.

By ferry Currently the only ferry connection from Belgium to the UK is from Hull to Zeebrugge, 25km east of Ostend.

By train Brussels (twice an hour; 1hr 30mins), Bruges (3 times an hour, 14mins), Ghent (twice an hour; 40mins). The grand railway station is a 10-minute walk from the tourist information office and town.

By tram On the coast tram, get off at Marie-Joséplein or at the railway station, where you'll also find the De Lijn ticket office. De Haan (20mins), Knokke (1hr 5mins) and Nieuwpoort (38mins) are all close at hand.

Getting around

By bus The bus station is on the right-hand side as you exit the railway station. Bus 1 into town departs every 30 minutes from platform 1; a single journey costs €3.

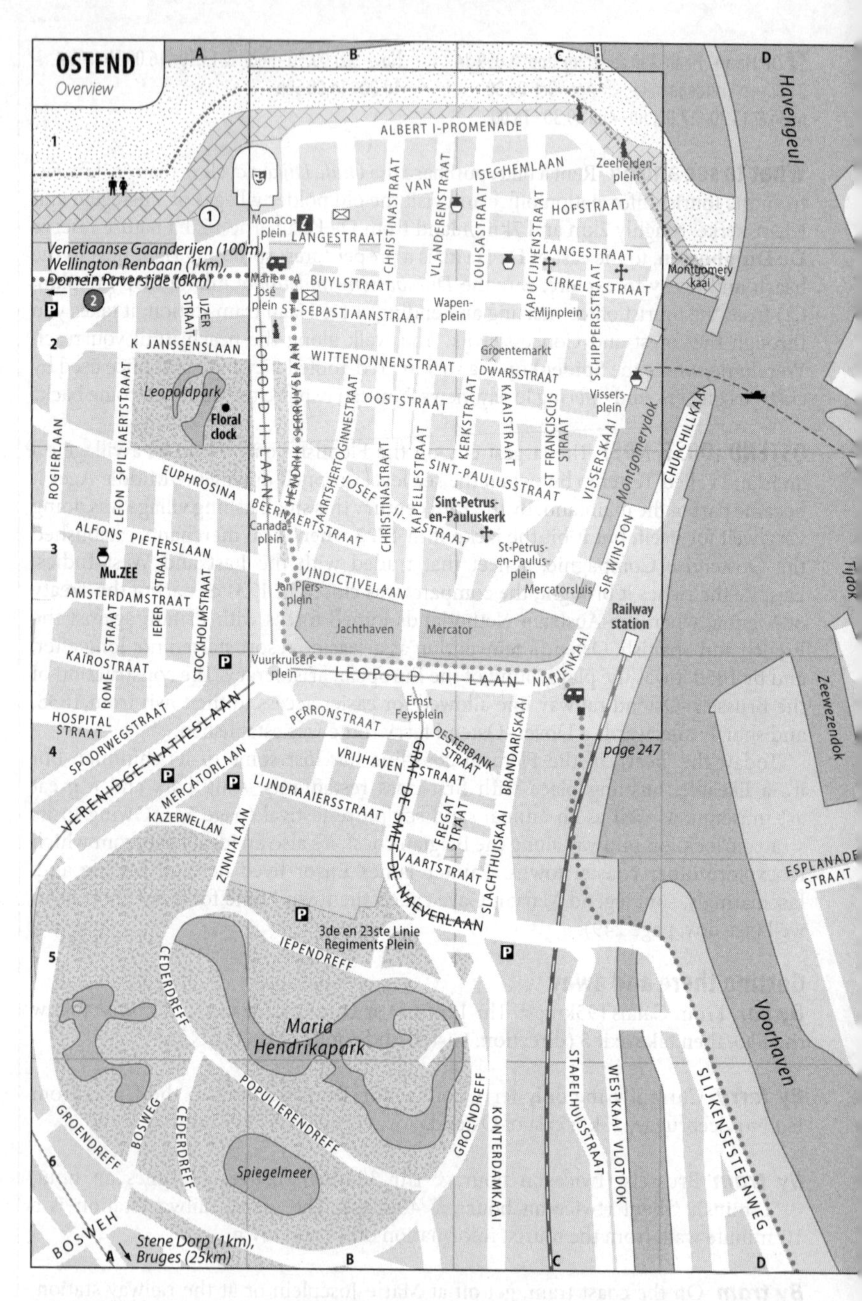

By ferry A free ferry service (w welkombijvloot.be; Oct–Mar 07.45–12.40 & 13.30–18.15, last departure west–east 17.55 & east–west 18.05; Apr–Sep more frequent departures – as late as midnight in high summer – check website) ferries passengers back and forth between the centre and Oosteroever (East Bank), home to sights like Fort Napoleon (page 248). Departs from Visserskaai next to the aquarium [247 D3] and deposits you at Maritiemplein in under 15 minutes.

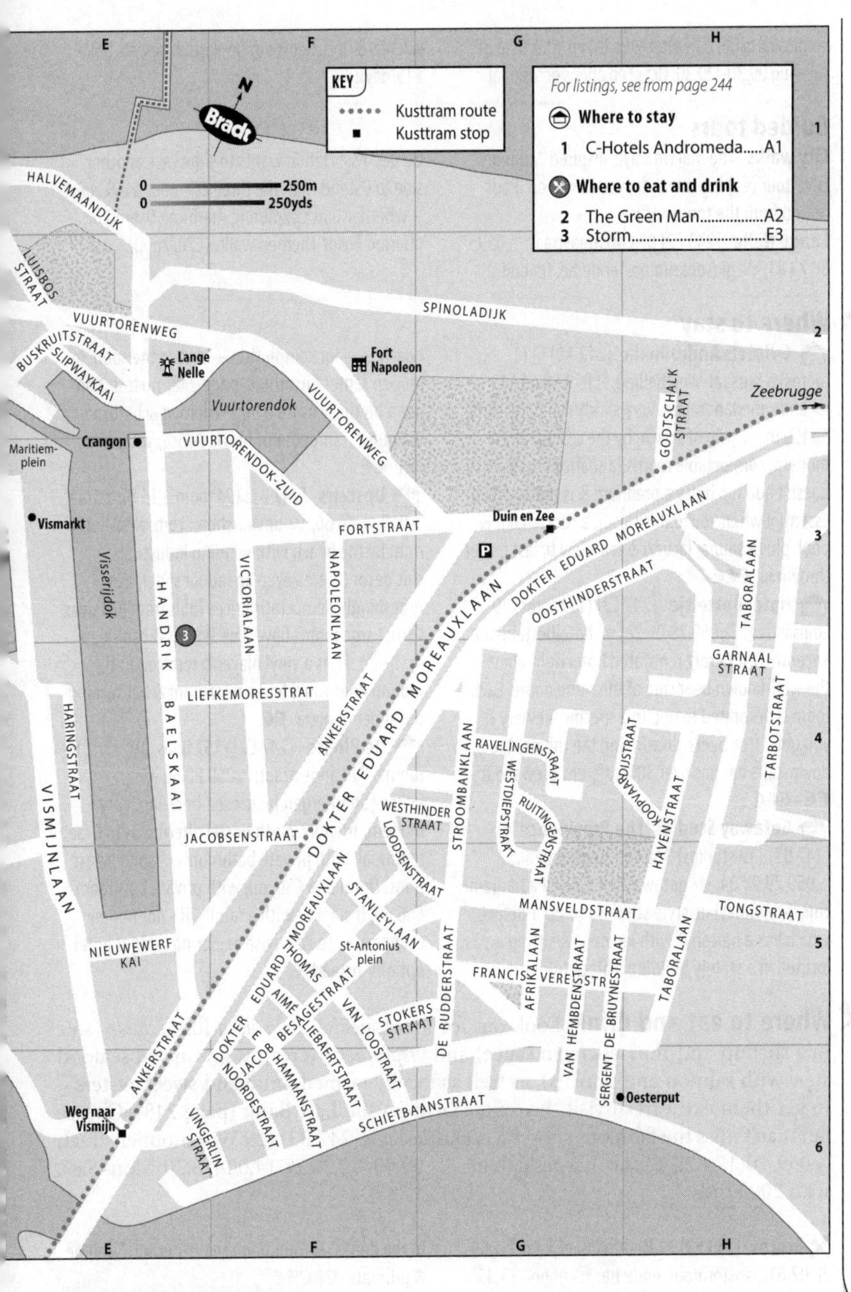

Tourist information

Tourist office [247 A2] 2 Monacoplein; 059 70 11 99; w visitoostende.be; Apr–Jun & Sep–mid-Nov 10.00–18.00; Jul–Aug 09.00–19.00; mid-Nov–Mar 10.00–17.30. This is a large office situated opposite the casino that sells tickets for De Lijn buses & trams, runs a Marvin Gaye tour (page 244) & can provide free maps of street artworks.

Bike rental [247 B1] Nico – Fun on Wheels, 44 Albert 1-Promenade, 059 23 34 81;

w nicokarts.be; ⏲ Easter–Jun & Sep 10.00–18.30; Jul–Aug 09.30–20.30; Oct–Feb opens occasional w/ends & hols. Rents out go-karts, bikes, etc (bike €15/day).

Guided tours

City walks The Marvin Gaye-inspired 'Midnight Love' tour (€5) is a must-do; you play it on iPods rented from the tourist office.

Lange Nelle [243 E2] 67 Christinastraat; ☎ 059 80 73 81; w gidsenkringoostende.be. Ostend Guides' Association wants to showcase another side to Ostend than the three Zs – *zon*, *zee* & *zand* – whether that's exploring maritime Ostend or offering Ensor-themed walks (€70/2hrs).

Where to stay

C-Hotels Andromeda [242 A1] (111 rooms) 5 Kursaal-Westhelling; ☎ 059 80 66 11; w andromedahotel.be. Very slickly run hotel right on the main strip of beach, by the casino. Offers modern, comfortable rooms (a seafront room doesn't add too hefty a premium & is pretty much essential when you're this close), a cocktail bar & pool, plus a sauna, jacuzzi & sea-view b/fast buffet thrown in. **€€€**

Hotel Botteltje [247 C2] (15 rooms) 19 Louisastraat; ☎ 059 70 09 28; w hotelbotteltje.be. Recently & superbly renovated hotel right above the well-known beer café of the same name. Each room is decorated to nod to a specific brewery & you get 2 free beers. Continuing the theme, the downstairs bar has over 300 different brews to try. **€€–€€€**

Getaway Studios 'The Providence' [247 B2] (49 studios) 36a Van Iseghemlaan; ☎ 059 79 99 04; w getaway.be. A bit of a bargain: chic, Scandinavian-style studios (go for a 'deluxe', which has a balcony) with kitchens & sitting areas located in a stately building a block from the beach, & – for completists – next to the soon-to-reopen James Ensorhuis (page 248) no less. Can get a bit noisy as it's a busy-ish road & bathrooms are quite cramped. But for this price, you can't lose. **€€**

Upstairs [247 B1] (94 rooms) 15 Hertstraat; ☎ 059 46 66 66; w upstairshotel.com. New hotel right by the beach with winning industrial-chic décor (there's even an indoor slide!) but refreshingly democratic prices (dbls from just over €50). Large rooms have 2 bedrooms & can sleep 4; The Roof has a vinyl player & terrace. On the ground floor you'll find a restaurant & bar turning out superior pizza. **€€**

De Ploate [247 C2] (157 beds, 49 rooms) 72 Langestraat; ☎ 059 80 52 97; w jeugdherbergen.be; closed Dec–Jan. Very modern, friendly youth hostel offering 2- to 6-bed rooms, all with private bathrooms. A solid b/fast is inc. Dorm bed €30, dbl with private bathroom €66.60. If staying with a family, it's not hugely economical, so I'd advise exploring budget hotel options instead. **€**

Where to eat and drink

Look out for local specialities *sole à l'ostendaise* (sole in a shrimp-and-mussel cream sauce) and *vispannetje* (creamy, gratinated seafood stew with salmon and prawns), as well as locally farmed, mild and sweet oysters – to get them extra fresh visit the oyster farm on the East Bank (page 248). Cheese fans can't miss the fabulous shop Kaas Haspeslagh [247 B3] (29 Wittenonnenstraat; ☎ 059 70 17 82; w kaas-haspeslagh.be; ⏲ 09.00–12.30 & 14.00–18.30 Mon–Sat), with 200 kinds.

Storm [243 E3] 21 Hendrik Baelskaai; ☎ 059 28 02 61; w stormoostende.be; ⏲ noon–13.45 & 19.00–20.45 Mon–Tue & Thu–Sat. The most exciting new fine dining spot in town & herald of the reinvention of the East Bank area. Chef Michiel Rabaey pays tribute to oft-overlooked species of North Sea fish (2-course lunch €39; 4- or 5-course dinner €59/69), cooks with seawater & picks herbs in the dunes surrounding the restaurant. Sublime & intimate. **€€€€€**

Bistro Mathilda [247 A3] 1 Leopold II-laan; ☎ 059 51 06 70; w bistromathilda.be; ⏲ noon–14.30 & 18.00–22.00 Wed–Sun, closed 3 wks mid-Feb, mid-Jun & mid-Nov. According to French newspaper *Le Monde*, this bistro fixture serves the best steak in the world. Quite a claim, but it's hard not to be impressed when the *rundvlees Blonde d'Aquitaine* is cooked at your table. €€€€–€€€€€

Brasserie du Parc [247 A2] 3 Marie-Joséplein; 059 51 13 05; w brasserieduparc.be; Jul–Aug 08.00–21.00 Tue–Sun, winter 08.00–21.00 Wed–Sun. Ostend's most beautiful restaurant – Art Deco heaven & incredibly well preserved. The menu does play 2nd fiddle to the décor, inevitably, but you can eat perfectly well or simply have a Cava or cake, while feeling like you're in another time. €€€

Wijnbistro diVino [247 C3] 2 Wittenonnenstraat; m 0473 87 12 97; w wijnbistrodivino.be; 18.00–22.00 Wed–Sun. Very convivial bistro on a foodie street. Regularly changing specials & a limited fixed menu spanning memorable tapas, pastas & Serrano ham; superb world wines to go with it. €€€

Kombuis [247 C1] 24 Van Iseghemlaan; 059 80 16 49; 11.00–15.00 & 18.00–23.00. Long hailed as the best place in town to eat mussels – piled high, served in white bowls & accompanied by frites – not much more to add. Usually crammed full & the tired, slightly odd interior is all part of the experience. €€–€€€

't Waterhuis [247 C5] 35 Vindictivelaan; 059 80 32 73; w waterhuisoostende.be; 11.00–22.00. Ostend's oldest restaurant was 1 of only a few places allowed to sell water to sailors & breweries until the town was connected to the potable water of the Bocq river in 1923. Today, locals head here for the excellent pasta & good selection of beers. €€–€€€

Passe-Vite [247 D3] 10 Nieuwstraat; 059 51 39 13; 09.00–18.00 Mon–Sat. Two-floor staple turning out healthy & affordable salads, pastas & soups. One of the best options for a swift & satisfying lunch not too far from the beach. €€

Sanseveria Bagelsalon [247 B3] 36 Wittenonnenstraat; 059 41 17 40; w sanseveria.be; 09.00–17.00 Mon & Wed–Sat, 10.00–17.00 Sun. Cutely decorated living room-style bagel parlour – a spin-off to the Bruges original. Irreproachable bagels spanning sweet b/fast options ('Oscar' is topped with speculaas paste) & more conventional but still delicious lunch options. Also serves quiches & salads. €

Lafayette Music Bar [247 A2] 12 Langestraat; m 0473 89 55 24; w lafayette.be; 14.00–02.00. You'll spot a portrait of Marvin Gaye on the wall of this glorious old-school bar – the master very much informs the vibe & musical selection of this joint, which attracts an interesting mix (many oldies & soul-music lovers) & results in questionable dancing but a good-time vibe.

The Green Man [242 A2] 64 Koningstraat; m 0476 30 55 01; w thegreenman.be; generally 18.00–23.00 Fri & 15.00–23.00 Sat but check website. Set in an 1898 house, this hugely characterful bar offers 1,000 single malt & blended whiskeys; the owner is a fount of knowledge, & previously launched a Belgian whiskey trail. Look at the website for details of special tasting evenings.

What to see and do

Mercator [247 A5] (Mercatordok; 049 51 43 35; w zeilschip-mercator.be; 10.00–17.00; adult/Kustpas/4–12/under 4 €5/4/3/free) Designed by Antarctic explorer Adrien de Gerlache and built in Scotland, the 78m Mercator – named after the 16th-century cartographer Gerardus Mercator – took to the seas in 1932. Designed mainly as a Belgian Navy training ship, in 1935 she sailed all the way to Easter Island to collect a Belgian research team, who brought back two colossal Moai statues as souvenirs; in her late 60s, she won the 1960 Oslo–Ostend tall ships' race. Now retired, she shimmers on Ostend docks after a recent restoration. It's great fun roaming the commander's cabin, wood-panelled officers' mess – smarter than the rest, as it was used to host dignitaries – and decks, dwarfed by her mighty mast.

Amandine [247 C5] (35 Vindictivelaan; 049 451 43 35; w zeilschip-mercator.be; Apr–Dec 10.00–17.00 Mon–Sun; Jan–Mar 10.00–17.00 Sat–Sun; adult/Kustpas/4–12/under 4 €5/4/3/free) From 1974 to 1995, this fishing trawler sailed 1,000 nautical miles between Ostend and the fishing grounds off southern Iceland

NEW YEAR'S DIVE

Balls of steel? Join the locals, many clad in wacky costumes, on the first Saturday of January for a bracing dip in the North Sea. On the day take the tram west to Koninginnelaan and head to the Stedelijk Zwembad (Municipal Swimming Pool) to sign in and collect a wristband that will give you access to the beach. Registrations start at 11.30, after which a Red Bull-organised party kicks off. There's a warm-up on the sand at 14.30, and then the starting gun goes off at 15.00, at which point everyone runs shrieking and squealing into the water. You may well end up on local TV! Warm up with a hot chocolate or a tot of gin afterwards; check the website (**w** nieuwjaarsduik.be) for details about overnight deals and warm-up packages.

to catch cod, sea bream, haddock and red mullet. The crew of eight were confined to the boat for months on end and worked in freezing conditions. However, Ostend's status as a major fishing port effectively ended overnight in 1995 when Iceland extended its protected-water boundaries, forcing trawlers like the *Amandine* out of good fishing grounds. They've done a great job bringing 'life on board' to, well, life: the smell of fish and the cries of gulls permeate the sorting bays in the hull, and the smell of bacon wafts from the galley kitchen.

Visserskaai [247 D4] Lined with restaurants and fish stalls, this stretch north of the railway station hosts the jetty for the free ferry to Ostend's East Bank and Fort Napoleon. Have a peek at the small but appealing Vistrap (Fish Market) [247 D3] (35 Visserskaai; ⌚ daily), where locals come to buy fresh North Sea shrimp and fish.

Seafront At the northern end of the quay, on Zeeheldenplein, you can't miss the Arne Quinze sculpture [247 D1] (Zeeheldenplein & Albert I Promenade). Installed in 2012, the same year the square was hugely expanded to guard against flooding, this series of ten orangey-red metal shapes is entitled 'Rock Strangers', and cost the city a cool €400,000. It looks like rubbish – literally – but is bizarrely appealing. You can go for a bracing walk along the breakwater that stretches out in front of you, or head west along the **Albert I Promenade**, built to link the centre and Wellington Renbaan (see below). The first major icon you'll spot, after a few minutes' walk, is the sweeping, modernist **casino** and adjoining **Kursaal** exhibition and concert centre [247 A1], dating from the 1950s. The building contains some stunning murals by Paul Delvaux, but irritatingly they can't be visited at present. If you're not the gambling type, a fun time to visit is during the Bal Rat Mort in March (page 52).

Venetiaanse Gaanderijen [242 A2] Keep heading west past hotels and restaurants and you'll come across these classical Venetian-style galleries, with their elegant portico and art exhibitions. Though they sit next to a rather sweet statue of King Baudoin (page 13), they were actually built by Leopold II, whose fingerprints are all over Ostend's grandest sites. Another 10-minute walk west, past the very imposing, very large Thermae Palace hotel, dating from 1933, will bring you to **Wellington Renbaan (Wellington Racetrack)** [242 A2] (10 Koningin Astridlaan; ☎ 059 80 60 55; **w** oostendekoerse.be; ⌚ races Jul–Aug every Mon). Built in 1883, and named after the Duke of Wellington, this track was regularly attended by

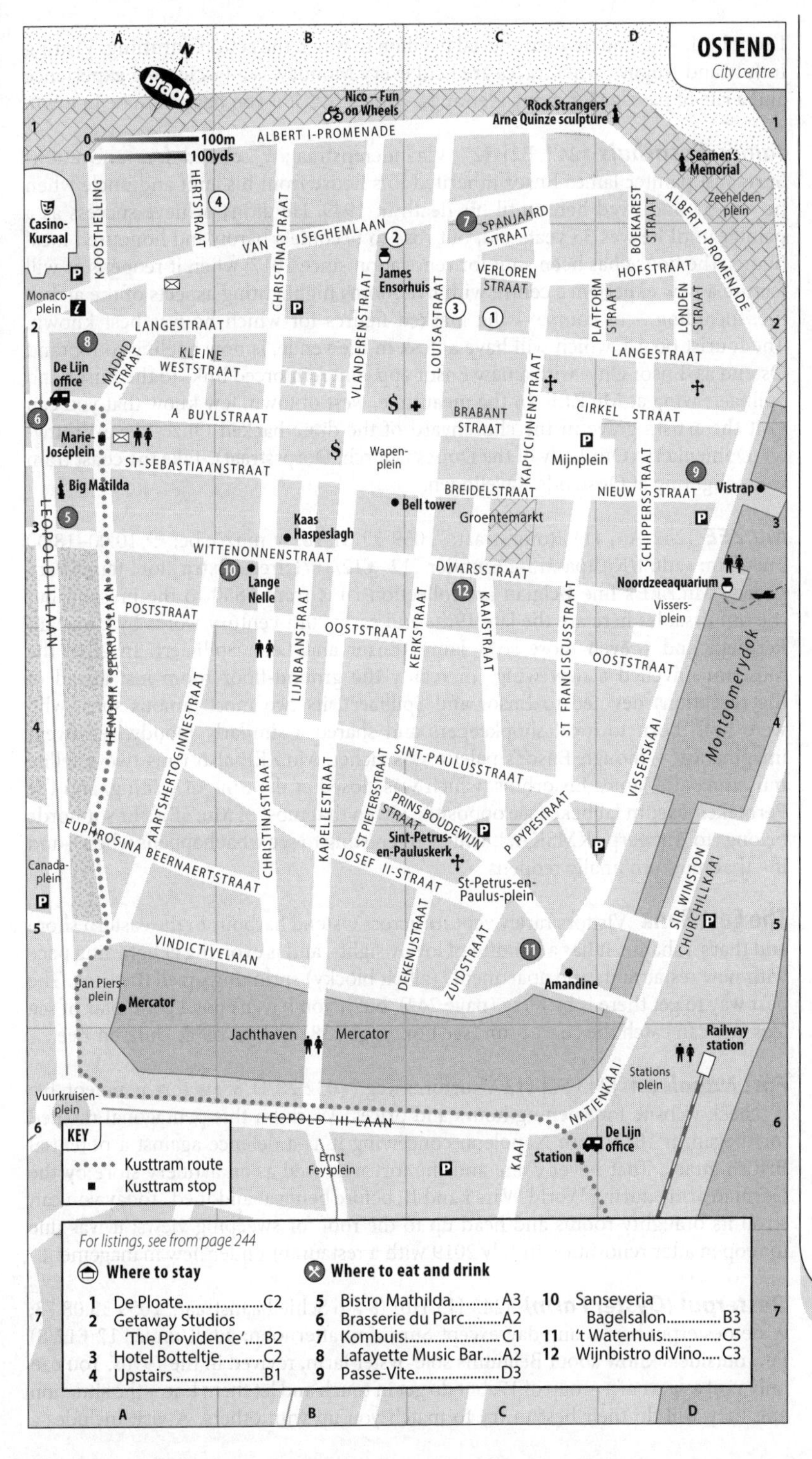
OSTEND
City centre
For listings, see from page 244
Where to stay
1 De Ploate C2
2 Getaway Studios 'The Providence' B2
3 Hotel Botteltje C2
4 Upstairs B1
Where to eat and drink
5 Bistro Mathilda A3
6 Brasserie du Parc A2
7 Kombuis C1
8 Lafayette Music Bar A2
9 Passe-Vite D3
10 Sanseveria Bagelsalon B3
11 't Waterhuis C5
12 Wijnbistro diVino C3
KEY
Kusttram route
Kusttram stop
Nico – Fun on Wheels
'Rock Strangers' Arne Quinze sculpture
Seamen's Memorial
Casino-Kursaal
James Ensorhuis
Big Matilda
Bell tower
Kaas Haspeslagh
Lange Nelle
Noordzeeaquarium
Sint-Petrus-en-Pauluskerk
Amandine
Mercator
Railway station
De Lijn office
Station
Vistrap
Albert I-Promenade
Van Iseghemlaan
Langestraat
Groentemarkt
Wapenplein
Mijnplein
Montgomerydok
Jachthaven
Leopold II-Laan
Leopold III-Laan
Vindictivelaan
Natienkaai
Sir Winston Churchillkaai
Visserskaai
Stationsplein
Ernst Feysplein
Vuurkruisenplein
Canadaplein
Monacoplein
Marie-Joséplein
Zeeheldenplein
Vissersplein
St-Petrus-en-Paulus-plein
Jan Piersplein

Leopold II, who had his own special pavilion to watch the action unfurling. Visiting in July and August, when races are held every Monday, is a fascinating experience and a rite of passage for many Flemings – don't miss it if you happen to be in town.

James Ensorhuis [247 B2] (27 Vlaanderenstraat; ⌚ closed for renovation) Surrealist painter James Ensor inherited this house from his aunt and uncle when he was 57 and lived here until his death in 1949. He didn't achieve success as a painter until he was 35 years old, but rose to become a baron and honoured local figure. The house has been shut for renovation since 2017; when it reopens, it will feature a new experience centre with five rooms highlighting aspects of the artist's life, including – of course – the masked figures for which he was best known. The tourist board, which will have a desk in the venue, is now angling to rebrand Ostend as 'Ensor City', with a new Ensor app, and reinforced links to the Ensor and Spilliaert wing at Mu.ZEE. In the meantime, west of town, few know that you can visit the artist's grave in the churchyard of the dune-backed Onze-Lieve-Vrouw-ter-Duinenkerk (Our Lady of the Dunes Church; Dorpsstraat). Take the coast tram west, alighting at Oostende Ravelingen.

Mu.ZEE [242 A3] (11 Romestraat; ☎ 059 50 81 18; **w** muzee.be; ⌚ 10.00–18.00 Tue–Sun; adult/Kustpas/13–26/under 12 €12/10/1/free, extra for temporary shows) Mu.ZEE's fine Belgian art collection runs from 1850 to the present, but the unmissables here are the late 19th- and early 20th-century works by Constant Permeke and – even more so – James Ensor and Léon Spilliaert. In 2016 the museum unveiled a new wing (in reality the ground-floor room just ahead of the reception) devoted to Ensor and Spilliaert, its two most famous sons, who were both born to local shopkeepers and shared a similarly moody, sea-swept imagination – though Ensor's palette was richer. Mu.ZEE also runs two satellite museums: the James Ensorhuis, which was closed at the time of writing, and the Permekemuseum Jabbeke (see opposite). Given that most of Mu.ZEE's Ensor horde belongs to Antwerp's KMSKA, it will be interesting to see what happens when – and if – that museum finally reopens.

The East Bank Visitors rarely venture across Ostend harbour to the eastern shore and that's a shame. It has a handful of lovely sights, and is evolving at lightning pace with new restaurants and apartments (albeit blocky) springing up all the time. The best way to get there is by ferry (page 242), but if you haven't got a good pair of sea legs you can catch the coast tram (see box, page 238) and get off at Duin en Zee.

Fort Napoleon [243 F2] (13 Vuurtorenweg; ☎ 032 26 31 85; **w** fort-napoleon.be; ⌚ check website for opening hours and prices) Work on this pentagonal moated fort began in 1811, with Napoleon conceiving it as a defence against a potential British attack. That never came and the fort was used as an artillery store by the German army during World Wars I and II, before being abandoned. Today you can stroll its draughty rooms and head up to the roof for sweeping views; it was due to reopen after renovation in July 2019 with a restaurant under new management.

Oesterput (Oyster Farm) [243 H5/H6] (84–6 Schietbaanstraat; ☎ 059 33 08 73; **w** de-oesterput.be; ⌚ any day except Sun/Mon afternoon; adult/under 12 €12/8) Few outsiders know about Belgium's sole oyster farm, revived in the 1990s. You can only visit as part of a group of 17, but do get in touch and let them know the situation and they will do their best to try to match you up with others. A visit includes a

SEXUAL HEALING

Did you know that soul legend Marvin Gaye penned his hit song 'Sexual Healing' while living in Ostend? It was December 1980 and Gaye's life and career had hit an all-time low: his relationship with Motown Records had soured after they'd rushed out an unedited album, he'd just split from his second wife Janis Hunter after only 18 months of marriage and he was in the throes of a serious drug addiction. He also owed the IRS millions in taxes. So when Ostend-born fan Freddy Cousaert invited him to come and stay at his house, Gaye accepted and turned up two weeks later on Valentine's Day 1981 with his son Bubby. Freddy and his wife organised an apartment for him and Gaye ended up staying for over a month. 'He loved the rain and the wind, the honesty of the sea,' recalled Freddy. A bronze statue of Marvin playing the piano graces the entrance of the casino and the tourist office runs a digital walking tour covering his favourite haunts.

presentation about the pearly beauties, a tour of the farm and the all-important taste test at the end with a lovely cold glass of wine. To get there, take the coast tram (direction: Knokke) and get off at Weg naar Vismijn, a 10- to 15-minute walk away.

***Shrimp fishing on the* Crangon** [243 E3] (2 Hendrik Baelskaai; **m** 0475 80 63 03; **w** crangon.be; departures 08.30 & 13.30; adult/under 12 €45/25) Fancy catching your own shrimp? Roll up your sleeves and board the *Crangon*, a traditional shrimp trawler named after the species' family name Crangonidae. On the 3½-hour round trip you'll be put to work sorting, washing and cooking the grey prawns, and at the end given a share of the haul as a reward.

Day trips

Permekemuseum Jabbeke [map, page 213] (341 Gistelsteenweg, 8490 Jabbeke; **t** 059 50 81 18; **w** muzee.be; ⏲ Apr–Sep 10.00–12.30 & 13.30–18.00 Tue–Sun; Oct–Mar 10.00–12.30 & 13.30–17.30 Tue–Sun; adult/13–26/under 13 €3/1/free) Located in the village of Jabbeke between Ostend and Bruges, this house was the home and studio of artist Constant Permeke. As per his wishes, it was opened as a museum in 1961 and with the aid of an iPad tour (you can also use your own smartphone) you can see over 100 of his dark and brooding paintings, as well as his sculptures – an art form he only started to explore in his 50s. To get there, take bus 54 from Ostend railway station and alight at Jabbeke Museum Permeke (⏲ 40mins).

Provinciedomein Raversyde ✷ [map, page 212] (636 Nieuwpoortsesteenweg; **t** 059 70 22 85; **w** raversijde.be; ⏲ mid-Mar–11 Nov 10.30–17.00 Mon–Fri, 10.30–18.00 Sat–Sun; combi-ticket adult/Kustpas/under 12 €10/8/free; Atlantikwall only €8/6/free, Anno 1465 only €6/5/free) This 50ha site, partially located in a protected dune area to the west of the city centre, comprises two main attractions, the foremost of which – Ostend's top tourist attraction, besides the beach – is the forbidding Atlantikwall, part of a series of coastal fortifications built by the Germans between 1942 and 1944. It ran from the French/Spanish border to the tip of Denmark and continued along Norway's coastline to northern Finland. Ostend's 2km stretch of superbly preserved bunkers, observation points and trenches is one of the most complete in Europe; in 2019 the Aachen Battery, a unique World War I German coastal battery, was due to be unveiled after restoration. Afterwards you can visit **Anno 1465**, the 'lost' medieval fishing village of Walraversijde, with its four reconstructed fishermen's dwellings. The lush 50ha park stretching east of both sites is great for a walk. To get there, take the coast tram west and get off at Domein Raversijde.

MIDDELKERKE AND WESTENDE Middelkerke and Westende are quiet resorts favoured by families. The former's wide beach attracts sandsurfers, horse riders and kite flyers.

Getting there and away On the coast tram alight at Middelkerke-Casino for Middelkerke centre, and Westende-Bad for Westende centre.

Tourist information

Middelkerke 1 Joseph Casselaan; 059 30 03 68; w middelkerke.be; Jun–mid-Sep 09.00–12.30 & 13.15–16.45; mid-Sep–May 09.00–12.30 & 13.15–16.45 Tue–Sat, 09.00–12.30 Sun

Westende 173 Henri Jasparlaan; 059 30 06 40, Jun–Sep 9.00–12.30 & 13.15–16.45; Oct–May 9.30–12.30 & 13.15–16.45 Sat & hols, 9.00–12.30 Sun

What to see and do Learn about the development of tourism on the coast at **Museum Kusthistories** (1 Joseph Casselaan; 059 30 03 68; w kusthistories.be; Jun–Sep & hols 09.00–12.30 & 13.15–16.45; Oct–May 09.00–12.30 & 13.15–16.45 Tue–Sat, 09.00–12.30 Sun; adult/Kustpas/under 12 €2/1/1), which shares a building with the Middelkerke tourist information centre. At Westende's tourist office you can see inside the Art Nouveau apartment **Villa Les Zéphyrs** (173 Henri Jasparlaan; 059 31 91 28; 11 Jun–15 Sep 09.00–12.30 & 13.15–16.45, 15 Sep–11 Jun same hours but Sat & hols only; adult/Kustpas/under 12 €2/1/1), designed by the famous Henri Van de Velde. Back in Middelkerke, comic-book lovers can spot several bronze statues of familiar characters along the sea dyke. The tourist office has maps of comic routes, including a selfie bench with Belgian female comic character Aunt Sidonia. Alternatively, take a stroll through **Warandeduinen** nature reserve, west of town. Towering over it is the unmissable **Warandetoren**, an old water tower that was reopened as a tourist attraction in 2018. Climb the corkscrew structure for a fantastic panoramic view of the coast, Middelkerke and Westende. Nearby there's a **sculpture park** (303 Zeedijk) housing several works from previous editions of the Beaufort art triennial, notably Belgian artist Wim Delvoye's *Caterpillar 5bis* (Zeedijk between Louis Logierlaan & Octave Van Rysselbergheplein). While the one you see is a copy (the original went to Ground Zero in New York), it's even more monumental than the real thing: a bizarre melding of a caterpillar tractor and a Gothic church.

NIEUWPOORT This elegant town played a critical role in World War I, when heroic locals intentionally inundated the surrounding polders to halt the German advance. Today it lays claim to the biggest yachting port in northern Europe, and is known for its well-heeled shops, brilliant fresh fish and unusually rich flora and fauna.

Getting there and away On the coast tram alight at Nieuwpoort-Stad for the historic centre and Nieuwpoort-Bad for the beach.

Tourist information

Main office 7 Marktplein; 058 22 44 44; w www.nieuwpoort.be; 09.00–noon & 13.30–16.30 Mon–Fri. Set in the town hall.

Beachside branch 11 Hendrikaplein; 058

23 39 23; w visit-nieuwpoort.be; ⌚ Apr–Jun 10.00–12.30 & 14.00–17.00; Jul–Aug 09.30–18.00; Sep–Mar 10.00–12.30 & 14.00–16.30. Pick up the free *Belevingsroute* map (11.8km), which takes you from Hendrikaplein over to the IJzermonding nature reserve, past the yacht marina to Westfront Nieuwpoort & the historic centre.

What to see and do Nieuwpoort revolves around its beach, where you can stroll along the beautiful sea dyke or just soak up the holiday atmosphere. Watch out for the golden Jan Fabre statue (13 Dienstweg Havengeul) of a kid sitting on a giant turtle. Officially titled *Searching for Utopia*, but known by all as 'The Turtle', it was produced during the first Beaufort triennial and was so popular that the city bought it.

Just to the east of where you stand, very unusually, the IJzer river flows directly into the North Sea, its fresh water mixing with salty seawater to create a uniquely rich biotope spanning mud flats, salt marshes and polders. Don't miss a stroll or bike ride through the **De IJzermonding Nature Reserve** (⌚ sunrise–sunset; free) located on the right bank; you might even spot seals early in the morning or at the end of the day. Reach it via a small ferry, *De Nieuwe Visie* (departs 5 Paul Orbanpromenade on the left bank and Oude Zeedijk on the right bank; ⌚ Apr–Sep 09.30–13.00 & 13.30–20.00 Sat–Sun, Oct–Mar 09.45–13.00 & 13.30–16.45 Sat–Sun, 15 Jun–15 Sep 09.30–13.00 & 13.30–20.00 daily; free).

At this point, set your compass south and stroll along the riverside promenade to the centre. A 45-minute walk (or swift coast tram ride) brings you to **De Ganzepoot**, a goose foot-shaped lock complex critical to water management in the Westhoek. Towering over it, you can't miss the 30m-wide, circular **monument to King Albert I** built in 1938, and reflecting his godly status among the military. At its foot is the visitor centre **Westfront Nieuwpoort** (2 Kustweg; ☎ 058 23 07 33; w westfrontnieuwpoort.be; ⌚ Feb–Jun & Sep–Dec 10.00–17.00 Tue–Sun, Jul–Aug 10.00–18.00 Tue–Sun; adult/Kustpas/7–25/under 7 €7/5.50/5/free), which recounts how, right at this spot, Karel Cogge (see box, page 258) and Hendrik Geeraert, among others, contrived to open the sluice gates and flood the area in order to halt the German advance during the Battle of Yser in World War I – and did it repeatedly to maintain optimum water levels throughout the war. You can see one of the handles that Geeraert used to raise the sluice of the mighty Noordvart, sort the myths from the facts, and take the lift up to the top of the monument for superb views of the site.

OOSTDUINKERKE Technically part of Koksijde, quaint and quiet Oostduinkerke is famous for its *paardenvissers* (horse fishermen), who trawl the shallows at low tide fishing for the grey North Sea shrimp used in dishes like *tomates-crevettes*.

Getting there and away The coast tram has four stops in Oostduinkerke; get off at Bad, which drops you in front of Astridplein, the central square facing the beach.

Tourist information

Tourist information 6 Astridplein; ☎ 058 51 13 89; ⌚ Easter, mid-Jun–mid-Sep & Ascension/Whitsun w/ends 10.00–noon & 13.30–17.00 Mon–Sat, 13.30–17.00 Sun, also open w/ends during hols, autumn & Christmas hols 10.00–noon & 13.30–16.00 Mon–Sat, 13.30–16.00 Sun

What to see and do A hundred years ago **horse fishermen** could be seen plying the shallows along the length of the Flemish coast, northern France, the Netherlands and the south of England. Today, despite numbers dwindling to three fishermen in living memory, and despite global warming bringing unwanted jellyfish and other catch close to the shore, Oostduinkerke is the only place in the world where the tradition lives on, hence UNESCO designating it as intangible cultural heritage in 2013. From spring to autumn, ruddy-cheeked, bearded fishermen (and, nowadays, one or two beardless fisherwomen) wearing yellow oilskins and sou'westers ride hefty Brabander horses up to their chests into the muddy North Sea. For 2 to 3 hours they wade up and down the beach pulling nets behind them and occasionally coming ashore to empty their catch into the wicker baskets slung either side of their saddles. Ask the local tourist office for the latest fishing demonstration times, or check w paardenvissers.be or f Paardenvissers; the dates marked with an asterisk end with shrimp-cooking on the sea dyke. You can wash off the juices by jumping in the 1950s-style outdoor heated pool here. Meanwhile, to find out more about the *paardenvissers*, head to **Navigo – Nationaal Visserijmuseum** (**National Fishery Museum**) (5 Pastoor Schmitzstraat; 058 51 24 68; w navigomuseum.be; Apr–Oct 10.00–18.00 Tue–Fri, 14.00–18.00 Sat–Sun; Nov–Mar 10.00–17.00 Tue–Fri, 14.00–17.00 Sat–Sun; adult/Kustpas/7–18/6 & under/1st Sun of month €7/5/2/free/free inc audio guide). The attached restaurant, **Estaminet de Peerdevisscher** (058 51 32 57; 10.00–20.00 Tue–Sun; €€–€€€), is run by horse fisherman Johan Casier and his wife and is set in an old fisherman's house for added authenticity. Another event to look out for is the **Garnaalfeesten** (**Shrimp Parade**), held on the last weekend of June.

KOKSIJDE AND SINT-IDESBALD These two family-orientated towns have two of the best museums on the coast, bar Ostend: the Abdijmuseum Ten Duinen and the former studio of artist Paul Delvaux, famous for his melancholy paintings of nudes. For a slap-up fish dinner in Koksijde, I highly recommend a visit to the chic **Julia Fish and Oyster Bar** (2 A Vanhouttelaan; 058 62 66 65; w julia-baaldje.be; noon–14.00 & 18.00–21.00 Thu–Mon; €€€€), run by the same team as the local fishmonger Mare Nostrum, which has been in business since 1919 and is now run by the fourth generation of a family of female fishmongers. The seafood is acclaimed by many as among the best on the coast, and the room is a lovely spot to devour it in.

Getting there and away On the coast tram alight at Koksijde-Bad for the centre; there's only one stop for Sint-Idesbald.

Tourist information

Koksijde 303 Zeelaan; 058 51 29 10; w visitkoksijde.be, Apr–Sep 09.00–noon & 13.30–17.30; Oct–Mar 09.00–noon & 13.30–16.30; closed year-round Sun morning

Sint-Idesbald 26a Zeedijk; 058 51 39 99; Easter, mid-Jun–mid-Sep & Ascension/Whitsun w/ends 10.00–noon & 13.30–17.00 Mon–Sat & 13.30–17.00 Sun; also open w/ends during hols, autumn & Christmas hols 10.00–noon & 13.30–16.00 Mon–Sat & 13.30–16.00

What to see and do In the last few years, harbour **seals** have returned to Koksijde and when the tide is high you can often see them basking on the stone barriers which point into the sea on the stretch of beach opposite Ster der Zee tram stop. Don't get too close. Koksijde is also home to the medieval **Abdijmuseum Ten Duinen** (**Ten Duinen Abbey Museum**) (2 Koninklijke Prinslaan; 058 53 39 50; w tenduinen.be; Apr–Oct 10.00–18.00 Tue–Fri, 14.00–18.00 Sat–Sun; Nov–Mar 10.00–17.00 Tue–Fri, 14.00–17.00 Sat–Sun; museum & abbey site: adult/Kustpas/7–18/under 7/1st Sun of month €7/5/2/free/free; tram stop: Koksijde-Ster der Zee), a fascinating archaeological site and museum built around the remains of an abbey founded in 1138 by a Cistercian hermit known as Ligerius. Also part of the complex, and a 2-minute walk south, is **Zuid-Abdijmolen** (van Buggenhoutlaan; 058 53 39 50; Apr–Sep 10.30–noon & 15.00–17.00 Mon–Fri, 10.30–noon Sat; adult/child €2/1, pay miller in cash), a working grain mill once owned by the Abbey of the Dunes and, incredibly, one of only eight of its kind found worldwide. Patrick Geryl – the only full-time miller in Belgium – is happy to lead you around.

To the east of Koksijde are the **Schipgatduinen** and **Doornpanne nature reserves**, the latter the site of **Hoge Blekker**, Belgium's highest sand dune at 33m. In **Sint-Idesbald** you can visit the studio of Surrealist painter **Paul Delvaux** (42 av Paul Delvauxlaan; 058 52 12 29; w delvauxmuseum.com; Mar–Sep 10.30–17.30 Tue–Sun, Oct–1st wk Jan 10.30–17.30 Thu–Sun; adult/Kustpas/under 7 €10/8/free), which hosts the largest collection of his hypnotic, erotic works worldwide.

DE PANNE Right up against the French border – many locals speak the lingo – De Panne has the widest beach on the coast, and you'll likely spot sand yachts whipping along it: the town is a big hub for the sport. It also has a pretty collection of early 20th-century holiday mansions and extensive sand dunes.

Getting there and away On the coast tram alight at De Panne-Kerk for the centre, or De Panne-Centrum for the beach. By train from Veurne (hourly; 7mins).

Tourist information

Tourist information 21 Zeelaan; 058 42 18 18; w toerisme.depanne.be; Sep–Easter 09.00–noon & 13.00–17.00 Mon–Sat, 10.00–12.30 Sun; Easter–Jun 09.00–noon & 13.00–17.00 Mon–Sat, 10.00–noon & 14.00–17.00 Sun; Jul–Aug 09.00–18.00 Mon–Sat. Tucked away in the town hall next to the local police office. Can organise accommodation & guided tours across the Westhoek & Oosthoek nature reserves. Sells the *Westhoekwandelroute* hiking map (10.4km; €2), dedicated to the latter. In Jul & Aug there's an extra info point on the beach.

Where to stay and eat

Esprit De Mer (3 rooms) 10 Visserslaan; 058 41 46 56; w espritdemer.be. Hosts Nathalie & Nico searched for a long time before striking upon their dream property, a former doctor's house in the genteel, protected Dumontwijk (see below). Rooms are stylish & spacious; Brise-Lames is the most romantic, under the eaves. €€€

Hostellerie Le Fox 2 Walckierstraat; 058 41 28 55; w hotelfox.org; noon–14.00 Mon, noon–14.00 & 18.00–21.00 Thu–Sun. Le Fox is pretty much in a league of its own as far as De Panne goes, having an impressive 2 stars from the Michelin men. Tasting menu or à la carte & seafood-centric. Don't wear shorts! They offer a €59 lunchtime tasting menu Thu–Sat & Mon. Also has a few smart rooms. €€€€

La Coupole 9 Nieuwpoortlaan; 058 41 54 54; w www.la-coupole.be. Stalwart, rather elegant, restaurant with a lovely terrace. Chef Jean-Paul Bonnez comes from a family of fishermen, so you can expect superior lobster & fish specials alongside a short but decent list of white wines. €€€

What to see and do In town have a wander around the **Dumontwijk** (**Dumont Quarter**), an area of streets bordered by Zeelaan, Duinkerkelaan and Witteberglaan that contains an array of intriguing English cottage-style houses conceived around 1900 by architect André Dumont. Back then, De Panne was little more than dunes, its metamorphosis into a resort having been stymied by a local landowner (he would have shuddered at the seafront blocks now). It's well worth arranging a guided tour through the tourist office; alternatively, they have a map of the highlights. While you're there, climb up to **Kykhill park,** an observation platform built on the site of Dumont's old Villa Kykhill, where fishermen's wives once looked for their husbands returning from fishing trips to Iceland. There are also attractive Art Deco properties scattered about.

Then explore the dune-rich 340ha **Westhoek** or 60ha **Oosthoek nature reserves**, home to an array of flora and fauna, including foxes, plovers, larks, nightingales and the short-eared owl, to name a few. You can book a guide through the tourist office or at **Domein Duinpanne** (2 Olmendreef; 058 42 21 51; 10.00–17.00 Tue–Sun, & Mon during school hols; free), a refurbished visitor centre with permanent and temporary shows about the sea, beach and dunes, as well as a café.

Just 2½km inland, in the village of Adinkerke, is **Plopsaland** (68 De Pannelaan, 8660 Adinkerke; 058 42 02 02; w plopsalanddepanne.be; Apr–Aug daily, closed Jan–Mar except hols, check website for other times; adult/Kustpas/child 85cm–1m/child under 85cm €36.99/31.50/12.50/free), a kids' theme park which centres around the world of TV gnome Plop and his friends – it's hugely popular with Flemish children. The Plopsa empire is growing – they also have a neighbouring water park, **Plopsaqua**, and were building a hotel at the time of writing. De Panne hosts festivals including **De Driedaagse Brugge-De Panne**, a three-day road cycling race in late March, and **Beach Endurance**, a mountain-bike race in November. Being so close to the border, if you fancy a foray into France, buy the *Cobergher* (47km; €2) cycle map from the tourist office; it starts from De Panne railway station and travels via Adinkerke and across the French border.

VEURNE

Just 6km from the French border and the North Sea coastline, Veurne – or Furnes as it's known in French – retains an ancient charm that Flanders' other coastal towns have lost. Established in the 9th century as part of a chain of fortified towns built to defend locals from pillaging Vikings, it benefited for a short while from the Hanseatic League, but when relations with London soured, the town entered a dark period and became embroiled in numerous wars. It also suffered under the thumb of the Spanish Inquisition, which held its court in the Landshuis. Peace and prosperity returned in the late 16th century, when Infanta Isabella and her husband Albert Archduke of Austria assumed control of the Spanish Netherlands. Many of the town's finest buildings date from this period. Indeed, Veurne boasts one of Flanders' most authentic market squares: it was situated 9km from the front line during World War I and, as a result, many of its 16th-century buildings avoided destruction. It's a lovely place to wander around and there are ample local specialities to tuck into too. The surrounding countryside, known as the Westhoek, is ideal cycling territory.

GETTING THERE AND AWAY

By car From Ypres follow the N8 northwest (32km; 35mins). From Ostend take the N33 south, merge on to the E40 (direction: Veurne/Nieuwpoort/Diksmuide) and take exit 1a, then follow Vaartstraat into town (34km; 27mins). From Bruges take the R30 then follow signs for the E40 and follow it west, taking exit 1a (55km; 40mins).

By train Bruges via Lichtervelde (hourly; 1hr); Ghent (hourly; 1hr); De Panne (hourly; 7mins).

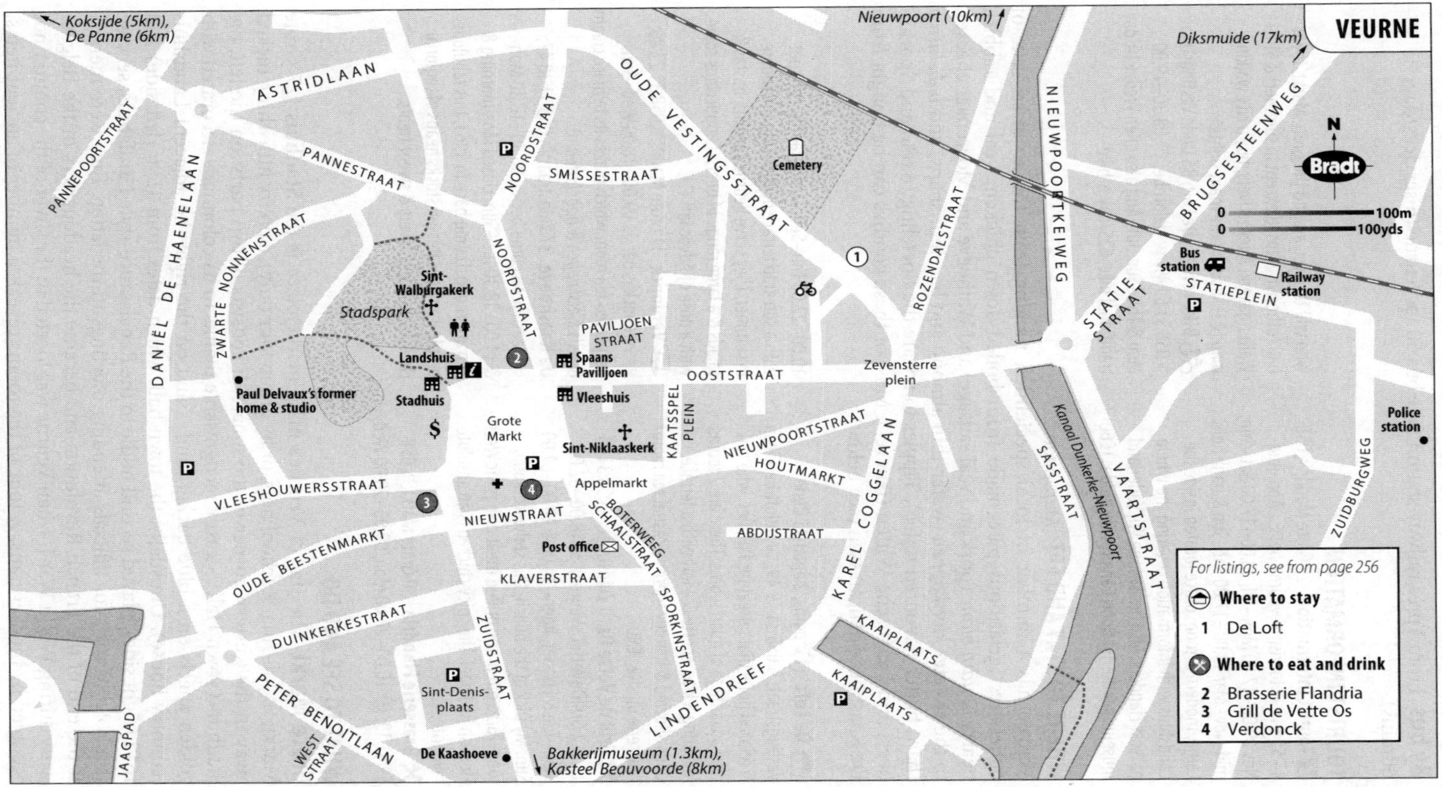

VEURNE

For listings, see from page 256

Where to stay

1 De Loft

Where to eat and drink

2 Brasserie Flandria
3 Grill de Vette Os
4 Verdonck

Koksijde (5km), De Panne (6km)
Nieuwpoort (10km)
Diksmuide (17km)
Bakkerijmuseum (1.3km), Kasteel Beauvoorde (8km)
0 100m
0 100yds
Bradt
N
ASTRIDLAAN
PANNEPOORTSTRAAT
PANNESTRAAT
NOORDSTRAAT
SMISSESTRAAT
OUDE VESTINGSSTRAAT
Cemetery
NIEUWPOORTKEIWEG
BRUGSESTEENWEG
DANIËL DE HAENELAAN
ZWARTE NONNENSTRAAT
Sint-Walburgakerk
Stadspark
Landshuis
Stadhuis
Paul Delvaux's former home & studio
PAVILJOEN STRAAT
Spaans Paviljoen
Vleeshuis
OOSTSTRAAT
Zevensterre plein
ROZENDALSTRAAT
STATIE STRAAT
STATIEPLEIN
Bus station
Railway station
Police station
Grote Markt
Sint-Niklaaskerk
KAATSSPEL PLEIN
NIEUWPOORTSTRAAT
HOUTMARKT
Appelmarkt
VLEESHOUWERSSTRAAT
NIEUWSTRAAT
BOTERWEEG
SCHAALSTRAAT
Post office
OUDE BEESTENMARKT
KLAVERSTRAAT
ABDIJSTRAAT
KAREL COGGELAAN
Kanaal Dunkerke-Nieuwpoort
SASSTRAAT
VAARTSTRAAT
ZUIDBURGWEG
DUINKERKESTRAAT
ZUIDSTRAAT
SPORKINSTRAAT
KAAIPLAATS
KAAIPLAATS
LINDENDREEF
Sint-Denis-plaats
PETER BENOITLAAN
WEST STRAAT
JAAGPAD
De Kaashoeve

By bus From Ypres railway station take bus 50 to Veurne (6 services/day; 45–60mins).

TOURIST INFORMATION

Tourist information 29 Grote Markt; 058 33 55 31; w toerisme-veurne.be; Apr–mid-Nov 09.00–17.00 Mon–Fri, 10.00–17.00 Sat–Sun; mid-Nov–Mar 13.00–17.00 Sat–Sun & bank hols. Large, modern 2-room office located inside the Landshuis with information covering the whole of West Flanders. Also houses the Vrij Vaderland museum on the 1st floor. Can provide guides (€60) who will take you around the Grote Markt, town hall (otherwise closed except in summer) & Sint-Walburgakerk. Alternatively, buy a city walking map (€2) showing the main sights.

Bike rental De Loft, 36 Oude Vestingstraat; 058 31 59 49; w deloft.be; 08.30–19.00 Mon & Thu–Sun; Jul–Aug also open Wed; €10/day traditional bike, €25/day e-bike

WHERE TO STAY AND EAT *Map, page 255*

Veurne has a number of local specialities, ranging from the acquired taste of *potjesvlees* (gelatinous pâté made from boiled-down chicken, veal and rabbit), hearty *boudin blanc* (pork and veal sausage) and Walhoeve and Moerenaar cheeses, to the sweeter *kletskoppen* (wafer-thin almond and hazelnut snaps) and *babelutten* (hard butter-flavoured toffee). Tipples to try are the Boeteling (6.6%) and Sporkin beers and Veurnsche Witten (jenever). Most of these goodies can be bought from De Kaashoeve delicatessen (see below).

De Loft (13 rooms, 2 apts) 36 Oude Vestingstraat; 058 31 59 49; w deloft.be. Clean & relaxed hotel that's great for families, who can take advantage of quad rooms. There are 2 rooms featuring a kitchenette & a loft with a terrace. Dogs allowed & handily there's a casual tea room/brasserie on site. **€€**

Grill de Vette Os 1 Zuidstraat; 058 31 31 10; GrillDeVetteOsVeurne; 18.00–02.00 Mon–Tue & Fri–Sat, noon–14.00 & 18.00–02.00 Sun. My pick of the bunch, this stalwart dining room turns out prime grilled meat dishes inc West Flemish Red beef. The spicy chicken is an absolute favourite. **€€€**

Brasserie Flandria 30 Grote Markt; 058 59 41 19; 10.00–20.00 Mon, 09.00–20.00 Wed, 10.00–22.00 Thu–Sun. Lovely family-run spot with a sun-trap terrace overlooking the square in summer. They serve Veurne specials, pastas & salads & a large range of beers. Cappuccinos come with a dose of Advocaat! **€€**

Verdonck 11 Grote Markt; 058 31 22 86; w verdonckijs.be; 09.00–18.00 Wed–Sun. Respected tea room which makes its own ice cream & sells *kletskoppen* & *babelutten*. **€**

De Kaashoeve 37 Zuidstraat; 058 31 18 47; w kaashoeveveurne.be; 08.30–12.30 Mon & 14.00–18.30 Tue–Sun, closed Mon morning & Sun afternoon. Dating back to 1963, this fabulous couple-run delicatessen stocks heaps of regional cheeses, beers, jenevers & sweet treats.

WHAT TO SEE AND DO

Grote Markt The star of Veurne's main marketplace is the **Stadhuis** (27 Grote Markt; Jul–Aug & school hols, or by group tour only), a pretty little thing tucked away in the western corner of the square. It consists of two parts: on the left, the Stadhuis (Town Hall) – easily recognisable thanks to its colonnade decorated with golden angels on a blue background – and on the right the adjacent Landshuis (country house). Unusually, the town hall, which dates from 1596 (left side) and 1612 (right side), played second fiddle to the Renaissance-style **Landshuis**, serving as a hotel of sorts for officials attending meetings in the latter. They were merged at the end of the French Revolution and became the headquarters of the Belgian army during World War I, when Veurne was located in the sliver of the country not occupied by the Germans. A tour of the rooms reveals a number of ancient items, including **Le Salon Bleu (Blue Room)**, where Austrian Emperor Joseph II slept in 1781, and the elaborate **Albert Hall** which King Albert I used as an office during World War I and where he met Britain's King George V. Above the fireplace hang portraits of Archduke Albert and Archduchess Isabella, and below is a portrait of local hero Karel Cogge (see box, page 258).

Over in the Landshuis, home to the tourist office, upstairs you'll find the discovery centre **Vrij Vaderland (Free Fatherland)** (🕘 as per tourist office; adult/7–18/under 7 €4/2/free), which may be rejigged during the lifetime of this guide. Rather than focusing on major World War I battles, it highlights Veurne's unusual position as part of the so-called unoccupied 'Belgian Sector', and the nerve centre of operations for Albert I, closely plotting the country's course in an attempt to spare Belgian troops from the huge casualty numbers of the Allies. There are interesting exhibits on health care: Marie Curie visiting Veurne with her X-ray machine, the mass influx of refugees and, in the former **Oude Zittingzaal (Court Room)**, the last ever beheading in Belgium, which took place in Veurne on 26 March 1918. Just off the Court Room, don't miss the 17th-century **chapel**, where the condemned could offer a last prayer before their execution; it's perhaps a fitting location for two paintings by Paul Delvaux, who lived the last 23 years of his life in Veurne at 19 Zwarte Nonnenstraat.

On the other side of the Grote Markt, flanking the entrance to Oostraat, are the **Vleeshuis (Butcher's Hall**, on the right) and the red-windowed **Spaans Pavilljoen** (on the left). The latter was built as the original town hall in 1530, but takes its name from when Spanish officers used it as their quarters in the 17th century.

Sint-Walburgakerk (St Walburga Church) (Sint-Walburgastraat, behind the Landshuis; 🕘 Apr–15 Nov 09.00–17.30; 16 Nov–Mar 09.00–17.00 Wed & Sat–Sun; free) This buttressed red-brick church dates mainly from the 14th century, but had its transept added in 1907. Numerous works of art are on show, but its pride and joy are the skull of St Walburga and a relic of the True Cross brought back from Jerusalem during the Crusades.

Sint-Niklaaskerk (St Nicholas's Church) (Appelmarkt; 🕘 08.30–18.30; free) Bulky 14th-century church plundered by French soldiers during the Revolution. They stole the medieval carillon, leaving only the heaviest bell, 't Bomtje, which dates from 1379 and is the bell you'll hear tolling solemnly during the Boetprocessie

BOETPROCESSIE

Veurne's famous Procession of the Penitents (w boetprocessie.be) has been held on the last Sunday of July since 1646. Its origins are debated, but it's either based on a tale of Robert II Count of Flanders returning from Jerusalem in 1099 with a fragment from Christ's cross (which currently resides in St Walburga Church), or a 1644 procession held by residents, re-enacting Christ carrying the cross before his crucifixion, in an effort to protect the town against an outbreak of plague. Either way, the event is unique because it's not performed for entertainment or as a tourist attraction; the participants apply to take part so they can atone for real sins.

Penitents don coarse brown robes and walk barefoot through the centre of town carrying heavy wooden crosses, marching to a slow and steady drumbeat. Meanwhile, members of the organisational group dress as characters from the New and Old Testaments.

A LOCAL HERO

Intent on completing the first phase of the Schlieffen Plan – to capture Paris – the German army advanced rapidly towards the Belgian coastline during the first few months of World War I. To halt their advance, Belgian troops established a front line 35km behind the river Yser, which ran from Nieuwpoort to Arras in France. However, during the Battle of the Yser the Germans crossed the river and it was feared the Allies were on the verge of losing their hold in Belgium.

Karel Cogge, a salt-of-the-earth Veurne local who worked for the water board, suggested they open the sluice gates at Nieuwpoort and slowly flood the area to halt the Germans. The idea was approved and on 26 and 29 October 1914 the gates were raised, creating a marshland that spread as far as Diksmuide and was over a mile wide. Cogge's plan had single-handedly prevented Belgium becoming fully occupied, and ended the Germans' Race to the Sea' for control of Calais and Dunkirk. In recognition of his services, Cogge was knighted in the Landshuis by King Albert I. His bust stands on Noordstraat. You can find out more about Cogge and his derring-do at the Nieuwpoort visitor centre, Westfront Nieuwpoort (page 251).

(see box, page 257). The new (relatively) 1960s set of bells plays concerts twice a week in summer (🕘 Jul–Aug 10.30–11.30 Wed, 20.00–21.00 Sun); the tower may reopen in the future.

Bakkerijmuseum (Bakery Museum) (2 Albert I-laan; ☎ 058 31 38 97; w bakkerijmuseum.be; 🕘 Sep–Dec & Feb–Jun 10.00–17.00 Tue–Fri, 14.00–17.00 Sat–Sun, Jul–Aug 10.00–17.30 Tue–Fri, 14.00–17.30 Sat–Sun, closed Jan; adult/6–12/under 6 €5/2/free, last tickets 1hr before closing time) A 25-minute walk from the Grote Markt, this bakery museum is contained within 17th-century farm buildings and aims to preserve traditional baking methods. The highlights are the bakery demonstrations held in the former barn and freshly made daily cake on sale in the café. To get there, take bus 56, 68 or 69 from Veurne railway station and get off at Veurne-Kliniek AZ West. From there it's a 5-minute walk to the museum.

Cycling Until 1627, the Moeren marshes on Veurne's eastern outskirts were unsafe and useless. That all changed when Antwerp engineer Wenceslas Coberger dug canals and drained them using a system of 22 windmills – the Charles Mill is the only original one to survive – transforming the region into a fertile plain, which is lovely to explore by bike. The tourist office sells the tailored *De Moeren* (37km; €2) map, which extends to the French border and takes in a handful of windmills; *Veurne-Ambacht* (48km; €2) is a longer route leading to Oostduinkerke; and *De Westhoek* (€8) covers the surrounding region and takes in the village of Lo (see opposite).

AROUND VEURNE

BEAUVOORDE The appeal of Beauvoorde district is the tiny hamlet of Wulveringem and its **Kasteel Beauvoorde (Beauvoorde Castle)** (10 Wulveringemstraat; ☎ 058 29 92 29; w kasteelbeauvoorde.be; 🕘 14.00–17.00 Wed, 10.00–17.00 Sat–Sun, public holidays 10.00–17.00 Wed–Sun; adult/6–11/under 6 €8/6/free, inc audio guide), which was built in 1408 but burned down 200 years later. The dark-grey 17th-century version seen today is built in Renaissance style and is surrounded by trees and a moat. It was lovingly restored by the last private owner, Arthur Merghelynck, who filled it with *objets d'art* and gifted it to the state after his death.

Getting there and away Beauvoorde Castle is clearly marked on the *De Westhoek* cycling map sold by Veurne tourist office. By car, follow Vaarstraat out of town and after 2.5km turn right on to Steengracht West. At its end turn left on to Ieperse Steenweg/N8. After passing a garden centre, turn right on to Gouden-Hoofdstraat and 2km later you'll see the castle on your right (8.1km; ⏲ 10mins).

LO The hamlet of Lo, 12km south of Veurne, was put on the map by none other than Julius Caesar. It's claimed he passed through the area in 55BC on the way to his Roman territories in Britain and rested at a very famous tree (see below). The pretty village has a smattering of other ancient sites too.

Getting there and away Lo is best visited by cycling from Veurne – buy the *De Westhoek* map from the tourist office – but you can also catch bus 50 (direction: Ypres) from Veurne station and return with the same bus from Lo's Eiermarkt (7 services/day in each direction from approx 07.00–19.00; ⏲ 25mins).

Tourist information

Tourist information 17a Markt; 058 28 91 66; w lauka.be; ⏲ Apr–Sep 09.30–noon & 13.00–17.00 Tue–Sat; Jul–Aug 09.30–noon & 13.00–17.00 Tue–Sat, 10.00–noon & 13.00–17.00 Sun; Oct–Mar 09.30–noon & 13.00–17.00 Mon–Fri. Tucked around the corner from the Markt. They offer lots of local information & you can also book a day tour.

Bike rental €12/day regular bike, €32/day e-bike from tourist office

What to see and do The village's highlight is **Caesarsboom (Caesar's Tree)**, a yew believed to be over 2,000 years old and a Belgian national monument. Legend has it that Roman emperor Julius Caesar tethered his horse to the tree and caught a few winks beneath its boughs. True or not, the ancient tree survives to this day and sits beneath the slender turret of **Westpoort**, the last remaining gatepost from Lo's 14th-century city walls, and next to **Het Damberd**, site of the town's former 1499 brewery. A 5-minute walk away, you'll find the **Duiventoren (Pigeon Tower)**, built in 1710 on the domain of Sint-Pietersabdij (St Peter's Abbey) and housing 1,132 pigeonholes; it was apparently a surprise gift for a newly arrived abbot!

Bezoekercentrum Jules Destrooper (5 Gravestraat; 058 28 09 33; w destrooper.be; ⏲ 09.30–12.30 & 13.30–17.30 Tue–Sat; adult/7–11/under 6 €5/3/free) This family-run bakery has been producing its Lo-speciality butter crisp, butter crumble and almond thin biscuits for over 130 years. Learn about their history and sample the main event.

DIKSMUIDE

Wandering around Diksmuide's pleasant Grote Markt listening to the golden-oldie tunes being softly piped out across the square, it's hard to imagine the intense conflicts played out here during World War I. From the very start, the town became embroiled in the Battle of the Yser, which effectively dismantled Germany's Schlieffen Plan and established the front line that would barely move for the next four years.

The main sites of interest are the IJzertoren peace monument and the preserved Dodengang trenches, but do take the time to buy some heavenly, custard-filled *IJzerbollen* and visit the town's tiny béguinage and art-filled Sint-Niklaaskerk.

GETTING THERE AND AWAY

By car From Ypres follow the N369 south (23km; 26mins); from Veurne follow the N35 eastwards (16km; 20mins); from Ostend take the N33 south and join the E40 (direction: Veurne), take exit 4 (direction: Middelkerke) and follow the N369 south (28km; 30mins); from Bruges follow the N31 south and merge with the E40 (direction: Ostend), take exit 4 (direction: Middelkerke) and follow the N369 south (49km; 43mins).

By train Bruges via Lichtervelde (hourly; 43–53mins); Ghent (hourly; 52mins); Veurne (hourly 10mins); Kortrijk via Lichtervelde (hourly Sat–Sun; 52mins).

TOURIST INFORMATION

Tourist information 6 Grote Markt; 051 79 30 50; w bezoekdiksmuide.be; Apr–Sep 09.00–17.00; Oct–Mar 10.00–noon & 13.00–16.00 Mon–Sat. Housed in the annex of the town hall, a friendly office which sells the 41km *IJzer 14–18* bike map (€2), passing by Vladslo German war cemetery. Can also arrange guided tours (€60/2hrs); in summer try to give a week's notice. Passing through the office, descend into the cellar for the new Treasure Trove (Apr–Sep 09.00–18.00; Oct–Mar 10.00–15.00 Mon–Sat; free), with exhibits on Diksmuide & the Westhoek.

Bike rental Catrysse, 56 Kaaskerkestraat; 051 50 46 70; 08.00–noon & 13.00–18.00 Tue–Fri, 09.00–noon & 13.00–17.00 Sat; €8/day, tandem €20/day

WHERE TO STAY AND EAT *Map, opposite*

The nearby brewery De Dolle Brouwers produces a number of speciality beers (page 262), and the local sweet treat is the delicious custard-filled doughnut known as *IJzerbol*.

B&B 't Withuis (12 rooms) 33 Grote Markt; 051 50 69 55; w withuisdiksmuide.be. Lovely old mansion (from the owners of neighbouring restaurant De Vrede) that was used by occupying German forces during World War II; you'll spot a bunker in the garden, which you cross to the modern, tasteful annex where rooms are located. B/fast is excellent & served in the mansion. €€€

Père et Mère 43 Grote Markt; 051 50 59 98; w pere-et-mere.be; noon–17.30 Wed–Fri & Sun, 14.00–21.00 Sat. Warm bistro run by Frans & Ria, whose children own the neighbouring businesses. Turns out ever-rarer classics such as pork cheeks in Trappist beer in generous portions. €€€

Bakker Bert 10 De Breyne Peelaertstraat; 051 51 17 35; w bakkerbert.be; 06.30–17.00 Mon & Sun, 06.30–17.00 Wed–Sat. Prepares lovely bread, pastries & *Diksmuidse boterkoeken* (butter cakes), invented by a German soldier during World War II.

SHOPPING

Markets

Farmers market Grote Markt; 14.00–17.00 Sat

General market Grote Markt; 08.00–noon Mon

WHAT TO SEE AND DO

Sint-Niklaaskerk (St Nicholas's Church) (Sint-Niklaasstraat; 08.00–18.00; free) This Gothic-style church boasts a number of artworks, the most interesting of which is the *Disbank*, a rarely seen charity bench, located to the left of the entrance, from which food would be dispensed to the needy at rich people's funerals. It's

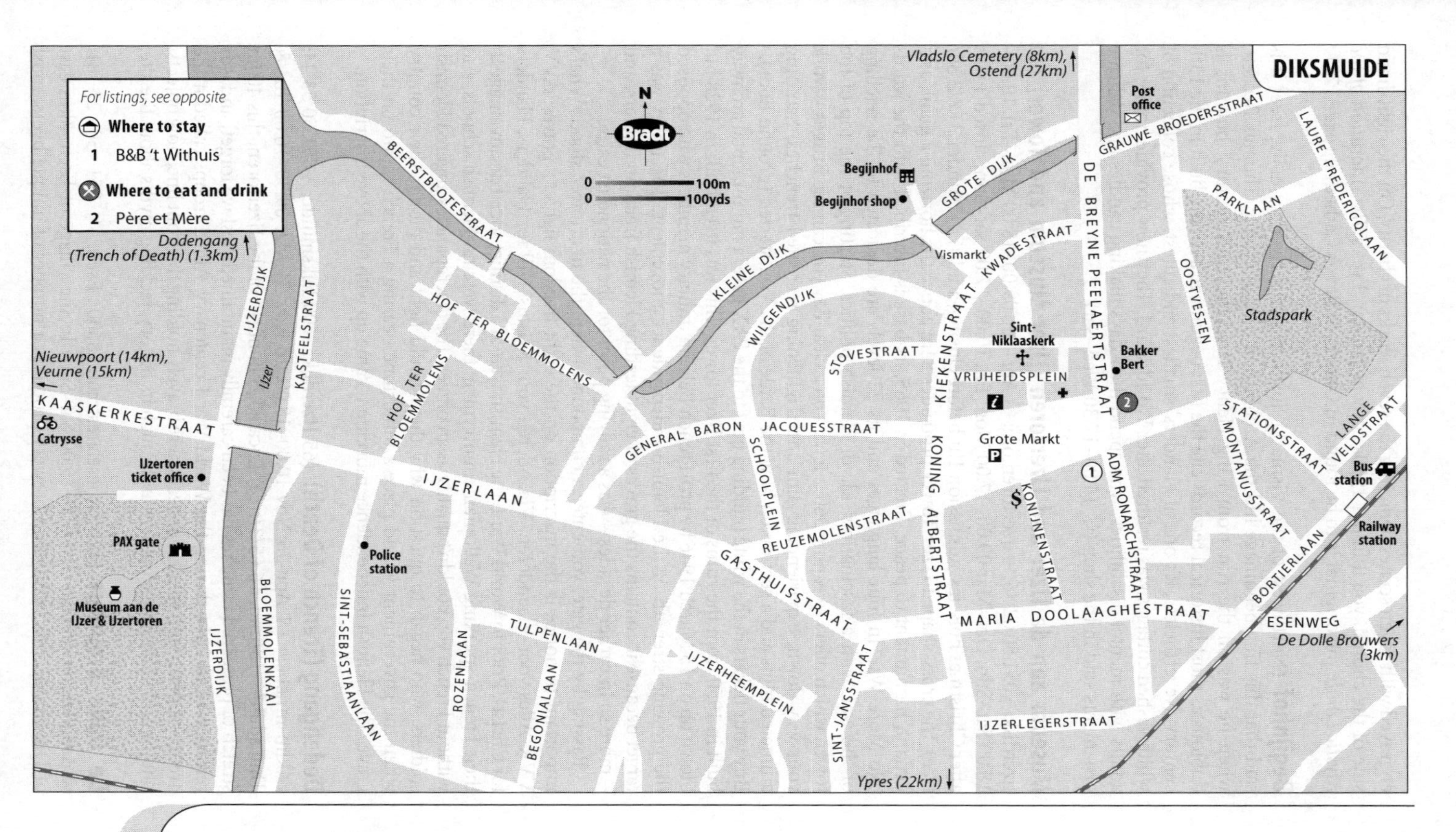
DIKSMUIDE
For listings, see opposite
Where to stay
1 B&B 't Withuis
Where to eat and drink
2 Père et Mère
Dodengang (Trench of Death) (1.3km)
Vladslo Cemetery (8km), Ostend (27km)
Nieuwpoort (14km), Veurne (15km)
Ypres (22km)
De Dolle Brouwers (3km)
N
Bradt
0 100m
0 100yds
Post office
Begijnhof
Begijnhof shop
Vismarkt
Sint-Niklaaskerk
Bakker Bert
Grote Markt
Stadspark
Bus station
Railway station
Catrysse
IJzertoren ticket office
PAX gate
Museum aan de IJzer & IJzertoren
Police station
IJzer
GRAUWE BROEDERSSTRAAT
LAURE FREDERICQLAAN
PARKLAAN
GROTE DIJK
DE BREYNE PEELAERTSTRAAT
KWADESTRAAT
KLEINE DIJK
BEERSTBLOTESTRAAT
OOSTVESTEN
WILGENDIJK
KIEKENSTRAAT
STOVESTRAAT
VRIJHEIDSPLEIN
STATIONSSTRAAT
LANGE VELDSTRAAT
IJZERDIJK
KASTEELSTRAAT
HOF TER BLOEMMOLENS
KAASKERKESTRAAT
GENERAL BARON JACQUESSTRAAT
SCHOOLPLEIN
KONING ALBERTSTRAAT
ADM RONARCHSTRAAT
MONTANUSSTRAAT
IJZERLAAN
KONIJNENSTRAAT
REUZEMOLENSTRAAT
BORTIERLAAN
GASTHUISSTRAAT
MARIA DOOLAAGHESTRAAT
ESENWEG
BLOEMMOLENKAAI
SINT-SEBASTIAANLAAN
TULPENLAAN
ROZENLAAN
BEGONIALAAN
IJZERHEEMPLEIN
SINT-JANSSTRAAT
IJZERLEGERSTRAAT

engraved with seven scenes depicting the seven works of charity. On the right-hand side of the church, you'll find a 1950s copy of Jan van Eyck's *The Adoration of the Mystic Lamb*; the original is to be found in Ghent's St Bavo's Cathedral (page 177).

Begijnhof (Northwest of the Vismarkt, just across the river; daily; free) It is said that this tiny béguinage hid the Archbishop of Canterbury, Thomas Beckett, when he was on the run from King Henry II in the 12th century, but this is dubious as most historical records cite the first béguinage as being built in the 13th century. Nevertheless, it's one of Flanders' smallest and cutest, whose collection of whitewashed cottages was restored after World War I. They now provide homes for adults with mental disabilities, who spend their days making candles and delicate ornaments sold in the shop (14.00–17.30 Wed–Sat).

Museum aan de IJzer and IJzertoren (IJzer Museum and Tower) (49 Ijzerdijk; 051 50 02 86; w ijzertoren.org; Apr–Sep 09.00–18.00 Mon–Fri, 10.00–18.00 Sat–Sun; Oct–Mar 09.00–17.00 Mon–Fri, 10.00–17.00 Sat–Sun, closed 3 wks after Christmas hols, last admission 1hr before closing; adult/7–17/under 7 €8/2.50/free) The cross-shaped **IJzer Tower** protrudes 84m above the horizon: a giant, and defiant, monument to peace. Erected in 1965, its base is inscribed with the words 'No More War' in four languages and its 22 levels are dedicated to the retelling of the war, with a fascinating side of Flemish politics. Starting at the top of the tower, which offers sweeping 360° views – on a clear day you can see Bruges – work your way down, experiencing dim and frightening recreated trenches, haunting animated films and a section on how the Battle of the Yser started (ground floor). Buy your tickets in the white building next to the **PAX gate**, a monumental archway built in 1950 from the ruins of the first IJzer tower. This was itself built in 1928 but blown up on 15 March 1946 by pro-French Belgian military members who opposed the growing strength of the Flemish independence movement. The tower was a target because it contains the graves of eight leading Flemish freedom fighters, and – more so in earlier decades – was a rallying point for the nationalist cause.

Passing by the gate, you enter a compound where the first tower stood. What's important to notice is the inscription on the eight freedom fighters' graves: AVV, VVK 'Alles voor Vlaanderen, Vlaanderen voor Kristus' (All for Flanders, Flanders for Christ). Prior to World War I, the Flemish were at a distinct social disadvantage to their French-speaking Wallonian countrymen: there were no Flemish schools, and without French you couldn't qualify as an officer. The discrepancies angered Flemish soldiers, who began to question why they should fight and die for their country when the government would place a tombstone bearing a French motto on their grave. The Flemish independence movement came up with the above inscription.

Dodengang (Trench of Death) (65 IJzerdijk, 8600 Diksmuide; 051 50 53 44; w klm-mra.be; 1 Apr–15 Nov 10.00–18.00; 16 Nov–31 Mar 09.30–16.00 Tue & Thu; adult/6–18/under 6 €5/3/free) Located 2km north of the IJzertoren, this 400m stretch of preserved trenches has been carefully maintained, 'lest we forget', and was refurbished in 2014 during the World War I centenary. Allied troops called it the 'trench of death' and spent four years here bravely holding the front line; now objects, photos and film footage guide you through its history, tackling myths about the site.

De Dolle Brouwers (12b Roeselarestraat, 8600 Esen; 051 50 27 81; w dedollebrouwers.be; 14.00–19.00 Sat–Sun) In the village of Esen, 3km east of Diksmuide, this family-run brewery produces a number of unique beers, most

BOTER-EN-KAASFEESTEN

Every year in May, on Whit Monday (six weeks after Easter), the residents of Diksmuide host a butter and cheese festival on the Grote Markt. A wonderfully pagan get-together of market stalls, music and cheese-hurling, it centres around the induction of new Knights of the Butter! Before being admitted, each of the prospective Dairy Knights is blindfolded and given various cheeses to taste. If he can name them and where they come from, he's placed on the scales and given his own body weight in butter as a prize. On the back of this tradition, the tourist office sells a special *Boterland* cycling map (44km; €2).

notably the additive-free Oerbier (7.5%), the pure-malt Arabier (8%), Boskeun, a special Easter beer, and the extremely sweet Stille Nacht (12%), which is only brewed at Christmas time. You can visit the café at the times listed opposite, but if you'd like a tour in English pitch up at 14.00 on Sunday; it costs €5 pp and includes a bottle of Oerbier.

Getting there and away Take bus 31 or 32 from Diksmuide railway station and get off at Esen Dorp (◷ 10mins). From there it's a 200m walk to the brewery.

German Military Cemetery, Vladslo (3 Houtlandstraat, 8600 Vladso-Diksmuide; ◷ daily; free) Over 25,000 soldiers are buried at this German war cemetery, which also contains the hugely moving *Grieving Parents* sculpture created by Käthe Kollwitz, whose 18-year-old son, Peter, was killed in the war and is buried here. To get there, you can drive, cycle or call the Belbus (📞 059 56 52 56) at least 2 hours before you want to go. It'll pick you up from an agreed spot and drop you on Houtlandstraat, a 300m walk from the cemetery. For more on the subject, nearby Koekelare, a 10-minute drive away, houses the **Käthe Kollwitz Museum** (w toerismekoekelare.be) and the **Lange Max Museum** (w langemaxmuseum.be), both of which focus on the German side of World War I and feature the eponymous German cannon.

YPRES (IEPER)

Ypres – or 'Wipers' as British soldiers pointedly called it – is a relatively small town with a very famous history. Most people associate it, of course, with World War I, but its great buildings – the Lakenhalle and Sint-Maartenskathedraal – were built on the back of its lucrative cloth trade with England. During the medieval period, Ypres was the third-largest city in Flanders after Ghent and Bruges – so important that Chaucer refers to it in *The Canterbury Tales*:

> A good wif was there, of biside Bathe, but she was somdel deef and that scathe. Of clooth-makyng she hadde swich an haunt, she passed hem of Ypres and of Gaunt.' (There was a wife of Bath, or a near city, who was somewhat deaf, it is a pity. At making clothes she had a skilful hand, she bettered those of Ypres and of Ghent.)

Close to the border, Ypres was caught up in various fights with the French, including the Battle of the Golden Spurs (pages 6 and 280) in 1302, and by the 16th century the cloth trade had died. The weavers left for richer pastures and the town gradually

MORE FROM BRADT

For more on World War I memorial sites, why not check out Bradt's *World War I Battlefields: A Travel Guide to the Western Front*? Visit **w** bradtguides.com/shop for a 10% discount on all our titles.

shrank from memory. Baedeker's 1901 edition of *Belgium & Holland* dedicates just two pages to the town, simply praising the 'many memorials of its golden period'. However, less than 13 years later World War I was declared and it wasn't long before these 'memorials' lay in ruin, flattened by artillery.

War arrived in Ypres on 7 October 1914 when 10,000 German troops entered the town, kidnapped the *burgomaster* (mayor), stole 62,000 francs from the city coffers and demanded that the local bakers prepare 8,000 loaves of bread to feed the soldiers. The next morning they released the mayor and marched west towards Vlamertinghe. Germans never entered the city again and residents felt safe enough to stay put until May 1915, when chlorine gas was deployed on the battlefields. As the war progressed, Ypres became a strategic defence point of the Ypres Salient (page 269) and was repeatedly battered by artillery fire. When locals returned at the end of the war, partly encouraged by the prospect of receiving subsidies, it was barely recognisable. It's said that you could sit on horseback and look over the town without a single building interrupting your view. While prominent figures like Winston Churchill put forward arguments for preserving the entire area in ruins as a memorial, residents weren't having any of it, and the city was painstakingly reconstructed in its original style.

GETTING THERE AND AWAY

By car From Dunkirk follow the E40, taking exit 1a (direction: Verne) and merging on to the N8 (53km; ⌚ 52mins). From Brussels, the quickest route is via the E40: head west towards Ghent, then take the E17/A19 to Kortrijk, exiting at junction 4 (direction: Ieper-Centrum) (123km; ⌚ 1hr 30mins).

By train Antwerp (hourly; ⌚ 2hrs 6mins); Bruges via Kortrijk (hourly; ⌚ 1hr 40 mins); Brussels via Ghent (hourly; ⌚ 1hr 58mins); Ghent (hourly; ⌚ 1hr 7mins); Kortrijk (hourly; ⌚ 33mins).

GETTING AROUND

By bus To get to Memorial Museum Passchendaele or Tyne Cot Cemetery, take bus 94 (direction: Roeselare) from Basculestraat, just east of the Meninpoort; for the former get off at Zonnebeke Klooster (⌚ 10mins); for the latter Passendale Tyne Cot (⌚ 15mins), both a few minutes' walk from the sites. Bus 95 (direction: Roeselare) links the Grote Markt and Langemark German Military Cemetery (⌚ 20mins).

By bike The Westhoek is wonderful for cycling, and it's quite possible to tour the World War I battlefield sites on two wheels – in fact, it's swifter than going by public transport, and gives you further chance to reflect. I'd recommend an afternoon ride to Hill 62/Sanctuary Wood and the Hooge Crater Museum, which are just beyond the city limits and take in some attractive countryside. The tourist office also sells two maps for longer rides including the battlefields: the 36km *Ieperboog* (Ypres Salient), and the 45km *Vredes* route (both are €2, and depart from the Grote Markt, but are well signposted in any case if you're on a very tight budget), the latter of which takes in Essex Farm Cemetery, Langemark, Vancouver Corner, Tyne Cot and Hill 62.

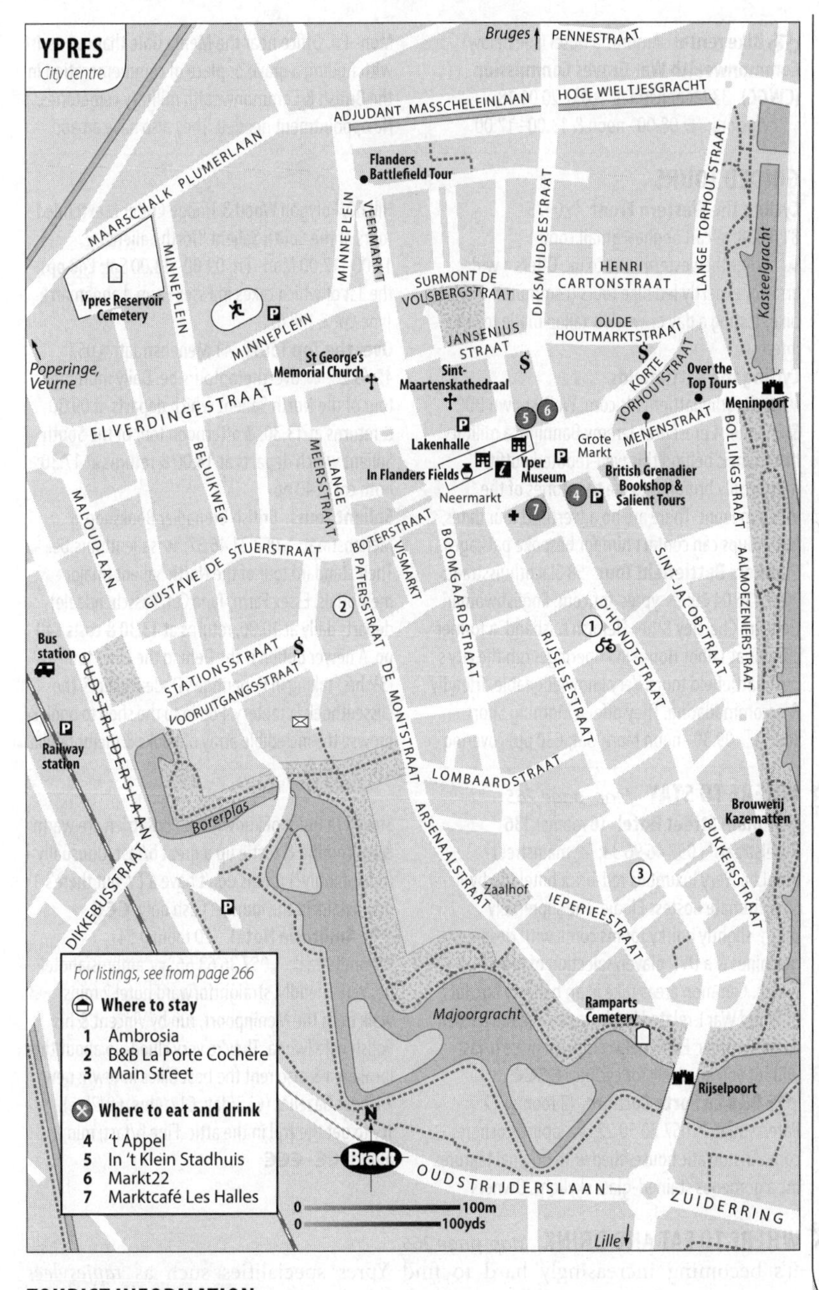

TOURIST INFORMATION

Tourist information Lakenhalle, 34 Grote Markt; 057 23 92 20; w toerisme-ieper.be; Apr–15 Nov 09.00–18.00 Mon–Fri, 10.00–18.00 Sat–Sun; 16 Nov–30 Mar 09.00–17.00 Mon–Fri, 10.00–17.00 Sat–Sun. Impressive office in the Lakenhalle with a proper bookshop stocking all the latest World War I tomes, many in English. Has info panels covering the local sights & can organise battlefield tours. Also sells a dizzying array of bike & car maps for Ypres & the Westhoek (see opposite).

Bike rental Ambrosia Hotel (see below)

Commonwealth War Graves Commission (CWGC) 33 Menenstraat; 057 20 01 18; w cwgc.org; 08.00–noon & 13.00–17.00 Mon–Fri. Office near the Menin Gate that can assist with finding a grave or place of commemoration in the British & Commonwealth military cemeteries. No appointment needed. They also have an app.

GUIDED TOURS

Cycling the Western Front 0475 81 06 08; e carl.ooghe@gmail.com; w cyclingthewesternfront.co.uk. Offers a wide array of expertly led bike tours (commuter or road bike) lasting a day or week & tailor-made to your interests.

Cycling the Battlefields w cyclingthebattlefields.com. Well-known BBC & Channel 4 presenter Jeremy Banning, a military historian, is behind this well-reputed outfit, masterfully bringing to life the stories of the Western Front. There are no advertised tour dates, but groups can contact him for bespoke packages.

Flanders Battlefield Tour 58 Slachthuisstraat; 057 36 04 60; w ypres-fbt.com. Englishwoman Genevra Charsley & her Flemish husband, a former curator at Talbot House in Poperinge, run the city's best battlefield tours. Very knowledgeable, friendly & accommodating. They offer a Morning Short Tour (09.30–noon Mon–Sat; €30 pp) covering Hill 60, Polygon Wood & Hooge Crater & extended tours of the South Salient/North Salient (13.00–17.00 Mon–Fri, 09.00–13.00 Sat; €40 pp), the 1st of which takes in Essex Farm, Langemarck, Tyne Cot & Hill 62.

Over the Top Tours 41 Menenstraat; 057 42 43 20; w overthetoptours.be. Daily morning tour of the North Salient which departs at 09.30 & returns at 13.30, & afternoon tour of the South Salient which departs at 14.00 & returns at 17.30; both cost €40 pp.

Salient Tours British Grenadier Bookshop, 5 Menenstraat; 057 21 46 57; w salienttours.be. Their standard tour of the North Salient (major memorials, Essex Farm, Tyne Cot, Passchendaele) departs daily at 10.00, returns at 13.30 & costs €40 pp. A newer option is the Behind the Lines tour (3½hrs) taking in Poperinge's Dodencellen & the Lijssenthoek Cemetery. Pop in to the shop to book & browse the incredible array of books & memorabilia.

WHERE TO STAY *Map, page 265*

Main Street Hotel (6 rooms) 136 Rijselstraat; 057 46 96 33; w mainstreet-hotel.be. Very luxurious red-brick hotel run by consummate hostess Elodie. The supremely plush, slightly quirky rooms come with Nespresso machines & a DVD player/selection of films to watch. Common areas take in an honesty bar, lots of World War I-related books to browse & a garden come summer. Extremely comprehensive b/fast will set you up nicely for cycling. **€€€€**

B&B La Porte Cochère (3 rooms) 22 Patersstraat; 057 20 50 22; w laportecochere.com. Aristocratic house filled with original features inc a gorgeous stained-glass skylight. Owners Steven (a fount of knowledge) & Katrien are warm & welcoming & rustle up a great b/fast. Unusually (refreshingly?) rooms don't have a TV, but there's 1 downstairs in the lounge. Cash only. **€€€**

Ambrosia Hotel (10 rooms) 54 D'Hondtstraat; 057 36 63 66; w ambrosiahotel.be. Very friendly, straightforward hotel 2 mins' walk from the Meninpoort, run by Vincent & his Polish wife Iwona. They're very clued-up about the local area & also rent the best bikes in town: new 24-gear Gazelles (€15/day, €12/4hrs, €9/2hrs). Try to get the trpl in the attic. Fine b/fast; min 2 nights. **€€–€€€**

WHERE TO EAT AND DRINK *Map, page 265*

It's becoming increasingly hard to find Ypres specialities such as *tapjesvlees* (bacon-infused braised pork or veal) and *kattenklauw* (a claw-shaped Danish pastry), but many shops have cat-themed chocolates or biscuits, and it's also worth drinking some of the local brews. Founded in 2013, **Brouwerij Kazematten** (1 Houten Paard; w kazematten.be; tours every 30mins between 15.00 & 17.00 Sat; adult/child €10/4 inc 3 beers) brews Wipers Times 14 and 16. They also run group tours on Saturdays; contact them and they'll try to add you to an existing

THE LAST POST

At the time of writing, the Last Post ceremony had been performed over 31, 300 times, having continued uninterrupted in its present location under the Meninpoort (Menin Gate) since 2 July 1928, except under German occupation during World War II when it was conducted in Brookwood Military Cemetery in Surrey. The tribute stems from the bugle call played in the British army (and that of other countries) to mark the end of the day's labours, and has come to represent the final farewell to the fallen. The Reveille, which closes the Last Post ceremony, and symbolises resurrection, was played at the start of the day to rouse troops. Every evening at 20.00, police halt traffic passing under the Menin Gate and three buglers play the simple but moving strain. Depending when you visit, you may see an extended ceremony where wreaths are presented. If you'd like to lay your own, contact the Last Post Association (w lastpost.be) in advance. No need to turn up early unless you want a front-row spot.

group. You might notice that all the addresses below are on the Grote Markt; note that Ypres's main square doesn't currently suffer from the same tourist trap issues as elsewhere!

In 't Klein Stadhuis 32 Grote Markt; 057 21 55 42; w inhetkleinstadhuis.be; noon–14.00 & 18.00–22.30 Tue–Fri, noon–14.30 & 18.00–23.00 Sat–Sun. Popular choice after attending the Last Post ceremony nearby, this 2-floor medieval-style establishment serves salads, soups & hearty Flemish stews & steaks. €€€

Markt22 22 Grote Markt; 057 20 99 97; noon–14.30 & 17.30–21.00 Mon, Tue, Thu–Sun. Taken over by the manager of the well-regarded Het Moment (which now opens by day only as a result) in 2018, this newcomer is particularly recommended for carnivores, with textbook steaks, stews & frites. €€€

Marktcafé Les Halles 35 Grote Markt; 057 36 55 63; w marktcafe-leshalles.be; 09.00–midnight Mon, Wed–Fri & Sun, 07.30–midnight Sat. Locals love to come to this buzzing, laidback brasserie & sink their teeth into the homemade hamburgers & Flemish stews. Very good prices & quality. €€€

't Appel 25 Grote Markt; 057 36 97 36; 08.00–20.00 Mon–Wed & Sat, 08.00–15.00 Thu–Fri, 11.30–20.00 Sun. Cheerful café right opposite the tourist office & In Flanders Field Museum. Perfect option for a fast & satisfying sit-down lunch (soup, pasta, toasties etc) that won't make a dent in the wallet. €–€€

WHAT TO SEE AND DO

Lakenhalle (Cloth Hall) (34 Grote Markt; 057 23 92 20) Ypres's original Cloth Hall was built in 1304, when it was one of the largest Gothic commercial buildings of the time – a tribute to the city's flourishing cloth trade. It was almost completely flattened by artillery fire during World War I, and then meticulously reconstructed between 1933 and 1967. Head inside and you'll find the tourist office, a café and two museums, the most important of which is the unmissable **In Flanders Fields Museum**, opened in time for the World War I centenary (w inflandersfields.be; 1 Apr–15 Nov 10.00–18.00, 16 Nov–Mar 10.00–17.00 Tue–Sun; adult/19–25/7–18/under 7 €10/6/5/free, combi-ticket with Yper Museum €13/8/6/free). Visitors receive a poppy bracelet and if you programme in your details at the start, you can receive tailored stories relating to soldiers from your region and, near the end of the museum, also learn how many people with your surname died in Belgium during the war. The exhibition takes you through all the major battles in the Ypres

KATTENSTOET

Every three years on the second Sunday of May, Ypres hosts the inimitable, utterly fascinating and – yes, rather odd – Kattenstoet or Cat Parade (w kattenstoet.be). Cats and Ypres go way back; in the Middle Ages, the city's Lakenhalle was overrun by mice, so cats were brought in to solve the problem – only to become a problem themselves when their numbers spiralled. Whether or not it's an apocryphal tale, one story goes that the only pest control the locals could think of was to throw the poor pusses off the top of the belfry; another interpretation might be that cats were considered an ill omen at the time. The last cat was thrown to its doom in 1817, though the tradition was revived in 1955 – this time, thankfully, with velvet moggies sating the crowds. During the festival, a parade of cat-themed flotillas and puppets weaves through town. The next events are in 2021 and 2024.

region, giving context on the run-up to war and reconstruction. Halfway through the display you'll find turnstiles leading up to the belfry (€2, pay in advance); it's worth climbing the 231 steps for views of the carillon and countryside, with battle sites indicated on information panels. If you'd like to find out more about World War I, meanwhile, the ground floor houses a **Research Centre** where you can consult extensive collections and a library.

War may be the main reason many travel to Ypres, but the city has another history and rich traditions – one of the reasons for the launch of the new **Yper Museum** (w https://www.ypermuseum.be; 🕘 1 Apr–15 Nov 10.00–18.00, 16 Nov–Mar 10.00–17.00 Tue–Sun; adult/19–25/7–18/under 7 €7 7/4/3.50/free), at the eastern end of the Cloth Hall, in 2018. Here, instead of a poppy bracelet, you're equipped with one featuring a cat's paw (kids get their own version, and can look out for cats and coins hidden about the space). Have a peek at the **Raadzaal** (**Council Chamber**) just before the entry gate; its beautiful stained-glass window, by Arno Brys, evokes the past glory of Ypres. Inside the slightly hectic but eminently kid-friendly space you'll find exhibits about Ypres's cat love, its cloth trade and a large array of medieval objects preserved in the surrounding flood zone.

Sint-Maartenskathedraal (St Martin's Cathedral) (Vandenpeereboomplein; 🕘 daily, closed noon–14.00; free) Like the Cloth Hall, the first version of St Martin's – which was built between 1230 and 1370 – was destroyed during the war and rebuilt with a cheekily taller tower to make it the then highest building in Belgium. Interestingly, the feast day of St Martin, also the patron saint of the medieval weavers' guild, falls on 11 November, chiming with when we pause and remember World War I. On that day, visitors to Ypres might see children running around excitedly with gifts, which they receive earlier than those provided elsewhere in Belgium by the more famous St Nick.

St George's Memorial Church (1 Elverdingsestraat; 🕘 Apr–Sep 09.30–18.00; Oct–Mar 09.30–16.00; free) This unassuming church was built by Sir Reginald Bloomfield – the architect behind the Menin Gate – in 1929. It's filled with brass plaques honouring fallen soldiers and furniture donated by victims' families. The stained-glass windows dedicated to various individuals and regiments are moving too, especially the window on the right above the baptistry, which remembers

Lieutenant Boyce Combe. He was killed on 11 November 1914 at the tender age of 26 and his name appears on the Menin Gate.

Meninpoort (Menin Gate) (Menenstraat) Erected in July 1927, the Menin Gate marks the spot where soldiers would leave town on their way to the front line. Carved into the interior walls are the names of 54,896 British and Commonwealth soldiers killed in World War I and whose graves are unknown. Soldiers who went missing after 16 August 1917 have their names inscribed on the walls at Tyne Cot Cemetery (page 274). As a mark of respect, the road is closed every evening at 20.00 and members of the local fire brigade sound their bugles in the Last Post (see box, page 267).

THE YPRES SALIENT

A salient is a military defence line that bulges into enemy territory and is surrounded on three sides. That which developed around Ypres during World War I was a result of the failure of the German Schlieffen Plan. Their aim was to avoid fighting a war on two fronts by invading France, then capturing its sea ports and Paris, via Belgium, before Russian troops could mobilise on the east German border. The attack relied on speed and the element of surprise. The Germans lost both when they were caught unawares by the Belgian resistance, who delayed them for over a month until French and British soldiers arrived. Both sides dug in: the Allies (British, French, Canadian, ANZAC troops and Belgians) defending the coastline and the Germans pushing towards it. Both built trenches that stretched for 644km from Nieuwpoort to the French/Swiss border, a line known as the Western Front. The contours of this line were established during the First Battle of Ypres, when Allied forces fought the Germans for control of the town and won, securing the last major settlement that stood between the Germans and the coast.

Over the next four years, this line – resembling an inverted 'S' – would barely move. Vicious trench warfare ensued, with increasingly bloody (and muddy) battles being fought in a bid to reach ridges, like Tyne Cot and Hill 60, that would provide elevated views of the battlefield and enemy lines. Ever more ruthless tactics were employed to weaken the enemy, including the use of chlorine and mustard gas, and casualties soared, culminating in the Third Battle of Ypres (see box, page 272), better known as the Battle of Passchendaele, which came to symbolise the Great War in its futile bloodshed (estimates of casualties tend to hover at around 500,000).

IN FLANDERS FIELDS

Lt Col John McCrae, 8 December 1915

In Flanders fields the poppies blow,
Between the crosses, row on row,
That mark our place; and in the sky,
The larks, still bravely singing, fly
Scarce heard amid the guns below.

We are the dead. Short days ago
We lived, felt dawn, saw sunset glow.
Loved, and were loved, and now we lie
In Flanders fields.

Take up our quarrel with the foe:
To you from failing hands we throw
The torch; be yours to hold it high.
If ye break faith with us who die
We shall not sleep, though poppies grow
In Flanders fields.

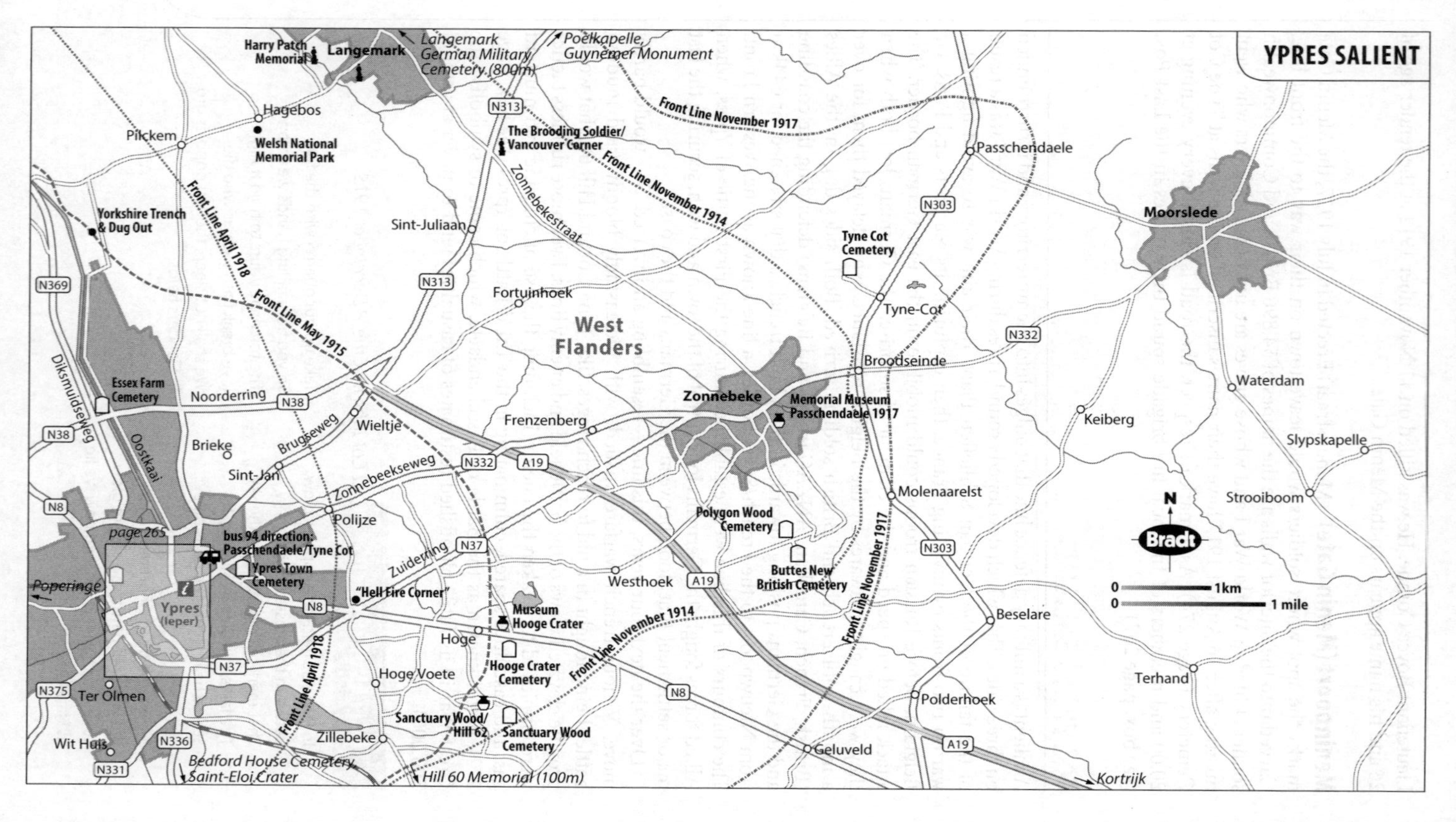
YPRES SALIENT
Harry Patch Memorial
Langemark
Langemark German Military Cemetery (800m)
Poelkapelle, Guynemer Monument
Hagebos
Pilckem
Welsh National Memorial Park
N313
The Brooding Soldier/ Vancouver Corner
Front Line November 1917
Front Line November 1914
Passchendaele
Moorslede
Yorkshire Trench & Dug Out
Front Line April 1918
Zonnebekestraat
Sint-Juliaan
N303
Tyne Cot Cemetery
N369
Front Line May 1915
Fortuinhoek
Tyne-Cot
West Flanders
N332
Broodseinde
Waterdam
Diksmuidseweg
Essex Farm Cemetery
Noorderring
N38
Zonnebeke
Memorial Museum Passchendaele 1917
Keiberg
Slypskapelle
Oostkaai
Wieltje
Brugseweg
Frenzenberg
Brieke
Sint-Jan
A19
Zonnebeekseweg
Molenaarelst
Strooiboom
N8
Polijze
Polygon Wood Cemetery
page 265
bus 94 direction: Passchendaele/Tyne Cot
N37
Zuiderring
Bradt
Ypres Town Cemetery
Westhoek
Buttes New British Cemetery
Poperinge
Ypres (Ieper)
"Hell Fire Corner"
0 1km
0 1 mile
Museum Hooge Crater
Beselare
Hoge
Hooge Crater Cemetery
Terhand
N375
Ter Olmen
Hoge Voete
Polderhoek
Sanctuary Wood/ Hill 62
Sanctuary Wood Cemetery
Wit Huis
N336
Zillebeke
Geluveld
N331
Bedford House Cemetery
Saint-Eloi Crater
Hill 60 Memorial (100m)
Kortrijk

By the time the Armistice was signed on 11 November 1918, 1½ billion shells had been fired on the Western Front and hundreds of thousands of soldiers had lost their lives in the Salient (quite how many no-one can say). The entire area was a wasteland of death, decay and liquid mud – the only sign of life being the flash of red poppies, whose long-dormant seeds had been brought to the surface. Today the area is somehow beautiful despite all, and dotted with cemeteries honouring the fallen soldiers. Since the centenary, three entry points or 'gateways' at strategic sights – including the Museum Hooge Crater (page 273) – have displays with films and maps of battle sites.

ESSEX FARM CEMETERY Just 2km north of Ypres city centre, near the village of Boezinge, the Essex Farm bunker sat 1.8 km from the front line and was used as an advance dressing station. It was here, on 3 May 1915, that Canadian surgeon Lieutenant Colonel John McCrae penned one of the most notable poems of World War I, *In Flanders Fields* (see box, page 269), after witnessing the death of his friend Alexis Helmer the day before. Helmer's name appears on panel ten of the Menin Gate. The poem was sent to *The Spectator* magazine in London, but rejected and eventually published by *Punch* on 8 December 1915. You can visit the bunkers where McCrae tended the wounded and the adjacent cemetery, where you should look for the grave of rifleman Valentine Joseph Strudwick, killed by a shell two

BOEZINGE

Most people have heard of Passchendaele and Messines and the great battles associated with them, but few have heard of Boezinge, a small village north of Ypres on the banks of the Ieperlee canal. In April 1915, during the Second Battle of Ypres, the German army was forcing French troops back across Pilkem Ridge. The French dug in just before reaching the canal and held the Allied line until the British 4th Division relieved them in June. They began advancing across no man's land on 6 July 1915. They sustained heavy losses, but were able to push the Allied line forward until it was less than 100m from the Germans. General Sir Herbert Plumer claimed that 'the attack … [was] one of the great battles of the campaign'.

When the war ended, the fighting ground was left fallow and forgotten until 1992, when a local volunteer group of archaeologists and historians called The Diggers obtained a permit to excavate. After digging barely 1m they uncovered trenches, dugouts, thousands of artefacts and undetonated bombs (incredibly, the Belgian Armed Forces still uncover 180 tonnes every year). Most poignantly, behind the Boezinge Industrial Estate, they found the remains of 155 British, German and French soldiers believed to have died in a gas attack. They lay hunched on the ground, still holding their guns and wearing their helmets. Sadly, only one could be identified: French soldier François Metzinger. Their remains were reinterred in the surrounding cemeteries. Surreally, situated amid the industrial estate today, you can visit a section of the reconstructed trench – known as the 'Yorkshire Trench' – with plenty of English information boards on its history (the dugouts were closed due to flooding at the time of writing). The Ypres tourist board has maps which include the Yorkshire Trench; otherwise, it's a 10-minute drive north of Ypres on Bargiestraat; there is parking in two lay-bys immediately alongside the site.

months before his 16th birthday. His tale was true of many poor boys who lied about their age for the chance of regular meals, pay and clothes. You'll notice that in many of the cemeteries the spacing and orientation of the headstones change. This indicates that the cemetery sat close to, or on, the front line, and rather than incorrectly marking the resting place of soldiers whose graves had been destroyed by artillery fire, gaps were left.

HILL 60 This manmade hillock – no higher than a second-floor window – was formed in the 1850s during the creation of the Ypres–Comines railway. The steam trains had struggled with the slight incline, so locals flattened the land and dumped the leftover earth in a pile by the side of the tracks. Prior to the war, the grassy bump was known as Lovers' Knoll, popular with courting couples. But it was these views that made it the source of intense fighting between the Allied and German forces, and by 1915 it was one of the most feared places on the front line. Control of the hill passed back and forth between the French – then British – and Germans in a series of suicidal attacks and counter-attacks, mostly played out underground. The biggest breakthrough came in June 1917, during the Battle of Messines, when British tunnellers created one of the largest manmade explosions in the pre-nuclear era under German lines, killing as many as 10,000 men. It was, as they went, a major success for the Allied armies – a battle over within a week, as against the war of attrition that characterised so much of World War I.

To get there, troops had to march past **Hell Fire Corner**, an infamous intersection (now roundabout) on the Menin Road providing a perfect target for German gunners. It was once known as the most dangerous spot on the Western Front.

SANCTUARY WOOD/HILL 62 (26 Canadalaan; 057 46 63 73; w hill62trenches.be; 09.00–18.00, closed 20 Dec–20 Jan; adult/under 14 €8/5) For a long time

THE THIRD BATTLE OF YPRES

The infamous Third Battle of Ypres – also known as the Battle of Passchendaele – was one of the bloodiest battles of World War I. In the summer of 1917, fighting on Germany's eastern border had unexpectedly stopped due to the Russian Revolution and the Germans were able to redeploy all their troops west. Faced with this imminent surge in German military strength, Britain knew it had to act quickly. Sir Douglas Haig developed a plan whose main aims were to reclaim the high ground at Passchendaele and to push the Germans back from the coast in order to destroy their submarine bases, which continually threatened Britain's supply lines and the American reinforcements arriving by ship. Buoyed by success at the Battle of Messines in June, the plan was given the go-ahead and, to 'clear the way' for his troops, Haig ordered a massive two-week bombardment. Then, on 31 July 1917, Haig sent Allied troops over the top, but a few days later the heavens opened and the worst deluge of rain to hit the region in 30 years turned Flanders' fields into a quagmire. Tanks got stuck, gun mechanisms jammed and crater holes that used to provide shelter from enemy fire filled with water. Men and horses drowned in the worst sections. Haig called off the attack, but stubbornly issued another on 16 August, another on 20 and 26 September, and yet another on 4 October. By the time Allied forces reached Passchendaele on 6 November, by some estimates 275,000 Allied soldiers and 220,000 German troops had lost their lives for the sake of 8km of land. To give you a sense of the scale of the loss, tourists to this private café-museum were shocked by the blatantly profiteering, lazy attitude of the owner – the grandson of the farmer who reclaimed this land back in 1919 – but his passing several years ago means that it's now (inevitably) in better hands. There's still a slightly abandoned air to the place, mind you, and debates will continue to rage over the exact level of authenticity of its (very rare) surviving trench system, but the museum's collection is simply superb – bursting with rifles, shell casings, helmets and, best of all, stereoscopes containing original 3D war photographs. From here it's a very quick cycle ride to Museum Hooge Crater (see below).

MUSEUM HOOGE CRATER (467 Meenseweg; 057 46 84 46; w hoogecrater.com; 2 Feb–23 Dec 10.00–18.00 Tue–Sat, 10.00–21.00 Sun; closed 2nd week Aug; adult/child €5/2) Housed in a 1920s chapel, this small-scale attraction definitely has a more professional approach than its fellow museum-café, Sanctuary Wood/ Hill 62 – proudly toting its 'best private museum in Flanders fields' status. They certainly do have an impressive collection of clothing, helmets and shells, as well as a 1916 ambulance and Fokker DR1 German warplane, all displayed in dioramas, to the soundtrack of classic British wartime songs. Outside you'll find an information point with a film and maps of the local area – there's plenty to explore in the environs if you have time, though the Hooge Crater, created by the British during the Second Battle of Ypres when they smuggled 1,700kg of explosives under German lines and detonated them in July 1915, was filled in during reconstruction. Weeks after the Hooge Crater formed, the area became the first location to witness the use of flamethrowers (or 'liquid fire'), which the Germans employed against British positions. Before the war, Hooge had housed a château; it was reduced to rubble and the site now somewhat incongruously houses Belgium's oldest theme park.

it is estimated that for every square metre gained, 435 men died. Aerial photographs of Passchendaele after the war show a pockmarked lunar expanse of complete devastation (see right).

In an attempt to gain an advantage before American troops arrived in Europe, the German army embarked on the Lys Offensive in April 1918 and in the space of three days pushed the Allies all the way back to the outskirts of Ypres, reoccupying the land taken by the Allies during the Third Battle of Ypres. However, the effort exhausted the final reserves of the German army and it was unable to resist the Allies' Hundred Days Offensive in August 1918. Months later, on 11 November, the Armistice was signed in a railway carriage in Compiègne forest, north of Paris.

Aerial photographs of Passchendaele taken before and after WWI

MEMORIAL MUSEUM PASSCHENDAELE 1917 (5a Berten Pilstraat, Zonnebeke; ☎ 051 77 04 41; w passchendaele.be; ⊕ Feb–mid-Dec 09.00–18.00; adult/7–18/under 7 €10.50/5/free inc audio guide except for under 7) Inside the striking, rather quaint-looking Kasteel Zonnebeke, a 1920s mansion, this highly professional museum presents the story of World War I, and in particular the 100-day Battle of Passchendaele (see box, page 272) that claimed the lives of hundreds of thousands of soldiers in 1917. The first sections provide an overview of the battles around Ypres. You then visit the immersive dug-out 'experience' complete with corrugated-iron walkways, bunker rooms, dim lights and eerie soundtrack, and emerge into reconstructed trenches. At the entrance you'll find the Zonnebeke tourist office and a room containing leaflets of the many walks and bike rides departing from here; there are free brochures of ANZAC and Canadian remembrance trails, and you can also buy World War I biking and hiking maps.

TYNE COT CEMETERY (Vijfwegestraat) Tyne Cot is the world's largest Commonwealth war grave cemetery and the final resting place of 11,954 souls. The sight of its uniform graves stretching into the distance is utterly humbling. Over 70% of them belong to unidentified British or Commonwealth soldiers and simply bear the words 'Known unto God'. The cemetery takes its name from a barn that once stood at the centre of this German stronghold, and which British troops presumably thought resembled a Tyneside cottage. The Germans had a handful of blockhouses or 'pillboxes' here, the largest of which was big enough to serve as an advance dressing station. Several have been preserved, including that beneath the mighty Cross of Sacrifice erected in 1922. Gently climb a few of its steps, and you get a glimpse of the Germans' advantageous viewpoint overlooking the British lines and Passchendaele. It was this high ground that the British fought for at the Battle of Ypres (see box, page 272). Spend a few minutes in the visitor centre (⊕ Feb–Nov 10.00–18.00) where a young girl hauntingly narrates the names of the fallen. The walking path to Zonnebeke, home to the Memorial Museum Passchendaele, is clearly signposted at the foot of the cemetery.

VANCOUVER CORNER This small garden is dominated by the statue of ***The Brooding Soldier***. Carved from a single piece of granite, it was erected in memory of the First Canadian Division, which was wiped out by a gas attack on 24 April 1915. The ferns planted round about are meant to symbolise the creeping green-tinted gas.

LANGEMARK GERMAN MILITARY CEMETERY Dotted with oak trees – the national symbol of Germany – Langemark is one of four German cemeteries left in Flanders. Originally there were 68, but many of the graves were consolidated or the bodies reinterred back home. Hitler visited the cemetery in June 1940 while Flanders was under German occupation following the Battle of France.

Inside the entrance arch, carved into oak panels, are the names of the original soldiers buried in the cemetery, which is also known as the **Cemetery of Student Soldiers**: university students who volunteered to join the war, but were given only six weeks' training before being sent to the Western Front – and often the worst parts.

Behind the entrance hall sits a square mass grave containing the remains of 24,000 soldiers – many are unknown, but you'll see the names of some 17,000 of them on the black stones here. Upon this mass grave is the statue of the ***Mourning Soldiers***, four slumped figures modelled on a 1918 photograph of the Reserve Infantry Regiment 238 mourning at the graveside of their comrade (see photo).

On a ridge to the southwest of Langemark (catch bus 40 from Langemark Markt) you'll also spot a resplendent red dragon in the middle of an area conquered by Welsh troops on 31 July 1917. The surrounding **Welsh National Memorial Park** (158 Boezingestraat) honours Wales's contribution to the Great War – it's worth noting that, proportionally, the country lost more of its population than any other.

German soldiers of the 238 Reserve Infantry Regiment mourning the death of a comrade. The second soldier from the right was killed in action two days after the photograph was taken.

HARRY PATCH MEMORIAL (97 Boezingestraat, just off the Pilkem–Langemark road) This simple stone marks the spot where Harry Patch (the 'Last Fighting Tommy') – who died at the age of 111 in 2009 as the last surviving combat soldier of World War I – and his comrades of the 7th Battalion Duke of Cornwall's Light Infantry crossed the Steenbeek river in the early hours of 16 August 1917 (as part of the Third Battle of Ypres) to reconquer Langemark – whose church steeple can be seen in the distance – from the Germans.

POPPY CENOTAPH (Adjacent to Langemark Cemetery) This 7m-high memorial was forged on the cobblestones of Ypres in 2016 by an international group of blacksmiths and farriers. Surrounded by 2,106 metal poppies, it also has a ring of panels featuring their interpretation of the war.

POPERINGE

Like its neighbours, the middle-sized town of Poperinge joined the cloth trade in the 14th century and flourished until competition with Ypres forced it to bow out and resort to cultivating hops for use in the production of beer. However, it wasn't enough and the town slipped into economic depression until the 18th century, when the region came under Austrian control.

Of course, Poperinge is most famously associated with World War I. Like Veurne, it was one of the few towns to remain under Allied control throughout the war and, as a result, was a haven for soldiers travelling to and from the front line. Troops referred to it affectionately as 'Pops'. Talbot House, in particular, became a legendary place of respite where soldiers could take much-needed rest and let off steam. The compact town, which incidentally boasts some of the best regional dishes in Flanders, makes an excellent day trip from Ypres and shouldn't be missed.

GETTING THERE AND AWAY

By car From Ypres follow the N308 west (12km; ⌚ 18mins). From Veurne follow the N8 south and when you reach the village of Oostvleteren turn right on to the N321 to Poperinge (29km; ⌚ 35mins).

By train Ypres (hourly; ⌚ 8mins); Kortrijk (hourly; ⌚ 42mins); Ghent (hourly; ⌚ 1hr 16mins).

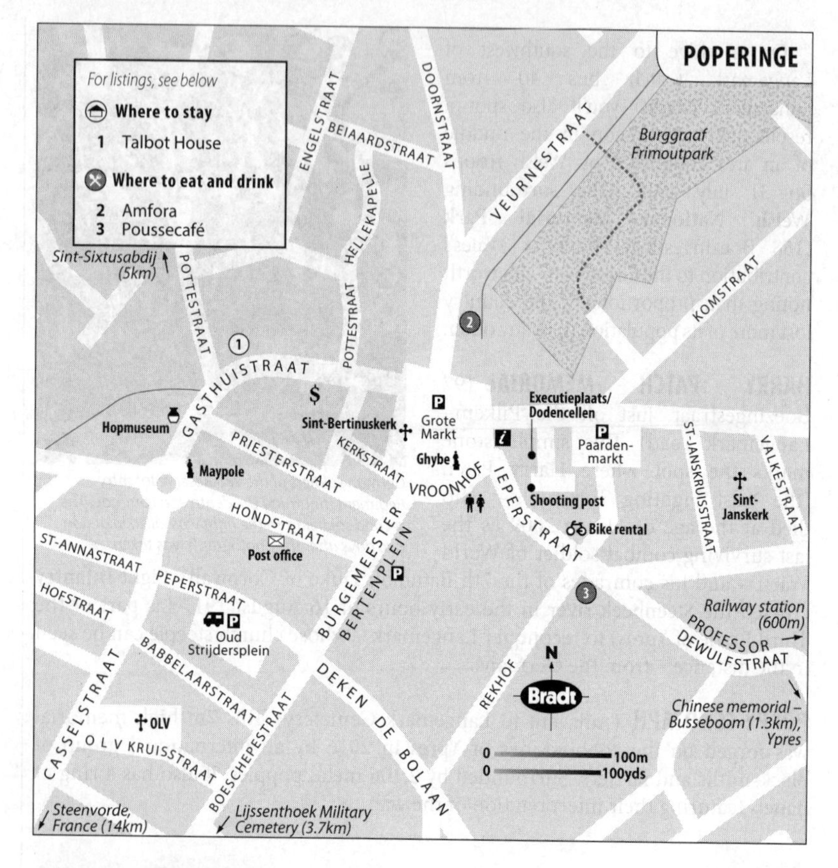

TOURIST INFORMATION

Tourist information 1 Grote Markt; 057 34 66 76; w toerismepoperinge.be; Apr–Sep 09.00–noon & 13.00–17.00 Mon–Fri, 09.00–noon & 13.00–16.00 Sat–Sun; Oct–Mar 09.00–noon & 13.00–17.00 Mon–Fri, 09.00–noon & 13.00–16.00 Sat. Narrow office in the basement of the town hall. Has created a Poperinge 14–18 app, with bike, hiking & car routes around the Great War sites, available in the App Store or Google Play. Long on detail, it's well worth downloading to get the inside track on the town.

Bike rental Hotel Palace, 34 Ieperstraat; 057 33 30 93; w fietsverhuurpoperinge.be; 08.00–22.00; city bike €11/day (with €25 deposit), electric bike €30 (€100 deposit). Can deliver bikes to your hotel for a supplement.

WHERE TO STAY AND EAT *Map, above*

Poperinge is a champion of regional food, having been named *Vlaanderen Lekkerland* – 'most tasty town' – in the past decade, and having won the coveted Vlaamse Streekvork for the best regional dishes in Flanders. Look out for *potjesvlees* (also known as *hennepot*), literally 'potted meat' made from boiled-down veal, chicken and rabbit; *kabeljauw aan de Schreve,* cod in a beer and cream sauce; *hopscheuten*, fresh hop shoots available in March; and *mazarinetaart,* a dense cinnamon-flavoured syrup-soaked cake.

Talbot House (7 rooms) 43 Gasthuisstraat; 057 33 32 28; w talbothouse.be. Talbot House is steeped in history & offers a once-in-a-lifetime opportunity to stay in an authentic World War I soldiers' house. The wardens who run it are mostly British volunteers & make you feel extremely welcome. No meals provided & few mod cons, but you can cook in the kitchen & b/fast is included in the generous room price (sgl €40–7, dbl €72–86), with the option to pay an extra €5 for a cooked English b/fast. Just wonderful. See below for further details. €

Amfora 36 Grote Markt; 057 33 94 05; w hotelamfora.be; Mon & Thu–Sun 08.00–21.00 (last orders). Superior, smart hotel restaurant serving lots of regional dishes, including *Poperinigse hennepot*, hop shoots & St Bernardus Tripel. On Mon, Thu & Fri they lay on a €16 lunch with soup & a main. €€–€€€

Poussecafé 45a Ieperstraat; 057 36 87 80; w poussecafe-pops.be; 10.30–20.00 Wed–Thu & Sun, 09.30–21.30 Fri, 10.30–21.30 Sat. Always busy with locals who come for the homemade *mazarinetaart* prepared in the bakery next door. Run by Kurt & Sabrina, who speak perfect English, & named after his Siamese cat. Bargain €15 w/day lunch; also serves as a tea room Wed–Sun afternoon. €

WHAT TO SEE AND DO

Executieplaats/Dodencellen (Execution Spot/Death Cells) (1 Guido Gezellestraat; 06.00–22.00; free) Accessed by a signposted door around the corner from the town hall, this point marks a very dark chapter in British military history. British soldiers who refused to return to the front line or were caught deserting – often as a result of trauma – were held in these two cells and executed at the post standing at the back of the courtyard. A priest would read them their last rites, the attending medical officer would place a white cloth over their heart and a line of six riflemen would face the accused – although only one of the guns was loaded. Now a memorial, one cell still bears the etchings of prisoners; the other hosts a lifelike, chilling projection. Four soldiers are believed to have been executed here; in total the British army carried out 346 executions during World War I, including of Canadian and ANZAC troops. The last execution took place on 8 May 1919.

Talbot House ✷ (43 Gasthuisstraat, entrance via Pottestraat; 057 33 32 28; w talbothouse.be; 10.00–17.30 Tue–Sun, last ticket 16.30; adult/7–22/under 7 €9/6/free, combi-ticket with Hopmuseum €10.50) A very special living museum that was established in December 1915 by Reverend Philip Clayton – AKA 'Tubby' – and chaplain Neville Talbot. The idea was to create an 'everyman's club' that would, unusually, make no distinctions according to rank, and instead offer soldiers a wholesome refuge from the horrors of the front line.

Tubby was born in Queensland, Australia, in 1885, but after losing their property several times to floods the family moved back to England when Tubby was two years old. He was a brilliant student, but decided to become a priest; when World War I broke out he was assigned to the 6th Division as an army chaplain and posted to the Salient. He visited the trenches and narrowly escaped death on a number of occasions, which provided the inspiration for the opening of Talbot House as a place of 'light, warmth and laughter' where soldiers could shelter from the ugliness of war. Here they could make as much noise as they liked, play card games and have an undisturbed night's sleep. Indeed, the 'real sheets' room (the General's Room) was famous as the only room in the house with a bed sheet – a luxury which cost five francs and was the prize of many a card game. By the summer of 1917, it's estimated that 5,000 soldiers a week were passing through the house in preparation for the Third Battle of Ypres (see box, page 272).

Tubby – who wasn't especially tubby, curiously – was a jovial landlord, famous for his love of humorous adages (or 'Tubbisms'), such as 'Never judge a man by his umbrella, it might not be his'. In the chapel, which sits on the fourth floor of the house beneath the eaves, he baptised 50 soldiers, performed 800 confirmations and delivered communion to tens of thousands of soldiers.

The house is filled with original items, but the two most poignant artefacts are found in the hallway on the ground floor. The first is 'Friendship corner', pages from a visitors' book where soldiers would leave messages for friends, or notes asking others if they knew of their whereabouts. The second is a map of the area. Poperinge and Ypres have been wiped away by the fingerprints of soldiers pointing to where they were stationed or had lost friends – you can even make out the salient, marked by a smudgy bulge. In the garden, you'll find the museum and shop; on the other side of the path, a small room is dedicated to temporary shows.

After the war, Tubby was made an honorary citizen of Poperinge. He returned to England in March 1919, accompanied by his dog Chippy, and became the vicar of All Hallows' Church near the Tower of London. Talbot House was a hugely important place of remembrance for World War I veterans, like Harry Patch – the last surviving soldier to have fought in the trenches during World War I – who visited the house before his death in 2009 and was able to sit in the same lounge chair he'd last sat in while talking to friends in 1917. With the last of these veterans gone, it's even more essential to remember them through a visit here – whether a descendent of someone who fought or not. Take your time to wander around and soak up the atmosphere, or spend the night (page 276) to really get a sense of the place's continuing hospitality. The place is so anchored in the veterans' memory that they even adopted the neighbour's cat, which – as I can attest – will be more than happy to share your billet.

Hopmuseum (71 Gasthuisstraat; 057 33 79 22; **w** hopmuseum.be; Mar–Nov 10.00–17.30 Tue–Sun; closed Dec–Feb, but open 14.00–17.00 during Christmas hols; adult/6–25/under 6 €6/2.50/free; last ticket 16.30) Poperinge sits at the centre of Hoppeland, Belgium's main hop-growing region, and until the 1960s this building was the *Stadsschaal* or municipal scales, the main headquarters for inspecting, weighing and pressing the hops. An interactive museum now explains the various stages of production.

Sint-Janskerk (St John's Church) (St-Janskruisstraat; 07.30–19.00; free) This Gothic church is venerated thanks to the miraculous statue of the Virgin Mary, which stands bathed in candlelight on the ornate Lady Altar on the left-hand side of the church. In 1479 a local, Jacquemyne Bayaerts, gave birth to a stillborn son, who had to be buried in unconsecrated ground because he hadn't been baptised. Distraught, the parents prayed to the Virgin Mary and pleaded for the child to be disinterred. Three days later their wish was granted and the child was found alive. They were able to quickly baptise the infant before it died an hour later. The miracle

KEIKOPPEN

Poperinge residents are nicknamed *keikoppen*, or 'pigheads', as a mark of their stubborn refusal to stop producing linen when the city of Ypres threatened them for impinging on their trade. The statue of Ghybe riding a donkey backwards, which stands in front of Sint-Bertinuskerk, is a satirical representation of the rivalry. The jester making an – pardon the pun – ass out of the donkey represents the three cloth towns of Ypres, Ghent and Bruges.

was recognised by the Pope in 1481 and has been celebrated ever since at the annual Maria-Ommegang in March.

Sint-Bertinuskerk (St Bertinus's Church) (Vroonhof; ⌚ 09.00–18.00; free) This 15th-century late-Gothic church with curling blue paint on the walls has a large oak-panelled entrance which holds the organ. It contains a number of artworks, but look out for the baldachin, a white and gold 18th-century Rococo procession canopy, in the right-hand chapel and, embedded above it, a Christmas-themed stained-glass window.

Lijssenthoek Military Cemetery (35a Boescheepseweg; ⌚ 09.00–18.00; free) Just 2.5km west of Poperinge, Lijssenthoek is the second-largest Commonwealth cemetery in the world after Tyne Cot (page 274). Originally a farm, it became the biggest evacuation hospital on the Ypres Salient and now contains over 10,700 tombstones representing both Allied and German troops, as well as Chinese workers. The low-lying visitor centre fills you in on the hospital's daily life, has a tear-off calendar recounting the story of one of the victims who died on that particular day, and hundreds of portraits on the wall revealing the faces behind the headstones. As you take it in, you'll notice voices seeming to whisper from behind the walls. There are databanks to search for relatives as well.

Chinese memorial – Busseboom (Corner of Sint-Jansstraat & Visserijmolenstraat; free) During World War I, both the British and French armies employed Chinese contract workers to build railways, restore roads and, eventually, to clean up the battlefields. At least 2,000 Chinese workers died during the period (mostly of flu or pneumonia); 35 of them are buried in the Lijssenthoek Military Cemetery and, as of 2017, 1.5km from Poperinge's limits, you'll find two monuments honouring them.

Day trips

Sint-Sixtusabdij (Sint-Sixtus Abbey) (12 Donkerstraat, 8640 Westvleteren; **w** sintsixtus.be) Whisper 'Westvleteren' into the ear of any beer enthusiast and they'll be putty in your hands. Sitting in seclusion 7km north of Poperinge, this small village is home to the revered Sint-Sixtus Abbey. Inside its walls, Cistercian monks brew award-winning Trappist beers, including the elusive no 12 – repeatedly ranked as the best in the world. The recipe of this beer remains shrouded in secrecy, and the brewery itself is off limits. However, visitors can find out more about the abbey in the **Claustrum** information centre (⌚ Sep–Jun 14.00–17.00 Mon–Wed & Sat–Sun, Jul–Aug 14.00–17.00 Mon–Thu & Sat–Sun), located in the **In de Vrede** café (☎ 057 40 03 77; **w** indevrede.be; ⌚ Sep–Jun 10.00–19.00 Mon–Wed & Sat–Sun, Jul–Aug 10.00–19.00 Mon–Thu & Sat–Sun), where you can also taste the beers. Choose from the bitter blonde 6 (5.8%), the cult brown 8 (8%), or the surprisingly sweet and oh-so-smooth no 12 (12%). Orders of the Abbey cheese with mustard and homemade pâté are essential nibbles to enhance the flavour of the beers. It's a great place to marvel at the elderly ladies who pitch up every day and knock back three or four of the no 12s. You can buy small mixed cases of the beer from the café shop, but if you join the ranks of addicts and want to get your hands on a crate then you'll have to go on the website, check when you can book and which beers are in stock, then call the beer hotline well in advance (☎ 070 21 00 45); a crate of 24 bottles costs from €35 to €45, not including a deposit for the crate. The system was born after a queue of over 400 cars made national news in 2005.

You'll be given a date and time for collection and have to go to a side entrance located to the west of the abbey.

Getting there and away

By bike Poperinge tourist office offers the free, beer-themed *Tournée Locale* cycling map, with several routes taking you past Sint-Sixtus Abbey, including the Poperinge–Ypres circuit (38–46.5km) and the Poperinge Vleteren route (33km), both starting at the town's Hopmuseum. For bike rental, see page 276.

By car From Poperinge take the N308 west out of town and turn right on to Diepemeers/N347; after 750m turn left into Krombeekseweg and take the fourth right into Nonnenstraat; follow it round and turn left into Donkerstraat; the café is on your left (7km; ⌚ 10mins).

KORTRIJK

The course of Flemish history was changed forever in the Groeninge fields on the outskirts of Kortrijk in July 1302. A group of lightly armed Flemish foot soldiers went head to head with a cavalry of professional French knights – and won. Known as the Battle of the Golden Spurs (pages 6 and 280), it was the first time in history a horseback army had been defeated by footmen and is considered by many the reason why Dutch is still spoken in Flanders today. In revenge, the city was razed by French King Charles VI in 1382 but Kortrijk bounced back by joining the cloth trade, and despite suffering severe damage during World Wars I and II it still has 200 listed monuments dotted around town.

The city is very close to the Wallonian border, and consequently is quite French with good shopping and a burgeoning café culture. It also blends old and modern very well, from the traditional Sint-Elizabeth Begijnhof and Broeltorens (Broel Towers) to its design biennial Interieur (**w** interieur.be) and seven modern bridges, which link Buda Island to the city centre and span the newly straightened and widened river Leie. Extensive works on the latter have seen citizens reunited with the water again: the area now boasts parks, buzzing eateries and city beach BudaBeach come summer.

GETTING THERE AND AWAY

By car From Ghent follow the E17 southwest and take exit 2 (direction: Hoog Kortrijk) and follow signs for Kortrijk Centrum (49km; ⌚ 35mins). From Bruges follow signs for the R30 out of town and join the E403, then follow it south for 45.8km and, at the interchange 1-Morseel, stay on the right and follow signs for the A19 towards R8/Kortrijk; follow the R8 and take exit 12 (direction: Marke) and follow Pottelberg into the centre of town (54km; ⌚ 41mins).

By train Ghent (twice an hour; ⌚ 30mins); Bruges (twice an hour; ⌚ 50mins); Brussels (twice an hour Mon–Fri, ⌚ 1hr 16mins; hourly Sat–Sun, ⌚ 1hr 23mins); Ypres (hourly; ⌚ 28mins).

TOURIST INFORMATION

Tourist information [281 D3] Begijnhofpark; ☎ 056 27 78 40; **w** toerismekortrijk.be; ⌚ May–Sep 10.00–18.00; Oct–Apr 10.00–17.00. In the same building as Kortrijk 1302 (page 284). Can organise a guide (€75/2hrs) so you can visit the belfry, medieval crypt & Broel Towers & can provide a free city walking map filling you in on Kortrijk's metamorphosis (or download the audio version from their website).

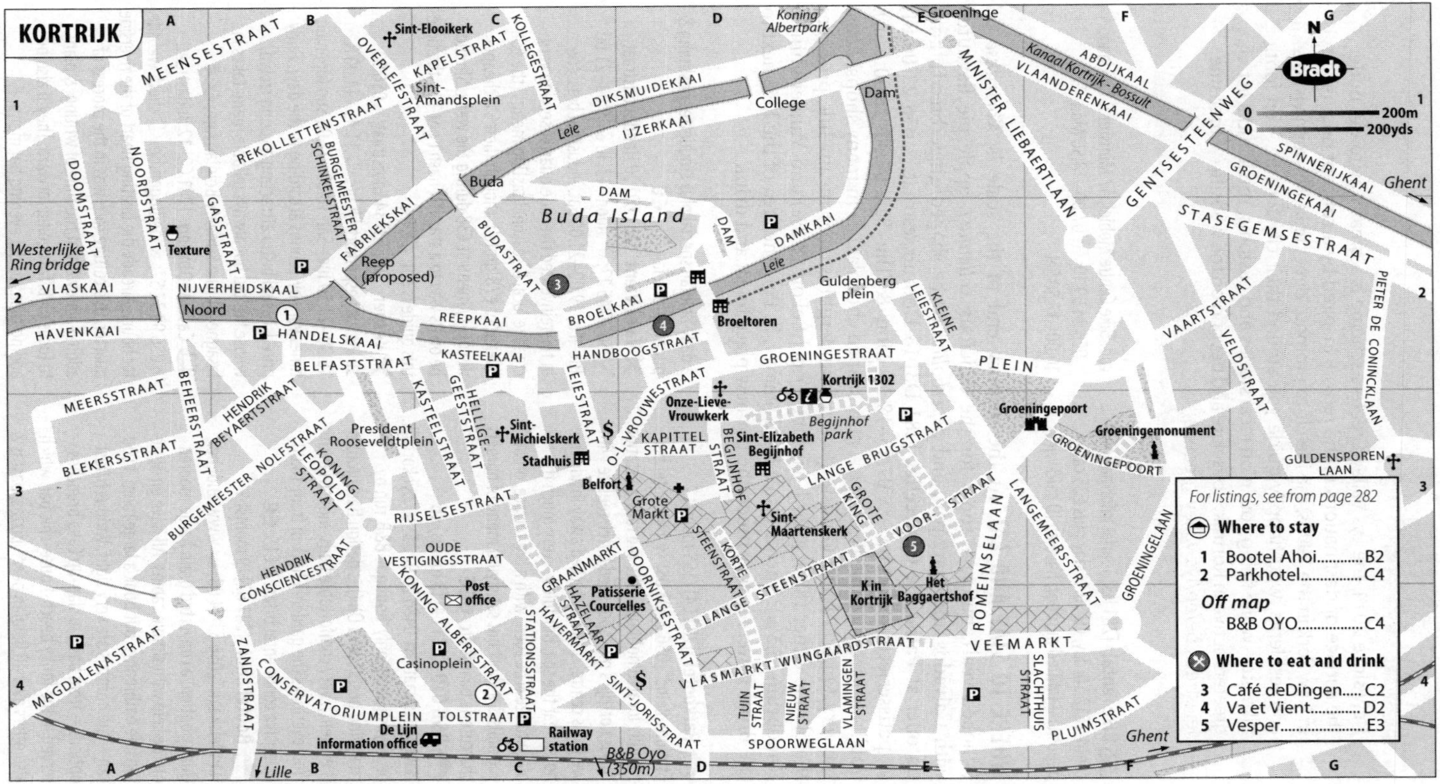
KORTRIJK
Bradt
N
200m
200yds
Kanaal Kortrijk - Bossuit
ABDIJKAAL
VLAANDERENKAAI
MINISTER LIEBAERTLAAN
GENTSESTEENWEG
SPINNERIJKAAI
GROENINGEKAAI
STASEGEMSESTRAAT
PIETER DE CONINCKLAAN
Ghent
Groeninge
Koning Albertpark
Dam
College
DIKSMUIDEKAAI
IJZERKAAI
Leie
Buda
DAM
Buda Island
DAMKAAI
MEENSESTRAAT
Sint-Elooikerk
KAPELSTRAAT
KOLLEGESTRAAT
OVERLEIESTRAAT
Sint-Amandsplein
REKOLLETTENSTRAAT
BURGEMEESTER SCHINKELSTRAAT
DOOMSTRAAT
NOORDSTRAAT
GASSTRAAT
Texture
Westerlijke Ring bridge
FABRIEKSKAI
Reep (proposed)
BUDASTRAAT
VLASKAAI
NIJVERHEIDSKAAL
Noord
HAVENKAAI
HANDELSKAAI
REEPKAAI
BROELKAAI
Broeltoren
Guldenberg plein
KLEINE LEIESTRAAT
VAARTSTRAAT
VELDSTRAAT
KASTEELKAAI
HANDBOOGSTRAAT
GROENINGESTRAAT
PLEIN
BELFASTSTRAAT
MEERSSTRAAT
HENDRIK BEYAERTSTRAAT
BEHEERSTRAAT
BLEKERSSTRAAT
President Rooseveldtplein
KASTEELSTRAAT
HELLIGE-GEESTSTRAAT
Sint-Michielskerk
Stadhuis
LEIESTRAAT
O.-L.-VROUWESTRAAT
Onze-Lieve-Vrouwkerk
Kortrijk 1302
Begijnhof park
Sint-Elizabeth Begijnhof
KAPITTEL STRAAT
BEGIJNHOF STRAAT
Groeningepoort
Groeningemonument
GROENINGEPOORT
GULDENSPOREN LAAN
BURGEMEESTER NOLFSTRAAT
KONING LEOPOLD I-STRAAT
RIJSELSESTRAAT
Belfort
Grote Markt
LANGE BRUGSTRAAT
GROTE KING
Sint-Maartenskerk
VOORSTRAAT
ROMEINSELAAN
LANGEMEERSSTRAAT
GROENINGELAAN
OUDE VESTIGINGSSTRAAT
HENDRIK CONSCIENCESTRAAT
KONING ALBERTSTRAAT
Post office
GRAANMARKT
DOORNIKSESTRAAT
KORTE STEENSTRAAT
Patisserie Courcelles
HAZELAAR STRAAT
HAVERMARKT
LANGE STEENSTRAAT
K in Kortrijk
Het Baggaertshof
VEEMARKT
STATIONSSTRAAT
MAGDALENASTRAAT
ZANDSTRAAT
CONSERVATORIUMPLEIN
Casinoplein
TOLSTRAAT
SINT-JORISSTRAAT
VLASMARKT
WIJNGAARDSTRAAT
TUIN STRAAT
NIEUW STRAAT
VLAMINGEN STRAAT
SLACHTHUIS STRAAT
PLUIMSTRAAT
SPOORWEGLAAN
De Lijn information office
Railway station
B&B Oyo (350m)
Lille
For listings, see from page 282
Where to stay
1 Bootel Ahoi............B2
2 Parkhotel...............C4
Off map
B&B OYO.................C4
Where to eat and drink
3 Café deDingen.....C2
4 Va et Vient............D2
5 Vesper.....................E3

MEET AND GREET

New since 2014, the Lys Valley Greeters scheme is a great way to get under the surface of destinations in the region. Inspired by a concept originating in New York in the 1990s, the idea is to promote direct links between visitors and residents, who happily guide you around their city for free – on foot, bike etc – while filling you in on local stories and customs. You'll find a list of greeters active in Kortrijk, Roeselare and beyond on the website (w toerisme-leiestreek.be/en/lys-valley-greeters).

Bike rental [281 D3] Tourist information centre (€12.50/day, €9.50/½ day plus €25 cash deposit) – limited number; have an ID card with you. Bike Centre Mobiel, 57 Minister P. Tacklaan; 056 24 99 10; 07.00–18.50 Mon–Fri, 10.00–17.50 Sat

WHERE TO STAY AND EAT At the savoury end of the scale is *Kortrijkse bil* (smoked veal), but save room for the delicious *kalletaart*, apple pie flavoured with Calvados and marzipan, and *peperbollen* (cube-shaped gingerbread), both on offer at **Patisserie Courcelles** [281 D3] (8 Doorniksestraat; 056 22 06 81; w patisseriecourcelles.be; 07.45–18.30 Mon & Thu–Sat, 07.30–18.00 Sun). You'll also see adorable *begijntjes* – nun-shaped chocolates – in many shops. Local brewery Omer Vander Ghinste (w omervanderghinste.be) meanwhile produces the blonde Omer (8%), award-winning Tripel LeFort (8.8%) and VanderGhinste Roodbruin (5.5%). There's also a local jenever, St Pol. The area of the Leie next to the Broel Towers is very much the hot new place to eat and drink.

Parkhotel [281 C4] (155 rooms) 2 Stationsplein; 056 22 03 03; w parkhotel.be. Handily located right opposite the railway station, this is Kortrijk's most polished hotel, replete with wellness centre, bistro &, tucked away inside the hotel near the spa, Bar Jules – very much the place to see & be seen, with a big terrace, great cocktails & a short but satisfying menu of burgers, charcuterie boards etc. **€€€**

B&B OYO [281 C4] (3 rooms) 46 Hoveniersstraat; m 0486 26 92 25; w oyokortrijk.be. Stylish adult-only 'boutique B&B' run by charming hosts Lan & Oli (his design background is evident). Very comfortable beds; industrial-chic 'Yoo' overlooks the garden. Check in from 16.00; extensive continental b/fast is €15. **€€**

Bootel Ahoi [281 B2] (9 rooms) 1 Handelskaai; 056 53 14 68; w www.ahoi.be. Quirky option: a converted grain barge moored on the Leie with simple cabins. All have en-suite capsule bathrooms, but book a large room if you can – the normals are very tight. Various b/fast options – from basic to slap-up Cava brunches – served in the funky beach-house-chic bar, which also offers over 40 Belgian beers, pizzas, pastas & a daily Belgian special plus croquettes or shrimp & pudding for a fair rate. **€€**

Va et Vient [281 D2] 20 Handboogstraat; 056 20 45 17; noon–13.30 & 19.00–21.00 Tue–Fri, 19.00–21.00 Sat. Industrial brasserie in the reinvented riverside quarter serving very creative local & seasonal tasting menus (the €58 'kleine' or €78 'grote'), though there's a cheaper discovery menu at €38 during the week. Should be on its way to a star, if it hasn't got 1 by the time this guide is out. **€€€€**

Vesper [281 E3] 34 Voorstraat; 056 90 30 98; w vesperkortrijk.be; 11.45–14.00 & 18.30–21.30 Tue–Sat, 18.00–21.00 Sun (opening times vary by 30mins according to the day). Fairly priced, casual bistro attracting a young crowd, whose limited but always reliable menu takes in lasagne, quiche & meaty Belgian fare. **€€€**

Café deDingen [281 C2] 12 Budastraat; 056 90 72 57; w dedingen.be; check website for hours. Already the beating heart of the riverside quarter, this 'culture café' was in the process of adding a brewery at the time of writing, & plans to focus on b/fast going forward. They'll also be adding tapas to the evening bar menu. **€**

WHAT TO SEE AND DO

Grote Markt Unusually, Kortrijk's **Belfort (Belfry)** [281 D3] stands alone in the middle of the Grote Markt; a squat red-brick affair that dates from the 13th century. It belonged to the former Cloth Hall destroyed in 1944, and today houses a 48-bell carillon. Near the top stand Kalle (of apple pie fame) and Manten, the hourly bell ringers. Also on the square is the 15th-century **Stadhuis (Town Hall)** [281 C3] (54 Grote Markt; ⌚ Jul–Aug 15.00–17.00 Tue, Thu & Sat; free), a traditional late Gothic-Renaissance building studded with sculptures of the Counts of Flanders. Inside, its **Schepenzaal (Aldermen's Hall)** and **Raadzaal (Council Chamber)** have impressive chimneys, but can only be visited with a guide.

Sint-Maartenskerk (St Martin's Church) [281 D3] (Sint-Maartenskerkstraat; ⌚ Apr–Nov 07.30–18.00 Mon, 10.00–18.00 Tue–Sat, 10.30–after 18.00 mass Sun; Oct–Mar 07.30–17.00 Mon–Sat; free) Just off the Grote Markt, this beautiful 15th-century church has an intricately carved entrance and 83m-high Brabantine-Gothic tower. To the left of the entrance hang ten modern paintings depicting the life of St Martin; elsewhere are paintings by students from the school of Rubens. The **treasury** in the **Sint-Elooikapel (St Eligius Chapel)** (⌚ Easter–Aug Sun afternoon, & before/after services on festive days, as well as by request) displays silver brocade liturgical robes and a silver collection spanning three centuries.

Sint-Elizabeth Begijnhof (St Elizabeth Béguinage) ✷ [281 D3] (Begijnhofstraat; m 0473 86 26 88; ⌚ summer 07.00–21.00; winter 07.00–20.00; free) Kortrijk's béguinage is uniquely fascinating: a totally secluded cobblestone enclave full of nooks and crannies that is now gleaming after a lengthy restoration begun in 1984 and set to complete in 2019. The works have added a number of new houses to rent; if you're interested and over 40 (the sole stipulation) I'm pleased to say that the rates are rather favourable!

The béguinage was probably founded in 1238 by Joan of Constantinople, Countess of Flanders, whose statue you see in the courtyard at the entrance. Despite its tranquillity today, over the centuries it served as a field hospital, a barracks and – much to the béguines's horror – a brothel, until the 'Grand Mistress' of the day (a democratically elected position) put a stop to all the drama in the 19th century. Adding to its importance, it was also home to the last béguine in the world, Marcella Pattyn, who died in 2013 at the age of 92, ending an 800-year-old tradition.

Stop at the **visitor centre** (⌚ 10.00–17.00 Tue–Sun) just outside the gate for an English booklet/map; I strongly advise that you shell out for the €2 audio guide to really get the most from a visit, but I've briefly resumed some key points below.

Facing the entrance courtyard, on your extreme left you'll see the **Kapel Sint-Matthews (St Matthew's Chapel)** (2 Begijnhof; ⌚ 13.00–17.00 Tue–Sun), whose 1678 organ is the second-oldest of its kind in Flanders. Straight ahead, dominating the square, the brick-fronted gabled house you see was the home of the Grand Mistresses who ran the béguinage. It now houses a lovely coffee shop, **Huis van de Grootjuffrouw** (31 Begijnhof; m 0498 76 16 24; w huisvandegrootjuffrouw.be; ⌚ 13.30–18.30 Wed–Fri, 11.00–18.30 Sat–Sun; €), offering cake, aperitifs, a simple soup at weekends, and – charmingly – a free chocolate *begijntje* served with your coffee.

Follow the path around to the left of St Matthew's Chapel and you'll find the **Saint Anna room**, now an impressive-looking **experience centre** but with little information in English. Outside is a *tiny* statue of Marcella Pattyn; reportedly she wasn't quite this diminutive in real-life! Retrace your steps to the café and head through the alley to its left; you could easily miss the **Chapel of Our Lady of the Snow** (named after a miracle) on your left – it's utterly dominated by the two huge churches that bracket the béguinage. Continue further down the path here to the gardens, then exit the béguinage, heading left on the gravel path that leads towards the squat **Artillery tower**, one of the last remaining remnants of the city's medieval defences.

Onze-Lieve-Vrouwekerk (Church of Our Lady) [281 D3] (Deken Zegerplein; ⌚ 08.00–18.00 Mon–Fri, 09.00–18.00 Sat, 11.00–18.00 Sun; free) This beautiful 13th-century church boasts a lavish Baroque interior. To the left of the entrance there's a plaque for poet-priest Guido Gezelle; further down the *Raising of the Cross* by Van Dyck; and above the choir gallery a ceiling covered in Flemish lions. However, the real treasure is the **Counts' Chapel**, built as the mausoleum of Count Lodewijk van Maele and decorated with stained-glass windows and 18th-century murals.

Texture [281 A2] (28 Noordstraat; ☎ 056 27 74 70; **w** texturekortrijk.be; ⌚ May–Sep 10.00–18.00 Tue–Sun; Oct–Apr 10.00–17.00 Tue–Sun; adult/under 12 & 1st Sun of month €6/free) This three-room museum, set in an old 1912 flax depot, tells the story of the region's renowned flax and linen industry – with 'Courtrai flax' still sought after today. Okay, flax probably doesn't sound like the most immediately fascinating subject, but we use it every day without even thinking about it, as you'll discover in the cabinet of curiosities. There's also a chamber with beautiful damask and lace, and a very superior bistro, Kaffee Damast (**€€€**), with regional products and live jazz gigs.

Kortrijk 1302 [281 A3] (Begijnhofpark; ☎ 056 27 78 50; **w** kortrijk1302.be; ⌚ May–Sep 10.00–18.00 Tue–Sun; Oct–Apr 10.00–17.00 Tue–Sun; adult/under 12 & 1st Sun of month €6/free) Engaging museum in the tourist office that explains the Battle of the Golden Spurs (pages 6 and 280), which took place on the outskirts of Kortrijk on 11 July 1302 and was the first time in history that foot soldiers (Flemish) had beaten a horseback army. The audio guide is narrated by a historical character, Gilles le Muisit, Abbot of St Martin's Abbey in Tournai, who wrote the original history of the battle – later spun and re-spun by those who saw in it the rallying cry (or should that be roar) of Flemish nationalism (including Hendrik Conscience, who wrote an epic novel on the topic – see page 18). Even the name of the battle, referencing the gilded spurs worn by the French knights, was only invented in the 18th century, so nothing is as it seems. The short film at the end of the museum is well worth watching if you've even a passing interest in this thorny subject.

Groeningepoort and monument [281 F3] (Plein) A 5-minute walk east on 't Plein, a 17th-century military training ground, you'll find the **Groeningepoort (Groeninge Gate)**, which was installed in 1908 to commemorate the Battle of the Golden Spurs. Follow the path through the park and you'll come to the gilded **Groeningemonument** of the Virgin of Flanders – a symbol of freedom – keeping a lion at bay.

Het Baggaertshof [281 E3] (37 Sint-Jansstraat; ⌚ 26 Mar–24 Oct 14.00–18.00 Tue–Thu & Sat–Sun; 25 Oct–25 Mar 14.00–17.00 Tue–Thu & Sat–Sun; free) This tiny béguinage was established in 1638 by the three Baggaert sisters, who wanted to provide lodging for poor widows and their daughters. In the rectangular courtyard, surrounding a medicinal herb garden, you'll still see a dozen original little houses and a chapel with a polychrome statue of Holy Mother Ter Olmen. A true hidden gem. Pause to sniff the rosemary-scented air.

Broeltorens (Broel Towers) [281 D2] (Broelkaai) Alongside the Artillery Tower, these chunky watchtowers spanning the river Leie are all that remains of the city's medieval walls. That on the right, known as the **Speytorre**, was built in 1385 to control traffic on the Leie; on the left, the **Ingelburghtorre** was a weapons depot built in 1415. Here you'll see the lowered banks of the river Leie, which bring you right up close to the water. Spend some time strolling around **Buda Island**, which you'll reach by crossing the bridge next to the Broel Towers; the area hosts a city beach in summer. As part of the Leie's transformation, six (of an eventual seven) bridges have already redrawn the local skyline, and are suspended 7m above the surface of the water.

ROESELARE

Roeselare is a commercial town where even the locals are nicknamed *Nieuwmarkters* because of their love of shopping. The main reason to visit, though, is its association with cycling lore: besides local boy Odiel Defraeye, the first Belgian to win the Tour de France (in 1912), it has turned out an epic four world champions – Benoni Beheyt, Patrick Sercu, Freddy Maertens and Jean-Pierre Monseré – and is the kickoff point for the Dwars door Vlaanderen semi-classic race in spring. In September 2018, former cycling museum WieMu reopened in a new, spruced-up guise as **KOERS** (page 286). Happily, another local icon, Brouwerij Rodenbach (133 Spanjestraat; 051 27 27 00; rodenbachbeer; tours €10 to be paid in cash), known for its red-brown beer, has now started welcoming individual visitors; check their Facebook for dates, or contact visit co-ordinator Nancy on nancy.verschaete@swinkelsfamilybrewers.com.

GETTING THERE AND AWAY

By car From Kortrijk follow the E403 north and take exit 7 (direction: Izegem) (26km; 28mins).

By train Kortrijk (twice an hour; 20mins)

TOURIST INFORMATION

Tourist information 15 Polenplein; 051 26 96 00; w visitroeselare.be; Mar–Sep 10.00–17.00 Mon–Sun; Oct–Feb 10.00–17.00 Mon–Sat. Very friendly office set in the excellent new KOERS museum. Naturally it offers cycle rental, but also an 8.5km city-walk brochure (€2) taking you via the local highlights.

WHAT TO SEE AND DO

Sint-Michielskerk (St Michael's Church) (Sint-Michielsplein; 051 26 96 00; Jun–Sep 09.00–11.00 & 14.30–18.00 Mon–Fri; Oct–May 09.00–11.30; free) This 18th-century church houses a handful of art treasures, including the tomb of 17th-century Flemish painter Jan van Cleef and his wife, and the largest organ in West Flanders, which is put to use every Thursday at the weekly **carillon concert** (20.30–21.30).

KOERS (15 Polenplein; 015 26 96 00; w koersmuseum.be; Oct–Feb 10.00–17.00 Tue–Sat; Mar–Sep 10.00–17.00 Tue–Sun; adult/3–18/under 3 €7/1/free) A must for cycling enthusiasts, this newly rejigged museum takes you on an interactive ride through the history of the sport in Flanders, via a collection of the earliest and most cutting-edge bikes in the Hall of World Champions, a room dedicated to local legend Jean-Pierre Monseré – aka 'Jempi' – tragically killed in a collision with a car while racing in 1971, and a host of nostalgia-inducing jerseys and paraphernalia.

NORTHERN BELGIUM ONLINE

For additional online content, articles, photos and more on Northern Belgium, why not visit w bradtguides.com/northernbelgium?

7

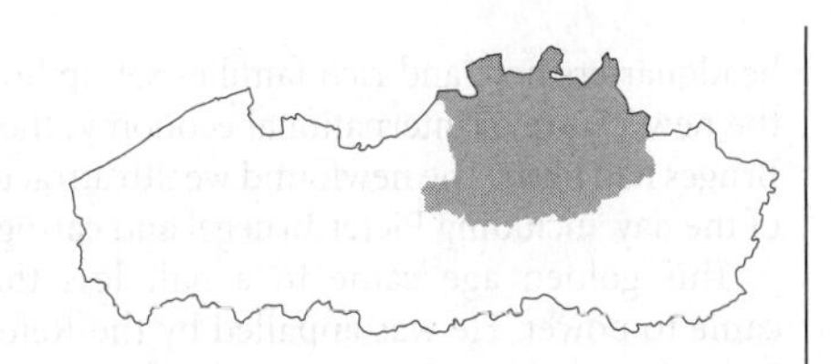

Antwerp

Home to over 1.8 million people, Antwerp is Flanders' most populous region and shares its northern border with the Netherlands. Most of the action is weighted in the west, where the dynamic city of Antwerp clusters around Europe's second-biggest port, its golden age treasures vying for attention with more contemporary pleasures. To the south, oft-overshadowed Mechelen is reinventing itself apace. Move east for De Kempen, a relatively undeveloped region of moors and wetlands popular with cyclists following the *Provincie Antwerpen* biking network. Also dotting the landscape are the untapped cities of Turnhout, Herentals and Geel – not forgetting charming Lier with its Zimmer clock tower.

ANTWERP

Flanders' de facto capital is handsome, hip and idiosyncratic, juggling edgy fashion boutiques, atmospheric museums and more than its fair share of Michelin-starred restaurants. Small it might be – there are around 520,000 residents, and it's easy to get by without looking at public transport – but self-effacing it's not, with locals labelling it 't Stad (the City), as though no other even existed. They may have a point: it was here that Sir Thomas More conceived his *Utopia*, that William Tyndale wrote the first English translation of the Old Testament, and where the world's first stock exchange was established. Antwerp was home to famous Baroque artist Peter Paul Rubens and pioneering printer Christophe Plantin. It's also the world's biggest diamond centre, and its port ranks right up there globally.

Curled around that centre of industry like an inverted 'C', Antwerp's medieval core is animated by carillon chimes and buzzing brown bars. The well-heeled crowds of chi-chi 't Zuid in the south cede to the clatter of heels in the red-light district – beyond that is the new museum quarter, 't Eilandje. Unspooling towards the ring road, elegant 19th-century neighbourhoods, a new Green Quarter and vibrant multi-cultural areas contribute to Antwerp's impressive balancing act – a city that's proud of its past but not looking back.

HISTORY Antwerp was settled during the 4th century by the Germanic Franks, a group of united Germanic tribes under forced conscription by the Romans. By the time the Empire's clutch in the north began to weaken around AD500, the tribes had built a fortified town. This was destroyed by the Vikings in AD836 and expansion was limited until the end of the 15th century, when the town suddenly began to blossom. The Zwin canal that fed trade to Bruges had begun to silt up, and as a result sea traffic was forced north to Antwerp. The city soon became Europe's sugar capital, and in the first half of the 16th century over a hundred ships a day were passing through the port, while more than 2,000 carts laden with pepper, silver and silks were unloaded at the docks. Foreign and domestic trading companies had all moved their headquarters here and rich families set up home in grand mansions. All flocked to the new 'centre of international economy', then Europe's richest city, eclipsing what Bruges had been. The newfound wealth attracted the best artists and scientific minds of the day, including Pieter Bruegel and cartographer Gerardus Mercator.

This golden age came to a halt less than a century later, when Philip II came to power. He was appalled by the Reformation riots sweeping through the Low Countries at the time and, when Protestants destroyed the inside of the city cathedral during an Ommegang Procession in 1566, he sent in his troops and the Inquisition to banish or hang participants. After nine years, the unpaid Spanish troops mutinied on 4 November 1576 and went on a three-day rampage, known as the Spanish Fury, that left 800 homes burned and over 8,000 citizens dead. They were expelled, but returned in 1585, forcing Antwerp's incorporation into the Spanish Netherlands. Part of the negotiations involved Antwerp becoming a Catholic city, and thousands of Protestants had to cross the border into the United Provinces (Holland). The loss of these skilled workers weakened the city's economy further and by 1800 the population had fallen from 100,000 to just 42,000.

There was a slight revival in 1609 when the Twelve Years Truce between the United Provinces and Spanish Netherlands was signed. However, during this period the Dutch increased their hold over the waterways and when the Treaty of Munster (part of the Peace of Westphalia agreement) was signed in 1648, the newly independent Dutch closed the Scheldt to all foreign shipping. The agreement ended the Thirty Years War between Protestants and Catholics, but sounded the economic death knell for Spanish-controlled Antwerp. The city didn't regain some of its glory until 1797, when Napoleon came to power and the French rebuilt parts of the docks for use as a military naval base. The Scheldt finally opened again in 1863 and Antwerp regained its prosperity.

The Germans occupied the city in both world wars. During World War II, their armies were finally forced out by the British in September 1944, but post-liberation the city was battered by hundreds of V1 and V2 rockets seeking to sever supply links to Allied soldiers. After the war, Antwerp quickly picked up the pieces, rising to become one of Europe's key ports, consolidating its role as the world's diamond trade hub, and unexpectedly morphing into a breeding ground for edgy fashion.

GETTING THERE AND AWAY

By plane Most visitors arrive via Brussels Airport Zaventem, 30 minutes from Antwerp by train, but the city has its own dinky airport, 6km from the centre in Deurne, and served by **Flybe** (**w** flybe.com) and **Tui** (**w** tui.com). Buses 51, 52 and 53 depart outside for Berchem station, a brief train, tram or bus ride away from the centre of town.

By train Antwerp has two mainline stations, Berchem and Centraal. You want the latter for the centre, a 15-minute walk away. Trams 3, 5, 9 and 15 run from the Diamant stop by Centraal Station to the centre (alight at Groenplaats). From Centraal Station trains depart for: Bruges (🕘 hourly; 1hr 29mins); Brussels (🕘 every 15mins; 50mins); Ghent (🕘 3 times an hour Mon–Fri, twice an hour Sat–Sun; 1hr).

By bus **Flixbus** (**w** flixbus.com) and **Eurolines** (**w** eurolines.eu) both serve Antwerp. From Brussels Zaventem the Airport Express (**w** airportexpress.be) departs for Antwerp every hour on the hour, terminating by Centraal Station.

By car Antwerp is at the junction of several European motorways, with easy access from Brussels and North Coast resorts such as Ostend. Paris is 4 hours away; Amsterdam half that. Note that Antwerp is now a Low-Emission Zone, so check that your vehicle is permitted before you travel (w lez.antwerpen.be). See box, page 41 for more details.

GETTING AROUND

By bus, metro or tram De Lijn (w delijn.be) operates a slick integrated bus, metro and tram system. A one-way ticket, purchased from the driver, De Lijn office at Centraal Station or select ticket machines, is €3 with unlimited travel for 1hr; a 24hr pass is €7. If you've bought a Belgian SIM card, text 'DL' to the number 4884 (€2.25) and hop aboard.

By bike Pocket-sized Antwerp is best explored on foot – or on two wheels. City-bike scheme Velo Antwerpen offers €4/day passes (book online via credit card only, w velo-antwerpen.be; charge after the first 30mins) and has stations throughout the city.

By scooter Antwerp's latest craze is for electric scooter rental scheme Bird (w bird.co). Download the app on to your phone and off you go – there's a small fee per minute of use.

By taxi Taxis can be hard to find beyond Centraal Station and Groenplaats. Call Antwerp-Tax (03 238 38 38, w antwerp-tax.be). The company also has an app.

TOURIST INFORMATION

Tourist information [295 C2] 13 Grote Markt; 03 232 01 03; w visitantwerpen.be; 10.00–17.00. Visit Antwerp's main branch (there's another in Centraal Station) offers myriad tours & booklets. Their historic city walks run every w/end (Jul–Aug daily), leaving the office at 14.00 (€8/10 on the day). They can also arrange private guided tours from €75/2hrs; give 2 weeks' notice. Be aware that there are plans to move the tourist office to Het Steen in 2020 (page 302).

GUIDED TOURS

Antwerp by Bike 7 Steenplein; m 0497 18 53 45; w antwerpbybike.be. Well-regarded group offering guided bike tours spanning the highlights, as well as more specialist itineraries such as Jewish Antwerp. English-language highlights tour departs Steenplein Mar–Oct 11.00 Sat–Sun; €17 if you bring a bike/€22 with hire.

De Ruien 21 Suikerrui; 03 344 07 55; w ruien.be; 10.00–17.00 Tue–Fri, 10.00–18.00 Sat–Sun. Kitted out in loaned green wellies, it's possible to take a tour of Antwerp's sewers or *ruien*. You can opt for a quick 15min boat tour (age 3 & up, €5) or 90min tablet tour (adult/10–16/City Card €17/11/14.50). You'll see old bridges & even an underground cathedral where hip aristos once partied in private.

Street Art Antwerp m 0487 755 898; w streetartantwerp.com. The city now has a thriving street art scene; run by Tim Marschang, this excellent venture, which has a full list of murals online, has offered 2hr tours of the hidden spots in Berchem & the centre since 2017 (€12 in advance/€15 on the day; details listed on f).

WHERE TO STAY Antwerp is one place where it pays to avoid the chains and take advantage of the vast array of arty B&Bs and boutique hotels. Add in larger hotels with gourmet restaurants and a clutch of great independent hostels, and it's well set-up for tourists, though it's hard to find a true bargain in the city centre (don't be scared of venturing further afield – Antwerp is a village, and sights are never far away).

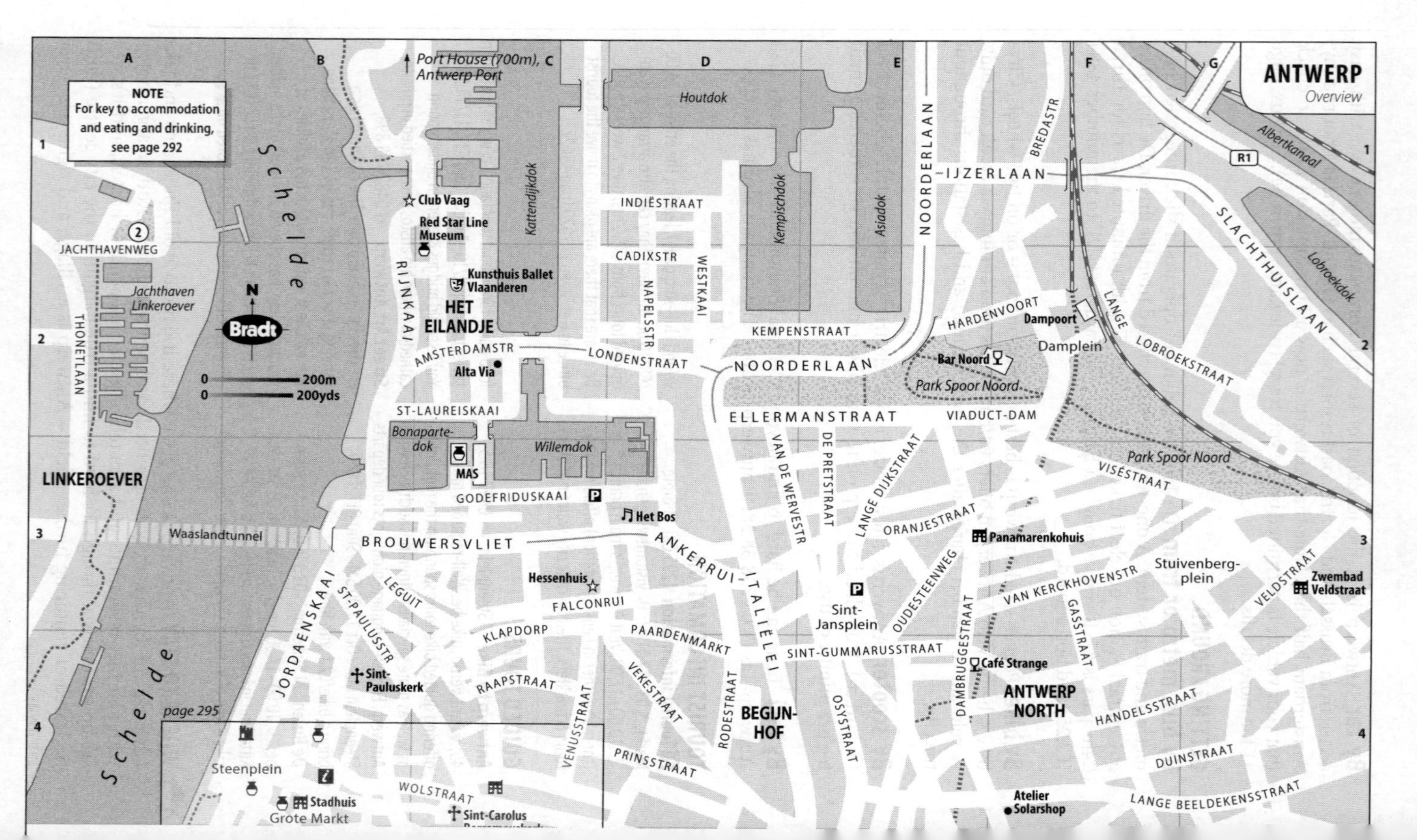

ANTWERP
Overview
NOTE
For key to accommodation and eating and drinking, see page 292
Port House (700m), Antwerp Port
Schelde
Club Vaag
Red Star Line Museum
Kattendijkdok
Houtdok
Kempischdok
Asiadok
Albertkanaal
Lobroekdok
R1
NOORDERLAAN
IJZERLAAN
BREDASTR
SLACHTHUISLAAN
INDIËSTRAAT
CADIXSTR
NAPELSSTR
WESTKAAI
Jachthaven Linkeroever
JACHTHAVENWEG
THONETLAAN
Kunsthuis Ballet Vlaanderen
HET EILANDJE
RIJNKAAI
AMSTERDAMSTR
LONDENSTRAAT
KEMPENSTRAAT
HARDENVOORT
Dampoort
Damplein
LANGE
LOBROEKSTRAAT
Bar Noord
Park Spoor Noord
Alta Via
200m
200yds
ST-LAUREISKAAI
ELLERMANSTRAAT
VIADUCT-DAM
Bonaparte-dok
MAS
Willemdok
LINKEROEVER
GODEFRIDUSKAAI
VISÉSTRAAT
Het Bos
Waaslandtunnel
BROUWERSVLIET
ANKERRUI
ITALIËLEI
VAN DE WERVESTR
DE PRETSTRAAT
LANGE DIJKSTRAAT
ORANJESTRAAT
Panamarenkohuis
Stuivenberg-plein
VELDSTRAAT
Zwembad Veldstraat
Hessenhuis
FALCONRUI
Sint-Jansplein
OUDESTEENWEG
VAN KERCKHOVENSTR
GASSTRAAT
JORDAENSKAAI
ST-PAULUSSTR
LEGUIT
KLAPDORP
PAARDENMARKT
SINT-GUMMARUSSTRAAT
DAMBRUGGESTRAAT
Café Strange
Sint-Pauluskerk
RAAPSTRAAT
VEKESTRAAT
RODESTRAAT
BEGIJN-HOF
OSYSTRAAT
ANTWERP NORTH
HANDELSSTRAAT
page 295
VENUSSTRAAT
PRINSSTRAAT
DUINSTRAAT
Steenplein
WOLSTRAAT
Stadhuis
Grote Markt
Sint-Carolus
Atelier Solarshop
LANGE BEELDEKENSSTRAAT

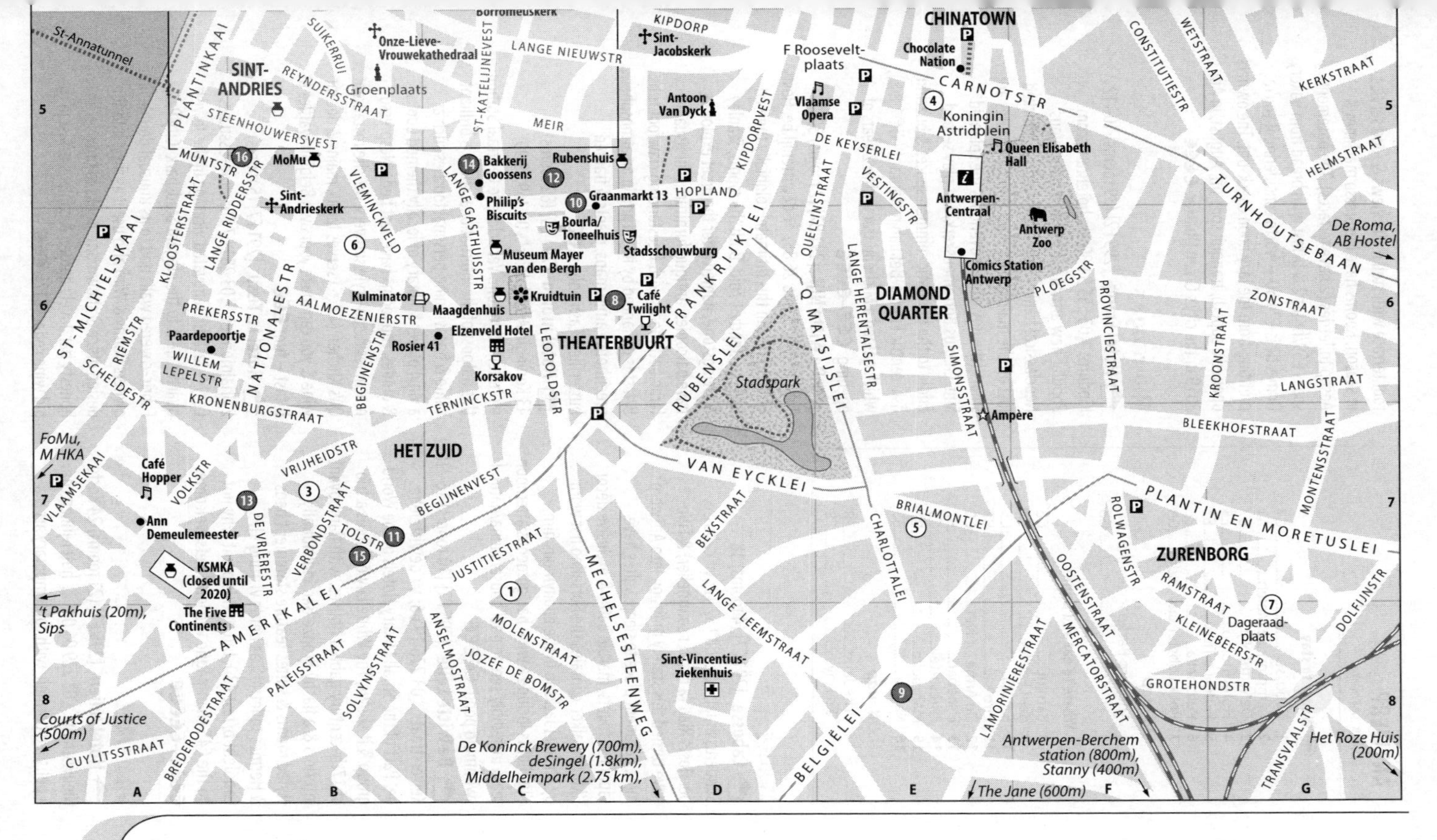
CHINATOWN
SINT-ANDRIES
THEATERBUURT
DIAMOND QUARTER
HET ZUID
ZURENBORG
St-Annatunnel
PLANTINKAAI
STEENHOUWERSVEST
REYNDERSSTRAAT
SUIKERRUI
Groenplaats
Onze-Lieve-Vrouwekathedraal
Borromeuskerk
ST-KATELIJNEVEST
LANGE NIEUWSTR
MEIR
KIPDORP
Sint-Jacobskerk
Antoon Van Dyck
F Rooseveltplaats
Vlaamse Opera
Chocolate Nation
CARNOTSTR
Koningin Astridplein
Queen Elisabeth Hall
Antwerpen-Centraal
Antwerp Zoo
Comics Station Antwerp
CONSTITUTIESTR
WETSTRAAT
KERKSTRAAT
HELMSTRAAT
TURNHOUTSEBAAN
De Roma, AB Hostel
DE KEYSERLEI
VESTINGSTR
QUELLINSTRAAT
KIPDORPVEST
HOPLAND
MUNTSTR
MoMu
16
Bakkerij Goossens
14
Rubenshuis
12
Philip's Biscuits
Graanmarkt 13
10
Bourla/Toneelhuis
Stadsschouwburg
LANGE RIDDERSSTR
Sint-Andrieskerk
VLEMINCKVELD
LANGE GASTHUISSTR
Museum Mayer van den Bergh
Kulminator
Maagdenhuis
Kruidtuin
Café Twilight
8
Elzenveld Hotel
Korsakov
Rosier 41
Paardepoortje
KLOOSTERSTRAAT
ST-MICHIELSKAAI
NATIONALESTR
PREKERSSTR
AALMOEZENIERSTR
BEGIJNENSTR
LEOPOLDSTR
FRANKRIJKLEI
RUBENSLEI
Stadspark
Q MATSIJSLEI
LANGE HERENTALSESTR
SIMONSSTRAAT
Ampère
PLOEGSTR
PROVINCIESTRAAT
ZONSTRAAT
KROONSTRAAT
LANGSTRAAT
BLEEKHOFSTRAAT
MONTENSSTRAAT
RIEMSTR
WILLEM LEPELSTR
SCHELDESTR
KRONENBURGSTRAAT
TERNINCKSTR
FoMu, M HKA
VLAAMSEKAAI
Café Hopper
VOLKSTR
VRIJHEIDSTR
13
DE VRIÈRESTR
Ann Demeulemeester
VERBONDSTRAAT
TOLSTR
11
15
BEGIJNENVEST
KSMKA (closed until 2020)
The Five Continents
't Pakhuis (20m), Sips
AMERIKALEI
JUSTITIESTRAAT
MECHELSESTEENWEG
VAN EYCKLEI
BEXSTRAAT
CHARLOTTALEI
BRIALMONTLEI
PLANTIN EN MORETUSLEI
ROLWAGENSTR
RAMSTRAAT
Dageraadplaats
KLEINEBEERSTR
DOLFIJNSTR
OOSTENSTRAAT
MERCATORSTRAAT
GROTEHONDSTR
LAMORINIERESTRAAT
LANGE LEEMSTRAAT
Sint-Vincentius-ziekenhuis
MOLENSTRAAT
JOZEF DE BOMSTR
ANSELMOSTRAAT
SOLVYNSSTRAAT
PALEISSTRAAT
BREDERODESTRAAT
CUYLITSSTRAAT
Courts of Justice (500m)
De Koninck Brewery (700m), deSingel (1.8km), Middelheimpark (2.75 km),
BELGIËLEI
Antwerpen-Berchem station (800m), Stanny (400m)
The Jane (600m)
TRANSVAALSTR
Het Roze Huis (200m)
A
B
C
D
E
F
G
5
6
7
8

ANTWERP *Overview*
For listings, see below

Where to stay

Where to eat and drink

Luxury

Cabosse [291 C7] (4 rooms) 18 Sanderusstraat; 03 689 52 12; w cabosse.be. Hosts Riad (a master sommelier) & Filip have turned this stately mansion into Antwerp's most decadent place to sleep. Suites have Japanese toilets, marble baths & exclusive décor ('Moonwalker' contains the Borsalino hat worn by Michael Jackson in the eponymous film). Highlights include a wine bar, gorgeous afternoon tea & incredibly serene pool house/sauna/natural swimming pond. **€€€€€**

De Witte Lelie [295 F1] (10 rooms) 16–18 Keizerstraat; 03 226 19 66; w dewittelelie.be. Part of the Small Luxury Hotels of the World group & it shows, The White Lily occupies a trio of 17th-century gabled houses, with flamboyant interiors & a flashy Bronze Bar. Individually styled rooms & suites feature statement beds & Hermès toiletries, as befits visiting VIPs. Candlelit b/fast €30, but at this point why not do the €45 champagne version?! Pets welcome. **€€€€–€€€€€**

Upmarket

Hotel Julien [295 E2] (21 rooms) 24 Korte Nieuwstraat; 03 229 06 00; w hotel-julien.com. A polished bolthole with contemporary art & a roof terrace with stellar city views & food service in season. Rooms have Nespresso machines & Aesop toiletries (2 have terraces). The basement spa is €59/hr for 2 & b/fast with bread from bakery Domestic is €24.50 – worth considering if you're profiting from the lazy noon check-out. The owners opened a superb, tranquil spin-off, August, in Apr 2019 in the city's Green Quarter. **€€€€**

Mid-range

Hotel Franq [295 F2] (39 rooms) 10–12 Kipdorp; 03 555 31 80; w hotelfranq.com. Popular new arrival occupying a sumptuous Neoclassical bank – hence the name – & tucked just off the main tourist drag. Rooms & suites are smart (the Royal Suite overlooks the splendid Sint-Carolus Borromeuskerk) but play second fiddle to the dramatic common spaces & buzzing, fish-centric Franco-Belgian restaurant (€€€€€), which gained a Michelin star within 2 years of opening. **€€€–€€€€**

De Witte Nijl [291 B7] (2 rooms) 35 Tolstraat; 03 336 26 85; w dewittenijl.be. Hosts Gino & Erik run this intimate, colonially themed B&B, in trendy 't Zuid. Both the rooms, Stanley & Livingstone, named after the great explorers, have balconies, antique furniture & unusually large bathrooms with freestanding clawfoot tubs. B/fast is enhanced by its setting in an atmospheric greenhouse amid maps, plants & framed butterflies. Cash only. **€€€**

Hotel Indigo [291 E5] (82 rooms) 43 Koningin Astridplein; 03 369 59 99; w hotelindigo.com. Very close to Centraal Station, this outpost of the international chain is brilliant value & has winning personal touches such as a vinyl player & library of locally themed books & guides. Hip rooms have vast beds, Nespresso machines & spa-style showers. On-site restaurant QA's Kitchen (€€€) serves tapas, mains & decent wine & you can make your own Belgian waffles at b/fast – fun! **€€€**

Hotel Le Tissu [291 E7] (5 rooms) 2 Brialmontlei; 03 281 67 70; w le-tissu.be. Cosy & tasteful renovated vicarage in the Jewish quarter, next to the elegant Stadspark (City Park). Fabric-covered walls nod to its unusual double life: owners Danny & Wim also use it as their interior design office & showroom. Books to browse, an honesty bar, lovely garden & copious b/fast in the old wine cellar (€17). **€€€**

Hotel Rubens [295 D1] (36 rooms) 29 Oude Beurs; 03 222 48 48; w hotelrubensantwerp.be. For location it's hard to beat this polished hotel, almost on top of the Grote Markt, but remarkably quiet. Rooms are bright & comfortable with all mod cons (deluxe garden rooms have leafy terraces, some suites are enormous) & they throw in an excellent b/fast buffet. In summer, you can take it on the patio scoping the hotel's 16th-century *pagaddertoren* (watchtower). **€€€**

Budget

Rock Lobster City Lodge [291 G8] (5 rooms) 1o Kreeftstraat; m 0476 56 64 07; w rocklobster.be. Just off Zurenborg hotspot Dageraadplaats, music journo Bart & human rights activist Eva's welcoming home from home has 5 music-themed rooms with theme-appropriate CDs to check out. Choose between the Glamrock room's gold accents, serene Icelandic room or minimal Electronic room. Occasional small concerts in the living room, also with rock photography & a vinyl corner! **€€**

Shoestring

Antwerp Backpackers (AB) Hostel [291 G6] (7 rooms) 110 Kattenberg; m 0473 57 01 66; w abhostel.com. Superb small hostel in multi-cultural Borgerhout that gets it just right: rooms have arty touches & there are ample facilities from hammocks & a BBQ in the garden to a book exchange, movie corner & well-stocked kitchen. Prices include towels, bedding & b/fast (pancakes, mmm!). Dorms €20, dbl €47. **€**

Pulcinella [291 B6] (47 rooms) 1 Bogaardeplein; 03 234 03 14; w jeugdherbergen.be. Sleek, minimal hostel affiliated to Hostelling International in a prime central location. A mix of 2-, 4- & 6-bed en-suite dorms (inc sgl-sex) with individual reading lights & lockers. Designer bar/lounge downstairs, free Wi-Fi throughout, bike shed & table tennis (no kitchen). Family-friendly & wheelchair accessible. Good b/fast & sheets included, but bring a towel (or buy 1 there for €6). Dorms €30, dbl €66. **€**

Camping De Molen [290 A1] (80 places, 4 cabins) 6 Jachthavenweg; 03 219 81 79; w camping-de-molen.be; Mar–Oct. Basic but functional campsite, also with cabins, in a field on the left bank of the Scheldt. Hot showers & an easy 30min walk into town via the Sint-Anna tunnel. Sint-Anna beach & a swimming pool close by. Tent €16, c/van €23, cabin €50, electricity €5/day. Cards only, unusually! **€**

WHERE TO EAT AND DRINK

WHERE TO EAT AND DRINK Antwerp's food scene is better than ever, combining hip cocktail joints, serious coffee shops and more fine-dining spots than a glutton could stomach. Hearty Flemish cuisine dominates, but you don't have to go far to find foreign flavours courtesy of the city's many nationalities, and there's a growing veggie scene too. Local specialities to try include *palingen in groene saus* (eels in green sauce), *filet d'Anvers* (smoked beef cured with salt, herbs and juniper berries) and *Antwerpse handjes* (see box, page 296). Top tipples are bright-yellow Elixir d'Anvers, made with 32 herbs, and the De Koninck Brewery's flagship bolleke beer (page 310).

Restaurants

Expensive

The Jane [291 E8] 1 Paradeplein; 03 808 44 65; w thejaneantwerp.com; noon–22.00 Tue–Sat. Antwerp's most oversubscribed restaurant since it opened in 2014, in a stunning former chapel replete with stained-glass windows & a giant skull installation. Chef Nick Bril oversees the globetrotting, rock 'n' roll, fine-dining menu, awarded 2 Michelin stars. Downstairs, offering a €160 10-course tasting menu, is notoriously hard to get in to; the Upper Room Bar, which offers both à la carte dishes from downstairs & Japanese pub-style *izakaya* dishes, is way more approachable, & arguably more fun. **€€€€€**

Sir Anthony van Dijck [295 C3] 16 Oude Koornmarkt; 03 231 61 70; w siranthonyvandijck.be; noon–14.00 & 18.30–22.00 Tue–Sat. Dries van Noten's favourite restaurant enjoys an exclusive courtyard location in the Vlaeykensgang (page 302). Earthy, eclectic décor courtesy of designer Axel Vervoordt is matched by note-perfect, classic French-Belgian food. The 3-course lunch (€42) makes less of a dent in the wallet. **€€€€–€€€€€**

Above average

Ciro's [291 B7] 6 Amerikalei; 03 226 63 30; w ciros.be; 11.00–22.00 Tue–Fri & Sun, 17.00–22.00 Sat. A fine mid-century interior nods to the pedigree of this old-school venture, established in 1962. It's a treat for carnivores (veggies should avoid); you'll find Belgian classics like waterzooi, but the Ciro's steak is particularly epic. €€€€

Fiskebar [291 B7] 11 Marnixplaats; 03 257 13 57; w fiskebar.be; noon–22.00. On happening Marnixplaats, Nikolaj Kovdal's restaurant – well-established but still hip – buzzes with satisfied diners feasting on razor clams & North Sea crab. Watch out for their brand-new fishermen's cabin-style seafood spot, Fiskeskur, in 't Eilandje. €€€€

Mid-range

Bourla [291 C5] 7 Graanmarkt; 03 232 16 32; w bourla.be; 11.00–23.00 Mon–Thu, 11.00–midnight Fri–Sat. Reliable & rather glam veteran brasserie in the theatre district with considerable buzz & a scenic, spacious terrace come summer. Best stick to the classics: endless steaks & immaculate double-baked fries. €€€

De Arme Duivel [291 C5] 1 Armeduivelstraat; 03 232 26 98; w armeduivel.be; noon–14.30, 17.30–22.00 Mon–Fri, noon–22.00 Sat, noon–18.30 Sun. Authentic bistro delivering the city's best Flemish beer stew & with a small patio area amid the chi-chi shops on Schuttershofstraat. Reserve ahead. €€€

Mampoko [291 B7] 8 Amerikalei; 03 257 77 10; w mampoko.be; 10.00–22.00 Mon–Fri, 09.00–22.30 Sat, 09.00–21.00 Sun. Atmospheric neighbourhood staple with colonial vibes noted for its brunch & useful on sleepy Sun nights. €€€

Cheap and cheerful

Native [291 B5] 8 Muntstraat; 03 437 08 25; w native.bio; noon–15.00, 18.00–21.00 Sat & Tue–Fri. Vegetarians & vegans adore this intimate organic café just off Kloosterstraat & offering a range of very superior soups, salads & sandwiches & sharing plates by night. Ideal for a quick lunch (also serves meat). €€

Stanny [291 F8] 1 Stanleystraat; 03 289 54 67; f cafestanny; Sep–Jun 17.00–01.00 Mon–Thu, 17.00–03.00 Fri–Sat. Once a run-down drinking hole, this homely neighbourhood haunt near Berchem station serves generous portions of simple, wholesome food & is justly busy. €€

ViaVia Reiscafé [295 E2] 43 Wolstraat; 03 226 47 49; w viavia.world; Oct–Jun 11.30–12.30 Mon–Sat, 15.00–midnight Sun, Jul–Sep 11.30–12.30 Tue–Sat. Branches of this friendly traveller's café grace Dakar, Entebbe & Buenos Aires. Foreign banknotes on pillars & a world map on the wall. Decent global food at traveller-friendly prices. €€

Shoestring

Beni Falafel [291 E8] 188 Lange Leemstraat; 03 218 82 11; w benifalafel.be; 11.30–22.00 Mon–Fri, noon–22.00 Sun. You might find yourself surrounded by Orthodox Jews at this out-of-the-way Jewish district joint, offering flavoursome falafel in a full or half pitta with hummus, salad & amazing spicy sauce, plus *bourekas* (baked filled pastries) etc. €

Fish a'gogo [295 C2] 1 Handschoenmarkt; m 0495 24 27 36; w fishagogo.be; noon–21.30 Mon & Thu–Sun. A beacon amid city-centre tourist traps: prop up a barrel for lip-smackingly fresh fish (€5–8 per small dish) & crisp white wines. €

Frites Atelier [291 C5] 32 Korte Gasthuisstraat; 03 430 38 72; w fritesatelier.com; 11.00–22.00 Mon–Thu & Sun, 11.00–23.00 Fri–Sat. A Dutch chef (Sergio Herman again) teaching Belgians how to make fries? Yup, & somehow a hit. While pricey for the genre, they're more meal than snack, with haute toppings like kimchi & beef stew. A few tables in & outside. €

Cafés

Barnini [291 C6] 10 Oudevaartplaats; 03 485 82 69; f barniniantwerp; 08.00–19.00 Mon–Sat, 08.00–17.00 Sun. Cute, retro café whose packed bagels & real hot chocolate topped with Smarties etc are a hit with students in the week & shoppers browsing the w/end market on adjacent Theaterplein. It has a little sister, Kaffeenini, on Nationalestraat. €

Cuperus Koffie [295 E3] 51 Sint-Katelijnevest; 03 233 25 89; w cuperuskoffie.be; 08.30–18.00 Mon–Sat. Just off the Meir, this 3-storey space has been serving great, democratically priced coffee (it's also a shop) since 1823, though it's moved home a few times since then! Super pastries & cakes too. Sit upstairs. €

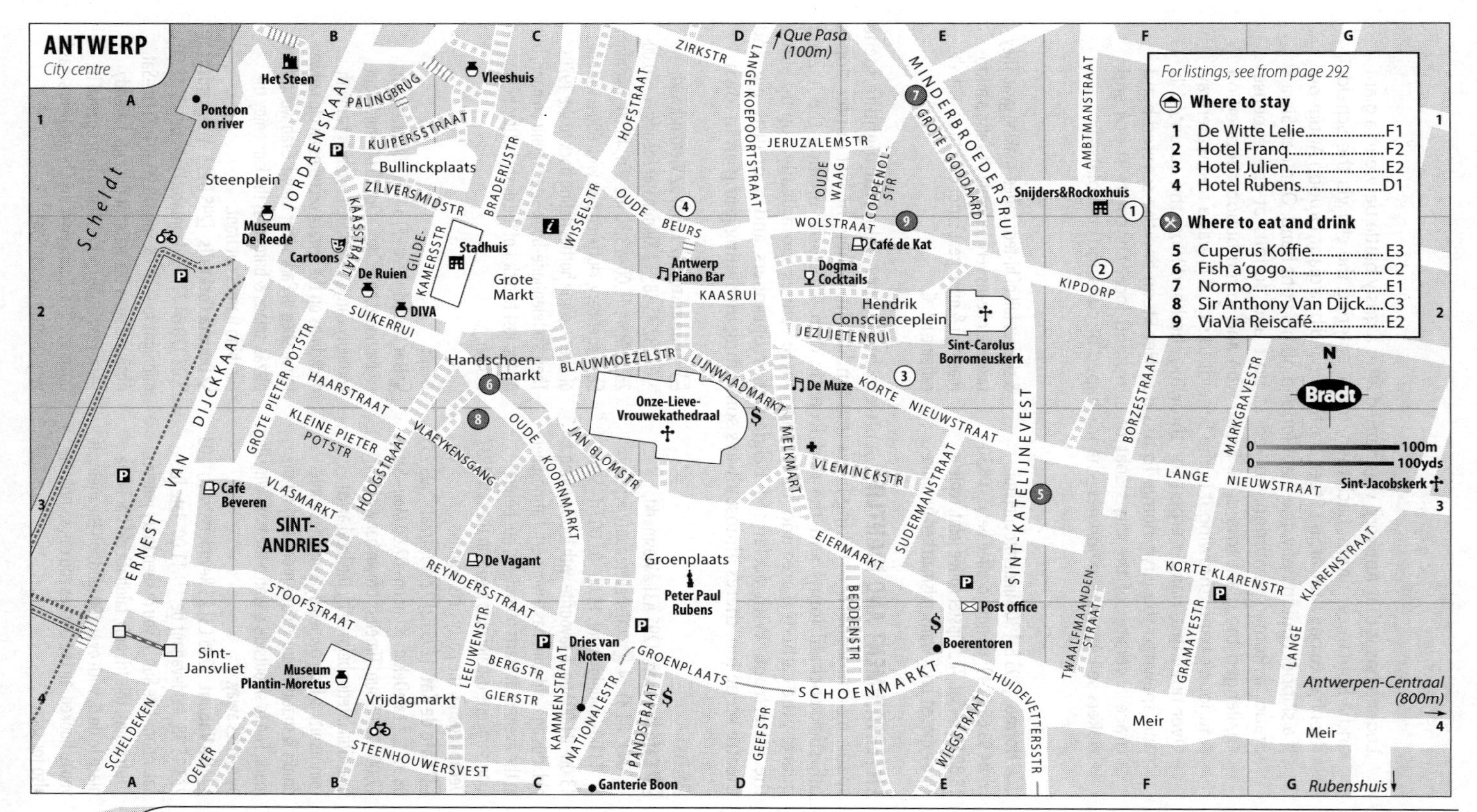
ANTWERP
City centre
For listings, see from page 292
Where to stay
1 De Witte Lelie F1
2 Hotel Franq F2
3 Hotel Julien E2
4 Hotel Rubens D1
Where to eat and drink
5 Cuperus Koffie E3
6 Fish a'gogo C2
7 Normo E1
8 Sir Anthony Van Dijck C3
9 ViaVia Reiscafé E2
Bradt
0 100m
0 100yds
Scheldt
Pontoon on river
Het Steen
Vleeshuis
Steenplein
Museum De Reede
Cartoons
De Ruien
DIVA
Stadhuis
Grote Markt
Bullinckplaats
Handschoen-markt
Onze-Lieve-Vrouwekathedraal
Antwerp Piano Bar
Dogma Cocktails
Café de Kat
Hendrik Conscienceplein
Sint-Carolus Borromeuskerk
Snijders&Rockoxhuis
De Muze
Café Beveren
SINT-ANDRIES
De Vagant
Groenplaats
Peter Paul Rubens
Dries van Noten
Post office
Boerentoren
Museum Plantin-Moretus
Sint-Jansvliet
Vrijdagmarkt
Ganterie Boon
Sint-Jacobskerk
Antwerpen-Centraal (800m)
Rubenshuis
Que Pasa (100m)
Meir
JORDAENSKAAI
PALINGBRUG
KUIPERSSTRAAT
ZILVERSMIDSTR
KAASSTRAAT
GILDE-KAMERSSTR
BRADERIJSTR
HOFSTRAAT
WISSELSTR
OUDE BEURS
ZIRKSTR
LANGE KOEPOORTSTRAAT
JERUZALEMSTR
OUDE WAAG
COPPENOL-STR
WOLSTRAAT
KAASRUI
JEZUIETENRUI
MINDERBROEDERSRUI
GROTE GODDAARD
AMBTMANSTRAAT
KIPDORP
SUIKERRUI
BLAUWMOEZELSTR
LIJNWAADMARKT
KORTE NIEUWSTRAAT
MELKMART
VLEMINCKSTR
SUDERMANSTRAAT
SINT-KATELIJNEVEST
BORZESTRAAT
MARKGRAVESTR
LANGE NIEUWSTRAAT
EIERMARKT
BEDDENSTR
KORTE KLARENSTR
KLARENSTRAAT
GRAMAYESTR
LANGE
TWAALFMAANDEN-STRAAT
ERNEST VAN DIJCKKAAI
GROTE PIETER POTSTR
HAARSTRAAT
KLEINE PIETER POTSTR
VLAEYKENSGANG
HOOGSTRAAT
OUDE KOORNMARKT
JAN BLOMSTR
VLASMARKT
REYNDERSSTRAAT
STOOFSTRAAT
LEEUWENSTR
BERGSTR
GIERSTR
KAMMENSTRAAT
NATIONALESTR
PANDSTRAAT
GROENPLAATS
SCHOENMARKT
GEEFSTR
WIEGSTRAAT
HUIDEVETTERSSTR
SCHELDEKEN
OEVER
STEENHOUWERSVEST

ANTWERPSE HANDJES

Legend has it that Antwerp was named after a grisly battle between a giant and a Roman centurion. Back then, traffic entering the city via the Scheldt river had to pay a toll at Het Steen bastion levied by a giant, Druoon Antigoon. If a skipper couldn't pay, the giant lopped off his right hand. One day Silvius Brabo, a Roman centurion, arrived at port and, furious at the expense, challenged the giant to a duel. Brabo won and in retribution chopped off Antigoon's hand, throwing it in the Scheldt to signal it was a free waterway. Over time, this 'Hand-werpen' (or 'throwing the hand') lost the accented 'h' and spawned the city's name. To this day, Het Steen and the severed hand grace a version of the city's coat of arms, and local chocolate shops and bakers sell *Antwerpse handjes* – hand-shaped biscuits and chocolates.

Normo [295 E1] 30 Minderbroedersrui; m 04 95 65 72 43; w normocoffee.be; 08.30–18.30 Mon–Sat. *The* hipster coffee joint, replete with exposed-brick walls, mismatched furniture & shelves full of hi-tech coffee-making gear. They take their beans very seriously (it's also a micro-roastery) & offer great carrot cake to go with the caffeine hit. €

ENTERTAINMENT AND NIGHTLIFE Antwerp has a very colourful nightlife scene spanning atmospheric drinking holes that tend to shut when the last punter slopes off, slick cocktail joints and the odd frenetic club. Hotspots include the 't Zuid quarter, the cathedral area and 't Eilandje, where venues sporadically pop up along the waterfront. With acclaimed Belgian choreographers and a healthy gig and theatre scene too, there's almost always something intriguing going on in town.

Pubs

Café Beveren [295 A3] 2 Vlasmarkt; m 0495 81 81 34; cafebeverenantwerpen; 13.00–midnight Thu, 13.00–03.00 Fri–Sat, 13.00–01.00 Sun. A favourite with locals young & old, this age-old joint has a wonderful atmosphere in the evening. It starts off quietly, but before long someone usually puts a euro in the rare 1937 Decap organ & the party gets going!

Café de Kat [295 E2] 22 Wolstraat; 03 233 08 92; cafeDeKat; noon–02.00 Mon–Sat, 17.00–02.00 Sun. Timeless brown bar with a beautiful interior beloved by the local artist community & long owned by women. Simple drinks & snacks (soup, croque monsieur) hit the mark. Fun to sit outside & watch the tram whizzing by metres away.

De Vagant [295 C3] 25 Reyndersstraat; 03 233 15 38; w devagant.be; 11.00–late Tue–Sat, noon–late Sun. If you're keen to try jenever (Dutch gin), this friendly, laidback old bar is the place to do it, with over 200 kinds on the menu. If you're hooked, all the bottles you can sample are also for sale.

Kulminator [291 B6] 32 Vleminckveld; 03 232 45 38; Kulminator.friends; 20.00–23.30 Mon, 16.00–23.30 Tue–Fri, 16.00–midnight Sat. Legendary, cluttered pub with 600+ varieties of beer – some bottles dating back to the 1970s. There's a telephone-book-sized menu on hand, but it's fun just to pick 1 of the dusty bottles behind the bar.

Bars

Bar Noord [290 F2] 64–80 Viaduct-Dam; w barnoord.be; Apr–Oct 10.00–midnight. Formerly Cargo, this chilled summer bar with deckchairs on the terrace occupies an old railway repair shed in Park Spoor Noord. Grab wood-fired pizzas, salads & burgers as the kids enjoy the climbing frames out front.

Dogma Cocktails [295 D2] 5 Wijngaardstraat; 03 770 64 77; w dogmacocktails.be; 18.00–midnight Tue–Thu & Sun, 18.00–01.00 Fri–Sat. Absinthe laces the water at this super-trendy speakeasy-style cocktail bar, which opened its doors in 2013. Loungeworthy Chesterfield sofas & very creative concoctions.

Korsakov [291 C6] 1 Sint-Jorispoort; m 485 46 45 06; f vokasrov; 14.00–late Mon–Fri, noon–late Sat–Sun. Reliably busy corner bar with 1950s vibes & a mix of students & workers from the local fashion houses. Smoking room upstairs.

Sips [291 A7] 8 Gillisplaats; 0478 31 08 66; w sips-cocktails.com; 17.00–01.00 Mon–Sun. Classy cocktail bar near photography museum FoMu run by superstar Manuel Wouters, who used to mix drinks on the QE2 & knows over 1,000 cocktail recipes by heart. Well, if they're good enough for Tom Cruise & Dolly Parton ...

Nightclubs

☆ **Ampère** [291 E7] 21 Simonsstraat; 03 232 09 23; w ampere-antwerp.com; depends on club nights. Under the tracks near Centraal Station, Belgium's first eco-friendly club (est 2015) is very much the place to be. Eclectic line-up of local DJs, techno icons etc. Great sound system, normal prices & lockers readily available.

☆ **Club Vaag** [290 B1] 4 Rijnkaai; 03 295 54 65; f; Thu–Sat 23.00–late. Techno heads in the know rave about this hidden basement in Eilandje. Relatively cosy but with a powerful sound system & impressive interiors, it's an award-winning venue that's flying the flag for Antwerp's party scene.

Live music

♫ **Antwerp Piano Bar** [295 D2] 33 Grote Markt; 03 225 05 36; f antwerppianobar; 21.00–04.00 Mon–Thu, 21.00–05.00 Fri–Sat. A live pianist adds to the joys of this über-kitsch haunt on the Grote Markt – like being on a cruise ship or in a vintage Scorsese flick (while quaffing textbook cocktails).

♫ **Café Hopper** [291 A7] 2 Leopold De Waelstraat; 03 248 49 33; w cafehopper.be; 10.00–late. Stylish spot inspired by Edward Hopper on 't Zuid's main square & long hosting intimate jazz concerts Mon at 21.00 & Sun at 16.00.

♫ **De Muze** [295 D2] 15 Melkmarkt; 03 226 01 26; w jazzcafedemuze.be; 11.30–01.00 Mon–Thu, 11.30–03.00 Fri–Sun. Mythic 3-floor jazz bar with live performances almost every night & great beers. It faced closure in 2014 but was saved by locals who couldn't bear to see it go.

♫ **Het Bos** [290 D3] 5–7 Ankerrui; 03 238 23 32; w hetbos.be; bar noon–midnight Wed–Sat, 09.00–04.00 Sun, gigs usually Fri–Sat. The follow-up to beloved squat-like venue Scheld'apen is a bohemian, multi-tasking hangout combining regular concerts, record fairs & dinners/Sun brunch by the excellent Otark Productions.

LGBT+ ANTWERP

Antwerp's LGBT scene is the most active and accepted in Flanders. To find out what's on, visit Het Roze Huis (1 Draakplaats; 03 288 00 84; w hetrozehuis.be; 13.00–16.30 Mon–Fri), an umbrella organisation for local LGBT associations that also houses the popular Café Den Draak, and participates in August's annual Antwerp Pride bash (w antwerppride.eu), organising its own queer arts festival.

Café Strange [290 E4] 161 Dambruggestraat; m 0474 42 49 01; w cafe-strange.be; 19.00–02.00 Tue–Sun. Antwerp's oldest gay café, but welcoming to all & run by octogenarian Armand; tiny dance floor & reasonably priced drinks, but you go there for the gritty, sometimes surreal vibe. A remarkable spot!

Café Twilight [291 D6] 4 Nieuwstad; m 0477 83 41 93; f TwilightAntwerpen; 14.00–late Wed–Fri, 10.00–late Sat–Sun. Lovely, relatively new gay bar whose expansive terrace on Theaterplein is a real hit in summer (grab an Aperol Spritz & people watch).

Que Pasa [295 D1] 1 Lange Koepoortstraat; w cafe-que-pasa.be; 20.00–05.00 Tue & Thu–Sun. Fun, borderline trashy late-night gay bar on the threshold of the red-light district. Drag shows Tue & Thu, Latin beats Sat & happy hour from 23.00–midnight.

☆ **Hessenhuis** [290 C3] 59 Falconrui; 03 231 13 56; w hessenhuis.com; 16.00–late Tue–Fri, 20.00–late Sat. Old 2-floor converted warehouse near the docks; serves as a café for workers by day, but morphs into a spirited bar by night (DJs at the w/end).

Theatres and concert halls

De Roma [291 G6] 286 Turnhoutsebaan; 03 292 97 40; w deroma.be. They don't make them like this any more. Fabulous Italian-style theatre with wooden stage & red velvet seats. Indie & mainstream films, plus concerts of the good & great.

deSingel [291 C8] 25 Desguinlei; 03 248 28 28; w desingel.be. Modernist arts centre on the ring road with a heavyweight programme of theatre, dance & music.

De Vlaamse Opera [291 E5] 1 Frankrijklei; 07 022 02 02; w operaballet.be. The Flemish Opera & Royal Ballet of Flanders (the latter led by Sidi Larbi Cherkaoui) perform in this fine early 20th-century building, as well as in Ghent.

Queen Elisabeth Hall [291 E5] 26 Koningin Astridplein; 07 079 00 13; w elisabethcenter.be. World-class new concert hall by Centraal Station with regular stints from the Antwerp Symphony Orchestra, but also big pop gigs & ballet.

Stadsschouwburg [291 D6] 1 Theaterplein; 03 400 69 69; w stadsschouwburgantwerpen.be. Big, brutalist theatre for well-known musicals, theatre & dance productions. It's also home to the Het Paleis children's theatre.

Toneelhuis [291 C6] 18 Komedieplaats; 03 224 88 44; w toneelhuis.be. AKA Bourla, Antwerp's most elegant theatre is run by a co-op of 5 theatremakers led by Guy Cassiers & often produces topical or literary theatre. Nice café too.

Cinemas

Cartoons [295 B2] 4 Kaasstraat; 03 232 96 32; w cinemacartoons.be. The city's most characterful cinema, showing mainstream & arthouse flicks. Have a wine or craft beer in the basement cellar while you're there.

Cinema Zuid [291 A7] 47 Waalsekaai; 03 242 93 57; w cinemazuid.be. Located inside photography museum FoMu [291 A7], this cosy venue has a great line in forgotten films, classics & silent movies with live musical accompaniment.

SHOPPING Antwerp is a superb city for fashion, notably the Sint-Andries district, which pivots around Nationalestraat, also taking in the independent shops along nearby Kammenstraat, Lombardenvest and Steenhouwersvest. Kloosterstraat is an antiques strip worthy of investigation, especially on Sundays when many shops are shut; Wolstraat is great for secondhand books. High-street names line the main shopping street the Meir, while De Wilde Zee is a charming, cobbled pedestrian zone known as Antwerp's larder. It's home to Antwerp's oldest bakery, **Bakkerij Goossens** [291 C5] (31 Korte Gasthuisstraat; 03 226 07 91; 07.00–19.00 Tue–Sat), and **Philip's Biscuits** [291 C6] (39 Korte Gasthuisstraat; 03 231 26 60; 10.00–18.00 Mon–Sat). Nearby, the classy **Theaterbuurt** [291 C6] (notably Schuttershofstraat) houses Delvaux and other luxury icons, and one of the city's best markets, dedicated to exotic food, on Theaterplein (08.00–16.00 Sat). Join the locals for Cava and oysters!

Alta Via [290 C2] 29 Nassaustraat; 03 293 87 33; w altaviatravelbooks.be; 10.00–17.30 Mon–Wed & Fri–Sat, 10.00–13.00 & 14.00–19.30 Thu. Excellent travel bookshop with a great selection of maps & guides, good service & coffee.

Ann Demeulemeester [291 A7] Leopold de Waelplaats; 03 216 10 33; 10.30–18.30 Mon–Sat. The most romantic, goth-compatible member of the Antwerp Six (page 58). The clothes hang, like artworks, inside a minimalist studio.

Atelier Solarshop [291 F5] 48 Dambruggestraat; m 0487 16 75 70; w ateliersolarshop.be; noon–18.30 Wed–Sat. 'Slow fashion' designer Jan-Jan Van Essche co-runs this unique store, housing 'beautiful stuff' (fashion & homewares, vintage & new) in a former solar panel shop – hence its name.

Dries van Noten [295 C4] 16 Nationalestraat; 03 470 25 10; w driesvannoten.be; 10.00–18.30 Mon–Sat. Few designers can boast such a home as Het Modepaleis, housing the famed Antwerp Six star's clashing, patterned clothes & beautiful shoes.

Ganterie Boon [295 C4] 2 Lombardenvest; 03 232 33 87; w glovesboon.be; 10.00–18.00 Mon–Sat. Wonderful 120-year-old artisanal shop selling handmade gloves in all colours; staff are so

JOIN THE FASHION PACK

Antwerp's fashion might be world-famous, but it's not something that leaps out at you as you stroll around. Short of attending a fashion department graduation show (see box, page 58), one great way to get to grips with it is by attending the biannual stock sales (usually Nov & Apr, w belmodo.be/fashiondays), little advertised events offering discounts of up to 70% on designers from Dries to younger talents. Sticking with the bargain Belgian fashion theme, try second-hand gems Rosier 41 (41 Rosier; 03 225 53 03; w rosier41.be; 10.30–18.00 Mon–Sat) and Labels Inc (95 Nationalestraat; 03 232 60 56; w labelsinc.be; 11.00–18.00 Mon–Sat).

experienced that they can measure you up on sight.

Graanmarkt 13 [291 C5] Graanmarkt 13; 03 337 79 91; w graanmarkt13.com; 10.30–18.30 Mon–Sat. Haute restaurant, gallery & concept store rolled into 1 fine townhouse, this venue continues to define Antwerp cool.

OTHER PRACTICALITIES

$ Bank [295 E4] KBC, 20 Eiermarkt, 09.00–12.30 & 14.00–16.30 Mon–Wed & Fri, 09.00–12.30 & 14.00–19.30 Thu

Luggage storage Self-service lockers in Centraal Station [291 E5] under the arches near the ticket office, €4.50–5.50/24hrs

Pharmacy [295 D3] 33 Melkmarkt, 03 226 08 97, 08.30–18.30 Mon–Fri, 09.30–17.30 Sat. At the w/end, on-duty branches are listed in pharmacies' windows.

Post office [295 D4] 33–5 Eiermarkt, 10.00–18.00 Mon–Fri, 10.00–15.00 Sat

WHAT TO SEE AND DO

Historic city centre

Grote Markt [295 C2] The focus of Antwerp's city centre, this triangular town square is dominated by the extravagant **Stadhuis** (**Town Hall**) and towering **Brabo Fountain**, which was sculpted by Jef Lambeaux in 1887 and depicts the legend which gave the city its name (see box, page 296). Round about sit smart guildhouses topped with gold figurines depicting the various trades, the majority restored 19th-century constructions. The town hall (1 Suikerrui; closed to public) celebrated its 450th anniversary in 2015, having survived the Spanish Fury, wars of the Habsburgs and French Revolution. Since April 2018 it has been undergoing a major interior and exterior renovation, set to complete in 2020, when it will revert to its historic role as the beating heart of the local political scene and an *open huis* (open house) whose ground floor will be accessible to the public. In the meantime, illustrated cloths by artist Fatinha Ramos telling the story of the city shroud the façade.

Handschoenmarkt [295 C2] Leaving the Grote Markt from the south corner leads you into the cobbled Handschoenmarkt square. Sitting in the shadow of Onze-Lieve-Vrouwekathedraal (Cathedral of Our Lady), it was used as a cemetery until the 16th century and then developed into a fur and glove market. Just off centre is a well topped with a statuette of town legend Brabo. The saying on the ironwork, 'the smith who came to be a painter out of love', has led many to believe that it's the work of Renaissance artist Quinten Matsijs, who started out as a blacksmith, but learned to paint so that he might court Catherina Heyns (either to please her father or to woo her, no-one can quite agree). A newer addition is Ghent artist Batist Vermeulen's adorable marble sculpture of Nello and his dog Patrasche, asleep

MAD FOR MUSEUMS?

The tourist offices sell the Antwerp City Card – a must if you're planning even the most basic sightseeing. Valid for 24, 48 or 72 hours (€27/35/40), it includes free access to 17 major museums, 4 monumental churches and the De Koninck City Brewery, alongside travel on the De Lijn network. You'll also get discounts on many other attractions, bike rental and even chocolate! Be aware that many venues issue their last tickets at 16.30. Not all have abundant information in English; the free Antwerp Museum App, available on the app store, is thus well worth downloading.

beneath an ingenious blanket of curving cobblestones. It nods to the 1872 novel *A Dog of Flanders*, about an Antwerp orphan and an abandoned cart dog, which is seen as a children's classic in Asia.

Onze-Lieve-Vrouwekathedraal (Cathedral of Our Lady) [295 D2/3] (Handschoenmarkt; ☎ 03 213 99 51; **w** dekathedraal.be; ⏲ 10.00–17.00 Mon–Fri, 10.00–15.00 Sat, 13.00–17.00 Sun; adult/under 12 & City Card €6/free) A chapel has stood on this spot since the 12th century, but work on the current version started in 1352. Original plans envisaged two towers, but the south spire was never completed. Perhaps this was a blessing in disguise because the cathedral and its exceptional 123m-high north tower alone took 169 years to complete. Even today, it is the largest Gothic church in the Low Countries. In 1533 the lavish interior was ruined by fire, in 1566 it was plundered during the Iconoclastic Fury, and in 1794 it was looted by French Republicans. Very little of the original Gothic interior therefore remains, but an ongoing restoration, due to finish in 2019, presents the Baroque additions and airy, seven-aisled interior at its best.

Luckily, the cathedral's treasures have survived its tumultuous past. The finest works on display are Peter Paul Rubens's (page 21) four masterpieces: *The Assumption of the Virgin* over the altar, *The Resurrection of Christ* in a right-hand side chapel, *The Raising of the Cross* in the left transept, and luminous, world-famous triptych *The Descent from the Cross* in the right transept. Painted after Rubens's return from Italy in 1612, and commissioned by the Guild of Arquebusiers, which wanted an altarpiece for their patron saint St Christopher (whose name means 'bearer of Christ'), it depicts mourners including Mary and John the Baptist struggling to lower Christ.

Since 2015, the Bishop of Antwerp's seat has housed a more contemporary wonder: *The Man Who Bears the Cross* by well-known Antwerp playwright/artist/theatre director Jan Fabre. The first artwork the cathedral had purchased in over a century, the glinting bronze figure depicts the 'everyman' (with Fabre's face) balancing a giant cross in his hand – a symbol of humankind's search for faith. It's not the only unusual feature here: make your way to the sacristy, and an unmarked door leads to De Plek (open during regular cathedral hours), a brand-new Gothic-inspired bar serving the cathedral's own dark and blonde beers. There aren't many places in the world where you can drink in a UNESCO cathedral! You'll find details of free daily tours of the cathedral on a board outside. There is a mass in English every Saturday at 17.00 and carillon concerts every Monday, Wednesday and Friday between noon and 13.00, and Monday from 20.00 to 21.00 in July and August. You don't buy a ticket: stand anywhere in the city centre and you'll hear a brilliant free performance – sometimes of modern numbers by Metallica etc!

Hendrik Conscienceplein [295 E2] Head east to Hendrik Conscienceplein, the prettiest square in the city, lined with buildings funded by the Jesuits in the 17th century. It's named after the Antwerp-born writer Hendrik Conscience, who is best remembered for *De Leeuw van Vlaanderen* (*The Lion of Flanders*) and whose statue sits in an alcove of the **Hendrik Conscience Heritage Library** (4 Hendrik Conscienceplein; ☎ 03 338 87 10; w conscienciebibliotheek.be; ⌚ only open during exhibitions, check the website; adult/under 12/City Card €5/3/free). The latter conceals a hidden gem: the period Nottebohm Room, housing cartographer Willem Blaeu's glorious celestial and terrestrial globes.

Sint-Carolus Borromeuskerk (St Charles Borromeo Church) [295 E2] (Hendrik Conscienceplein; ☎ 03 231 37 51; w topa.be; ⌚ 10.00–12.30 & 14.00–17.00 Mon–Sat; free) Dominating the square, this splendid Baroque church was built by the Jesuits from 1614 to 1631 (look for their 'IHS' monogram on the façade) and hailed as 'heaven on earth'. It once bore Rubens's stamp everywhere, from the 39 ceiling paintings to the tower and façade, but lightning struck the wooden roof in 1718 and all was destroyed in the ensuing fire. There are still joys: the Onze Lieve Vrouwekapel (Chapel of Our Lady) on the right-hand side is an eye-popping ode to the Virgin Mary, and the church's painting-switching mechanism is ingenious. In 2012 they also recovered Rubens's *The Return of the Holy Family from Egypt* after endless peregrinations. Do avail yourself of the brilliant free tours (just ask at the reception), full of colourful detail on how the church's design was meant to demotivate Protestant 'dragons'! (The church also houses a less spectacular lace museum, open on Wednesday only.)

Boerentoren (KBC Tower) [295 E4] Standing 97m tall on the corner of Eiermarkt and Schoenmarkt, and marking the boundary between the historic centre and the Meir, is the eye-catching 'farmers' tower'. Designed by Jan van Hoenacker for the 1930 World Exhibition in Antwerp, the blockish but elegant building was Europe's first skyscraper – and still dominates the local skyline alongside the higher, finer spire of the Cathedral of Our Lady. It's now used as the city headquarters of banking giant KBC, and is home to a number of the city's start-ups.

Groenplaats [295 D3/4] Also known as Groen Kerkhof (or 'Green Cemetery'), this not-so-green square atop an underground car park is where the dead were buried until the 18th century, when the Austrian occupiers abolished cemeteries inside the city walls. Now lined with cafés, bars and the neo-Baroque Hilton Hotel, it serves as a transport hub enlivened by a bronze statue of Baroque artist extraordinaire Peter Paul Rubens at its heart.

Vrijdagmarkt [295 B4] A few minutes' walk away, this 16th-century square was created to host a secondhand clothes market – a statue of St Cathérine, patron saint of haberdashers and spinners, stands in the middle – and still hosts a weekly market (⌚ 09.00–13.00 Fri) for furniture and other secondhand goods. It's a scenic, buzzing spot for lunch, but the main lure is the Museum Plantin-Moretus in the west corner.

Museum Plantin-Moretus ✱ [295 B4] (22 Vrijdagmarkt; ☎ 03 221 14 50; w museumplantinmoretus.be; ⌚ 10.00–17.00 Tue–Sun; adult/12–25/under 12 & City Card €8/6/free) This wonderfully creaky museum (the only museum in the world to boast UNESCO status) occupies the former home of Christophe Plantin, a

French bookbinder who moved to Antwerp in 1549 and six years later founded his publishing house, the Officina Plantiniana. A shrewd businessman, Plantin secured contracts for all Spain's liturgical publications from King Philip II, also indulging his love of humanism by publishing the works of Latin scholar Justus Lipsius. As a result, the business rose to become the largest printer-publisher in the Low Countries. When Plantin died, his son-in-law, Jan Moretus, took over, then his son Balthasar, a close friend of Rubens, whose portraits of the family still hang here. The family sold the building to the city in 1876 and it quickly reopened as a museum. Today visitors can wend though the offices, printing room and libraries – most of the heavy shutters remain closed for preservation reasons – accompanied by an immaculately produced novel-length guide recounting Plantin's many passions and feats. Reproductions of his famous works appear alongside rare type specimens and other fascinating printing tools. The whole house breathes history, not least the world's two oldest printing presses, located downstairs in the print room under the statue of Mary, and the world's second-oldest printed Bible, masterminded by Plantin's acquaintance Gutenberg, who invented moveable type printing.

Vlaeykensgang, and Grote and Kleine Pieter Potstraat Connecting Hoogstraat, Oude Koornmarkt and Pelgrimstraat, the Vlaeykensgang [295 C3] is a quaint, much-Instagrammed 16th-century alleyway originally lined with cobblers' shops. It once housed the city's poorest families and faced demolition in the 1960s, but was thankfully saved by a wealthy antiques dealer, Axel Vervoordt. Today it houses the exclusive restaurant Sir Anthony van Dijck (page 293) and is a popular spot for listening to carillon concerts in summer – or simply feeling like you've fallen down a rabbit hole into medieval times. Exiting on to Hoogstraat, stroll across the street (veering slightly to the left) and enter Kleine Pieter Potstraat [295 B3], which forms a T-junction with Grote Pieter Potstraat [295 B2/3]. These two streets are the oldest in Antwerp. They're named after wealthy 15th-century banker Pieter Pot, who funded the construction of the Priory of St Salvador, of which only the chapel remains (it sits on the corner of the two streets and is now inhabited by a furniture and bedding store).

The waterfront From Grote Pieter Potstraat stroll a block north to Suikerrui, connecting the Grote Markt and riverfront Steenplein, with its raised walkway and excellent views of the Scheldt. Steenplein is home to Antwerp's oldest building, fortress castle **Het Steen** ('steen' meaning 'stone' or 'fortress') [295 B1], which was built around 1200 to repel Viking raiders. Having served as a prison and maritime museum – its collection is now at MAS – it is currently being converted into a cruise terminal and visitor centre due to open in 2020, which doesn't sound immediately promising, but fingers crossed. Most of the fortress was destroyed during the 19th century, when the quays were expanded, and its main draw now is a rude bas-relief of Scandinavian god Semini above the entrance gate. Local mothers worshipped Semini as a fertility symbol (replete with erect phallus), though he was reviled by later clergy and his statue castrated by outraged Jesuits, so the years haven't been too kind!

DIVA [295 B2] (17–19 Suikerrui; 03 360 52 52; w divaantwerp.be; 10.00–18.00 Thu–Tue; adult/under 26/under 12 & City Card €10/7/free) The city's bling-tastic diamond museum opened in May 2018 to much fanfare. The focus is on interactivity, with the ticket including an audio guide narrated by über-camp butler Jérôme, who leads visitors through six rooms – a boudoir, a trading room etc –

revealing how Antwerp rose to become the world's diamond-processing hub. There are some brilliant silver objects and jewels on display (I loved the peculiar windmill cups, once popular at drinking parties), though be aware that there's a lot more information about diamonds than there are real diamonds. High-profile temporary shows by luminaries such as Axel Vervoordt are definitely worth a look – as is the gift shop, featuring DIVA gin (containing carob seeds, long used to measure the carat weight of diamonds).

Museum De Reede [295 B1] (7 Ernest van Dijckkaai; 03 434 03 04; w museum-dereede.com; 11.00–17.00 Thu–Tue; adult/13–18/under 13/City Card €8/3/free/free) Antwerp's first museum dedicated solely to the graphic arts, and opened in 2017 by a Dutch collector, is a beguiling place. Upstairs, the core of the collection comprises 150 works by three graphic masters: Francisco Goya (seen as the founder of modern art), Félicien Rops (a Belgian whose delirious etchings favour erotic and Satanic themes) and Edvard Munch, represented mostly by intense lithographs – often based on his more famous paintings. Regularly changing downstairs shows on lesser-known graphic artists can be a revelation.

Vleeshuis (Butchers' Hall) [295 C1] (38 Vleeshouwersstraat; 03 292 61 01; w museumvleeshuis.be; 10.00–17.00 Thu–Sun; adult/12–25/under 12/City Card €5/3/free/free) The imposing red-and-grey brick butchers' guildhouse with its two turreted towers dates from 1504 and was the tallest private building in the city throughout the 16th century. The butchers' guild was abolished in 1793 under French occupation, and the venue now houses a 'sounds of the city' museum charting 600 years of music and dance in Antwerp. Highlights upstairs include rare 17th-century harpsichords and clavichords (some by eminent local workshop Rucken) and the last existing 16th-century contrebasse flute. Downstairs focuses on brass bands and gargantuan bells from Belgium's last carillon factory, which closed its doors in 1980. There's not much detail in English so keep the dedicated website open on your phone (w vhapp.be) to call up information on exhibits and hear instruments being played. Staff readily kickstart the exotic-looking Verbeeck organ.

North of the centre: Schipperskwartier, the University Quarter and 't Eilandje A short walk from the historic centre lie three neighbourhoods with distinctly different vibes. The gritty **Schipperskwartier** (Sailors' Quarter) is home to Antwerp's red-light district, now contained within three streets: Verversrui, Vingerlingstraat and Schippersstraat. Its crown jewel remains 'Europe's most high-tech bordello', Villa Tinto (17–19 Verversrui), with 51 windows, a biometric scanner to identify workers and panic buttons under the beds. Emerging on to Brouwersvliet, watch out for Dutchman Joost Swarte's new vice- and virtue-themed mural. If you feel the need to repent, the area also contains the wonderful **Sint-Pauluskerk**. Centring on cobbled squares such as Stadswaag, by the venerable Royal Academy of Fine Arts, the neighbouring **University Quarter** abounds in cheap drinking holes and a few highlights: Antwerp's only béguinage, the newly rejigged Snijders and Rockoxhuis museum and lavish Sint-Jacobskerk. Antwerp's famous docks, known as **' t Eilandje** (The Little Isle), sit in the far north and extend well beyond the city limits. Neglected as recently as the 1950s, the area has been significantly gentrified particularly in the last decade, with obvious targets like the iconic MAS museum, newer Red Star Line Museum and attention-grabbing diamond-shaped Port House Authority by late starchitect Zaha Hadid, plus buzzing bars and cafés.

Sint-Pauluskerk (St Paul's Church) [290 B4] (14 Veemarkt; 03 232 32 67; w topa.be; Apr–Oct 14.00–17.00 daily; Nov–Mar 14.00–17.00 Sat–Sun; free) Memorably dubbed 'a Baroque treasure in a Gothic shrine', this dignified church was built for the Dominicans in the 16th century. The project stalled during a period of Calvinist rule in 1578, but the following decade, after the Spanish recaptured the city, the Dominican monks returned and set about refashioning the church in Baroque style. The 15 paintings lining the nave's north aisle, the 'Rosary Cycle', are a fine-art comic strip recounting the lives of Jesus and Mary. They were completed in 1620 by artists including van Dyck, Jordaens and Rubens, behind the bloody *Scourging at the Pillar*. The church's organ is one of Europe's finest, animating Mass during celebrations.

Begijnhof [290 D4] (39 Rodestraat; 03 202 84 30; 08.00–18.00) On the eastern edges of the university district, Antwerp's only béguinage is exceptionally well preserved, and a place of utter calm, its crooked cobbled streets encircling a private garden. Originally in the south of the city, it was destroyed by the French in 1542, but soon re-established in its current location. Around 40 old béguine houses remain, mostly from the 17th century, occupied by elderly residents after the death of the last béguine in 1986. Have a glimpse in the small church as you stroll around.

Snijders and Rockoxhuis [295 F1] (10–12 Keizerstraat; 03 201 92 50; w rockoxhuis.be; 10.00–17.00 Tue–Sun; adult/under 26/under 18 & City Card €8/6/free) In February 2017, former Mayor Nicolaas Rockox's 17th-century townhouse, 'Den Gulden Rinck', was combined with 'De Fortuyne', the adjoining property of his long-time neighbour Frans Snijders. Both men were key figures in the Baroque era. An avid patron of the arts, Rockox was friends with Rubens, humanist Justus Lipsius and publishers Jan and Balthazar Moretus (page 302), and as president of the Arquebusiers' Guild commissioned Rubens to paint *The Descent from the Cross* now hanging in the Cathedral of Our Lady. Snijders was a renowned painter of animals and still lifes. Banking giant KBC acquired both houses in 1970. The beautifully restored rooms are dark, so opt for the iPad tour, which leads you through a treasure trove of art, from early landscape artist Joachim Patinir's *St Christopher Bearing the Christ Child* to Pieter Brueghel the Younger's chaotic illustration of over 100 Flemish proverbs highlighting human folly. Just to the right of the entrance, Snijders's home is dominated by his gorgeous, gleaming animal portraits and still lifes, spanning hunting scenes and fish markets. Watch out for the cats constantly hovering on the edge of the frame!

Sint-Jacobskerk (St James's Church) [291 D5] (73 Lange Nieuwstraat; 03 232 10 32; w topa.be; 14.00–17.00; adult/under 12/City Card €3/free/free) The resting place of Rubens, and a short stroll north of his house museum, was over 150 years in the making – long enough for its Gothic bones to spawn the decadent Baroque interior you see today, and containing over 100 types of marble. Notably, it was one of the few churches in the city not to have been plundered by the French, so still contains many of the treasures and tombs of the Antwerp elite who poured money into the construction of family side chapels and the artworks that adorn them. Of particular interest are the burial vault belonging to the Rockox family, located in the third chapel from the transept, and Rubens's tomb, which lies behind the main altar in the Chapel of Our Lady, beneath his painting *Our Lady and the Christ Child Surrounded by Saints*. Interestingly, the faces of St George, St Jerome, the Virgin Mary and Mary Magdalene are purported to be portraits of Rubens, his father, Isabella Brant (his first wife) and Hélène Fourment (his second wife). Visit in summer and you might see crowds of pilgrims asking for benediction for their journey (and receiving a shell to hang around their neck): it has long been a pitstop on the pilgrimage route to Santiago de Compostela. Find out more from the volunteer guides, who are happy to give free tours. Parts of the church are closed for an ongoing restoration.

Bonapartedok and Willemdok 't Eilandje's two central docks were constructed on the orders of Napoleon towards the end of the French occupation; he wanted the port to be like 'a pistol aimed at the heart of England'. The Bonaparte (or 'museum dock') was completed in 1803 and named after the diminutive French general, but the Willemdok ultimately took the name of the country's new ruler, William I of the Netherlands. Pleasure yachts, historic barges and a vintage crane cement its maritime atmosphere.

Museum aan de Stroom (MAS) [290 C3] (Hanzestedenplaats; 03 338 44 00; w mas.be; 10.00–17.00 Tue–Fri, 10.00–18.00 Sat–Sun; adult/12–25/under 12 & City Card €10/8/free, or €5/3/free if no temporary show) The stunning MAS – constructed from red Indian sandstone and waves of perspex – has become one of Antwerp's most enduring symbols, and a hallmark of 't Eilandje's gentrification, since opening in 2011. Reuniting the collections of the former Ethnographic, National Maritime and Folk museums, it offers themed permanent and temporary displays very loosely investigating the Belgian port's past and place in the world – via Pre-Columbian art and a second-floor 'visible storage' room. Its main draw is the 10th-floor roof terrace, offering superb panoramic views of the city (there's no charge to access the building's common parts). One floor down is exclusive two-star Michelin restaurant 't Zilte (chef Viki Geunes co-runs a hotel, U Eat & Sleep Antwerp, at the building's foot), and another floor down local artist Guillaume Bijl's jaunty *Saluting Admiral Couple* statue perched on a terrace outside the building's windows. On the square in front, Luc Tuymans has created a vast skull mosaic as a nod to the plaque for Quinten Matsijs on the façade of the the Cathedral of Our Lady. You'll also find pavilions with various displays on the port and its arts.

Red Star Line Museum [290 B2] (3 Montevideostraat; 03 298 27 70; w redstarline.be; 10.00–17.00 Tue–Sun; adult/12–26/under 12/City Card €8/6/free/free) A 10-minute walk north from MAS, this very engaging museum (est 2013) recounts the story of transatlantic shipping company the Red Star Line, which carried over 2 million passengers (including Albert Einstein) from the warehouses where the museum now stands to the US and Canada from 1873 to 1934. Beautiful vintage posters advertising the service line the museum's walls, but it's the audio testimonies of passengers – increasingly Jewish refugees from Eastern Europe – that really hit home, with many embarking on Herculean quests merely to reach Antwerp. There's a charming café at the exit of the permanent collection and they often host excellent free temporary displays in the old baggage shed on the ground floor.

Port House [290 C1] (1 Zaha Hadidplein; 03 205 20 11; w portofantwerp.com) The headquarters of the Antwerp Port Authority previously served as a fire station which, courtesy of British-Iraqi architect Zaha Hadid's office, now bears a stunning diamond-like extension floating above it, and projecting towards the Scheldt. With no public transport connections, getting to it means an unlovely 15-minute walk north (or shorter bike ride) from the Red Star Line Museum. You'll pass the city limits (!) and a park looking over at Sint-Anna beach before it hoves into view. The glittering facets of the building and view back into town are mesmerising, but I would only recommend it to very keen architecture buffs. The tourist office holds regular 90min tours – in Dutch only, so gather a group for an English tour (€80). For now, perhaps best admired from afar!

South of the centre: Sint-Andries, Het Zuid and the Theaterbuurt

Stretching south from the city centre, these three neighbourhoods developed during the latter half of the 19th century and are home to most of the city's museums, theatres and galleries, as well as its best shopping. **Sint-Andries** was once known as the 'Parish of Hardship', but it only takes a glimpse of Nationalestraat, which runs due south from Groenplaats, and Kloosterstraat, which runs parallel to it, to see that those days are long gone. Posh **Het Zuid** is Antwerp's answer to Paris, with striking squares and Art Nouveau architecture. The **Theaterbuurt**, AKA Antwerp's Latin Quarter, sits off to the east and is one of the city's most delightful neighbourhoods, known for its theatres, exclusive boutiques and weekend market, as well as its tranquil botanical garden.

ModeNatie This bright-white corner building at 28 Nationalestraat is ground zero for Antwerp fashion, housing the fabled Royal Academy of Fine Arts fashion department, headed by designer Walter Van Beirendonck, and Flanders DC, promoting the Flemish creative industries. Since 2002, it has been home to fashion museum **MoMu** [291 B5] (03 470 27 70; w momu.be; closed until autumn 2020), now shut for renovation. The plan is to display far more of the museum's collection – it's the largest in the world for contemporary Belgian fashion – and to focus on the story of the Antwerp Six (page 58) as well as more recent graduates. In the meantime, the wonderful attached bookshop **Copyright** (03 232 94 16; w copyrightbookshop.be; 11.00–18.30 Tue–Sat, 14.00–18.00 Sun) remains open.

Paardepoortje [291 A6] In the south of Sint-Andries, at 14 Willem Lepelstraat, a horse marks the entrance to the hidden Paardepoortje alleyway – a white, flower-lined enclave that's one of the last examples of 19th-century working-class housing in the city. Another rare sight, round the corner from the KMSKA at 1 Plaatsnijdersstraat, is **The Five Continents** [291 B8], a jaw-dropping 1901 Art Nouveau building commissioned by a shipwright who added a ship's bow to the original design – hence its nickname, *het bootje* ('the little boat'). It now houses the Chilean consulate.

M HKA (Museum of Contemporary Art) [291 A7] (32 Leuvenstraat; 03 260 99 99; w muhka.be; 11.00–18.00 Tue–Wed & Fri–Sun, 11.00–21.00 Thu; adult/under 26/under 13 & City Card €10/1/free) Antwerp's Museum of Contemporary Art is housed in a vast 1920s converted grain silo. Since spring 2017, the entrance hall has morphed into a stylish library/reading room after the intervention of Belgian designer Axel Vervoordt and Japanese architect Tatsuro Miki. M HKA's heart lies with the happenings of the 1970s and 1980s, and in particular with American Gordon Matta-Clark, once active on the local scene. It was initially hoped that the museum could incorporate his 1977 action *Office Baroque*, in which he cut geometric shapes out of a building on the city's riverfront, but only a door from the project remains in the small ground-floor permanent collection, also with works by luminaries Luc Tuymans, Jan Fabre and Marina Abramović. Try to time a visit with the opening of a temporary show, which is a big social event locally, with attendees spilling out on to the terrace of the fourth-floor café.

FoMu (Photo Museum) [291 A7] (47 Waalsekaai; ☎ 03 242 93 00; w fotomuseum.be; ⏲ 10.00–18.00 Tue–Sun; adult/under26/under 18 & City Card €10/3/free) Easily combined with nearby M HKA, this well-respected, warehouse-bound photography museum has a collection of over 915,000 items – negatives, antique cameras, art and documentary photography – mainly focused on Belgium, but not just. The permanent collection, due to be rejigged, slightly misses a trick, but the temporary exhibitions are spot on, taking in radical image-makers, confirmed names and the odd megastar. Upcoming Belgians like Max Pinckers and Bieke Depoorter are especially well supported.

KMSKA – Koninklijk Museum voor Schone Kunsten (Royal Museum of Fine Arts) [291 A7] (Leopold de Waelplaats; ☎ 03 224 95 50; w kmska.be; ⏲ closed until 2020) Undergoing renovation since way back in 2011, the city's KMSKA is (tentatively) set to reopen in 2020, with the addition of 10 rooms completely altering the nature of the stately late 19th-century building. In the meantime, parts of its exceptional collection, including major works by Rubens, the world's top James Ensor collection (now at Mu.ZEE in Ostend) and the largest horde of paintings by Rik Wouters, are travelling in Belgium and beyond.

Justitiepaleis (Courts of Justice) [291 A8] (20 Bolivarplaats) At the foot of 't Zuid, and opened in 2006, Antwerp's exceptionally striking, environmentally friendly law courts look like the wind-blown sails of a ship, owing to the jutting, rakish shape of the roofs. Richard Rogers, also behind Paris's Pompidou Centre, designed the complex.

Museum Mayer van den Bergh [291 C6] (19 Lange Gasthuisstraat; ☎ 03 338 81 88; w museummayervandenbergh.be; ⏲ 10.00–17.00 Tue–Sun; adult/12–25/under 12 & City Card €8/6/free) Some 19 of the paintings, sculptures, drawings and other *objets d'art* in this 5,000-strong private art collection currently figure on the Flemish *Topstukkenlijst* (Masterpieces List), reflecting its might. All belonged to self-taught collector Fritz Mayer van den Bergh (1858–1901), who hailed from a family of rich merchants and died at the age of just 43. Mayer van den Bergh had a real eye for art and picked up some incredible bargains: he bought Pieter Bruegel the Elder's apocalyptic *Dulle Griet* (*Mad Meg*) for €12 at an auction in Cologne in 1897, and was one of the first to spot the talent of the then unknown artist. Recently restored, *Dulle Griet* remains a highlight here, rounded out by other sublimely wintery works by the master. Van den Bergh's mother – and housemate until his death – had the Gothic Revival property built especially for the collection and opened it as a museum in 1904. An English audio guide was due to be introduced in October 2019, adding to the charms of the unusually intimate building – less plagued with tourists than the nearby Rubenshuis.

Maagdenhuis (Maidens' House) [291 C6] (33 Lange Gasthuisstraat; ☎ 03 338 26 20; w maagdenhuismuseum.be; ⏲ 10.00–17.00 Mon–Fri, 13.00–17.00 Sat–Sun; adult/12–26/under 12 & City Card €7/1/free) From 1552 to 1882, the Maidens' House was an orphanage for girls. Often the girls did have families, but their parents were either too poor to raise them, or felt the skills (sewing, lace-making etc) they learned here would serve them better later on in life. Babies were often left in purpose-built compartments, known as 'drawers', which were dug into the façade of the orphanage. The intention for many was to reclaim the child once things had improved; to identify them later on, a token – often a playing card – was ripped in half. One portion was given to the parents, the other to the child; if the child was reclaimed the pieces were joined together as proof of a legitimate reunion. Examples of these sit in a cabinet near the entrance (amazingly, the practice still continues in Antwerp). Other rooms contain paintings by van Dyck, Jordaens and Rubens. The old chapel to the right of the entrance has a display of majolica porridge bowls – the precursor of Delft Blue porcelain – used by the girls, and wonderful documentary-style oil paintings of their daily lives by Joannes De Maré.

Rubenshuis (Rubens's House) [291 D5] (9–11 Wapper; 03 201 15 55; w rubenshuis.be; 10.00–17.00 Tue–Sun; adult/12–25/under 12 & City Card €10/8/free) Rubens did for Antwerp what Elvis did for Memphis, so it's no surprise that the artist's palazzo, between the Theaterbuurt and Meir, is the city's top sight. Rubens (page 21) bought the courtyard complex in 1611 and lived, taught and entertained here until his death in May 1640. Visits take in his studio, living quarters and phenomenal personal art gallery, with a landscaped garden in the centre. The town failed several times in its attempts to acquire the complex after the artist's death, and when it finally did in 1937 it was little more than a ruin. Careful restoration ensued and period furniture brought in to furnish the rooms; the newly restored Roman-style portico and garden pavilion are the only original elements. A selection of the maestro's own works includes one of just four self-portraits he ever produced, in which the then 53-year-old sports a hat to conceal his baldness; there's also a playful, early *Adam and Eve*, and *The Annunciation*. An interactive Rubens Experience Centre, containing facilities the current building is ill-equipped to offer, is due to open here in 2022.

Centraal Station area The area around Centraal Station forms another major focal point, humming with crowds shopping for diamonds or kicking back at the cafés on De Keyserlei. Until the 19th century, social and business affairs in Antwerp had focused on the river, but when the Scheldt was reopened in 1863 the port had to be expanded to cope with the boom in shipping traffic. Hundreds of riverside buildings were demolished (only Het Steen castle was saved) and the 16th-century city walls were pulled down. A new railway was built and residential neighbourhoods such as Zurenborg and Stuivenberg sprang up. The dynamics of the metropolis had changed forever. Today, the area's main attractions are the station itself, Antwerp Zoo and the adjacent Diamantkwartier (Diamond Quarter), the largest of its kind in the world.

Centraal Station [291 E5/6] Completed in 1905, this stunning, cathedral-like building cannot fail to impress – appearing 'more suitable … for a state ceremony than as a place to wait for the next connection to Paris or Oostende', as the narrator of W G Sebald's novel *Austerlitz* memorably puts it. The building displays all the pomp you'd expect from an era when Belgium, under King Leopold II, was asserting its might through dubious colonial adventures in the Congo. Soaring to a height of 44m, the great iron and glass trainshed was designed by Clement van Bogaert, while Bruges-born architect Louis Delacenserie masterminded the stone-

A DIAMOND IN THE ROUGH

Procuring a genuine diamond without getting scammed is far easier since the City of Antwerp and Antwerp World Diamond Centre came up with the 'Antwerp's Most Brilliant' (w antwerpsmostbrilliant.be) label, only awarded to companies with impeccable ethics and standards. Look for the stickers in shop windows, or pick up a brochure from the tourist office.

clad terminus buildings and spectacular domed waiting room. The extraordinarily eclectic design nods to the Italian Renaissance, but also strikes Byzantine and Moorish notes, as well as boasting medieval turrets – a fusion of styles that propels it to the top of lists of the most beautiful railway stations in the world.

In 2017, theme park **Comics Station Antwerp** (Kievitplein; 03 232 33 08; f; noon–17.00 Wed, 10.00–17.30 Sat–Sun; over 3s/under 3s/City Card €21.50/free/25% off) moved into the southern end of the building. The attractions, based around Belgian cartoon characters, are simple but good for a few hours of fun, and the star is the 'Mega Twister' – Europe's longest indoor slide!

ZOO Antwerp [291 F6] (26 Koningin Astridplein; 03 202 45 40; w zooantwerpen.be; Jan–Feb & Nov–Dec 10.00–16.45; Mar–Apr & Oct 10.00–17.30; May–Jun & Sep 10.00–18.00 but until 19.00 Sun in Sep; Jul–Aug 10.00–19.00; adult/12–17/3–11/under 3/City Card €26.50/24.50/21.50/free/25% off) Right by Centraal Station, and marked by an eye-catching verdigris statue of a black boy atop a dromedary camel, Antwerp Zoo was founded in 1843, making it one of the oldest in the world. Old buildings including an Egyptian temple add to its charms, but it's not stuck in the past: in recent years it has worked hard to enlarge its compounds, replicating animal habitats wherever possible; attractions include a new savannah zone for buffalo and a 'Hippotopia' pool, as well as a magical butterfly garden.

The Diamond Quarter [291 E6] Flanked by Pelikaanstraat, Lange Herentalsestraat and Vestingstraat, Antwerp's surprisingly low-key diamond district covers one square mile to the southwest of Centraal Station. While much of the gem cutting and polishing has moved elsewhere, an astonishing 84% of the world's rough diamonds, and around half of its cut diamonds, still pass through this neighbourhood. It's home to around 380 workshops and 3,500 brokers, merchants and diamond cutters, the Antwerp World Diamond Centre, which co-ordinates operations from Hoveniersstraat, and four trading exchanges. Orthodox Jews traditionally ran the show, but are increasingly making way for Jain Indians. While business takes place behind closed doors, one thing you *can* do here is shop: diamond boutiques abound on Pelikaanstraat and Vestingstraat, offering rare riches for those with deep pockets.

Outer districts

North: Antwerp North Long a forgotten backwater of the city, this district to the north of Centraal Station has become a popular spot with young families, and offers a glimpse of multi-cultural, working-class Antwerp that feels notably different to the rest of the city. One route in is via the bright-red pagoda on van Wesenbekestraat, the boundary of Belgium's only official **Chinatown** [290 E4], next to brand-new attraction Chocolate Nation [291 E5] (w chocolatenation.be), with 14 rooms uncovering the story of Belgian chocolate – early reports were very positive. Chinese families settled in Antwerp after World War II, though today it's more of an Asiatown, sheltering multiple nationalities from Koreans to Thai and Nepalese. The contiguous districts of Amandus-Atheneum and Stuivenberg (the latter now often called Seefhoek, after the ancient beer Seef, which is made here) make up the rest of Antwerp North, and are home to Portuguese near Sint-Jansplein, Africans near De Coninckplein and Moroccans by souk-like Handelsstraat.

There aren't any major sights per se, but rather handsome old 'public service' facilities set up for poor labourers in the 19th century, and the odd hip shop or café occupying converted industrial buildings. The **Zwembad Veldstraat** (83 Veldstraat; ☎ 03 290 55 55; **w** sportoase.be; ⌚ 07.00–22.00 Mon–Fri, 08.00–18.00 Sat–Sun; adult/4–26/under 3 €3/1.50/free) is a stunning Art Deco pool dating back to 1933, also housing steam baths and a spa. Another must, rarely visited by tourists, is the **Panamarenkohuis** [290 E3] (2 Biekorfstraat; bookings via **w** muhka.be; ⌚ tours currently at 13.30 twice a month on Sat, with plans to extend in 2019; €20). The original house and studio of Belgian artist/inventor Panamarenko, who retired in 2005 and dedicated the property to M HKA, is a glorious showcase of his zany, non-functional vehicles – zeppelins, flying backpacks, submarines – and lifelong quest to untether himself from earth.

When the sun is out, make like the locals and head up to **Park Spoor Noord** (27 Damplein). Formerly an abandoned railway marshalling yard, this sprawling plot has been embraced since reopening as a park in the late 2000s, and offers barbecues, games and a popular seasonal bar, as well as fountains for cooling off.

Southeast: Zurenborg, Haringrode and Middelheim Divided in two by a railway line, **Zurenborg** is the Belle-Époque jewel in Antwerp's crown. Here, between 1894 and 1914, the city's richest citizens commissioned an architectural Disneyland that made the district famous throughout Europe. Every style from Art Nouveau to neo-Gothic and Tudorbethan is on show along the eponymous Cogels-Osylei and side streets. Buildings to look out for are the Art Nouveau De Morgenster (55 Cogels-Osylei), the Baroque Witte Paleizen (Circus Cogels-Osylei) and the Greek Neoclassical Euterpia – also a restaurant popular with creatives (2 Generaal Capiaumontstraat). With tree-lined streets and prim gardens, the area is still one of the most exclusive places to live in the city, and its heart, Dageraadplaats, and the smaller Draakplaats, are packed with great bars and restaurants.

Bordering Zurenborg and Berchem, the **Haringrode** neighbourhood is of note for two things. First, the car-free Groen Kwartier (Green Quarter), formerly home to army barracks, and now juggling sustainable residences, restaurant The Jane (page 293) and **PAKT** (1 Regine Beerplein, **w** pakt-antwerpen.be), a complex of eco-friendly renovated warehouses housing numerous eateries. Next to the Koning Albertpark, where criminals were once hanged, the **De Koninck Brewery** (291 Mechelsesteenweg; ☎ 03 866 96 90; **w** dekoninck.be; ⌚ 10.00–18.00 Tue–Sun, last entry 16.30; adult/4–15/3 and under & City Card €12/6.50/free) has been going just three years less than Belgium has been a country. In 2015, they added high-tech tours, which kick off with a glass of their Triple d'Anvers, take you along a 4m-high walkway right above the brewery, and top you up with their flagship *bolleke* (the word refers to the glass it's served in, but has become a standby for the beer itself). It's a fun if manic experience – many customers were sozzled on my visit – that terminates, naturally, in a bar. A food court has sprung up around it too; watch out for BBQ restaurant Black Smoke and De Koninck's co-tenants

Van Tricht, among Europe's top cheesemongers, who run their own wine and cheese bar.

In the outskirts, and utterly worth the bracing 15-minute or so bike ride to get there, Middelheim's three parks – Den Brandt, Middelheim and Vogelenzang – are the legacy left by rich nobility who once owned them as private grounds. Middelheim itself is home to a world-class open-air sculpture park, **Middelheim Museum** (61 Middelheimlaan, 03 288 33 60; w middelheimmuseum.be; Oct–Mar 10.00–17.00, Apr & Sep 10.00–19.00, May & Aug 10.00–20.00, Jun & Jul 10.00–21.00; free). As you stroll around, you'll find works by Auguste Rodin, Ai Weiwei and Henry Moore. Watch out for Erwin Wurm's *Misconceivable*, a yacht that drips over a bank into the water with the flexibility of a Dalí clock.

West: Linkeroever (Left Bank) Projected as the solution to a local housing crisis around 1900, the west bank of the Scheldt, or Linkeroever, never quite took off, and today only 15,000 people live there. There are two good reasons to travel to the oft-ignored area, however: stellar views of Antwerp's skyline, and the journey – through the stunning **Sint-Anna pedestrian tunnel** [291 A5] under the river. To find it, look for the 1930s brick building on St-Jansvliet square. Inside, the original wooden Art Deco escalators take you down to the footpath, from which it's a 15-minute walk to the other side (or swift bike ride). On exiting, Linkeroever park sits right in front of you. Pause to appreciate the scenery, then head north towards De Molen, an open-air pool with nearby restaurants serving good mussels. At the headland lies Sint-Anna beach, a stretch of white shingle popular with locals in the season.

MECHELEN

Mechelen (Malines in French) is one of Flanders' most underrated cities, and as the seat of the archbishop, it is to Belgium what Canterbury is to the UK. Equidistant between Brussels and Antwerp, it might be overshadowed by its neighbours now, but in the late 15th century it was the most important town in the southern Netherlands. Charles the Bold, Duke of Burgundy, established parts of his administration here in 1473; future Holy Roman Emperor Charles V lived here as a child with his aunt Margaret of Austria, under whose governorship the city peaked. Its glow faded when Margaret died in 1530, and the royal court moved to Brussels. Mechelen later reinvented itself as Belgium's ecclesiastical hub; more recently it has won plaudits for its integration policy under Bart Somers, who was voted World Mayor of the Year in 2016, owing to his success at uniting 86,000 inhabitants of 138 nationalities. While it is a manageable day trip, Mechelen merits a longer stay: with more UNESCO sights than any other art city in Flanders, it's home to atmospheric museums and restaurants – and two important, albeit dark, World War II sites.

GETTING THERE AND AWAY

By car Mechelen is 35 minutes (30km) from Brussels and 30 minutes (27km) from Antwerp. For both, follow the E19 taking, respectively, exit 10 (Mechelen-Zuid) or exit 9 (Mechelen–Noord). From Leuven it's 35 minutes (25km); follow the N26. There's free parking on Douaneplein, a 10-minute walk from the Grote Markt.

By train Brussels (every 10mins; 25mins); Antwerp (every 10mins Mon–Fri, every 15mins Sat–Sun; 20mins); Ghent (every 12mins; 1hr); Leuven (every 15mins; 30mins). Mechelen's two railway stations, Mechelen and Mechelen-Nekkerspoel, are around 15 minutes' walk from the centre; not all trains stop in

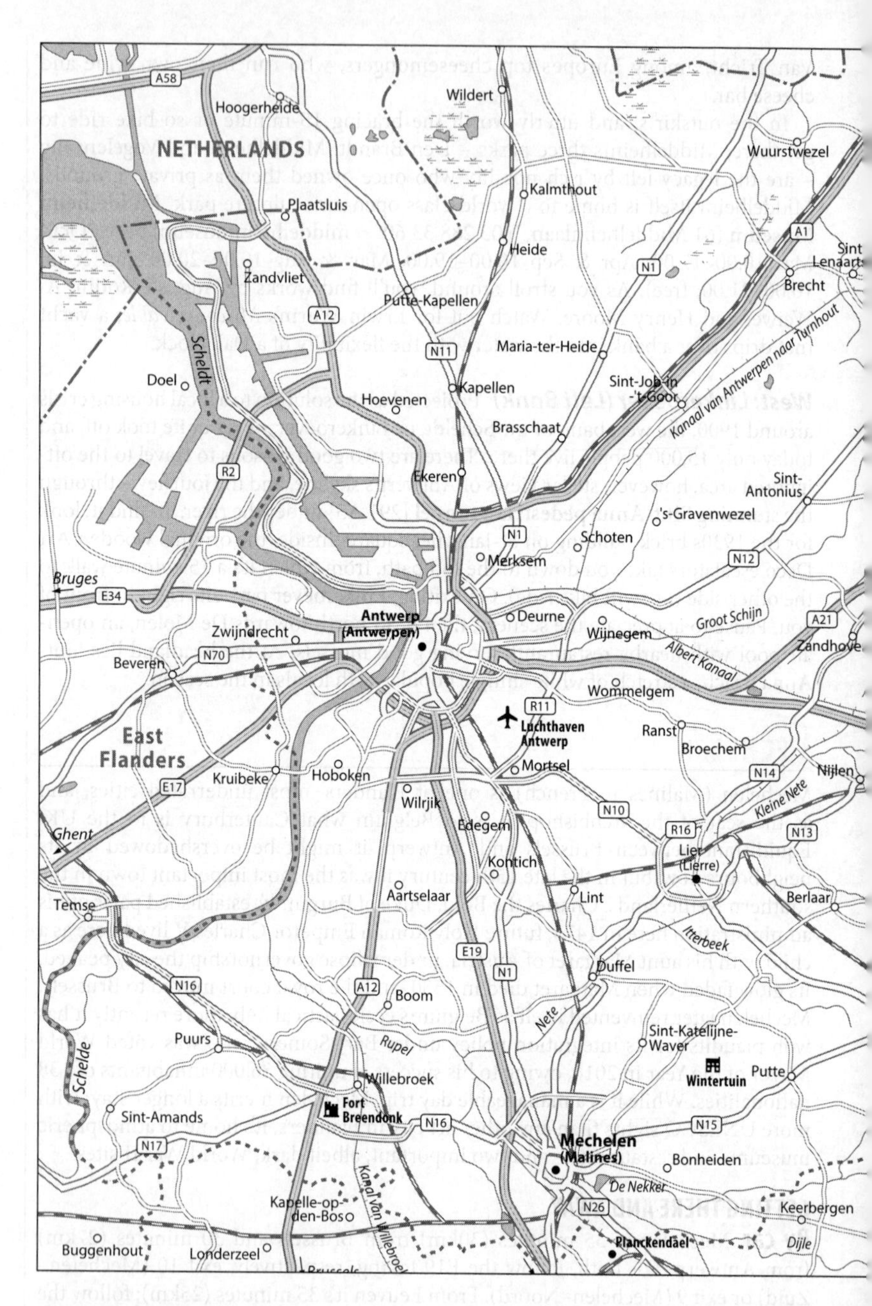

Mechelen–Nekkerspoel. One good reason to get out there is the **Speelgoedmuseum** (**w** www.speelgoedmuseum.be), with one of the largest collections of toys in Europe.

GETTING AROUND

By bus Bus 1 links Mechelen railway station with the Grote Markt every 8 minutes. De Lijn operates the local service; a single ticket is €3; a day ticket is €10.

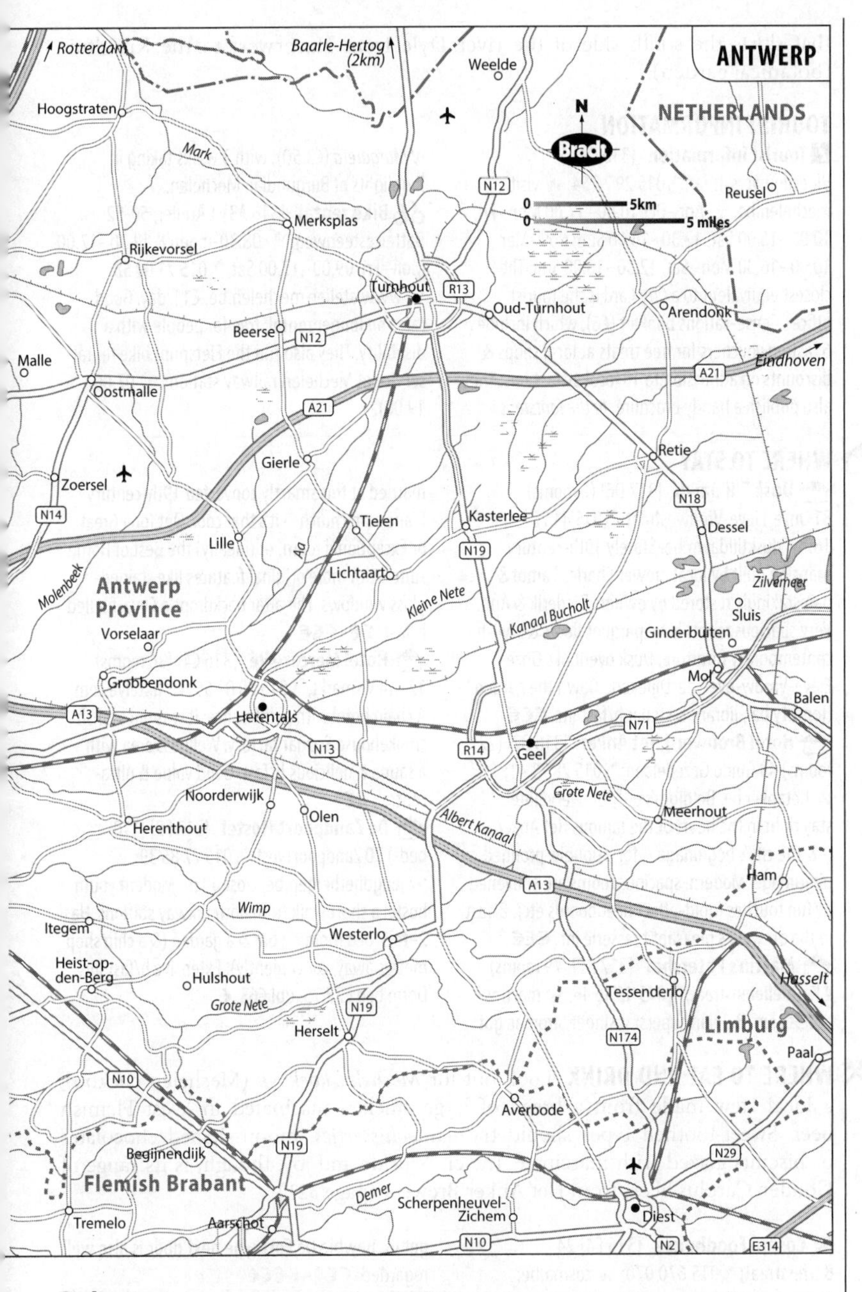

By boat Explore the city's canals on an informative 40-minute boat trip (Haverwerf; 03 213 22 54; **w** bootjesinmechelen.be; Mar & Nov departures Sat, Apr–Nov daily; adult/4–12/3 & under €6.50/4.50/free, cash only if you pay on board).

By foot Mechelen is a very compact town and easy to explore on foot. When you visit, be sure to have a wander along the **Dijlepad** (**Dyle Path**), a tranquil walkway that skirts the south side of the river Dyle from Haverwerf to the Kruidtuin (botanical garden).

TOURIST INFORMATION

Tourist information [316 D4] 6 Vleeshouwersstraat; 015 29 76 54; w visit.mechelen.be; Apr–Oct 10.00–17.00 Mon–Fri, 10.00–16.00 Sat, 12.30–16.00 Sun; Nov–Mar 10.00–16.00 Mon–Sat, 12.30–16.00 Sun. The closest equivalent to a City Card is the tourist office's Sense-sations booklet (€6), which includes 6 tasting vouchers for free treats at local shops & discounts on admission to 10 local attractions. They also publish a handy brochure, *In the footsteps of Margareta* (€3.50), with 3 walks taking in highlights of Burgundian Mechelen.

Bike rental [316 A3] 't Atelier; 50-52 Battelsesteenweg; 08.30–noon & 12.30–17.00 Mon–Fri, 09.00–17.00 Sat; 015 71 09 58; w www.atelier-mechelen.be; €11/day. Good rates on longer rental; free for people with a disability. They also run the Fietspunt bike rental service at Mechelen railway station (07.00–19.00).

WHERE TO STAY

Dusk Till Dawn [317 D6] (2 rooms) 81 Onze-Lieve-Vrouwestraat; 015 41 28 16; w dusktilldawn.be. Stately 19th-century mansion built by local brewer Charles Lamot & painstakingly restored by owners Diederik & Ann. Very spacious rooms have parquet floors & stylish contemporary furniture; Dusk overlooks Onze-Lieve-Vrouw-over-de-Dijlekerk, Dawn the garden. Honesty bar, library & stellar b/fast inc. **€€€**

Hotel Brouwerij Het Anker [316 B2] (22 rooms) 49 Guido Gezellelaan; 015 28 71 41; w hetanker.be. Belgium's only brewery hotel: stay right in the heart of the famous Het Anker – & the city's béguinage – for a double-pronged pilgrimage. Modern, spacious rooms are enlivened by fun touches (gold-effect headboards etc). B/fast in the brewery's pleasant brasserie inc. **€€€**

Martin's Patershof [317 B5] (79 rooms) 4 Karmelietenstraat; 015 46 46 46; w martins-hotels.com. Belgian superstar singer Stromae got married at this smartly converted 19th-century Franciscan church – it's that cool. Opt for a Great or Exceptional room, or (ideally) the Best of Home suite, with more original features like stained-glass windows. The altar backdrops a Cava-fuelled b/fast. **€€–€€€**

Hotel Mercure Vé [316 C4] (36 rooms) 12–14 Vismarkt; 015 20 07 55; w hotelve.com. A chain hotel with a difference: it was once a fish smokehouse & cigar factory. Wellness area with a sauna & delicious b/fast. Good value & ultra-central. **€€**

De Zandpoort Hostel [317 F5] (110 beds) 70 Zandpoortvest; 015 27 85 39; w jeugdherbergen.be; closed Jan. Modern youth hostel a short walk from both railway stations. Has 2- to 5-bed rooms, a bar & a garden (& a chip shop metres away, conveniently). Extensive b/fast inc. Dorm bed €27.75, dbl €63. **€**

WHERE TO EAT AND DRINK

Look out for *Mechelse koekoek* (Mechelen cuckoo), a local stew made from a breed of large chicken marinated in West Flemish beer. Sweet-toothed types should try *maneblussertjes*, moon-shaped chocolates or biscuits glazed with marzipan. The city's pride and joy, though, is its range of Gouden Carolus beers from Het Anker Brewery (page 321).

Cosma Foodhouse [316 E4] 24 Befferstraat; 015 670 070; w cosma.be; noon–15.00 & 18.00–22.00 Wed–Sat. Metro-chic brasserie, deli & shop in an old bakery that brings London glamour to Mechelen. 'Fancy finger food' to start, then inventive fish, meat & vegetables cooked on their hi-tech 'Big Green Egg' grill. Great for veggies. If you can't get in, newbie De Fortuyne next door is also well regarded. **€€€–€€€€**

Graspoort [316 C4] 28 Begijnenstraat; 015 21 97 10; w graspoort.be; 18.00–22.00 Tue–Sat. Health-conscious, veggie-friendly restaurant with a leafy terrace. Pastas, fusion dishes & delicious raw vegetable salads on offer. **€€€**

Het Anker 49 Guido Gezellelaan; 015 28 71 41; w hetanker.be; 10.00–23.00. Buzzing brasserie belonging to the brewery (see opposite) where you can spoil yourself with the many varieties of Gouden Carolus beer alongside filling, reasonably priced local dishes like *Mechelse koekoek*. €€€

Sava [316 D4] 13 Grote Markt; 015 64 70 90; w savamechelen.be; 09.00–late. A great option on the Grote Markt serving superior, reasonably priced tapas in good portions & Cava. Popular in summer when crowds spill on to the terrace. €€–€€€

Bokes & Co [317 C6] 53 Korenmarkt; m 0468 34 44 64; w bokes-co.be; 09.00–17.00 Tue–Sat. Appealing café launched by siblings Vicky & Seppe, & filled with mismatched furniture & vintage knick-knacks. Pastries or full b/fasts but also tasty sandwiches, soups & burgers. €€

Kafee Zapoi [317 D6] 115 Onze-Lieve-Vrouwestraat; m 0495 70 28 23; w kafeezapoi.be; 16.00–midnight Tue–Fri & Sun, noon–02.00 Sat. Fantastic alternative eetcafé offering good, local food for bargain prices (food service from 18.00–21.30 Wed–Sat). They play vinyl & hold regular gigs. €€

Kaffee-Ine [317 C5] 6 Onze-Lieve-Vrouwestraat; m 0475 48 58 14; 09.00–17.00 Tue–Sat. Mechelen's first serious coffee bar is still a hit. Enjoy the funky décor & cool music as you sip delicious filter coffees or decadent-topped lattes. €

ENTERTAINMENT AND NIGHTLIFE Mechelen is a city for enjoying good beers, bars and banter, rather than late-night dancing – ideally around the Vismarkt, a small square by the Dyle that was rundown not so long ago but is now the city's trendiest hangout spot. Mechelen also has a healthy gig scene, and a great arts centre, **Nona** [316 C4] (19 Begijnenstraat; w nona.be), offering edgy theatre and experimental jazz. From the first week of June until mid-September, don't miss live carillon concerts on Mondays at 20.30; Cultuurplein has big screens showing the players in action.

't Ankertje aan de Dijle [316 C4] 20 Vismarkt; 015 34 60 34; f hetankertjeaandedijle; 16.00–midnight Mon–Fri, noon–02.00 Sat, 14.00–20.00 Sun. On the Vismarkt, a convivial brown café in a late-Baroque building serving all Het Anker Brewery's beers (there's also a shop); upstairs is decorated with advertising panels from the 30 breweries that once called Mechelen home.

De Gouden Vis [316 C4] 5–7 Nauwstraat; 015 20 72 06; w degoudenvis.be; noon–late Mon–Fri, 14.00–late Sat, 10.00–late Sun. This Art Nouveau staple is one of Belgium's nicest boozers with authentic décor, a canalside terrace & lengthy beer menu. Old couples sipping coffee by day; a younger crowd by night.

De Hanekeef [316 E3] 8 Keizerstraat; 015 20 78 46; 09.00–03.00. Mechelen's oldest pub (est 1886) retains its pretty tiled floor & beamed ceiling. You'll stumble across locals reading the paper or playing games; if you're wondering about all the cockerel paraphernalia, it nods to the sale of roosters & chickens on adjoining Veemarkt.

Kuub [316 C3] 3a Minderbroedersgang; m 0472 60 00 81; w dekuub.be; noon–midnight Tue–Fri, noon–02.00 Fri–Sat, 10.00–midnight Sun. You can't miss this golden cube – literally. It bills itself as a culture café, which translates as regular concerts, parties & other happenings.

Unwined [316 C4] 22 Steenweg; 015 41 81 85; 17.00–midnight Tue–Thu, noon–midnight Fri–Sat, 15.00–22.00 Sun. The team behind this unpretentious bodega trained at leading wine school Wine & Spirit Education Trust & want to eliminate the snobbery surrounding wine bars. Huge selection across various price points & tasty tapas to soak it up.

SHOPPING Mechelen's shopping district pivots around the pedestrianised triangle of de Bruul, IJzerenleen (which holds a thriving market, 08.00–13.00 Sat) and Onze-Lieve-Vrouwstraat, where artisanal stores offset the high-street brands.

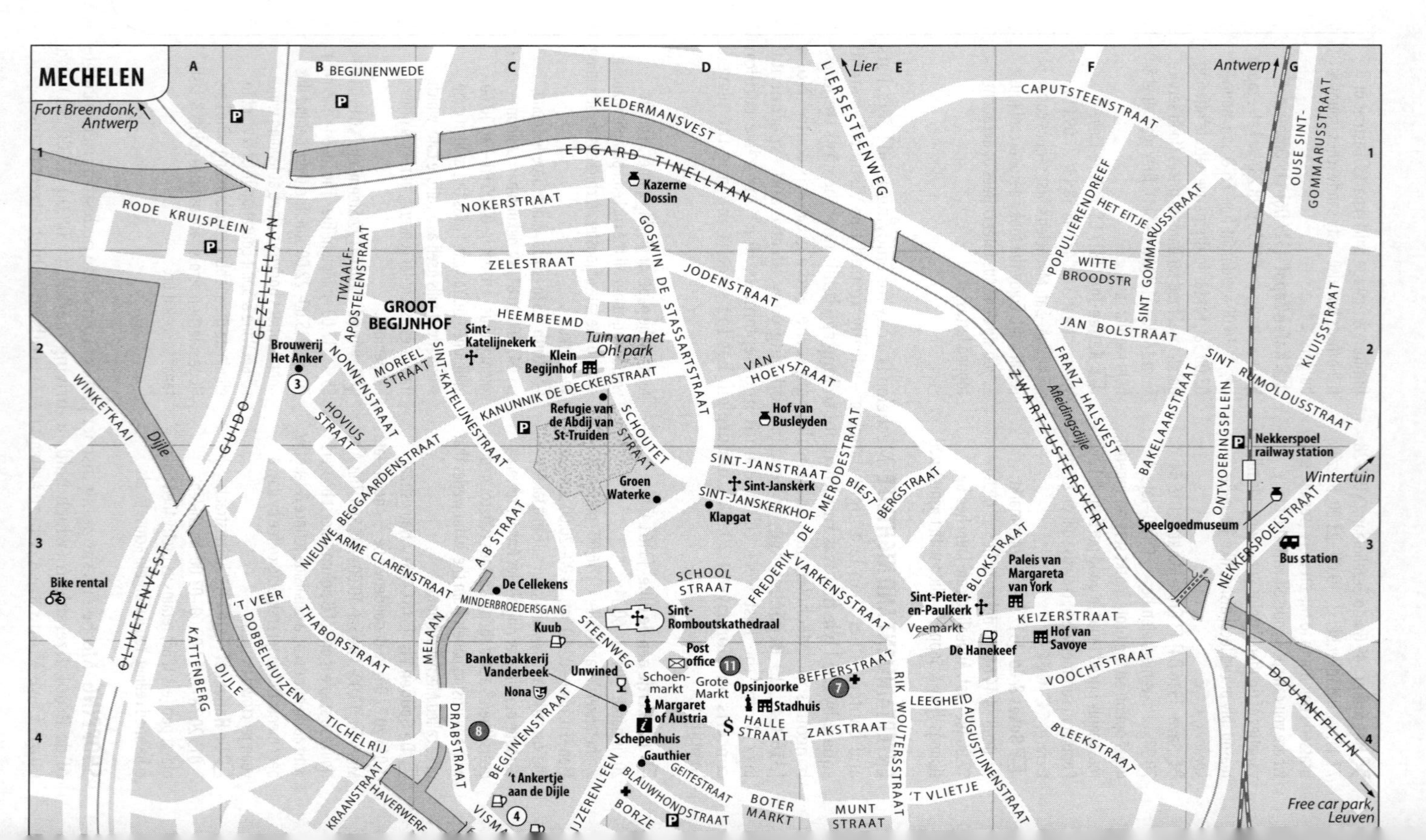

MECHELEN
Fort Breendonk, Antwerp
Lier
Antwerp
BEGIJNENWEDE
KELDERMANSVEST
EDGARD TINELLAAN
LIERSESTEENWEG
CAPUTSTEENSTRAAT
OUSE SINT-GOMMARUSSTRAAT
RODE KRUISPLEIN
GEZELLELAAN
GUIDO
NOKERSTRAAT
Kazerne Dossin
ZELESTRAAT
GOSWIN DE STASSARTSTRAAT
JODENSTRAAT
POPULIERENDREEF
HET EITJE
WITTE BROODSTR
SINT GOMMARUSSTRAAT
TWAALF-APOSTELENSTRAAT
GROOT BEGIJNHOF
HEEMBEEMD
Sint-Katelijnekerk
Tuin van het Oh! park
Klein Begijnhof
JAN BOLSTRAAT
KLUISSTRAAT
Brouwerij Het Anker
NONNENSTRAAT
MOREEL STRAAT
SINT-KATELIJNESTRAAT
KANUNNIK DE DECKERSTRAAT
VAN HOEYSTRAAT
FRANZ HALSVEST
Afleidingsdijle
ZWARTZUSTERSVERT
SINT RUMOLDUSSTRAAT
BAKELAARSTRAAT
ONTVOERINGSPLEIN
Nekkerspoel railway station
WINKETKAAI
Dijle
HOVIUS STRAAT
Refugie van de Abdij van St-Truiden
SCHOUTET STRAAT
Hof van Busleyden
SINT-JANSTRAAT
Sint-Janskerk
BIEST
BERGSTRAAT
Wintertuin
NIEUWE BEGGAARDENSTRAAT
Groen Waterke
SINT-JANSKERKHOF
Klapgat
FREDERIK DE MERODESTRAAT
Speelgoedmuseum
NEKKERSPOELSTRAAT
Bus station
OLIVETENVEST
ARME CLARENSTRAAT
A B STRAAT
Bike rental
De Cellekens
SCHOOL STRAAT
VARKENSSTRAAT
BLOKSTRAAT
Paleis van Margareta van York
'T VEER
MINDERBROEDERSGANG
Sint-Romboutskathedraal
Sint-Pieter-en-Paulkerk
KEIZERSTRAAT
DOBBELHUIZEN
THABORSTRAAT
MELAAN
Kuub
STEENWEG
Veemarkt
Hof van Savoye
Post office
De Hanekeef
KATTENBERG
Banketbakkerij Vanderbeek
Unwined
Schoenmarkt
Grote Markt
Opsinjoorke
BEFFERSTRAAT
VOOCHTSTRAAT
DIJLE
Nona
Margaret of Austria
Stadhuis
LEEGHEID
RIK WOUTERSSTRAAT
DOUANEPLEIN
TICHELRIJ
DRABSTRAAT
BEGIJNENSTRAAT
HALLE STRAAT
ZAKSTRAAT
AUGUSTIJNENSTRAAT
BLEEKSTRAAT
Schepenhuis
Gauthier
IJZERENLEEN
GEITESTRAAT
'T VLIETJE
KRAANSTRAAT
HAVERWERF
'tAnkertje aan de Dijle
BLAUWHONDSTRAAT
BOTER MARKT
MUNT STRAAT
Free car park, Leuven
VISMA
BORZE

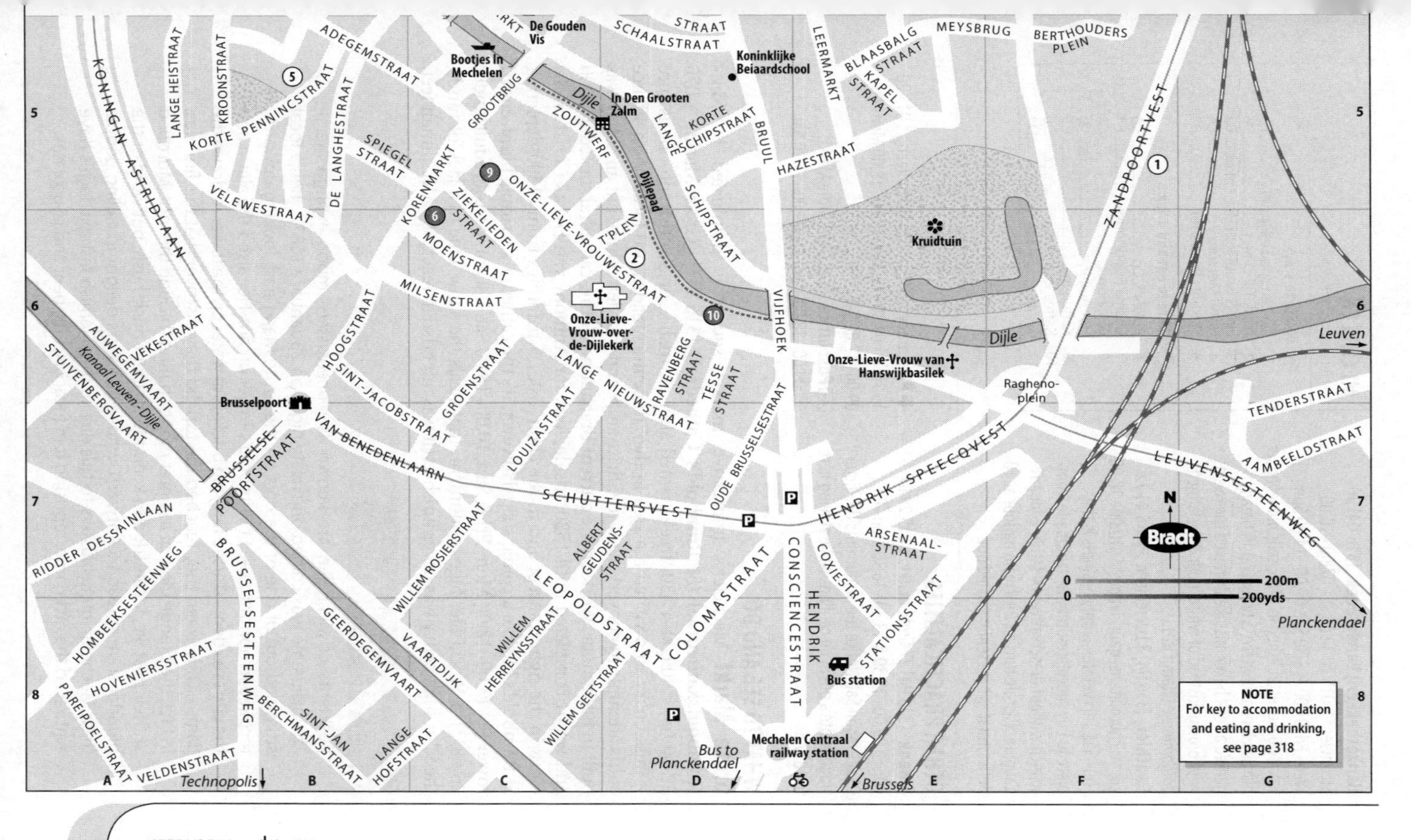
De Gouden Vis
SCHAALSTRAAT
Koninklijke Beiaardschool
LEERMARKT
BLAASBALG STRAAT
KAPEL STRAAT
MEYSBRUG
BERTHOUDERS PLEIN
KONINGIN ASTRIDLAAN
LANGE HEISTRAAT
KROONSTRAAT
KORTE PENNINCSTRAAT
ADEGEMSTRAAT
Bootjes In Mechelen
Dijle
In Den Grooten Zalm
GROOTBRUG
ZOUTWERF
LANGE SCHIPSTRAAT
KORTE SCHIPSTRAAT
BRUUL
HAZESTRAAT
ZANDPOORTVEST
DE LANGHESTRAAT
SPIEGEL STRAAT
KORENMARKT
ZIEKELIEDEN STRAAT
ONZE-LIEVE-VROUWESTRAAT
Dijlepad
SCHIPSTRAAT
Kruidtuin
VELEWESTRAAT
MOENSTRAAT
T'PLEIN
MILSENSTRAAT
Onze-Lieve-Vrouw-over-de-Dijlekerk
VIJFHOEK
Leuven
VEKESTRAAT
AUWEGEMVAART
Kanaal Leuven - Dijle
STUIVENBERGVAART
HOOGSTRAAT
SINT-JACOBSTRAAT
GROENSTRAAT
LANGE NIEUWSTRAAT
RAVENBERG STRAAT
TESSE STRAAT
Onze-Lieve-Vrouw van Hanswijkbasilek
Ragheno-plein
TENDERSTRAAT
Brusselpoort
BRUSSELSE-POORTSTRAAT
VAN BENEDENLAARN
LOUIZASTRAAT
OUDE BRUSSELSESTRAAT
HENDRIK SPEECQVEST
AAMBEELDSTRAAT
LEUVENSESTEENWEG
SCHUTTERSVEST
N
Bradt
RIDDER DESSAINLAAN
WILLEM ROSIERSTRAAT
ALBERT GEUDENS-STRAAT
ARSENAAL-STRAAT
COXIESTRAAT
HOMBEEKSESTEENWEG
BRUSSELSESTEENWEG
LEOPOLDSTRAAT
COLOMASTRAAT
HENDRIK CONSCIENCESTRAAT
STATIONSSTRAAT
0 200m
0 200yds
Planckendael
HOVENIERSSTRAAT
GEERDEGEMVAART
VAARTDIJK
WILLEM HERREYNSSTRAAT
Bus station
PAREIPOELSTRAAT
SINT-JAN BERCHMANSSTRAAT
LANGE HOFSTRAAT
WILLEM GEETSTRAAT
NOTE
For key to accommodation and eating and drinking, see page 318
VELDENSTRAAT
Technopolis
Bus to Planckendael
Mechelen Centraal railway station
Brussels
A
B
C
D
E
F
G
5
6
7
8

Banketbakkerij Vanderbeek [316 D4] 36 Steenweg; 015 20 32 66; 07.00–18.00 Wed–Fri, 07.00–18.30 Sat, 07.00–14.00 Sun. Family baker established in 1766; sells *maneblusser* biscuits & *potdommeke*, a brown raisin bread so named after a baker mistakenly mixed the raisins with brown, instead of white, flour & exclaimed *potdommeke* ('damn it!').

Gauthier [316 D4] 3 IJzerenleen; 015 41 72 46; w chocolaterie-gauthier.be; 10.00–18.00 Thu–Sat. This veteran family business is the place to buy chocolates: they're handmade from scratch without preservatives by father Edouard; daughter Pascale runs an ice-cream parlour at 10 Befferstraat, where senior started out.

MECHELEN

For listings, see from page 314

Where to stay

1	De Zandpoort Hostel	F5
2	Dusk Till Dawn	D6
3	Hotel Brouwerij Het Anker	B2
4	Hotel Mercure Vé	C4
5	Martin's Patershof	B5

Where to eat and drink

6	Bokes & Co.	C6
7	Cosma Foodhouse	E4
8	Graspoort	C4
	Het Anker	(see 3)
9	Kaffee-Ine	C5
10	Kaffee Zapoi	D6
11	Sava	D4

OTHER PRACTICALITIES

$ Bank [316 D4] 27 Grote Markt; 015 29 82 00; 09.00–12.30 & 13.30–16.30 Mon–Fri, 09.00–noon Sat. Notice the plaque outside: Victor Hugo wrote a poem on carillons while staying here in 1837.

Pharmacy [316 D4] 25 IJzerenleen; 015 20 15 74; 09.30–12.30 & 13.00–18.00 Mon–Fri, 09.00–17.00 Sat

Post office [316 D4] 1 Grote Markt; 09.00–18.00 Mon–Fri, 09.00–12.30 Sat

WHAT TO SEE AND DO

Grote Markt Mechelen's impressive market square is dominated by **Sint-Romboutskathedraal (St Rumbold's Cathedral)** [316 D3] (Grote Markt; 070 22 00 08; 09.00–17.30; free), named after an Irish – or Scottish, no-one is sure – missionary who visited the area in the 7th century. Sadly, two locals took offence at his attempts to convert them to Christianity and murdered him, but an abbey was built in his honour. Work on the current Brabantine Gothic cathedral started in 1200 and wasn't completed until 1520. Inside, look for Anthony van Dyck's *Christ on the Cross* in the right transept and in the choir aisle 25 paintings from c1500 depicting St Rumbold's life like a comic strip. However, it's the cathedral's soaring, blunt-ended **tower** (13.00–18.00 Mon–Fri & Sun, 10.00–18.00 Sat, last entry 16.40; adult/under 26 €8/3), a World Heritage monument, that steals the show. Due to a lack of funds, the 97m-high belfry was never finished (it was intended to reach 600 Mechlinian feet,

MOON EXTINGUISHERS

Residents of Mechelen are known as *maneblussers* (moon extinguishers). The nickname was coined one misty night on 28 January 1687, when a local stumbled out of one of the bars on the Grote Markt and, looking upwards, recoiled in horror to see St Rumbold's Tower on fire. He raised the alarm and the city's residents started ferrying buckets of water up the tower to douse the flames. Only when they reached the top did they discover that the 'fire' was, in fact, the orange glow of a winter moon shining through the mist. Mortified at their mistake, locals tried to keep the incident hush-hush, but word of the blunder soon spread to Antwerp, whose residents delight in calling people from Mechelen *maneblussers* to this day. In true Flemish fashion, locals have embraced the nickname, reprising it in local biscuits, beer and chocolates.

FOR WHOM THE BELL TOLLS

Bell towers have played a prominent role in Flanders for centuries, originally serving to spread warnings about attacks or fires. They were also the original time-keeping devices, and most still sound out the hours, with Mechelen's bell tower also striking each quarter hour, and even the midway 7½-minute point, known as the *Mechelen halfke* ('Little Mechelen half'). Many people mistake carillons for bell towers, but in fact the word denotes the world's heaviest musical instrument, made of a series of bells of different sizes, each producing a different note. St Rumbold's houses Belgium's finest carillon, a 49-bell contraption, with each bell having its own name (the most notable is Salvator, weighing 8,884kg). Thirty-nine steps above this set of bells is a second complete carillon on which concerts are played (catch hour-long performances on Saturdays at 11.30 and Sundays at 15.00, as well as Monday nights in summer). Carillon-playing nearly died out in the 19th century – it was seen as too fusty – but Mechelen was central to its revival, not least city carillon player Jeff Denyn, who went on to found the Koninklijke Beiaardschool (Royal Carillon School) in 1922. The first of its kind in the world, it's still turning out *carilloneurs* in its new home on de Bruul. Every five years the school holds the Queen Fabiola international carillon competition.

or 167m), but it's still Belgium's highest Gothic tower. There are 538 steps leading to the top and it's not an easy climb (though far less crowded than the Bruges belfry), but there are six rooms to explore at intervals and recover your breath, including the Crane Room where you can see two carillons. At the top, a glass Sky Walk offers 360° views of the town, and on a clear day you can see Brussels and Antwerp. Watch out for the peregrine falcons – they recently returned to the tower!

To the east is the UNESCO-listed **Stadhuis (Town Hall)** [316 D4] comprised of the former cloth hall, with its unfinished belfry and, to its left, the Palace of the Great Council. The belfry is, in fact, hollow; funds for its completion dried up when the cloth trade dipped in the 14th century, and St Rumbold's Tower was used as a belfry instead. The Palace of the Great Council was also only ever such in name – the council never convened here, confusingly! Look for the 36 medallions on the Befferstraat side of the building, portraying rulers such as Philip the Good, Duke of Burgundy (1478–1506). A bronze statue of **Opsinjoorke** (see box, page 320) stands in front of the town hall; there's a fun yellow version of it for kids to climb in Sint-Romboutskerkhof nearby.

North of the Grote Markt Head east along Befferstraat to Veemarkt, site of the newly restored, beautiful Jesuit **Sint-Pieter-en-Paulkerk (Church of St Peter and St Paul)** [316 E3] (44 Veemarkt; ⌚13.00–16.00 Thu–Tue; free). You'll find richly carved confessional boxes, a pulpit recounting the missionary work carried out by St Francis Xavier, and a lead urn near the altar containing relics of Margaret of Austria.

Next door, on Keizerstraat, is the **Paleis van Margareta van York (Palace of Margaret of York)** [316 F3]. Margaret was the third wife of Charles the Bold, Duke of Burgundy. She moved to Mechelen after being banished from Ghent for meddling in the affairs of her stepdaughter Mary of Burgundy, who was left in charge when Charles died in 1477. You can still glimpse Margaret's diamond-shaped coat of arms on the façade; the building now houses the Stadsschouwburg (City Theatre). Next to it you'll find *Golden Boy*, a new brushed-bronze statue of a boy on a rocking horse by famous Scandinavian artist duo Elmgreen and Dragset; it depicts the childhood of Charles V, who lived with his sisters in Margaret of York's palace and was raised by his aunt Margaret of Austria. Her palace, the **Hof van Savoye (Court of Savoy)** [316 F3], stands diagonally opposite. Designed by local architects the Keldermans family – also behind St Rumbold's Tower – it was one of the first Renaissance-style buildings in the Low Countries. Walk through the green door on the left and you enter a regal courtyard lined with box hedges.

Retrace your steps slightly to Veemarkt and follow it as it becomes Biest and hits Frederik de Merodestraat. Here, in summer 2018, the home of Hieronymus van Busleyden, an advisor to Charles V, reopened as **Hof van Busleyden** [316 D2] (65 Frederik de Merodestraat; 015 29 40 30; w hofvanbusleyden.be; 10.00–17.00 Mon–Tue & Fri–Sun, 10.00–22.00 Thu; adult/13–26/12 & under €11/5/free), a high-tech museum devoted to Mechelen's glory days around 1500, when it was the de facto capital of the Burgundian Netherlands. Despite a confusing layout, fine exhibits bring the period to life, as well as Mechelen's love for Margaret of Austria, who reshaped its fortunes. For me the highlights were the stunning 16th-century retable cabinets the *Besloten Hofjes* (Enclosed Gardens), whose teeming interiors embody early modern religious beliefs. Local Augustinian nuns who ran a hospital nearby for 500 years used to guard Europe's largest collection of retable cabinets.

A 2-minute walk south, **Sint-Janskerk (St John's Church)** [316 D3] (Sint-Janskerkhof; Apr–Oct 13.00–17.00 Thu–Tue, Nov–Mar 13.00–16.00 Thu–Tue; free) was the stomping ground of members of the Great Council – hence its great number of treasures, including Rubens's triptych *The Adoration of the Magi* above the altar. In 2008, exquisite 14th-century murals of St Christopher and St George were uncovered at the foot of the western tower and can be visited with a guide.

Opposite the church is the tiny **Klapgat (Gossip Alley)** [316 D3], so called because churchgoers used to gather for a natter there after Mass (*klappen* means to chat in Dutch). At the end of it, just to the left, admire the **Groen Waterke (Green Water)** [316 D3], an area of the exposed Melaan canal (page 322) named after the duckweed that grows there.

At this point you can walk north for 5 minutes to the tip of the city and the unmissable **Kazerne Dossin (Dossin Barracks)** [316 D1] (153 Goswin de

OPSINJOORKE

Mechelen and Antwerp enjoy a light-hearted rivalry, but things weren't always so amicable. Tensions arose in 1301 when Antwerp lost is *staplerechten* (staple rights) to Mechelen, meaning that all fish, salt and corn brought in by boat had to be offered for sale in the city markets for three days before it could be reloaded and taken to Antwerp. However, the rivalry reached new heights on 4 July 1775 while Mechelen was celebrating its annual procession of *Sotscop* (Dumbhead), a doll representing abusive, drunken husbands, who were symbolically humiliated as the doll was paraded through town and tossed in the air, before being caught in a cloth. On this occasion, the doll landed in the crowd and an onlooker from Antwerp was accused of trying to steal it. The crowd was furious and the poor chap had to attend a court hearing. He was eventually cleared, but as the Sotscop had fallen on a *Sinjoor* – Sinjoor being a version of the Italian *signor* used by Maneblussers to mock Antwerpenaars for their snobby stance – it has been called *Opsinjoorke* ever since.

Stassartstraat; ☎ 015 29 06 60; w kazernedossin.eu; ⌚ 09.00–17.00 Mon–Tue & Thu–Fri; 09.30–17.00 Sat–Sun; adult/10–21/under 10 €10/8/4), opened in 2012. From 1942 to 1944, more than 26,000 Jews, Roma and Sinti were deported from the Dossin Barracks to Auschwitz-Birkenau. Only 5% of them survived. The city was chosen due to its proximity to both Brussels and Antwerp, which were home to large concentrations of Jews. Across its first, second and third floors, the museum charts the backdrop to the Holocaust and, in particular, Belgium under Nazi occupation, focusing on the stories of five people directly implicated in the round-ups, deportations – and worse – of the period. The fourth floor overlooks the former barracks itself, which lies opposite. While it's now an apartment complex, bizarrely, you can stroll over the road and enter the building, finding a small **memorial museum** on your right, which was due to reopen in September 2019 after renovation (check Kazerne Dossin website for details). I'd advise pausing to reflect in the stark courtyard where arrivals were processed.

Another option from Green Water is to take Schoutetstraat – the first left if you're heading north. You'll pass the **Refuge of Tongerlo Abbey** [316 C2], built by Norbertine monks from Tongerlo in 1484. Since 1986, the refuge and its lovely Renaissance garden have belonged to tapestry restoration company **De Wit** (7 Schoutetstraat; ☎ 015 20 29 05; w dewit.be; ⌚ tours Jan–Jun & Aug–Dec 10.30 Sat; adult/12–18/under 12 €8/4/free). I realise it's a subject that doesn't initially get everyone excited, but De Wit is the world's best – restoring tapestries for the Louvre. Their guided tours are oddly fascinating; you'll glimpse their prestigious collection of ancient and modern tapestries and get to grips with warp and weft during a demonstration.

Right next to De Wit, just off Kanunnik de Dekerstraat, and along Klein Begijnhofstraat, is the city's **Klein Begijnhof (Small Béguinage)** [316 C2]. Spruced up by the city a few years back, it's worth a wander, as is the adjacent Tuin van het Oh! park, featuring a tranquil strip of canal.

A 5-minute walk west will bring you to the main event, the UNESCO-listed **Groot Begijnhof (Large Béguinage)** [316 B2/C2], spanning Nonnenstraat, Conventstraat, Hoviusstraat and Acht-Zalighedenstraat. Originally it stood outside the city walls but these buildings were destroyed in 1578 during the religious wars, so the béguines moved closer to the centre, buying existing property and building a few new houses as well. This led to a mix of architectural styles that make Mechelen's béguinage unique in Flanders – others follow a uniform layout.

On its western flank sits the **Brouwerij Het Anker (Het Anker Brewery)** [316 B2] (49 Guido Gezellelaan; ☎ 015 28 71 41; w hetanker.be; ⌚ tours 11.00 Tue–Sun; & 13.00 Fri–Sun; 14.00 & 15.00 Sat–Sun; €9). Béguines began brewing beer on this site in the Middle Ages. In 1872 the brewery was taken over by the Van Breedam family and renamed Het Anker; it has remained in the family ever since. Though there were 30 local breweries in the 1940s, Het Anker is the sole survivor, best known for its Gouden Carolus range, notably the Gouden Carolus Classic (8.5%), which has won several gold medals at the World Beer Awards; I also recommend the Cuvée van de Keizer, a knee-buckling 11% brew released on 24 February every year to commemorate Charles V's birthday. Tours of the brewery take in the old copper kettles in the brewing hall, lead you past barrels of maturing whiskey – they opened a distillery, De Molenberg, 8km away in 2010, which you can also visit (combi-ticket €19; w/end shuttle between sites) – and end in a tasting of two beers in the brasserie.

Head back into the centre via Arme-Clarenstraat. At its end glimpse through the gate at **De Cellekens** [316 C3], once an almshouse for poor single women; the current owner is an artist, and you can admire her dancing sculptures in the pretty garden. Then cross the **Melaan**, a tributary of the river Dyle covered in 1913 to prevent the spread of disease, but restored to its former glory in 2007.

South of the Grote Markt The Grote Markt merges into the Schoenmarkt, and on its southern side stands a statue of Margaret of Austria [316 D4]. When Belgium gained its independence in 1830, the government ordered every city to raise a statue of a local hero and, interestingly, Mechelen is the only town that chose a woman. *Ons Margriet* – as she's affectionately known – used to stand in the centre of the square, but was ignominiously moved to the side in 2005 to make way for an underground car park. Just behind the statue is the elegant 13th-century **Schepenhuis** (**Aldermen's House**) [316 D4] (6 Vleeshouwersstraat; ⌚ Apr–Oct 10.00–17.00 Mon–Fri, 10.00–16.00 Sat, 12.30–16.00 Sun; Nov–Mar 10.00–16.00 Mon–Sat, 12.30–16.00 Sun), where the Great Council of Mechelen, the Netherlands's highest court, once met. Now it houses the tourist office and marks the beginning of **IJzerenleen**, a broad pedestrianised shopping street leading south of the Grote Markt. This was once a stream linked to the Dyle river, and the site of the city's fish market. Margaret of Austria complained about the smell, but it was only filled in after her death in 1531. Today it's lined with smart boutiques with (fake) 16th-century façades.

Walk to the end of IJzerenleen, turn right and enter the **Vismarkt** [316 C4], a trendy café-lined square that was originally – as you can probably guess from the name – the city's fish market; indeed, there are still one or two shops selling their fishy wares. Cross over the river to the **Haverwerf** (**Oats Wharf**) [316 B4]; on the corner by the Kraanbrug you'll find three stunning 16th- and 17th-century houses with biblically themed façades. Also on this stretch is the former **Lamot brewery**, which was active until the 1980s; its handsome sign lingers, but the site is now a conference centre, alas.

Retrace your steps, passing over the 13th-century **Grootbrug**, a sandstone bridge that's often claimed to be the oldest of its kind in Flanders. The embankment on your left is known as **Zoutwerf** (**Salt Wharf**), where salt used to preserve fish and meat was traded. Look for two wooden façades: **De Waag** (**The Weighhouse**, no 7) where the salt was weighed, and **De Steur** (**The Sturgeon**, no 8), where the salt was stored. The former fishmongers' guildhouse, **In Den Grooten Zalm** (**In The Large Salmon**, no 5), sits beside them and is easily identified by the gilded salmon above its door.

Return to the bridge and head south, through the Korenmarkt, until you reach the outer ring road. In the centre stands **Brusselpoort** (Kruispunt Hoogstraat) [317 B6/7], the only remaining gate from the city walls that surrounded the town in the 13th century.

If you follow the main road around to the left, it's a 10-minute walk to **Onze-Lieve-Vrouw van Hanswijkbasilek** (**The Church of Our Lady of Hanswijk**) [317 C/D6] (Hanswijkstraat; ⌚ Apr–Oct 09.00–17.00; Nov–Mar 09.00–16.00; free), an atmospheric soot-stained basilica that arose as a result of a miracle. In AD988 a barge ran aground at this very spot. Only when a statue of the Virgin Mary, among its cargo, was moved to dry ground did the barge lift free. Locals took it as a sign that Mary wanted to stay where she was, and built a church in her honour. The episode is marked by the Hanswijk Procession (w hanswijkprocessie.be) every year on the Sunday before Assumption. Far rarer is the horse-fuelled Hanswijk Cavalcade, taking place every 25 years (next edition: 2038!) and usually rounded off by Mechelen's own Ommegang.

Day trips

Fort Breendonk ✷ (57 Brandstraat, Willebroek; ☎ 03 860 75 24; **w** breendonk.be; ⏱ Sep–Jun 09.30–17.30; Jul–Aug 09.00–18.00; adult/6–18/under 6 €11/10/free) You've heard of Auschwitz, but few people know that Belgium had its own equivalent of a concentration camp – a moated fort that, while small, was certainly deadly. Between 1940 and 1944, 3,500 prisoners passed through its gates; 184 were shot, 23 were hanged and 100 died of torture or exhaustion. Unusually, the site is incredibly well preserved and still whispers of the horrors that took place there, especially during winter, when damp drips from the walls; an excellent audio guide leads you through the nightmarish barracks, torture room and out to the execution site, while casting light on the lives of those unfortunate enough to be interned there.

Getting there and away Willebroek station is a short train ride from Mechelen (hourly; ⏱ 12mins). From there it's a straightforward 20-minute walk to the fort.

Technopolis (Technologielaan; ☎ 015 34 20 00; **w** technopolis.be; ⏱ 09.30–17.00; adult/4–11/under 4 €17/13.50/free) Interactive science museum that explains all those things you never learned in school, and allows kids to slide down a pole like firefighters, stand inside a giant soap bubble or sleep on a bed of nails.

Getting there and away It's a 10-minute bus ride from the city; buses 282 and 682 depart every 30 minutes from the main station.

Wintertuin Ursulinen (Ursulines's Wintergarden) ✷ (9 Bosstraat, Onze-Lieve-Vrouw-Waver; ☎ 015 75 77 28; **w** visitwintertuin.be; ⏱ tours mid-Jan–mid-Dec 14.00 Sun; adult/3–11 €12/free) This former Catholic boarding school, established in 1841 by progressive Ursuline nuns keen to provide an education for young women (albeit so they could impress their farmer husbands) is an astonishing sight in the middle of the Flemish countryside. The Art Nouveau winter garden, intended to impress prospective pupils' parents, is the stunning showpiece, but fascinating 2-hour tours (dress warm in winter as the enormous school, still in action, isn't heated at weekends) also cover the history of the Ursulines, their views on education and an incredible gallery with 35 pianos!

Getting there and away Take bus 511 from Mechelen–Nekkerspoel (the stop you want faces a Chinese restaurant). After 10 minutes, alight at Onze-Lieve-Vrouw-Waver Kerk.

ZOO Planckendael (582 Leuvensesteenweg, Muizen; ☎ 015 41 49 41; **w** zooplanckendael.be; ⏱ Jan–Feb & Nov–Dec 10.00–16.45; Mar–Apr & Oct 10.00–17.30; May–Jun & Sep 10.00–18.00; Jul–Aug 10.00–19.00; adult/12–17/3–11/under 3 €28/25.50/21.50/free) Normally I don't recommend zoos, but Planckendael is a little different: it's a 40ha safari park which runs a research and conservation programme with ZOO Antwerp (page 309). Animals are split into five continent-themed zones and have plenty of room to roam. Highlights include a treetop walk over the park.

Getting there and away It's a 10-minute journey via bus; take buses 284, 285 or 686 from outside Mechelen railway station. In summer, the zoo lays on an express bus with an on-board host offering explanations during the 10-minute journey (⏱ Apr–May w/ends & select w/days; Jun & Sep w/ends; Jul–Aug daily). Buses depart from behind Mechelen railway station every 15 minutes from 09.45; the last shuttle leaves Planckendael 15 minutes after the park closes.

LIER

It's a hard heart that isn't charmed by Lier. This small town, equidistant between Antwerp and Mechelen, is officially older than Brussels, having received its town charter in 1227, 15 years prior to the capital. It was also the stage for one of the most famous marriages in history. To prevent arguments breaking out between the competing cities of Ghent, Brussels, Bruges and Antwerp, it was decided that Philip the Fair and Johanna of Castille would marry in Lier. The story goes that they fell in love at first sight – she was 16, he was 18 – and Philip insisted that the marriage took place that very evening, presumably so the lustful teenager could consummate the marriage as soon as possible! Among their six children was Charles V, who would rise to become Holy Roman Emperor.

The town has a strong association with lace – between 1820 and 1950 3,000 women were employed at home making it – and you can watch local lace-making clubs hard at work in the pretty béguinage. You also shouldn't miss Lier's pride and joy, a 90-year-old clock tower known as the Zimmertoren. If you can, visit in spring when the surrounding orchards are in full bloom and a racing-pigeon market animates the Grote Markt on Sundays (until mid-April) – such markets are very rare these days.

GETTING THERE AND AWAY

By car From Antwerp follow signs for the R10, then join the N1 and follow it south for 3km, then turn right on to the N10 to Lier (23km; 40mins). From Mechelen follow the N14 north (18km; 30mins).

By train Antwerp (every 15mins; 18mins); Mechelen (hourly Mon–Fri; 16mins; twice an hour Sat–Sun; 40mins); Leuven (twice an hour; 40mins); Brussels (twice an hour Mon–Fri; 45mins, via Antwerp, twice an hour Sat–Sun; 1hr).

TOURIST INFORMATION

Tourist information 58 Grote Markt; 03 800 05 55; w visitlier.be; Apr–Oct 09.00–16.30 Mon–Fri, 09.00–12.30 & 13.00–16.00 Sat–Sun; Nov–Mar 09.00–12.30 & 13.30–16.30 Mon–Fri. Smart office on the ground floor of the town hall, with handy free tourist maps of all the sights inc information in English.

Bike rental Fietspunt, 32 Leopoldplein (railway station); 03 488 18 51; Apr–Sep 07.00–19.00 Mon–Fri, 09.00–13.00 Sat–Sun; Oct–Mar 07.00–19.00 Mon–Fri; €9/day or €5/ from 13.00. Or, in the same location, try Blue Bike (page 59).

WHERE TO STAY AND EAT *Map, opposite*

The best place to try local speciality *Lierse vlaaikes* – small, round spiced cakes – is **Hendrickx Bakkerij** (130 Antwerpstraat; 07.00–18.00 Wed–Sat, 07.00–14.00 Sun). To sample local brew Caves and St Gummarus beers, make for old waterside café **St Gummarus** (2 Felix Timmermansplein; 10.00–01.30 Mon–Fri, 09.00–01.30 Sat, 11.00–midnight Sun).

Best Western Plus Zimmerhof (23 rooms) 2 Begijnhofstraat; 03 490 03 90; w zimmerhof.be. Lier is too small to have much in the way of hotels, but this is the pick of the bunch – a 1902 brick ex-retirement home right in the centre & with smart, modern courtyard

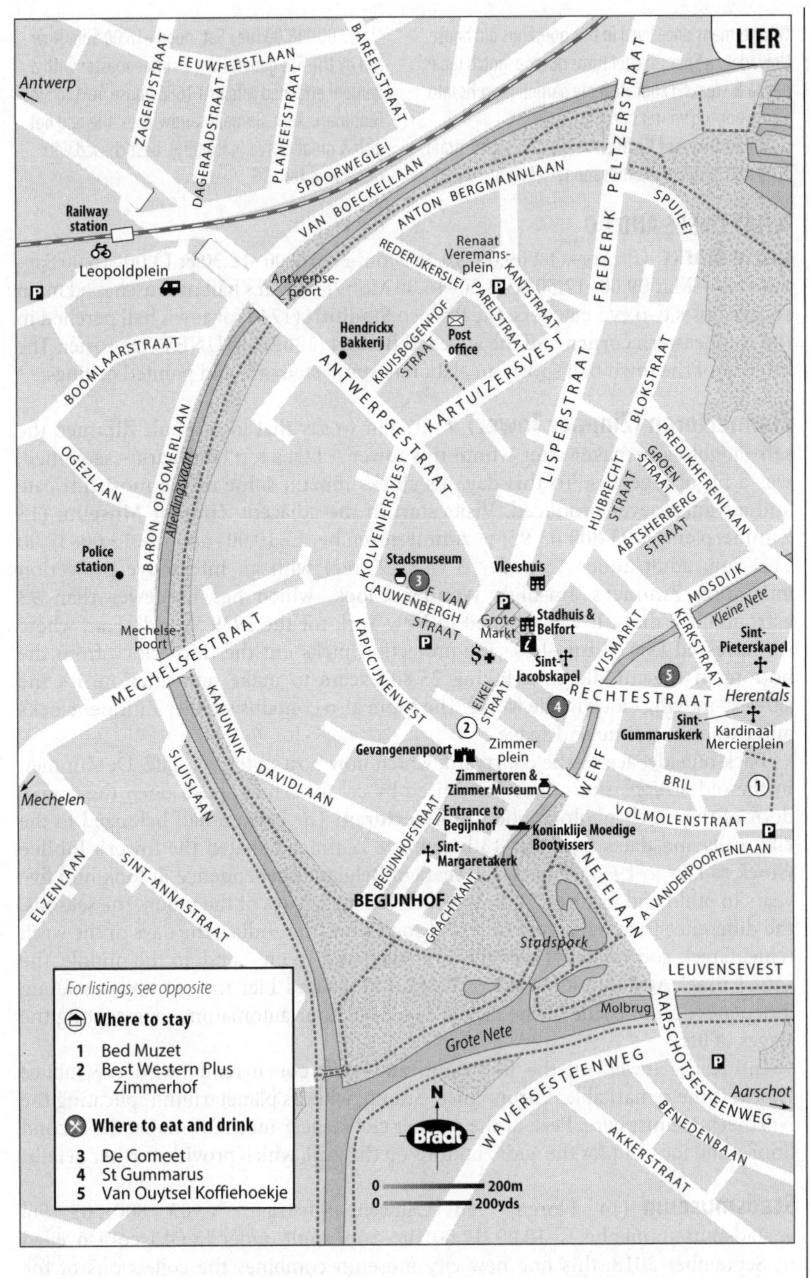

rooms. Great b/fast inc – with free Cava on Sun! €€€

Bed Muzet (27 rooms) 65 Volmolenstraat; 03 488 60 36; w bedmuzet.be. Newish 'culture hostel' in a renovated convent & aimed at creative types (there are rehearsal rooms etc) but all are welcome. Lovely garden, basic b/fast & linens inc. Popular café Bar Muza right opposite, next to Lier's music school. Sgl €27, dbl €64. €

De Comeet 16–18 Florent Van Cauwenberghstraat; 03 297 27 24; w decomeet.be; 17.30–22.00 Tue–Sun. Author Felix

Timmermans once lived in this gorgeous old house. Nowadays a Spanish chef turns out top-notch tapas, paella & steaks. Exquisite leafy garden morphs into a cosy pop-up winter bar. €€€–€€€€

Van Ouytsel Koffiehoekje 27 Rechtestraat; 03 480 29 17; w koffievanouytsel.com; 09.00–18.00 Tue–Sat, noon–18.00 Sun. Now run by the 5th generation, a coffee roaster with a genteel attached café in a 1686 house next to Sint-Gummaruskerk. Bargain sandwiches, the odd hot dish & great coffee (naturally), best chased with *Lierse vlaaikes*. €€

WHAT TO SEE AND DO

Grote Markt (Apr–Oct 09.00–16.30 Mon–Fri, 09.00–12.30 & 13.00–16.00 Sat–Sun; Nov–Mar 09.00–12.30 & 13.30–16.30 Mon–Fri) Lier's half moon-shaped main square hosts two eye-catchers: the Rococo **Stadhuis** (1740) or town hall perched in the southeastern corner, and the attached **Belfort** (1369), on UNESCO's roster. The interior of the town hall sports an elaborate spiral staircase and painted ceilings.

Zimmertoren (Zimmer Tower) ✷ It's fair to say that local Louis Zimmer, the self-taught clockmaker after whom this tower – Lier's top landmark – is named, was a bit of a genius. To this day, his clocks remain some of the most intricate and advanced ever produced. Visits start in the adjacent **Zimmer Museum** (18 Zimmerplein; 03 800 03 95; w zimmertoren.be; 10.00–noon & 13.00–17.00 Tue–Sun; adult/under 16/under 6 €4.50/2/free) with an interactive projection animating Zimmer's 4m-high **Wonder Clock**, which has no fewer than 93 astronomical dials. It was shipped to New York for the 1939 World's Fair, where it impressed Einstein no less. The projection picks out the third clock from the bottom in the middle row: taking 25,800 years to make one rotation, it's the slowest-moving clock in the world. The room also contains smaller Zimmer clocks and exhibits on time and space.

Back outside, across the courtyard, which now hosts a terrace café, De Zimmer, in the old *Schippershuis* once patronised by eel fishermen, push open the creaky door of the much-photographed **Zimmertoren**. The bottom half belonged to the city walls and dates from the 13th century. Zimmer donated the tower's **Jubilee Clock** to Lier in 1930 to mark 100 years of Belgian independence. It took him five years to build and features 13 dials, which tell the phases of the moon, the seasons, the difference between actual time and solar time, the zodiac, the days of the week (clue: Greek god Jupiter stands for Thursday) and so on – and, in the middle, the actual time! At noon, a parade of Belgian kings and Lier mayors appears fêting independence; one side of the façade also hosts four automatons representing the stages of life.

Inside the tower, on the first floor, and built concurrently with the Jubilee Clock, is the remarkable Astronomical Studio, with its planetarium replicating the Northern Hemisphere. Peek at the mother clock's gear mechanisms on the second floor – and look out for the audio buttons on the wall, which provide further details.

Stadsmuseum (14 Florent van Cauwenberghstraat; 03 800 03 96; w stadsmuseumlier.be; 10.00–17.00 Tue–Sun; adult/under 18 €4/free) Unveiled in September 2018, this fine new city museum combines the collections of the Wuyts-Van Campen and Baron Caroly Municipal Museum, which formerly stood on site, and the Timmermans-Opsomerhuis, which housed works by local artists. Themed sections over three rooms bring to life the story of the city and its inhabitants: *Schoon Lier* (Beautiful Lier) references a book by famous local author Felix Timmermans (page 18), while *Lierke Plezierke* (Fun-loving Lier) details Lier's giant parades and *Pallieteren*, or nature walks. The third room, modelled

SHEEP HEADS

In the 14th century, John II, Duke of Brabant, wanted to thank town residents for their loyalty during fights with neighbouring Mechelen. As a reward they could choose to have a cattle market or a university. They opted for the cattle market, at which point the duke is claimed to have sighed: 'Oh, the sheep heads!' The market brought great wealth initially, but university privileges were bestowed on Leuven instead and it became famous worldwide. How different Lier's fortunes might have been! A herd of bronze sheep can be found wandering along Schapenkoppenstraat to mark the event. You can also buy sheep's head pralines – including ones made of ruby chocolate, a new type of chocolate created in Belgium in 2017 – from Chocolaterie Dom (70 Grote Markt; 03 337 48 44; w chocolateriedom.be; 10.00–18.00 Tue–Sat).

on collector Baron Caroly's Antwerp home, houses Pieter Brueghel the Younger's *Spreekwoorden* (Proverbs, 1607), based on his father's work of the same name, and Rubens's *modelo* of a bigger painting on display in Antwerp, *The Vision of Holy Theresia of Avila*. You literally can't miss the looming replica of a mammoth skeleton found in Lier in 1860.

Begijnhof (Begijnhofstraat; 24hr; free) Entered via a blue-doored archway, Lier's béguinage (the second of two local UNESCO sites) was founded in 1212 and is very pretty indeed. You'll soon come across the 17th-century Rococo-style Sint-Margaretakerk (during services), but more fascinating are the workshops run by four local lace-making societies (the Lier Municipal Fine Arts Academy is also working hard to safeguard the dying art). The tourist office has a list of the clubs, and can book tours. Ghislain at **'t Pladdeke** (13 Oude-Kerkhof; 13.00–17.00 Mon & Fri; free) speaks good English, and is happy to explain all about Lier's unique tulle lace, made with a fine hook, as his female co-members delicately go about their work.

Sint-Gummaruskerk (St Gummarus Church) (Kardinal Mercierplein; w sintgummaruskerktelier.be; Easter–Oct 10.00–noon & 14.00–17.00 Tue–Fri, 14.00–16.30 Sat, 14.00–17.00 Sun–Mon; admission to choir & treasury adult/18 & under €3/free) Construction of this splendid Brabantine Gothic church began in 1378 and took 200 years. In 1496 it hosted the wedding of Philip the Fair and Johanna of Castille. Its rich interior houses the relics of St Gummarus, a knight who died in AD774 after performing several miracles and who is honoured as Lier's patron saint – a healer of both broken bones and broken marriages. His relics are paraded through town every year on the first Sunday after 10 October. Of the church's many artworks, perhaps the most beautiful are the intricate stained-glass windows gifted by Maximilian I of Austria on the appointment of Charles V as Duke of Brabant.

Sint-Pieterskapel (St Peter's Chapel) (Heilige-Geeststraat; 09.00–17.00; free) In the shadow of St Gummarus Church and dating from 1225, this is likely the oldest building in Lier. It stands on the site of a wooden chapel founded by St Gummarus when he arrived in Lier in the 8th century (his empty tomb lies behind the altar).

Boat trip Created in 1932, the **De Koninklije Moedige Bootvissers (Royal Company of Brave Fishermen)** is an association of Lier fishermen who historically patrolled the Neter river catching eels from barges and selling their haul at the local fish market. The practice was banned in 1974 and the fishermen now run boat tours on the old barges (Schapekoppenstraat; 03 480 80 75; w bootjevareninlier.be; Apr–Oct 14.00–18.00 Sat–Sun & bank hols; adult/under 12 €3.50/2).

Cycling Lier's surrounding countryside is particularly beautiful in springtime when the fruit orchards come into bloom. Hop on to the saddle and follow the *Fietsen tussen bloesems en fruit* or Orchard Route (41.7km), a bike trail starting from Lier railway station that takes you through the fruit-growing villages of Ranst, Broechem, Emblem, Vremde and Wommelgem. You can buy fruit along the route. The longer *Pallieteren Langs de Nete* (49.5km) route follows the Nete and leads you to the quaint village of Gestel. You can download the maps (in Dutch) for free on Visit Lier's website. The tourist office can also prepare picnic hampers; order at least 48 hours in advance.

Alternatively, join a self-guided **cycling dinner tour** (Apr–Sep Wed–Sun; adult/under 11 €35/20), which starts with breakfast on the Grote Markt, followed by three further courses as you make your way towards either Mechelen or Oelegem along the Nete. You don't need to make a reservation – just pitch up between 09.15 and 11.00 at the tourist office – but you'll need to rent bikes prior to starting.

HERENTALS

Herentals once had a thriving textile trade and you can still see the 16th-century Lakenhal and old city gates, but today this small-scale city in the Kempen region is an unassuming place that quietly goes about its business.

GETTING THERE AND AWAY

By car From Antwerp take the E19/E34 then follow signs for the E313; take exit 21 (direction: Herentals) (36km; 40mins). From Mechelen follow the N1 then R6 north to Lier, and then take the N13 to Herentals (37km; 43mins). There is free parking on Belgiëlaan and Augustijnenlaan.

By train Antwerp (twice an hour Mon–Fri, hourly Sat–Sun; 32mins); Lier (4 times an hour Mon–Fri, twice an hour Sat–Sun; 14mins); Mechelen (hourly Mon–Fri; 32mins; via Antwerp, hourly Sat–Sun; 54mins).

TOURIST INFORMATION

Tourist information 35 Grote Markt; 014 21 90 88; w herentals.be; Jul–Aug 09.00–noon Mon, 09.00–noon & 13.30–16.00 Tue–Fri, 10.00–14.00 Sat & Sun. With at least 3 weeks' notice, the English-speaking staff can arrange a guide (€50/2hrs). They also offer a free historical walking map in English.

Bike rental Fietspunt, 1 Stationsplein (railway station); 014 32 14 45; w fietsenatelier.be; 11.00–19.00 Mon–Fri. Phone ahead to reserve; €9/day.

WHERE TO EAT AND DRINK Local Brewery **Leysen** (w brouwerijleysen.be; tours 1st Thu of the month) makes blonde, double and triple Baskwadder, named after a barbed wire-munching monster rumoured to wander the Kempen at night!

Brasserie den Engel 1 Kerkstraat; 014 72 44 42; w brasseriedenengel.be; 11.00–21.00 Tue–Sat. Old mansion in the centre of the action with a smart, contemporary interior. Friendly service & more than solid brasserie classics. €€€

Vinhmm 5 Kerkstraat; 014 22 22 10; vinhmm; 11.00–18.00 Mon & Sat–Sun; 11.00–22.00 Thu–Fri. Cosy, buzzing wine bar with a huge variety of wines by the glass (inc Belgian), charcuterie & cheese plates & a lovely terrace.

WHAT TO SEE AND DO The **Lakenhal** (**Cloth Hall**) (Grote Markt; with guide or during exhibitions) dominates the Grote Markt, having been built by wool weavers and cloth makers in the 16th century (its octagonal belfry has UNESCO status). To the north of the square, marked on the free tourist map, you'll find Herentals's small and still quaint **béguinage**, established in the 17th century. In the middle stands the beautiful Gothic **Sint-Katharinakerk** (**St Catharine's Church**) (May–Sep 14.00–17.00 Fri–Sun). In a positive new development, the former infirmary at number 13 is also now a museum, with a guide on hand to provide explanations (May–Sep 14.00–17.00 1st Sun of the month). Outside these seasonal openings, contact the tourist office, which can arrange a guide.

To the south of the Grote Markt, **Sint-Waldetrudiskerk** (**St Waldetrudis Church**) (11 Kerkstraat; May–Sep 14.00–17.00 Wed–Sun; free) boasts works by Jordaens and a remarkable retable of saints Crispin and Crispian set to shine in 2019 via the Flemish Masters in Situ scheme, which aims to put the spotlight on hidden gems.

If you fancy a mini-adventure, head to the 22m-high **Toeristentoren De Paepekelders** (Heistraat; w toeristentoren.be; May–Sep 10.00–18.00, Oct–Apr 10.00–16.00 Sat–Sun; adult/under 13 & over 55 €1/0.70), a wooden lookout tower and café built in 1958 to chime with the Brussels World's Fair – though woodworm and lightning put paid to it, and the current version dates from 1985; on a clear day locals say you can see that event's icon, the Atomium. To get there take bus 305 (direction: Turnhout) from Kerkstraat, alighting at Herentals AZ Sint-Elizabeth. From here it's a 17-minute walk north to the tower via Nederij – home to pretty Château Le Paige (during exhibitions; free) – Lichtaartseweg and Heistraat.

Alternatively, also from Kerkstraat, you can take bus 305 south (direction: Leuven) to **Art Center Hugo Voeten** (23 Vennen; m 0475 55 51 25; w artcenter.hugovoeten.org; during tours 10.30 & 14.00 1st Sun of the month; €10), an ex-grain factory turned nine-level art showcase housing works by famous Belgians, Rodin – and, oddly, the largest gathering of Bulgarian art outside that country!

East of town is major theme park **Bobbejaanland** (45 Olensteenweg; 014 55 78 11; w bobbejaanland.be; Apr–Oct 10.00–17.00 & Jul–Aug until 18.00, but regular closures for hols etc, so check website; adult/child 1m–1.40/under 1m €34/29/free). Bus 215 departs from Herentals station and drops you outside the park.

GEEL

In the 13th century the sarcophagus of martyr St Dymphna (see box, page 330), the patron saint of mental disorders, was unearthed in Geel. The town became a major pilgrimage site and it wasn't long before a hospital was established to care for the many patients who came to the town seeking a cure. When the hospital became too crowded, the people of Geel began taking in visitors – and so began Geel's renowned system of family nursing, still a model of psychiatric care. The city also boasts a smattering of fine Art Nouveau homes; the tourist office has a brochure (text in Dutch only, unfortunately).

GETTING THERE AND AWAY

By car From Antwerp follow the E313 east and take exit 23 (direction: Geel-West), then take the N19 to Geel (49km; ⏱ 50mins). From Leuven take the N19 north, past Aarschot (47km; ⏱ 1hr). From Hasselt follow the E313 and take exit 24 (direction: Laakdal), following signs for Geel (43km; ⏱ 40mins).

By train Antwerp (hourly; ⏱ 45mins); Lier (hourly; ⏱ 27mins); Leuven (via Lier 3 times an hour Mon–Fri; ⏱ 1hr 25mins; via Lier hourly Sat–Sun; ⏱ 1hr 43mins); Hasselt (hourly Mon–Fri; ⏱ 57mins; via Lier hourly Sat–Sun; ⏱ 1hr 38mins).

TOURIST INFORMATION

Tourist information 1 Markt; 014 56 63 80; w visitgeel.be; ⏱ 10.00–14.00 Tue & Sat–Sun, 10.30–12.30 & 13.30–16.00 Wed–Fri. Friendly office whose website is due to be translated into English in 2019.

WHERE TO STAY AND EAT Geel bakeries prepare one of my favourite regional cookies, *Geels hartjes*: two heart-shaped butter biscuits filled with apricot jam and marzipan. The local beer is Zeuntbier (7.5%), a light blonde that goes well with the Zeuntpaté and bitter Zeuntkaas (pâté and cheese).

Hotel Verlooy (12 rooms) 117 Pas; 014 57 41 70; w verlooy.be. Very hospitable boutique hotel, close to the main square & offering chic, minimal rooms & a pleasant garden. Superior continental b/fast – well, they do run the next-door bakery, selling the best *Geels hartjes* in town. **€€€€**

Brasserie de Post 53 Markt; 014 58 06 48; ⏱ 07.00–17.00. The speciality of this stalwart spot is *postgras* – various meats buried beneath a mountain of skinny fries (get 1 per 2 people or face the consequences). You won't leave hungry! **€€€**

Da Corrado 15 Markt; 014 58 46 84; ⏱ noon–14.00 & 18.00–22.00 Wed–Fri, 18.00–22.00 Sat, noon–14.00 & 17.00–22.00 Sun. Small & cute Italian offering excellent value for money & textbook *osso bucco*. **€€€**

Cultuurcafé De Werft 34 Werft; 014 89 27 26; w cafedewerft.be; ⏱ 09.00–14.00 Tue, 10.00–21.00 Wed–Fri, 07.00–14.00 Sat. This relaxed coffee house attached to a cultural centre turns out excellent veggie dishes &, in keeping with Geel's inspiring social mandate, often hires staff with disabilities. **€**

THE LEGEND OF ST DYMPHNA

Dymphna was the daughter of a 7th-century Irish king. When she was 14 years old her mother died and her father, having loved his wife deeply, sought to replace her with a similar-looking woman. When one couldn't be found he began to pursue his daughter, who apparently was the spitting image of her mother. He was determined to marry her, but when Dymphna heard of her father's intentions she fled the castle with her tutor Gerebernus and sailed to Europe. She landed at Antwerp and made it as far as Geel, but was inadvertently betrayed by an innkeeper in Westerlo who told the king's agents where she was. Gerebernus was murdered and when Dymphna refused to travel home with the king, he cut off her head. Locals buried them both in a cave and in the 13th century her white sandstone sarcophagus was uncovered; a piece of it can be seen in the Gasthuismuseum (see opposite). If you're dubious about the verity of the legend, bear in mind that in 1974 the relics were carbon dated and found to be the thigh bones of a young woman and an elderly man who died between AD700 and 800.

WHAT TO SEE AND DO

Gasthuismuseum (Hospital Museum) (1 Gasthuisstraat; 014 56 68 40; w www.gasthuismuseumgeel.be; 13.30–17.00 Wed–Sun; adult/6–18/under 6 €3/1.50/free, inc audio guide) A 10-minute walk east of the Grote Markt, this serene, must-visit museum is housed in the old St Dymphna Hospital, which was founded in 1286 on the spot where St Dymphna was martyred (see box, opposite), and run by Augustinian nuns until 1552. You can wander through the original rooms, including the kitchen, pharmacy, former bakery and sick wards. Since a facelift in 2017, there is now a handy audio guide in English recounting the stories of nurses and patients, and featuring more of a focus on St Dymphna herself. The tour ends in a splendid chapel.

Sint-Dimpnakerk (St Dymphna's Church) (St-Dimpnaplein; Apr–Sep 14.00–17.00 Tue & Thu–Sun; free) Built 1349–1570, this beautiful church contains the relics of St Dymphna and Gerebernus and five works on the Flemish Masterpieces list, notably an enormous multi-panel retable carved from wood depicting the saint's legend above the altar.

TURNHOUT

Just shy of the Dutch border, and serving as the unofficial capital of the Kempen region, Turnhout might be under the radar now, but it certainly didn't suffer from a lack of visitors in the past: the Dukes of Brabant built a castle here so they had somewhere to stay during hunting trips to the Kempen forest, and Maria of Hungary later used it to host lavish parties. By the end of the 16th century, Turnhout had been left impoverished by outbreaks of war, fire and plague, but got back on its feet in the 19th century by carving out a niche as the world's foremost producer of playing cards. It's an appealing, small-scale place with a handful of fascinating sights.

GETTING THERE AND AWAY

By car From Antwerp follow the E19, merge on to the E34 and take exit 23 (direction: Turnhout-West) (45km; 45mins). From Geel take the N19 north (20km; 30mins).

By train Antwerp (hourly; 50mins); Lier (twice an hour Mon–Fri; hourly Sat–Sun; 32mins); Geel via Herentals (hourly Mon–Fri; 32mins; hourly Sat–Sun; 41mins).

TOURIST INFORMATION

Tourist information 44 Grote Markt; 014 44 33 55; w toerismeturnhout.turnhout.be; 09.00–16.30 Mon–Fri, 09.00–14.00 Sat. Can organise various guided tours (€55) with a week's notice. Their *diversiteitswanderling* (Diversity Walking Tour) takes in churches, a mosque & Turkish shops. They also have a *biertroefroute* where you visit 3 cafés, taste a local beer & play a game of cards.

Bike rental Fietspunt, platform 1 of the railway station; m 0484 16 01 22; 07.00–10.00 & 15.00–18.30 Mon–Fri; €10/day

WHERE TO STAY AND EAT

Bon-Bon Nuit (3 rooms) 10 Victoriestraat; m 0494 78 88 37; w bonbonjournuit.be. A quaint chocolate shop with décor inspired by 1930s Paris. Choose from the traveller-themed Le Transatlantique, metro-themed Le Voyage with a balcony & views of Heilig-Hartkerk, or the romantic

THE WORLD'S WEIRDEST BORDER TOWN

A short bus-ride from Turnhout lies what might be the most remarkable village on earth: **Baarle**. Worldwide there are 62 enclaves – portions of one territory surrounded by the territory of another state – and Baarle houses 30 of them, known either as Baarle-Hertog (the Belgian bits) or Baarle-Nassau (the Dutch ones). Strolling around is surreal, as you cross between the Netherlands and Belgium multiple times!

The geopolitical anomaly was first mentioned in AD922; in 1198 the enclave mess began, as local aristocrats began dividing up parcels of land. The situation worsened when Belgium declared independence; some 15 attempts to resolve the problem having failed, the borders were at last finalised in 1995.

The situation has resulted in a rare bureaucratic nightmare: Baarle has two mayors, two police forces and two post offices – just imagine that! But many businesses profit from the legal loopholes: a former bank on the border simply moved its paperwork from one side of the building to the other when the different country's tax inspectors called! Meanwhile, Dutch teens can't drink until they're 18, but Belgium, where the legal age is 16, is just over the street – you can figure out the implications of that one.

As you walk around, watch out for the 'NL' and 'B' markers on the streets, and one house right on the border bearing two different house numbers – one with a Belgian flag and one with a Dutch one!

To get there, take bus 260 from Turnhout railway station – it then passes through the city centre – to the stop Baarle–Hertog Molen (25mins), right next to Baarle's **tourist office** (1 Singel; +31 013 507 99 21; w toerismebaarle.com; Jan–Apr & Oct–Dec 11.00–15.00 Tue–Sat, noon–15.00 Sun; May–Sep 10.00–16.00 Tue–Sat, 11.00–15.00 Sun; also open Jul–Aug noon–16.00 Mon). With advanced reservation, they can provide guided tours (€50/1hr). They also offer free cycling maps of the enclave route, as well as the Baarlezine, a brochure mixing local history and a walking route. Don't miss it: Baarle is a rare showcase of the virtues of compromise – something that the world needs so badly right now.

Le 7ième Ciel in the attic with a claw-foot bath. They have an infrared cabin for fatigued travellers (€12/30mins) & b/fast, inc in the price, is served in the shop. **€€€**

Cachet de Cire (3 rooms) 23 Guldensporenlei; 014 42 22 08; w cachetdecire.be. Run by fabulously helpful hostesses Fee & Greet, this highly regarded, reasonably priced gastro restaurant (€€€) also has 3 comfortably furnished rooms. B/fast served 04.00–11.00 – now that's flexibility! **€€–€€€**

Café St Pieter 60 Grote Markt; 014 41 10 50; 08.00–midnight Mon–Fri, 07.00–midnight, 11.00–19.00 Sun. Friendly, laidback café on the main square run by the Smulders family since 1906. Lots of dark wood, roaring fire, good beers & light meals. **€€**

De Penge 45 Lindekensstraat; 014 41 29 24; w depenge.be; 14.15–01.00 Tue & Thu–Sun. Originally for workers, Turnhout's oldest brown bar (est 1890), under a new owner, is a gorgeous tiled spot with the best beer list in town.

WHAT TO SEE AND DO

Sint-Pieterskerk (St Peter's Church) (Grote Markt; 08.30–17.00 Tue–Sat, 09.30–17.00 Sun; free) This sober red-brick church was built in the 13th century and has undergone several enlargements – all that remains of the medieval church is the lower half of the 62m-high tower. In the more elaborate interior you'll find a remarkable 19th-century pulpit featuring fishermen hauling in their catch; and – in the St Anna chapel behind the altar – a 16th-century triptych depicting the martyrdom of St Apollonia (centre) and St Agatha (right), and the decapitation of another saint (left).

Kasteel van de Hertogen van Brabant (Castle of the Dukes of Brabant)

(1 Kasteelplein; ⌚ with guide only) Northwest of the main square, this grand moated castle was built in 1110 and used as a lodge by the Dukes of Brabant when they went hunting in the Kempen forest. Under the Habsburgs, Maria of Hungary used it as a pleasure palace – then, in a volte-face, it served as a prison under the French, before falling into decay. Restored in the early 20th century, it now houses law courts.

✷Begijnhof (Begijnenstraat) A 5-minute walk north of the Grote Markt, Turnhout's UNESCO-listed béguinage (⌚ 07.00–22.00; free) is one of Flanders' finest. It was founded in 1300 and in the 18th century housed 350 béguines; the last béguine, Joanna de Boer, died in 2002. The St John Convent houses a fascinating **museum** (56 Begijnhof; ☎ 014 42 12 48; w begijnhofmuseum.be; ⌚ 14.00–17.00 Tue–Sat, 11.00–17.00 Sun; adult/under18 & Wed in Jul–Aug €5/free). After an introductory video in English, you explore a scullery, infirmary etc housing the world's largest collection of béguine-related artefacts. Elsewhere in the compound is a simple café, **De Meerloop** (44 Begijnhof; ⌚ 14.00–17.00 Sun–Fri; €), and a dinky new bistro, **Begijnhof 65** (65 Begijnhof; m 0468 05 32 72; ⌚ 11.00–18.00 Tue–Thu, 11.00–22.00 Fri, 09.00–17.00 Sat; €€), offering quirky lunches, homemade *macarons* and local herbal liqueur *Begijntje*. On 24 December the atmosphere is magical as the béguinage's streets are lit with candles.

Taxandriamuseum (28 Begijnenstraat; ☎ 014 43 63 35; w taxandriamuseum.be; ⌚.14.00–17.00 Tue–Sat, 11.00–17.00 Sun; adult/under 18 €5/free) Housed in the Huis metten Thoren, a stately 16th-century burgher mansion, this museum has an engaging albeit confusingly named permanent collection, Hotel Taxandria, which is not at all about hotels but instead charts local history through themed rooms stuffed with hunting paraphernalia, coins, paintings, fashion and relics.

Nationaal Museum van de Speelkaart (National Playing Card Museum)

(18 Druivenstraat; ☎ 014 41 56 21; w speelkaartenmuseum.be; ⌚ 10.00–17.00 Tue–Fri, 11.00–17.00 Sat–Sun; adult/under 18 €5/free) Turnhout is the largest manufacturer of playing cards in the world. The first were printed here in 1826; in 1970, several local manufacturers merged to form the card and game company, Cartamundi. Expanded over the years and now with a café, this fun museum is stuffed with printing presses and tools, and explores the various facets of cards, from their use as propaganda to their role in fortune-telling and magic acts. Try not to blush at the *very* naughty Victorian cards!

8

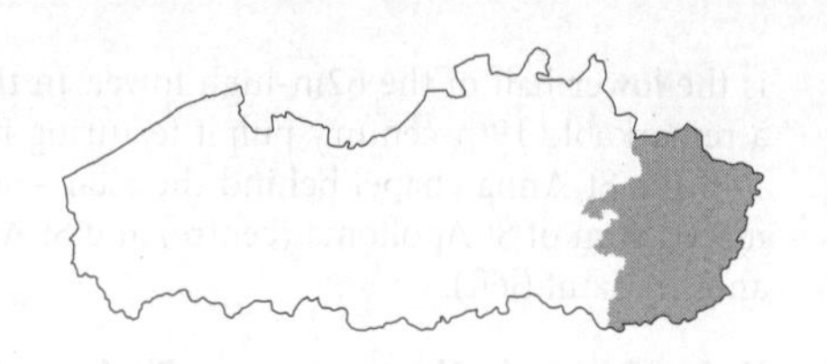

Limburg

Flemish Primitive Jan van Eyck and fashion designers Martin Margiela and Raf Simons all hail from Limburg – Flanders' least populated, most overlooked province. It might always have remained a 'land of farmers', if it weren't for one thing: coal, which was discovered in the Kempenland north of the province in 1901. Between 1917 and 1938, seven mines opened, growing to become some of the biggest in Europe and, at their peak, employing 70% of Limburg residents, as well as a vast population of Italians and Turks, many of whom settled permanently. The last mine closed in the 1980s and, refreshingly, in recent years, instead of knocking down these industrial behemoths, the government has given them protected monument status, contributing millions of euros to transform them into tourist attractions.

From the 'Sahara' of northerly Lommel, to the pine woods and heather-laden moors of Hoge Kempen, Belgium's only national park, Limburg is a land of radically different landscapes. With French-speaking Liège, and Maastricht, in the Netherlands, both close at hand, the area is a real melting pot with its own distinct spirit – you'll find most locals claim to feel Limburgish first and Flemish second.

To the south sit fashionable regional capital Hasselt, known for its jenever; the fruit-growing town of Sint-Truiden; and Tongeren, Belgium's oldest settlement. Nearby Genk once housed three mines and is at the heart of the area's post-industrial makeover. Add in a handful of offbeat, award-winning tourist initiatives and an impressively expanded cycling network (pick up a map of regional routes at local tourist offices for €9.50) and Limburg's fortunes are only set to rise.

HASSELT

The capital of Limburg province, Hasselt was founded in the 7th century and is a small-scale but appealing city associated with the production of jenever, a highly alcoholic grain spirit (page 48) made here since the 19th century and celebrated in mid-October at the Jeneverfeesten festival (page 55). Fashion fans will be pleased to discover that Hasselt has fine boutiques, mostly car-free shopping streets and a fashion museum to keep Antwerp on its toes. It's also proud of its 80 graffiti and street artworks, which you can locate with the aid of a free tourist office map.

GETTING THERE AND AWAY

By car From Brussels follow the E40 east out of the city and take the exit for the E314 (direction: Genk/Hasselt); after passing junction 26 turn off the motorway on to the E313 and take exit 27 (direction: Hasselt-West) for the centre (82km; ◷ 1hr). From Antwerp follow the E313 east and take exit 27 (direction: Hasselt-West) (83km; ◷ 1hr). You can catch buses 20a, 36 and 45 free of charge from the car park on Boudewijnlaan (bus stop: Hasselt Administrative Center) into the city centre.

By train Brussels (twice an hour Mon–Fri, hourly Sat–Sun; ⌚ 1hr 15mins); Antwerp (twice an hour Mon–Fri, ⌚ 1hr 40mins; hourly Sat–Sun, ⌚1hr 13mins); Leuven (3 times an hour Mon–Fri, twice an hour Sat–Sun; ⌚ 45mins). A light rail link to Maastricht, over the border in the Netherlands, is due to go into service in 2021, cutting the journey time to 36 minutes.

GETTING AROUND

By bus Hasselt's pioneering free inner-city public transport scheme sadly no longer operates, but the 48hr City Card (see box, page 340) grants you free bus transport as far afield as Domein Bokrijk (page 344); activate it on board during your first ride. The city is also pedestrian-friendly, with all the sights clustered within the small ring road.

TOURIST INFORMATION

Tourist information 59 Maastrichterstraat; 011 23 95 40; w visithasselt.be; ⌚ 10.00–17.00 Mon–Sat, 10.00–15.00 Sun. Friendly, modern office selling hiking & cycling maps, regional produce & myriad free English-language leaflets: *Exclusive Hasselt*, *Alternative Hasselt*, *Trendy Hasselt* (spot the theme?) & the Taste Route, with elements of all of the above. Can provide English-speaking guides (€70/1½hrs) tailored to your interests. A fun new innovation is the Babbelfiets (w babbelfiets.be) or 'Chat Bike', combining a sightseeing tour & local anecdotes (25-min tour departs tourist office; ⌚ summer hols Thu–Sun 11.00–15.00, term-time 11.00–15.00 Sat–Sun; adult/4–12/City Card €10/5/free); it can also shuttle you from the tourist office to the Japanse Tuin, the railway station or your hotel (€5/2.50).

Bike rental Fietspunt (railway station); ⌚ mid-Mar–mid-Oct 07.00–19.00 Mon–Fri, 09.00–13.00 Sat–Sun. Another handy rental location is Abdijsite Herkenrode (page 341); ⌚ mid-Mar–mid-Oct 10.00–17.00 Tue–Sun; both locations €10/day.

WHERE TO STAY *Map, page 338*

Hassotel (50 rooms) 2–10 Sint-Jozefsstraat; 011 23 06 55; w hassotel.be. Trendy sibling to the nearby Century Hotel, with very slick, minimalist rooms – & 3 spectacular penthouses with gorgeous terraces featuring a fireplace. The cosy, perennially buzzing restaurant (**€€€–€€€€**) offers generous, high-quality 3-course business dinners (€32) & a satisfying b/fast. **€€€**

't Hemelhuys (8 rooms) 15 Hemelrijk; 011 35 13 75; w www.hemelhuys.be. Rustic B&B tucked away in a quiet corner but right in the centre of town. Set up by friends Liesbeth & Ann, they offer a very warm welcome & the snug rooms are tastefully decorated with lots of oak, quality linens & antique writing desks. L'Occitane products in the bathroom & homemade croissants & bread served at b/fast – in the garden if weather permits. **€€–€€€**

WHERE TO EAT AND DRINK *Map page 338*

Hasselt is best known for its jenever and speculaas biscuits – the latter far thicker and tastier than the free ones you get in cafés, and best sampled at cosy Fijnbakker Cools (page 339). Keep an eye out for the Herkenrode Abbey beers, and Hasselt pâté, which includes jenever and occasionally hazelnuts – hazelnuts being the symbol of the city – which you'll find at butchers' shops on Maastrichterstraat and Zuivelmarkt. The tourist office has created a Taste Route (€9) with coupons to sample local gems; on Sundays it's dedicated to sweet stuff. With numerous young chefs shaking up the fine dining scene, Hasselt is a great place to splash out.

Rosch 34 Dorpsstraat; 011 18 27 93; w rosch.be; ⌚ noon–13.15 & 19.00–21.00 Mon–Fri (closed Mon lunch). Small fine dining spot run by a young couple – he's a chef, she's a pâtissier – who met working at Belgium's fabled Hof van Cleve. The €27 lunch menu is a steal & the

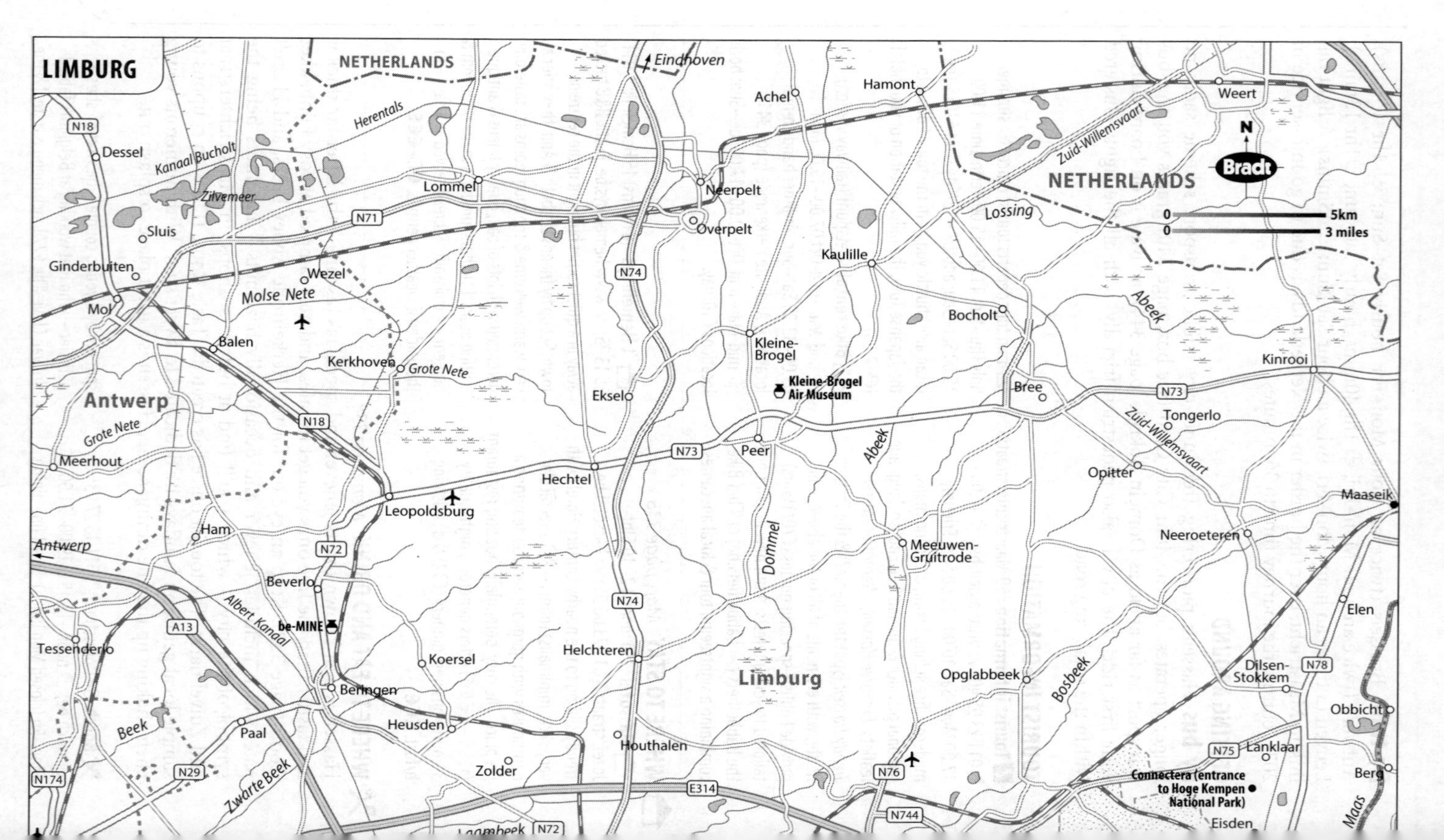
LIMBURG
NETHERLANDS
Eindhoven
Achel
Hamont
Weert
N
Bradt
NETHERLANDS
Zuid-Willemsvaart
Lossing
0 5km
0 3 miles
Herentals
N18
Dessel
Kanaal Bucholt
Zilvermeer
Lommel
Neerpelt
N71
Overpelt
Sluis
Ginderbuiten
Wezel
Molse Nete
N74
Kaulille
Abeek
Mol
Bocholt
Balen
Kleine-Brogel
Kerkhoven
Grote Nete
Kinrooi
Kleine-Brogel Air Museum
Eksel
Bree
N73
Antwerp
Tongerlo
Grote Nete
Zuid-Willemsvaart
N18
Abeek
Peer
Meerhout
N73
Opitter
Hechtel
Maaseik
Leopoldsburg
Ham
Meeuwen-Gruitrode
Neeroeteren
Antwerp
N72
Dommel
Beverlo
N74
Albert Kanaal
Elen
A13
be-MINE
Tessenderlo
Helchteren
Koersel
Limburg
Opglabbeek
Bosbeek
Dilsen-Stokkem
N78
Beringen
Obbicht
Beek
Paal
Heusden
Houthalen
N75
Lanklaar
Zolder
N76
N174
N29
Zwarte Beek
E314
Connectera (entrance to Hoge Kempen National Park)
Berg
N744
Maas
Laambeek
N72
Eisden

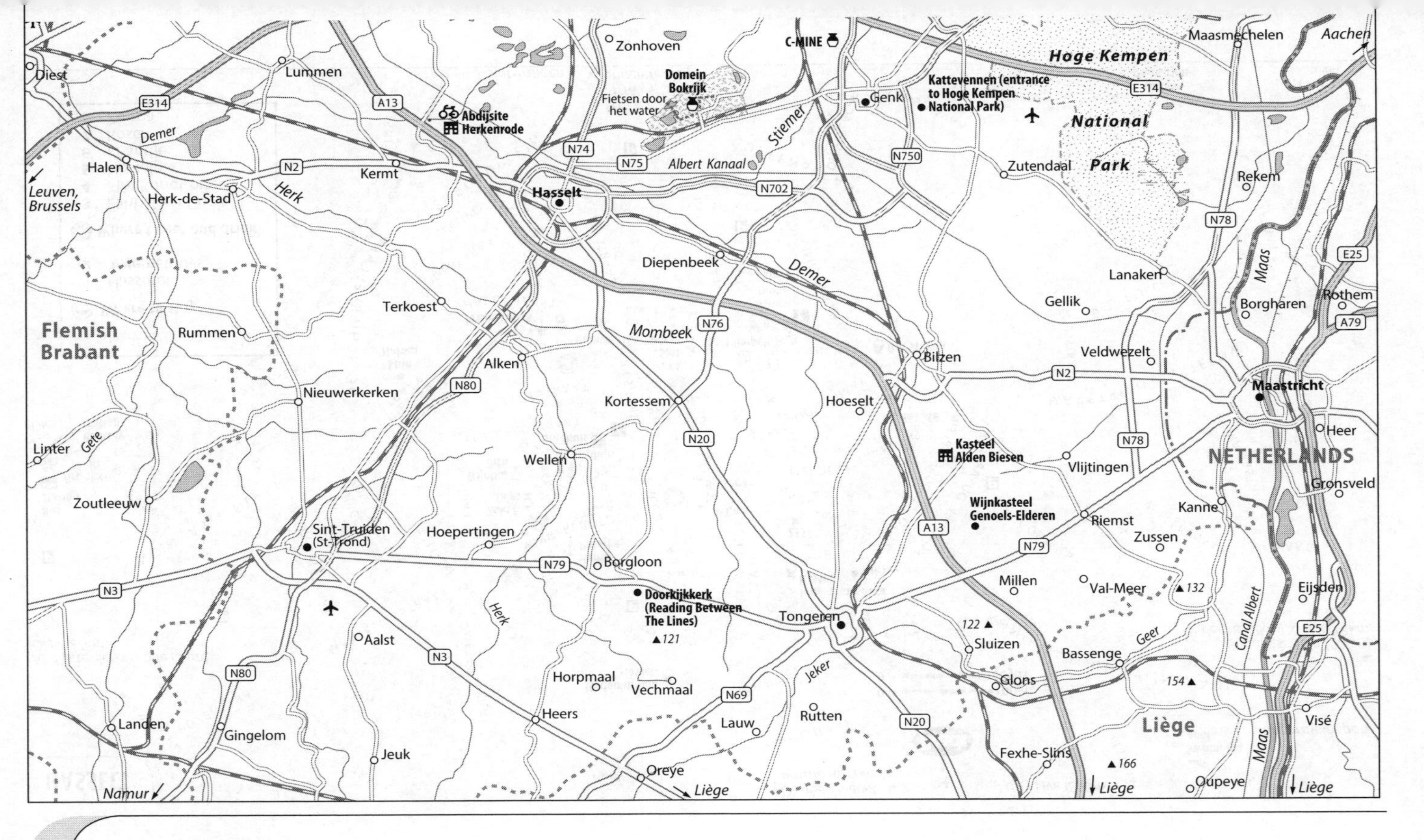
Hoge Kempen
National
Park
Kattevennen (entrance to Hoge Kempen National Park)
C-MINE
Domein Bokrijk
Fietsen door het water
Abdijsite Herkenrode
Maasmechelen
Aachen
Zonhoven
Lummen
Diest
Genk
Zutendaal
Rekem
Lanaken
Gellik
Borgharen
Rothem
Maastricht
Heer
NETHERLANDS
Gronsveld
Eijsden
Visé
Oupeye
Liège
Halen
Leuven, Brussels
Herk-de-Stad
Kermt
Hasselt
Diepenbeek
Terkoest
Rummen
Flemish Brabant
Alken
Nieuwerkerken
Kortessem
Hoeselt
Bilzen
Veldwezelt
Vlijtingen
Kasteel Alden Biesen
Wijnkasteel Genoels-Elderen
Riemst
Kanne
Zussen
Val-Meer
Millen
Linter
Zoutleeuw
Wellen
Sint-Truiden (St-Trond)
Hoepertingen
Borgloon
Doorkijkkerk (Reading Between The Lines)
Tongeren
Sluizen
Bassenge
Glons
Aalst
Horpmaal
Vechmaal
Heers
Lauw
Rutten
Fexhe-Slins
Landen
Gingelom
Jeuk
Oreye
Namur
Demer
Herk
Stiemer
Albert Kanaal
Mombeek
Gete
Jeker
Geer
Canal Albert
Maas
E314
A13
N2
N74
N75
N702
N750
N78
E25
A79
N76
N80
N20
N79
N3
N69
132
122
121
154
166

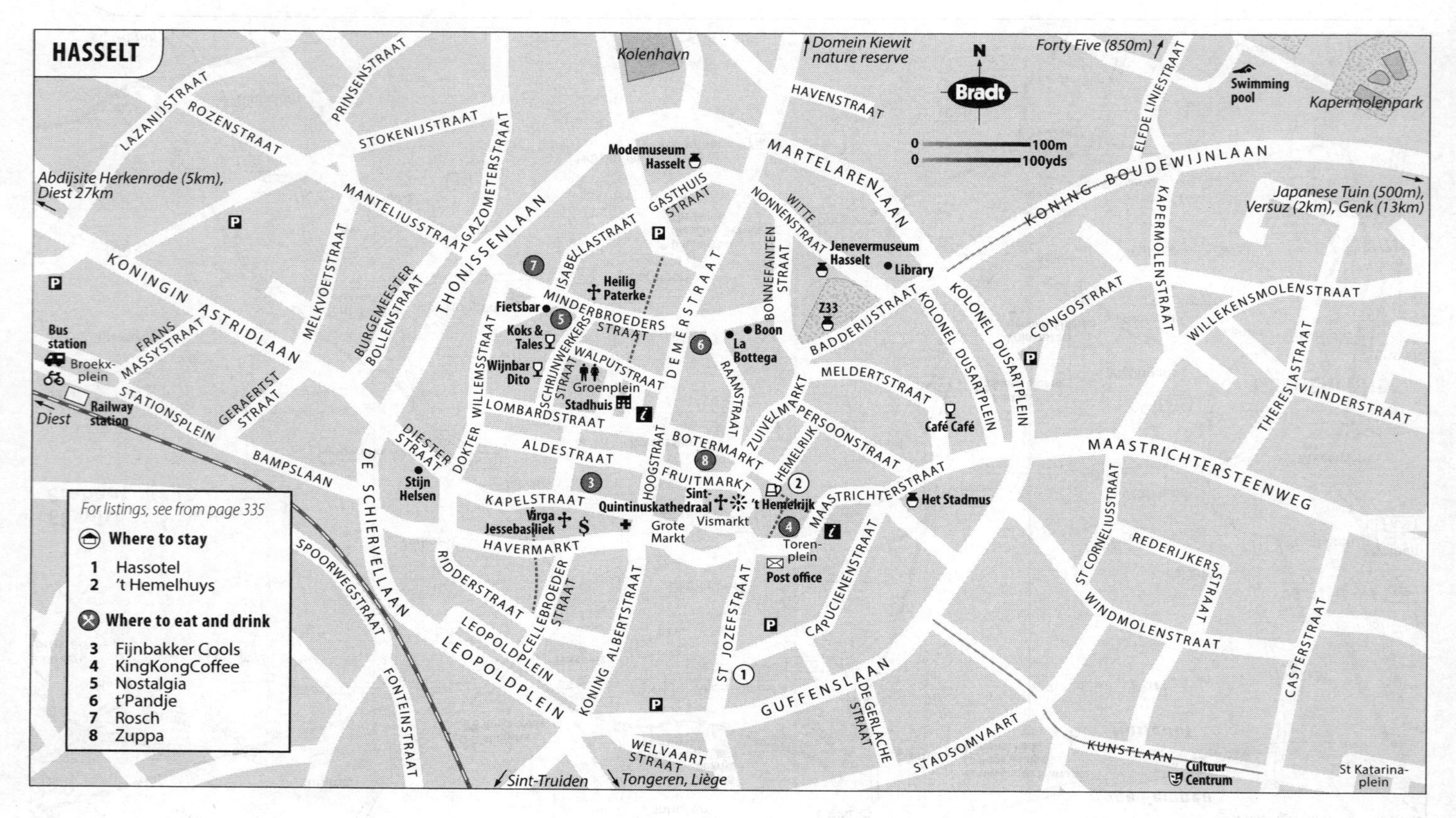
HASSELT
For listings, see from page 335
Where to stay
1 Hassotel
2 't Hemelhuys
Where to eat and drink
3 Fijnbakker Cools
4 KingKongCoffee
5 Nostalgia
6 t'Pandje
7 Rosch
8 Zuppa
Bradt
N
0 100m
0 100yds
Kolenhavn
Domein Kiewit nature reserve
Forty Five (850m)
Swimming pool
Kapermolenpark
Abdijsite Herkenrode (5km), Diest 27km
Japanese Tuin (500m), Versuz (2km), Genk (13km)
Diest
Sint-Truiden
Tongeren, Liège
LAZANIJSTRAAT
ROZENSTRAAT
PRINSENSTRAAT
STOKENIJSTRAAT
MANTELIUSSTRAAT
GAZOMETERSTRAAT
HAVENSTRAAT
MARTELARENLAAN
ELFDE LINIESTRAAT
KONING BOUDEWIJNLAAN
KAPERMOLENSTRAAT
WILLEKENSMOLENSTRAAT
CONGOSTRAAT
THERESIASTRAAT
VLINDERSTRAAT
MAASTRICHTERSTEENWEG
KONINGIN ASTRIDLAAN
MELKVOETSTRAAT
BURGEMEESTER BOLLENSTRAAT
THONISSENLAAN
ISABELLASTRAAT
GASTHUIS STRAAT
WITTE NONNENSTRAAT
BONNEFANTEN STRAAT
Modemuseum Hasselt
Jenevermuseum Hasselt
Library
Z33
BADDERIJSTRAAT
KOLONEL DUSARTPLEIN
Heilig Paterke
Fietsbar
MINDERBROEDERS STRAAT
DEMERSTRAAT
Boon
La Bottega
Koks & Tales
Wijnbar Dito
SCHRIJNWERKERS STRAAT
WALPUTSTRAAT
Groenplein
Stadhuis
RAAMSTRAAT
MELDERTSTRAAT
Café Café
Bus station
Broekx-plein
FRANS MASSYSTRAAT
GERAERTST STRAAT
Railway station
STATIONSPLEIN
BAMPSLAAN
LOMBARDSTRAAT
DOKTER WILLEMSSTRAAT
DIESTER STRAAT
ALDESTRAAT
BOTERMARKT
ZUIVELMARKT
PERSOONSTRAAT
HEMELRIJK
FRUITMARKT
HOOGSTRAAT
Stijn Helsen
KAPELSTRAAT
Sint-Quintinuskathedraal
't Hemelrijk
Vismarkt
MAASTRICHTERSTRAAT
Het Stadmus
Virga Jessebasiliek
Grote Markt
Toren-plein
Post office
HAVERMARKT
DE SCHIERVELLAAN
SPOORWEGSTRAAT
RIDDERSTRAAT
CELLEBROEDER STRAAT
KONING ALBERTSTRAAT
ST JOZEFSTRAAT
CAPUCIENENSTRAAT
ST CORNELIUSSTRAAT
REDERIJKERSSTRAAT
WINDMOLENSTRAAT
CASTERSTRAAT
LEOPOLDPLEIN
FONTEINSTRAAT
GUFFENSLAAN
DE GERLACHE STRAAT
WELVAART STRAAT
STADSOMVAART
KUNSTLAAN
Cultuur Centrum
St Katarina-plein

à la carte far from ruinous – very much a sign of the new wave of adventurous-but-relaxed food reshaping the local scene. €€€€

Nostalgia 46 Minderbroedersstraat; 011 22 78 43; **w** grillrestaurantnostalgia.be; 17.30–midnight Thu–Mon. No-nonsense, reasonably priced restaurant turning out Greek & Slavic dishes, many singed on the charcoal grill & served with perfect jacket potatoes. Good atmosphere & you won't leave hungry! €€€

Zuppa 13 Botermarkt; 011 42 65 76; **w** zuppasoupbar.be; 10.00–16.00 Mon–Sat. Swift & satisfying city-centre lunch option: they offer 7 or so incredibly filling, superior soups & throw in hearty bread & an apple. €

t'Pandje 3 Paardsdemerstraat; 011 22 38 37; **w** pandje.be; 10.00–18.30 Mon–Thu, 10.00–19.30 Fri–Sat. Interior design shop with a long-running 25-seat café at the back serving blackboard specials, waffles & homemade pies. €€

Fijnbakker Cools 27 Kapelstraat; 011 22 39 31; **w** coolshasselt.be; 10.00–17.45 Mon, 08.00–17.45 Tue–Sat. Lovely, high-end café/bakery founded back in 1856. Their speculaas are wonderfully crisp & tasty, & if you happen to drop in around celebrations (Christmas, Valentine's Day) they produce some exquisite cakes. €

KingKongCoffee 58 Maastrichterstraat; **m** 0496 15 19 45; 10.00–17.45 Tue–Sat. Very cool, alternative coffee shop always full of the locals (not least as it's a dinky place); you can get textbook espresso etc, but also more madcap creations such as the 'Zombie Whoof' (a latte with dark chocolate & honey). €

ENTERTAINMENT AND NIGHTLIFE

Café Café 40 Meldertstraat; 011 72 08 70; **w** cafecafe.be; 18.00–01.00 Wed & Sun, 18.00–04.00 Thu–Sat. Small & crowded converted syrup factory that's long been a staple on the local scene. Hosts regular concerts & generally free DJs/club nights at the w/end that attract a surprisingly wide age group.

't Hemelrijk 11 Hemelrijk; **m** 0483 45 14 44; 15.00/16.00–late. Old-school pub offering hundreds of Belgian beers served in the proper glass for added authenticity.

Koks & Tales 9 Schrijnwerkersstraat; **m** 0491 11 94 30; **w** koksandtales.com; 18.00–23.00 Tue–Thu, 17.00–01.00 Fri–Sat. Snug 1930s-style cocktail bar where Rob Biesmans makes superb seasonal drinks from a list spanning classics & wacky libations like the Ginger Beard!

Wijnbar Dito 8 Schrijnwerkersstraat; 011 91 70 95; **w** wijnbardito.be; 18.00–23.00 Mon, 16.00–23.00 Thu & Sun, 16.00–midnight Fri, 14.00–midnight Sat. Tiny 22-seat wine bar offering a huge array of bottles at democratic prices, with 20 wines to try by the glass each month according to a theme (eg: grape variety, region, winemaker). Also has a limited kitchen turning out cheese & charcuterie.

☆ **Forty Five** 9 Bootstraat; 011 23 13 13; **w** fortyfive.be; generally 22.00–05.00 on club nights. Electronic music hangout forming the epicentre of Limburg music life alongside the on-site Muziekdroom, which is a great place to catch a gig.

☆ **Versuz** 70 Gouverneur Verwilghensingel; 011 22 26 95; **w** versuz.be; 23.00–06.00 Mon, 22.00–06.00 Thu, 22.30–07.00 Sat; entrance €8 (Thu) or €15 (Sat/Mon), 50% discount with City Card. Voted 1 of the world's top 100 clubs by DJ Mag, this palatial spot has a champagne & cigar bar & a patio with a pool! Glam Ibiza-style nights but remains student-friendly with affordable door prices. Check the website for hotel deals including tickets & late checkout (you'll need it).

SHOPPING Hasselt is a lovely place to browse. If you mean business, I'd advise picking up the tourist office's four shopping route maps. Otherwise the best spots to check out are Kapelstraat and Aldestraat, for high-end fashion and shoes, and the fast-changing Dorpsstraat and environs for hipper wares. Here are some favourites.

Boon 13 Paardsdemerstraat; 011 42 21 99; **w** chocoladehuisboon.be; 10.30–18.00 Tue–Sat. The best chocolate shop in town – enter & you can spy on chocolatiers Patrick Mertens & Tom Theysmans going about their work. Sadly their café proved too popular for its own good & recently closed, but you can still sample Boon chocolates & coffee at neighbouring La Bottega (page 340).

FietsBar 54 Minderbroedersstraat; **m** 0484 61 96 62; **w** fietsbar.com; 08.00–18.00 Tue–Fri, 10.00–18.00 Sat–Sun. A trendy but winning concept: a bike shop where you can get repairs done while you hang out in the attached café serving cake, hot chocolate & light lunches.

La Bottega 9 Paardsdemerstraat; 011 23 20 33; w labottega.be; 10.00–18.00 Mon–Sat. You'll probably spot locals with La Bottega bags as you stroll around town – not only does the ex-storage space have a vast women's department (especially shoes), it also runs to homewares & kids' toys too. The on-site bistro (**€€–€€€**) is a very popular place for a luxury b/fast (€25) or tasty lunch.

Stijn Helsen 10 Diesterstraat; 011 24 27 07; w stijnhelsen.com; 10.00–18.00 Mon–Fri, 09.30–18.00 Sat. Hasselt's pride & joy trained with Valentino & Vivienne Westwood, & designed the *Spiderman* costumes for Toby Maguire. I've given the address of his concept store, combining his own – smart, high-quality – collection with likeminded labels; he also has women's & tailoring shops nearby.

Markets

Antiques & vintage market Kolonel Dusartplein; Apr–Oct 08.00–13.00 Sat

General market Kjolonel Dusartplein; 08.00–13.00 Tue & Fri

OTHER PRACTICALITIES

$ Bank KBC, 7 Havermarkt; 09.00–12.30 & 13.30–16.30 Mon–Fri, 09.00–noon Sat

+ Pharmacy In het Zwaard, 3 Grote Markt; 011 22 33 90; 08.30–18.00 Mon–Fri, 08.30–17.30 Sat. Set in a wonderful historic building – you can't miss it.

Post office 49 Maastrichterstraat; 09.00–18.00 Mon–Fri, 09.00–15.00 Sat

WHAT TO SEE AND DO

Jenevermuseum Hasselt (19 Witte Nonnenstraat; 011 23 98 60; w jenevermuseum.be; 10.00–17.00 Tue–Sun; adult/12–26/under 12/City Card €7/5/free, inc complimentary shot except for under 12s) Hasselt once had about 20 jenever distilleries; this one, active since the 1800s, houses a museum teaching you the differences between gin and jenever, displaying old posters, bottles, labels etc and letting you enjoy a cheeky tot in the tasting room afterwards.

Modemuseum Hasselt (Fashion Museum Hasselt) (11 Gasthuisstraat; 011 23 96 21; w modemuseumhasselt.be; 10.00–17.00 Tue–Sun; adult/12–18/under 12/City Card €8/3/free/free) In an atmospheric 17th-century ex-monastery, this small but very impressive fashion museum has a strong collection with an accent on such Limburg designers as Martin Margiela and Raf Simons. There's no permanent display, but worthy temporary shows, so do check what's on before you go.

Het Stadsmus (Stadmus City Museum) (2 Guido Gezellestraat; 011 23 98 90; w hetstadsmus.be; 10.00–17.00 Tue–Sun; free, audio guide €1) Small, free museum charting the city's history. It's mostly of note for having the oldest known monstrance (vessel for exhibiting objects of piety) in the world.

Heilig Paterke (Museum Father Valentinus) (19 Minderbroedersstraat; 011 24 10 63; 09.00–11.30 & 13.30–16.00 Mon–Fri, 09.45–11.30 & 13.30–

MAD FOR MUSEUMS?

It's well worth picking up the tourist office's 48-hour City Card (€19.50), which grants you a massive 75 benefits, including free bike rental for a day, free travel on public transport, free access to local museums and even a free breakfast and earrings (rather unusual!). They also produce a fun version for kids (€3), packed with activities and gifts. Pick it up at the tourist office or participating museums, attractions and hotels.

16.00 Sat–Sun; free) The funeral chapel of Valentinus Paquay, a friar who lived in Hasselt from 1854 until his death in 1905 and was beatified by Pope John Paul II in 2003. Very memorable to see believers sitting in reflection around his tomb, or touching his hands and feet before they leave – gives you an idea of his significance for *Hasselaars*. There's also a museum where you can listen to stories about his life and see his personal effects.

Japanse Tuin (Japanese Garden) (23 Gouverneur Verwilghensingel; 011 23 52 00; JapanseTuinHasseltBE; 31 Mar–3 Nov 10.00–17.00 Tue–Sun; adult/under 12/City Card €6/free/free) You don't have to go to Hasselt's sister city, Imati, for a piece of Japan – the city has had its own very Zen cherry tree-, carp- and Bonsai-filled garden since 1992. You're welcome to bring your own picnic. To get there, take bus 45 (direction: Maaseik/Maastricht), 36 (direction: Genk) or 20a (direction: Lanaken/Maastricht), alighting at Hasselt Rijksadministratief Centrum. Cross the street, take the steps down and follow the bike path to the garden entrance.

Day trips

Abdijsite Herkenrode (Herkenrode Abbey) (4 Herkenrodeabdij; 011 23 96 70; w abdijsiteherkenrode.be; visitor centre & shop: 10.00–17.00 Tue–Sun; garden: Apr–Oct 10.00–17.00 Tue–Sun, & Mon in Jul–Aug; combined entry adult/12–18/under 12/City Card €7/4/free/free inc 1 beer) Founded around 1180 by the Count of Loon, this monastery – located 4km northwest of town – was once the richest women's abbey of the Low Countries, and key to Hasselt's growth, but fell into disrepair when the nuns were expelled during the French Revolution. Today its interactive museum tells the story of these ups and downs, with a beautiful 2ha herb garden and nature walks right from the door. In recent years it has also produced three abbey beers that are well worth a try – you can buy them in the attached shop or sample one in the self-service brasserie, De Paardenstallen (€€–€€€). Also in the area are **Limburg Lavendel** (w limburglavendel.be) – aka Provence transported to Hasselt – and garden architect **Dina Deferme's garden** (w deferme.be).

Getting there and away To get there, take buses 51, H01 or H12 (15mins) from Hasselt railway station, alighting at Kuringen Herkenrode Brug/Kuringen Heerstraat, from where the abbey is a 10- to 15-minute walk. If you're hoping to tackle cycle path *Fietsen door het Water* (page 344), the abbey is an ideal starting point – it offers bike rental and a free car park.

be-MINE (201 Koolmijnlaan, 3580 Beringen) At 32ha, the former Beringen mine is the biggest industrial heritage site in Flanders and also Western Europe's best-preserved mine, still equipped with its original coal washeries (one of which is set to morph into a hotel). Your first point of call should be the **tourist information** office in the reception (011 42 15 52; w toerismeberingen.be; 10.00–17.00), which can arrange guided tours of the be-MINE site (€60/1½hrs, €125/day); I highly recommend the services of ex-teacher Ivo Coomans. They also have information on the wider Limburg region. For now, the main draw for tourists is the **Mijn Museum** (**Mining Museum**) (w mijnmuseum.be; 10.00–17.00; adult/6–18/under 6 €6/4/free, inc tablet/audio-tour, tickets from tourist office), with nine rooms charting life underground, the mine's turbulent closure and future plans for the site. There's also a fabulous indoor **climbing centre**, Alpamayo, in the ex-control room of the power station, an **'adventure mountain'** (the impressively converted old slag heap) and – most dramatically – **TODI** (w todi.be), a state-of-the-art indoor diving and snorkelling centre in the former coal silos, where you can dive amid thousands of tropical freshwater fish. In 2021, a €20 million experience centre is due to open in the mine's vast ex-bathing complex, aiming to put you in miners' shoes.

Getting there and away By car, follow the E313 from Hasselt, taking exit 26 to Beringen (25 km; ◷ 26mins). So far, public transport links are a little cumbersome: the quickest way is to catch the train from Hasselt railway station to Beringen station, then bus 58 (direction: Lommel) to Koersel Beringen Mijnen, a minute from the mine's entrance.

GENK

Despite being the second-most populous city in Limburg after Hasselt, most English-speaking tourists never make it to Genk – perhaps unaware of it, or only aware of its industrial past. In fact, it's a fascinating, surprisingly multi-cultural place to visit, with over 85 nationalities calling Genk home – largely as a result of its mining history. Its main asset is the former Winterslag mine, now design and cultural hotspot **C-mine**; neighbouring **Vennestraat** is also home to wonderful restaurants and shops, while the wider Genk area contains two must-visit sights. I'm limiting myself to the essentials here, but if you have more time, friendly Genk is definitely worth an overnight stay.

GETTING THERE AND AWAY

By car From Hasselt follow the N2 east out of the city and then head north on to the N702; watch out for signs for the N76, and follow it all the way into town (16km; ◷ 20mins).

By train Hasselt (hourly; ◷ 19mins); Sint-Truiden (hourly; ◷ 38mins); Tongeren (hourly; ◷ 1hr).

TOURIST INFORMATION

Tourist information 10 C-mine; 089 65 44 90; w visitgenk.be; ◷ 13.00–17.00 Mon, 10.00–17.00 Tue–Sun. Located in C-mine (see opposite).

WHERE TO STAY AND EAT *Map, opposite*

Carbon Hotel (60 rooms) 38 Europalaan; 089 32 29 20; w differenthotels.be. Recipient of a major design prize, this is 1 of 3 local properties run by Limburg chain Different Hotels. The name references the local coal industry, with suitably macho (but comfortable) rooms to match. There's a stunning minimal-chic spa & impressive brasserie, though b/fast isn't exactly a bargain at €19. **€€€**

Casa Paglia 110 Vennestraat; 089 35 36 77; w lapostagenk.be. The Paglia family's former grocery shop now juggles a pizzeria & this lovely trattoria serving textbook pasta & other Italian specialities & 200 wines by the bottle. **€€€**

Peppe's 2 Bochtlaan; 089 25 31 78; w peppes.be; ◷ 08.30–20.00 Thu–Mon. TV chef Peppe Giacomazza's buzzing restaurant & gourmet grocery shop is rammed with authentic Sicilian produce. It's great for a panini, fresh pizza or pasta, or an aperitif & early dinner. The chef also runs a swankier restaurant, La Botte (**€€€€**), if you want to splurge. **€€–€€€**

WonderBar 41 Winterslagstraat; 089 25 68 23; w wonderbargenk.be; ◷ 16.00–00.30 Tue–Sun. Very atmospheric *Alice's Adventures in Wonderland*-inspired cocktail bar with a great list of gins & cocktails (eg: the Queen of Hearts).

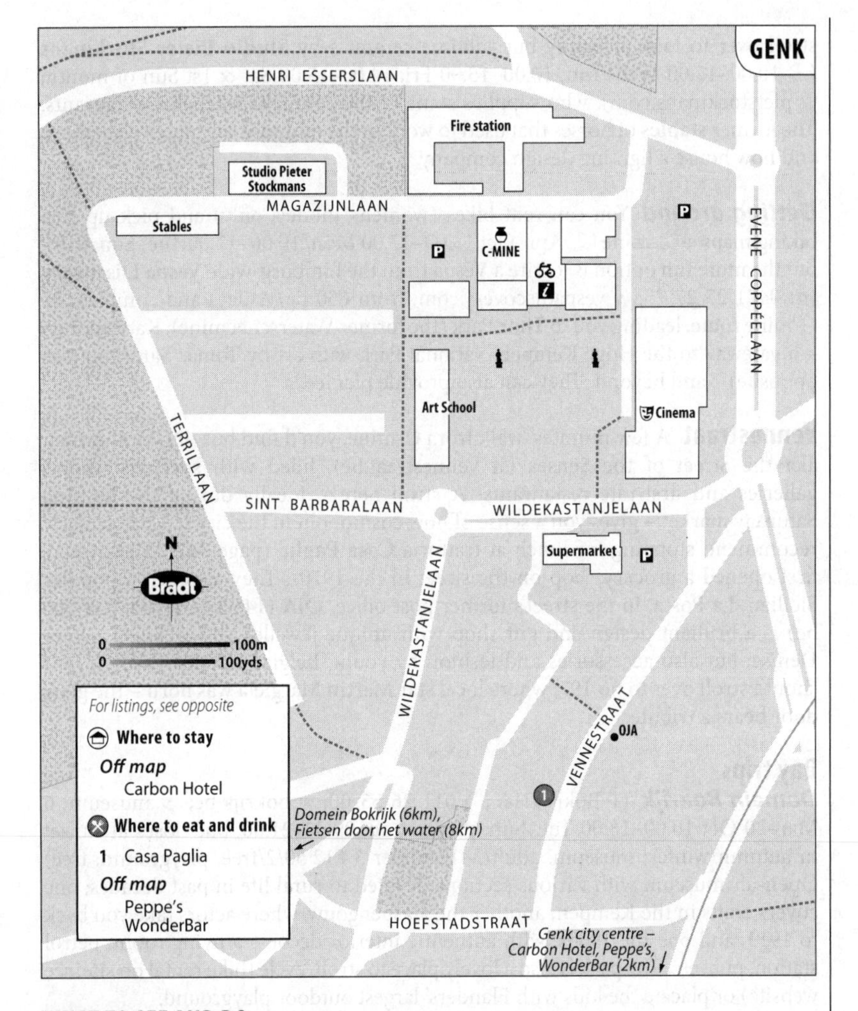

WHAT TO SEE AND DO

C-mine Opened in 1914, making it the first mine in the Kempen basin to go into production, Winterslag employed 6,250 workers at its peak, and produced over 1.6 million tonnes of coal before it was shuttered in 1988. Today the 'C' stands for 'creativity' (as against be-MINE's sporting appeal), with the site housing top arts school LUCA, concert halls and an exhibition space that hit the headlines in 2018 when it hosted a show by director Tim Burton. The best part, though, is exploring the wonderfully preserved buildings. Start at the information office by the entrance, and pick up an iPod tour and paper map (€6), which lead you around the main **Energy Building**, including the stunning compressor hall (you'll need a guide to access all the rooms). Then explore **C-mine expedition** (🕘 10.00–17.00 Tue–Sun; adult/6–18/under 6 €8/5/free), a subterranean passage with artworks and virtual reality-enhanced exhibits bringing the mine to life. If you have energy you can climb up one of the headframes, from which you'll have a great view of the huge steel **maze** built here by architect duo Gijs Van Vaerenbergh (also responsible for Borgloon's stunning see-through church, see page 352) in 2015. While you're there, stroll over to look at pricey but sublime ceramics by **Studio Pieter Stockmans** (🕘 10.00–17.00 Wed–Thu, 10.00–15.00 Fri, 14.00–15.00 Sat & 1st Sun of month; w pietstockmans.com), who supplies some of the country's Michelin restaurants. The former **stables** of horses that used to work in the mine are a minute's walk away, and now house a lighting design company.

Getting around You can rent bikes (women's models only) and pick up free biking maps at C-mine (🕘 Apr–Oct 13.00–17.00 Mon, 10.00–17.00 Tue–Sun; €10), but the more fun option is to hire a Vespa from the Limburg-wide **Vespa Discovery** (m 0471 27 27 75; w vespadiscovery.com; from €50 pp/½ day) and complete its C-mine route, leading you to Thor Park (the former Waterschei mine), Kattevennen – a gateway to the Hoge Kempen National Park with art by Tomás Saraceno (see opposite) – and beyond. They can also provide picnics.

Vennestraat A few minutes' walk from C-mine, you'll find buzzing Vennestraat aka the Street of the Senses (w vennestraat.be), filled with specialist shops, galleries and first-rate restaurants. A stroll here – ideally during the buzzing Saturday market – gives you a sense of how cosmopolitan the city is. I particularly recommend stopping for lunch at trattoria **Casa Paglia** (page 342). The owners first opened a grocery shop on the street in the 1970s. They also run a popular Sicilian, La Posta, in the street's former post office. **OJA** (145 Vennestraat; w oja.be) is a brilliant design and gift shop with unique jewellery by architect owner Denise, but also accessories and fashion by young Belgian talents. Fashion fans should stroll over to no 197, where local star Martin Margiela was born – the glass door bears a tribute.

Day trips

Domein Bokrijk (1 Bokrijklaan; ☎ 011 26 53 00; w bokrijk.be; 🕘 museum: 6 Mar–20 Oct 10.00–18.00 Tue–Sun, playground: 09.00–21.00, but closes at sunset in autumn/winter; museum: adult/3–12/under 3 €12.50/2/free, playground: free) Open-air museum with various sections devoted to rural life in past decades; one covers crafts in the Kempen, another the Haspengouw, where actors take you back to 1913, and one the 1960s, with authentic interior décor – a living room, petrol station, pub, etc. The park is also a lovely place to stroll, cycle (bike rental on site, see website) or placate the kids with Flanders' largest outdoor playground.

Fietsen door het Water (Cycling Through Water) Riding high after being voted one of the world's 100 greatest places to visit by *Time* magazine in 2018 – quite a coup for Limburg – this 212m-long track cuts through a large pond in the De Wijers nature reserve. It's exciting to cycle along as it dips so low that you're at eye level with the water – not to mention the grand curious swans, swimming inches away. Completed in 2016, it has been such a success that the tourist board is further expanding the scheme. 'Cycling through Trees' was due to open in July 2019; this will be joined by 'Cycling Through the Heath' (early 2020) and 'Cycling Underground' (currently in the design phase). To get there, rent a bike (see below) and make for junction 91 of the Limburg cycle route network; you can download a free 22km route past it starting and ending in Hasselt from w visitlimburg.be.

Hoge Kempen National Park [map, page 337] (w nationaalpark.be; 🕘 sunrise–sunset; free) To the east of Genk spreads Flanders' only national park, which was established in 2006. The Hoge Kempen is 5,700ha of moorland covered in purple heather, pine woods and lakes, and home to deer, snakes, frogs, toads and goshawks. There are several trails; the **Kattevennen** yellow walk (11.5km) passes through pine forests, but you can also follow the **75km self-guided trail** that skirts the circumference of the park, with shorter loops if you lose heart. The finest route in the whole park is the **Mechelse Heide**, with panoramic views of moorland. If you'd like to see the area properly, hire a ranger for a 2-hour guided walk (€60/70; book three weeks ahead).

Getting there and away The park has six gates, with the easiest access point – and the only one that's viable with public transport – being Kattevennen, near Genk (19 Planetariumweg, 3600 Genk; ☎ 089 65 55 55; ⌚ visitor centre: 09.00–17.00 Mon–Fri, 13.00–17.00 Sun, Apr–Oct also Sat 13.00–17.00), which hosts a planetarium and offers bike rental from Easter to mid-October. You can easily reach it on foot, or by bus or bike from Genk. If you're going by car, the park's main gate, Connectera, by Maasmechelen, is on the site of the former Eisden mine and has numerous attractions.

SINT-TRUIDEN

The pleasant town of Sint-Truiden owes its success to the crumbling abbey at its centre, built in the 7th century by Frankish nobleman St Trudo, who is claimed to have cured a woman's blindness. When he died his relics were interred in his self-named abbey and it became an important site of pilgrimage. The steady flow of visitors brought wealth and involvement in the linen-production trade. The town lost its standing in the mid 15th century when Charles the Bold took charge and destroyed the city walls. Its monuments suffered further damage during the French Revolution and World War I. However, you can still visit the three most important buildings – the Stadhuis, Abdij and Onze-Lieve-Vrouwekerk, marked by their three towers. Finally, Sint-Truiden is a well-known fruit town. The Haspengouw – an area of countryside on its eastern outskirts, also encompassing Tongeren – is particularly beautiful in spring when the orchards blossom, and during the September and October harvest. Rent a bike or put on your hiking shoes and explore!

GETTING THERE AND AWAY

By car From Hasselt follow the N80 southwest (20km; ⌚ 24mins). From Leuven follow the N3 east past Tienen (38km; ⌚ 45mins).

By train From Hasselt (hourly; ⌚ 15mins); Leuven (hourly; ⌚ 31mins); Brussels (hourly; ⌚ 58mins).

TOURIST INFORMATION

Tourist information Grote Markt; ☎ 011 70 18 18; w visitsinttruiden.be; ⌚ Apr–Oct 09.00–17.00; Nov–Mar 09.00–12.30 & 13.00–17.00 Mon–Sat, 10.00–12.30 & 13.00–16.00 Sun. Set in the old Stadhuis, it has a well-stocked regional produce shop & walking & cycling maps. Sells the economical Trudopas (Apr–Oct adult/under 26/under 12 €4/3/free, Nov–Mar adult/under 26/under 12 €3/2/free), which you'll need to visit most local sights. You can also buy it at the Begijnhofkerk (page 347).

Bike rental Stationsplein 65 (railway station); ☎ 011 69 24 29; ⌚ 15 Mar–15 Oct 07.00–19.00 Mon–Fri, 09.00–17.00 Sat–Sun; 16 Oct–14 Mar 07.00–19.00 Mon–Fri; €10/day

WHERE TO STAY AND EAT Fruit – especially apples and pears – features heavily in Sint-Truiden's diet thanks to the surrounding orchards. Look for PIPO apple juice, *kattekop* (apple cake) and *stroop*, a thick kind of marmalade. Brouwerij Kerkom offers several varieties of Bink beer just south of town, and is particularly known for its seasonal Blossom Bink (7.1%) with honey and local pear syrup.

Hotel Stayen (77 rooms) 168 Tiensesteenweg; 011 68 12 34; w hotelstayen.com. Hotel meets football pitch at this budget property set inside the local soccer stadium, with some rooms – modern but unremarkable – actually overlooking the pitch. SkyBox Rooms in the West Tribune come with a kitchenette & private dining area. Be aware that it's a cavernous place (with 4 restaurants), so you'll spend some time schlepping along the corridors. €€

De Gebrande Winning 7 Zepperenweg; 011 68 20 47; w degebrandewinning.be; 11.30–14.00 & 17.30–late Tue & Thu–Sun. Heralded as the best beer restaurant in Belgium, this brick-walled establishment elevates grandmother-style cooking into 'brand new old dishes' (ie: more refined than granny used to make). They have a beer club & offer fantastic beer-pairing menus with some very exclusive bottles. Their €37 tasting menu is great value. €€€–€€€€

Het Begijntje 62 Begijnhof; 011 69 57 53; w hetbegijntje.be; 11.00–18.00 Mon–Fri, 10.00–20.00 Sat–Sun. Located inside the béguinage. On the down side it has rather modern décor – bar some old wooden beams – but on the plus side they serve very solid Sint-Truiden-specific dishes like *haspengouw stoofpotje* (pork & bacon stew simmered in Bink beer & apple). €€

Venise 12 Grote Markt; 011 65 46 81; w ijssalon-venise.eu; 08.00–18.30 Mon & Wed–Fri, 08.00–19.30 Sat–Sun. A bit dated but locals – particularly the elderly – flock to this cosy tea room for its ice creams, pancakes & *kattekop*. €

SHOPPING

Market Grote Markt; 07.00–13.00 Sat. Still going strong after 600 years with its mix of food, textiles & flowers.

WHAT TO SEE AND DO

Stadhuis (Grote Markt; Apr–Oct 09.00–17.00; Nov–Mar 09.00–12.30 & 13.00–17.00 Mon–Sat, 10.00–12.30 & 13.00–16.00 Sun; free) The façade of Sint-Truiden's distinctive orangey-red Spanish-style town hall dates from the 18th century and was built around the medieval hall and belfry, which were erected in 1606 and house a 50-bell carillon. The surrounding Grote Markt has numerous cafés where you can listen to the carillon, and is also the site of the Gothic 12th-century Onze-Lieve-Vrouwekerk (**Church of Our Lady**) (09.00–17.00; free), with its beautiful fresco of the Last Judgement, historic organ and **schatkamer** (**treasury**) (14.00–16.30 Sat, 14.00–17.00 Sun; free), containing the relics of St Trudo.

Sint-Trudoabdij (St Trudo Abbey) Just around the corner, you'll find the remnants of St Trudo Abbey, largely destroyed during the French Revolution, but still living on through its Baroque gateway and Romanesque bell tower, or Abdijtoren (1 Diesterstraat; 09.00–17.00; free with Trudopas). Thanks to a metal staircase, you can climb the 196 steps to the top – five rest areas contain information – for wonderful views of the main square (note that you are not allowed to enter the tower alone, and children under 18 must be accompanied). The Trudopas also grants you access to the underground **chapel and crypt**, which belonged to the Romanesque church that once stood on the site and contains spooky coffin slots carved into the brick. The entrance is directly across the patch of lawn down a small ramp. The chicken coop here might seem odd, but it belongs to celebrated artist Koen Vanmechelen, an honorary citizen of Sint-Truiden. You can also visit the sumptuous **Keizerszaal (Emperor's Hall)** (🕘 Apr–Oct 14.00–17.00 Sat–Sun; free with Trudopas), covered in 18th-century frescoes, then take a small path leading to the auditorium, the **Academiezaal (Academy Hall)** (Apr–Oct 14.00–17.00 Sat–Sun), designed by architect Louis Roelandts, behind the Opera Gent building.

Sint-Agnesbegijnhof (St Agnes Béguinage) (Entry via Speelhoflaan & Schurhoven; 🕘 Apr–Oct, 10.00–12.30 & 13.30–17.00 Mon–Fri, 13.30–17.00 Sat–Sun; free) Founded in 1258, Sint-Truiden's béguinage is unique thanks to its preserved farm and Romanesque **Begijnhofkerk (Béguinage Church)**, whose walls bear 38 stunning murals and pillar paintings from the 13th to the 17th centuries. It also houses a Baroque organ. Next to the Romanesque Church, don't miss the **Festraetsuurwerk** (🕘 Apr–Oct entry at 10.45, 11.45, 13.45, 14.45 & 15.45 Mon–Fri, or 13.45, 14.45 & 15.45 Sat–Sun; free with Trudopas), a studio housing watchmaker Kamiel Festraets's hugely accomplished astronomical clock, finished in 1942.

Cycling and walking The countryside to the east of Sint-Truiden is particularly beautiful between April and May when the apple, pear and cherry orchards are in full bloom. The tourist office sells maps tailored to visiting the prettiest parishes; pick from walking routes (€1), cycling routes (Fietsen tussen Bloesems en Fruit; 35-49km; €3) or driving circuits (Toeren door Haspengouw; 75–102km; €3).

TONGEREN

Flanders' oldest city, Tongeren was home to the Eburones, a Gallic tribe who protested furiously when the Romans arrived and tried to take over. Their king, Ambiorix, rose to fame for his bravery on the battlefield and even impressed Julius Caesar, who described him in his memoirs as the 'bravest of all Gauls'. Of course, this didn't stop Caesar crushing the tribe and forcing them into slavery. Ambiorix managed to escape and, consequently, is embraced as a Flemish hero. The Romans named the town Atuatuca Tungrorum, and when Brussels was still no more than a few dirt lanes, Tongeren was a bustling Roman trading outpost connected to the imperial highway. It was also one of the first towns in the Low Countries to adopt Christianity after the appointment of Bishop St Servatius in AD342. Under the protectorship of Liège, it continued to thrive, allowing for the construction of the medieval city walls. However, a huge fire reduced the centre to rubble in 1677, and the town didn't enjoy a revival until Belgian independence in 1830.

Today Tongeren is an instantly likeable place which has embraced its Roman history with gusto. It now boasts one of Europe's best museums and the largest antiques market in Benelux (🕘 07.00–13.00), with 350 stalls and 40 shops spanning Leopoldwaal, Clarissenstraat and Maastrichterstraat on Sundays, and a huge covered antiques hall near the Moerenpoort. The tourist office has a free brochure pinpointing all the stalls. Expect to rub elbows with experts and amateurs from around the world.

GETTING THERE AND AWAY

By car From Hasselt follow the N20 south (20km; 🕘 29mins).

By train From Hasselt (every 15 mins Mon–Fri, hourly Sat–Sun; 🕘 23mins); Leuven (via Hasselt/Liège every 15 mins Mon–Fri, twice an hour Sat–Sun 🕘 1hr 25mins).

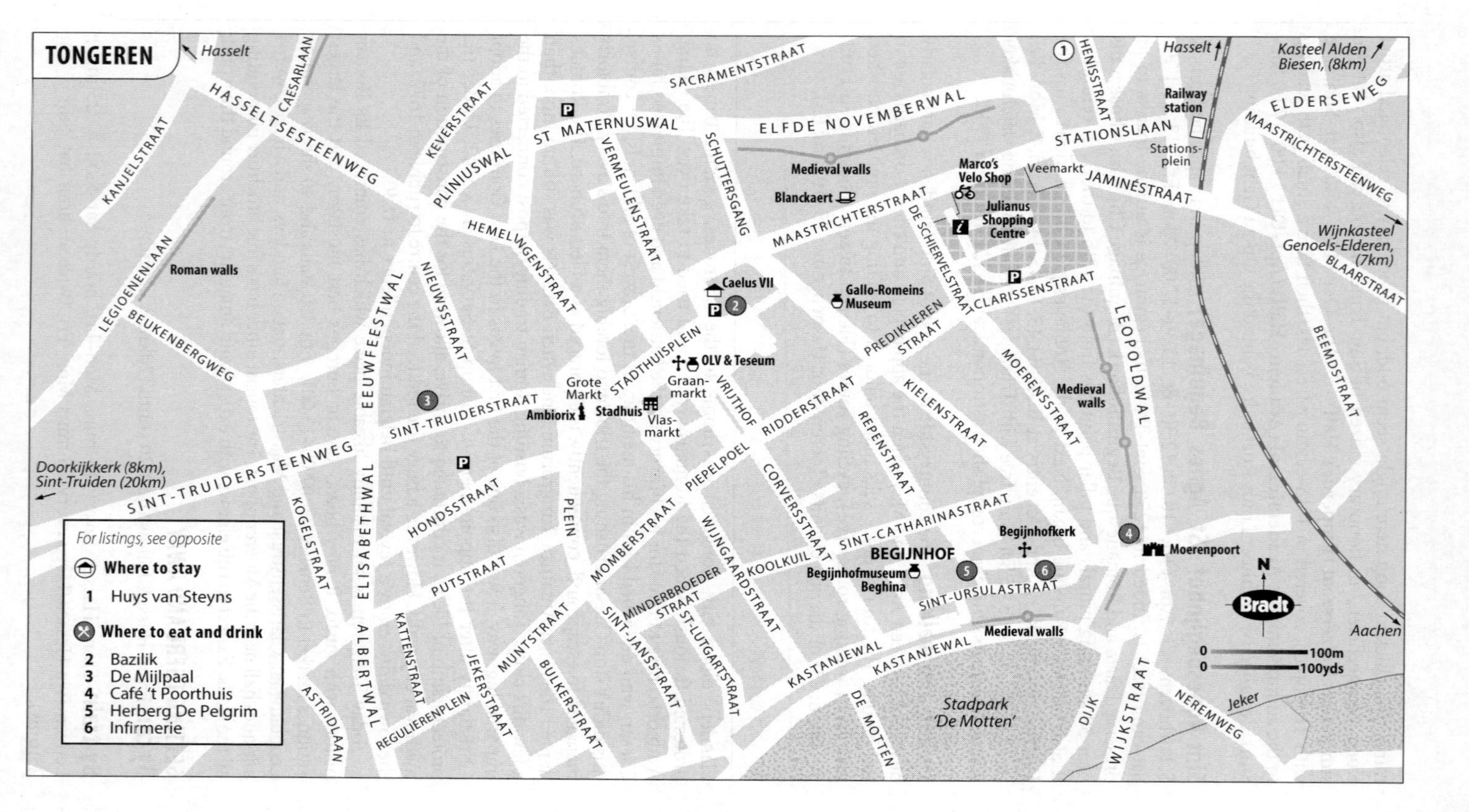
TONGEREN
Hasselt
Kasteel Alden Biesen, (8km)
Wijnkasteel Genoels-Elderen, (7km)
Aachen
Doorkijkkerk (8km), Sint-Truiden (20km)
Railway station
Stations-plein
ELDERSEWEG
MAASTRICHTERSTEENWEG
BLAARSTRAAT
BEEMDSTRAAT
HENISSTRAAT
STATIONSLAAN
JAMINÉSTRAAT
Veemarkt
Marco's Velo Shop
Julianus Shopping Centre
CLARISSENSTRAAT
LEOPOLDWAL
MOERENSSTRAAT
Medieval walls
Moerenpoort
Begijnhofkerk
BEGIJNHOF
Begijnhofmuseum Beghina
SINT-CATHARINASTRAAT
SINT-URSULASTRAAT
KOOLKUIL
KASTANJEWAL
Stadpark 'De Motten'
DE MOTTEN
DIJK
WIJKSTRAAT
NEREMWEG
Jeker
SACRAMENTSTRAAT
ELFDE NOVEMBERWAL
ST MATERNUSWAL
SCHUTTERSGANG
Blanckaert
MAASTRICHTERSTRAAT
DE SCHIERVELSTRAAT
Gallo-Romeins Museum
PREDIKHEREN STRAAT
KIELENSTRAAT
REPENSTRAAT
RIDDERSTRAAT
CORVERSSTRAAT
WIJNGAARDSTRAAT
MINDERBROEDER STRAAT
ST-LUTGARTSTRAAT
SINT-JANSSTRAAT
Caelus VII
OLV & Teseum
Graan-markt
VRIJTHOF
STADHUISPLEIN
Grote Markt
Stadhuis
Vlas-markt
Ambiorix
PIEPELPOEL
MOMBERSTRAAT
PLEIN
MUNTSTRAAT
BULKERSTRAAT
JEKERSTRAAT
REGULIERENPLEIN
KATTENSTRAAT
PUTSTRAAT
HONDSSTRAAT
SINT-TRUIDERSTRAAT
SINT-TRUIDERSTEENWEG
NIEUWSSTRAAT
HEMELINGENSTRAAT
VERMEULENSTRAAT
PLINIUSWAL
KEVERSTRAAT
EEUWFEESTWAL
ELISABETHWAL
ALBERTWAL
KOGELSTRAAT
ASTRIDLAAN
HASSELTSESTEENWEG
CAESARLAAN
KANJELSTRAAT
LEGIOENENLAAN
BEUKENBERGWEG
Roman walls
P
N
Bradt
0 100m
0 100yds
For listings, see opposite
Where to stay
1 Huys van Steyns
Where to eat and drink
2 Bazilik
3 De Mijlpaal
4 Café 't Poorthuis
5 Herberg De Pelgrim
6 Infirmerie

TOURIST INFORMATION

Tourist information 2 Via Julianus; 012 80 00 70; w toerismetongeren.be; Oct–Mar 08.30–noon & 13.00–17.00 Mon & Wed–Fri, 10.00–noon & 13.00–17.00 Tue, 10.00–16.00 Sat, 10.00–14.00 Sun; Apr–Jun & Sep 08.30–noon & 13.00–17.00 Mon & Wed–Fri, 10.00–noon & 13.00–17.00 Tue, 10.00–16.00 Sat–Sun; Jul–Aug 08.30–17.00 Mon–Fri, 10.00–16.00 Sat–Sun. Striking office & regional products shop inside the old chapel of the St Jacobusgasthuis (St Jacob's Guesthouse), where pilgrims stopped en route to Santiago de Compostela. Has created an engaging *Milestone Route* brochure leading you past the major sights (€5 or free with city pass).

Bike rental Marco's Veloshop; 99 Maastrichterstraat; 012 39 39 66; w marcosveloshop.com; 09.00–18.00 Tue–Sat (Sun & Mon by appointment). Electric bikes €25/day, city bikes €10. You can collect your bike from 08.00 & return it until 21.00. The tourist office sells the *Bicycle routes in & around Belgium's first city* map (€2.50) with 4 circular routes (information in Dutch only); the *Fietsen rond Tongeren* (36km) loop takes you past Château Genoels-Elderen.

WHERE TO STAY AND EAT *Map, opposite*

Tongeren bakeries produce two local biscuits: the *Tongerse moppen* (with honey, aniseed and herbs) and dodecahedron-shaped *caëderkükse*, based on an artefact in the Gallo-Romeins Museum (buy both at Blanckaert, 62 Maastrichterstraat; 012 23 14 78; 07.00–18.00 Tue–Sat, 07.00–14.00 Sun). You'll also spot speculaas biscuits and chocolates nodding to local hero Ambiorix; and Dagelyckx Beer, produced by the Begijnhofmuseum Beghina.

Huys van Steyns (7 rooms) 20 Henisstraat; 012 69 88 99; w huysvansteyns.be. Stunning boutique hotel set in a renovated 19th-century shoe factory once belonging to the brand Ambiorix, still active today. Rooms have high ceilings, crystal chandeliers & rich wallpaper. There's a genteel reading room & a decadent b/fast is served in the sun room. If it's full, try the owners' sister property Hotel Caelus VII, which was the top dog locally before this hotel. **€€–€€€**

De Mijlpaal 25 Sint-Truiderstraat; 012 26 42 77; w demijlpaal.org; noon–14.00 & 19.00–21.00 Mon, Thu–Fri & Sun, 19.00–21.00 Sat. Michelin-starred kitchen run by a husband-&-wife team. It's intimate, clean & classic & the delicate portions delicious. The 3-course mid-week lunch is €42 a head. **€€€€€**

Infirmerie 11 Sint-Ursulastraat; 012 44 10 44; w infirmerie.be; 11.30–22.00 Wed–Sat, 09.30–22.00 Sun. The swisher of the 2 béguinage restaurants has a stately setting in the former béguines' infirmary, next to the St Ursula Chapel, which now hosts concerts. Serves polished brasserie staples. Wed–Fri lunch there's a bargain €18.50 business lunch with soup, a main & coffee. **€€€–€€€€**

Bazilik 1 Kloosterstraat; 012 21 33 24; w www.bazilik.be; 11.00–22.00 Mon–Wed & Fri, 09.00–22.00 Thu & Sat–Sun. Charming Victorian-style brasserie a few steps from the Gallo-Romeins Museum. Has a sweeping staircase, tiled floor & please-all menu of salads, pastas, fish & meat. **€€€**

Herberg De Pelgrim 9 Brouwersstraat; 012 26 26 66; w herbergdepelgrim.be; 11.30–14.30 & 17.30–21.00 Wed–Sun. Characterful, long-running venue in a 1632 house inside the béguinage, run by Stefan & Ine in recent years. **€€€**

Café 't Poorthuis 112 Kielenstraat; 012 23 56 68; 15.00–23.00 Mon, 10.30–23.00 Thu–Sat, 06.30–23.00 Sun. Buzzing brown café which sits in the shadow of Moerenpoort & attracts market traders on Sunday; look for the portraits of old customers on the walls. Offers sandwiches, snacks & pancakes. **€–€€**

WHAT TO SEE AND DO

Grote Markt At the centre of the Grote Markt stands a bronze 19th-century statue of Gallic warrior **Ambiorix** gazing sternly at the Gothic **Onze-Lieve-Vrouwebasiliek (Basilica of Our Lady)** (09.00–17.00; free), whose first stones were laid in 1240 and which took 300 years to finish – though numerous on-site

MAD FOR MUSEUMS?

The tourist office's city pass (€14) includes access to the permanent collection of the Gallo-Romeins Museum, the Teseum treasury and archaeological site, the Béguinage Museum Beghina and Moerenpoort. You'll also receive the *Milestone Route* brochure or a walking and cycling map. Pick it up at the tourist office or Teseum.

churches had preceded it, remnants of which you can glimpse in the Teseum (see below). In front of the altar, you'll find a beautiful 15th-century **statue of Mary** in walnut; in 1889 the Pope granted locals permission to crown the statue, kickstarting the Coronation Celebrations (Kroningsfeesten), when she is paraded about town; it still takes place every seven years, attracting around half a million visitors (next edition: July 2023).

At the exit you'll find the reception centre for new museum site the **Teseum** (🕘 10.00–17.00 Tue–Sun; combi-ticket schatkamer & archaeological site: adult/6–26/under 6/city pass €10/2/free/free, entry to each site: €6/1/free/free inc iPod guides), combining the schatkamer (treasury) and an **archaeological site**. Opened in 2016, the **treasury** is one of the richest in Benelux, hosting 250 objects. According to an ancient catalogue, they've hung on to 85% of the collection since 1516! At the entrance you'll see a 6th-century Merovingian jewelled buckle and an 11th-century wooden sculpture of Christ's head. Upstairs are 14 silver relics of saints, active during the Coronation Celebrations.

As of 2018, you can also now head 3m below ground to explore an atmospheric **archaeological site**, offering glimpses of the seven churches located under the current basilica, as well as a tower that was part of a 4th-century Roman wall. It has been a mighty effort to excavate the site without toppling the basilica above, and it's mind-boggling to stroll back through centuries of the city's past. The brightly coloured stucco wall murals are the greatest treasure here – some were originally 5m high. If you'd like to know more, the tourist office can arrange guides for the Teseum/basilica (€60/2hrs, €90/3hrs) and sells a very detailed three-in-one guidebook (€12).

Gallo-Romeins Museum (Gallo-Roman Museum) (15 Kielenstraat; 📞 012 67 03 30; **w** galloromeinsmuseum.be; 🕘 09.00–17.00 Tue–Fri, 10.00–18.00 Sat–Sun; permanent & temporary shows adult/4–18/under 4 €15/1/free, permanent collection free with city pass) Worthy winner of the 2011 European Museum of the Year Award, this impressive building charts Tongeren's past from prehistoric times (hunter-gatherers) to its heyday, when the Romans arrived in 10BC. Its motto, borrowed from Marcus Aurelius, is 'What follows is always related to what preceded it'. You get an audio guide providing an overview of major exhibits. Temporary shows are often expertly curated, and accompanied by creative workshops to keep kids busy.

Sint-Catharina Begijnhof (St Catharina Béguinage) (Sint-Ursulastraat; 🕘 daily; free) Consisting of just seven streets, Tongeren's béguinage certainly squeezes a lot in. As well as the béguinage church, you'll find a scruffy but functional youth hostel, Begeinhof (**w** begeinhof.be), with its glaring neon sign, and two good restaurants (page 349). However, the real gem here is a preserved 17th-century béguine's house which hosts the **Begijnhofmuseum**

Beghina (Béguinage Museum) (12 Onder de Linde; ☎ 012 21 32 59; w begijnhofmuseumtongeren.be; ⌚ 14.00–17.00 Tue–Sun; adult/12–18/6–12/under 6/city pass €4/2.50/1.50/free/free). Start in the attic, used to store grain and dry laundry, and work your way down. Aside from the nook-and-cranny charm of the place, there are some elaborate Liège stucco mosaic-tile fireplaces on the first floor, a 16th-century triptych of *The Adoration* and a 14th-century statue of St Catherine of Alexandria, the patron saint of the béguinage. When you join a guided tour (€12 pp plus €60/guide, min six people), you can try a glass of the béguinage beer – the béguines used to drink up to four litres a day instead of the disease-ridden local water – and a slice of apple and quince *begijnentaart*. Not suitable for travellers with disabilities.

Moerenpoort (Moeren Gate) (Leopoldwal; ⌚ 10.00–16.00, but closes 13.30 Sun Oct–Mar; get the access code from the tourist office or Teseum; free) This squat watchtower is the last survivor of the city's six medieval gates and dates from 1379. It houses displays on the city's military history and its near total destruction during the Great Fire of 1677. Climb to the top of the tower for superb views of the béguinage.

Ancient city walls Sections of Tongeren's medieval city walls can be see along Elfde Novemberwal and Leopoldwal and behind the béguinage on Kastanjewal. Construction of towers posted at regular intervals along the wall was funded by individual guilds. The tower seen on Kastanjewal is known as Lakenmakerstoren (Cloth Maker's Tower) and was built by the cloth weavers. Sections of surviving Roman walls can be found further out along Caesarlaan and Legioenenlaan.

Day trips

Alden Biesen (6 Kasteelstraat; ☎ 089 39 96 10; w alden-biesen.be; ⌚ visitor centre: Apr–Sep 09.00–17.00 Mon–Fri, 10.00–17.00 Sat–Sun; Oct–Mar 10.00–17.00 Mon–Fri, 10.00–16.00 Sat–Sun, castle: 10.00–17.00 Tue–Sun during exhibitions, or with guide; adult/18–26/7–18/under 7 €5/4/2.50/free) This huge castle complex features a moat-surrounded 13th-century fortress and formal rose gardens. Without a guide it's possible to visit the estate, the visitor centre, with its permanent exhibition on the castle, the French garden and English park (the latter open Apr–Nov only). You can also see the moated castle during temporary exhibitions. Otherwise you'll need to book a guide – the visitor reception offers numerous options (count around €70 per guide), some adding the local town of Bilzen, famous for having hosted a mythic jazz festival. They also sell a €10 English walking guide to the complex. To get there, take the train to Bilzen station and then either a taxi (the castle is 5km away), or the Belbus (☎ 011 85 03 00; reserve in advance). By car follow the N758 from Tongeren, turning left on to Bammestraat after 5.5km (8km; ⌚ 9mins).

Wijnkasteel Genoels-Elderen (9 Kasteelstraat, 3770 Riemst; ☎ 012 39 13 49; w wijnkasteel.com; ⌚ 09.00–18.00 Mon–Sat; €5 for 1 tasting, but you can pay more for a larger selection of wines, or €5 to join group tour) The Romans brought their viticulture with them and successfully grew grapes on the slopes surrounding Tongeren. The practice died out in the 17th century when Europe entered a mini Ice Age, as depicted in the frosty paintings of Flemish artists at the time. Genoels-Elderen's first vines were planted in the 1990s, and it now produces world-class Chardonnay and Pinot Noir (and particularly wonderful sparkling wines). On

2-hour guided tours you visit the castle, distillery, vineyards (Belgium's largest) and ancient cellars, finishing with a tasting session. Reservations are essential, as they need to match individual visitors with other groups. To get there by car follow the N79 east out of Tongeren; when you cross the motorway take the first left to Sint-Maartenstraat and carry straight on until you reach the castle (6km; ⏱ 8mins).

Doorkijkkerk (Reading Between The Lines) (Walkway between Sint-Truidersteenweg & Roman Kassei, 3840 Borgloon; free) Created in 2011 as part of a project run by Hasselt contemporary art centre Z33, this stunning see-through church is the work of Belgian architects Pieterjan Gijs and Arnout Van Vaerenbergh, also behind the maze at C-mine (page 343). With 100 steel sheets stacked on top of each other, it weighs a whopping 30 tons; it was meant to be temporary, but moving it was too costly so it has remained, much to the joy of all. Nice nature walks in the area and it's great for a picnic, but considering it's in the middle of nowhere, it gets crowded! The site can only be reached on foot or by bike; a 10km drive from Tongeren, you'll find a car park on Sint-Truidersteenweg between Grootloonstraat and Neremstraat, from which you follow the signs. You can also catch bus 23a from Tongeren station to Borgloon Grootloonstraat (⏱ 18mins); from there it's a 13-minute walk.

Further afield If you're travelling by car, I highly recommend exploring **De Voerstreek** (w voerstreek.be), about a 30-minute drive east of Tongeren. Comprising six villages, notably the three S's – 's-Gravenvoeren, Sint-Pieters-Voeren and Sint-Martens-Voeren – this is one of Flanders' most beautiful walking and cycling areas, and hosts the region's highest point. From the 1960s on, the Voerstreek hit the news when it became the subject of heated language debates between Flemings and Walloons; in 1963 it became an exclave of Limburg – ie: geographically detached from the rest of Flanders. The area hosts 125km of signposted walks; Flemish TV viewers voted its *Bronnenwandeling* route the most beautiful in Flanders.

MAASEIK

Hugging the Dutch border, Maaseik is rarely covered by guidebooks and what a shame. Birthplace of artist Jan van Eyck, subject of a year-long celebration in Flanders in 2020, its pretty market square is lined with medieval houses (you'll spot a statue of Jan and his brother Hubert), while the local church conceals the oldest hand-painted gospel in the Low Countries. What's more, you can weave across the border and explore the waterways or visit Hoge Kempen National Park.

GETTING THERE AND AWAY

By car From Hasselt take the N702 towards Genk, then follow signs for the N76. At Genk, join the N75/Europalaan and then take the N78 to Maaseik (43km; ⏱ 50mins).

TOURIST INFORMATION

Tourist information 45 Markt; 089 81 92 90; w toerisme.maaseik.be; ⏱ Apr–Oct 10.00–17.00 Mon–Fri, 10.00–12.30 & 13.30–17.00 Sat–Sun; Nov–Mar 10.00–16.00 Mon–Fri, 10.00–12.30 & 13.30-16.00 Sat–Sun. Friendly office & main location of Musea Maaseik, housing 2 on-site museums. Has walking & cycling maps, local products & information on the wider region.

Bike rental Fietsen De Leemhoek, 38a Stationsstraat; 089 71 19 80; w fietsendeleemhoek.be; ⏱ 09.00–noon & 13.00–18.00 Mon–Fri, 09.00–17.00 Sat. Large shop renting bikes, e-bikes, mountain bikes & children's bikes.

MAASEIK

For listings, see from page 354

Where to stay

1 Het Agnetenklooster
2 Hotel Van Eyck

Where to eat and drink

3 Café Majestic
4 Melk en Suiker
5 Tiffany's

Bus stop
N78, boat trip to Thorn
N773 Neeroeteren
Fietsen De Leemhoek (350m), N78, Hoge Kempen NP, Genk, Hasselt
A2/E25, Maastricht
KONING ALBERTLAAN
ACHT MEILAAN
SLACHTHUISSTRAAT
BURGEMEESTER PHILIPSLAAN
ROSMOLEN STRAAT
MAASTRICHTERSTEENWEG
PELSERSTRAAT
LOERSTRAAT
CAPUCHIENENSTRAAT
ELKERSTRAAT
HERTSTRAAT
KONINGSSTRAAT
Post office
KLEINE KERKSTRAAT
PRINSENHOFLAAN
ROZENBOOMGAARDSTRAAT
PLANTAGE
RUEEELSTRAAT
BOSSTRAAT
HALSTRAAT
VOSSENBERG STRAAT
BOOMGARDSTRAAT
Musea Maaseik
Markt
Catharinakerk
GROTE KERKSTRAAT
Jan & Hubert Van Eyck
TORREN STRAAT
MONSIEIGNEUER KONINGSSTRAAT
SIONSTRAAT
KAARTRIDDERSTRAAT
MALBROEKSTRAAT
MUNNIKEN STRAAT
HEPPERSTRAAT
MARKTSTRAAT
VULLERSTRAAT
WALSTRAAT
EVERTSTRAAT
HOUTSTRAAT
BLEUMERSTRAAT
De Gapert
De Drie Marieen
SCHILLINGSTRAAT
KONING BOUDEWIJNLAAN
SCHANSBERG
Maas
Pater Sangersbrug
EERSTE STRAAT
HEPPERSTEENWEG
TWEEDE STRAAT
N
Bradt
0 100m
0 100yds

WHERE TO STAY AND EAT *Map, page 353*

Maaseik is known for its *knapkoek*, butter biscuits sprinkled with large sugar crystals and offering a satisfying snap.

Het Agnetenklooster (3 rooms, 2 suites) 17 Sionstraat; 089 56 43 27; w hetagnetenklooster.be. Historic former infirmary, stylishly renovated in 2010. My favourite rooms are the regal Bibliotheeksuite & the Agnes up in the attic. **€€€**

Hotel Van Eyck (31 rooms, 2 suites) 48 Markt; 089 86 37 00; w hotel-vaneyck.be. Pleasant hotel on the main square – rumoured to have been van Eyck's birthplace, though it's not proven! Rooms are spacious & contemporary; the 2 suites have stunning oak-beamed ceilings & infrared cabins. There's also a sauna & fitness area. **€€€**

Tiffany's 19 Markt; 089 56 40 89; w tiffanysmaaseik.blogspot.com; noon–13.30 & 18.00–20.30 Wed–Fri & Sun, 18.00–20.30 Sat. Run by Fabia & Philippe since 1984, this homely dining room has touches of Art Nouveau, fine glassware & porcelain plates. The menu revolves around a competitively priced daily set menu & there's a good wine list too. **€€€**

Café Majestic 10 Bospoort; 089 56 40 53; w majestic-maaseik.be; 10.30–late Wed–Sun. Looks just like a normal house, but this bar is a real local hangout. Time your visit correctly & it'll be alive with locals singing carnival songs in the local Mezeik dialect. **€€**

Melk en Suiker 37Bleumerstraat; 089 24 67 80; w melkensuiker.be; 10.00–18.30 Mon & Fri–Sun, 09.00–18.30 Wed. Friendly, contemporary café delivering the town's best coffee – either alongside superb b/fast granola or some of their textbook homebaked biscuits. They also serve ice cream & brunch dishes. **€€**

WHAT TO SEE AND DO In addition to the sites below, there are two 17th-century houses worth visiting: **De Drie Marieen** (77 Bleumerstraat) and **De Gapert** (47 Bleumerstraat).

Musea Maaseik (45 Markt; 089 56 68 90; w museamaaseik.be; Apr–Oct 10.00–17.00 Tue–Fri, 10.00–13.00 & 13.30–17.00 Sat–Sun; Nov–Mar 10.00–16.00 Tue–Fri, 10.00–13.00 & 13.30–16.00 Sat–Sun; combi-ticket RAM, Apotheekmuseum & Kerkschatten adult/8–18 €6/2) Set in the same building as the tourist office, the Musea Maaseik spans the Regionaal Archeologisch Museum (RAM) and Apotheekmuseum, and also Sint-Catharinakerk, a 3-minute walk away. The **Apothecary Museum** is a colourful 18th-century room lined with hundreds of drawers and porcelain bottles, and was Belgium's oldest privately owned apothecary. **RAM** is meanwhile a well-maintained archaeology museum with recreated scenes, interesting artefacts and a hands-on education centre for kids in the basement.

Sint-Catharinakerk (St Catherine's Church) (Kerkplein; Apr–Oct 13.00–17.00 Tue–Fri & Sun, 13.00–16.30 Sat; Nov–Mar 13.00–16.00 Tue–Sun; free) A modern-looking neo-Baroque church which houses elaborate confession boxes and an old carillon machine. However, the real treasure is found in the **kerkschatten** or treasury (via Musea Maaseik combi-ticket, as above), down a flight of stairs to the left of the altar. On display is a very rare 8th-century gospel – the oldest of its kind in the Low Countries – known as the *Codex Eyckensis*. It was written and painted by St Harlindis and St Relindis – the daughters of Frankish Lord Adelard, who founded the town – who became abbesses at the Aldeneik hamlet convent to the west of Maaseik. Split into two books, the pages are incredibly fragile and the colour and detail exquisite. A video presentation shows how the books were restored, and an adjoining room contains a number of religious treasures, including the arm-shaped relics of Harlindis and Relindis – odd cases with hands carved from wood and panels of glass showing the radius and ulna.

Day trips

Watermills The surrounding area has 16 watermills, 12 of which still remain in working order. The village of Neeroeteren, 6km west of Maaseik, has two: **Neermolen** (Langerenstraat 8; ⌚ May–Jun & Sep 14.00–17.00 1st & 3rd Sun of the month; Jul–Aug 14.00–17.00 Sat–Sun; €2), which was built in 1330 and grinds grain, and **Klaaskensmolen** (Kleeskensmolenweg 20; ⌚ May–Jun & Sep 14.00–17.00 2nd & 4th Sun of the month; Jul–Aug 14.00–17.00 Sat–Sun; €2), which dates from 1548 and is Flanders' last working water-powered saw mill. You can drive there, but why not rent bikes and follow the extensive watermill cycling route included in the Kempen-Broek cycling map (€3 from Tourisme Maaseik, or via w kempenbroek.eu).

Cross-border trips In summer you can enjoy a tour of the waterways aboard the Paep van Meinecom III (☎ 089 56 75 03; w marec.be; ⌚ Jul–Aug Wed & Sat–Sun departs Ophoven at 13.30, 15.30 & 17.30, departs Thorn 14.30, 16.30 & 18.30; return ticket: adult/child €9.50/8), which departs from Harbour De Spaanjerd in Ophoven, 4km north of Maaseik, and takes 1 hour to sail via Stevensweert to historic **Thorn**, a pretty Dutch village of whitewashed cottages across the border.

Alternatively, create your own cross-border trip using the *Grensoverschrijdend* Fietsroutenetwerk (35km; €6) map, which includes Thorn, Wessem, Maasbracht and Stevensweert. To get across the water you can use the foot passenger ferry (⌚ Apr–Oct) at Veerpont and the car ferry (⌚ all year) at Berg.

Hoge Kempen National Park See page 344.

Limburg MAASEIK 8

Appendix 1

LANGUAGE

DUTCH (FLEMISH) With its strings of consonants and conjugated vowels, Dutch makes for bewildering pronunciation sessions and the complex series of growls, slurs and throat-clearing sounds necessary for proper pronunciation are difficult to replicate. As a general rule, place stress on the beginning of a word, devoice consonants at the ends of words and try to listen to a native speaker and follow their vocalisations whenever you can.

The pronunciation of vowels in Flemish is broadly the same as in English. However, Flemish is littered with diphthongs (double sounds) that involve complicated contortions of the mouth and tongue; it's nearly impossible to find the proper equivalent sounds in English words, but here are the fundamentals:

Vowels

a	like 'a' in 'allotment'	ie	like 'ee' in 'free'
aa	like 'ar' in 'arrow'	ieu	pronounced ee-oo
ae	like 'ar' in 'cart'	ij	like 'ei' – see above
au	like 'ow' in 'cow'	oe	like 'oo' in 'stool'
ee	like 'ai' in 'sail'	oo	like 'oa' in 'coat'
ei	like 'ay' in 'way'	ou	like 'ou' in ' about'
eie	like 'ay' in 'hay'	ui	like 'ui' in 'alleluia'
eu	like 'err' in 'herring'	uu	like 'oo' in 'soot'
eeu	pronounced ay-ooh		

Consonants

ch	like 'ch' in 'chip'	v	like 'f' in 'follow'
kh	like 'ch' in Scottish 'loch'	w	like 'v' in 'vacuum'
g	like 'g' in 'grow'	sch	like the 'sk' in English 'skip' - 's' is soft, but 'k' is pronounced with throat-clearing as if you're about to spit.
j	like 'y' in 'yes'		
ng	like 'ng' in 'string'		
nj	like 'nio' in 'onion'		

FRENCH You'll need to speak some French while staying in Brussels. The pronunciation of French letters and diphthongs is very similar to English. Some variants are listed below:

Vowels

a	like 'a' in 'back'	è	ever so slightly different to 'e', it sounds like 'e' in 'envoy' with a descending tone
e	like 'e' in 'pet'	eu	like 'u' in 'yurt'
é	like 'a' in 'say'		

i	like 'e' in 'email'	ou	is pronounced as 'oo' in 'mood'
o	like 'o' in 'pot'	u	say 'ee', but shape your mouth to say 'oo'
au	is pronounced as 'o' in 'over'		

Consonants

ch	is pronounced as 'sh'	ll	is often not pronounced
c	is pronounced as 's' in 'c'est' and 'k' in 'combien'	w	is pronounced as 'v'
h	is silent	r	roll the tongue – imagine Sean Connery saying 'really'
th	the 'h' is not pronounced, so it's just 't'		

ENGLISH	DUTCH	FRENCH
Essentials		
Hello	*Hallo*	*Bonjour*
Goodbye	*Tot ziens*	*Au revoir*
Good morning	*Goedemorgen*	*Bonjour*
Good afternoon	*Goedemiddag*	*Bonjour*
Good evening	*Goedenavond*	*Bonsoir*
Good night	*Goedenacht*	*Bonne nuit*
My name is …	*Mijn naam is …*	*Je m'appelle …*
I am from …	*Ik ben van …*	*J'habite à …*
How are you?	*Hoe gaat het?*	*Ça va?*
Very well, thank you	*Goed, dank u wel*	*Très bien, merci*
And you?	*En met u?*	*Et toi?/Et vous?*
Nice to meet you	*Aangenaam kennis te maken*	*Enchanté(e) m/f*
See you later	*Tot straks*	*À bientôt*
Thank you	*Dank u wel*	*Merci (beaucoup)*
What's your name?	*Wat is u naam?*	*Comment vous appelez-vous?/Comment tu t'appelles?*
I don't understand	*Ik begrijp het niet*	*Je ne comprends pas*
Do you speak English/French/Spanish?	*Spreekt u engels/frans/spans*	*Parlez-vous anglais, français/espagnol?*
I don't speak French/Dutch	*Ik spreek geen Frans/Nederlands*	*Je ne parle pas français/néerlandais*
Could you speak more slowly please?	*Kunt u wat langzamer preken, a.u.b?*	*Pouvez-vous parler plus lentement, s'il vous plaît?*
What is this called?	*Hoe noemt dit?*	*Comment ça s'appelle?*
What is that?	*Wat is dat?*	*Qu'est que c'est ça?*
Could you repeat that?	*Zou u dat kunnen herhalen?*	*Pouvez-vous répéter ça?*
Could you write it down?	*Kunt u het opschrijven?*	*Pouvez-vous écrire ça?*
Yes	*Ja*	*Oui*
No	*Nee*	*Non*
No, thank you	*Nee, dank u*	*Non, merci*
Please	*Alstublieft (a.u.b)*	*S'il vous plait*
You're welcome	*Graag gedaan*	*Je vous en prie*
Excuse me	*Pardon*	*Excusez moi*
I'm sorry	*Sorry/het spijt me*	*Désolé(e)/pardon*
I don't like …	*Ik hou niet van …*	*Je n'aime pas …*
Cheers!	*Proost!*	*Santé!*

Requests

I would like …	*Ik wil …*	*Je voudrais …*
Can I have …?	*Kan ik krijgen, alstublieft (a.u.b) …*	*Est-ce-que je peux avoir …*
Where is …?	*Waar is … ?*	*Où est … ?*
Where are …?	*Waar zijn … ?*	*Où sont … ?*
When do you …?	*Wanneer gaat u …?*	*Quand vous …?*
I like …	*Ik hou …*	*J'aime bien …*

Time

today	*vandaag*	*aujourd'hui*
tonight	*vanavond*	*ce soir*
tomorrow	*morgen*	*demain*
yesterday	*gisteren*	*hier*
morning	*de morgen*	*matin*
afternoon	*de middag*	*après-midi*
evening	*de avond*	*soir*
night	*de nacht*	*nuit*
now	*nu*	*maintentant*
next	*volgende*	*puis*
early	*vroeg*	*tôt*
late	*laat*	*tard*
later	*later*	*plus tard*
What time is it?	*Hoe laat is het?*	*Quelle heure est il?*
When do you close?	*Wanneer sluit u?*	*À quelle heure vous fermez?*
When do you open?	*Wanneer opent u?*	*À quelle heure vous ouvrez?*
one minute	*een minuut*	*une minute*
one hour	*een uur*	*une heure*
half an hour	*een half uur*	*une demi-heure*
a day	*een dag*	*un jour*
a week	*een week*	*une semaine*
a month	*een maand*	*un mois*
a year	*een jaar*	*une année*

Numbers

0	*nul*	*zéro*
1	*een*	*un(e)*
2	*twee*	*deux*
3	*drie*	*trois*
4	*vier*	*quatre*
5	*vijf*	*cinq*
6	*zes*	*six*
7	*zeven*	*sept*
8	*acht*	*huit*
9	*negen*	*neuf*
10	*tien*	*dix*
11	*elf*	*onze*
12	*twaalf*	*douze*
13	*dertien*	*treize*
14	*veertien*	*quatorze*
15	*vijftien*	*quinze*
16	*zestien*	*seize*

17	*zeventien*	*dix-sept*
18	*achttien*	*dix-huit*
19	*negentien*	*dix-neuf*
20	*twintig*	*vingt*
21	*eenentwintig*	*vingt et un*
30	*dertig*	*trente*
40	*veertig*	*quarante*
50	*vijftig*	*cinquante*
60	*zestig*	*soixante*
70	*zeventig*	*soixante-dix*
80	*tachtig*	*quatre-vingt*
90	*negentig*	*quatre-vingt dix*
100	*honderd*	*cent*
1,000	*duizend*	*mille*
first	*eerste*	*premier*
second	*tweede*	*deuxième*
third	*derde*	*troisième*
fourth	*vierde*	*quatrième*
fifth	*vijfde*	*cinquième*
sixth	*zesde*	*sixième*
seventh	*zevende*	*septième*
eighth	*achste*	*huitième*
ninth	*negende*	*neuvième*
tenth	*tiende*	*dixième*

Days of the week

Monday	*maandag*	*lundi*
Tuesday	*dinsdag*	*mardi*
Wednesday	*woensdag*	*mercredi*
Thursday	*donderdag*	*jeudi*
Friday	*vrijdag*	*vendredi*
Saturday	*zaterdag*	*samedi*
Sunday	*zondag*	*dimanche*

Months/seasons

January	*januari*	*janvier*
February	*februari*	*février*
March	*maart*	*mars*
April	*april*	*avril*
May	*mei*	*mai*
June	*juni*	*juin*
July	*julli*	*juillet*
August	*augustus*	*août*
September	*september*	*septembre*
October	*oktober*	*octobre*
November	*november*	*novembre*
December	*december*	*décembre*
spring	*de lente*	*printemps*
summer	*de zomer*	*été*
autumn	*de herfst*	*automne*
winter	*de winter*	*hiver*

Family

mother	*moeder*	*mère*
father	*vader*	*père*
sister	*zus*	*soeur*
brother	*broer*	*frère*
son	*zoon*	*fils*
daughter	*dochter*	*fille*
husband	*man*	*mari*
wife	*vrouw*	*femme*
stepbrother	*stiefbroeder*	*beau-frère*
grandmother	*grootmoeder*	*grand-mère*
grandfather	*grootvader*	*grand-père*
stepsister	*stiefzuster*	*belle-soeur*
boyfriend	*vriend / lief*	*ami*
girlfriend	*vriendin / liefje*	*amie*
I am single	*Ik ben vrijgezel*	*Je suis célibataire*
I am married	*Ik ben getrouwed*	*Je suis marié(e)*
friend	*vriend*	*ami(e)*

Countries/nationalities

I am …	*Ik ben …*	*Je suis …*
I come from …	*Ik kom uit …*	*Je viens d' …*
Britain/British	*Groot Brittannië/Brits*	*Grande-Bretagne/ britannique*
England/English	*Engeland/Engels*	*Angleterre/anglais(e)*
Scotland/ Scottish	*Schotland/Schots*	*Ecosse/ecossais(e)*
Wales/Welsh	*Wales/Welsh*	*Pays de Galles/gallois(e)*
Ireland/Irish	*Ierland/Iers*	*Irlande/irlandais(e)*
America/American	*Amerika/Amerikaans*	*Amérique/américain(e)*
Canada/Canadian	*Canada/Canadees*	*Canada/canadien(ne)*
Australia/Australian	*Australië/Australisch*	*Australie/australien(ne)*
New Zealand	*Nieuw-Zeeland/ Nieuw-Zeelander*	*Nouvelle-Zélande/ néo-zélandais(e)*
South Africa	*Suid Afrika/ Suid Afrikaans*	*L'Afrique du Sud/ sud-africain(e)*
Belgium	*België/Belgisch*	*Belgique/belge*
France/French	*Frankrijk/Frans*	*France/français(e)*
Germany/German	*Duitsland/Duits*	*Allemagne/allemand(e)*
Flanders/Flemish	*Flaanderen/Vlaams*	*Flandre/flamand(e)*
The Netherlands	*Nederland/Nederlands*	*Les Pays-Bas/hollandais(e)*

Public transport

I would like a ticket to …	*Ik zo graag een ticket naar …*	*Je voudrais un billet pour …*
single	*enkel*	*simple*
a return	*heen en terug*	*aller-retour*
How much is it?	*Hoeveel kost het?*	*C'est combien?*
What time does the … leave?	*Om welk uur vertrekt de …?*	*À quelle heure le … part?*
Will you tell me when to get off?	*Wil je me zeggen wanneer ik mag afstappen?*	*Pouvez-vous me dire quand je dois descendre?*
delayed	*vertraging*	*retardé*

cancelled	*geanuleerd*	*annulé*
first class	*eerste klas*	*première classe*
second class	*tweede klas*	*deuxième classe*
platform	*peron*	*quai*
ticket office	*kaartjes balie*	*bureau de vente*
timetable	*uurrooster*	*horaire*
from	*van*	*de*
to	*naar*	*à/pour*
How far is …?	*Hoe ver is …?*	*C'est loin …?*
How do I get to …?	*Hoe geraak ik van naar …?*	*Comment je peux aller à …?*
Where is the …?	*Waar is de …?*	*Où est/sont le/la/les …?*
Is it near?	*Is het kort bij?*	*C'est près?*
bus station	*busstation*	*gare routière*
railway station	*treinstation*	*gare*
airport	*luchthaven*	*aéroport*
port	*haven*	*port*
bus	*bus*	*bus*
train	*trein*	*train*
plane	*vliegtuig*	*avion*
boat	*boot*	*bateau*
ferry	*ferryboot*	*ferry*
taxi	*taxi*	*taxi*
arrivals	*aankomst*	*arrivées*
departures	*vertrek*	*départs*

Private transport

I'd like to rent …	*Ik zou graag een … huren*	*Je voudrais louer …*
car hire	*auto verhuur*	*location de voitures*
driving licence	*rijbewijs*	*permis de conduire*
Where is the nearest service station?	*Waar is het dichst bijzijnde benzinne station?*	*Où est la station service la plus proche?*
diesel	*diesel*	*gazole*
leaded petrol	*gellode benzine*	*essence super*
unleaded petrol	*loodvrijë benzine*	*essence sans plomb*
car	*auto*	*voiture*
motorbike	*moto*	*moto*
bicycle	*fiets*	*vélo*
car park	*parkeerplaats*	*parking*
traffic lights	*werkeerslichten*	*les feux*
level crossing	*oversteekplaats / zebrapad*	*passage à niveau*
roundabout	*rond punt*	*rond-point*
I've broken down	*Ik heb auto pech*	*Je suis en panne*
I've run out of petrol	*Ik zit zonder benzine*	*Je suis en panne d'essence*
I have a puncture	*Ik heb een punctuur*	*J'ai une crevaison*

Directions

Is this the road to …?	*Is dit de weg naar …?*	*Est-ce que c'est la route pour …?*
Where is it?	*Waar is het?*	*C'est où?*
straight ahead	*rechtdoor*	*tout droit*
right	*rechts*	*à droite*

left	*links*	*à gauche*
north	*noord*	*nord*
south	*zuid*	*sud*
west	*west*	*ouest*
east	*oost*	*est*
behind	*achter*	*derrière*
in front of	*rechtover*	*devant*
near	*dichtbij*	*près de*
opposite	*tegengesteld*	*en face*

Signs

entrance	*ingang*	*entrée*
exit	*uitgang*	*sortie*
push	*duwen*	*poussez*
pull	*trek*	*tirez*
open	*open*	*ouvert*
closed	*gesloten*	*fermé*
toilets	*toiletten/wc*	*toilettes*
information	*informatie*	*information*

Accommodation

Where is a cheap/good hotel?	*Waar is een goedkoop/ goed hotel?*	*Où je peux trouver un hôtel pas cher/un bon hôtel?*
Could you write the address?	*Kan je het adres opschrijven?*	*Pouvez-vous écrire l'adresse?*
Do you have any rooms available?	*Heeft u nog kamers vrij?*	*Vous avez des chambres?*
I'd like …	*Ik zou graag …*	*Je voudrais …*
a single room	*enkele kamer*	*une chambre simple*
a double room	*dubbele kamer*	*une chambre double*
a room with two beds	*een kamer met twee bedden*	*une chambre avec deux lits*
a room with an en-suite bathroom	*slaapkamer met douche*	*une chambre avec salle de bain*
I have a reservation	*Ik heb een reservatie*	*J'ai une réservation*
Is breakfast included?	*Is het ontbijt inbegrepen?*	*Est-ce que le petit déjeuner est inclus?*
Which floor?	*Welk verdiep?*	*Quel étage?*
What room number?	*Welk kamer nummer?*	*Quel numéro de chambre?*
Do you have a quieter room?	*Heb je een rustigere kamer?*	*Est-ce que vous avez une chambre calme?*
Do you have a room with air conditioning?	*Heb je een kamer met airconditioning?*	*Est-ce que vous avez une chambre avec climatisation?*
key	*sleutel*	*clé*
porter	*portier*	*porteur*
reception	*receptie*	*réception*
I would like to check out	*Ik zou graag uitboeken*	*Je voudrais régler la note*

Eating out

Do you have a table for … people?	*Heeft u een tafel voor … personen?*	*Est-ce-que vous avez une table pour … personnes?*
I would like to reserve a table	*Ik zou gaar één tafel*	*Je voudrais réserver une table,*

	reserveren, alstublieft	*s'il vous plaît*
breakfast	*ontbijt*	*petit-déjeuner*
lunch	*middagmaal*	*déjeuner*
dinner	*diner*	*dîner*
snack	*snack*	*casse-croûte*
Please may I see the menu?	*Kan ik de kaart krijgen alstublieft?*	*Est-ce-que je peux voir le menu?*
Do you have a children's menu?	*Heb je een kindermenu?*	*Vous avez un menu pour enfants?*
smoking/non-smoking	*rokers/niet rokers*	*fumer/non fumer*
I am a vegetarian	*Ik ben vegetarisch*	*Je suis végétarien(ne)*
waiter	*kelner*	*monsieur*
waitress	*serveerster*	*madame/mademoiselle*
dish of the day	*dagschotel*	*plat du jour*
soup	*soep*	*potage*
starter	*voorgerechten*	*entrée*
main course	*hoofdgerechten*	*plat principal*
dessert	*nagerechten*	*dessert*
Please may I have …	*Kan ik … krijgen, a.u.b*	*Est-ce que je peux avoir …*
glass	*glas*	*un verre*
cup	*kop/tas*	*une tasse*
knife	*mes*	*un couteau*
fork	*vork*	*une fourchette*
spoon	*lepel*	*une cuillère*
plate	*bord*	*une assiette*
the menu	*menu*	*le menu*
the wine list	*de wijn kaart*	*la carte des vins*
Where are the toilets?	*Waar zijn de toiletten?*	*Où sont les toilettes?*
I'm full	*Ik zit vol*	*J'ai assez mangé(e)*
It's delicious	*Het is heel lekker*	*C'est délicieux*
Enjoy your meal	*Smakelijk*	*Bon appétit*
Please may I have the bill	*De rekening, alstublieft*	*L' addition, s'il vous plaît*
tip	*drinkgeld*	*un pourboire*

Basics

bread	*brood*	*(du/le) pain*
butter	*boter*	*du/le beurre*
olive oil	*olijfolie*	*l'huile d'olive*
pepper	*peper*	*du/le poivre*
salt	*zout*	*du/le sel*
sugar	*suiker*	*du/le sucre*
vinegar	*azijn*	*du/le vinaigre*
cheese	*kaas*	*du/le fromage*
egg	*ei*	*l'oeuf*
jam	*konfituur*	*de la confiture*

Preparation

rare (bloody and practically kicking)	*saignant*	*saignant*
medium rare	*a point*	*à point*
well done	*bien cuit*	*bien cuit*

plain (without sauces)	*natuur (zonder saus)*	*nature (sans sauces)*
minced	*fijngehakt*	*haché*
stuffed	*gevuld*	*farci*
steamed	*gestoomd*	*à la vapeur*
roasted	*gebraden*	*rôti*
boiled	*gekookt*	*bouilli*
stewed	*gestoofd*	*mijoté*
fried/baked	*gebakken*	*frit/au four*
smoked	*gerookt*	*fumé*
grilled	*gegrild*	*grillé*
Fruit	***vruchten***	***fruits***
apple	*appel*	*pomme*
banana	*banaan*	*banane*
blackcurrant	*zwarte bes*	*cassis*
grapes	*druiven*	*raisins*
lemon	*citroen*	*citron*
orange	*sinaasappel*	*orange*
peach	*perzik*	*pêche*
pear	*peer*	*poire*
pineapple	*ananas*	*ananas*
raspberry	*framboos*	*framboise*
strawberry	*aardbei*	*fraise*
Vegetables	***groenten***	***légumes***
asparagus	*asperges*	*asperges*
beans	*haricots*	*bonen*
broccoli	*brocoli*	*broccoli*
cabbage	*chou*	*witte kool*
carrot	*carotte*	*wortel*
chicory	*endive*	*witloof*
chips	*frites*	*frieten*
garlic	*ail*	*look*
green beans	*haricots verts*	*prinssessebonen*
leek	*poireau*	*prei*
lettuce	*laitue*	*kropje*
mushroom	*champignon*	*champignon*
onion	*oignon*	*ui*
peas	*petits pois*	*erwten*
potato	*pomme de terre*	*aardappel*
rice	*riz*	*rijst*
spinach	*épinards*	*spinazie*
tomatoes	*tomates*	*tomaat*
Fish and seafood	***vis en schaaldieren***	***poisson et fruits de mer***
bass	*zeebaars*	*loup/bar*
cod	*kabeljauw*	*morue*
crab	*krab*	*crabe*
eel	*paling*	*anguille*
fish	*vis*	*poisson*
haddock	*schelvis*	*églefin*

herring	*haring*	*hareng*
lobster	*kreeft*	*homard*
mackerel	*makreel*	*maquereau*
mussels	*mosselen*	*moules*
oyster	*oester*	*huître*
plaice	*schol*	*plie/carrelet*
prawns	*garnaal*	*crevettes*
salmon	*zalm*	*saumon*
sardines	*sardine*	*sardines*
scallop	*Sint - Jacobschelp*	*coquille St-Jacques*
sole	*zeetong*	*sole*
squid	*inktvis*	*seiche*
trout	*forel*	*truite*
tuna	*tonijn*	*thon*

Meat	***vlees***	***viande***
beef	*rundsvlees*	*boeuf*
chicken	*kip*	*poulet*
duck	*eend*	*canard*
goose	*gans*	*oie*
ham	*hesp*	*jambon*
horse	*paardevlees*	*cheval*
kidney	*nier*	*rognon*
lamb	*lam*	*agneau*
liver	*lever*	*foie*
pork	*varkensvlees*	*porc*
rabbit	*konijn*	*lapin*
sausage	*worst*	*saucisse*
snails	*slakken*	*escargots*
steak	*steak*	*steak/bifteck*
turkey	*kalkoen*	*dinde*
veal	*kalfsvlees*	*veau*
venison	*ree(bok)*	*cerf/chevreuil*

Dessert	***dessert***	***dessert***
cake	*taart*	*gâteau*
ice cream	*ijskreem*	*glace*
pancake	*pannekoek*	*crêpe*
waffle	*wafel*	*gaufre*
whipped cream	*slagroom*	*crème fouettée/Chantilly*

Drinks	***drankjes***	***boissons***
white wine	*witte wijn*	*vin blanc*
red wine	*rode wijn*	*vin rouge*
medium	*half droog*	*demi-sec*
sweet	*zoet*	*doux*
dry	*droog*	*sec*
house wine	*huiswijn*	*vin de table*
a bottle of wine	*een fles wijn*	*une bouteille de vin*
still water	*platwater*	*eau plate*
sparkling water	*bruisentwater*	*eau gazeuse*

beer	*bier*	*bière*
coffee	*koffie*	*café*
tea	*thee*	*thé*
milk	*melk*	*lait*
decaffeinated	*caffeïne vrij*	*déca*
hot chocolate	*warme chocomelk*	*chocolat chaud*
orange juice	*sinaasappelsap*	*jus d'orange*
ice	*ijs*	*glaçons*

Sightseeing

How much is admission?	*Hoeveel is de inkom?*	*Combien est l'entrée?/ C'est combien l'entrée?*
castle	*kasteel*	*château*
church	*kerk*	*église*
art gallery	*kunst gallerij*	*galerie d'art*
museum	*museum*	*musée*
cemetery	*begraafplaats / kerkhof*	*cimetière*
palace	*paleis*	*palais*
square	*plein*	*place*
town hall	*stadhuis*	*mairie*
theatre	*theater*	*théâtre*
library	*bibliotheek*	*bibliothèque*
ticket please	*ticket alstublieft*	*billet, s'il vous plaît*
student	*student*	*étudiant(e)*
adult	*volwassen*	*adulte*
child	*kinder*	*enfant*

Shopping and practicalities

How much does this cost?	*Hoeveel kost dit?*	*Combien ça coûte?*
Do you have ...?	*Heeft u ...?*	*Est-ce que vous avez ...?*
Do you have this in ...? *see Colours*	*Heeft u dit in ...?*	*Est-ce que vous avez ça en ...?*
chemist/pharmacist	*apotheek*	*pharmacie*
market	*markt*	*marché*
newsagents	*nieuwsagentschap*	*magasin de journaux*
bookshop	*boekhandel*	*librairie*
bakery	*bakkerij*	*boulangerie*
grocers	*kruidenierswinkel*	*épicerie*
clothes store	*kledij winkel*	*magasin de vêtements*
larger	*grooter*	*plus grand(e)*
smaller	*kleiner*	*plus petit(e)*
too big	*te groot*	*trop grand(e)*
too small	*te klein*	*trop petit(e)*
I am looking for a ...	*Ik zoek een ...*	*Je cherche un(e) ...*
bank	*bank*	*banque*
post office	*postkantoor*	*poste*
church	*kerk*	*église*
embassy	*ambasade*	*ambassade de ...*
money exchange office	*geldwisselkantoor*	*bureau de change*
tourist office	*touristenkantoor*	*office du tourisme*
internet café	*internet café*	*café internet*

stamp	*postzegel*	*timbre*
phonecard	*belkaart*	*carte de téléphone*
postcard	*ansichtkaart*	*carte postale*
lace	*kant*	*dentelle*

Colours

black	*zwart*	*noir(e)*
blue	*blauw*	*bleu(e)*
brown	*bruin*	*marron*
green	*groen*	*vert(e)*
orange	*oranje*	*orange*
red	*rood*	*rouge*
white	*wit*	*blanc/blanche*
yellow	*geel*	*jaune*

Adjectives

cheap	*goedkoop*	*pas cher/chère*
expensive	*duur*	*cher/chère*
ugly	*lelijk*	*laid(e)*
beautiful	*mooi*	*beau/belle*
bad	*slecht*	*mauvais(e)*
good	*goed*	*bon(ne)*
difficult	*moeilijk*	*difficile*
easy	*gemakkelijk*	*facile*
old	*oud*	*vieux/vieille*
new	*nieuw*	*nouveau/nouvelle*
boring	*saai*	*ennuyeux*
interesting	*interessant*	*intéressant(e)*
big	*groot*	*grand(e)*
bigger	*groter*	*plus grand(e)*
small	*klein*	*petit(e)*
smaller	*kleiner*	*plus petit(e)*
hot	*heet*	*chaud(e)*
cold	*koud*	*froid(e)*
slow	*langzaam*	*lent(e)*
quick	*snel*	*rapide*
empty	*leeg*	*vide*
full	*vol*	*plein(e)*

Health

I need a doctor	*Ik zoek een dokter*	*J'ai besoin d'un médecin*
dentist	*tandarts*	*dentiste*
It hurts here	*Het doet hier pijn*	*J'ai mal ici*
Do you have anything for …?	*Heb je iets voor …?*	*Est-ce que vous avez quelque chose pour …?*
headache	*hoofdpijn*	*mal à la tête*
sore throat	*keelpijn*	*mal à la gorge*
blocked nose	*verstopte neus*	*nez bouché*
cough	*hoest*	*toux*
pain	*pijn*	*douleur*
skin rash	*huiduitslag*	*éruption de boutons*

EMERGENCY

Help!	*Help!*	*Au secours!/aidez-moi!*
Call a doctor!	*Bel een dokter!*	*Appelez un docteur!*
There's been an accident	*Er was een ongeluk*	*Il y a eu un accident*
I'm lost	*Ik ben verloren*	*Je suis perdu*
Go away!	*Laat mij gerust/Ga weg!*	*Partez!*
police	*politie*	*police*
fire	*vuur*	*feu*
ambulance	*ambulance/ziekenwagen*	*ambulance*
thief	*dief*	*voleur*
hospital	*ziekenhuis*	*hôpital*
I'm not feeling well	*Ik voel me niet lekker*	*Je ne me sens pas bien*
I'm hurt	*Ik ben gekwetst*	*Je suis blessé(e)*

constipation	*geconstipeert/verstopt*	*constipation*
upset stomach	*maagpijn*	*mal au ventre*
sunburn	*zonnebrand*	*coup de soleil*
diarrhoea	*buikloop/diaree*	*diarrhée*
nausea	*onwel*	*nausée*
prescription	*voorschrift*	*ordonnance*
pharmacy	*apotheek*	*pharmacie*
paracetamol	*paracetamol*	*paracétamol*
antibiotics	*antibiotica*	*antibiotiques*
antiseptic	*antiseptisch*	*antiseptique*
tampons	*tampon/OB*	*tampons*
condoms	*condoom*	*préservatifs*
contraceptive	*voor behoedsmiddel*	*contraceptif*
sunblock	*zonnen craime*	*écran total*
I am …	*Ik ben …*	*Je suis …*
asthmatic	*astmatisch*	*asthmatique*
epileptic	*epeleptie*	*épileptique*
diabetic	*diabeetisch*	*diabétique*
I'm allergic to…	*Ik ben alergies aan …*	*Je suis allergique à …*
penicillin	*penicilline*	*pénicilline*
nuts	*nooten*	*noix*
bees	*bijen*	*abeilles*

Travelling with children

Is there a …?	*Is er een … ?*	*Est-ce qu'il y a …?*
baby changing room	*babyverschoonkamer*	*une pièce pour changer le bébé?*
a children's menu?	*kindermenu*	*un menu enfants?*
Do you have …?	*Heb je een …?*	*Est-ce que vous avez …?*
nappies	*pampers*	*couches*
potty	*potje*	*pot de bébé*
babysitter	*kinder oppas*	*babysitter*
highchair	*kinderstoel*	*chaise haute/chaise bébé*
Are children allowed?	*Zijn kinderen toegelaten?*	*Est-ce que les enfants sont acceptés?*

Appendix 2

GLOSSARY

FLEMISH

abdij	abbey
begijnhof	convent occupied by béguines (members of a sisterhood living as nuns without vows; they retain the right to return to the secular world)
belfort	belfry
beurs	stock exchange
brouwerij	brewery
burgher	upper-class merchant
burgomaster	mayor
dienst voor toerisme	tourist office
eetcafé	café serving snacks
grote markt	central town square
hal	hall
huis	house
jenever	juniper-flavoured liquor
kaai	quay
kasteel	castle
kerk	church
koning	king
korenmarket	corn market
kunst	art
lakenhalle	cloth hall
markt	market
ommegang	procession
o.v.(originele versie)	non-dubbed film
paleis	palace
polder	low-lying land reclaimed from the sea
poort	gate
plaats	square or open space
schone kunst	fine arts
stadhuis	town hall
steen	fortress
toren	tower
toeristische dienst	tourist office
tuin	garden

Appendix 3

FAMOUS FLEMINGS ... THERE ARE MORE THAN YOU THOUGHT

It's a long-standing joke: how many famous Belgians can you name? Quite a few it turns out – not least when it comes to Flanders (though I've also snuck in a few notable *Brusselaars*, and who could leave out Brussels-born Audrey Hepburn?). Nobel Prize winners, designers, film stars: Flanders has produced them all.

JACQUES BREL (1929–78) Cheekily adopted by the French as one of their own, this talented singer-songwriter was born in Schaarbeek, Brussels. He achieved fame following the release of *Quand on n'a que l'amour* in 1956. He occasionally wrote songs for his Flemish homeland, most notably *Le Pays Plat*. Renowned for his deep emotional singing voice and occasional film roles, he died of lung cancer in 1978 and was buried metres from painter Paul Gauguin on the Marquesas Islands in French Polynesia.

PIETER BRUEGEL THE ELDER (1525–69) Unlike his contemporaries, Dutch-born Bruegel chose not to incorporate Renaissance themes into his work. Despite visiting Italy twice, he preferred to stick with northern painting traditions and became famous for immortalising the Flemish landscape and its people. His early work is intricate in design and detail and painted from a bird's-eye view, while his later pieces depict just one or two figures seen at eye level and are larger in scale. His sons Pieter Brueghel the Younger and Jan Brueghel became renowned artists in their own right.

KIM CLIJSTERS (1983–) Born in Bilzen, near Hasselt, and affectionately nicknamed 'Kimmeke' by the Flemish, Clijsters rose to fame at Wimbledon in 1999. She would go on to win four Grand Slam singles titles, and rise to become the women's world number one in both singles and doubles before retiring in 2012. *Time* magazine has named her one of the '30 legends of women's tennis'.

ANNE TERESA DE KEERSMAEKER (1960–) The Mechelen-born choreographer first found fame in 1982 with *Fase, four movements to the music of Steve Reich*. Austere and demanding, it caused an immediate sensation. The next year she founded her dance company Rosas, known initially for all-female casts and its striking mix of discipline and expressionism. By the end of the decade she had almost single-handedly launched Belgium's contemporary dance scene, with experimentalists like Wim Vandekeybus, Jan Fabre and Sidi Larbi Cherkaoui following in her wake.

JAMES ENSOR (1860–1949) A founding member of Les XX (see box, page 24), Baron Ensor spent most of his life in his hometown of Ostend. Forbidden by his family to marry the love of his life and frustrated by his lack of success, Ensor became increasingly morbid. In his paintings, skeletons and masks are coupled with warped perspectives to create incredibly unsettling, macabre compositions. His masterpiece, *Christ's Entry into Brussels*, reflects his seething contempt for his peers and Belgian politicians – with Ensor himself posing as the ignored Messiah. Rejected by Les XX, he only managed to unveil it 30 years later – though it ended well: when the painting was finally shown in 1929, Ensor received a knighthood.

AUDREY HEPBURN (1929–93) Edda van Heemstra Hepburn-Ruston was born in the Ixelles district of Brussels, the only child of an Englishman and a Dutch baroness. A talented ballerina, the elfin brunette turned to acting after the severe malnutrition she suffered during World War II put a dent in her dancing career. Her wit, charm and intelligence quickly caught the attention of studio directors and in 1953 she won an Academy Award for her role in *Roman Holiday*. Also famous for her roles as Holly Golightly in *Breakfast at Tiffany's* and Eliza Doolittle in *My Fair Lady*, Hepburn became one of Hollywood's leading actresses throughout the 1950s and '60s.

VICTOR HORTA (1861–1947) Born in Ghent, Horta was Europe's foremost Art Nouveau architect, incorporating the Impressionist and Pointillist styles he had picked up while studying interior design in Paris into 'biomorphic whiplash' buildings. After entering the Royal Academy of Fine Arts, he was taken on as an assistant by his professor, Alphonse Balat – architect to King Leopold II. Four of Horta's buildings are UNESCO World Heritage sites, and his fingerprints are all over Brussels – not least his world-famous Hôtel Tassel, considered the first Art Nouveau building.

JACKY ICKX (1945–) Brussels-born Jacques Ickx was a Formula One racing driver active between 1967 and 1979. He notched up 25 podium appearances and won the 24 Hours of Le Mans race six times. At the 1970 Spanish Grand Prix his car crashed; Ickx managed to escape but received serious burns. He retired in 1979, but still participates in historic races as a driver, often for Porsche or Ferrari.

GEORGES LEMAÎTRE (1894–1966) The Roman Catholic priest proposed the Big Bang theory and expansion of the universe in 1927, two years before Edwin Hubble.

RENÉ MAGRITTE (1898–1967) Renowned for his quirky, thought-provoking art, Magritte began to draw aged 12 and went on to train at the Royal Academy of Fine Arts of Brussels. When he was 14 his mother committed suicide; the sight of her body, dredged from the river, haunted many of his early paintings. His first exhibition in 1927 was critically panned and, smarting from the failure, he briefly moved to Paris where he met Surrealist co-founder André Breton. With renewed inspiration, he returned to painting after World War II and enjoyed far greater success.

MARTIN MARGIELA (1957–) The Genk native graduated from the fashion department of Antwerp's Royal Academy of Fine Arts in 1979, a year before the Antwerp Six. After a stint under Jean-Paul Gaultier, he started his own label with Jenny Meirens – with the *maison*'s shows and deconstructionist aesthetic (oversized proportions, raw hems etc) going on to have a lasting influence on fashion. Despite never giving a single interview and refusing to pose for photographs, the 'ghost' of fashion's fame has only grown, long since his departure from his own label.

GERARDUS MERCATOR (1512–94) Born Gheert Cremer, the Flemish cartographer, better known by his Latin name, developed the Mercator projection in 1569: a flat chart showing the lines of latitude and longitude which revolutionised nautical navigation.

He is also credited with producing the first globes – made from papier-mâché and tinted with watercolours – and the first modern atlas.

EDDY MERCKX (1945–) The greatest cyclist of all time, Merckx – nicknamed 'the cannibal' for his tendency to ride flat out during races – won the Tour de France five times, the Giro d'Italia five times and was crowned world champion three times. In 1969 he was involved in a crash that killed his pacer and left Merckx with a twisted pelvis and cracked vertebrae; he returned to cycling but was plagued by constant pain. He retired from the professional circuit in 1978 and today runs a road-bike brand.

GEORGES REMI (1907–83) Better known by his *nom de plume* **Hergé** – the French pronunciation of his reversed initials – Remi was born in Etterbeek, Brussels. After leaving school, he joined the staff of the Catholic newspaper *Le XXe Siècle* and was put in control of its children's supplement. Dissatisfied with its existing comic strips, he came up with Tintin, a character inspired by his brother Paul (an officer in the Belgian army). Hergé pioneered the use of bold colours and the *ligne claire* style that rendered Tintin ageless. He used the intrepid reporter, accompanied by his lovable fox terrier Snowy, as a vehicle to explore contemporary issues. *The Adventures of Tintin* has been translated into over 70 languages and sold over 230 million copies.

PETER PAUL RUBENS (1577–1640) Born in Germany, the leading Flemish Baroque luminary moved to Antwerp with his mother as a child. He began painting at the age of 14 and was declared a master painter at 21. Visits to Italy and Spain followed, where he encountered and studied the works of the great Renaissance artists. The death of his mother in 1608 saw him return to Antwerp and set up a workshop to satisfy the widespread demand for his vigorous, sensual history paintings and portraits. Rubens's personal contribution to the 2,000 works he is said to have produced was sometimes limited to painting hands and faces, with his apprentices completing the rest – some of them, including Jan van Eyck, going on to become famous in their own right.

RAF SIMONS (1968–) The Flemish designer has travelled a long way from Neerpelt, where he was born to an army nightwatchman and a cleaner. Initially studying industrial design in Genk, he interned for Antwerp Six member Walter von Beirendonck and was converted to fashion by a 1991 Martin Margiela show. Self-trained, his eponymous, Antwerp-based menswear label, drawing on subcultures, has had a formidable impact on the industry – as have his stints as creative director of labels Jil Sander, Christian Dior and, most recently, US giant Calvin Klein.

LUC TUYMANS (1958–) One of the most influential painters working today, Tuymans was born in Mortsel, near Antwerp, to a mother whose family was in the Dutch resistance and a father who had brothers in the Hitler Youth. Around jobs as a railway guard and bouncer, he studied fine arts, and made his mark in the 1980s when he began to make figurative paintings tackling major historical events, such as the Holocaust, or politics of the Belgian Congo, in his trademark harsh yet elegant style.

JEAN-CLAUDE VAN DAMME (1960–) Renowned for his martial arts prowess and his ability to do full splits while performing stunts, the 'Muscles from Brussels' – or 'JCVD' as he's also known – enjoyed Hollywood success during the 1990s with action films like *Timecop* and *Universal Soldier*. He's equally famous for his perfect posterior, which he flashed in his breakthrough film *Bloodsport*.

HENRI VAN DE VELDE (1863–1957) This neo-Impressionist painter – who was invited to become a member of Les XX (see box, page 24) – is famous for pioneering the Art Nouveau movement in Belgium, along with Victor Horta. He designed the Boekentoren university library in Ghent.

ROGIER VAN DER WEYDEN (1399–1464) Born in Tournai, van der Weyden was originally known as Rogier de la Pasture, but converted to the Dutch equivalent when the reigning Dukes of Burgundy awarded him the title of Brussels's *stadsschilder* (town painter). His popularity increased when, aged 51, he made a pilgrimage to Rome, picking up commissions from the Medici and Este families along the way. By his death in 1464, van der Weyden was one of Europe's richest, most celebrated painters.

JAN VAN EYCK (1390–1441) Born near Maaseik, van Eyck was court painter to Philip the Good, Duke of Burgundy, and travelled widely on diplomatic missions. Renowned for his unparalleled application and layering of oil glazes, van Eyck's work is incredibly detailed and incandescent. His most famous work is *The Adoration of the Mystic Lamb*, aka the Ghent Altarpiece; 2020 is 'van Eyck Year' in Flanders, with celebrations and exhibitions across the region.

DRIES VAN NOTEN (1958–) Born into a family of garment makers, van Noten graduated from Antwerp's famous fashion department in 1980, and made his mark as a member of the Antwerp Six (page 58). Though he briefly fell out of fashion in the minimalist 1990s, his extraordinarily rich, patterned clothing – often with ornate embroidery or clashing colours – has been a watchword for style ever since.

AXEL VERVOORDT (1947–) Often called a 'tastemaker extraordinaire', the antiques dealer and interior designer began to buy up and restore Antwerp's 16th-century alley the Vlaeykensgang while still in his twenties. Best known for his wabi-sabi philosophy, privileging earthy, rough-hewn spaces that bear the marks of time, his clients include Robert de Niro and Kanye West. In 2017 Vervoordt launched Kanaal, a former gin distillery turned housing and arts complex in Wijnegem, just outside Antwerp; he and his wife May continue to live in sumptuous castle's-Gravenwezel, not far away.

Appendix 4

FURTHER INFORMATION

BOOKS

History and culture

Blom, J C H (ed) *History of the Low Countries* Berghahn Books, 2006. A thorough examination of Belgium, Luxembourg and the Netherlands's collective history, from the Merovingian dynasty to the present. Peppered with paintings by artists of the day.

Drozdiak, W *Fractured Continent: Europe's Crises and the Fate of the West* Norton, 2017. Addressing the rise of Trump and fall of the EU, this expert book by an ex-*Washington Post* editor has a chapter devoted to EU hub Brussels.

Holt, T & V *Major and Mrs Holt's Battlefield Guide to Ypres Salient* Pen & Sword Books Ltd, 1997. An easy and invaluable read that covers the Salient in detail and contains good itineraries, maps and anecdotes. The most recent edition came out in time for the World War I centenary – you'll find it at Ypres tourist information office.

Hochschild, A *King Leopold's Ghost* Mariner Books, 1999. Hard-hitting examination of Belgium's savage colonial adventure in the Congo – a largely undocumented genocide that the country still hasn't reckoned with.

Pearson, H A *Tall Man in a Low Land* Abacus, 2000. One man's laugh-out-loud account of his travels around Belgium with his wife and young daughter.

Swan, L *The Wisdom of the Beguines: The Forgotten Story of a Medieval Women's Movement* Bluebridge, 2016. Thorough exploration of pioneering independent laywomen the béguines, who once flourished in Flanders and the Netherlands.

Tuchman, B *The Guns of August* Penguin, 2014. Pulitzer Prize-winning account of the outbreak of World War I on the Western Front, originally published in the 1960s.

Literature and art

Alpers, S *The Making of Rubens* New Haven, 1995. An unconventional critique of the master's art.

Bronte, C & E *The Belgian Essays* Yale University Press, 1997. The Brontë sisters visited Brussels in 1842; their experiences there helped to shape their writing careers. All 28 essays feature in the original French accompanied by an English translation.

Charney, N *Stealing The Mystic Lamb* PublicAffairs, 2010. The American art historian charts the incredible adventures of Ghent's much-stolen *The Adoration of the Mystic Lamb* altarpiece (page 178) in a manner akin to a Tom Clancy thriller.

Claus, H *The Sorrow of Belgium* Penguin Books Ltd, 1994. This seminal work tells the story of a Flemish child (Claus's alter ego) caught up in the German occupation of Belgium in World War II.

Coe, J *Expo 58* Viking, 2013. The popular English author reanimates the intrigues of the Brussels World's Fair, and iconic Atomium, in this retro comic caper.

Conrad, J *Heart of Darkness* Oxford University Press, 2007. The classic tale of Marlow's journey up the Congo river and into the soul of man – a creative take on life in the Congo under Belgian rule.

Conscience, H *The Lion of Flanders* Fredonia Books, 2003. A historical romance hailed as one of Hendrik Conscience's masterpieces.

Dernie, D *Victor Horta* Wiley-Academy, 1995. A treat for architects, this volume covers 19 of Horta's Art Nouveau projects and includes design plans and photos.

De Vos, D *The Flemish Primitives: The Masterpieces* Princeton University Press, 2003. Lavishly illustrated, De Vos assesses and brings to life the new techniques employed by these masters of art.

Gablik, S *Magritte* Thames & Hudson Ltd, 1985. Gablik lived in Magritte's house for six months, 20 years prior to writing this book, which examines the artist's work and philosophies. There is a disappointing lack of colour photos.

Harbison, C *Jan van Eyck: The Play of Realism* Reaktion Books, 1995. Explores the characters that appear in van Eyck's masterpieces.

Hollinghurst, A *The Folding Star* Chatto & Windus, 1994. A gay Englishman moves to Flanders to teach – falling in love with one student, and getting embroiled with another's father, who curates a museum of Symbolist art by an Ensor-like figure.

Rodenbach, G *Bruges-la-Morte* Dedalus, 2009. A melancholic middle-aged widower sees his dead wife's double in the streets of Bruges; the sleeping city itself is the star.

Royle, N *Antwerp* Serpent's Tail, 2004. An American-Belgian making a documentary on Delvaux gets embroiled with a serial killer; there are references to real-life Belgian movie director Harry Kümel, whose videotapes are left at the scene.

Sebald, W G *Austerlitz* Hamish Hamilton, 2001. The prize-winning novel meditating on time, memory and the Holocaust starts memorably with an ode to Antwerp Centraal Station, and is full of micro-detail about the region, besides its literary brilliance.

Thompson, H *Tintin: Hergé and his Creation* John Murray, 2011. A dual biography of cartoon character Tintin and his creator Hergé.

Verhulst, D *Christ's Entry into Brussels* Portobello Books, 2014. The literary take on James Ensor's namesake painting – a fierce, brilliant rant against Belgium.

General

Blyth, Derek *Hidden Belgium* Luster, 2017. Longtime Belgium-based journalist Derek Blyth unearths wacky places to visit in the country. He has also written listings-style books on the hidden secrets of Antwerp, Brussels, Ghent and Bruges.

Webb, T *Good Beer Guide Belgium* Campaign for Real Ale, 2009. The definitive guide to Belgian beer – it covers all the breweries, the best cafés and beer festivals.

Other European guides For a full list of Bradt's European guides, see **w** bradtguides.com/shop.

Bird, Angela and Stewart, Murray *Pays de la Loire: The Vendée* 1st edn, Bradt, 2018.

Lambert, Anthony *Switzerland Without a Car* 6th edn, Bradt, 2017.

Phillips, Laurence *Lille* 4th edn, Bradt, 2015.

Skelton, Tim *Luxembourg* 4th edn, Bradt, 2018.

Stewart, Murray *The Basque Country and Navarre* 2nd edn, Bradt, 2019.

Thomson, Emma and Ruler, John *World War I Battlefields: A Travel Guide to the Western Front* 2nd edn, Bradt, 2017.

WEBSITES

w belgiancoast.co.uk Official English-language West Flanders tourism website

w belgiantrain.be Booking website for all train travel in Belgium

W camping.be List of campsites in Flanders
W delijn.be Public transport network in Flanders
W eurostar.com Official website for Eurostar trains from London to Brussels
W eurotunnel.com Official website for car trains from Folkestone to Calais
W flanderstoday.eu Main English-language paper (online) covering Flanders
W newplacestobe.com Website covering hip new openings across Flanders
W stib.be Public transport network in Brussels
W thebulletin.be Veteran Brussels-based English quarterly and website
W thewordmagazine.com Cool English-language magazine focusing on Brussels
W tov.be Official East Flanders tourism website
W use-it.be Funky website for young travellers. Excellent printable maps too
W visitbrussels.com Official Brussels tourism website
W visitflanders.com Official Flanders tourism website
W visitlimburg.be Official Limburg tourism website
W westtoer.be Official West Flanders tourism website

NOTES

NOTES

Index

Entries in **bold** indicate main entries; entries in *italics* indicate maps